STUDIES IN THE EARLY HISTORY OF BRITAIN

General Editor: Nicholas Brooks

Bradford & Ilkley Community College
LIBRARY

The Origins of Anglo-Saxon Kingdoms

The Origins of Anglo-Saxon Kingdoms

Edited by Steven Bassett

Leicester University Press   1989
(a division of Pinter Publishers)
London and New York

Copyright © Leicester University Press, 1989

First published in Great Britain in 1989 by
Leicester University Press (a division of Pinter Publishers Ltd)

Trade and other enquiries
25 Floral Street, London WC2E 9DS

Editorial office
Fielding Johnson Building, University of Leicester,
University Road, Leicester LE1 7RH

British Library Cataloguing in Publication Data

A CIP catalogue record of this book is available
from the British Library

Library of Congress Cataloging-in-Publication Data

The Origins of Anglo-Saxon kingdoms.
 (Studies in the early history of Britain)
 Bibliography: p.
 Includes index.
 1. Great Britain—History—Anglo-Saxon period,
449–1066. 2. Anglo-Saxons—Kings and rulers—History.
3. Monarchy—Great Britain—History. I. Bassett, Steven.
II. Series.
DA152.075 1989 942.01 89–8009
ISBN 0–7185–1317–7 HDK ✓

Set in Linotron 202 Trump by Wyvern Typesetting Ltd, Bristol
Printed and bound in Great Britain by SRP Ltd, Exeter

Contents

Foreword

Preface

List of figures

List of Tables

1

1   In search of the origins of Anglo-Saxon kingdoms   3
Steven Bassett

2   Early medieval kingships in the British Isles   28
Thomas Charles-Edwards

3   The origins of barbarian kingdoms: the continental evidence   40
Edward James

2

4   The creation and early structure of the kingdom of Kent   55
Nicholas Brooks

5   The kingdom of the South Saxons: the origins   75
Martin Welch

6   The Jutes of Hampshire and Wight and the origins of Wessex   84
Barbara Yorke

7   Frithuwold's kingdom and the origins of Surrey   97
John Blair

8   The Middle Saxons   108
Keith Bailey

9   Essex, Middle Anglia and the expansion of Mercia in the
South-East Midlands   123
David Dumville

10   Kingship and material culture in early Anglo-Saxon East Anglia   141
Martin Carver

11   The formation of the Mercian kingdom   159
Nicholas Brooks

12   Defining the Magonsæte   171
Kate Pretty

13   The early history of western Mercia   184
Margaret Gelling

14 Lindsey   202
    Bruce Eagles

15 The origins of Northumbria: some aspects of the British
    background   213
    David Dumville

    3

16 The Tribal Hidage: an introduction to its texts and their
    history   225
    David Dumville

17 The Chertsey resting-place list and the enshrinement of
    Frithuwold   231
    John Blair

    Notes   237

    Index   289

Foreword

The aim of the *Studies in the Early History of Britain* is to promote works of the highest scholarship which open up virgin fields of study or which surmount the barriers of traditional academic disciplines. As interest in the origins of our society and culture grows while scholarship yet becomes ever more specialized, interdisciplinary studies are needed more urgently, not only by scholars but also by students and by laymen. The series will therefore include research monographs, works of synthesis and also collaborative studies of important themes by several scholars whose training and expertise has lain in different fields. Our knowledge of the early Middle Ages will always be limited and fragmentary, but progress can be made if the work of the historian embraces that of the philologist, the archaeologist, the geographer, the numismatist, the art historian and the liturgist – to name only the most obvious. The need to cross and to remove academic frontiers also explains the extension of the geographical range from that of the previous *Studies in Early English History* to include the whole island of Britain. The change would have been welcomed by the editor of the earlier series, the late Professor H.P.R. Finberg, whose pioneering work helped to inspire, or to provoke, the interest of a new generation of early medievalists in the relations of Britons and Saxons. The approach of this series is therefore deliberately wide-ranging. Early medieval Britain can only be understood in the context of contemporary developments in Ireland and on the continent.

This volume is the second collaborative study to appear in the series. No less than thirteen scholars here combine to consider both the general problems of English state formation and the particular problems of the individual Anglo-Saxon kingdoms. The group, gathered together under Steven Bassett's initiative and meticulous editorship, bring diverse skills – historical, archaeological, topographical and philological – to the work. What is exciting, however, is the frequency with which these studies throw light on each other and reach fresh and unexpected insights from a new look at familiar evidence. Without seeking to impose a single methodology or a uniform interpretation of English state formation, this volume addresses both the general issue and the individual kingdoms from new angles and with rigorous scholarship. Not only those who seek to construct an interpretative model to explain the origins of kingdoms, but also those whose interests are focused on a particular territory will find here food for thought that is rich indeed.

N.P. Brooks
Birmingham University
October 1988

Preface

The desire to know how Anglo-Saxon kingdoms originated is one that has possessed me from my undergraduate days, when I first impertinently decided that historians had little reliable to say on the matter (and had first said it too long ago) and archaeologists nothing at all. Yet it seemed a question that was still worth trying to answer – or, rather, to answer again, for the few notable efforts I knew of had mostly been made early in the century. Further enquiry seemed to have been deterred by a slowly increasing awareness of how little could reliably be told of Britain's history in the first post-Roman centuries. But in view of the wealth of new information about the Migration Period in Britain that was being produced by the efforts of historians, archaeologists and placename scholars alike, I felt that it was high time for them to ask again where Anglo-Saxon kingdoms, and kingship, had come from.

My chance came in 1986 when Trevor Rowley kindly allowed me a platform on which to organize a public discussion of the question. A conference on 'The Origins of Anglo-Saxon Kingdoms' was duly held in Oxford on 12–14 December 1986 under the auspices of the University's Department for External Studies. Its stated aim was to pay particular attention to the small kingdoms – that is, the less successful ones that never achieved the size or longevity of Northumbria, Mercia or Wessex, the big three which eventually subsumed them. My belief was that most, possibly all, of these small kingdoms had also reached their greatest extent by similar expansion over yet smaller, weaker neighbours. If so, they must represent the earliest well-documented stage in a long process of state formation – one beginning early in the Migration Period and culminating in the tenth century in a single kingdom of England. By highlighting the small ones, and at the same time concentrating on the earliest discernible stages in the growth of Northumbria, Mercia and Wessex, the conference would, I hoped, illuminate the broader question of how Anglo-Saxon kingship and kingdoms began. It would also put the discussion of their origins in a wider, western European context.

The present volume directly arises out of that (for me) most stimulating and pleasurable occasion. Almost all of those who gave a paper then are represented in it (with two of them providing additional chapters), together with one new contributor. They have cheerfully put up with the foibles and idiosyncracies of my editorship and I thank them all for that, as I also do for their assistance individually in specific matters. To one of them, Nicholas Brooks, I owe a further debt of gratitude for the help, advice and encouragement he has given me, in his capacity as General Editor of the series in which this volume appears, at every stage in its preparation. I am also very grateful to Susan Martin at the Leicester University Press and, on its acquisition by Pinter Publishing, to Patrick Armstrong for their expert assistance; to Henry Buglass who drew all the maps from the authors' originals; and to Philippa Bassett for her work on the index. Finally the publishers and I wish to thank the British Library Board and the Curators of the Bodleian Library for permission to reproduce photographs of manuscripts in their care.

Steven Bassett
Birmingham
August 1988

List of figures

Fig. 1.1   Winchcombeshire.   7
Fig. 1.2   Lands in the kingdom of the Hwicce granted in all surviving
           charters (to 821).   9
Fig. 1.3   Lands in the kingdom of the Hwicce granted in spurious
           charters (to 821).   10
Fig. 1.4   Lands in the kingdom of the Hwicce granted in all essentially
           reliable charters (to 821).   11
Fig. 1.5   Lands in the kingdom of the Hwicce granted by its rulers,
           with or without a Mercian king associated in the grant (to
           821).   12
Fig. 1.6   Lands in the kingdom of the Hwicce granted by a Mercian
           king acting alone (to 821).   13
Fig. 1.7   Lands in the kingdom of the Hwicce granted before 727 by a
           Mercian king acting alone.   14
Fig. 1.8   Lands in the kingdom of the Hwicce granted between 727
           and 821 by a Mercian king acting alone.   15
Fig. 1.9   Lands in the kingdom of the Hwicce granted in lost but
           reliably reported charters (to 821).   16
Fig. 1.10 The probable extent of the regio of the Stoppingas.   19
Fig. 1.11 The Rodings area of west-central Essex.   22
Fig. 1.12 Parishes in the vicinity of Great Chesterford on the Essex–
           Cambridgeshire border.   25
Fig. 2.1   Northern Ireland c. 900.   35
Fig. 4.1   Early Kent: physical and ecclesiastical divisions.   56
Fig. 4.2   Early Kent: administrative divisions.   70
Fig. 5.1   Early Anglo-Saxon Sussex: sixth-century sites.   76
Fig. 5.2   Early Anglo-Saxon Sussex: seventh-century sites.   77
Fig. 5.3   Early Anglo-Saxon Sussex: fifth-century sites.   82
Fig. 6.1   The Jutish province in southern Hampshire.   85
Fig. 7.1   The early subdivisions of the three Wealden counties.   99
Fig. 7.2   Surrey: manorial and parochial outliers.   101
Fig. 7.3   The Chertsey estate and its environs.   102
Fig. 7.4   The Thames valley in the seventh and eighth centuries.   104
Fig. 8.1   The Middle Saxon province.   109
Fig. 8.2   Middle Saxon groups and major centres.   116
Fig. 10.1 East Anglia and its environs.   145
Fig. 11.1 Mercia and its neighbours.   161
Fig. 12.1 The topography of the West Midlands, showing Roman
           towns and early Anglo-Saxon cemeteries.   173
Fig. 12.2 The Welsh border in the Anglo-Saxon period.   180

Fig. 13.1 Warwickshire: placenames which are pre-English or of
related significance.   194
Fig. 13.2 Staffordshire: placenames which are pre-English or of related
significance.   195
Fig. 13.3 Herefordshire: placenames which are pre-English or of
related significance.   196
Fig. 13.4 Cheshire: placenames which are pre-English or of related
significance.   197
Fig. 13.5 Shropshire: placenames which are pre-English or of related
significance.   198
Fig. 13.6 -sæte names along Offa's Dyke.   200
Fig. 14.1 Lindsey and its environs, showing Romano-British and early
Anglo-Saxon sites.   203
Fig. 16.1 The Tribal Hidage: Recension A.   226
Fig. 16.2 The Tribal Hidage: Recension B.   228
Fig. 17.1 John Leland's excerpts from the Chertsey resting-place list. 231

List of Tables

Table 4.1   The primitive *regiones* of Kent.   73

Table 17.1   Comparison of the Chertsey resting-place list with related
             texts.   232

Part 1

1 In search of the origins of Anglo-Saxon kingdoms

STEVEN BASSETT

How did kingdoms first come into being in Anglo-Saxon England?[1] There are several possibilities. The concept of the kingdom could have been imported by Germanic immigrants in the fifth and sixth centuries, so that those who had been kings (or their equivalent) on the continent could expect, and be expected, to forge something similar in Britain. The Old Saxons were said not to have had kings in Saxony, but realistically we know next to nothing about forms of government in the Anglo-Saxon homelands on the eve of the migration.[2] Or perhaps the idea of kingship was newly learned or invented in the first years of the English settlement in Britain. If it was, then what stimulated the immigrants to abandon their old forms of social control so soon? In either case, how successful were these new kings? Did any of their kingdoms last long enough to be known to us? On balance that seems unlikely; the meagre clues we have suggest sixth-century origins for most of the kingdoms that survived, that is, the most successful of the ones whose names we know.[3]

This allows, then, for a third possibility. Whether or not kingship of Offa's and Alfred's sort had existed in the Germanic homelands, perhaps the new-comers to Britain did not find it a suitable institution for the circumstances of their settlement there, or may not at first have had the opportunity to choose their own systems of government. In that case, when kingdoms were eventu-ally formed, what would they have replaced, and by what means? What sort of people became their first rulers?

Asking these questions may seem like whistling in the dark. That is to say, they are not unreasonable ones to ask, but they cannot of course be answered because there simply is not the evidence available to allow us to do so. When we first have anything substantive to judge by – and that is generally for the earlier seventh century – kingship is already an established institution, no matter how precarious its practice may have been for individual rulers. We quickly perceive a number of extensive kingdoms, some of them relatively impressively organized and all looking more or less fully formed. Yet their origins, which could not have been all that remote then, at first sight seem completely invisible to us. Kingdoms such as Kent, Wessex and Mercia evolved or were forged in the first century and a half of the English settlement, which is an effectively prehistoric period so far as the study of early Anglo-Saxon institutions is concerned.

But the picture is not so black as some have painted it. Now that historians, archaeologists, and placename scholars do talk to each other, increasingly coordinate their studies and combine the results, the Migration Period in lowland Britain is no longer an impenetrable Dark Age. We are gaining a much better understanding of the condition of the Britons in the fifth century, of the varying contexts and the progress of the Anglo-Saxon settlement amongst them, and of the eventual creation of a hybrid society, Anglo-Saxon in name and language but in blood and culture a successful fusion of the two peoples.[4] And so there is no longer any excuse for our saying that the Anglo-Saxon kingdoms doubtless emerged out of some sort of primordial barbarian chaos, and then suppressing a delicate shudder as we turn to more genteel developments in the seventh century and later. It is true that we will never know any details, often not even the bare outline, of most historical kingdoms' beginnings. But we do have several important leads, and by following them we may be able to reach a general explanation of how and why Anglo-Saxon kingship originated; we will also learn something of the geography of the earliest kingdoms. In so doing we may discover that our sources have left far more clues to the location, extent and raison d'être of those kingdoms than we realized. Finally, we can hope to have reduced still further the gap in our understanding of the transition from Roman Britain to Anglo-Saxon England.

But first a word of caution. If we do find that we can see the earliest stages of state formation in Anglo-Saxon England, are we sure that we will recognize the products as kingdoms? And will their rulers look anything like our mental picture of an Anglo-Saxon king? Our present perception of what the very first kings and kingdoms must have been like is heavily conditioned by the historical, literary and archaeological sources of the seventh century and later. We may find, then, that for several reasons our ability to imagine and explain their origins is impaired. For instance, the influence of the Christian Church on seventh-century kingship may well have brought about substantive changes to its pre-Christian form. Similarly, the Church's prime involvement in producing the written sources on which we rely so much for our first views of Anglo-Saxon kings and their kingdoms may have led to an idealized portrayal of them. One recalls Bede's efforts as an historian to encourage the rulers of his day to be true kings – even, perhaps, to think of their power as God-given rather than in any sense deriving from those whom they ruled. Rather less easy to spot may be a tendency I detect in Bede to think no Anglo-Saxon kingdom worth mentioning (except in passing) unless or until it had a bishop of its own.

A third problem with our sources for kingship is that the kings themselves may frequently have falsified them. For example, David Dumville and others have shown that royal genealogies were particularly prone to manipulation for political ends.[5] They could be lengthened or shortened as current needs altered a ruler's perception of his dynasty's or his kingdom's past. Separate genealogies could be artificially linked, usually to give the ruling dynasty an appearance of greater legitimacy in its own kingdom or in that of a weaker neighbour over which it had gained a measure of control. Sometimes two genealogies were dovetailed completely, as two separate kingdoms permanently coalesced; this might enhance the new state's sense of unity and give it the spurious appearance of longevity as a single unit. Other sources, both historical and literary, could be devised (or revised) to suit current political needs, to glorify the ruling dynasty or to provide a kingdom with the earlier history it had either forgotten or never had. (It is hard to resist wondering if the exciting picture we get from the poem Beowulf of kingship in action was not crafted to compensate for some extremely mundane processes of state formation in its audience's real life.)[6]

So, with no written sources for Anglo-Saxon kings and kingdoms before the seventh century, and nothing substantive until the early eighth, we rely heavily on retrospection for their beginnings; the sources we do have, therefore, need the most careful handling. Archaeology too presents problems. It is very easy to project our preconceptions about Anglo-Saxon kingship on to sites like Sutton Hoo and Yeavering – and to suspect nothing when the sites confirm them. 'Archaeologists', Philip Rahtz has observed, 'usually find what they're looking for.' To approach the archaeology of kingship with an open mind, however, is to find how little it can yet distinguish early kings from their aristocrats, or the nobility in general from the rest of earlier Anglo-Saxon society.

Placenames may at first seem to have little to offer us here, apart from clues in some kingdoms' own names to the contexts of their formation. For instance, both Deira and Bernicia have names of British origin; and Kent and Lindsey are names that hint at the continuing political role of two major late Roman administrative centres, Canterbury and Lincoln.[7] We may find, nevertheless, that placenames are of great importance in tracing the nature and extent of the earliest politically distinct land-units (though there will no doubt continue to be wide divergences of opinion on the use of such evidence).

These, then, are the sorts of problems that have always confronted students of the early history of Anglo-Saxon power and politics. Many scholars have shied away from them; one or two others might have served us better if they had done so too. Otherwise there have in the main been three sorts of approach to the question of origins.

The first of them, still rare, is the comparative approach. There are two sources for this. One is the usually much fuller material that exists for kingship and state formation in the rest of early medieval Britain (that is, beyond the limits of Anglo-Saxon settlement), and in the nearer parts of the continent among other Germanic peoples who migrated into the Western Empire. We neglect such obvious comparisons at our peril. The other source is modern social anthropology. Many pre-industrial societies of today have been studied whose economic and social circumstances seem in certain ways broadly similar to those of the Migration Period communities in lowland Britain discovered by archaeology. It is reasonable, then, to look at their political organization and its development for possible analogies, or simply so as to broaden our perception of what was possible in early Anglo-Saxon England. The second approach is essentially thematic: the study of one or more particular sorts or sources of evidence for all early kings and kingdoms. The value of the exercise is epitomized by James Campbell's published papers on the terms Bede used to distinguish between the differing status of rulers and between different sorts of peoples, territories and settlements;[8] and, second, by David Dumville's discussions of royal genealogies and king lists.[9] The third approach to the question of origins is through the detailed study of a single kingdom or its equivalent. Here one thinks at once of Brian Hope-Taylor's magisterial essay on the origins of Bernicia[10] and, for instance, of the advances made in our understanding of the formation of the kingdom of Wessex by H.E. Walker, David Kirby, Martin Biddle and Barbara Yorke.[11]

A kingdom at which we can profitably look in some detail is the one named after some of its inhabitants, the Hwicce. A lot has already been written about this relatively unimportant kingdom in the West Midlands, with a seminal article from A.H. Smith in 1965, a recent book from Della Hooke, and another soon to be produced by Patrick Sims-Williams.[12] One could be forgiven for thinking that there is little left worth saying on the subject, but some new points can be made which may throw light on the question of the origins of such kingdoms. In the latter part of this chapter a general explanation of the processes of Anglo-Saxon state formation will be proposed and illustrated.[13] As this was prompted by work on the Hwicce among other things, that kingdom is an appropriate place to start.

First, some general information is required about the kingdom of the Hwicce. Its extent is roughly indicated by land charters and other sources which tell us that certain places lay within it, and by the distribution of placenames incorporating the name Hwicce.[14] A more precise indication comes from the late medieval boundary of the dioceses of Worcester and Gloucester combined, which can be mapped.[15] The original, undivided diocese of Worcester was created for the Hwicce in 679 or 680,[16] and would presumably have been coterminous with the kingdom; indeed, it may have helped to stabilize its boundaries. Long after the kingdom had disappeared in both name and layout, the diocesan geography still perpetuated its late seventh-century outline with only minor alterations.

The formation of the kingdom of the Hwicce has generally been seen as the work of king Penda of Mercia in or just after 628,[17] though there is precious little evidence for this view. It has also been assumed that, in doing so, he imposed a uniform control over many mixed British and Anglo-Saxon communities in the West Midlands. But the question of what this new kingdom replaced is usually begged for lack of information. Penda may indeed have formed a distinct political unit in the area; but it seems more likely that, if he did so, he merely hastened the process by which such a kingdom was already being created. An amalgamation of smaller kingdoms was probably in process of being forged there by the Anglo-Saxon rulers of one of them, a people (perhaps already called the Hwicce) whose territory was centred on Winchcombe.[18] Penda may well have lent them some assistance, or perhaps defeated them, so as to have a manageable buffer state on Mercia's south-western flank; but it is doubtful if he did any more than that. Finberg's suggestion, following Stubbs, that he planted lesser members of the Bernician royal family on the Hwicce to be their rulers is both unlikely and unnecessary.[19]

As Stenton showed, the later history of the kingdom, until the last trace of it disappears in the late eighth century, is one of steady decline in status *vis-à-vis* its neighbours the Mercians.[20] After its complete absorption by Mercia the area of the kingdom persisted for two centuries or so as one of a number of major administrative subdivisions of the enlarged Mercian state, each controlled by its own ealdorman. By the end of the tenth century that pattern had been destroyed under the influence of the West Saxon kings of the by then united kingdom of England. The area of the former kingdom of the Hwicce was divided up between four newly created shires – the bulk of it in Worcestershire and Gloucestershire, a chunk in Warwickshire, and a small but highly significant part forming the short-lived Winchcombeshire.[21]

The last-named of these shires survived only until about 1017, when it was taken into Gloucestershire. However, despite its very brief life, its extent can be reliably reconstructed (fig. 1.1) from information given in two unimpeachable eleventh-century sources. One of them is what Finberg entitled the *Liber Wigorniensis*, the earlier eleventh-century part of what is better known as Hemming's Cartulary;[22] the other source is Domesday Book.[23] But there are several indications that the area which briefly became the shire of Winchcombe had already had a separate identity for a long time. These point to its having formed the heartland of the kingdom of the Hwicce, and to its having previously been a kingdom in its own right, controlled by the family who later on became rulers of the far larger, historically attested kingdom.

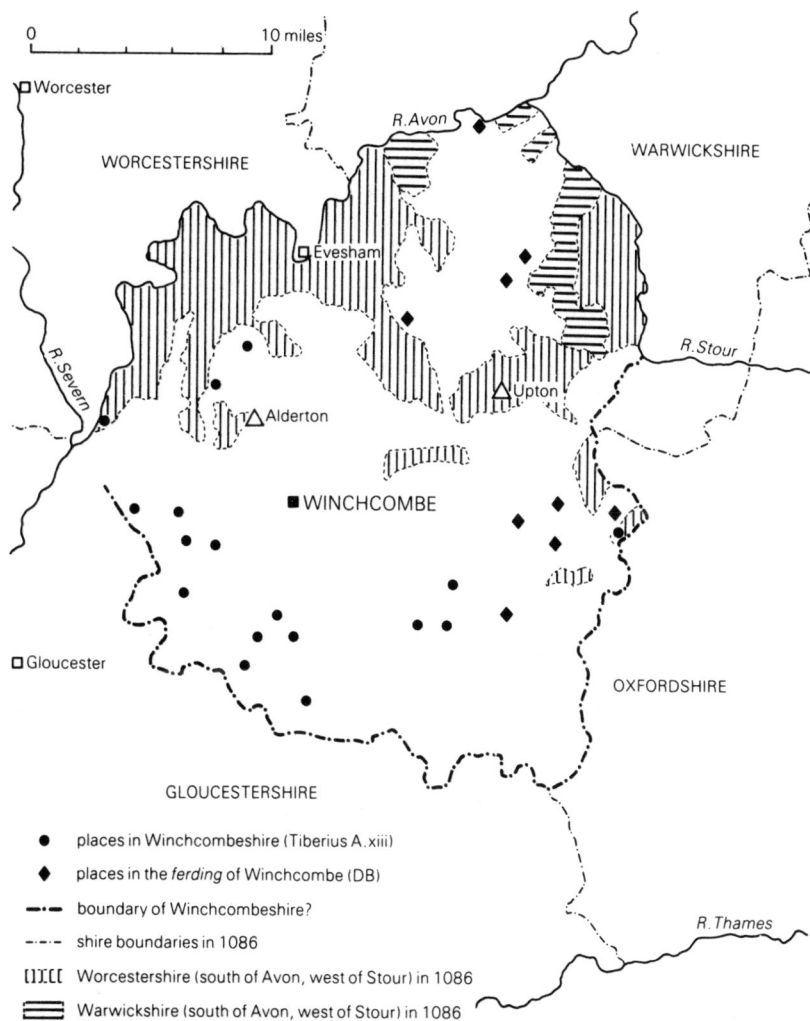

Figure 1.1. **Winchcombeshire.** (Based on Hill, *Atlas of Anglo-Saxon England* (1981), map 178, with additions.)

An authentic charter of 897 records the details and outcome of a dispute which arose between the churches of Worcester and Winchcombe, concerning an estate at Upton in Blockley.[24] Its interest to us here is that it cites a stipulation by king Coenwulf of Mercia (who died in 821) in respect of his 'hereditary land belonging to Winchcombe'.[25] The extent of that land is not recorded, but one of Coenwulf's own charters shows that Alderton (fig. 1.1) also lay within it.[26]

It is significant that Coenwulf calls the land his *hereditas*, since it gives greater meaning to what we know of his personal links with Winchcombe. It has been shown elsewhere that the place was a royal *tun* of the Hwicce and then of the Mercian kings, and that Offa and Coenwulf were both major patrons of its church – one which had no doubt been founded by the Hwiccian royal house.[27] Coenwulf's daughter Cwoenthryth was abbess of this monastic church; he buried his son Cynhelm in it, and was later on buried there himself – the pair of them probably in a freestanding stone mausoleum of the sort known from Repton.[28]

Coenwulf had succeeded Offa's sickly son Ecgfrith on the throne of Mercia in 796. We know nothing helpful about his title to succeed, and so can only speculate on how his 'hereditary land belonging to Winchcombe' came into his hands.[29] But clearly that land had once been of prime importance to the rulers of the Hwicce themselves, as a study of land grants in their kingdom shows.

The separate dots on fig. 1.2 mark the location of all grants of land made by charter in the kingdom of the Hwicce up to 821, the time of Coenwulf's death. Of them all, those on fig. 1.3 mark ones granted by charters which are considered too unreliable to be included in this analysis.[30] These spurious charters bear eloquent witness to the industry of the monks of Evesham in the twelfth century. Excluding them leaves those shown on fig. 1.4, which represent all known grants of land by 821 which are recorded in basically sound charters. There are probably just enough sound ones to allow us to say something worthwhile about the distribution of the land grants in both time and space.

They can be usefully divided into two categories. Those shown on fig. 1.5 represent lands given out by rulers of the Hwicce, with or without the association of the contemporary Mercian king in the grant.[31] They are fairly widely distributed, with something of a concentration in the area of the future Winchcombeshire (but nothing statistically significant).

However, the telling information comes from the evidence of the other category of sound charters – those issued by 821 which record grants made by a Mercian king acting on his own. These (fig. 1.6) must represent lands in the kingdom of the Hwicce that had become the private property of the kings of Mercia or, at the very least, that had come under their direct control. Fig. 1.7 shows all land grants of this sort made before 727.[32] Not one of them concerns land within the area known by the start of the eleventh century as Winchcombeshire. But when the later grants made by Mercian kings alone are plotted – that is to say, those made from 727 onwards (to 821) – they show a quite remarkable concentration within the future Winchcombeshire (fig. 1.8).[33] The distribution of lands conveyed by lost but reliably reported charters (fig. 1.9) reinforces this contrast.[34] Clearly by the later 720s the rulers of the Hwicce had lost their sole control even of this part of the kingdom.[35]

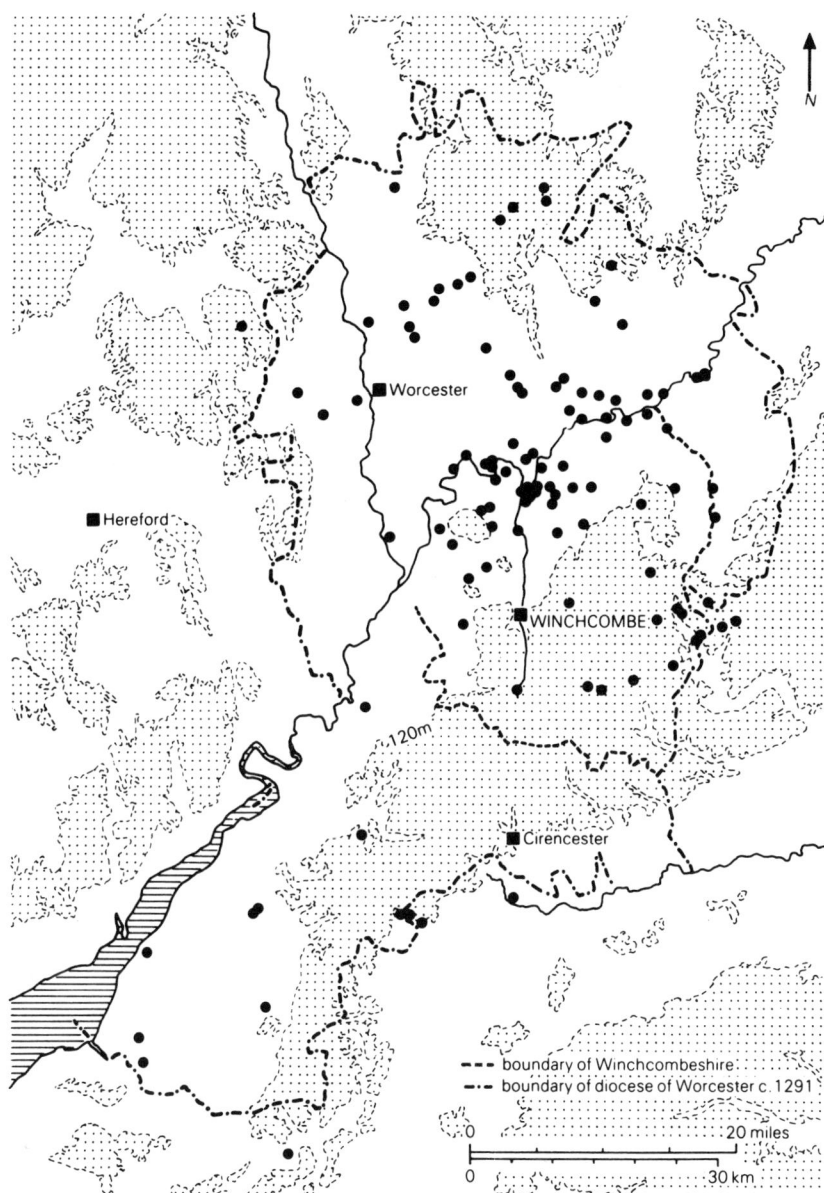

Figure 1.2. Distribution map of lands in the kingdom of the Hwicce granted in all surviving charters (*to 821*).

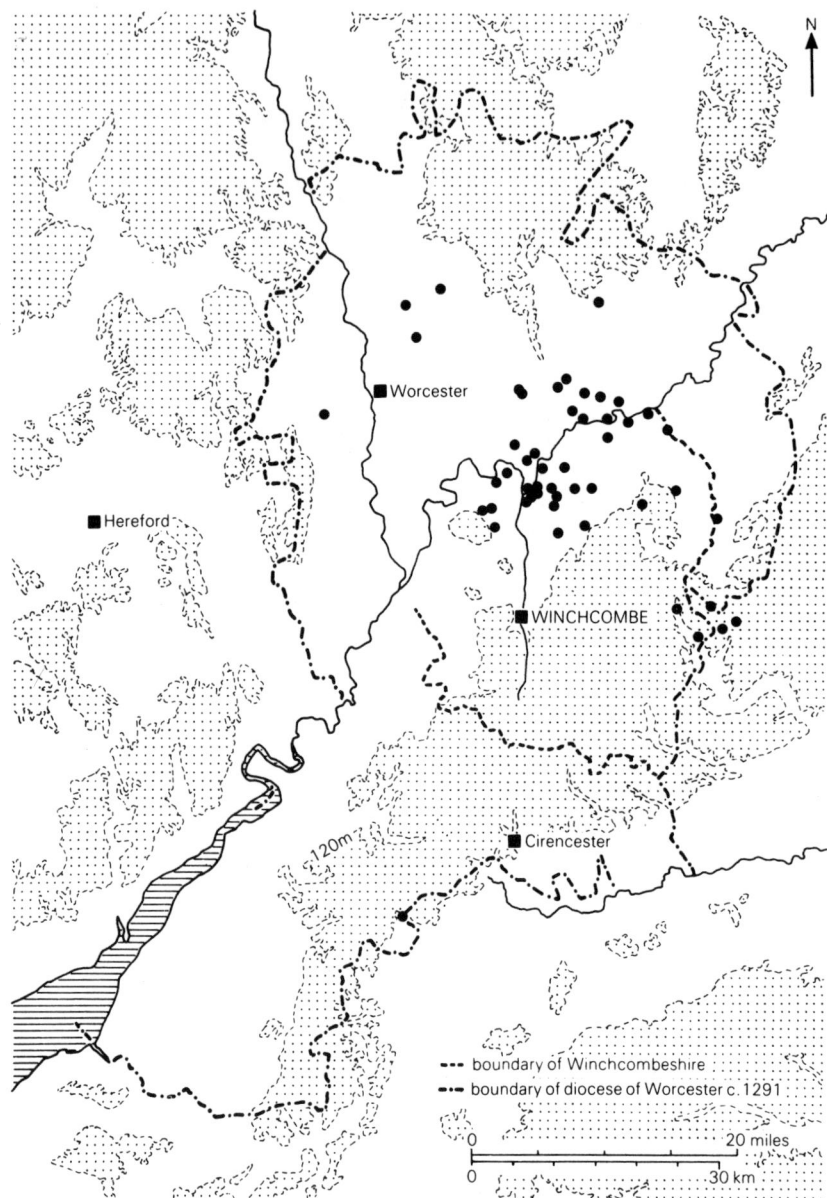

Figure 1.3. Distribution map of lands in the kingdom of the Hwicce granted in spurious charters (*to 821*).

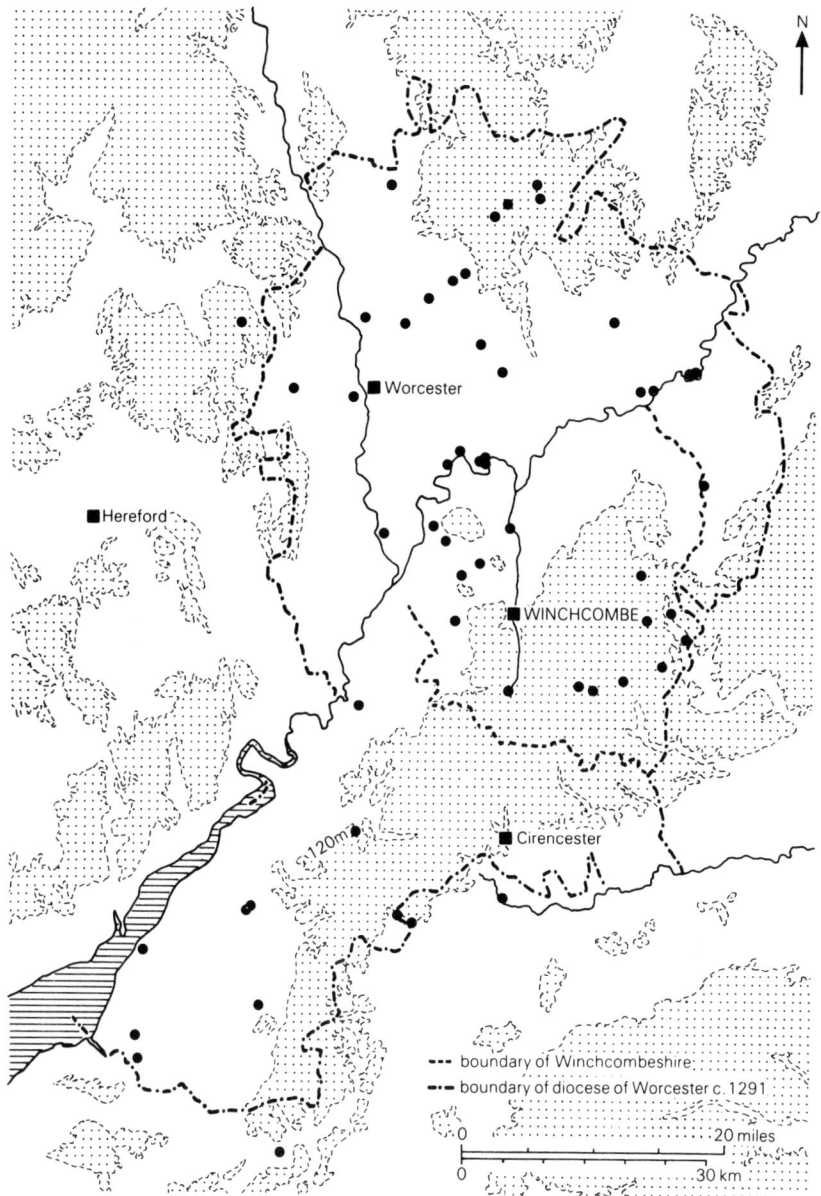

Figure 1.4. Distribution map of lands in the kingdom of the Hwicce granted in all essentially reliable charters (*to 821*).

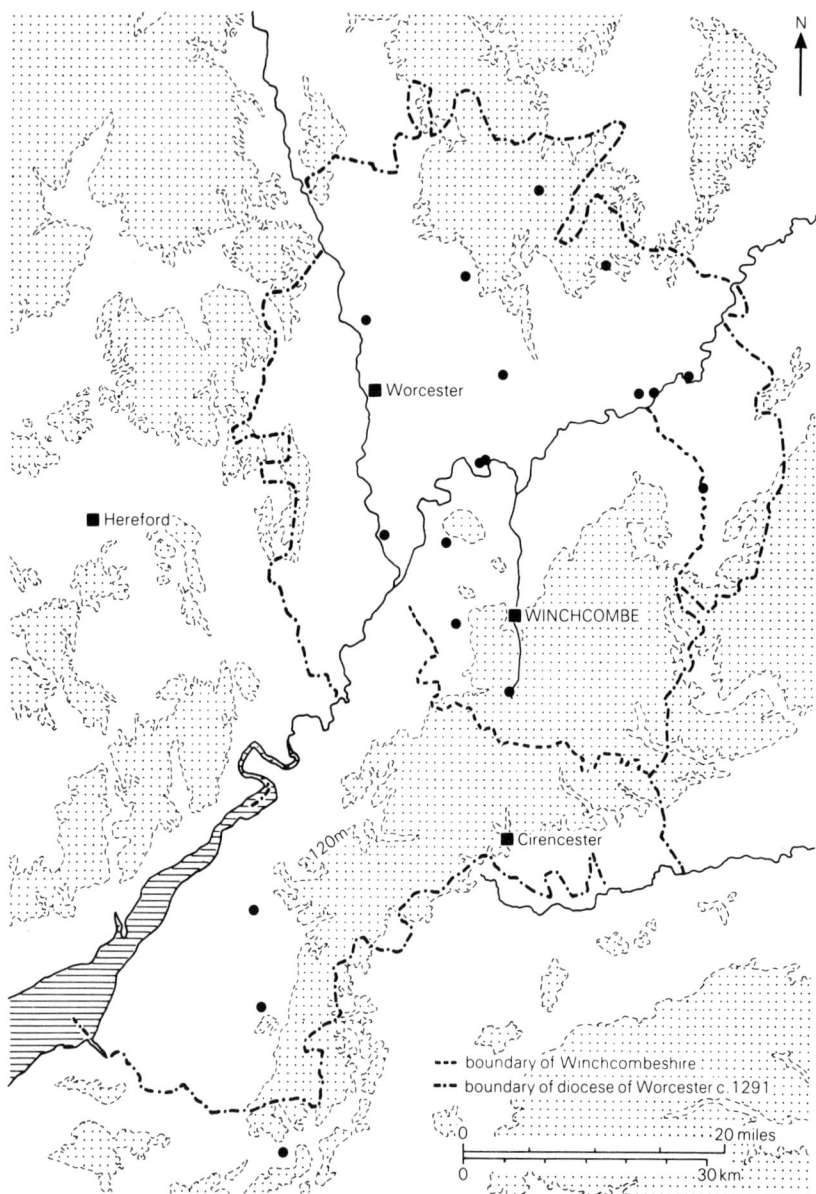

Figure 1.5. Distribution map of lands in the kingdom of the Hwicce granted
by its rulers, with or without a Mercian king associated in the grant (*to 821*).

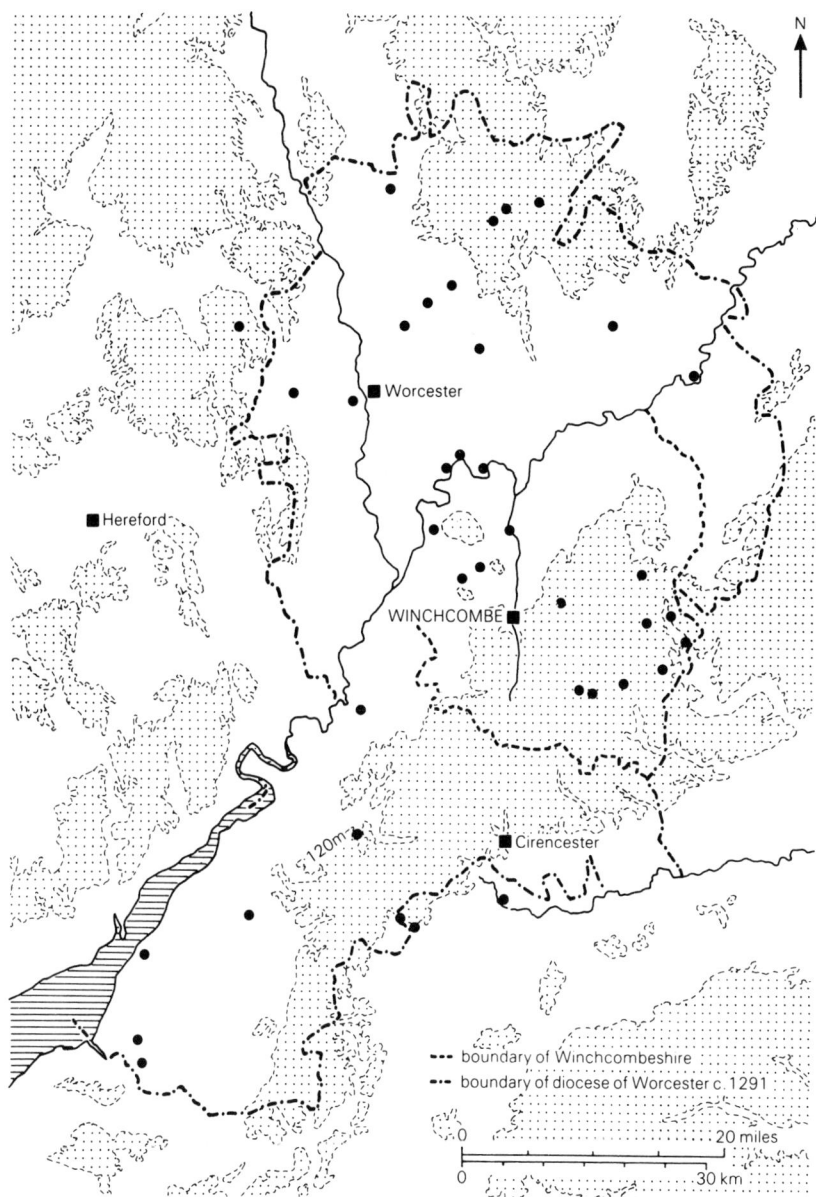

Figure 1.6. Distribution map of lands in the kingdom of the Hwicce granted by a Mercian king acting alone (*to 821*).

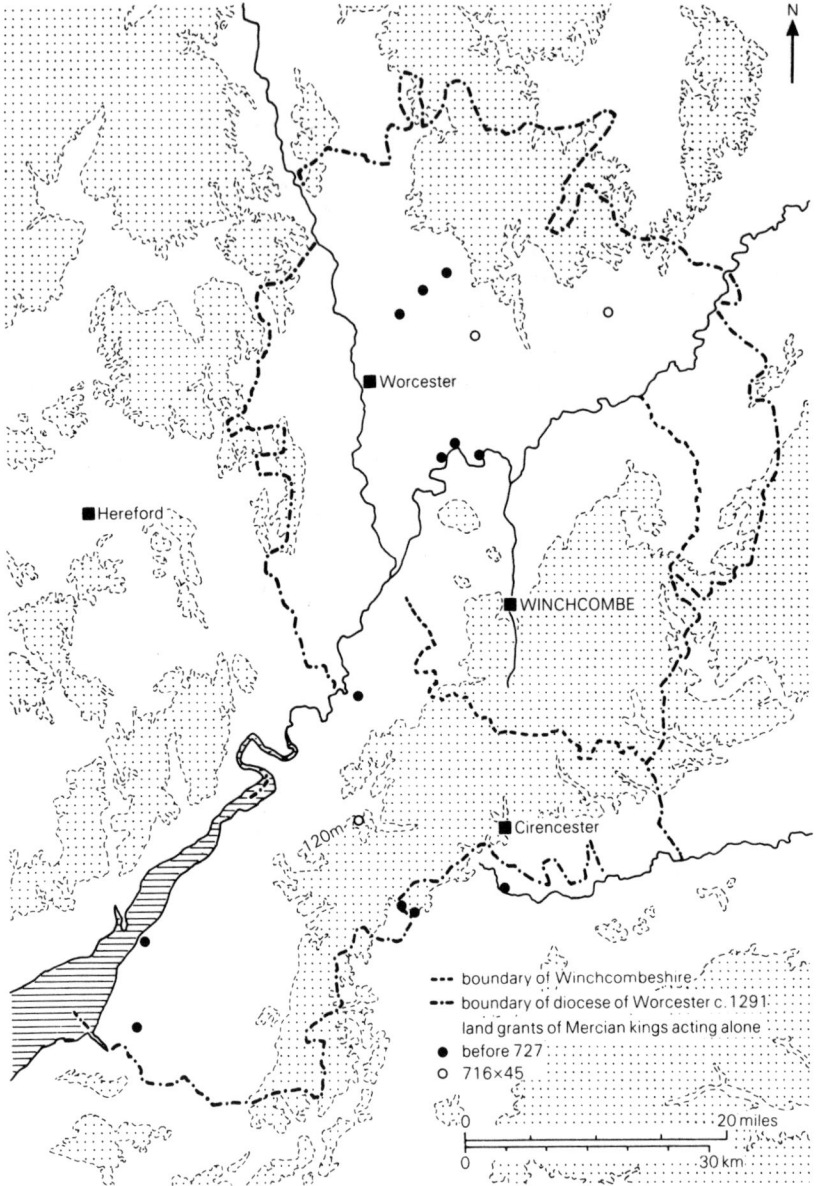

Figure 1.7. Distribution map of lands in the kingdom of the Hwicce granted *before* 727 by a Mercian king acting alone.

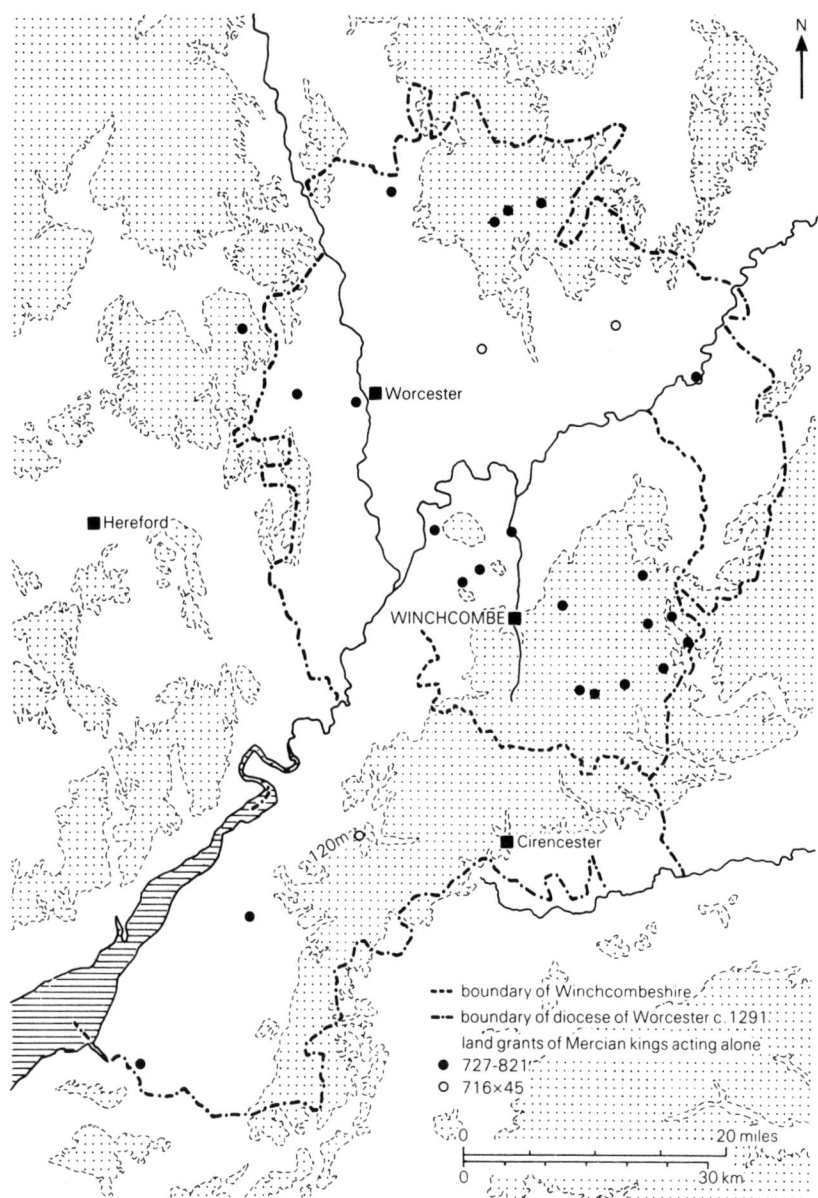

Figure 1.8. Distribution map of lands in the kingdom of the Hwicce granted *between 727 and 821* by a Mercian king acting alone.

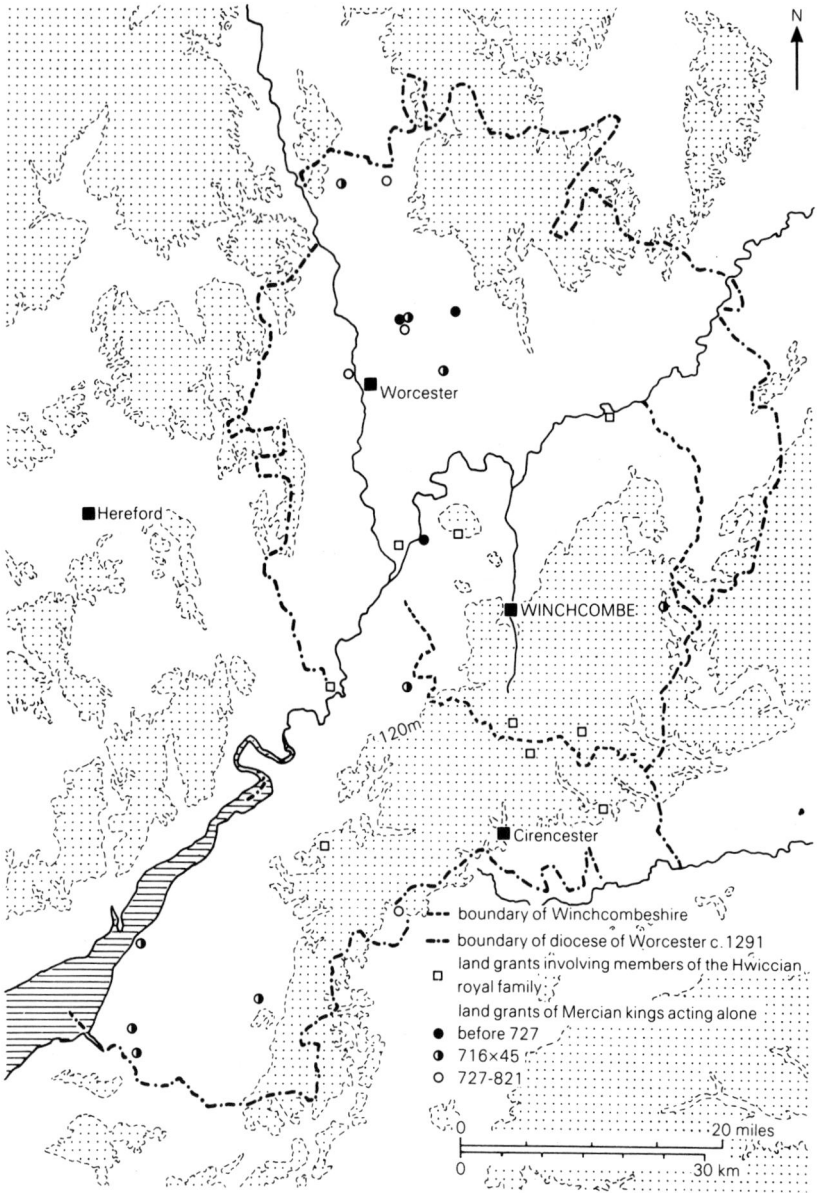

Figure 1.9. Distribution map of lands in the kingdom of the Hwicce granted in lost but reliably reported charters (*to 821*).

This area, then, identifies itself as what Coenwulf called his 'hereditary land belonging to Winchcombe' – the area which remained longest in the private ownership of the Hwiccian royal dynasty and which, even at the end of the ninth century, was still subject to strict leasing regulations. The total absence of reliable charters granting lands in this area before the 720s does not of course mean that the Hwiccian kings had little or no land there, but that it was *all* in royal hands. It was their most prized and anciently held land, their patrimony which was to be kept intact at all costs. So far as we can tell, few grants of it were made by members of the dynasty until well into the eighth century, and the few we know of were to their own family churches.[36] In none of them did a Mercian king take any part.

By the tenth century much of the land in question had been given to the church of Worcester, with the result that it became part of Worcestershire rather than of Winchcombeshire.[37] However, there can be little doubt that in its original, complete form this territory would have been geographically coherent, with its northern limits on or near the Rivers Avon and Stour.

The territory's special status within the kingdom of the Hwicce is enough to identify it as a land-unit of the sort described in Latin sources of the middle Saxon period as a *regio*, or sometimes as a *provincia*. These were large, discrete areas with some administrative autonomy which in the middle Saxon period often formed major components of the well-known kingdoms (themselves called *provinciae* on occasion).[38] Bede, for instance, tells us that both Mercia and Northumbria were composed of such *regiones*.[39] We learn of others apparently not yet firmly linked to a major kingdom when they first appear in our sources. In the East Midlands in particular in the seventh century there seem to have been many of these units of no greater size or importance than the one around Winchcombe, which (unlike the latter) were still in most respects politically independent.[40]

There are apparently two reasons why we do not nowadays refer to these small, still largely autonomous units as kingdoms. Firstly, we are rarely told enough about them for us to know anything of their rulers. However, the one or two such rulers who do appear in early sources clearly have royal attributes, if nothing like so many as their contemporaries in the major kingdoms; they are Bede's *principes*, and the *reguli* and *subreguli* of early charters. Secondly, the impact of these small units on our sources is so ephemeral that they are easily overlooked. For most of them their first appearance there is also their last.

But these two reasons are not good enough ones for not calling such smaller political units by the name 'kingdom'. For many of them their sole appearance in written sources is in the seventh- or possibly eighth-century document known as the Tribal Hidage.[41] This looks to be a list of the tribute assessments which one of the major kingdoms – very probably Mercia – claims from all other political units of the day south of the Humber by virtue, one assumes, of its overlordship.[42] All the well-known kingdoms are there, and the list seems to give us some sort of league table of them in terms of their size and ability to pay. But besides these there are a great many small fry. Some of them we hear of in other sources (if merely a repeat of their name) or else in the form of a placename; but many are otherwise unknown to us. Yet there they are in the Tribal Hidage, each one separately assessed in the same way as East Anglia, Kent and Wessex.

Can territories so short-lived and dimly perceived really have been of any importance, let alone political units worthy of the title 'kingdom'? Historians have usually answered that they cannot have been; but in early sources the major kingdoms *and* these smaller units are referred to in the same terms – that is, as *provinciae* and *regiones*. One may view them, then, as appropriately described as kingdoms, though small ones on the point of extinction. They figure in the Tribal Hidage as units already under the heavy hand of Mercian overlordship. After a short time they had been effectively annexed. Like the Hwicce and many others on Mercia's borders, they survived thereafter only as administrative units of greater or lesser size and importance within a much enlarged Mercian state.

The same early sources which give us a brief glimpse of these smaller, less successful kingdoms have something further to reveal about the origins of the whole process of state formation. For they use the two terms *provinciae* and *regiones* for yet tinier land-units. These were much smaller ones than the territory which eventually became Winchcombeshire; indeed, the latter seems to have comprised at least eleven such land-units (though none of them figures in early sources).[43]

One such was the *provincia* of *Husmerae*, now known to have lain at the northern end of the kingdom of the Hwicce, around modern Kidderminster.[44] Another, around Wootton Wawen in the same kingdom, was the *regio* of a group known as the *Stoppingas*, of whom we know only from an incidental reference in an earlier eighth-century charter of king Æthelbald of Mercia.[45] The charter permits a senior member of the Hwiccian royal family to give 20 hides of land in the *regio* of the *Stoppingas* to the monastic church which he had founded (or intended to found) there. We still have the church, which the charter specifically places at Wootton [Wawen], in its late Anglo-Saxon rebuild.[46] The extent, too, of the *regio* can be hypothesized, as the church can be reasonably assumed to have taken it as its parish. Like most minster parishes, this one had fragmented into many smaller parishes by the thirteenth century. But there are enough clear echoes of its fission in later medieval sources for the outline of the minster parish, and so the *regio* too, to be reconstructed (fig. 1.10).[47]

It would certainly be going too far to suggest that a tiny area such as this should be called a kingdom, even though it too was termed a *regio* in Bede's day. But it is from considering the nature of these smallest units, and – even more important – what eventually became of them, that we will learn most about the origins of Anglo-Saxon kingdoms.

The *Stoppingas* themselves are long lost, and probably already were (except in name) in the eighth century. They were a people who sound like an extended family, perhaps with Stoppa as their founder or the earliest remembered common ancestor.[48] They are in other words what used to be called a tribe or kindred, or in Ireland a *tuath*.[49] The *regio* of Æthelbald's charter had presumably been their defined area of settlement. That is not to say that such an extended family still occupied the area in Æthelbald's day – though many families ultimately descended from it doubtless did, along with others of different descent – or even that its members had been the only occupants of the land-unit. Nor indeed would all who came to view themselves as *Stoppingas*

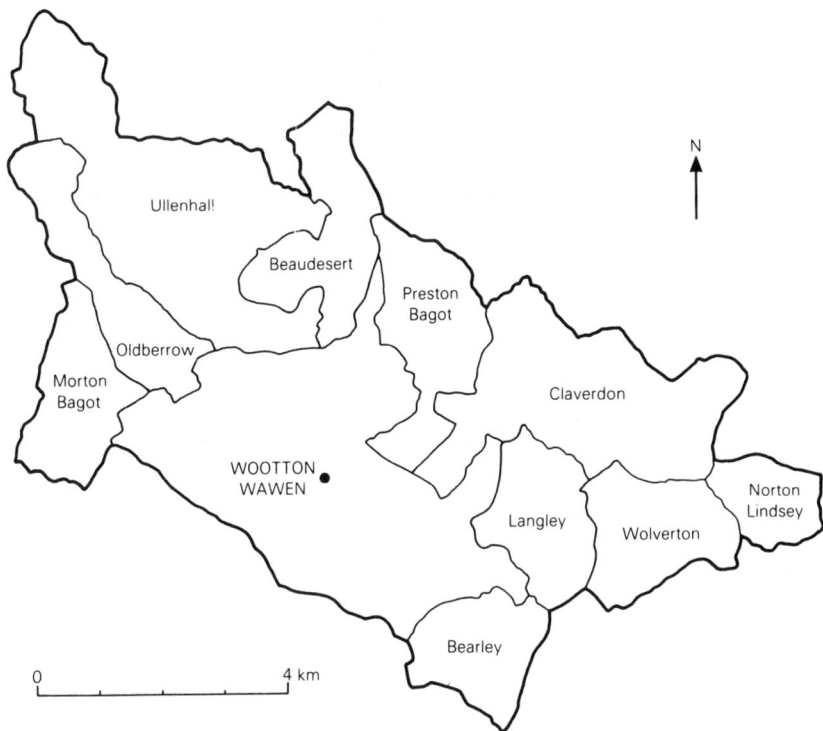

Figure 1.10. The probable extent of the *regio* of the *Stoppingas*. (Parish boundaries as shown on Inclosure and Tithe Award maps.)

have been true descendants (or their spouses) of the founding family.

Whatever their precise ethnic composition, what such early groups did have is a well-defined settlement area. Whatever powers each group's leaders had, it was within that area that they exercised them. In so far, then, as Anglo-Saxon kingship evolved from the normal circumstances of settled agrarian communities in the Migration Period, the *regio* of the *Stoppingas* and all other such settlement areas should be recognized as distinct polities – indeed, embryonic kingdoms.

But how are we to identify these early settlement areas? Luckily, not all of them require us to have middle Saxon charters to hand, as they can often be rediscovered from much later evidence which relates to their eventual breakdown into smaller units. They were in fact typically the land-units on which minster churches were set up in the seventh and eighth centuries. By then, as the example of Wootton Wawen shows, they appear much more readily to us as huge economic units centred on a major settlement – a king's *tun* or its equivalent.[50] It was out of them that middle Saxon kings and a few other people carved blocks of land for endowing churches and, increasingly, giving their officials payment for services to be rendered. These two effectively equivalent mechanisms – the creation, so to speak, of spiritual and secular benefices – operated, together with a third one, to bring about a permanent fragmentation of the early settlement areas as economic units. The third mechanism was the normal (i.e. non-testamentary) practices of partible inheritance and other subdividing of a family's land among various of its members.[51] The three together account for the emergence of manorialism in Anglo-Saxon England.

It should be noted that use of the words 'estate' and 'manor' for any of the land-units discussed here has been carefully avoided. There is, it needs to be said, no evidence of that particular form of agrarian organization in England during the centuries in which the early kingdoms developed, nor is there a likely context for it. This is the chief of several compelling reasons why the concept of the multiple estate should be rejected as unhistorical.[52] The notion of the manor, and of the landlord–tenant relationship, developed as kings ceded land to private persons and to the Church, whose idea of control was more proprietary. Land was being privatized.

The Church knew well about 'Roman' estate relationships and came of course to be a very substantial holder of lands carved out of the early settlement areas. The granting of them to the Church, and of powers over their inhabitants (i.e. ones inherent in the Church's right to enjoy the lands, and other powers additionally diverted to it), gave it ample opportunity to convert the lands into estates proper. Furthermore, the increasingly common practice of granting such lands to laymen allowed the same processes to operate as in the Church's case, doubtless usually by deliberate imitation.

The third mechanism involved in the emergence of Anglo-Saxon manorialism is perhaps the most important of all, while certainly being the hardest one to observe. It would no doubt have operated in response to the increasing size of the tribe (the extended family). Eventually the concept of tribal ownership, administered on behalf of all by the patriarch(s) and enjoyed in terms (it seems) of each separate nuclear unit using a parcel of the tribe's land freely, subject to the patriarch's overall control, would have given way to the accustomed pattern of middle Saxon land-holding. This is a pattern characterized by all lands in a kingdom being subject to a certain extent to its king, who seems able to demand a variety of dues and services from everyone holding a parcel of it and to divert them to the holder by booking it. There is no need for kings to *own* all land, and certainly not in the sense of Roman law; but they do seem to have had a wide range of rights over all of it. Those who were not kings could hold land of two sorts: bookland – by its very nature an estate proper – and allodial land, which may be equivalent to (or may at least include) 'folkland'. One imagines that as the closeness of the relationship, in both kin and personal/geographical terms, between patriarch(s) and all other members of the tribe diminished through time, so would the strength of the concept of tribal land (enjoyed but not owned by those who farmed it) have diminished too. This concept can be presumed to have been replaced by one of actual ownership subject to certain limitations (the king's rights), with alienation becoming increasingly normal.[53]

These then were probably the essential elements in the splitting up of early settlement areas and the concomitant spread of manorialism in Anglo-Saxon England. We can see the emergence of large numbers of separate manors in the later Anglo-Saxon period, and (at a rather slower pace) of a parochial geography which mirrored the manorial one.[54] However, over the same period of time the land-units of local administration generally did not alter to anything like the same extent, so that the hundreds and wapentakes of Domesday England may often reflect something of the outlines of one or more early land-units. Even the many exceptions to this often provide important clues. The use of evidence of these sorts, and of other sources (including placenames) which there is not the space to catalogue, allows many of the early settlement areas to be rediscovered. And even if individual attempts may sometimes be overoptimistic, the pattern that results is reliable enough to use.[55]

In some instances it is very easy to achieve this rediscovery. There is, for example, a group of eight ecclesiastical parishes in central Essex called the Rodings, on which Maitland was the first to comment.[56] Roding is a name in *-ingas* which means 'the people of Hrotha',[57] Hrotha being the hypocoristic form of several Anglo-Saxon personal names – rather like 'Ed' today. There were already eight parishes there as early as 1291 (fig. 1.11). At the end of the Middle Ages they served nine separate manors, with Roding Morrell lying in White Roding parish.[58] However, in Domesday Book we find no fewer than sixteen estates, each of them called simply *Rodinges* (or *Roinges*).[59] Clearly pre-Conquest manorial fragmentation had been extreme there. Yet because of the name they shared, it is not hard to rediscover the outline of the original land-unit (give or take some minor changes to its boundary) out of which the sixteen estates were created. And because of the sort of name it is, that land-unit can be identified as an early settlement area, one directly analogous to the *regio* of the *Stoppingas*.

I imagine it to have existed, fully formed, long before the middle Saxon period, even though we hear nothing of it until the eleventh century. What is so striking about it is not merely its basically regular shape, but the extent to which it conforms to the prevailing natural topography. It comprises a discrete block of the valley of the River Roding in its middle course (fig. 1.11), and clearly contains a cross-section of all available local resources: it is geographically coherent. The same is true of the *regio* of the *Stoppingas*.[60] These areas, then, are exactly what one would expect a well organized, self-contained community living under an economy of subsistence and exchange to have occupied.

Very little indeed can be said for sure about the origins and likely composition of early groups of this sort that we recognize in names like *Stoppingas* and the Rodings and in better-known examples such as Hastings, Reading, Sonning and Barking. What we do know, however, about Britain in the Migration Period suggests the following hypothetical scenario. The Anglo-Saxons seem to have found the Britons still working the agrarian landscape of earlier centuries in extensive areas of lowland Britain. Most former estates may have remained in use as agricultural territories, though the old landlord–tenant relationship had probably been ended and they would no longer have been worked at anything like their late Roman levels of productivity.[61] The newcomers would have settled on the estates, sometimes no doubt by force of arms but often by agreement with the existing occupants – this is the clear conclusion to be drawn from the physical evidence of the period.[62] Thereafter intermarriage would steadily hybridize successive generations of inhabitants (both Germanic and British) of the various settlements within a given district – presumably a bloc of contiguous estates of an appropriate size and geographical

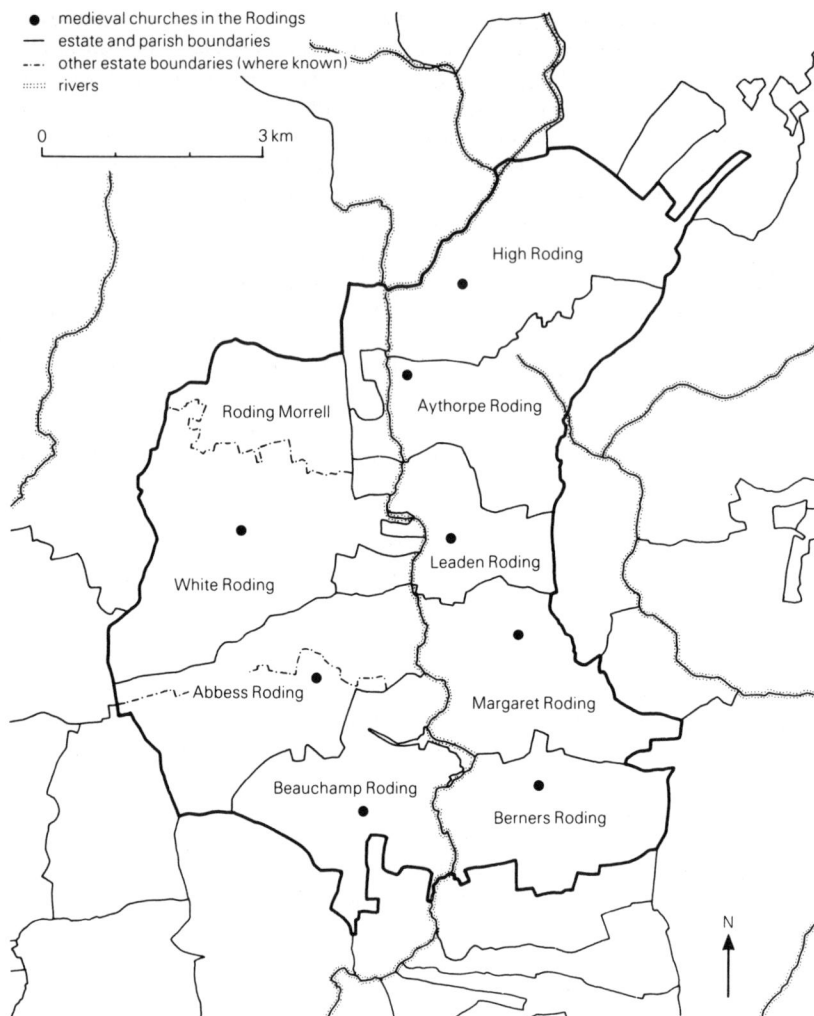

Figure 1.11. The Rodings area of west-central Essex. (Parish boundaries as shown by the 1st edn. O.S. Six Inch Survey.)

composition. It is likely that this would lead in time to the emergence of a tribe (i.e. extended family) identifiable as the dominant group within that district. Doubtless not all inhabitants of the district may have been members, but they would increasingly become identified with the tribe by the world beyond. Indeed a growing sense of territorial identity might lead it to project its history further back in time than it was entitled to do (a common enough trait among self-aware groups that are developing political control).

The district that was the tribe's settlement area would therefore (according to the hypothetical scenario) comprise the land of a number of former estates. Its limits would often coincide very closely with the common boundary of those estates, i.e. where old boundaries had been consciously retained, or else where there had been minimum shrinkage of land in regular agricultural use. Sometimes its limits would lie well inside that external boundary for one reason or another (but usually because of the abandonment of land in circumstances of a much reduced demand for surplus agricultural produce). Where that was so, there would no doubt at first be vacant land between tribal settlement areas; it would soon be absorbed, however, as often as not to a line more or less that of the common external boundary of the formerly separate estates. Within these emergent settlement areas, it is suggested, the *internal* Roman boundaries would decrease in importance, though no doubt some parts of them would be perpetuated (or revived) in whatever internal divisions the areas may have had – the divisions which would become those of townships, and which would eventually be re-established in many instances once the process of fragmentation began.[63]

Of course not all the peoples of this sort of whom we know from early sources, and in particular from -*ingas* placenames, would have been ones of the size of the *Stoppingas* and *Hrothingas*. Some would undoubtedly have been smaller, representing the cadet branches which developed distinctive self-awareness within an enlarging tribe (becoming in the process identified with one part of the settlement area, a future township).

So how did kingdoms first come into being in Anglo-Saxon England? Two ideal types of formation can be proposed (though they are not necessarily the only two types). The first involves the steady coalescence of adjacent settlement areas, a process accompanied by the translation of the leaders of dominant tribes into kings. This will have been well advanced long before the end of the Migration Period, though at different rates of speed in different areas; and it could no doubt have begun long before there were Anglo-Saxons in the area. The second type involves the takeover, by an outside group, of an existing territory in the early post-Roman period.

The first ideal type proposes that kingship is likely to have evolved in many instances through the development of increasingly hierarchical leadership within the larger extended families. Sometimes it would have lain at the end of a process starting with the leadership of a family being held by its most senior suitable members in partnership. The evidence we see of multiple kingship in some early Anglo-Saxon contexts may well reflect such an origin.[64] Otherwise, or eventually, a single leader might emerge, not necessarily through his own determination rather than by popular selection. So, wherever that man's powers customarily passed first, on his death, to younger members of his generation, before his own sons got their turn, we may again be seeing a form of kingship with its origins in the extended family.[65] There are good Irish parallels for this.[66] No doubt some dynasties were formed by men operating outside the normal rules of society – people epitomized by Stenton's comment on Penda of Mercia: 'for all that is known to the contrary, he may have been merely a landless noble of the Mercian royal house fighting for his own hand.'[67] Men of that sort (though I do not accept that Penda was one of them) would have satisfied their ambitions by forcibly installing themselves at the head of tribal communities of the sort I have been describing.

The process of state formation presumably began in earnest when the settlement areas of these communities started to coalesce. Once adjacent ones were contiguous and resources became the object of determined competition, or once inter-community rivalry became socially entrenched for other reasons, then the process of amalgamation would begin.[68] Some areas would be conquered by their neighbours, and their lands and goods absorbed. The successful leaders would quickly become 'the best of earthly kings . . . the best of those who bestowed gold', and every fighting man of the community a 'warrior, proudly adorned with gold . . . exulting in his treasure'.[69] On a different social plane, intermarriage would play an important if less dramatic part.

At different rates in different areas, but equally inexorably, this slow steady process would have been under way from well within the Migration Period. Each stage was represented by the further aggrandizement of the successful at the expense of their weaker neighbours. Amalgamation did not need to progress far before family leadership in an original settlement area would be transformed among the fittest into full-blown kingship of Offa's and Alfred's sort. By then it would be attended by an aristocracy composed of members of cadet branches of the ruling dynasty or, on occasion, representatives of other, absorbed, families whose services could be retained as local governors in their own once independent settlement areas. The etymology of Old English *cyning* could cover all these stages. It may have originally meant 'son of the family' with special reference to its ruling line.[70] Eventually *cyning* became synonymous with 'king' in its modern sense, a monarch whose power is in no sense representative.

Of course there is nothing particularly new about many aspects of this first ideal type of formation; several of them are antediluvian to a degree. But they are ripe for renewed consideration. Our views on what happened in lowland Britain in the Migration Period have changed a great deal in recent decades.[71] In particular we have made progress in understanding what 'the transition from Roman Britain to Anglo-Saxon England' meant to local societies. The new input from medieval archaeology and placename studies, and most recently from landscape history, should force us to look at such old ideas again. Some of them are well worth reviving, not least those relating to the creation of new extended families during the Migration Period, each eventually having its own recognizable settlement area.

On occasion, however, a quite different mechanism could be involved in the creation of an Anglo-Saxon kingdom. This – the second of the two ideal types outlined above (p. 22) – is the takeover of an existing post-Roman (i.e. British) territory of one sort or another by an outside group. Some of these outsiders would perhaps have been mercenaries, hired in the first instance by civilian authorities whom they eventually succeeded, or supplanted, as wielders of whatever political authority the central settlement still retained over its hinterland. Suggestions of this sort in respect of Canterbury, Winchester, and York have been put forward at different times in studies of the origins of Kent, Wessex, and Deira respectively.[72] Similarly the kingdom of the East Saxons may represent a transmutation of the late Roman *civitas* of the Trinovantes into an Anglo-Saxon state.[73] (Within it settlement areas such as that of the *Hrothingas* would doubtless have evolved as they did elsewhere, but would presumably not have been allowed to coalesce.)

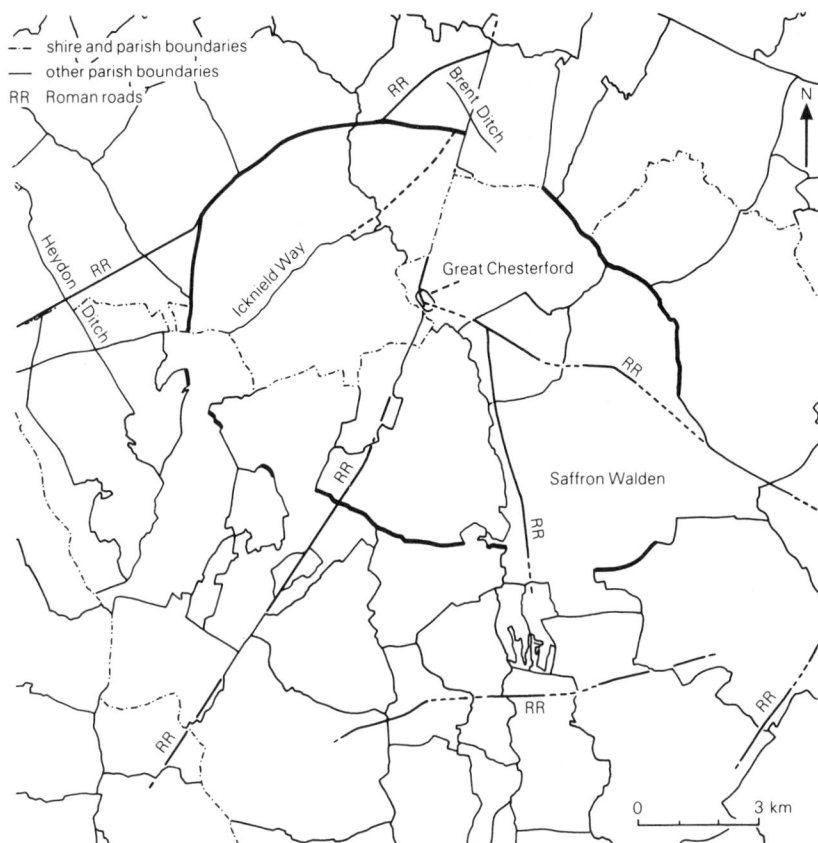

Figure 1.12. Parishes in the vicinity of Great Chesterford on the Essex-Cambridgeshire border. (Parish boundaries as shown by the 1st edn. O.S. Six Inch Survey.)

Elsewhere there may have been a takeover (by new immigrants or by a settled community nearby) of a former Romano-British town and its immediate hinterland. In the main such occurrences are only likely to be detected through topographical studies. A good example is provided by the small walled Roman town at Great Chesterford on the north-western border of the county of Essex.[74] Its cemeteries[75] appear to show a peaceful fusion of the town's latest Roman population and a group of Germanic newcomers, many of them perhaps mercenaries. Ecclesiastical parish boundaries (fig. 1.12) still perpetuate the outlines of a territory of sorts around the town which, it can be shown, must be of late Roman or immediately post-Roman creation. Just to the south of it is Bonhunt, which has a Latin loanword in its name.[76] Here Keith Wade has excavated a high status middle Saxon settlement[77] which can be identified as a royal *tun*. The associated land-unit has been rediscovered from later evidence;[78] and the close topographical relationship it bears to Great Chesterford and its encircling territory cannot be due to mere coincidence. The settlement and land-unit of Bonhunt were evidently developed in relation to them, and the inhabitants of Bonhunt were presumably already (or would soon be) in control of the town and its hinterland. This example is of something superficially very different from the settlement areas of extended families which have been described here, but it is without doubt of similar significance in terms of the earliest stages of state formation.

In conclusion, then, what are we to make of early kingdoms and their equivalents which were of such differing sizes and political importance, yet all similarly referred to as *provinciae* and *regiones*? Can there be a general explanation of their origins which holds good for the whole of Anglo-Saxon England? James Campbell helped greatly by posing this question accurately for the first time, and went quite a way to providing an answer to it: he suggested that the ambivalences he found in the meaning of *provincia* and *regio* in Bede's Ecclesiastical History – or what he called the 'messiness and ambiguities' of Bede's use of them – reflected 'something of the world he described'.[79] One can go further. Bede, reviewing the political events of the century and a half before 731, was looking at the processes of Anglo-Saxon state formation in action. He was, to introduce a new metaphor, watching the earlier rounds of a fiercely contested knock-out competition.

This metaphor is worth developing, since it seems particularly helpful in understanding the origins of Anglo-Saxon kingdoms. As we have seen in the case of the Hwicce, it is usually possible to map the approximate extents of middle Saxon dioceses and thereby to discover something of the outlines of English political geography in the late seventh century. That is the first time when we have written sources to show us the knock-out competition in progress. The document called the Tribal Hidage probably belongs then or not long afterwards. It is like the *Sports Pink* newspaper which reports the winners of, say, the fifth round of the F.A. Cup. Most of the little teams have long gone; there are a few potential giant-killers left – the Spalda, the Arosætna, the East and West Willa[80] – survivors only because they have so far avoided being drawn against the major teams. But the next round will see them off; they have had their brief moment of glory and no more will be heard of them.

These recent casualties are, of course, the larger of those discrete areas with some considerable political autonomy which will continue to exist as major and identifiable administrative subdivisions within the well-known historical kingdoms. They are, for instance, the many distinct groups in the Tribal Hidage which are together styled the Middle Angles in other sources. Previous rounds of the knock-out competition have seen off what may be no more than embryonic kingdoms, such as the area which eventually became Winchcombe-shire – an area jealously protected by the ruling dynasty of the Hwicce, who presumably had begun building their kingdom from a home base at Winch-combe. There are other possible casualties of earlier rounds that one might suggest: for example, the 'north folk' and the 'south folk' of the kingdom of East Anglia, each of them still important enough for much of the seventh century to merit its own bishop, and each likely to have produced some of the kings of East Anglia from amongst its own formerly independent royal dynasty.[81]

From the end of the seventh century the competition proceeds apace as the number of Anglo-Saxon kingdoms steadily declines, and the most active and successful of the survivors grow mightily in size. On the eve of the Cup Final Mercia is hot favourite to take the prize. But suddenly the clever money switches to Wessex, as serious crowd troubles in the eastern half of England throw the Mercians right off their game. And so the West Saxons, through blatant gamesmanship and scoring fewer own goals, win the final game and carry off as their trophy a united kingdom of England.

Thus ended a competition which had lasted for three to four centuries, and whose earlier rounds passed entirely unrecorded. But the historical materials are to hand with which we can rediscover them, if we are prepared to go far enough beyond the written sources in our search for the origins of Anglo-Saxon kingdoms.

2 Early medieval kingships in the British Isles

THOMAS CHARLES-EDWARDS

In the early Middle Ages powerful forces were at work to limit the spatial extent of effective political authority. These forces are seen at their clearest in Ireland; indeed Irish historians have been at pains to stress the primacy of the small-scale kingdom with undeveloped administrative resources, whereas in England the historical limelight has often been monopolized by the major kingdoms.[1] Patrick Wormald has, however, recently maintained in a courageous and penetrating article that the oddness of Celtic kingship has been exaggerated.[2] Once the different emphases of the surviving evidence have been taken into account, the reality, he suggests, was not so very different in Ireland, Wales or England. I shall skirt round issues of ideology and of the origins of institutions so as to confine myself to two themes central to our understanding of early medieval kingship and to the relationship between small and large political units: royal food renders and dynastic segmentation.

FOOD RENDERS AND THE ROYAL CIRCUIT

In the whole of the British Isles all but very minor kings kept on the move in order to survive: itineration was an essential economic basis of kingship. No large household could stay in one place for more than a few weeks without a long-distance trade in all essential foodstuffs. Such a trade had sustained major capitals in the Roman Empire, above all Rome itself and Constantinople, but away from the sea and major rivers there was, even in the heyday of the Empire, very little movement of food beyond local markets.[3] This was not a matter of coinage; in Ireland before the Vikings there was no native coinage, but silver and to some extent gold were used, alongside cattle and slaves, as media of exchange, being valued according to weight.[4] The same appears to have been true of Celtic Britain.[5] But, with coins or without coins, it made much more sense to take a royal household to the food rather than the food to the royal household. In Ireland and in Wales this itineration was known as the king's circuit.

The king's circuit might be organized in two ways. On the one hand, the king might have his own halls and appurtenant buildings distributed around his kingdom – the *villae regis* of Bede are an example – or, on the other hand, he might expect to enjoy the hospitality of magnate or monastery.[6] Bede's remarks about the austere feeding provided at Lindisfarne for secular magnates and even the king himself in the days of Aidan, Fínán and Colmán suggest that in 731 monasteries were expected to offer more ample fare.[7] Bede's kings, therefore, lived partly on the food renders collected at their own *villae*, partly on the hospitality of others. The alienation of land to the Church did not necessarily make much difference to the pattern of the circuit.

It must be admitted that our sources for seventh- and eighth-century England never quite give us a grandstand view of the royal circuit, but sideways glances are to be obtained from many texts including charters, laws and narrative sources.[8] I shall take it for granted that the institution existed and go on to examine its ramifications.

The king's circuit allowed men to approach the king. The young Wilfrid, when he came to the age of 14, left home and went to be presented to Eanfled, Oswiu's queen and Edwin's daughter.[9] He could do this partly because he had received arms, horses and clothing for himself and for his servants so that he could properly stand in the royal presence, but also because he had, as a boy, ministered to *regales socii*, noble companions of the king, in his father's house. It was they who recommended and presented him to Eanfled. The movement of kings, queens and their households could thus establish links with local noble families and offer local ambition its opportunity to place its sons in the royal household. It also gave the royal household powerful leverage: the young aspirant to a noble career must pass its test of arms, clothing, horses and attendants. Even for someone of the self-confidence of the young Wilfrid, the approach was best conducted indirectly by the intercession of noble patrons in the household. Such men, therefore, had ample opportunity to confer favour. The young Wilfrid came to court up a ladder of benefit and counter-benefit.

As soon as kingdoms grew beyond a certain size, the king's circuit could no longer embrace the whole territory with ease. Though Paulinus might accompany Edwin and his queen to Yeavering in Bernicia and stay for over a month in the *villa regis*, or go with Edwin to Littleborough in Lindsey, he stayed more often with the king in Deira.[10] Edwin belonged to the Deiran dynasty and appears to have spent more time there than in his outlying territories south of the Humber or north of the Tees. This preference for Deira was no doubt political, but also there had to be a limit to how many loaves of bread, vats of honey, ambers of ale, wethers, geese, hens, cheeses and other foodstuffs the households of the king and the queen could consume in a year. A choice might have to be made and the pattern of a king's circuit may thus enable us to distinguish between the core of a kingdom and its periphery; in the core the king and his household will itinerate regularly, in the periphery occasionally. It is very clear, for example, that the core of Charlemagne's territories lay in Austrasia; most of the lands in his empire were visited rarely, if at all, and then usually by the king on campaign, not at peace.[11] In just the same way the core of Edwin's dominions lay in his ancestral kingdom of Deira.

Some kings subdued territory in which they probably never had an established circuit at all. Ecgfrith received tribute from Mercia for a few years in the 670s, just as Oswiu had exacted tribute from the Picts and the Irish of Dál Riata.[12] These are cases of tribute taken from the people of another kingdom even though there were still native rulers. Such tribute was perceived by both Bede and the Life of Wilfrid as making the conquered people servile.[13] I suspect that the reason for this was not merely that the tribute was paid to an alien king, though that was part of it, but also that the tribute was of a different character from normal food renders paid to a native ruler. The food rents said in the late seventh-century West Saxon laws of Ine to have been due from ten hides may plausibly be thought of as a royal food render.[14] If so, they roughly reflect the ordinary diet, for they comprise both a grain and a meat element, both solid food and drink. The simplest division of early medieval food renders was into bread, *panis*, an accompaniment to bread, *companaticum* or *pulmentum*, and drink, *potus*. Ine's food render has items under all three hea 'ings. But the tribute paid by the Saxons to the Franks in the late sixth and early eventh centuries is said by Fredegar to have consisted of 500 cows.[15] As late as the twelfth century the tributes paid by Welsh kings to their Anglo-Norman or Angevin overlord consisted of so many hundreds of cows.[16] When such tributes came to table they would have been only *companaticum*, either meat or dairy products.

The distinction these scraps of evidence suggest is a simple one: in an economic regime of food renders a king will receive renders within his own kingdom which reflect all the broad categories into which the contemporary diet was divided; but from outside his kingdom he will usually receive livestock as tribute. The reason is not far to seek. Within his own kingdom a king goes on circuit with his household and must be maintained by food renders which are likely to meet all their main needs. But he will not normally go on circuit round the territory of another people in only loose subjection to him, even though they owe him tribute. In this case, then, the food must come to him since he will not go to the food. The only convenient way in which this can be done is to make the food travel on its own hoofs – that is to say, it must be livestock.

When the Mercians paid tribute to Ecgfrith in the 670s, they may well, therefore, have paid it in the form of livestock, just as the Thuringians were still expected to pay 500 pigs each year to the Saxon emperor at the beginning of the eleventh century.[17] Refusal to pay might only lead to the tribute being taken forcibly in a cattle raid. In Celtic countries there appears to have been a close relationship between cattle tribute and cattle raid. At irregular intervals the Uí Néill tried to enforce the cattle tribute due from the Leinstermen by means of invasions leading to the forcible removal of cattle.[18] It was the recognized custom for a new king to establish his position as overlord by means of a *crech ríg* or royal cattle raid.[19] Similarly, in Northumbria one reason for Ecgfrith's use of small forces of horsemen in operations against the Picts may have been the intention of carrying off cattle so as to compel the payment of tribute.[20] When, therefore, early Welsh poetry praises a king as 'a driver of cattle', it is thinking no doubt of the cattle raid, but perhaps also of the imposition of cattle tribute. Thus a poem in praise of Cadwallon, the killer of Edwin and victim of Oswald, declares that Cadwallon's cattle have not bellowed before the goads, or spear points, of Edwin's men, implying successful rejection of the demands for tribute which Edwin made in the days of his power.[21] In the tenth century a poem, probably composed to urge the Welsh to rise up against Athelstan, denounces the tributes paid to the officials of the overking and prophesies a turning of the tables on the English. The Welsh will be led by 'two conquerors of the Saxons . . . two noble raiders of a country's cattle'.[22] No more will the English feast at the expense of the Welsh but rather the Welsh will gather to the ale feast.[23] The association of cattle raid and cattle tribute thus accentuated the military subjection, even humiliation, of the people compelled to pay such renders. They paid an emblem of military defeat.

Furthermore, cattle tribute was probably demanded every year, whereas ordinary food renders could hardly have been exacted unless a royal household actually appeared to eat them. Before *c.* 700 I doubt whether one had to pay the *feorm* of one night unless a royal household was there to be fed. The normal kind of food render, embracing the whole diet, could hardly be transported far, so that, if no one appeared to eat it, that was presumably the end of the obligation for that year. Whereas cattle tribute was pure tax, ordinary food renders thus retained an honourable link with hospitality.

A regime of food renders, therefore, was common to the Celtic and Germanic parts of the British Isles in the centuries after the departure of the Roman army and Roman mints. It was a regime in which primary kingship, as opposed to military hegemony, was naturally small-scale. Moreover only small-scale kingship could be honourable to king and subject alike. Only in the core of their territories could even the wielders of military hegemonies be seen frequently, travelling round on circuit. Only in the core, therefore, was the obligation to feed the king and his household matched by frequent access to his presence and his favour. In the periphery rarer visits made both the burdens and the rewards less important. Finally, beyond the boundaries of the royal circuit, in lands where the overking only came with an army at his back, livestock had to be paid as tribute without the compensation for the nobility of normal access to the royal household. The suggested pattern is thus threefold: in the core of his territories an overking is often seen and often maintained; in the periphery he is little seen but also little maintained; in his subject kingdoms he is hardly ever seen in peace, but his tribute departs on the hoof every year. This third relationship is understandably seen as servile, for the exchange is all one way.

Though this model is helpful, it is oversimplified, since it suggests that there was only one royal household which went on circuit. For seventh-century Northumbria, at least, this assumption is false. First, there is clear evidence that the queen sometimes had a separate household from that of the king. The Life of Wilfrid suggests that Eanfled, the wife of Oswiu, acted as a focus of noble loyalty distinct from that of her husband. Wilfrid as a boy left home and went to her rather than to Oswiu.[24] His early career appears to have been mainly under her patronage rather than that of the king.[25] Before 664 she and her household could celebrate Easter at a different time from that adopted by the king.[26] Then there are also sub-kings and joint-kings. When Wilfrid celebrated the consecration of his new church at Ripon at some time in the 670s, he invited the *reges* (the brothers Ecgfrith and Ælfwine) and also *subreguli.*[27] Moreover, the Life of Wilfrid inserts between the *reges* and the *subreguli* a further category, that of the *praefecti.* The latter are evidently considerable men, whose status can easily be grossly underestimated if *praefectus* is translated 'reeve'. One *praefectus*, Berhtfrith, was in charge of military operations against the Picts in 711.[28] Presumably the same Berhtfrith was described by the Life of Wilfrid as *secundus a rege princeps,* 'a leader second in rank to the king', and as being the first to give his advice at the council by the River Nidd in 706.[29] Berhtred, who died fighting against the Picts in 698 as a *dux regius,* may have been a brother or kinsman to judge by his name, rank and sphere of operation.[30] Berhtred has been shown to be identical with the Berht who led an army to Ireland in 684.[31] Irish annals, probably deriving from the Iona Chronicle, give his father's name as Beornheth; he is likely to be the person of that name described by the Life of Wilfrid as a *subregulus* and as aiding Ecgfrith against the Picts in the 670s.[32] It is very possible that these men, *subreguli*, *praefecti* or *duces regii*, provided the main royal presence in Lothian and had the right to a local royal circuit. In Northumbria, therefore, there was not just one person, the king, ma intaining himself and his household through the regime of food renders and the royal circuit. There were also the queen, sub-kings, royal *duces* and *praefecti*.

Some of these royal or semi-royal figures had local associations. I have already suggested as much for Berhtfrith, Berhtred and the latter's father Beornheth. The sphere of authority of Alhfrith, Oswiu's eldest son and for a time his joint-king, appears to have been within the kingdom of Deira or coterminous with it.[33] Since the queen sometimes had a separate household it is possible that Rhiainfellt, Oswiu's British wife, provided a focus of loyalty for the British nobility of Rheged after it had been incorporated into Northumbria.[34] Similarly, Eanfled, the daughter of the Deiran Edwin, may have offered a natural point of access to royal favour for the Deiran nobles after the death of their native king Oswine. Such queens were in a position – being necessarily allied to the Bernician king though not themselves of the Bernician dynasty – to ease the transition between outright hostility to Bernician rule and incorporation into a united Northumbria. There were therefore ways, whether through under-kings, joint-kings, *praefecti* or queens, for separate loyalties to be accommodated. The unity of the kingdom was sometimes threatened by secondary royal households, as shown by Oswiu's difficulties with his nephew Ethelwald and his son Alhfrith.[35] Nor is it surprising that Wilfrid's 'ecclesiastical kingdom' should make even so powerful a ruler as Ecgfrith nervous.[36] But it appears to have been preferable to run such risks rather than have one household attempting to provide access to royal presence and favour for the nobility of all Northumbria.

A further oversimplification in the model of the political structure of a kingdom such as Northumbria is that it has been assumed that kings simply lived off food renders and hospitality. By the end of Bede's lifetime this was already untrue. The clearest evidence is provided by Bede's letter to Ecgberht, bishop, and shortly to be archbishop, of York, written in 734. Ecgberht was a member of the royal kindred; his brother would succeed to the throne in 737.[37] Bede looks forward to the day when Ecgberht can rule Northumbria as a metropolitan with twelve bishops under him, for only so will it be possible for all villages to receive an episcopal visitation once a year.[38] But, though this is indirect confirmation of the suggestion that no Northumbrian king could go on circuit round all of his territories, Bede adds that even villages in the mountains, which have never seen a bishop for several years, pay episcopal *tributa*.[39] It is thus possible to pay tribute even if the recipient is not present to consume food renders on the spot. Perhaps such tribute may have taken the form of cattle or other livestock, especially since the villages lay in the mountains where livestock farming is likely to have been important. In that event upland areas were being treated almost as if they were subject kingdoms. But it is also possible that the Northumbrian coinage, some of which was minted for Ecgberht himself, may have been used to exact such tribute.[40] In that case the upland villages will presumably have had to sell some of their cattle in lowland markets in order to acquire the necessary cash. Tribute may thus have stimulated inter-regional trade. In any event trade and coinage were already making an impact in Bede's own lifetime on the economic basis of kingship.

Much of this picture may be true for early medieval Wales, though the evidence is pitifully slight. The sources do not become tolerably informative until the twelfth century, which in Wales is the last century in which a regime of food renders predominates. One or two scraps of evidence from the documents written into the Lichfield Gospels, probably in the ninth century, and from the charters appended to the Life of Saint Cadog indicate that the pattern of food renders revealed in the later laws goes back in its essentials before the Norman invasion.[41] Here also there are two main categories: hospitality owed to the king or queen and food renders paid to a royal centre.[42] The same pattern obtains for the Church: the abbot of St Illtud's church is said, in his twelfth-century *vita*, to have received *annua tributa* and also to have been entertained to *annua convivia*.[43] Compulsory billeting of royal servants is clearly separated from hospitality dues for, while hospitality is an honourable obligation, servants are billeted on bondmen.[44] By the twelfth century hospitality dues appear to have been largely converted into food renders paid to the royal hall which was the focus of the commote, the local administrative district. By then the king went on circuit largely round his own halls, whereas at an earlier date hospitality provided by the nobles was of greater importance.

In general, however, the difference between the economic bases of Anglo-Saxon and Celtic kingships cannot be understood until we have tackled our second theme, the structure of royal dynasties. This can best be approached by taking first the situation in Ireland.

THE STRUCTURE OF ROYAL DYNASTIES

The Irish perception of political units is much more dynastic than the English and rather more so than the Welsh. Kingdoms and peoples are regularly identified by means of their ruling dynasties.[45] Thus a kingdom on the Irish sea coast of Leinster is known as 'The Descendants of Enechglas', Uí Enechglais, the name of its royal kindred.[46] Such royal kindreds are sometimes mobile. The earliest evidence for the Uí Enechglais is an inscription whose language would fit the fifth century recording the burial of a certain MacCaírthinn, descendant of Enechglas (MAQI CAIRATINI AVI INEQAGLASI).[47] The site of this inscription is, however, close to the River Boyne, well to the north of the early medieval province of Leinster.

In England, by contrast, names of kingdoms are normally those of peoples or subdivisions of peoples rather than of dynasties; for example Mierce, East Engle. Some have been inherited from the Romano-British past, such as Lindsey, but most are entirely Germanic. It is strange that when one turns to such texts as Beowulf or, still more, Widsith, it appears as though the Germanic world from which the English had migrated was full of kingdoms named after dynasties.[48] To give just one example, the Danes ruled over by Hrothgar are the Scyldingas, named after the dynasty descended from the legendary Scyld Scefing, whereas in The Fight at Finnesburh there is another kingdom, focused upon its ruling dynasty the Hocingas.[49] The way of distinguishing kingdoms whose population consists of only part of a people such as the Danes is thus to refer to the people of the kingdom by the name of the ruling dynasty. There are similarly named dynasties in England – the Oiscingas of Kent, Wuffingas of East Anglia and the Iclingas of Mercia – but apparently these dynastic names were not applied to the relevant kingdoms, even though they formed part of such peoples as the Engle, just as the Hocingas were part of the Dene.[50] This is particularly strange if the ethnicity of the people was ever a consequence of the ethnicity of the dynasty, that is to say, if a mixed immigrant population came to be regarded as, say, Anglian because the dynasty was Anglian.[51] Given this disparity between the English and continental Germanic worlds, it may be important that names of the Hocingas type are common among the smaller groupings recorded in the Tribal Hidage and elsewhere, for example the Feppingas.[52]

In Ireland there is a clear distinction between major population groups (corresponding to the Angles or the Saxons in Britain) and the populations of kingdoms (corresponding, say, to the Hwicce in England). In the seventh century Irishmen seem to have thought that there were three main peoples in Ireland: the Féni, the Ulaid (men of Ulster) and the Laigin (Leinstermen).[53] If we take the most extreme case, that of the Féni, it is possible to enumerate dozens of separate kingdoms among the one people. Moreover, there was no single overking who exercised authority over them all. The sense of identity of the Féni is quite independent of kingship. It may be compared with the sense of identity of the Anglians of Bede's day, for they too recognized no single overking.

What created and preserved small kingdoms among the seventh-century Irish was a combination of geography and dynastic segmentation.[54] The primary base of the typical Irish king was a territory of small extent, often a single area of well-cleared land, called a *mag* or *campus*. Thus in Inishowen, on the north-west side of Lough Foyle, there is one kingdom in Mag Tóchuir and another in the Brétach, the coastal strip running along the side of the lough.[55] Larger political units such as Cenél nÉogain (fig. 2.1) were conglomerations of such small kingdoms with client kings subordinated to an overking (*ruiri*, 'great king'). Topography made small basic units inevitable, but it did not ensure that they retained the status of distinct kingdoms. A principal reason for the fragmentation of power was the tendency of dynasties to split up into distinct branches which then took control of separate small territories. If a dynasty acquired power over several small territories, its success would not lead to the formation of a unitary kingdom embracing all the conquered lands. Instead it enabled the dynasty to maintain the royal status of more of its branches as kings of small kingdoms. I shall take one outstanding example to illustrate the point: Cenél nÉogain, 'the kindred of Éogan'. The distribution of kingdoms belonging to Cenél nÉogain on the map has been reconstructed on the basis partly of hagiographical evidence, Tírechán in the seventh century and the Tripartite Life *c.* 900, partly on the basis of a genealogical tract no earlier than *c.* 1000.[56] The evidence is not all as strong as one could wish, but even the genealogies can be corroborated to some extent.

Once they have been put up against the hagiographical and the annalistic

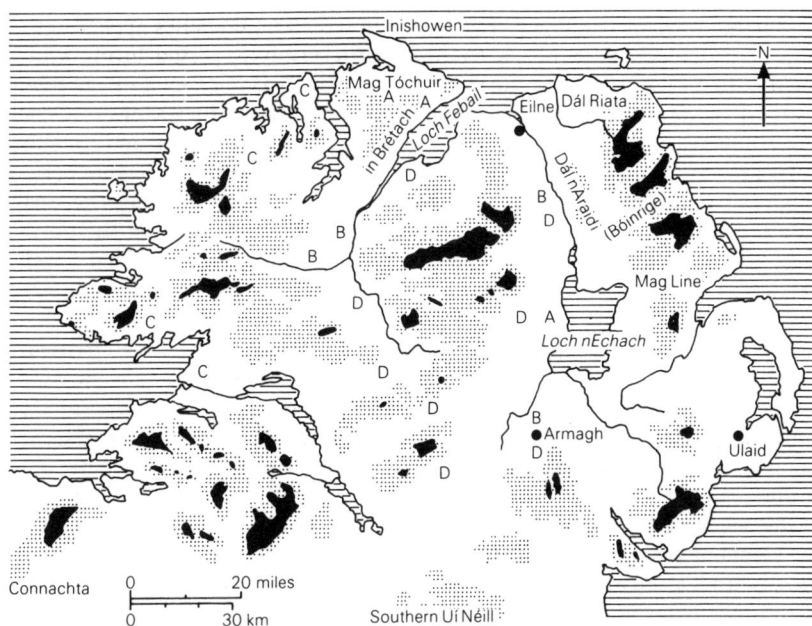

Figure 2.1. Northern Ireland *c.* 900. A = kingdoms of Cenél nÉogain ruled
by early branches of the dynasty; B = kingdoms of Cenél nÉogain ruled by
late branches of the dynasty; C = kingdoms of Cenél Conaill; D = kingdoms
of the Airgialla.

sources, the genealogies tell an interesting tale. By the late seventh century it
was accepted that Éogan, the eponymous ancestor of Cenél nÉogain, was one
of the sons of Niall, whom the Uí Néill, 'descendants of Niall', claimed as their
common ancestor.[57] Branches of the Uí Néill ruled kingdoms in an arc from
Inishowen in the north to Brega between the Liffey and the Boyne. They thus
dominated the basin of the Foyle and also the Midlands from the Shannon to
the Irish Sea. Cenél nÉogain was ultimately the most successful branch of the
northern Uí Néill. Whether their pedigree from Niall was genuine does not for
the moment matter at all. Their political stance in the seventh century and
thereafter was that they were a branch of the Uí Néill. They are in any case a
splendid example of an expanding dynasty.

The territorial conquests of Cenél nÉogain may be summarized in the phrase
'from Inishowen to Tyrone'.[58] Inishowen up in the far north-west is Inis
Eóghain, 'the island/peninsula of Eóghan'. It is named dynastically after the
eponymous ancestor. So too is Tyrone, Tír Eóghain, 'the land of Eóghan'. This,
however, is a considerably later name and came into existence only as a result
of territorial aggrandizement in the period from the eighth to the tenth
century. On fig. 2.1 are distinguished two phases of expansion, A and B. In the
genealogies the ruling families of the A kingdoms are in general early branches,
in other words relatively remote collaterals of the overking of Cenél nÉogain.
Cenél nÉogain appears to the genealogists like a tree from whose main branch
there were several branches near the base, then nothing for a bit until, higher

up, further branches emerged. The period in which no branches appear in the genealogical record coincides with the seventh century, a period during which the dominant power among the northern Uí Néill was not Cenél nÉogain but its rival Cenél Conaill. During much of the seventh century kings of Cenél Conaill were, indeed, the leading rulers among all the Uí Néill, and thus the most powerful kings in the northern half of the country. At the same period abbots of Iona were normally members of Cenél Conaill.[59] From the early eighth century, however, Cenél Conaill lost its predominance in the north-west to Cenél nÉogain and the latter then resumed its expansion south-eastwards at the expense of the Airgialla; thus it created, in the long run, Tyrone.

The most important lesson to derive from this story is that territorial expansion and dynastic segmentation – or branching – went hand in hand. Royal kindreds segmented in the genealogical record because they were able to confer high status on their branches; in the extreme case, such as that of Cenél nÉogain, it had to be royal status. When, therefore, Cenél nÉogain was not able to conquer new kingdoms, its collateral branches lost status and so passed out of the genealogical record. This is the reason for the curious pattern by which the Cenél nÉogain genealogical tree branched near the bottom, then not at all for a period, after which it branched vigorously. It is clear from all this that Irish royal dynasties could expand as much as any Anglo-Saxon counterpart, but that their need to maintain the status of as many as possible of their branches ensured that the primary kingdoms remained small.

The same phenomenon can be exemplified further east, in the lands running from north to south on the eastern side of the River Bann, namely the territories of the Cruithni (or Cruithin).[60] Here the most powerful dynasty was the ruling kindred of Mag Line, the valley of the Antrim Water running down to Lough Neagh. It is a good example of a primary kingdom. But by the mid- to late seventh century it had expanded to the north to incorporate the neighbour-ing kingdom of Bóinrige. It was in Bóinrige that seventh-century Patrician writers proposed to place the period of Patrick's slavery.[61] They could do so because it was an eminent example of a kingdom which had perished, a fitting end for a land whose druid king had held Patrick in slavery and defied Christianity. In the course of the seventh century the kingdom of Eilne further north between Bann and Bush also fell under the control of the dynasty of Mag Line.[62] They installed a collateral branch to rule the new acquisition, whereas Bóinrige appears to have been incorporated into Mag Line. The secular subjection of Eilne brought an ecclesiastical subjection in its train. Adomnán knows of a bishop of Coleraine (Cúl Raithin) in the time of Columba, but, according to Tírechán, it no longer had a bishop in the second half of the seventh century and many of its churches were now subject to the church of Connor to the south, within the sphere of the king of Mag Line.[63] The ecclesiastical dominance of Eilne by Connor is likely to have helped the king of Mag Line to maintain the client status of his kinsman the king of Eilne.

In Ireland, then, dynasties expanded only to segment, whereas the rulers of expanding English kingdoms were careful to deny the royal aspirations of their fellow kinsmen. Admittedly the contrast is not absolute. Some collateral lines of the Bernician dynasty survived with enough of a power base somewhere so that they were able to take the kingship in the eighth century after having been excluded for over a century.[64] Several lines of the royal kindreds of Wessex and of Mercia disputed the succession in the seventh and eighth centuries.[65] We have already met joint-kingship and *subreguli*; fragmented kingship is also attested in Wessex between 672 and 685.[66] Earlier Cenwalh had been obliged to concede a royal appanage within Wessex to his brother's son Cuthred.[67] Yet the general tendency is to maintain a united kingship.

St Guthlac is a good example of a member of the royal kindred of Mercia, an Icling, who tried but failed to gain the kingship. The method was to recruit a warband or *comitatus* and use it to raid neighbouring kingdoms.[68] For some, such as the West Saxon Cædwalla or the Mercian Penda, this was the way to royal power.[69] Guthlac was less successful and turned to the life of a hermit. His failure is all the more instructive because the main resources of his father Penwalh lay not in Mercia proper but among the Middle Angles.[70] Penwalh flourished in the days of Æthelred (675–704), in other words in a crucial period of Mercian expansion. Penwalh's career, as an Icling and yet also a Middle Anglian magnate, must lie at the centre of the story of Mercian expansion to the south-east. If he had been an Irishman, he would very probably have been a king, subordinate to the king of the Mercians but with his own territory. Yet Guthlac's ambition does not seem to have been directed at becoming a Middle Anglian *subregulus* or *princeps*, but rather king of the Mercians; though the descendants of Penda were in Penwalh's day dominant within the Iclingas, collateral lines would take the kingship after 716.[71] Guthlac's bid for power is perhaps a symptom of the dynastic uncertainty at that period which offered the opportunity for members of collateral branches to recover power.

Early medieval kingship was naturally small-scale. Yet there are many examples of kings whose dominions extended far beyond the compass of any royal circuit. Other men – joint rulers, client kings, *praefecti*, *duces*, *principes* – had to rule outlying provinces. Major rulers therefore had to face the problem of preserving their control over such provinces and at the same time of securing their own positions from challenge by collateral kinsmen within the royal dynasty. Kingship was as much a status with privileges as an office with duties; for members of royal dynasties it was a status enticingly close to their grasp. The boundary between royal and noble status was probably, however, drawn in one place in Ireland and in a different place in England. In Ireland the fundamental rule was that, if a man was not himself king, royal descent did not confer royal status.[72] There was no class of 'royals' enjoying royal status by birth even if they were not kings. In England, however, Mul, the brother of Cædwalla, king of the West Saxons, was regarded as of royal status even though he was not king, for the wergeld paid by the men of Kent for his killing in 687 was royal.[73] The *duces regii* of Bede are thus probably 'royal *duces*' rather than '*duces* of the king'. There may have been little, if any, difference in status between the *dux* Berhtred and his father Beornheth, *subregulus*.

If an Irish *ruiri*, 'great king', needed to gratify the desire of his kinsmen to enjoy royal status, he had to allow them the status of client kings or even the prospects, however remote, of succeeding him as *ruiri*. The first course led to the dynastic expansion and segmentation which we have seen exemplified in Cenél nÉogain; the second lay behind the succession of collaterals, the 'circuit' of the kingship 'round the branches of the kindred' often found in Irish dynasties, and the designation of royal aspirants as 'material of a king'.[74] From the point of view of these kinsmen there was every reason to exert all available pressure to secure a turn in 'the circuit round the branches of the kindred'. If a branch of a royal lineage failed to secure the kingship for two generations, they had little chance of ever gaining it again.[75] It was not, therefore, surprising if, while they retained the necessary power, they made their support for the current king conditional upon his offering them prospects of succession.

Dynastic pressures and the impossibility of effective direct rule over a wide area conspired to make Irish kings govern through client rulers and acknowledge that these client rulers possessed royal status. The same pressures were not so strong in England for an English king's kinsmen could enjoy royal status without securing the kingship itself or even the recognized prospect of kingship. It is symptomatic of these different approaches that, whereas a major Irish king might claim to be a 'great king', *ruiri*, or even a 'king of great kings', *rí ruirech*, he did not deny the claims of his client rulers to the full status of king, *rí*. In the Irish terminology the local, small-scale king is the norm; his superiors have titles based upon his (*rí→ruiri→rí ruirech*). In England the opposite approach is normal: the *rex* is the major ruler while his inferiors are imperfect kings, *subreguli*, 'royal leaders', *duces regii*, or 'chief men', *principes*. Even the Berhtfrith who is *secundus a rege* in Northumbria is a *princeps* rather than a full king.[76] This second approach does appear in Ireland, too, from the eighth century; but only client rulers who are not considered to be kinsmen of the overking are demoted to the status of *duces, toísig*.[77]

Although segmentation of the dynasty dictated the shape of Irish politics, therefore, not all client kings were collateral kinsmen of their overkings. The assumption appears to have been that those who were his kinsmen would be in a privileged position; their subjection was less onerous and more honourable. The effect of the assumption was to stimulate falsification of royal pedigrees so as to claim such privileges. An excellent example is provided by the kingdoms of the Airgialla (D in fig. 2.1). In a text, probably of the early eighth century, the Airgialla claimed kinship with the Uí Néill and set out their privileges as favoured client kings.[78] The most notable are as follows: the Uí Néill may claim military service from the Airgialla for six weeks, but only once in three years; the Airgialla are not obliged to join a hosting in spring or at harvest time; they must give hospitality to the principal kings of the Uí Néill 'when travelling the roads, except that the company of a king which extends to hundreds is not maintained'.[79] An implication is that they do not owe food renders but only limited hospitality.

From less favoured client kingdoms, however, food renders are demanded, and there is some evidence that these might take the form of payments of cattle.[80] Moreover, within their own kingdoms rulers were also able to control the landed resources of those 'subject to the king's tribute' (*sub censu regis*) and to billet their followers in the houses of their subjects.[81] The first right was the more important: those *sub censu regis* had to leave a third of their land to the king at their death and a third to the Church.[82] They may also have been subject to a share-cropping arrangement during their lifetimes.[83] Only a section of the population was singled out for such treatment.[84] In conformity with the usual genealogical scheme this semi-servile element in the population was sometimes regarded as unrelated to the ruling dynasty and its free subjects.[85] These rights were sometimes extended to subject kingdoms if they lacked such privileged status as that claimed by the Airgialla.[86]

In early Irish kingship there is a contrast between a multitude of royal prerogatives and a paucity of servants to enforce them. The contrast can be pushed too far: the Irish king had his steward, his counsellors, his royal freedmen, *amuis ríg*, his messengers, his judge.[87] Yet his prerogatives make a far more imposing list. Several are still there adorning the Scottish kingship of the twelfth and thirteenth centuries; its Irish roots were far from being an obstacle to the aspirations of David I to establish a strong royal government on contemporary lines.[88] Apart from military service, tribute and hospitality dues the Irish king has rights of purveyance, of billeting, of a share of debts enforced with his aid, of special exactions on defeated subjects. He can confer his protection (equivalent to the Germanic *mund*).[89] Road work is a public obligation (though fortress work is an obligation of royal clients not of the people as a whole).[90]

The principal differences between Ireland and England in the area of royal dues appear to be, first, that in Ireland hospitality dues were relatively more important than in England. This affected overkings, for they demanded hospitality from their client kingdoms.[91] The difference is associated with the structure of their dynasties, since hospitality predominated among client kingdoms ruled by collateral kinsmen of the overking. A highly segmented dynasty in which several branches retained royal status thus favoured hospitality dues at the expense of food renders. The Airgialla were anxious to claim that they were closely related to the Uí Néill, for it offered them a way to retain the status of favoured clients. Secondly, there is no evidence of a network of local royal centres to which food renders were delivered. On this score England and Wales agree in having such centres as against Ireland.[92]

There is therefore a very real contrast between Irish and English kingship in the seventh and eighth centuries. In both countries there were powerful reasons why political authority should have been small-scale. In Ireland these forces were decisively aided by the pattern of dynastic segmentation. This does not of itself make Ireland the odd man out in Western Europe. The Merovingians too tended to segment into distinct branches retaining royal status; so, apparently, had the Alamanni in the fourth century. The Welsh exhibit much the same pattern: the descendants of Rhodri Mawr (ob. 878) came to rule much of Wales in the tenth century, but their success only led to segmentation between a Gwynedd branch and a Dyfed branch.[93] The old kingdoms reasserted themselves. The degree of segmentation in Ireland was, however, unusual. The best guess at present is that this was the effect of a lack of a network of local royal centres such as the *villae regis* of Bede. It is notable that, while it remained west of Druim Alban, Dál Riata was as fragmented as any Irish dynasty; but as soon as one of its segments, Cenél nGabráin, had established its power over the Pictish lands north of the Forth and south-east of the Highland Line, the foundations began to be laid of a united kingdom of the Scots.[94] This, however, was in a region where local royal centres probably already existed in Pictish times.

3 The origins of barbarian kingdoms: the continental evidence

EDWARD JAMES

The presence of this chapter in a volume on Anglo-Saxon kingdoms is, I suppose, a result of the knowledge that over the last generation some of the most useful advances in our understanding of Anglo-Saxon England have been made by those who have looked at the problems from a continental viewpoint and in a continental context. I am thinking above all of Michael Wallace-Hadrill, but could also mention James Campbell or Patrick Wormald. This is not of course to deny the equally valuable approach of studying England in its British and Irish context, as has been done and is still being done by scholars such as Thomas Charles-Edwards, Wendy Davies, David Dumville, Clare Stancliffe and the ubiquitous Wormald.

> Winds of the World, give answer! They are whimpering to and fro –
> And what should they know of England, who only England know?[1]

An external viewpoint not only sets England in context and highlights its uniquenesses (if any); it also gives access to a great deal of additional source material, and shows us in the full glare (or flicker) of the sources the origins of kingdoms, which in England are concealed in the all but impenetrable gloom of Gildas and the Anglo-Saxon Chronicle. What I want to do here, therefore, is to look at a little of what we know of the origins of barbarian kingdoms on the Continent, which may shed some reflected light on conditions in England.

The first, second and third division kingdoms of the Continent in the fifth and sixth centuries (to continue Steven Bassett's football analogy, above p. 26) probably thought that the English kings were amateurs knocking a ball around in some corner of a foreign field, or hooligans looking for a game to disrupt; or, more worryingly, thought that the English were playing cricket. To change to a more appropriate sporting analogy, they despised the English for playing cricket rather than organizing chariot races. As soon as the Franks took over Provence, said Procopius with avuncular amusement, they started going to the circus at Arles. And that great Romanizing Frankish king of the sixth century, Chilperic – detested by Gregory of Tours, who thought that barbarians ought not to pretend to be anything but barbarian – built or restored circuses at Soissons and Paris. Continental kings wanted to be a part of *Romanitas*: comparisons between England and the Continent may be very unhelpful, because of the all-pervasive influence of Rome upon all those continental kingdoms about which we know anything at all.

In terms of the origins of kingdoms we may perhaps think of three main areas: the territories beyond the Rhine and in the North, where no Roman political units had been created (and where there is precious little evidence before the eighth century); west of the Rhine and south of the Danube, where Roman political units (such as *civitates*) survived; and England, where Roman political or administrative units may or may not have survived. (The problem of the possible influence of Rome upon the earliest Anglo-Saxon kingdoms, which once so exercised such scholars as Jolliffe or Finberg, has interestingly been largely side-stepped by the contributors to this volume, save in Bassett's comments on Great Chesterford and Bonhunt, above.)

The origins of kingdoms are of course inseparable from the origins of another institution, the people. To quote from Susan Reynolds's splendid book on medieval kingdoms and communities:

> A kingdom was never thought of merely as the territory which happened to be ruled by a king. It comprised and corresponded to a 'people' (*gens, natio, populus*) which was assumed to be a natural inherited community of tradition, custom, law, and descent.[2]

She is referring to conditions at the end of the early Middle Ages, and that equation is one which is only just emerging in the earlier period. But the definition and origins of the *gens, natio* or *populus* is one thing we have to think about. A second is the usage of the various words for 'king', which has actually received reasonable attention from historians. A third is the usage of words for 'kingdom', which has not. It nevertheless does surely tell us something about political concepts of the late Roman period when we realize that *regnum* can be used of the Empire as well as of a barbarian kingdom, or that *regna* was also used of the Empire or indeed of a landowner's private estates. This is perhaps just as revealing as the fact that in the Carolingian period the word in the singular could refer to a kingdom, or a duchy, or a county. 'Kingdom' is therefore a flexible term; 'king', in some senses, is even harder to pin down.

One of the first historians to study the origins of a particular barbarian kingdom, Gregory of Tours, was also the first to come up against the fact that a large part of the problem was that of translating Germanic words for Germanic institutions into Latin vocabulary – although arguably he failed to recognize the fact. Gregory, writing in the late sixth century, used now vanished fifth-century Latin historians to investigate the early history of Frankish kingship.[3] It is one of the few early medieval texts where we can see a historian attempting to compare and analyse the documents in front of him. Sulpicius Alexander, he notes, does not refer to *reges* among the Franks but *duces*. But then, Gregory says, Sulpicius writes about Marcomer and Sunno, *regales Francorum*. Gregory remarks that 'when he says *regales* we do not know whether they were kings or if they held a *regnum* in place of a king'. Later still Gregory finds that Marcomer and Sunno were called *subreguli*. Then his source Sulpicius, 'giving up all talk of *duces* and *regales*', as Thorpe's translation has it,[4] speaks of the *reges Alamannorum et Francorum*, leaving out, however, as Gregory notes with exasperation, the name of the Frankish king. Gregory found no mention of Frankish kings in his other source, Renatus Profuturus Frigeridus, and is forced to rely on tradition for what he recounts of the first kings: 'It is commonly reported that . . . the Franks crossed the Rhine . . . and set up in each *pagus* and *civitas* long-haired kings chosen from their first and, so to speak, most noble family.'

I shall return to this passage later. It introduces us to our first problem: to think what a Roman writer expected to find in a German leader before he would bestow the title *rex* on him. It is a problem that traditionally goes back to that prime source of all information, and much misinformation, on the early Germans, Tacitus. His famous phrase 'reges ex nobilitate duces ex virtute sumunt' has been repeated again and again, and variously interpreted, by modern historians: 'they take kings according to their noble birth, military leaders according to their ability.'[5] From Tacitus it is fairly clear what distinguishes a king from a temporary military leader: he is for life, he takes part in religious and political matters as well as military ones, and he comes of a royal family. But, to confuse matters, it seems likely that a successful *dux* could found a royal line or even become king himself.

It is tempting to think that the confusion in Gregory of Tours's sources results from the difficulty of Romans knowing whether the Frankish military leaders they were dealing with or fighting were military leaders purely and simply or whether they were kings in the Tacitan sense; indeed, Wallace-Hadrill remarked that these chapters in Gregory read 'rather like an unconscious gloss on the famous distinction of the Roman historian'.[6] Ammianus Marcellinus's passages referring to the Alamans or the Quadi are other pointers to the difficulty that Romans had actually relating their own political vocabulary to the Germanic reality: viz. what Edward Thompson had to say about this in *The Early Germans*.[7]

> At the battle of Strasbourg in 357 the Alamannic warriors were led by two men, Chonodomarius and his brother's son Serapio, who are not known to have held any exceptional position in time of peace. [They are called 'kings higher than all the rest in authority' by Ammianus: xvi.12.23.] Subordinate to this pair were five 'kings nearest in power' to them (*reges proximi potestate*), and an unknown number of similar 'kings' (*reges*) who took no part in the campaign: these were the leaders of the tribes (*pagi*). Under the five *reges* stood ten 'petty kings' (*regales*) whose powers and functions are unknown. Finally our authority tells how one of the *reges* invited to a banquet 'all the *reges* and *regales* and *reguli*' in his neighbourhood, though without mentioning the difference between the *regales* and the *reguli*. Similarly, among the fourth-century Quadi, we hear of a *rex*, a *regalis*, and a *subregulus* as well as optimates and judges.

This multiplication of words for royalty is, of course, very like what we meet in some of the earliest Anglo-Saxon charters – like those of Uhtred, *regulus* of the Hwicce, which are witnessed by a *rex*, a *regulus* and a *subregulus*.[8] We have no way of knowing if there was a recognized Alamannic or Anglo-Saxon vocabulary for such gradations of royalty – as there was, in the law-tracts at least, among the Irish. But we might suspect that there was, and that lesser men had rather more *royal* or *regal* aspects to them than is implied by the colourless 'ealdorman' or 'reeve' used by the Colgrave and Mynors translation of Bede's *Ecclesiastical History* for *duces regii*, *principes* or *praefecti*. Perhaps, as Bassett suggests above for the leaders of the *Husmerae* or the *Stoppingas*, such men were the 'real' kings. All these Alamannic kings had something regal about them to Roman eyes and presumably to Alamannic eyes as well. The question 'What makes someone a *king?*' is thus a crucial one, which is rarely asked by Anglo-Saxon historians, who are mostly too ready to carry on the discussion in the terminology established by Bede.

One theory which may help us understand Tacitan distinctions is that propounded by a number of historians in Germany and Austria: that Germans did indeed have two words for king. In Gothic these were *thiudans* and *reiks* (pronounced 'rix' or 'rex'). The former is the traditional king, with his concerns in religious and political as well as military matters; the latter is the military leader. Procopius said that the Ostrogoth Theodoric was a *rhix*, 'for thus barbarians are accustomed to call their leader'.[9] And in his Gothic Bible Ulfila used the word *reiks* to translate *archon*, governor or military commander, while he used *thiudans* of Christ and the Roman emperor.[10] In a West Germanic language like Old English we find a similar distinction, the theory runs, though the opposition is between *theoden*, a word rarely used, and above all of Christ, and *cyning* (later German *könig*). Beowulf is called by an amalgam of the two words on several occasions (e.g. line 2579): *thiod-cyning*. This is, Herwig Wolfram suggests, the exact equivalent of the East Germanic *thiuda-reiks* or Theodoric – one of the commonest of Germanic royal names – symbolizing the coming together of traditional royal functions with that of supreme war leader. Although in the conditions of the Migration Period it is the *reiks*-king who comes to predominate, the *thiudans*-king may have greater prestige. In Ulfila's view, after all, *thiudans* translated both earthly emperor and king of heaven.

The complexities of kingship among the Visigoths are best illustrated at the time of Athanaric.[11] When the Visigoths lived north of the Danube, said Eunapius, they were divided into various tribes – *phylai* in Greek – whose chiefs were called in Greco-Roman sources by such diminutives as *regalis*, *regulus*, *archon*, *basiliskos*. In 364, however, crisis brought a leader of the whole people to the fore, who lasted at least until the settlement of the Goths in Moesia in 382. This was Athanaric, referred to not as *basileus*, 'king', but as judge: *iudex*, *dikastes*. He was certainly not of undistinguished background; his father had been so powerful, according to Themistius, that Constantine had appeased him by erecting his statue in Constantinople.[12] But when the Romans once addressed him as king (*basileus*), he objected, saying that he should not be called 'king' but 'judge', 'for the former term implied authority, but the latter wisdom'.[13] St Ambrose called him *iudex regum*, 'judge of kings'. He clearly bore a title superior to a mere *rex*, in the same way that an emperor did, and it is probable that in Gothic he was called *thiudans*.

These distinctions of types of kingship may work for the Goths; it is not clear that they apply to other Germanic peoples on the Continent. But the discussion does usefully remind us that our one English word 'king' may translate at least two, and perhaps several, different concepts of kingship and different levels of royal rule among the barbarian peoples. We might better understand what a king is by looking at some of these very different types of king (and hence very different origins of kingdoms) as they appear in actual historical contexts.

The first type of king we must reckon with is the tribal king – the Germanic equivalent of the *rí tuaithe*, usually called by some diminutive of *rex* in Latin sources such as Ammianus Marcellinus or Bede (*regulus*, *subregulus*) but apparently equivalent to the *rex* of Tacitus. Of the origins of this type of king we can know nothing, although we may conclude that it is an institution which has its origins in distant prehistory, just as the word used for it in Irish, Latin and Sanskrit (*raj*), has its origins in prehistoric Indo-European (although, as we have seen, its Gothic equivalent *reiks* may have had a different meaning). We might justifiably assume that all Germanic peoples had such kingship. Bede, of course, said that the continental Saxons did not have kings but had *plurimos satrapas*, who elected a war leader in times of crisis.[14] But Bede was using the word *rex* in his History in the sense that later became common in western Europe: the ruler of a whole people. As Judith McClure has shown, he was also deeply influenced by the *reges* of the Old Testament, who were primarily military leaders.[15] Bede did not use the word *rex* of the tribal kings of the West Saxons or the Mercians (who once, presumably, ruled over all the various kingdoms in Mercia listed in the Tribal Hidage) any more than he did of the 'satraps' of the Old Saxons. But we must, I am sure, nevertheless take them to be the most basic form of Germanic kingship. They are the *Kleinkönige* of German historiography.

Our second type of king, then, must be the *Heerkönig*, the warrior king (called *reiks* by the Goths). In times of crisis, said Tacitus of the Germans and Bede of the Old Saxons, Germans were inclined to elect a leader, *ex virtute*. Migration of course, whether or not followed by settlement within the Empire, entailed perpetual crisis. When we talk about the origins of barbarian kingdoms, we are usually talking about those new forms of kingship and kingdoms which arose in this period of perpetual crisis in the last two centuries of the Western Roman Empire; they mostly arose directly or indirectly out of relationships between the Romans themselves and various Germanic groups. The Old Saxons had no such relationships. Their institutions evolved centuries later directly out of their relationship with the new Empire of Charlemagne. All this is drastically simplifying of course; it is impossible to deny that internal processes of which we are unaware may have been operating among the various Germanic peoples in the course of the fourth and fifth centuries, to produce the new forms of kingship which we can discern. But it is nevertheless likely that most of those processes had a good deal to do with the proximity of the Romans, the economic developments encouraged by that proximity, the Roman diplomatic policy of favouring individual Germanic allies (witnessed to archaeologically, perhaps, in burials full of luxury imported goods), or the opportunities offered by warfare either against the Romans or in alliance with them. It was distinctly to the advantage of Roman authorities to support the emergence of single kings within each Germanic people, since it made their own dealings with that people very much easier.

Heerkönige, then, arose out of military necessity of one sort or another. Their association with Romans may have made them think of their role as much in Roman terms as in Germanic ones; they may have been very unlike the older tribal kings with their religious and ritual obligations. And some of them may have sealed this difference and their separation from the past by converting to Christianity – Arian Christianity in most cases, but nevertheless an abandonment of the old gods. It was a *Heerkönig*, Genseric, who, in one of the few episodes in late Roman history that actually looks like an unambiguous barbarian conquest of Roman territory, led the Arian Vandals into

Carthage and founded a kingdom in one of the richest provinces of the Western Empire.

One way the Romans had of allying themselves closely with individual Germanic kings was to create the third type of king we might deal with: those Germanic kings who were Roman officials. There are numerous examples of Germanic *magistri militum* in the East as well as the West in the fourth century; consulships were held by not a few of them.[16] These were in most cases not kings; they had no position within their native Germanic society.[17] But from the late fourth century onwards we find examples of Germanic kings who enhance and perhaps extend their royal power by Roman titles. Theodoric, king of the Ostrogoths, is no doubt the best example. The first mention of him in Procopius's Gothic Wars is as 'a man who was of patrician rank and had attained the consular office in Byzantium'.[18] This was perhaps of little direct concern to the Ostrogoths whom he led, but was undoubtedly of major importance to the Romans in Italy who formed the bulk of his subjects (and tax payers), and hence considerably increased his power. It was of importance particularly because *patricius* and *consul* were civilian titles, giving him authority over the Roman bureaucratic structure, as his title of king gave him authority over his Visigoths. It is interesting that once he arrived in Italy he did not use the title *rex Ostrogothorum* along the lines of other western barbarian kings; he was *Flavius Theodoricus rex*, a title which emphasized his imperial connections and arguably the all-inclusive nature of his kingship, which was not restricted to Goths. Another German to be given the title *patricius* was Gundobad, a Burgundian *magister militum* who was made *patricius* in Italy after the death of his uncle, the emperor-maker Ricimer, and who returned to Gaul to become *rex Burgundionum*. It was arguably as *patricius* that he was able to act as judge and legislator for Romans as well as Burgundians.

As our final example of a Roman official-made-king there is perhaps one who has been revealed by archaeology: the Frank Childeric, whose grave was discovered in 1653, whose gold fibula suggests his official status and whose seal ring announced his title as *Childericus rex* – like Theodoric's, without the normal ethnic qualification. His exact constitutional position is unknown, although we know something of his close association with Roman authorities. His son Chlodovechus (or Clovis) was, it seems, made patrician in 508 by the emperor Anastasius: so at least proclaims the chapter heading in Gregory of Tours's Histories, even if the chapter itself describes the impossible title of 'consul aut Augustus'.[19] Shortly afterwards he established his main residence in Paris; called a council of bishops; drew up a written law code in Latin; and in short began to use the Roman political structure for his own ends – from the point of view of Anastasius, or a Gallo-Roman, a perfectly natural and desirable conclusion to the story.

What Clovis did next was, however, far more important from the point of view of the origins of the Frankish kingdom. We see in a series of dramatic episodes the kind of political process which might have occurred in total obscurity in several parts of Anglo-Saxon England in the sixth century. Gregory of Tours tells us (with some glee, apparently) that Clovis used his new authority to get rid of all other Frankish kings, most of them his own relatives, and to unite the Frankish people with himself as sole king. He did this in various underhand and colourful ways; at the end of his life he used to sit on his throne and complain about how lonely it was to be without relatives, doing this, explained Gregory, in order to flush out any survivors and kill them.[20] Precisely who these rival kings were is not clear. As we have seen, Gregory had explained (at ii, 9) that when the Franks had crossed the Rhine they 'set up in each *pagus* and *civitas* long-haired kings chosen from their first and, so to speak, most noble family'. But we may, I think, justifiably doubt whether all Frankish kings were indeed related to the Merovingians; this is part of Gregory's (or his contemporary Frankish kings') attempt to portray the Merovingians as the only natural ruling family of the Franks. What we do see in Clovis's career, much more clearly than with any Anglo-Saxon kingdom, is the elimination of the tribal kings and their replacement by one ruler for the whole people or nation. In the case of England some of these tribal royal dynasties apparently survived as *subreguli*. Although the *thunginus* of the Lex Salica may, as Wenskus suggested, be the survival of the old Frankish tribal kings, and although the prince buried under Cologne cathedral c. 530 may be a surviving member of the Rhineland Franks' royal family, it seems likely that Clovis had indeed successfully wiped out all royal opposition to him.[21] Subsequently of course the Franks wiped out other royal lines too, such as those of the Alamans, and substituted subordinate dukes or *principes* for these kings. It is a measure of the unique prestige of the Merovingian kings that these subordinate and non-royal rulers – in Alamannia, Bavaria, Aquitaine and elsewhere – seem never to have usurped the royal title. The *princeps* of Aquitaine, in the early eighth century more powerful than any Anglo-Saxon or indeed Frankish king, nevertheless does not (it seems) call himself king.[22] The picture we have of kingship in Francia is thus one in which there may be non-royal rulers who were (by the eighth century) more powerful than Frankish kings;[23] kingship, however, was until 751 restricted to one family for reasons of the pressures of historical tradition. Within the *regnum* of the Franks, however, there might be at any one time several *regna*, each ruled by a king from that same family.

Childericus rex had once, according to Gregory, been deposed by the Franks and replaced as king by the former *magister militum*, the Roman Aegidius. What we are to make of this statement is, and has been, anybody's guess. Was Aegidius really *rex Francorum* (a possibility some commentators have entertained)? Or was he perhaps, like Childeric, a *rex* without ethnic qualification – raised on a shield as *rex* by his Germanic warriors just as in the fourth century the emperor Julian had been? Aegidius at least introduces us to our fourth, very tentative category of kings in this period: Roman kings. Romans were perfectly accustomed to the idea that different (non-Roman) peoples each had their king; from there it was but a step to think of Romans in a particular area themselves having their own ethnic king. The earliest known is from North Africa: at the same time as there was a *rex Vandalorum et Alanorum* sitting in Carthage, further west there was Masuna, *rex gentium Maurorum et Romanorum*. And in northern Gaul there was Aegidius's son Syagrius, whom Gregory of Tours calls *rex Romanorum*. I have recently published an article arguing that Syagrius's kingship was an invention of Gregory's, and that his political importance in northern Gaul in the late fifth century is largely an invention of twentieth-century scholars.[24] But consistency is a sign of small-mindedness, and I throw Syagrius in as a reminder of the possibility at least that a new idea of ethnic kingship was emerging which could encompass Romans as well. This is not an unimportant possibility, when one thinks of the political institutions which emerged in post-Roman Britain among the 'Welsh'.

I quoted Susan Reynolds earlier, as saying that by the central Middle Ages it was regarded as the norm that a people should form a kingdom under a king and that peoples, in Regino of Prüm's phrase, 'differed between themselves in descent, manners, language and laws' (*genere, moribus, lingua, legibus*). The titles of early medieval kings only confirm this idea that kings are rulers of peoples or nations: we have the *reges Francorum, Langobardorum, Burgundionum* and so on. Royal titles are almost invariably ethnic or national titles rather than territorial ones. And even our early medieval sources present us with the idea that national kingship is normal and natural. The origins of kingdoms might thus be regarded as easily discovered – in the origins of peoples. But what was a people? What were the Franks, the Alamans, the Visigoths, the Thuringians, the Saxons, or the political groupings into which all these 'peoples' were divided in pre-migration or even, in some cases, post-migration times? It is clear, to start with, that these groupings were very fluid, above all in the Migration Period. As Wolfram put it, in ethnographic terms a *gens* was not a state of being but an on-going process: 'a *gens* was in migration, in *peregrinatio*, in order to develop from a polyethnic group into a people that represented a kingdom and converted before long to the true faith.'[25] Peoples did not produce kings – Bede's *reges*; kings produced peoples. As historians have come to see, since the work of Wenskus above all,[26] an early medieval people is not an ethnic or genetic, let alone racial, entity; it is a grouping brought about by political means, which ended in the disruption of the old Germanic tribal groupings and frequently in the incorporation into this new 'people' of the Roman population.

Despite Wenskus, the racial theory of ethnic origination still lurks behind the explanations of some early medieval historians and archaeologists. The theorists of nationalism in the nineteenth century, who influenced historians of the Middle Ages at the time and who still condition our own thinking, imagined that a people was a group of men and women with a common language, a common culture and a common racial type who could be clearly distinguished from their neighbours. They portrayed the settlement of the Anglo-Saxons in Britain, and that of the Franks in Gaul, as an invasion of a long-skulled 'Nordic' race into an area inhabited by broad-skulled 'Celts'. Some believed that the later French monarchy and aristocracy could trace their origins directly back to the military race of the Franks; the French Revolution was 'the final victory of the Gauls over the Franks'.[27] That is why some historians of the Franks have been so interested in establishing whether particular individuals in sixth- or seventh-century Gaul had 'Frankish blood', whether a particular institution was 'Roman', 'Gallic' or 'Frankish', or by what stage the two races of Gauls and Franks had largely 'fused' through intermarriage. But historians today can see that 'peoples' are much more fluid than were once thought; they can combine into new groups, take on new names, or impose those names on to others. Early medieval peoples are not biological entities, like races; sometimes they appear to be no more than men and women who are temporarily grouped together, by others, by themselves or, more commonly, by their leaders. They may have a common language, a common culture, a common way of dressing (which can be discovered by the archaeologist), but if they have, all these things may have been imposed on them by conquest or cultural domination, as happened to the Celts in pre-Roman times.

There are semantic problems involved as well, revealed, for instance, if we ask the innocent question 'who were the Franks?'[28] It is a question which demands at least two more questions in reply: 'What period do you want to know about?' and 'Do you want to know about it from the point of view of insiders or outsiders?' As far as the Franks themselves are concerned the name itself presumably originates with them, since 'Frank' meant something like 'fierce' in their own language. But for the first two and a half centuries of the history of the Frankish people we have to rely on the perceptions of outsiders as to who were Franks and who were not; we only have Roman sources to inform us. It is not until the beginning of the sixth century that we have the first historical (but highly problematical) source which might conceivably have been written by a Frank: the earliest version of their law code, called the *Pactus Legis Salicae* by those modern historians who have tried to reconstruct it. But the *Pactus Legis Salicae* does not use the word 'Frank' at all. The people for whom the *Pactus* was intended were Salians, the group from which Clovis emerged to unite the various other tribal groups under the banner of 'Frank'. 'Frank' was a political designation, therefore, rather than a natural focus of loyalty or community. Loyalty to the tribe rather than to the whole confederation may have lasted among some Franks, particularly those who remained east of the Rhine, until as late as the eighth century.

In the time of Clovis it was probably fairly easy for a Gallo-Roman cleric to know who was a Frank and who was not. They could probably be distinguished by dress, by name, by social position and function and perhaps by language (although some Frankish families may have been living among Romans and speaking Latin for generations). Gregory of Tours is not nearly so concerned with distinguishing Frank from Roman as many historians have been; perhaps in his day it was clear that 'Frank' was primarily a political label. The only time he mentions the ethnic identity of a particular German is when he points out that he is a Saxon, a Thuringian or a Burgundian. We are perhaps right to assume that most of the others with Germanic names were Franks, but it is also clear that Gregory does not consider it necessary constantly to point out that 'this man is a Frank; this man is a Gallo-Roman'. We cannot even be sure from his account who was the first Frank to become a bishop. It may have been Bertechramnus (Bertram) of Bordeaux, because Gregory mentions almost as an aside that he was related to the Frankish kings. However, Bertram may have been the product of a 'mixed marriage'. His Frankish name alone does not indicate Frankish parentage, for by the sixth century it was becoming quite fashionable for Romans, even aristocratic Romans, to take Germanic names; Gregory himself had a great-uncle called Gundulf. Patrick Geary has recently argued for the eighth century how fluid ethnic categories were:

> No one characteristic, be it law, language, custom, or birth, can be considered a sufficient index by which to assign ethnicity, nor was it any

different for contemporaries. Self-perception, and perception of others, represented a choice in a variety of somewhat arbitrary characteristics, which could be seen differently by different people. The real, although not entirely impenetrable, barriers were between slave and free, free and noble. Within the elite a person or faction could be Burgundian by birth, Roman by language, and Frankish by dress. Likewise, someone born of a father from Francia and a mother from Alamannia could properly be termed a Frank or an Alamannian by different authors considering him from different perspectives. His own perception of himself might change during his lifetime, depending on how he viewed his relationship to the Frankish king and his local faction.[29]

The 'emergence' of a people, and hence often the origins of a kingdom, are thus a complex cultural and political process which is seldom easily discernible. A curious passage in the History of the Gothic Wars by the Greek historian Procopius has often been related to this process; it is indeed the only passage in any early medieval source which describes how a new people came into being. Procopius explains more than once that the Germans 'are now called Franks', but he uses the more classical word here; he tells how the Germans went against their neighbours the Arborychoi, whom most commentators believe to be the Armoricans, the inhabitants of north-west Gaul.

> But the Arborychoi proved their valour and loyalty to the Romans and showed themselves brave men in this war, and since the Germans were not able to overcome them by force, they wished to win them over and make the two peoples kin by intermarriage. This suggestion the Arborychoi received not at all unwillingly; for both, as it happened, were Christians. And in this way they were united into one people, and came to have great power. Now other Roman soldiers had been stationed at the frontiers of Gaul to serve as guards ... [They] gave themselves, together with their military standards and the land which they had long been guarding for the Romans, to the Arborychoi and Germans; and they handed down to their offspring all the customs of their fathers, which were thus preserved, and this people has held them in sufficient reverence to guard them even up to my time. For even at the present day they are clearly recognised as belonging to the legions to which they were assigned when they served in ancient times, and they always carry their own standards when they enter battle, and always follow the custom of their fathers. And they preserve the dress of the Romans in every particular, even as regards their shoes.[30]

Procopius is far from being the most reliable of observers, above all when it comes to the customs of barbarian peoples. But if this strange story relates to anything, it must refer to the Franks at the time of Childeric and/or Clovis. (Procopius himself seems to place it before the accession of Clovis, except that he portrays the Franks as Christians.) And it shows us the acceptance by Romans of Frankish royal authority, and subsequently the acceptance of the title 'Frank', so that by the seventh century most people descended from Romans in northern Gaul accepted themselves to be Franks, and by the eighth century were devising historical explanations for this – suggesting for instance that in the fifth century the Franks had killed all the Romans in northern Gaul, after, that is, having learnt to speak their language. If only we knew more about the process by which the British of eastern Britain were incorporated into the Anglo-Saxon kingdoms, and the effect which this may have had upon concepts of kingdom and people in England.

If we want to look more closely at the means by which two political and cultural groups might merge to form a new people and kingdom we might examine one mechanism much discussed in recent years: the 'techniques of accommodation' experienced in those kingdoms founded under the institutions known as *hospitalitas*. Since the pioneering work of Gaupp in 1844 historians have generally regarded these settlements which established a relationship of *hospitalitas* between Romans and settling Germans as deriving from the normal procedures of military billeting. There was indeed a legal obligation upon Roman citizens to provide shelter for individual soldiers if called upon to do so, although this involved no food or other payments. But Walter Goffart's book of 1980, *Barbarians and Romans, AD 418–584: the Techniques of Accommodation*, brought a brusque end to this consensus, which had hitherto been marred only by discussion of details of practice. Goffart tried to show that certain Germanic peoples were given a living within the Empire in a way that had little to do with billeting, save in the occasional use of this word *hospitalitas* to refer to both systems. Historians had always recognized that the settlements involved more than shelter, but they assumed that the idea of dividing houses between host and billeted soldiers was expanded to encompass the division of estates between landowners and Germanic federates. The more perceptive historians worried about the practical details. Why was there not a single cry of protest from Roman landowners in the sources? How could Ennodius have written to Liberius, the man in charge of this partition in northern Italy under the Ostrogoths, and said 'You have enriched the countless hordes of Goths with generous grants of lands, and yet the Romans have hardly felt it. The victors desire nothing more, and the conquered have felt no loss'?[31] Goffart supplied a deceptively satisfying answer. In essence he argued that what was ceded to the barbarian newcomers was not land but the right to collect taxation directly. Instead of imperial officials collecting taxes which were then paid out to their barbarian allies, the barbarians were individually assigned the public taxes paid by one or more tax payers, and the collection was their responsibility.

The ideal situation from the Roman point of view was something like the assignation in 440 of *deserta rura* in southern Gaul to the Alans – that is, in Goffart's view, lands from which the Romans had for whatever reason been unable to collect tax. In other cases the central government did lose the proceeds of taxation, but they also handed over the obligation of defending that area and the cost of tax collection, and the local tax payer lost nothing. Goffart argued that there was no set system which was used every time; each settlement was negotiated individually. In 418 the Visigoths were settled in Aquitanica Prima, and all the tax from that area went to the barbarians, one-third to the king and two-thirds to individual Visigoths. In 443 the Burgundians were settled in Sapaudia, and the tax revenues from half the lands worked by the landowners themselves went to individual barbarians, while tax from *terrae cum mancipiis*, lands worked largely by registered bondsmen on behalf of a great landowner, were assigned to the king himself. In Ostrogothic Italy one-third of the tax receipts were paid into a separate fund, the *illatio tertiarum*, and reassigned in multiples of tax units, called *iuga* or *millena*, to individual Goths. The settlement of the Lombards, Goffart argues, was in two stages: in 573 the taxes of surviving Roman nobles were assigned to a number of Lombard 'guests', and in 584, with the restoration of the monarchy, there was a division of resources between the dukes and the king, and the tax payments of all bondsmen were assigned to Lombards of lesser rank.

Goffart's idea is seductive. Reassignment of tax revenues was politically and administratively possible in the way that confiscation of property could never have been. And as an idea about the origins of some barbarian kingdoms – basically those of southern Europe, although it is not impossible that the Franks or even, dare I say it, some groups of Angles or Saxons may have experienced such a settlement – it offers some intriguing possibilities. It would mean that effectively these barbarian kings were installed in their new kingdoms as direct substitutes for Roman emperors, surrounded by the propaganda of 'hospitality' deliberately designed, suggests Goffart, to encourage acceptance of these newcomers into Roman society. Germans were given an incentive to protect the Roman structure, from which they benefited considerably; Romans were placed in a very direct relationship with the army which lived in their vicinity. The main trouble with this expedient of course was that it encouraged also the transfer of loyalty from the Empire to a nearer and much more effective government; an imperial province became gradually a barbarian kingdom. Hence Goffart's neat and much quoted dictum: 'When set in a fourth-century perspective, what we call the Fall of the Western Empire was an imaginative experiment that got a little out of hand.'[32] And the barbarian kingdoms that were created were of a particular kind, exhibiting many of the principal features of the post-Roman constitution on the Continent: the withdrawal of much of the business of tax collection from the state, which helped the process of what Goffart apologetically calls debureaucratization; the growing confusion between public taxation and land rents; and the emergence of a group, barbarian landowners and Romans who had commuted their taxes by payment of a lump sum, who paid no public taxes at all.

The trouble with this picture lies in the details, which rest on scanty and intransigent evidence, which are extremely hypothetical, and which are often established only by analogy with equally hypothetical conditions elsewhere or by assuming technical meanings for such ordinary Latin words as *terra* or *mancipium*. When the sources say that *terra* was divided up, all previous historians translated *terra* as 'land'; not so, says Goffart, it is an otherwise unattested appearance of the word as used by bureaucrats, meaning 'tax payment'. The evidence for the Burgundians uses *terra* in an apparently straightforward and literal way, and yet, says Goffart, it cannot be so. The evidence for the Lombards relies on two short passages from the source written two centuries after the events, Paul the Deacon's *Historia Langobardorum*; did Paul really have access to earlier bureaucratic jargon? (Similar problems arise with the argument that Gildas used the technical vocabulary of *hospitalitas* in describing the settlement of Saxons under agreement with the *tyrannus superbus.*) Building hypotheses out of highly fragmentary evidence is of course what fifth-century historians do every day of their lives; and Goffart does provide a consistent and plausible theory from the evidence, which is more than his predecessors had managed to do. And it concentrates our attention on one important aspect of the origins of a certain type of barbarian kingdom – that in which the barbarian elements are almost totally obscured by the surviving Roman structure. This is not to suggest that *hospitalitas* arrangements, or simplified versions of them, could not have been at the origins of one or more Anglo-Saxon kingdoms. But the only such arrangements we know of are in southern Europe, where our knowledge of fifth- and early sixth-century events are more extensive, and where the Roman tax machinery and bureaucracy may have functioned long enough to allow such relatively complex administrative reorganizations to take place.

We have seen a number of ways in which kingdoms originated on the Continent: through the traditional tribal kingships, as a development of the equally traditional war leadership, through close alliance with the Roman Empire or with the Roman inhabitants of part of the Empire. We have seen how successful kings like Clovis can create a new type of kingship, and a new type of people, by a ruthless policy of conquest or political intrigue; we have seen other kings, if we believe Goffart, moving smoothly into the seat vacated by the emperors. Whether we have found any parallels to the much more obscure processes going on in eastern Britain in the fifth and sixth centuries is another matter. The clearest connection between England and the Continent in this problem of the origins of kingdoms is not to do with the realities of political power but with the way in which English kings and their subjects came to regard kingship, as closer contact and eventually Christianity brought them the triple image of Roman emperor, Merovingian king and Hebrew monarch. As soon as we have written sources in England, that triple image dominates the literary version of kingship which is often all that we have to guide us, or mislead us. The continental evidence reminds us of the wide range of possibilities available to those who speculate on the realities, on the origins of Anglo-Saxon kingdoms; it teaches us also perhaps how flexible our concepts of 'kingship' and 'kingdom' actually have to be.

Part 2

4 The creation and early structure of the kingdom of Kent

NICHOLAS BROOKS

Historians of Anglo-Saxon England have been strangely reluctant to produce any general model of state formation. Interest in the creation of the early Anglo-Saxon kingdoms has been largely or solely in their role as precursors of the single (West Saxon) kingdom of England, rather than in the process of state formation itself, and has been limited to political and military developments. The early Middle Ages in England have been interpreted in terms of 'progress' towards a single monarchy. There has been virtually no expression here of the concern of Marxist historians to relate the rise of the state to the emergence of the feudal mode of production, that is to the rise of a land-owning aristocratic élite living off the rents or labour of an increasingly tied peasantry.[1] Eastern European historians[2] or 'new' archaeologists,[3] who are both accustomed to working with far less evidence, would find our lack of interest in theoretical models extraordinary. One would be more confident of justifying our empirical concentration upon the extant evidence and our rejection of models, were it not a reflection of the insularity of much English scholarship.

In any account of Anglo-Saxon state formation Kent will inevitably have a prominent place, since it was claimed to be the first English kingdom in existence. It was also the first to be converted to Christianity and has therefore an earlier 'historical threshold' – that is the period from which written sources first survive – than any other. The Kentish origin myth is preserved in various forms by Bede, by the *Historia Brittonum* and by the Anglo-Saxon Chronicle, whilst the Kentish royal genealogy is found in these same sources and in the 'Anglian Collection' of genealogies.[4] It has even been claimed that fragments of Kentish annals of seventh-century origin survive in later continental annals.[5] More certainly the law codes of seventh-century Kentish rulers – Æthelberht, Hlothhere and Eadric, and Wihtred – allow us to see the Kentish state in operation earlier than any other English kingdom.[6] Similarly Kent has preserved by far the largest number of early (seventh- and eighth-century) royal diplomas, both in contemporary form and in later copies,[7] which show something of how the ecclesiastical and lay aristocracy secured their hold on the land. If we add to all this the Kentish royal hagiographical legend whose eighth-century origins have recently been traced by Dr Rollason and the fact that Kent was predominant in the production of early coinage in England,[8] then it is clear that, relatively speaking, there is no shortage of written evidence for the early Kentish kingdom.

The unwritten sources for early Kent are equally impressive: namely the archaeological record and the evidence of the Kentish landscape itself. The pagan Anglo-Saxon cemeteries of Kent with their rich inhumation burials have long attracted scholarly study and thankfully are still graced by archaeologists who use the study of grave-goods to suggest answers to historical questions about the origins and chronology of invasions and about the development of social and political structures.[9] Most recently Kent's landscape and settlement history have been brilliantly analysed by Professor A. Everitt.[10] By distinguishing the six contrasting *pays* of Kent whose exploitation has been so very different throughout Kentish history (fig. 4.1), he has given us a key to an understanding of the peculiarities of Kent's early medieval archaeology and agriculture and of its political and administrative geography.

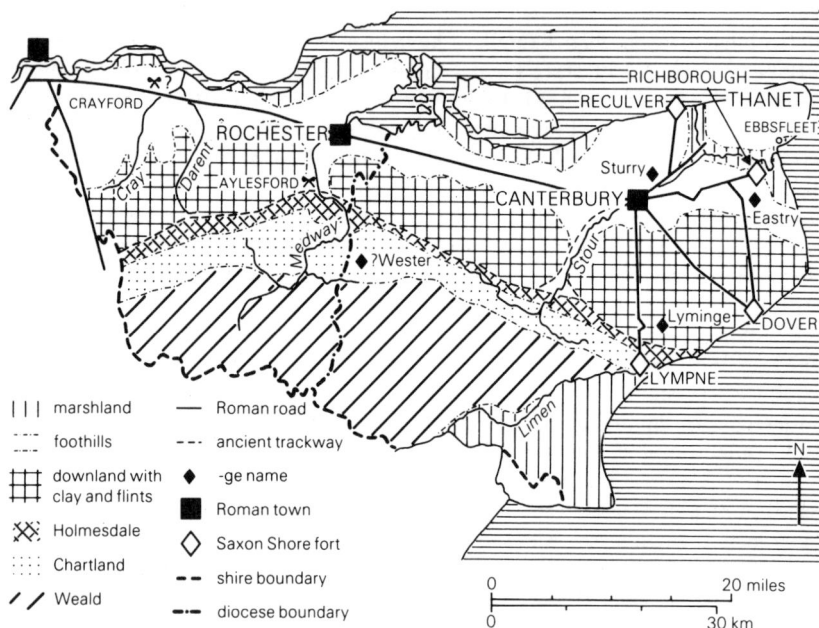

Figure 4.1. Early Kent: physical and ecclesiastical divisions. The physical regions or *pays* are taken from A. Everitt, *Continuity and Colonization: the Evolution of Kentish Settlement* (1986). The earliest evidence for the boundary between the dioceses of Rochester and Canterbury is of the mid-eleventh century (S1564).

A true synthesis of all these categories of evidence is much needed but would have to be of monograph length. Here it may be more useful to re-examine the written sources for the creation of the kingdom and for its early structure. Some of them have been subjected to critical, even hypercritical, analysis in recent years; others have come to bear an enormous superstructure of interpretation and conjecture that has been accepted widely and has been built into current models of settlement history. There is a need for a new assessment.

THE NAME 'KENT' AND THE ORIGINS OF THE KINGDOM

Alone of the southern English kingdoms Kent was already a kingdom, a state, long before the *adventus Saxonum*. It had indeed been a Celtic (Belgic) Iron Age principality and thereafter a Romano-British *civitas* with its capital at *Durovernum Cantiacorum* (Canterbury), which was the focus of the Roman road system of Kent.[11] The survival of Kent as a distinct political unit is paralleled by the survival of the name. *Καντιον*, *Cantium* and *Cantia* are the learned forms known to Ptolemy, Caesar and Bede respectively, but they probably all represent a monosyllabic *C(h)ant* or *Cænt* in the vernacular, whether British or Old English.[12] The survival of the name, perhaps paralleled in the northern English kingdoms of Deira and Bernicia,[13] may suggest that the Anglo-Saxon kingdom had been formed not simply by the coalescing of groups of English settlers, but that it had also inherited something of its structure from the Celtic and Roman past. The concentration of early Anglo-Saxon settlement in exactly those areas – the 'Foothills' and the 'Holmesdale' (fig. 4.1) as defined by Everitt – where the major Romano-British sites had been located reinforces the possibility of such continuity. So does the emergence of centres of Anglo-Saxon royal government at places like Lyminge, Wingham and Faversham which had been the sites of villas or temples or of metal-working in the Roman era.[14] So too does the influence of the Roman theatre in Canterbury on the emerging topography of the town in the early Middle Ages.[15] In this context it is also perhaps worth recalling the story in the *Historia Brittonum* of how the kingdom of Kent was transferred from the British king Gwyrangon to Hengist as the bride-price for Vortigern's marriage to Hengist's daughter.[16] This story may indeed be entirely mythical, but it is perhaps significant that it is a story of the transfer of a kingdom from British to English control by legal means, not a story of the forging of an English kingdom by warfare.

The name Kent was known to Strabo and Diodorus Siculus in the first century BC and it is probable that Kent had already been mentioned some three centuries earlier by the navigator Pytheas. At least as a geographical term 'Kent' is therefore very ancient.[17] According to Caesar the inhabitants of Kent in 55–4 BC were ruled by four kings, whom he names. Whether scholars have been correct to deduce that at this time Kent was divided into four territories which can be identified from the distribution of coins, pottery or hillforts seems very doubtful. Joint rule is surely equally possible. Rule by a single king well before the Claudian conquest of AD 43 is certainly suggested by the distribution of coins of one of the Belgic rulers named Dumnovellaunus.[18] It must be stressed, however, that there is really no evidence of the western extent either of the Celtic kingdom of Kent or of the Romano-British *civitas* of *Cantium*. Ptolemy indeed attributes three towns to the *Cantii*: London, *Durovernum* and *Rutupiae* (Richborough).[19] Scholars have unanimously refused to include London, but in rejecting it we are left without any proof that Romano-British *Cantium* included West Kent at all. Several have supposed that the Roman *civitas* was divided into two *pagi* based on the towns of Rochester and Canterbury, but that is no more than a guess derived from the existence of the towns and the later division of Kent into two halves. We have in fact no evidence of where the boundary between the *Cantiaci* and the *Regni* lay, though the Weald is certainly the only single geographical feature that could have served the purpose.

Whatever the extent of the pre-Anglo-Saxon unit, however, by the fifth century AD 'Kent' had had several centuries' existence both as a geographical term and as a tribal territory, and it may still have retained some memories of rule by Celtic kings. Two principal ways in which the name might then have been transmitted to the Anglo-Saxons can be suggested: (i) after the withdrawal of Roman armies, 'tyrants' or kings may have emerged once more as rulers in Kent, and their power may then have been transferred to, or seized by, English rulers; (ii) alternatively 'Kent' may simply have been known to 'Saxon' seafarers in the fourth century and have passed into the Germanic languages as a geographical expression. In this sense it could have served as a suitable name for an English kingdom when political and military developments created a unit of comparable extent.

THE KENTISH ORIGIN MYTH

Bede

It may well be doubted after the devastating criticism of Turville-Petre, De Vries, Dumville and Sims-Williams[20] whether the historian can find anything usable in the traditional stories of the arrival in Britain of the founders of the Kentish dynasty. But whilst the stories of Hengist and Horsa and of Oisc/Æsc and of their relations with Vortigern and his sons may be myth, it is important to locate, to date and to understand the various mythical elements as fully as possible. The first witness is Bede, writing in 731 in the famous Book I chapter 15 of his Ecclesiastical History. He begins by repeating Gildas's account of the British invitation to the *Saxones* to settle in 'the eastern part of the island', ostensibly to defend the Britons against their northern enemies. After a famous passage on the continental origin of the English, which was probably a late addition, Bede then says, 'Their first rulers are said (*perhibentur*) to have been two brothers Hengist and Horsa'. Bede goes on to record Horsa's death in battle and the existence in East Kent of a notable monument in his name, and he traces their descent from the Germanic war god, Woden (Uoden–Uecta–Uitta–Uictgisl–Hengist).[21] In a later chapter he gives the genealogy of the Kentish king Æthelberht, which traces his descent back to Oeric *cognomento* Oisc, the son of Hengist, and he states that Hengist and Oisc first entered Britain at the invitation of Vortigern as he had already related (*ut supra retulimus*).[22]

In fact, however, this is Bede's first mention of Oeric/Oisc; he has hitherto written of Hengist and *Horsa* as the first leaders of the 'Saxons' who arrived in response to Vortigern's invitation. Bede was here being uncharacteristically slipshod, but it is likely that he knew more stories about Hengist, Horsa and Oisc than he actually tells us. His concern after all was with *ecclesiastical* history; he needed only to say enough about them to explain the presence of pagan Anglo-Saxons in Britain. His use of the word *perhibentur* suggests that he was indeed following oral tradition, whose authority he could not check, rather than a written source or a first-hand witness whose personal authority was unimpeachable.[23] Technically Sims-Williams is correct to insist that Bede does not state that Hengist and Horsa landed, or even fought, in Kent.[24] He only asserts that Horsa's *monumentum* was there and that the kings of Kent were descended from Oisc, son of Hengist. It is therefore theoretically conceivable that the stories in the *Historia Brittonum* and the Anglo-Saxon Chronicle of the battles of Hengist, Horsa and Oisc with the Britons in Kent are simply post-Bedan inventions of later eighth-century or ninth-century authors, who jumped to the wrong conclusions from Bede's account.

But it is difficult to conceive who, apart from Bede's Kentish informants, would have been concerned about Hengist's and Oisc's descent from Woden, about Horsa's monument in East Kent and about the descent of the Kentish royal dynasty. Some version of the Kentish origin myth known to us from the later sources is therefore likely to have already been known in Kent in Bede's day. Moreover even in the story as we have it in Bede there are mythical elements already present. I refer here not just to the supposed ancestors of Hengist and Horsa – Uihtgisl, Uitta and Uecta – who, as Sims-Williams has argued, may represent a Kentish claim to the 'Jutish' settlement of the Isle of Wight (Latin *Uecta/Uectis*; O.E. *Uiht*);[25] nor just to the surely fictitious doubleton Hengist and Horsa (O.E. 'stallion' and 'horse'); nor to Hengist's fame in the Old English poetic record; but rather to Oisc. Bede reports that Oisc was the *cognomentum*, the distinguishing family name, of Oeric, Hengist's son, and that from him the Kentish kings were called *Oiscingas* ('the descendants of Oisc'). We are given no indication how an apparently undistinguished Eric acquired this surname, or why the dynasty should have remembered themselves as the sons of Oisc rather than of Oeric or indeed of Hengist. If *Oiscingas* was the dynastic family name, what was the force of Oeric's *cognomentum* Oisc? There is reason to suspect that at some early stage in the transmission of the Kentish origin myth Oeric has been identified with a divine founder figure, for philologists equate the name Oisc with (i) the *princeps* Ansehis, who according to the Ravenna Cosmographer had brought the 'Saxons' to Britain; (ii) the Norse word for a god *áss* and the O.E. personal-name element Os-; and (iii) the Gothic demi-gods *Ansis* whom Jordanes tells us stood at the head of the royal genealogies of the Goths. Indeed 'Hengist' may be a further (and later) duplication of the same god name,[26] or may have been borrowed from heroic tales originally quite distinct. Claims of descent from divine progenitors and the identification of the 'Founding Fathers' as gods are of course standard elements in the dynastic praise or 'oral tradition' of early Germanic peoples, as they are of many tribes throughout the world today.[27] It may be that the identification of Oeric as Oisc represents one stage in the evolution of the Kentish royal genealogy before the supposed generations from Hengist to Woden, another divine progenitor, were added. The dynasty would have been known as *Oiscingas* before descent from Woden, or from Hengist, was claimed.

In the form recorded by Bede the Kentish royal genealogy can therefore be seen to be a fiction of epic heroes, gods and demi-gods and of eponymous but invented Wight-men. It is likely to reflect the stories that were cultivated at the royal court of Kent by English court poets (*scopas*) in the early eighth century and which were passed on to Bede by his informant on Kentish matters, abbot Albinus of St Augustine's. Indeed if we were to accept Moisl's argument that descent from pagan gods is unlikely to be a feature of dynastic tradition that was invented after the conversion to Christianity, then some version of the descent of the *Oiscingas* from Woden and other gods may have existed in oral tradition at the Kentish court of Æthelberht before the arrival there of St Augustine in 597.[28] A case might be made that Oeric and Octha are less clearly mythical than the other names in the genealogy, but where our evidence is so slight no weight can be attached to that. If, then, the *dramatis personae* of the Kentish origin legend are largely or entirely fictional, we need to go on to consider whether any credence can be given to the elaborate details of their deeds recorded in the *Historia Brittonum* and the Anglo-Saxon Chronicle.

The Anglo-Saxon Chronicle

At first sight the Chronicle's account of the foundation of the kingdom, set in a brief annalistic framework, seems more credible. In essence it is a story of a landing, of four battles (three of which are named), of the death of Horsa and the succession of Hengist (in 455, that is) six years after the landing, and of the succession of his son Æsc (in 488) seemingly in the fortieth year after the landing. The chronology is attached to a first landing in 449, which was the year in which Bede recorded the accession of Marcian and Valentinian in whose time he believed the arrival of the English to have occurred. As Sims-Williams has pointed out,[29] the Chronicle's pattern of landing, of creation of the kingdom after five or six years, of three named battles and of the succession of the son some forty years later is exactly matched in its duplicated and equally artificial account of the origins of the West Saxon kingdom. Indeed elements of the same pattern recur in the account of the supposed establishment of Ælle (a warrior whose wider fame was known to Bede) and his sons in Sussex. There is little sense in attempting to determine whether the Kentish account is modelled upon the West Saxon, or the West Saxon upon the Kentish. The pattern is likely to have once been far more widely spread than our extant examples indicate. We are here in the presence of a recurrent origin myth,[30] whose form owes more to the court poet's, or *scop's*, concept of what a dynastic origin story ought to contain (and to the annalist's attempt to fit that concept into a chronological scheme) than it does to historical reality.

A number of loose ends in the Chronicle's story of the beginnings of Kent suggest that it is a late and composite account. Thus after the supposed battle of *Ægelesthrep* and the death there of Horsa (455), Hengist *and Æsc* are said to have 'succeeded to the kingdom' or 'taken power' (*feng to rice*). Yet in 488 Æsc 'succeeded to the kingdom' (*feng to rice*) apparently for a second time and then reigned a further twenty-four years. The Kentish placenames of the Chronicle's account are worrying too, since they just fail to be satisfactory forms of well-known Kentish places. The landing takes place at *Ypwinesfleot* (*Heopwinesfleot*) which seems to be significantly close to, but not the same as, *Yppelesfleot*, that is Ebbsfleet on Thanet; the first battle occurs at *Ægelesthrep*, an improbable placename form where we might expect *Ægelesford* for Aylesford; the next takes place at *Crecganford* which is close to, but not an acceptable form of, *Cræganford*, Crayford (fig. 4.1). The third battle, *Wippedes-*

fleot, cannot be identified but gains no credibility from the reputed death there of the eponymous thegn Wipped. We may regard all these four places as genuine but unidentifiable sites, but it is surely more likely – as Wallenberg argued[31] – that the first three are all mangled forms of the names Ebbsfleet, Aylesford and Crayford. Such consistent error suggests that the compilers of the Anglo-Saxon Chronicle were not following a Kentish written account of the origins of the dynasty, but rather drawing on oral tradition, which after the demise of the independent Kentish kingdom would have been kept alive through the ninth century only in a West Saxon context. The West Saxon dynasty of Egbert (802–39) may have had ancestors in the Kentish royal family,[32] and a West Saxon *scop*, ignorant of Kentish geography, could have garbled the placename forms in a way that would not have been acceptable to a Kentish audience.

Indeed the closer we search the common stock of the Anglo-Saxon Chronicle for authoritative information about the early kingdom of Kent, the more it vanishes before our eyes. There is indeed some record of West Saxon-Kentish hostilities: in 568 Ceawlin and Cutha are said to have defeated king Æthelberht of Kent in battle at *Wibbandun*; in 686 Cædwalla and his brother Mul are said to have ravaged Kent; and in 687 Mul is burnt there and Cædwalla takes his revenge. The weighting of this information suggests, as we might expect, that it derives from West Saxon rather than Kentish sources. Otherwise the only information that the Chronicle has about Kent before 731 was drawn from Bede's Ecclesiastical History and in particular from the chronological recapitulation in the final chapter.[33]

The inference would seem to be that the compilers had no Kentish written sources for the early kingdom at all. That reinforces the conclusion that the Chronicle's version of the Kentish origin story is oral tradition, and that it is an account of mythical founders creating a kingdom according to a set formula at dates and places that deserve no credence. That does not of course mean that dynastic oral tradition could not preserve memories of actual events, or even that written sources are necessarily more authoritative or less liable to manipulation than the oral record. It only means that the early medievalist does not normally possess the tools, sometimes available to the anthropologist/historian in modern Africa, to establish which parts of the tradition may be historical rather than mythical.[34]

The Historia Brittonum

In Kent, however, we are remarkably fortunate that we have another control on the Kentish origin myth in the version recorded in the *Historia Brittonum* of the early ninth century.[35] This account was claimed by John Morris to be 'a sixth-century source', which he termed 'the Kentish Chronicle' and which he believed to have been incorporated lock, stock and barrel by 'Nennius' into the *Historia* in the 820s.[36] David Dumville has since taught us to disbelieve every element of this interpretation: the author of the *Historia* was not 'Nennius'; he did not simply incorporate earlier written sources by 'making a heap of what he found'; there is no reason to suppose that the *Historia*'s chronological calculations were made in the sixth century rather than in the ninth.[37] None the less the relationship of the *Historia*'s account to that of the Anglo-Saxon Chronicle is of interest, and Morris was quite right to stress that there is a connection between the two:

Anglo-Saxon Chronicle		Historia Brittonum
449	Hengist and Horsa, invited by Vortigern, land at *Ypwines-fleot*.	c.31 Vortigern invites Heng st and Horsa and gives them 1 anet.
		c.44 Vortemir son of Vortigern fights four battles against Hengist and Horsa:
455	Hengist and Horsa fight against Vortigern at *Ægelesthrep* (?Aylesford). Horsa killed; Hengist and Æsc succeed to kingdom.	Second battle at ford called *Episford* (Brit. *Rithergabail*). Horsa killed and also Categirn, Vortigern's son.
456	Hengist and Æsc fight Britons at *Crecganford* (?Crayford) and kill 4000; Britons flee from Kent to London.	First battle on River *Derguentid* (Darent).
465	Hengist and Æsc fight Britons at *Wippedesfleot* and slay 12 British elders. Thegn Wipped also slain.	Third battle in field by shore of Gallic sea *iuxta lapidem tituli*. Barbarians flee to ships.
473	Hengist and Æsc fight Britons, capture spoils. Britons flee.	
488	Æsc succeeds to the kingdom and reigns 24 years.	c.45 After Vortemir's death, barbarians return through Vortigern's friendship. Treacherous slaying of 300 British elders. Vortigern cedes Essex, Sussex and Middlesex.

Like the Chronicle the *Historia Brittonum* tells of the arrival of Hengist and Horsa in East Kent; like the Chronicle it tells of four battles, but names only three; like the Chronicle it records the death of Horsa in one of the named battles; and like the Chronicle it records a series of battles which ends with the enemy fleeing. But beyond these similarities which indicate a common origin, the overall effect of the *Historia*'s account is of course the reverse of that in the Anglo-Saxon Chronicle. When the sequence of battles starts, the English (*Saxones*) are already in control of Kent as a result of Vortigern's marriage to Hengist's daughter (c.37); Vortemir fights them first in the extreme west of Kent at the River Darent – the Chronicler's second battle at Crayford is just two and a half miles from the Darent (fig. 4.1); then Vortemir fights them at the ford site, *Episford*,[38] perhaps equivalent to the Chronicle's *Ægelesthrep* (?Aylesford) since Horsa is killed at each; and the last named battle is on the English Channel (*mare Gallicum*), which may be identical with the battle that the Chronicle calls *Wippedesfleot* since the element -*fleot* in Kentish placenames is the standard term for a tidal creek in coastal marshes. The site could be in the marshes of the Wantsum channel or possibly in Romney Marsh.[39] The overall contrast between the two accounts is stark: the Chronicle has landing and battles apparently involving movement from east to west, and has the Britons fleeing to London; the *Historia Brittonum*'s three battles progress from west to east and culminate in the flight of the Saxons to their ships on the Channel.

Clearly we have here a single tradition which in one version has been slanted for the benefit of an English audience, in the other for a British audience. It is a splendid example of how myth can be adapted to serve diametrically opposed purposes by a relatively minor reordering of the chronology, the location of key events or the motivation of the key participants. Yet, as H.M. Chadwick pointed out long ago,[40] there can be no doubt that the *Historia*'s version of the story is of English origin. Hence we are given the English form of names first, followed by their British equivalents: *Tænet -- Ruoihin* (c.31), *Cantguaraland – Cent* (c.37), *Episford – Rit her gabail* (c.42); hence too the story of Vortigern's 300 counsellors being treacherously murdered by Hengist's Saxons at the conference/feast when Hengist ordered his men to produce their hidden knives with the cry, *Eure nimath seaxas* ('Draw your knives'). The *Historia*'s use of Old English here would itself suggest the origin, but it is confirmed when the same story is found with the same punch line, but with different participants, in the origin myth of the continental Saxons as recorded in part by Widukind of Corvey and more fully in the *Annales Stadenses*.[41] This is clearly a familiar Germanic folktale or formulaic myth which, suitably adapted, is likely to have been part of the stock repertoire of many an Anglo-Saxon or Germanic court *scop* or praise singer. That it is a story of treachery and could therefore readily serve British interests in the *Historia* does not weigh against its English or Saxon origin. The gap between base treachery and admirable cunning was not great, for earlier wrongs by the enemy could always be held to justify deception.

In the *Historia Brittonum*, then, we find English myth adapted for a British audience, but this does not mean that its evidence should simply be rejected in favour of the Anglo-Saxon Chronicle's seemingly more straightforward account. It may be significant that the flight of the Britons to London in the Chronicle follows only the second of the battles (*Crecganford*). Our impression of the westward progress of the English relies upon the fact that *Wippedesfleot* cannot be identified and that the fourth battle is unnamed. The oral tradition upon which the Chronicle's sparse annals draw may have been much more tumultuous and complex. Similarly we have already seen that both Bede and the Chronicle make Oisc (Æsc) the son of Hengist, which is difficult to square with the name *Oiscingas* for the Kentish royal dynasty and with the fact that the warrior king Oisc appears to be the name of a god. It is therefore of interest that in the *Historia* Oisc does not figure in the stories of the struggles of Vortigern and his sons with Hengist and his 'Saxons'. Moreover in its version of the Kentish royal genealogy, which the *Historia* draws from the so-called 'Anglian collection' of genealogies, the descent is given in the sequence: Hengist–Octha (Ocga)–Ossa (Oese), rather than: Hengist–Oisc (Æsc)–Octa as found in Bede and the Chronicle. If we bear in mind that these genealogies are also an essential part of the court praise preserved and developed orally by Anglo-Saxon *scopas*,[42] then we should not seek to explain one or other version as a product of a simple error in transmission, whether written or oral. Rather each may stand witness to different versions of the Kentish/English origin legends.[43] In this light the *Historia Brittonum* may be seen to preserve the fullest version of the sort of dynastic stories that were first told in the court of the Anglo-Saxon kings of Kent. They have been transmitted to us immediately by a British writer, and perhaps intermediately through a wider 'Anglian' context, and it remains difficult to be sure how much they may have been changed in the process. Their function, however, is clear. They serve to explain the tenure of the kingdom of Kent by Hengist and Octa, and therefore also by those whom the genealogy showed to be descended from them. Genealogy and origin story are together the essential constituents of the court propaganda of the Kentish kingdom.

THE ANGLO-SAXON KINGDOM

Irminric

If we move on down the Kentish royal genealogy (Hengist–Oeric/Oisc–Octa–Irminric–Ædilberct), we leave the realms of dynastic myth and approach those of history with Irminric or Iurminric, who bore the same name as Ermanaric, the Gothic warrior king of the fourth century, and is said to be the son of Octa in one version and of Oese (?=Oisc) in the other.[44] Writing in the early 590s Gregory of Tours refers to Irminric (without naming him) as 'a certain king in Kent' at a date which, as we shall see, seems to be in the late 570s or early 580s.[45] Beyond the divergent claims made for his ancestry in the genealogy nothing is known of Irminric's origin. It should be noted, however, that Irmin-/Eormen- is an uncommon element in Anglo-Saxon personal names. Apart from the infamous Northumbrian queen, Iurminburh, who fell out with St Wilfrid but whose origins are unknown, the only Anglo-Saxons whose names contain the element are from Kent, and almost all of them can be shown to have been members of the Kentish ruling house and therefore descendants of Irminric.[46] Though rare in England, Irmin- is a very common element in continental personal names, especially among the Franks.[47] Archaeologists have long recognized amongst the grave-goods from sixth-century Kentish burials a significant Frankish element, particularly of luxury items such as belt fittings, garnet jewellery, glassware and bronze bowls. Their significance and chronology have been much disputed;[48] but if we were looking for a moment when a Frankish element first entered Kentish dynastic history, it should perhaps be reckoned to have been under Irminric rather than his better-known son. Indeed to be accurate, this continental Germanic element presumably began with the parents who chose his name. Even so it is difficult to suppose that the naming of Irminric can (unless he were unusually long lived) have been quite as early as *c.* 500, the date preferred by Sonia Chadwick Hawkes for the beginning of the Frankish phase in the Kentish archaeological record. A date for Irminric's birth in the second quarter of the sixth century would seem most likely in view of the redating of the reign of his son Æthelberht that the contemporary evidence requires. But since we cannot identify Irminric's parents, and since archaeological dating is necessarily hazardous, to have brought the two categories of evidence within a generation of each other is as much as could be hoped.

Æthelberht

With king Æthelberht we cross the historical threshold more definitely. As the first Anglo-Saxon king to be baptized, as the most powerful English ruler of his day and as the progenitor of the later kings of Kent, there were good reasons for Æthelberht to be remembered. Moreover Bede, our principal but not our only informant, derived his information about Kent from Albinus, the abbot of the monastery of St Peter and St Paul at Canterbury – the church where Æthelberht and the subsequent Christian kings of Kent were buried.[49] It is therefore no surprise that Bede should be well informed about the deaths of Kentish kings of the seventh and early eighth centuries. That was above all the information that a royal burial-church like St Augustine's (as it was later to be called) would preserve. We must therefore take Bede's information about the length and dates of Æthelberht's reign seriously.

Bede tells us that Æthelberht died in 616, 'the twenty-first year from the sending of Augustine and his companions to preach to the English people'.[50] It is likely that Bede himself supplied the incarnation year, as was his practice in the Ecclesiastical History. There is no reason to suppose that Bede, or his informants, had calculated all the incarnation dates of sixth- and seventh-century Kentish kings from a regnal list in the manner that Bede was able to reckon the dates of every Northumbrian ruler back to the supposed accession of the dynastic founder Ida in 547.[51] Neither Bede nor the compilers of the Anglo-Saxon Chronicle seem to have had access to any such Kentish regnal list. Bede did indeed know that Egbert I, who died in the year of the synod of Hertford (673), had reigned for nine years and that his predecessor Earconberht's rule lasted twenty-four.[52] But unless he knew the length of Eadbald's reign, which he does not state, he could not have calculated the year of Æthelberht's death by working backwards in this fashion. In fact it would have been far simpler for Bede to reckon forward twenty completed years from the sending of Augustine in 596 and thus to reach 616. That Æthelberht's death and burial were indeed remembered at Canterbury in terms of the chronology of the mission is confirmed later in the same chapter when Bede returns to the subject: 'King Æthelberht died on 24 February, 21 years after receiving the faith, and was buried in the *porticus* of St Martin within the church of the blessed apostles Peter and Paul.'[53]

Whilst the interest in the mission of Augustine and in the location of the king's burial was natural enough for Bede's informant, abbot Albinus, it must be observed that this second presentation of the facts might lead us to calculate the king's death as 597+21=618, since Augustine probably actually arrived in Kent in Spring 597. 618 is indeed the year of Æthelberht's obit in the fragmentary early Kentish and Northumbrian annals preserved in later continental chronicles from St Germain des Prés, Fleury and elsewhere.[54] 618 also seems to be indicated by the 'E' version of the Anglo-Saxon Chronicle when it places Æthelberht's accession in 565 and attributes a reign of fifty-three years to him (though most scholars have preferred to suppose the annal misplaced and *liii* to be a misreading for *lvi*).[55] But Bede's confusion whether the *xxi* years after the mission should be an ordinal or a cardinal number, and whether they should be reckoned from the sending or the arrival of the Gregorian mission, certainly warns us against accepting his calculated date of 616 too firmly. 616×18 would seem a wiser estimate of Æthelberht's death.

In his first references to Æthelberht's death Bede also tells us the length of his reign: '. . . after the temporal kingdom which he had held most gloriously for 56 years, he attained the eternal joys of the heavenly kingdom.'[56] G.H. Wheeler sought to suggest that Bede is here contrasting Æthelberht's *life* on earth with his everlasting *life* in heaven,[57] and is therefore telling us that Æthelberht was 56 years old when he died. But the contrast between the earthly *rule* of kings and the eternal *rule* of God in heaven is such a favourite theme of monastic writers, and of Bede in particular,[58] that it is more probable that Bede meant that Æthelberht had *reigned* for fifty-six years. Whether he was correctly informed, or had understood his information correctly, is another matter. Fifty-six years would indeed be a reign of unusual length, some fifteen years more than the longest Anglo-Saxon reign otherwise known, that of Æthelbald of Mercia (716–57).[59] Indeed it would be longer than that of any other English rulers apart from George III (1760–1820) and Victoria (1837–1901).

Such doubts deserve attention because the supposed fifty-six-year reign conflicts with the evidence of a writer who was an exact contemporary of Æthelberht, namely Gregory of Tours. Writing Book IV of his History at some date in or before 581, Gregory described how the Frankish king Charibert had (in 561) succeeded to his share of the kingdom of his father Lothar and had then taken as his wife Ingoberga, by whom he had a daughter who later received a husband in Kent.[60] Reading this passage in the context of Gregory's account of the succession of Lothar's sons, it seems that Charibert was following standard Merovingian practice in taking a wife after acquiring his kingdom. Only the offspring of a king could succeed to the throne in Merovingian Francia, and ambitious Frankish princes therefore delayed marriage until they became king.[61] Gregory mentioned the marriage of Ingoberga's daughter again, when in the early 590s he described in Book IX how he had attended Ingoberga on her deathbed in 588–9 in order to hear her will. He explains her generous benefactions to the poor and to the church of Tours by the fact that she had no descendants save a single daughter whom 'the son of a certain king in Kent had married'.[62]

If historians have been correct in identifying this daughter as Bertha, the Frankish princess whose marriage to Æthelberht of Kent is recorded by Bede, then the chronological implications are clear. Bertha must have been born between late 561 and 568, since her father Charibert had died in 567. She would not have been old enough to marry Æthelberht before the mid-570s at the earliest, and she had evidently done so in or by 581, when Gregory first noted the fact. At the time of the marriage (*c.* 575×81) Æthelberht was apparently only 'the son of a certain king in Kent', a description inconceivable if he were already on the Kentish throne, let alone if he had been ruling since 560×2 as acceptance of Bede's fifty-six-year reign would imply. However, all the chronological problems disappear if Bede's '56 years' had originally applied not to

Æthelberht's reign but to his age at death. Æthelberht would then have been born in 560×2 and have been of very much the same age as his wife Bertha. Married when he was about 18–20 years of age, he had certainly gained the Kentish throne before the death of Ceawlin of Wessex in *c.* 593 since he had earlier been defeated by him at *Wibbandun* and driven back to Kent.[63] It is possible that Æthelberht may still not have been king in 588–9 when Ingoberga did not know of (or did not remember!) her son-in-law's accession; unfortunately we cannot tell how regularly Bertha had kept in contact with her mother in Tours or be sure that Gregory's ignorance therefore means that Æthelberht was not yet then king.

Thus the evidence of the contemporary Gregory of Tours enables us to correct Bede's interpretation of Kentish chronology and to assign the following dates to the first Christian king of Kent: born 560×2, married to Bertha *c.* 580, succeeded to the Kentish kingdom *c.* 580×93, became overlord *c.* 593×7, received the Augustinian mission 597, died 616×18. Here surely is a credible career, which does not compel us either to attribute to Æthelberht an entirely improbable longevity or to prefer the second-hand and later tradition recorded by Bede to the evidence of a disinterested and well placed foreign contemporary. One final point emerges from Gregory's evidence: nothing suggests that the marriage of Bertha and Æthelberht was of great significance at the time it was contracted. With the division of the Frankish kingdom in 511 and again in 561, and with so many Merovingian rulers entering successive marriages or alliances of whatever sort, Frankish royal princesses were not in short supply. Ingoberga, indeed, seems not to have retained Charibert's favour for very long, and after his death in 567 and the dismemberment of his kingdom it must have been clear that Bertha would have neither great inherited wealth nor significant political clout.[64] Similarly we do not know that Æthelberht was Irminric's only son or whether there were elder brothers, let alone uncles or cousins, to dispute his path to the Kentish throne. We must constantly beware the temptation to assume that a royal genealogy is in fact a regnal list of successive kings passing the throne from father to son. At the time of his marriage to Bertha Æthelberht was simply one Kentish *filius regis*. We cannot be sure how far the marriage enhanced his political prospects, since we do not know what other brides might have been available. Marriage to a West Saxon princess during the overlordship of Ceawlin might have been a far more ambitious act.

THE STRUCTURE OF THE KENTISH KINGDOM

Already in the laws of king Æthelberht we can see something of the structure of the early Kentish state. Amongst the compensations and penalties prescribed for a great range of injuries and offences, the laws specify the payment due to the king when one of his followers (*leode*) was injured; they also protect all those at a royal vill (*cyninges tun*) and those drinking with the king at the *ham* of one of his subjects. An itinerant royal household eating and drinking the food surpluses collected at his own estates and those of his subjects therefore lies at the core of the Kentish kingdom as of other early medieval states.[65] Thanks to the researches of Professor Everitt a high proportion of these early estate centres in Kent can be identified and their location in the 'old arable lands' of the county, the so-called 'Foothills' and 'Holmesdale', established.[66]

The king's protection or *mund*, whose breach led to a fine of 50 gold shillings, was also used to prevent the violation of his slave girls (c.10) and of the 'best' widows of noble rank (c.75). Even more remarkably the same sum was exacted by the king as 'lord-ring' (*drihtinbeage*) when a free man was slain (c.6), and probably also when a free man was the victim of robbery (c.9). Clearly royal lordship was already dominant in Kent and was being exercised over both the noble and the free classes. Both *eorls* and *ceorls* in Kent had their own estates (*tunas*), however, staffed by their own 'loaf eaters' (dependants) and female slaves who came under their *mund* of 12 and 6 shillings respectively (cc.13–17, 25, 27). Both the Kentish king and the noble and free lords therefore had a financial interest in doing justice. In the laws of Hlothhere and Eadric we hear of the court (*mædel þing*) where the judges of the Kentish people (*Cantwara deman*) imposed right on plaintiffs and defendants (c.8); we also meet the king's hall (*sele*) in the trading port of *Lundenwic* where witnesses could be brought before the king's *wic*-reeve to warrant disputed property that had been bought in the town (c.16). Presumably the kings had halls at other centres where reeves could fulfil the same function. In Canterbury it seems likely that the great Roman theatre, whose vast bulk dominated the early medieval town, long served as the assembly place for the Cantware.[67] The overall impression is of a highly centralized kingdom on which royal lordship had been firmly imposed.

However strongly governed Æthelberht's Kent may have been, it seems likely to have been an amalgamation of two kingdoms that had once been distinct. The creation of a second Kentish bishopric at Rochester as early as 604 is difficult to understand, unless there was a real sense in which the inhabitants of West Kent were still at that time a separate *gens*. No other seventh-century English kingdom had two sees until archbishop Theodore deliberately set out in the 670s to divide the vast East Anglian, Northumbrian, Mercian and West Saxon bishoprics. Until then diocese and kingdom were coterminous. Yet in the seventh and eighth centuries Kent was frequently ruled by two joint-kings and, as Dr Yorke has recently shown, it was common for one of these kings to be subordinate and sometimes (perhaps normally) to have authority only in West Kent. Some of these minor rulers in Kent were the sons or brothers of the king of the whole of Kent; others, such as Sæbbi, Sigehere and Swæfheard in the late 680s and early 690s, and Sigered in the early 760s, seem to have been either the contemporary kings of Essex or else cadets of the East Saxon royal house.[68] If we compare this evidence with that for the seventh-century subordinate Northumbrian kingdom of Deira, which – thanks to Bede – is somewhat better evidenced, then it is difficult to resist the suggestion that West Kent had been either a separate kingdom for which the rulers of (East) Kent and of Essex had competed or a part of a once larger East Saxon kingdom.

In this connection we need to remember that archaeologists have long recognized that the pagan archaeology of West Kent is distinct from that of the richer East; its links are with the cemeteries of the lower Thames valley, especially those of Surrey and Essex, not with those of East Kent with their

Jutish and Frankish connections.[69] One further indication of the early separation of East and West Kent may be found in the placename Wester in the parish of Linton in East Kent (fig. 4.1). If this name indeed contains the primitive element -*ge* (cf. German *Gau*), then this 'western district' was an exact parallel to Eastry ('the eastern *ge*').[70] A kingdom whose 'western *ge*' had its administative centre at Wester cannot have included West Kent. The implication would seem to be that the earliest Anglo-Saxon kingdom of Kent, presumably before the reign of Æthelberht, only comprised what is today East Kent, that is the medieval diocese of Canterbury. Hence *Durovernum* (Canterbury) could properly be termed in Old English *Cantwaraburh*, 'the borough of the people of Kent', that is of this smaller kingdom in the east. Whether West Kent was an autonomous kingdom for long or whether it was always disputed between the Kentish and East Saxon dynasties cannot be known. We may suspect, however, that a function of the Kentish origin legend was to show Æthelberht's purported ancestors operating in West Kent and in the vicinity of London so as to justify his claim to that half of the kingdom too.

If we wish to pursue the substructure of the early Kentish kingdom more deeply, then we have to tackle the thorny problem of the Kentish lathes. Domesday Book shows that in 1086 Kent was divided into administrative and jurisdictional districts whose Old English name, *læð*, was latinized by the Anglo-Norman scribes as *lest(um)*. In East Kent there were four lathes: *Wiwarlest* from *Wiwaralæð*, 'the lathe of the men of Wye'; *Borowartlest* from *Burhwaralæð*, 'the lathe of the men of the borough (i.e. Canterbury)'; *Limowarlest* from *Limenwaralæð*, 'the lathe of the men of Lympne' (or 'of the river *Limen*'); and *lest de Estrei*, 'the lathe of Eastry'. In West Kent there was one whole lathe of Aylesford (*lest de Elesford*) and two 'half lathes' of Sutton-at-Hone and Milton Regis (*dimidium lest de Sudtone, dimidium lest de Middeltune*). The geographical reality of the division of Kent into lathes is revealed by the fact that almost every Kentish manor in the survey is said to lie in a certain lathe and a certain hundred. Hence the Domesday lathes can be mapped (fig. 4.2). The men of the four lathes of East Kent sometimes met together as a single court, for they were asked by the Domesday commissioners to declare what laws or rights the king had over the *alodiarii* (the free peasants or gavelkinders) of the whole county. They replied that the king had a fine of 100 shillings for encroachments upon the king's highway (*publica via regis*), that he had *grithbryce* (the fine for breach of his especial peace) of £8 when the offence occurred on the road, but that all other royal fines (*forisfacturae*) were of 100 shillings.[71] Allowing for the differences in the units of account, we may surely see these eleventh-century 100 shilling fines as the successors of the fines of 50 Kentish gold shillings for *mundbryce* and *drihtinbeage* in Æthelberht's laws and as fulfilling much the same function. Whether we should place any weight upon the fact that the men of the lathes of East Kent appear to declare the law for the whole county and whether we may suppose that some form of lathe and lathe court already existed in Æthelberht's day for the exaction of such fines are more problematic issues.

The word *læð* is in fact only rarely found in pre-Conquest documents. Like O.E. *soc* ('soke') it may mean either 'jurisdiction' or a 'court' or the area over which authority is exercised. The one document where named lathes occur is

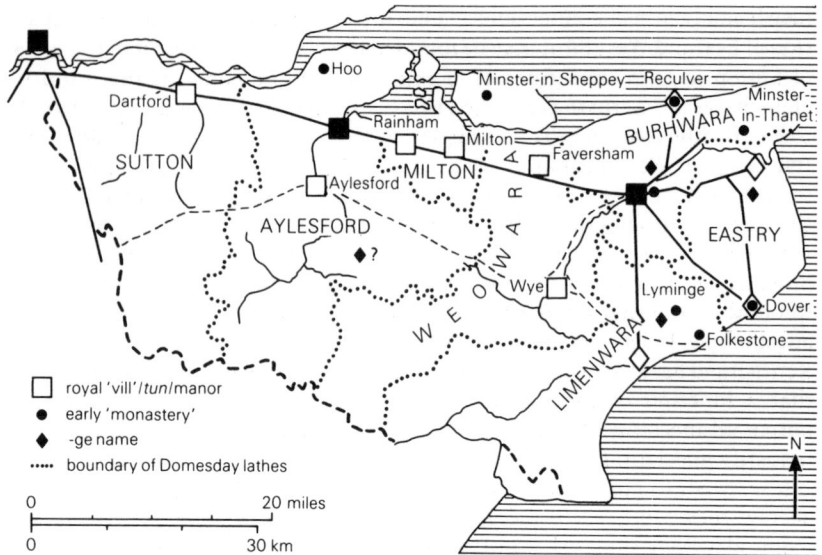

Figure 4.2. Early Kent: administrative divisions. The boundaries of the Domesday lathes in the Weald are largely conjectural. The royal 'vills' or manors are those recorded in Domesday Book or in pre-Conquest charters; the monasteries are those recorded before 900.

the Rochester bridgework list of *c.* 975.[72] The identification of all the contributory estates listed there, however, shows that 'Aylesford and all the lathe that belongs thereto' cannot refer to the Domesday lathe of Aylesford, but only to the royal manor of Aylesford itself; whilst the reference to 'Hollingbourne and all the lathe that belongs to it' is to the area that was later the Domesday hundred of Eyhorne. It seems clear that 'lathe' was not a technical term for a district of a particular size and function. Despite the richness of our documentation for Anglo-Saxon Kent, it would be foolish to attach much weight to the absence of any explicit reference to administrative territories that can be identified with the Domesday lathes. If the courts of the lathes are correctly understood as courts of the free peasants, the gavelkinders, of Kent,[73] then we should not expect our extant Kentish charters and dispute settlements, which only concern the nobility and emanate from the shire court(s) of East and West Kent, to refer to them.

The principal evidence that the Domesday system of lathes is indeed ancient is found in a number of diplomas of the eighth century granting estates in various parts of Kent that have detached woodland pastures ('denns') in the Weald ('the common wood'), which are said to lie *on limenweara wealde, on weowera wealde, in limen wero wealdo et in burh waro uualdo, in cæstruu-arouualth, on cæstersæta walda* and so forth.[74] By that time substantial areas of the Weald would seem to have already been assigned to the lathes of the *limenwara*, the *burhwara* and the *weowara* as commons for the pannage of herds of pigs; it would also seem that the *cæsterwara* or *cæstersæte*, 'the people of the chester' (i.e. of Rochester), may be an early name for a West

Kentish lathe which in Domesday Book is apparently represented in whole or in part by the 'lathe of Aylesford'. In other charters we meet estates located *in regione eastrgena, in regione easterege* and *in regione caestruuara.*[75] Such phrases might be translated as 'in the lathe of Eastry' and 'in the lathe of the men of Rochester', if *regio* here refers to a precise administrative district rather just the general vicinity.

Our understanding of such references and of the working and origins of the lathe system in Kent is dominated by the interpretation of J.E.A. Jolliffe, who approached the lathe from the legal and estate records of the thirteenth century and regarded it as a relic of the pre-feudal age.[76] For him the lathe was 'an embodied folk' administering customary law in its court and regulating customary communal use of outlying wealden and marshland pastures. At the centre of each lathe was a royal vill, administered by a *praefectus* or reeve, where the dues of the free peasantry were collected without the intervention of any intermediate lords. By analysing the assessment of Kentish manors in Domesday Book, Jolliffe deduced that each lathe was a territorial unit assessed at a round number of 80 or 160 sulungs for the purpose of securing the payment of food rents to the king.[77] This assessment was ancient, being already traceable in the reckoning of estates in terms of *aratra* in the earliest Kentish charters of the late seventh century. It followed that the five lathes and two half lathes of Domesday Book had in the seventh century been represented by some eleven or twelve original lathes with a uniform assessment in sulungs. Jolliffe believed that these original units could also be traced through the use of the Latin term *regio* and the vernacular *-ware* in early sources, as well as through the occurrence of the primitive element *-ge* in Kentish placenames (Eastry, Sturry and Lyminge). Thus for example it was possible to recognize early references to lathes of Sturry, Lyminge, Hoo, Rainham and Faversham.[78] The further back one traced the lathe, the smaller and more regular it became.

Jolliffe's interpretation of the lathe has been enormously influential. As he foresaw, scholars have detected similar pre-feudal territorial units based on royal vills very widely elsewhere in Britain: in the sokes of East Anglia, the 'shires' and 'thanages' of northern England and Scotland, in the 'multiple' or 'discrete' estates beloved by geographers and in primitive *regiones* in many parts of Anglo-Saxon England.[79] In Kent K.P. Witney, building on Jolliffe's work, identified a high proportion of the 500-odd outlying wealden 'denns' of Kentish manors and was able to go on to conjecture how the Weald had been divided between nine of the supposed twelve original lathes.[80] Before this dominant model is inscribed on the tablets, however, its foundations need to be examined.

The counting of sulungs (as of hides) is a horrible task on which no two scholars agree, and it is not surprising that before the age of the computer Jolliffe made slips and that his desire to find eighty-sulung units sometimes overrode the evidence or the geographical probabilities. K.P. Witney has corrected the grosser errors but his successive emendations of the details mean that there is no longer any clear overall pattern and therefore put the reality of the eighty-sulung units into question. Even more fundamentally, however, neither Jolliffe nor Witney sought to establish the antiquity of the Domesday assessments. Domesday Book itself shows that there were major changes in the assessment of estates between 1066 and 1086; yet we are asked to believe that the 1066 assessment was that of the seventh century, substantially without change. Whenever we examine particular estates in detail, we find evidence to the contrary. A single example must suffice. The cathedral church of Canterbury claimed to have been given twenty-six sulungs at Reculver by king Eadred in a charter which survives in a tenth-century manuscript. The detailed boundary clause establishes that the estate by then comprised the ecclesiastical parishes of Herne, Reculver and Hoath, as did the archiepiscopal manor of Reculver in the thirteenth century and subsequently.[81] Yet the assessment of the manor in Domesday Book and subsequently was only eight sulungs, not twenty-six. In fact amongst the authentic pre-Conquest charters of Christ Church, Canterbury, there is not one where the assessment of the estate is identical with that of the Domesday manor of the same name. Reductions of varying proportions are the rule.[82] Yet unless they were uniform and systematic throughout the county, such reductions will have made any attempt to reconstruct the seventh-century units from the Domesday assessments hazardous.

Equally unsatisfactory, as Gordon Ward demonstrated,[83] was Jolliffe's incomplete and selective discussion of the use of the term *regio* in early charters. When a charter states that a property is *in regione quae vocatur cert, in regione vocabulo bromgeheg* or *in regione quae dicitur westan widde*,[84] there can be little doubt that it is simply locating the land by reference to the nearest estate centre or notable topographical feature. We do not need to start inventing early lathes of Chart, Broomy or Westwood. For the same reason we should hesitate before accepting the reality of the supposed early lathes of Rainham or Faversham, unless we suppose that every royal estate had its lathe.[85] When the *regio* is a folk name – *in regione caestruuara, in regione merscuuariorum* – the case for regarding it as a 'lathe' is clearly stronger, particularly since we find the former people to have had woodland commons in the Weald, whilst the *Merscware* ('the people of Romney Marsh') were of sufficient importance for their devastation by king Coenwulf of Mercia to be mentioned alongside that of the *Cantware*.[86] We can only guess, however, whether the *Merscware* were a subdivision of the *Limenware*, an alternative name for the same lathe or a separate folk and lathe in their own right. More instructive is the case of the Hoo peninsula: the Domesday hundred of Hoo, which comprised estates assessed at fifty-seven sulungs, seems to have been the territory of *Howare* in the Rochester bridgework list and may be identical with the *regio* in which the neighbouring estate of Stoke lay in a charter of 738.[87] It would seem that *-ware*, like *læð* and *regio*, could be applied to areas or peoples of different size and different status.

There is therefore good reason to be much more cautious how we reconstruct the primitive *regiones* of Kent. A new analysis of the Domesday assessments without Jolliffe's preconceptions, a study of the parish and hundredal boundaries along the lines now proving so fruitful elsewhere, and the testing of the wide range of evidence that Professor Everitt has brought to bear on the development of Kentish settlement – all these are needed before we can hope to identify the early territorial units of Kent or to understand their role with any confidence. For the present it may be most helpful to summarize present knowledge in diagrammatic form (Table 4.1).

Table 4.1 The primitive *regiones* of Kent

Domesday Lathe	Royal Vill	*Ge*	*Wara* name	Monastery	*Regio*
Wiwaralæð	Wye (Faversham)		Wiwaraweald	Minster-in-Sheppey	
Burhwaralæð	Canterbury (Sturry)		Burhwaraweald	St Augustine's Minster-in-Thanet Reculver	
Limenwaralæð	Lympne	(Lyminge)	Limenwara-weald	Lyminge Folkestone	
Eastry	Eastry	Eastry		Dover	Eastry
Aylesford	Aylesford (Rochester)	(?Wester)	Cæsterware	(Hoo)	Cæsterware
Sutton (½)	Dartford				
Milton (½)	Milton (Rainham)				
			Merscware Howare	Hoo	Merscware Hoo
	Rainham Faversham				Rainham Faversham

This presentation of the evidence suggests that the four lathes of East Kent existed from the early days of the kingdom. Each was based upon a major royal vill; three of the four had a single -*ge* name in their territory; and three had woodland commons in the Weald mentioned in early charters. At present there does not seem to be any good evidence that there were ever more than four lathes in the East. A case has indeed been made for a lathe of Faversham; but it amounts to no more than that (i) there was a royal estate there in the ninth century as in Domesday; (ii) a nearby property could be described as 'in the region suburban to the king's *oppidum* which is called by the inhabitants there Faversham'; and (iii) Faversham had a detached wood at Kingsnoad in Ulcombe.[88] In West Kent there seems to be no evidence that the lathe of Aylesford or the half lathes of Sutton and Milton were ancient administrative units. We hear instead in pre-Conquest charters of a single unit based on Rochester, that is of the *Cæsterware*; later, perhaps when the kings had given away all their property in the city to the bishops, West Kent was reorganized into three unequal territories based upon the king's chief manors.

Such an interpretation of the early lathe system of East and West Kent is very much less ambitious than that of Jolliffe, but it does not do violence to the sources. It has the merit too of pointing to yet another way in which West Kent differed from the East. 'Men of Kent' and 'Kentishmen' were, it would seem, distinct in their organization, and the differences may go back to the incorporation of West Kent under the rule of the East Kentish dynasty – a process that is likely to have been prolonged, but to have reached a decisive stage in the reign of Æthelberht. It may have been at that time too that the Kentish origin legends and the Kentish royal genealogy were first formulated for the gratification of the itinerant king and his *leode*. The court of an ambitious and initially pagan overlord is exactly the place where we would expect there to be cultivated stories of his heroic and divine ancestors, claims of his descent from the first Anglo-Saxon leaders and accounts of their glorious activities in the most recently acquired part of his kingdom. In the English origin legend in its various forms may we not detect some of the political cement of the kingdom of Æthelberht?[89]

5 The kingdom of the South Saxons: the origins

MARTIN WELCH

The extent of the South Saxon kingdom can be seen on the maps showing the archaeological distribution of sixth-century cemeteries and settlements and the seventh-century cemeteries and barrow burials, some of which probably continue into the eighth century (figs. 5.1 and 5.2). In both maps we find a broadly similar distribution extending from the Apple Down cemetery in the Marden group of parishes in the west across the South Downs to Eastbourne in the east, with a few miscellaneous finds in the western coastal plain around Chichester and the occasional site along the Lower Greensand ridge to the north of the Downs. The Weald to the north and east of Eastbourne has produced no sites at all for the early Anglo-Saxon period. Only in the Hampshire border area is there any potential for confusion between South Saxon sites and those of their neighbours.

There is no reliable historical information about the South Saxon kingdom before the seventh and eighth centuries, and our principal sources then are the Life of St Wilfrid, Bede's Ecclesiastical History, the Anglo-Saxon Chronicle, the Tribal Hidage and the South Saxon charters.[1] The absence of a royal genealogy or king list for the South Saxon kingdom is noteworthy, for we might reasonably have expected one to be prepared in the monastery at Selsey during the eighth century; if so it has not survived. Such genealogies tend to present problems of interpretation, however, and it might not have added greatly to our understanding of the kingdom.

On the assumption that the Tribal Hidage describes a seventh-century situation,[2] it is not surprising to find that the assessment of the South Saxon kingdom at 7,000 hides matches the figure given by Bede,[3] who had bishop Daniel of Winchester as his correspondent for events in Wessex and Sussex.[4] It seems that the number of 7,000 hides had a symbolic value and was not to be taken too literally, for it is the standard description of a middle-sized kingdom or province in the Tribal Hidage.[5] King Hygelac presents Beowulf with 'seven thousand [hides], hall and throne',[6] showing this to be the appropriate endowment for a prince who has proved himself. Bede describes the South Saxon kingdom as extending 'south and west from Kent as far as the land of the West Saxons',[7] noting elsewhere that the Isle of Wight lies 'opposite the frontier between the South Saxons and the Gewisse separated from the mainland by a channel three miles wide, which is called the Solent'.[8] Bede's use here of the term *medium* for 'frontier' implies a buffer zone between the Gewisse or West Saxons and the South Saxons. This is perhaps the Jutish province defined by Barbara Yorke elsewhere in this volume, and at the very least it is the territory of the *Meanware* centred on the Meon valley in east Hampshire. Wulfhere of

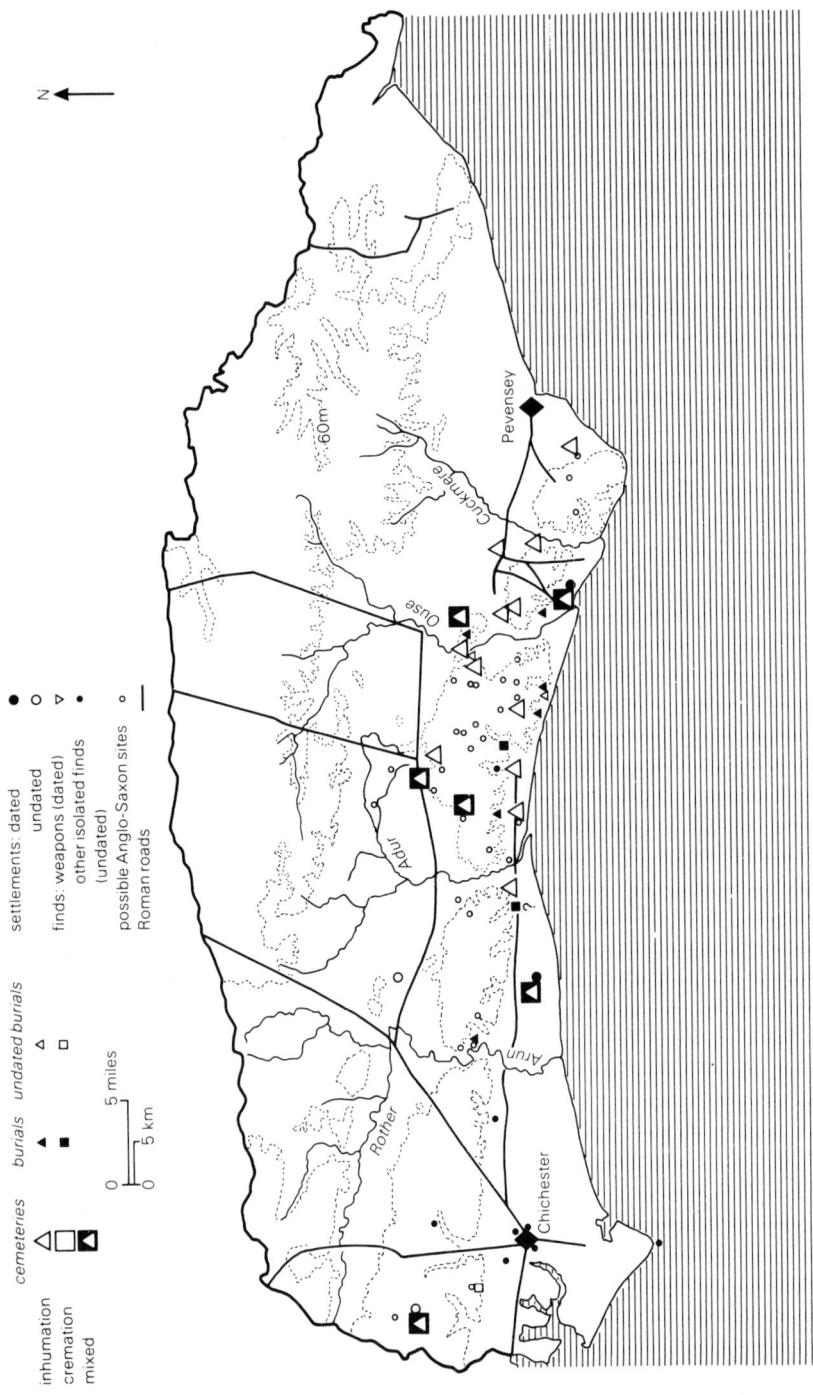

Figure 5.1. Early Anglo-Saxon Sussex: sixth-century sites.

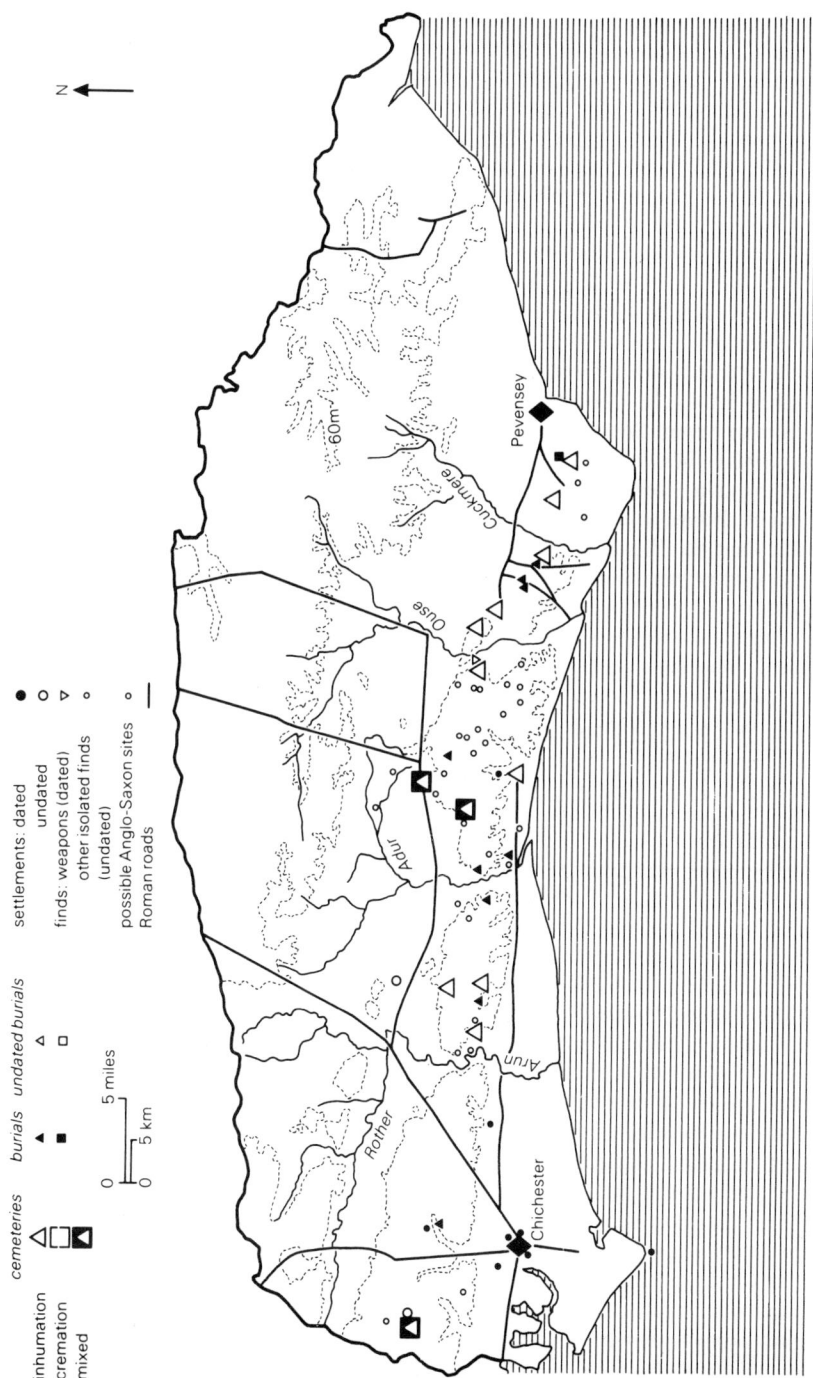

Figure 5.2. Early Anglo-Saxon Sussex: seventh-century sites.

Mercia gave the *Meanware* and the Isle of Wight to Æthelwealh, king of the South Saxons,[9] in the 660s or more probably in the first half of the 670s,[10] presumably as a reward for military assistance against the Gewisse. This surely implies that neither of these two provinces had hitherto formed part of the South Saxon kingdom; indeed both were to be annexed by the West Saxon king Cædwalla in the 680s.[11] Further definition of the western frontier is provided by Bede's assumption that the small monastic community at Bosham lay within the kingdom,[12] and the possibility that the name of the Marden group of parishes means 'boundary hill'[13] and refers to a frontier which runs close to the pre-1974 county boundary.

The Life of St Wilfrid attributes the failure of Christianity to take root among the South Saxons prior to Wilfrid's own mission to their kingdom's natural defences, 'its rocky coasts and thick forests'.[14] Although there is an element of exaggeration here, the lack of good natural harbours on the Sussex coast between Pagham Harbour near Chichester and the former lagoon by the late Roman Saxon Shore fort of *Anderitum* at Pevensey, together with the chalk cliff line between Brighton and Beachy Head, is being described here, as well as the great Wealden forest inland. In view of the 15,000 hides assigned by the Tribal Hidage to Kent, more than double the assessment for Sussex, it is possible that the Weald to the north and east of Pevensey, the later Rape of Hastings, may have been attached to Kent rather than to the South Saxon kingdom in the seventh century. The Roman road pattern in this region links it to Rochester, Canterbury, Lympne and Dover rather than to the South Downs and the *civitas* capital of Chichester.[15]

It seems that the *Hæstingas* who gave their name to this region were a small semi-independent tribal group, comparable to the peoples listed as occupying the East Midlands in the Tribal Hidage.[16] The *Historia Regum* reports the defeat of the *gens hestingorum* by Offa of Mercia in 771[17] and two eleventh-century entries in the Anglo-Saxon Chronicle testify that the Hastings folk still retained a separate identity on the eve of the Norman Conquest.[18] The three surviving placenames incorporating the personal name Hæst appear to occur on the margins of their territory at Hastingford in the west, Hastings itself on the south coast and Hastingleigh near Ashford in Kent in the east.[19] It seems reasonable to postulate that the *Hæstingas* may have originated in south-east Kent; and with the absence of any early Anglo-Saxon sites in the Hastings region, it seems that their colonization of the Weald took place relatively late, in the seventh to eighth centuries. We do not know the name or title of any of their rulers; and the suggestion that the Wattus *rex* who attests three charters[20] at the end of the seventh century and the beginning of the eighth was their king depends on a rather naïve interpretation of placenames and can be regarded as unproven.[21] Similarly we cannot be certain when the *Hæstingas* became attached to the South Saxon kingdom; but the charter evidence can be read as implying that this was achieved by Offa as a direct result of his victory in 771, and his decision to grant the Bexhill estate to bishop Oswald of Selsey in 772 apparently reflects this policy.[22]

The charter evidence is less helpful when it comes to defining the frontier between Sussex and Kent. The Old English bounds of the three hides of outland at Icklesham attached to Offa's Bexhill grant refer to the *cantwara mearc*. But Icklesham is located some one and a half miles south-west of New Winchelsea well within present-day Sussex. Next in a grant of fishing rights on the Lympne of *c.* 740, another charter refers to *terminos suthsaxoniae,* though the text survives in a copy probably datable to no earlier than the late eighth century.[23] Finally *suthsaxa lond* occurs on the eastern boundary of a ninth-century estate at Burmarsh in Kent.[24] It seems that we are looking at the bounds of outlying sections of estates held by either men of Kent or South Saxons, rather than at a well-defined boundary between two former kingdoms which in the ninth century became shires of greater Wessex. Sussex still lacked an exact northern boundary in 1086;[25] and it must be admitted that it is difficult to gauge the extent to which the five rapes of Sussex described in Domesday Book can be seen to reflect earlier regional divisions of the South Saxon shire, let alone of the earlier kingdom. The rapes of Domesday Book are Norman lordships, apparently created to defend the strategically important coastline facing Normandy, and probably bear little resemblance to any previous districts called rapes.[26]

Æthelwealh is the only king of the South Saxons of whom we can claim much knowledge. The ally of Wulfhere, as we have seen, he had to accept Christian baptism and marriage to a Hwiccian princess called Eafa or Eaba as well as the provinces of the *Meanware* and the Isle of Wight. It may be that the monastic community at Bosham provided Eafa with a private chapel and she lived to greet the exiled bishop Wilfrid when he sought refuge with Æthelwealh.[27] Wilfrid received an estate based on the Selsey peninsula, most probably at Church Norton, on which to found a monastery; his biographer states that it was the king's own *villa,*[28] i.e. a *villa regalis.* It seems then that Æthelwealh's power was centred in the region of the former Roman *civitas* capital of Chichester. In archaeological terms Chichester appears to have been virtually deserted between the fifth and ninth centuries,[29] when Alfred the Great established a *burh* there, making use of the Roman stone walled circuit, which provided the basis for a limited urban development in the tenth and eleventh centuries. If we wish to discover the location of a royal palace of the seventh to eighth centuries, we should probably look outside the town walls, perhaps at Kingsham in nearby Donnington parish. Munby has recently suggested that the *villa* granted to Wilfrid may well have been associated with a small trading settlement on Pagham Harbour by analogy with evidence for such trading establishments there later in the Middle Ages, and this would indeed have made the gift more attractive to Wilfrid.[30] Wilfrid certainly founded a monastery there, but he does not appear to have established a bishopric. It was not until a decade or so had passed after his departure from Sussex that a synod created a see for the South Saxons and abbot Eadberht of Selsey was elected the first bishop between 705 and 709.[31] The failure to set up the see at Chichester may well indicate the unimportance of the former Roman town.

An exiled prince of the Gewisse called Cædwalla, who was roaming the Wealden regions of *Ciltine et Ondred* in the early 680s, emerged to attack and kill Æthelwealh.[32] He in turn was driven out of the kingdom by two *duces regii,* Berthun and Andhun, but returned later as king of the Gewisse and killed Berthun.[33] The joint rule of the two *duces* may imply a division of the South Saxon kingdom,[34] in which case a west–east division presaging the modern counties of West and East Sussex might be envisaged. Berthun may well have ruled the western part centred around Chichester and Selsey, which would be why he was killed and not Andhun. Thereafter Sussex remained a West Saxon dependency for the rest of Cædwalla's reign and most of Ine's.[35] A South Saxon king called Nothhelm, whose name in one charter[36] is also given in an abbreviated form as Nunna, may well be the same Nun or Nunna described as fighting with Ine against the British in 710. He is also referred to there as Ine's *mæge* or kinsman;[37] and while it is possible that Nunna was a South Saxon married to a West Saxon princess, the term *mæge* implies that he was more probably a West Saxon of royal blood appointed by Ine to rule the South Saxons. Wattus *rex* apparently shared that authority with him, perhaps ruling the eastern half of the kingdom.[38] It has also been noted that most of those named as *reges*, or after 771 as *duces*, in the South Saxon charters have a name with either an *Æthel-* or an *Os-* stem,[39] which might imply two different royal dynasties.[40] Alternatively, as *Os-* stem names are common among Hwiccian rulers,[41] the *Os-* names may commemorate descent from the Hwiccian Eafa and the *Æthel-* names relate to Æthelwealh, implying just one family. Whichever the case, joint rule of two or more *reges* or *duces* is not uncommon; for example, Ealdwulf, Ælfwald and Oslac appear together as *reges* in a grant by Ealdwulf,[42] and Oswald, Osmund, Ælfwald and Oslac as *duces* all witness Offa's Bexhill charter.[43]

If we accept the possibility that the South Saxon kingdom was divided at the very least into two parts, with the western half ruled from the Chichester and Selsey area, is there a comparable centre which can be postulated for the eastern half? The Saxon Shore fort of *Anderitum* at Pevensey is one possibility. No modern excavations have been conducted there, but by analogy with Portchester castle in Hampshire,[44] an aristocratic if not a royal centre might be envisaged. A more convincing case can be made for the important Alfredian *burh* at Lewes, which later became the county town of East Sussex. It seems that in the late Anglo-Saxon period Lewes was a more successful town than Chichester, having two moneyers in the tenth century when Chichester and Hastings had only one each. A find of two iron weapons during building work in 1899 for an extension to what are now the County Courts may well indicate the presence of an important early Anglo-Saxon cemetery on the hilltop centre of Lewes. One of them, a throwing-axe of francisca type dated to the late fifth and early sixth centuries, is a relatively rare weapon, but not nearly as rare as the other, a long seax of the late seventh to eighth centuries.[45] This putative cemetery was flanked by two indisputable early Anglo-Saxon cemeteries on Malling Hill in South Malling to the east across the Ouse and at Saxonbury House (Kingston-by-Lewes) on the edge of the Southover suburb to the west.[46] To this we can add the case put that the eighty hide estate of South Malling held by the archbishop of Canterbury at the time of Domesday Book had been carved out of a much larger royal estate centred on Lewes.[47] The Malling estate included twenty-one haws or *hagae* in Lewes, but more significantly it was flanked by two royal estates centred on Beddingham to the south and Rother-field to the north.[48] If we turn next to the coinage of king Athelstan in the tenth century, we find that Lewes is one of the few towns to be described on coins as an *urbs*.[49] The other three are Oxford, Southampton and the as yet unidentified 'Darent'. Perhaps Lewes only obtained this status as a tenth-century *burh*, but it is possible that it was also a major royal centre: an *urbs* in the ninth-century reign of Alfred, the eighth-century reign of Offa and the seventh-century reign of Æthelwealh.[50]

This chapter began by considering the distribution of sixth- and seventh-century cemeteries and settlement sites in Sussex, but there are many fewer sites datable to the fifth century (fig. 5.3). These must now be related to the record of the activities of a Saxon military adventurer called Ælle in the second half of the fifth century, as it appears in the Anglo-Saxon Chronicle and Bede's Ecclesiastical History. Five cemeteries, one of which is associated with a contemporary settlement, are located in a restricted region of downland between the Rivers Ouse and Cuckmere in East Sussex, while a sixth cemetery and settlement occupy a strategic position in a hillfort at Highdown near Worthing, with commanding views of the West Sussex coastal plain. It has been tempting to interpret the Ouse–Cuckmere settlement as a block of territory ceded to the Saxons by the British authorities, and this may still be correct.[51] On the other hand, the recent discovery by a metal detector of an early fifth-century North German hybrid brooch related to the Saxon *Stützarmfibel* type, in an unexcavated cemetery in Keymer parish north of Brighton,[52] may indicate Saxon settlement in the fifth century spreading across the Downs from Highdown to the Cuckmere valley.

According to the first of the Chronicle's entries, Ælle landed with three ships, defeated the hostile Britons and drove them into the Wealden forest.[53] Clearly there are mythical elements in this account, such as the three ships and the naming of the beach on which they landed after one of Ælle's sons. The traditional interpretation of this entry has no merits, for it links the *Cumeneshora* of a tenth-century forged charter to the *Cymeneshora* of the Chronicle to identify the beach with one on the Selsey peninsula.[54] Chichester's capture would surely be a probable result of Ælle's victory if he had landed at Selsey, but it is not mentioned. Added to this is the absence of any fifth-century archaeological evidence in the Chichester–Selsey area, indeed west of Highdown. It is difficult to see how Ælle could drive his British assailants into the Weald after an opposed landing at Selsey, but there is no such difficulty if he landed in an area of many fifth-century sites, perhaps near Lewes on the Ouse estuary or near Alfriston on the Cuckmere. Next came the battle with the Britons near the banks of *Mearcredesburna*[55] which can be plausibly translated as 'the river of the frontier agreed by treaty' and thus related to the postulated cession of territory between the Ouse and the Cuckmere.[56] If the Cuckmere marks the eastern boundary of Ælle's territory, then he had good reason to storm the fort at *Anderitum* and massacre everyone there.[57] A hostile garrison able to attack his settlements at will and then hide behind the stone walls of Pevensey castle required and received decisive action.

The only other certain information we have of Ælle is Bede's statement that he was the first 'English king to rule over all the southern kingdoms which are divided from the north by the River Humber and the surrounding territory'.[58] This should not be read too literally, for we cannot be sure what Bede knew and what was merely supposition on his part. Ælle need not have held the title of *rex*, for Bede's assumption that he did may be no more than a guess on his part. Nor can we realistically equate the type of overlordship that Ælle might have exercised over others in southern Britain with the power exercised by a Ceawlin or an Æthelberht in the sixth century, let alone an Offa in the eighth

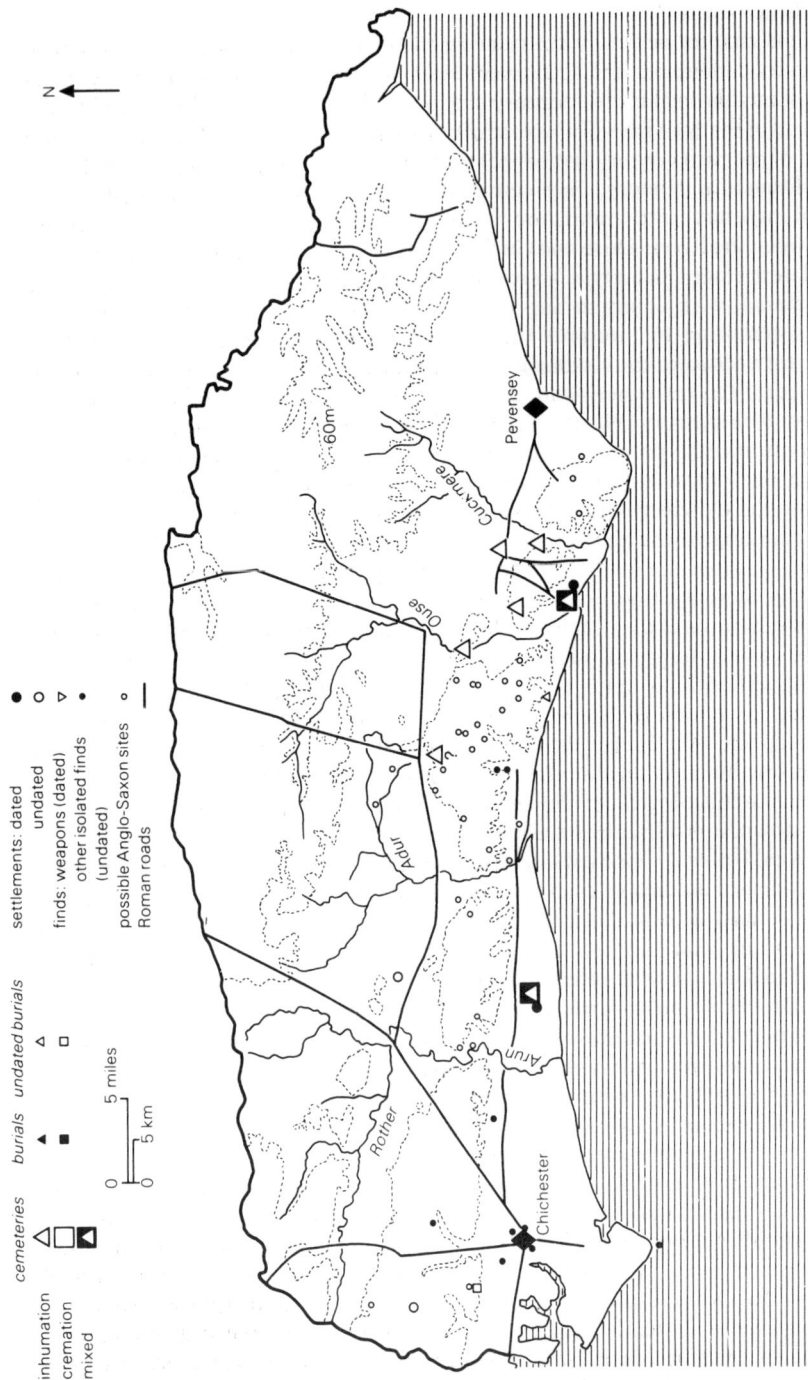

Figure 5.3. Early Anglo-Saxon Sussex: fifth-century sites.

century. We can accept that Ælle was an extraordinary military leader of great renown, but any attempt to map the territory he may have dominated is doomed to failure.[59] Finally, there is no particular reason to assume that Ælle founded a successful dynasty or that the seventh-century king Æthelwealh was his descendant. Historians writing after the Norman Conquest did their best to link the fifth-century myths surrounding Ælle and his sons to the historical kings of the later seventh and eighth centuries,[60] but their attempts are unconvincing.

In conclusion, it seems that the origins of the South Saxon kingdom can be sought in the fifth-century settlement of the South Downs. The archaeological evidence implies that this was centred in the eastern half of the Sussex downland with a westerly outlier on Highdown near Worthing. By the beginning of the sixth century at the latest this settlement had spread along the entire length of the South Downs in Sussex, as Ælle's successors took full control of the Roman *civitas* centred on the town of Chichester. By the second half of the seventh century it seems that South Saxon kings were ruling from centres in the Selsey and Chichester region. To add to the evidence already cited, there is the tale of Wilfrid's ship becoming grounded off the coast around Chichester harbour to the west of Selsey Bill around the year 666. An unnamed king arrived on the scene as a fourth attack was being prepared by the local South Saxon population,[61] in all probability implying a royal residence in the neighbourhood. For logistical reasons, it is difficult to believe that comparable royal centres did not exist in the eastern downland region, perhaps at Lewes or Pevensey. The evidence for joint rule by *duces* and *reges* is suggestive here, but all the evidence is circumstantial. It seems probable that the Hastings region of the Weald, the later rape of Hastings, was administered in the Roman period from the *civitas* town of Canterbury rather than from Chichester. The seventh-century kings of Kent may have ruled it, and its incorporation into the South Saxon kingdom may well be a late event, which need not antedate Offa's campaign of 771. It was Offa too who demoted the native South Saxon rulers to the status of *duces*. This marked the effective end of the kingdom, which thereafter was merely a shire.

6 The Jutes of Hampshire and Wight and the origins of Wessex

BARBARA YORKE

Any study of the origins of Wessex must begin by confronting the problems posed by the annals in the Anglo-Saxon Chronicle which describe the activities of Cerdic and Cynric. The annals provide the only narrative account of the foundation of the West Saxon kingdom; but although the events are said to have occurred in the late fifth and early sixth centuries, our source for them dates only from the late ninth century, and we do not know anything about the transmission of its Cerdic and Cynric material. One of the few definite things which can be said about the early West Saxon entries in the Chronicle is that they do at least tell us how some West Saxons of the later ninth century saw, or wished to see, the origins of their kingdom. The problem, of course, lies in trying to discern whether the ninth-century version of events bears any relationship to what actually may have occurred in the late fifth and sixth centuries.

Gone are the days when a historian felt able to write, to quote Charles Plummer, 'as if he had been present at the landing of the Saxons, and had watched every step of their subsequent progress'.[1] Archaeological discoveries helped to strengthen the suspicions of historians, like Plummer, who doubted whether a landing in the vicinity of the Solent in the last decade of the fifth century could provide an adequate explanation for the Anglo-Saxon settlement of the whole of Wessex.[2] Considerable ingenuity has been shown in attempts to reconcile the written and archaeological evidence,[3] but the difficulties of such reconciliation increase as the number of archaeological studies grows. Even if the annals are seen as only describing the activities of the dynastic founders, and not of the bulk of Saxon settlers in Wessex, difficulties abound, for as recent studies have stressed the early annals contain serious internal inconsistencies and chronological distortions.[4] This paper will review briefly some of the causes for suspicion with the Chronicle's version of events, before examining in greater detail the political and territorial claims which its annals appear to make.

One major cause for concern is that the account of the foundation of Wessex in the Chronicle bears many of the general characteristics of foundation legends to be found elsewhere in the Indo-European world.[5] A number of these characteristics are also to be found in the various versions of the foundation of Kent,[6] and there are some striking parallels between the Kentish and West Saxon accounts. In both Kent and Wessex a pair of closely related kinsmen with alliterating names is said to have arrived off the coast of Britain with a small number of ships and, after a few years battling against British armies, to have established a kingdom.[7] There is even in both instances, if one includes

Figure 6.1. The Jutish province in southern Hampshire, showing places mentioned in the text.

the Kentish account in the *Historia Brittonum*, a sub-plot in which the founders arrange for two kinsmen (Octha and Ebissa and Stuf and Wihtgar respectively) to take control of a different part of the country.[8]

The legendary element in the Chronicle's account of the foundation of Wessex is further enhanced by the close connection within the annals of personal names and placenames. Thus in 495 Cerdic and Cynric arrive and fight a battle at *Cerdicesora*, in 519 they fight at *Cerdicesford* and in 527 at *Cerdicesleaga*.[9] In 501 Port and two sons arrive and fight a battle at *Portesmuþa*, and in 508 we learn that the district *Natanleaga* was called after a British king called Natanleod whom Cerdic and Cynric defeated. The placename *Wihtgarabyrg* is said to have been the place of burial in 544 of Wihtgar, the ruler of *Wiht ealand*.[10] Such derivations are indicative of the type of folk etymology that Bede cited when he wrote that *Hrofæscæstræ* (Rochester) was named after a former chief named Hrof.[11] The actual existence of Port and Natanleod is as unlikely as Hrof's. The 'port' of *Portesmuþa* is most likely to derive from Latin *portus*, 'a harbour',[12] and 'Natan' in *Natanleaga*, represented today by Netley Marsh, from O.E. *næt*, 'wet'.[13] *Wihtgarabyrg* (or *Wiht-*

garæsbyrg as it appears in the annal for 530) has no modern equivalent, though attempts have been made to derive Carisbrooke from it.[14] The first element is clearly taken from the Old English version of the Latin name of the Isle of Wight (*Uecta/Uectis*),[15] and in the Tribal Hidage the men of Wight are the *Wihtgara*,[16] but it seems doubtful whether Wihtgar as such, or even his *byrg*, ever existed. If Port and Whitgar seem to have been created from placenames, can we place much reliance on their supposed companions Bieda and Mægla or on Stuf? Although some writers have been happy to reject Port, but retain his sons Bieda and Mægla, and to abandon Wihtgar, but still see Stuf as a genuine Jutish leader,[17] the identification of dubious elements in these early annals, which seem to belong to a genre of foundation legends, makes such selective treatment a doubtful exercise.

Other problems arise with the placenames which incorporate the name Cerdic. It is at least a personal name known to have been used by the West Saxons.[18] Cerdic himself is not as likely as the other eponymous leaders to take his existence from the places containing his name;[19] rather it is the places which appear insubstantial. Only *Cerdicesford* can be equated with a modern settlement name: Æthelweard believed it to be Charford on the River Avon (Hants).[20] Cerdic at least seems to have had an existence outside the pages of the Chronicle, though that does not necessarily mean that he existed in the way that the Chronicle portrays him. For once one gets past the problem of nomenclature there is the even greater hurdle of the chronology.

It has also been appreciated for some time that some of the earliest West Saxon annals duplicate events.[21] The West Saxons appear to arrive at *Cerdicesora* in 495 and again in 514; Cerdic and Cynric succeed to the kingship in 500 (according to Æthelweard's Latin version of the Chronicle and the West Saxon Regnal Table) and in 519;[22] the battle of *Natanleaga* in 508 may be mirrored by the battle of *Cerdicesleaga* in 527. All these duplications are nineteen years apart, that is, the length of a lunar cycle and of the separate cycles within the Easter tables of Dionysius. It has been suggested that events occurring in one Dionysiac cycle could have been erroneously transferred to another when two different forms of reckoning were brought together.[23] What is certain is that these observations decrease further the likelihood of the early annals telling us in what way, and at what time, the foundation of the West Saxon kingdom occurred.

The chronology of the early West Saxon annals has been undermined additionally by David Dumville's comparison of the length of reigns allotted in the Chronicle's framework with the reign lengths of another ninth-century compilation, the West Saxon Regnal Table.[24] The most striking variation is in the reign of Ceawlin, which is put at thirty-one or thirty-two years in the Chronicle's framework,[25] but is allocated only seven or seventeen years in the Regnal Table (unfortunately it is not clear from the variant manuscripts of the Regnal Table what the original reading for Ceawlin was). The Regnal Table places the beginning of Cerdic's reign later than the Chronicle, for when all the variations between the manuscripts containing the Regnal Table are taken into account, we arrive at the date range 527×40 for the beginning of Cerdic's reign.[26] The Regnal Table apparently preserves a ninth-century tradition that the kingdom of Wessex began in the second quarter of the sixth century. The Chronicle agrees with most of the reign lengths of the Regnal Table, so that its much earlier date for the foundation of the kingdom and the greatly extended length of Ceawlin's reign can only be regarded with the greatest suspicion.

Just as there are close parallels between aspects of the foundation accounts of Wessex and Kent, so there are also some close links between the supposed chronologies of the two kingdoms.[27] According to the annals relating to Kent in the Chronicle, Hengist and Horsa succeeded to the kingdom in 455, that is, six years after their *adventus* (for, misreading Bede, the Chronicle appears to take 449 as a firm date for their arrival).[28] In Æthelweard's version of the Chronicle and in the Regnal Table, Cerdic and Cynric arrived in 494 and became kings six years later in 500. In the Chronicle itself the gap between *adventus* and accession does not emerge so clearly. The advent of Cerdic and Cynric is placed in 495, but the equivalent of the 500 annal in Æthelweard is missing, and it is the arrival of Port and his sons which occurs six years later in 501.[29] The duplicating annal of the West Saxon *adventus* is placed in 514[30] (nineteen years after 495), and the second version of elevation to the kingship in 519. The gap here is five years, but nineteen years after 494 (the date of the *adventus* in Æthelweard and the Regnal Table) would have given 513 and a six-year gap.

In the Chronicle Æsc, son of Hengist, is said to have begun ruling in 488. As the Chronicle has already recorded that Æsc was previously ruling with his father, 488 is presumably intended to indicate the date at which Æsc began to rule alone, and so it must also have been the date of Hengist's death.[31] Therefore Hengist, according to the Chronicle's chronology, died in the fortieth year after his arrival in 449. Moving a few years later in the Chronicle, we see that Cerdic is said to have died in 534, the fortieth year after his arrival in 495. We can also note that Cerdic, like Hengist, was succeeded by a son who had previously been ruling with him.

The Kentish parallels can be continued into Ceawlin's reign which, as we have seen, was given thirty-one or thirty-two years in the Chronicle's framework, although only seven or seventeen in the Regnal Table. Ceawlin's accession is placed by the Chronicle in 560, which, according to Ecclesiastical History ii, 5, was the date at which Æthelberht of Kent began to rule. The Chronicle contains no notice of Æthelberht's accession, though it does imply that he was ruling in 568, when Ceawlin and Cutha are said to have defeated him at *Wibbandun*. In view of the other close connections which can be found between the chronologies of Kent and Wessex, it does look as if it was rather more than coincidence that the lengthening of Ceawlin's reign made it begin at the same time as that of Æthelberht of Kent. As Bede's list of overlords makes it clear that Ceawlin preceded Æthelberht as overlord of the southern English,[32] it may well have seemed to some West Saxons of the ninth century unlikely, or implausible, that Ceawlin should have begun to rule some years after Æthelberht's accession, as the reign lengths of the Regnal Table implied.[33] It would appear likely that a compiler or editor of the early West Saxon annals substituted the supposed date of Æthelberht's accession for the date for the beginning of Ceawlin's reign which could be derived from the Regnal Table, and that this was only one of several West Saxon dates which were revised in the light of Kentish chronology.

The earlier West Saxon dates in the Chronicle could have been calculated back from 560 on the basis of the information in the Regnal Table, for both 534 (the accession of Cynric) and 519 (the (second) accession of Cerdic and Cynric) are broadly compatible with the reign lengths of the Regnal Table, if 560 is taken as the date of Cynric's death.[34] However, there appears to have been a desire to place the origins of the West Saxon kingdom back further still, which was achieved by giving Cerdic a reign of thirty-nine years (like Hengist)[35] and placing the West Saxon *adventus* five or six years earlier (an interval of time which may also have been derived from a Kentish prototype).[36] It would appear that the West Saxons were affected by their knowledge of Kentish chronology when they produced a version of their early history for the Chronicle. Emulation of the history of Kent may provide an explanation for the apparent desire to extend West Saxon history further back into the past, though, as we shall see, there may have been additional reasons.

The legendary elements of the foundation narratives in the Chronicle and their suspicious chronology inevitably raise doubts about the historical validity of their subject matter. We must never forget that the Chronicle is a late ninth-century document, and that we do not know on what information the fifth- and sixth-century annals are based. They can only be accepted as genuine accounts if we can find verification for them in earlier records. Can we find any such support for the picture the Chronicle provides of the origins of the West Saxon kingdom? Exactly what claims were being made in the Chronicle are obscured by our inability to identify all the placenames, though the claim that the West Saxon leaders conquered the Isle of Wight and then delegated authority to two kinsmen emerges clearly enough. Bede's well-known statement that the men of Wight were of Jutish and not West Saxon stock is enough to throw suspicion on this part of the Chronicle's narrative.[37] The Chronicle does not state that Stuf and Wihtgar were Jutes, but Asser makes it clear that in ninth-century Wessex Stuf and Wihtgar were believed to be Jutish and the founders of the royal house of Wight.[38] Although it would not have been impossible for Cerdic to have Jutish nephews, it is not a claim which carries much conviction.

There is no source other than the Chronicle which even hints at such an early connection between the Isle of Wight and the kingdom of Wessex. Bede, of course, does not discuss the Germanic *adventus* in any detail, but in his famous addition to Gildas's narrative in *HE* i, 15 he does, by postulating a common Jutish origin for the inhabitants of Kent and Wight, open up the possibility that there was an important early link between the two kingdoms. This conclusion is reinforced by the appearance of the name Uecta (the Latin name of the Isle of Wight) as a son of Woden in the Kentish genealogy provided by Bede. The names of Uictgisl and Uitta, the father and grandfather of Hengest in the same source, could have a similar derivation,[39] and we can note in this context that Bede refers to the inhabitants of Wight as *Uictuarii*. We cannot be certain of the significance of the appearance of these names in the Kentish genealogy, but they do seem to suggest a perceived connection between the two royal houses and a joint tradition of a Jutish leader whose name was taken from that of the Isle of Wight.[40] The archaeological evidence also urges us to link the early history of the island with Kent rather than with Wessex. For it would appear that some of the early settlers in both areas did indeed come from Jutland, and that in the sixth century the provinces were linked by common aspects of their material cultures.[41] The aristocracies of the two kingdoms seem to have shared common tastes, which were in part derived from Francia and in part from Scandinavia. The richest grave so far known from the Isle of Wight, a female burial from the Chessell Down cemetery, bears such a close resemblance to female aristocratic burials from Sarre (Kent) that it may be evidence for inter-marriage between the two royal houses in the second half of the sixth century.[42]

Bede gives us every reason to believe that the Isle of Wight was a self-governing area of some significance before its conquest by Cædwalla of Wessex in 686. At the time of Cædwalla's conquest the island had its own royal family (the king, Aruald, and two sons were put to death by Cædwalla), and there is nothing in Bede's narrative to suggest that the West Saxons had any prior claim to the island. On the contrary, the island is said to have come under alien rule (*externae subiectionis*) when conquered by the West Saxons.[43] In v, 23, where he summarizes the condition of the church at the time he was writing, Bede comments that the *episcopatus Uectae* belonged to the bishop of Winchester, as if one might have expected the island, like other former kingdoms, to have had its own bishop, and as if, in spite of having been under West Saxon control since 686, the connection between Wight and Wessex still required comment.[44] Bishop Daniel of Winchester was, according to Bede's Preface, his chief informant for Wessex and Wight, and so the comment and the whole tone of the account of the conquest of Wight (which shows sympathy for the fate of the inhabitants) presumably reflect Daniel's own opinions. If so, it is of great interest to see a leading West Saxon apparently showing reservations about West Saxon claims over the island. The independence of Wight is also demonstrated by its inclusion in the Tribal Hidage, where it is assessed as an independent province.[45] The Chronicle is the only source which suggests a close connection between Wessex and Wight before 686.

We cannot be entirely certain what claims were being made in the Chronicle for a connection between the activities of Cerdic and Cynric and the lands of southern Hampshire which Bede also believed to be Jutish. The annal for 501 which records the battle of *Portesmuþa* contains the only reference to Port and his two sons Bieda and Mægla, and no link is made between them and Cerdic and Cynric. Nor do we know the location of *Cerdicesora* where Cerdic and Cynric are said to have landed and begun the activities which led to their assumption of the kingship. The only places associated with Cerdic and Cynric which can be identified are Netley Marsh, an area west of Totton and on the northern fringes of the New Forest, and Charford on the River Avon, even further west in the county and close to the Wiltshire border. If these identifications are correct it would appear that the Chronicle wished to place the origins of the kingdom of Wessex in Hampshire, but it should perhaps be noted that the evidence that this *is* what the Chronicle was claiming is not as clear cut as some later commentators have suggested. Once again we have to ask the question whether any of our earlier sources provides support for placing the origins of the kingdom of Wessex in Hampshire.

Bede evidently saw much of southern Hampshire as an area which was under West Saxon control at the time he wrote, but which still preserved its identity as a Jutish *natio* (*HE* i, 15) and had once been, like the Isle of Wight, an independent Jutish province. Bede does not provide an exact definition of the boundaries of the province, though his work does give several useful pointers.

The Jutish province was *contra ipsam insulam Uectam*, 'opposite the Isle of Wight'.[46] Conversely the island was *contra medium Australium Saxonum et Geuissorum*, and separated from the mainland by the Solent.[47] Bede cannot have meant by this that the Isle of Wight was opposite the border of the South Saxons and the West Saxons as it stood in 731, as that would mean that he thought the Isle of Wight and the Solent lay opposite the Sussex/Hampshire border which would hardly be an accurate description. Bede knew exactly where the Solent was as he knew its two tides met at the mouth of the Hamble,[48] and he was presumably indebted to bishop Daniel for the very exact knowledge he displays of Hampshire topography. Bede must have meant in this passage that the Isle of Wight lay opposite the border of the South Saxons, on the one hand, and of the Geuissae, on the other – in other words, that the eastern extremity of the island lay opposite the South Saxon border, and the western extremity opposite what had been at one time that of the Geuissae. The mainland territory between the South Saxons and the Geuissae must have been the Jutish province. Unfortunately although it may have been clear enough to Bede where the original Geuissae border ran, it is not so clear to us. However, if we used Bede's words to give us a rough location we would place the Jutish province between (approximately) Lymington and Hayling Island.

Bede does identify a number of areas within these bounds as Jutish, and his evidence can be supplemented by placenames and other material. When Æthelwealh of the South Saxons agreed to be converted to Christianity, his overlord Wulfhere of Mercia rewarded him by assigning him the two provinces of Wight and the Meonware.[49] This is the only time Bede refers to the Meonware and it is probably correct to see them as a Jutish province centred on the River Meon, but it is not necessary to see them as equalling the whole of the Jutish mainland territory. Later in the Saxon period the River Meon bisected the two minster parishes of Titchfield and East Meon, and the bounds of these two minster parishes may delineate the territory of the Meonware which Æthelwealh received.[50] Support for seeing this area as Jutish comes from the name *Ytedene*, 'valley of the Jutes', from a lost hamlet near East Meon.[51] *Portesmuþa* may also have been in the Titchfield *parochia* and thus in the province of the Meonware.[52]

Bede makes it clear that the Jutish territory extended further west. The River Hamble is said to run through the Jutish lands.[53] It separated the minster parish of Titchfield from the adjoining parish of Bishop's Waltham.[54] The account of the fall of the Isle of Wight to Cædwalla provides important additional information. Bede describes how two princes of the Isle of Wight fled from the island to the neighbouring province of the Jutes.[55] They were taken to a place called *Ad Lapidem* which is probably to be identified with the village of Stone, which lies on the peninsula of land between the River Otter and Southampton Water, rather than with Stoneham near Southampton.[56] Stone had probably been a crossing point between the Isle of Wight and the mainland in the Roman period, as a Roman road terminated there.[57] Furthermore when the princes were apprehended in or near Stone, it was the abbot of a monastery *in loco qui vocatur Hreutford* who intervened to have them baptized. The district name *Hreutford*, 'Reed ford', was later replaced by that of Redbridge, and Stone was in Redbridge hundred in Domesday Book and was probably in the minster parish of *Hreutford*.[58] Bede's account of the flight of the princes of Wight therefore provides valuable confirmation that the west bank of Southampton Water was within the Jutish province. The princes may have intended to move from Stone to the New Forest, though Bede does not indicate exactly where they hoped to hide. However, it would appear that the New Forest was Jutish territory, for 'Florence' of Worcester records that the New Forest was known in English as *Ytene*, 'of the Jutes'.[59]

The evidence collected so far supports Bede's generalized comment in i, 15 that the mainland province of the Jutes lay 'opposite the Isle of Wight', for it would appear to have included the New Forest and Redbridge hundred, to the west of Southampton Water, and the territory around the Rivers Hamble and Meon (the minster parishes of Bishop's Waltham, Titchfield and East Meon) to the east. Only the intervening area where the Rivers Test and Itchen flow into Southampton Water has not been covered. Logically we would expect this area also to have been Jutish, and supporting evidence comes from the name *Ytingstoc*, modern Bishopstoke, on the east bank of the River Itchen between Winchester and Southampton.[60] It would seem that the lower reaches of the River Itchen also ran through Jutish territory.

It would appear that a substantial section of the Hampshire coast lay within the Jutish province. The Jutes appear to have occupied all the low-lying coastal plain from (roughly) the western extremity of the New Forest to Hayling Island, though we cannot be certain exactly where the original western and eastern boundaries lay (fig. 6.1). The coastal plain would have been separated from the chalklands to the north by a band of woodland which was known as the Forest of Bere.[61] The area of the Meonware, however, did include an area of downland and the hillfort of Winchester Hill, though it is likely that a substantial belt of woodland also screened their territory from the lands to the north.[62] It does not appear that the Jutish lands extended into the areas associated with Cerdic in the Chronicle. *Cerdicesford*, 'Charford' on the River Avon, is west of the New Forest, and we have no evidence that the Jutish boundary extended that far. Netley Marsh lies on the northern extremity of the Forest. The soil is very poor here and the land boggy and so this area could have been a no man's land between two territories. Another place which could be relevant to the discussion is *Cerdicesbeorg*, near Hurstbourne Tarrant, which has been proposed as the place of Cerdic's burial.[63] It lies well to the north of the Jutish area and, like Charford, was very close to the later border with Wiltshire.

Bede clearly regarded the mainland Jutish province as having a very similar status to the kingdom of Wight. Both are described as a *gens* and the areas that they occupied were *provinciae*. The terms *gens* and *provincia* were habitually used by Bede to delineate areas that were political entities, that is self-governing territories usually with the status of a kingdom.[64] We have no definite evidence that the Jutish mainland area was ever ruled by kings, like the Isle of Wight, but the tradition of Port and his sons recorded in the Chronicle obviously could be taken as evidence that there had been a royal house at one time who claimed Port and one or other of his offspring as ancestors. Bede would hardly have written about the mainland Jutish province in the way that he did if it had not preserved its political distinctiveness into the Saxons' Christian era, that is, if it had not survived as a distinct unit well into the seventh century, like the kingdom of Wight. The placenames which describe parts of the province as Jutish also help to reinforce these conclusions.

These occur close to the boundaries of the province, and are presumably the result of a desire to distinguish Jutish from Saxon territory.[65] Archaeological evidence suggests that the material culture of the Hampshire Jutes was not strikingly different from that of their Saxon neighbours,[66] and it would be unrealistic to think that all, or even the majority, of the people in the province were actually of Jutish descent.[67] The distinction between Saxon and Jute is likely to have been more of a political than a cultural distinction, that is, a recognition that the Jutes were a different people because they had different rulers who were, or who claimed to be, of Jutish origin.

It might seem surprising, if this area was once an autonomous unit, that we do not have a name for it, and presumably Bede did not know a separate term. However, it may be that we do have a record of the name of this area if only we could recognize it. There are a number of names in the Tribal Hidage which have not been satisfactorily equated with a settlement area. Of particular interest are the names which follow that of the Wihtgara, and appear as Noxgaga and Ohtgaga in the O.E. version and as Hexgaga and Ochtgata/Octhgaga in the Latin.[68] These names have presumably been corrupted in transmission, but it is interesting to note in the form Ochtgata the name of another hypothetical Jutish leader, Octha, who appears variously as the son of Hengest and the grandfather of Æthelberht of Kent.[69] The Noxgaga and the Ohtgaga were assessed at 5,000 and 2,000 hides respectively, as opposed to 600 hides for the Wihtgara.[70] Davies and Vierck in their attempt to associate the Tribal Hidage entries with likely settlement areas concluded that there was no room for the Noxgaga and Ohtgaga north of the Thames, and tentatively suggested that they might be located in Surrey and Hampshire.[71] The area which Bede and the placename evidence suggest belonged to the Jutes conforms to the type of settlement area delineated by natural features which Davies and Vierck defined.[72] It is also not uncommon in the early Anglo-Saxon period to find cognate groups linked by a river and settled on its opposite banks.[73] In this instance it would appear that the Jutes of Wight and the mainland were linked by the Solent and had settled on its opposite banks.

The Jutish provinces seem to have come under permanent West Saxon control in the latter part of the seventh century. Bede described the conquest of the Isle of Wight by Cædwalla as occurring soon after his accession to the throne of Wessex,[74] and the Chronicle dates the campaign to 686 where it is linked with an attack on Kent.[75] The kingdom of Wight had already had its independence curtailed when Wulfhere had granted control of it and the province of the Meonware to king Æthelwealh of the South Saxons whom he had persuaded to accept baptism.[76] The Chronicle places Wulfhere's conquest of Wight in 661.[77] As we have seen, the Meonware occupied only the most easterly portion of the mainland Jutish province, and there is no reference to what happened to the western portion, though it might be a reasonable assumption that it came under West Saxon control at this time.

The removal of the West Saxon see from Dorchester-on-Thames to Winchester could be connected with acquisition of the western part of the mainland Jutish province. The Chronicle dates Wine's appointment to 660,[78] and we know from Bede that the transfer of the see took place at the time of his appointment.[79] However, the Chronicle's date may be slightly inexact, as it states that Wine was bishop for three years, but separate information in the

Ecclesiastical History shows that Wine was still bishop in 664 when he consecrated Chad with the assistance of two British bishops.[80] But it must have been at just about the time that Wulfhere was arranging the conversion of the Meonware that Cenwalh was establishing his new bishopric at Winchester which was only a few miles from the northern border of the mainland Jutes, if *Ytingstoc*/Bishopstoke can be seen as lying close to the province's northern edge.[81] Perhaps the new bishopric did not achieve the quick results Cenwalh had been hoping for, because Wine was expelled from his bishopric by the king after only three years. The next bishop, Leuthere, was apparently not appointed until 670.[82] Whether political assimilation proceeded as slowly as conversion must have done is not known, but the princes of the royal house of Wight still thought it worth their while to escape to the western half of the province in 686. Cædwalla's conquest and savage treatment of the Jutes of Wight seem decisively to have marked the end of Jutish independence.

The events of 686 must have been catastrophic for the Jutes, and there is every reason to think that they also marked an important stage in the development of Wessex. The transfer of the West Saxon see from the upper Thames valley to Winchester *c.* 660 could be seen as heralding a major geographical shift in West Saxon interests.[83] Of course their ambitions in the south were not only centred on the Jutish provinces. Surrey and Sussex were also on the shopping list, and these provinces were also conquered by Cædwalla, though the West Saxons had to wait longer to annex them permanently. There was also a continuing interest in expansion westwards, though it is hard to disentangle from the battles listed in the Chronicle the exact course of West Saxon advances into the British areas. But even with these other attractions the conquest of the Jutish provinces is likely to have been very significant. With their conquest the West Saxons of course acquired sizeable territories with good agricultural land, but they also, as Chris Arnold has emphasized, acquired ports with easy access to Francia and to long-established trade routes.[84] It is surely no coincidence that the new trading centre of *Hamwic* was founded, as the archaeological evidence suggests, soon after Cædwalla's conquest.[85] The West Saxons appear to have taken the earliest opportunity to build this large planned settlement, which has no known parallels in West Saxon territory but may be matched by older *wics* in Kent, at London and at Ipswich.[86]

The Ecclesiastical History contains some important evidence to support the idea that the final conquest of the Jutish provinces was a major milestone in the development of Wessex. After the reign of Cædwalla Bede ceases to use the term Geuissae as an alternative to 'West Saxon'.[87] Bede says that Geuissae was the name by which the West Saxons were formerly known (*antiquitus*).[88] He uses the term in a number of instances prior to 688, and Birinus and Agilbert who had their see at Dorchester-on-Thames are described as bishops of the Geuissae.[89] Cædwalla for the early part of his career is also of the Geuissae (particularly in the context of his conquest of the Jutes), but by the time of his abdication he is *rex Occidentalium Saxonum*.[90] In the epitaph on his tomb in Rome, which Bede reproduces, Cædwalla is described as *rex Saxonum*,[91] and, as this is also the title which is used in his charter for the foundation of a minster at Farnham, it was presumably the title which Cædwalla actually used.[92] It would appear that after his (permanent) conquest of the Jutes and (temporary) overlordship of the South Saxons and the men of Surrey, Cædwalla abandoned the old tribal name of his people for one which could be seen as expressing a wider hegemony over other Germanic peoples.

There is a sense in which the kingdom of the West Saxons could be seen as beginning c. 686–8; but the question of where the Geuissae came from, if they did not originate in Jutish Hampshire or the Isle of Wight, still needs to be answered. There are two main (and well-known) possibilities. If we set aside the references to the Jutish areas in the Chronicle, we discover that the places which can be associated with Cerdic and Cynric are in the vicinity of the River Avon, that is, in the extreme west of Hampshire and the south-east corner of Wiltshire. As we have seen, *Cerdicesforda*, the site of battles in 508 and 519, was identified by Æthelweard with Charford on the River Avon, and *Cerdicesbeorg*, the putative site of Cerdic's burial, is in the parish of Hurstbourne Tarrant in the north-west of Hampshire and close to a tributary of the Avon. Cynric as sole king of Wessex is said to have fought battles in the vicinity of Old Sarum and Barbury Castle in Wiltshire.[93] Cemetery evidence would support the idea of a concentration of sixth-century Saxons in the Avon valley, particularly in the Salisbury area, but caution must be exercised.[94] If part of the Cerdic and Cynric account is historically implausible, it would be illogical to claim that the rest of the Cerdic and Cynric annals could be accepted without demur. For it is possible that the Avon valley, like Jutish Hampshire and Wight, was an area of secondary rather than primary conquest.

The other area which the Chronicle associates with the early West Saxon kings is the upper Thames valley, and historians and archaeologists have been perturbed for some time about the apparent need to locate early West Saxon activity in this area as well as in Hampshire and Wiltshire.[95] The upper Thames area features in a number of annals connected with Ceawlin, son of Cynric, according to the Chronicle annals, which are not without problems; and the chronology of Ceawlin's reign as given in the Chronicle is suspect.[96] Nevertheless the annals are quite different from those associated with Cerdic and Cynric, and, it has been suggested, could derive from an oral poetic source.[97] Such a source might not seem much of an improvement on the Cerdic and Cynric annals, but it is only one of several pieces of information linking the early West Saxon kings with this area, and Ceawlin's military successes receive some support from the inclusion of his name in the list of overlords in the Ecclesiastical History ii, 5. The upper Thames was certainly a centre of early Saxon settlement and contains a number of Saxon 'princely burials',[98] but the evidence which really gives the Thames valley a case for serious consideration as the place where the royal family of the West Saxons originated is the foundation of the first West Saxon see at Dorchester-on-Thames in 635.[99] Although in the event the see was short-lived as a new bishopric was established at Winchester c. 660, it may be the best indicator we have of where the original heartland of the Geuissae lay.

If we put aside the ninth-century account of the origins of the West Saxon kingdom contained in the Chronicle, we can construct from earlier sources a rather different picture of the development of Wessex. In this alternative narrative the Isle of Wight and mainland Hampshire appear not as areas of primary West Saxon settlement, but as ones of secondary conquest by the Geuissae. The Chronicle is almost certainly misleading when it says that the

West Saxons controlled these areas in the late fifth and sixth centuries, though it is probably right to indicate, by focusing its early annals on the Jutish territories, that acquisition of these provinces was of the greatest importance in the growth of Wessex. And although Bede implies that the Jutes were treated harshly by their West Saxon conquerors, some Jutish families evidently retained important positions in the new West Saxon kingdom. People who could claim descent from the royal family of Wight were amongst the highest echelons of ninth-century West Saxon society. For king Æthelwulf of Wessex married Osburh, a woman of royal Jutish descent, and her father Oslac had the important position of *pincerna* in Æthelwulf's household.[100]

There are a number of theories which could account for the West Saxons' willingness to locate the activities of their founders in what was foreign territory until well into the seventh century. Of course in the absence of any earlier stages in the compilation of the West Saxon annals any solutions can only be hypothetical. One could argue that the stress on the Jutes arose from king Alfred's desire to celebrate both his paternal and his maternal ancestors, for Alfred, like the kingdom of Wight as depicted in the Chronicle, was the product of a West Saxon and Jutish union. On the other hand, the story of Cerdic and Cynric and Stuf and Wihtgar could be seen as growing out of a desire on the part of the West Saxons to justify Cædwalla's violent annexation of the Jutes. For the Chronicle's account stresses that the West Saxons had a prior claim to the Isle of Wight and that the founders of the royal house of Wight were kinsmen of the West Saxon rulers. If this were the pretext for the early annals, one would expect the myth that they embody to have been established at around the same time as Cædwalla's conquest.

The balance of the evidence suggests that the West Saxons annexed established traditions of Port and his sons and of Stuf and Wihtgar for their own purposes. Many of the perculiarities of the Cerdic and Cynric entries in the Chronicle could be explained if pre-existing accounts of the activities of the Jutish leaders had been adapted to serve West Saxon purposes. The duplication of events, for instance, could have arisen from a desire to model the careers of Cerdic and Cynric on those of the Jutish leaders, with Cerdic and Cynric of course taking priority. The activities of the Jutish leaders might have been recorded orally, but the West Saxons could also have received written notice of them. The Kentish and South Saxon annals for the late fifth century which are incorporated in the Chronicle were presumably derived from outside Wessex, and the most reasonable explanation would be that they came to Wessex, probably from Kent, already in annalistic form.[101] Such a source could also have included annals for the Jutish leaders of Hampshire and Wight, and in view of the close connections which apparently existed between Kent and Wight in the sixth century it would not be surprising to find the stories of Hengist and Horsa and Stuf and Wihtgar linked together. These hypothetical annals would also help to explain why a drastic revision of West Saxon chronology was necessary, for if it was discovered that Stuf and Wihtgar had apparently arrived many years before the traditional dates for the reigns of Cerdic and Cynric in the West Saxon Regnal List, there would have been a powerful incentive for extending West Saxon chronology further back into the past in order to give Cerdic and Cynric the priority which the West Saxons no doubt felt they deserved. As we have seen, the West Saxons seem to have turned to Kentish chronologies to provide workable timespans. Such a revision might in itself have necessitated a duplication of events to help fill the blank spaces the new chronology opened up, though the West Saxons were probably motivated primarily by a desire to make sure that their own founders anticipated the achievements of Jutish leaders.

Additional, older sources do not seem to support the contention of the Chronicle that the kingdom of Wessex had its origins in the conquest of Wight and areas of southern Hampshire in the sixth century. Bede seems quite clear that these areas were independent 'Jutish' provinces until the second half of the seventh century. The evidence for the kingdom of Wight is well known, but it has not always been appreciated that the Solent area of Hampshire seems to have been a province of similar status for almost as long. The existence of this Jutish province in Hampshire has an important bearing on the reasons for the removal of the West Saxon see from Dorchester-on-Thames to Winchester and for the foundation of *Hamwic*. Its recognition is also significant for the history of the shire system in Wessex. For it could be suggested that *Hamtunscir*, which was allotted to Sigebert in 757 when he was deprived by Cynewulf of control of the rest of Wessex,[102] was not the later shire of Hampshire but that part of it which was the former Jutish province. The later shire of Hampshire is clearly an artificial creation in which the Jutish province has been amalgamated with other areas whose early Saxon history is obscure. The amalgamation is perhaps most likely to have occurred in the ninth century when Winchester replaced *Hamtun* as the centre of royal authority.[103]

The origins of the West Saxons themselves – or the Geuissae as they should really be called before 686 – are obscure. Ceawlin is the first of their kings in whom any confidence can be placed and his base seems to have been in the upper Thames valley. It would probably be appropriate to see Ceawlin as a Penda figure, who was able to bring disparate groups of Saxon people together within a framework of military success. It may well have been the case that the Geuissae only became a substantial force following the activities of Ceawlin in the late sixth century. Ceawlin evidently achieved some kind of overlordship of a number of Saxon kingdoms, but more permanent conquests were the work of the seventh century. A priority seems to have been a place, if not exactly in the sun, then certainly on the south coast, and a campaign began under Cenwalh and was completed by Cædwalla to conquer the kingdoms of the Jutes. It is very significant that, according to evidence in the Ecclesiastical History, it is after this conquest that the kingdom of the West Saxons came into existence. When we search for the origins of Wessex we can find traces of the complex amalgamation of provinces which is so apparent in the histories of Northumbria and Mercia.[104]

7 Frithuwold's kingdom and the origins of Surrey

JOHN BLAIR

A text central to the themes of this volume is the charter, composed between 672 and 674, by which a Mercian sub-king named Frithuwold grants land to abbot Eorcenwold, later bishop of London, for the minster at Chertsey.[1] If genuine (and the writer accepts the arguments that basically it is genuine), it is one of the earliest Anglo-Saxon diplomas, one of the first pieces of primary evidence for the endowment of English monasteries, and probably the oldest English document which contains a description of precise local topography. It is also the source upon which some writers have based their case for an independent kingdom of Surrey. The central passages may be translated thus:[2]

> I, Frithuwold, of the province of the men of Surrey, sub-king of Wulfhere, king of the Mercians, of my own free will, being in sound mind and perfect understanding, from this present day grant, concede, transfer and assign from my rightful possession into yours, land for increasing the monastery which was first constructed under king Egbert [of Kent], 200 hides for strengthening the same monastery, which is called Chertsey, and five hides in the place which is called Thorpe. I not only give the land, but confirm and deliver myself and my only son in obedience to abbot Eorcenwold. And the land is, taken together, 300 hides, and moreover by the river which is called the Thames, the whole along the bank of the river as far as the boundary which is called the ancient ditch, that is *Fullingadic*; again, in another part of the bank of the same river as far as the boundary of the next province, which is called Sonning (*Sunninges*). Of the same land, however, a separate part, of 10 hides, is by the port of London, where ships come to land, on the same river on the southern side by the public way. There are, however, diverse names for the above-mentioned land, namely Chertsey, Thorpe, Egham, Chobham, Eaton, Molesey, Woodham and *Hunewaldesham*, as far as the above-mentioned boundary. I grant it to you, Eorcenwold, and confirm it for the foundation of a monastery, that both you and your successors may be bound to intercede for the relief of my soul – along with fields, woods, meadows, pastures, and rivers and all other things duly belonging to the monastery of St Peter, Prince of the Apostles, at Chertsey . . . And I, Frithuwold, who am the donor, together with abbot Eorcenwold, have formed the sign of the Holy Cross + on account of my ignorance of letters. Sign of the hand of Frithuric, witness + . . . [Eight other witnesses]. And in order that this donation may be secure and the confirmation stable, this charter is confirmed by Wulfhere, king of the

Mercians, for he both placed his hand on the altar in the residence which is called Thame and subscribed with the sign of the Holy Cross in his own hand +. These things are done at Frithuwold's vill, by the aforesaid ditch *Fullingadic*, about the Kalends of March.

The aim of this chapter is to suggest a context, political, topographical and religious, for the Chertsey charter. It will address three questions: first, what was the internal territorial structure of seventh-century Surrey? Second, how does the Chertsey case illuminate the process of minster foundation and endowment which seems so characteristic of the late seventh century? Third, who was Frithuwold, and can his control of Surrey under Mercian overlordship be reconciled with the hypothesis of a residual local autonomy?

THE INTERNAL ORGANIZATION AND IDENTITY OF ANGLO-SAXON SURREY[3]

The great woodland common of the Weald stamps on the three counties of Kent, Sussex and Surrey a broad geographical uniformity (fig. 7.1). All around it, near the coast and in the Thames valley, were early settled communities which looked inwards to the Weald as the mainstay of their pastoral economy. It was an extended, transhumant economy, with herds of swine driven down long, straight droveways to summer pastures deep in the woodland.[4] There is thus an obvious sense in which Kent, Sussex and Surrey divide naturally into broad swathes of land radiating out of the Weald. By the eighth century some of these swathes had acquired an administrative and economic identity. The lathes of Kent and the rapes of Sussex are discussed elsewhere in this volume by Nicholas Brooks and Martin Welch. Suffice it to say here that, whatever the hazards of reconstructing precise assessments and boundaries, the existence of tribal or provincial *regiones* similar to those now recognized throughout England, articulated to the distinctive geography of the Weald, can hardly be denied. The territories of the *Cæsterwara*, the *Weowara*, the *Limenwara* and the *Meallingas*[5] were as real as those of the *Husmera*, the *Stoppingas* and the Fenland tribes.

Surrey has fewer early sources than Kent, but its organization can be approached through analysis of post-Conquest manorial and parochial link-ages (figs. 7.2 and 7.3 on p. 101 and 102). Studies of other regions have shown that such linkages generally result from the division of land-units in a transhumance economy: as a territory was split up into manors, so too were its woods and commons fragmented into complex, interlocking archipelagos of individual pastures.[6] The outliers mapped on fig. 7.2 are recorded as swine-denns in late Anglo-Saxon charters, as detached farms in medieval manorial records, as chapelries of mother churches, and as fragments of parishes on the earliest detailed maps.[7] This evidence is miscellaneous, and some of it rather late; not every link is necessarily ancient. Yet the overall pattern is remarkably consistent with the view that subdivision proceeded within defined territories, approximating to groups of Domesday hundreds.

In central and eastern Surrey the direction of linkages is strongly and unambiguously from north to south. The organization of this area is exactly

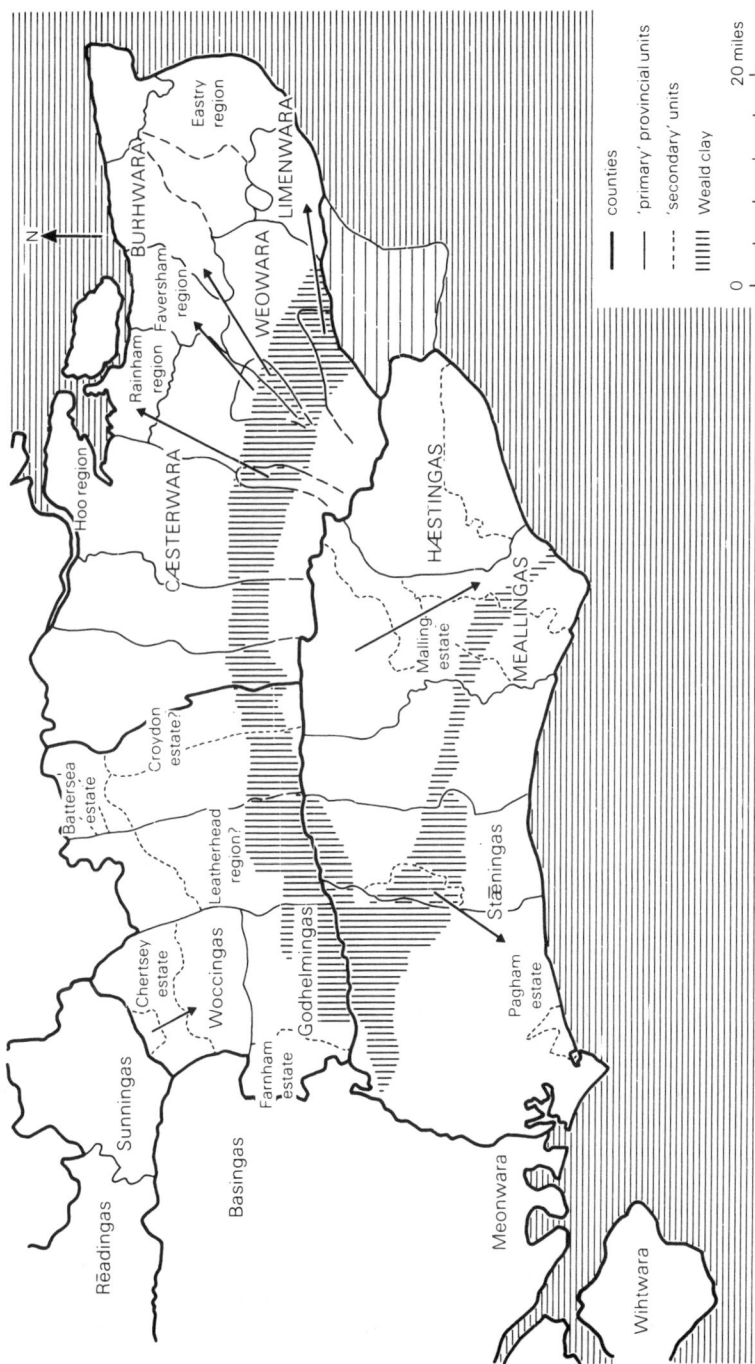

Figure 7.1. The early subdivisions of the three Wealden counties. (Kent after Witney, *Jutish Forest*, fig. 5; Surrey after Blair, *Early Medieval Surrey*, fig. 4. In the absence of reliable earlier data the Sussex rape boundaries are shown as in 1086.)

Labels appearing on the map:

Rēadingas

Sunningas

Basingas

Battersea estate

Croydon estate?

Leatherhead region?

Chertsey estate

Woccingas

Farnham estate

Godhelmingas

Meonwara

Pagham estate

Stǣningas

Wihtwara

MEALLINGAS

Malling estate

HǢSTINGAS

CESTERWARA

Hoo region

Rainham region

Faversham region

BURHWARA

Eastry region

WEOWARA

LIMENWARA

counties

'primary' provincial units

'secondary' units

Weald clay

N

0   20 miles

that of the western Kentish lathes which it adjoins; indeed, a north–south strip along the county boundary, including Croydon, may once have belonged to Kent.[8] It is arguable that central and eastern Surrey can be resolved into two large *regiones*, centred on Kingston and Wallington; but whatever the precise internal divisions of this zone its essential conformity to the Kentish system is obvious.

Very different is the structure of western Surrey. The Hog's Back and the Downs east of Guildford divide it into two halves: Woking and Godley hundreds northwards and Farnham, Godalming and Blackheath hundreds southwards. No manorial or parochial connections cross this boundary, and links are in general from west to east rather than from north to south. For reasons described below, Woking and Godley hundreds are clearly divisions of an earlier whole; they were centred on the royal vill of Woking, and can plausibly be interpreted as the *regio* of the *Woccingas*. The unity of the three southern hundreds cannot be demonstrated so clearly, but their combined area was roughly equivalent to that of the Woking territory, and they were self-contained to the extent that they included no satellites of manors outside them. The large royal manor of Godalming may be seen as the focus of a coherent territory, the *regio* of the *Godhelmingas* corresponding to that of the *Woccingas*. The linkages show how different was the pastoral economy of the Woking and Godalming territories from that of the territories further east: they looked not to the Weald but to the sandy heaths on the borders of Hampshire and Berkshire. In short, the central and eastern divisions of Surrey are of a piece with Kent, whereas the western divisions are of a piece with the Sonning and Reading *regiones* extending up the Thames valley.[9]

We now return to Frithuwold's charter. Apart from outliers at Eaton (in Cobham), Molesey and 'by the port of London where ships come to land', the estate lay in a large compact block (fig. 7.3). Its eastern boundary was an ancient landmark running southwards from the Thames: the 'antiqua fossa, id est *Fullingadic*'. The estate, as later defined,[10] extended as far east as Weybridge. Here a road-line runs southwards from the Thames to continue as a long, straight parish boundary between Byfleet and Walton-on-Thames, part of which is marked by substantial ditches on St George's Hill; the line continues as an intermittent bank across Wisley and Ockham commons, and then as a more substantial one between Blackheath and Wotton hundreds. In other words, it separates the Woking and Godalming territories from the 'Wealden' territories to their east. It seems a fair conclusion that this was the *Fullingadic*: a major boundary between two economic zones, already ancient by the early 670s. Once it had presumably defined a territory of the *Fullingas* or 'tribe of Fulla' – otherwise unknown unless, as seems possible, their leader's name is also preserved in that of Fulham (Middlesex).

Earlier writers on the origins of Surrey have wavered between two apparently conflicting facts: its name (*suðre ge*, 'the southern province') and its economic identity with Kent and Sussex.[11] It is tempting to conclude from the name that Surrey was once the southern half of a Middle Saxon kingdom larger than modern Middlesex. But, as Keith Bailey and David Dumville show elsewhere in this volume, the 'Middle Saxons' seem somewhat late and artificial: an amalgam of tribes, each with its own territory, which only acquired a common name and identity in the context of Mercian overlordship.

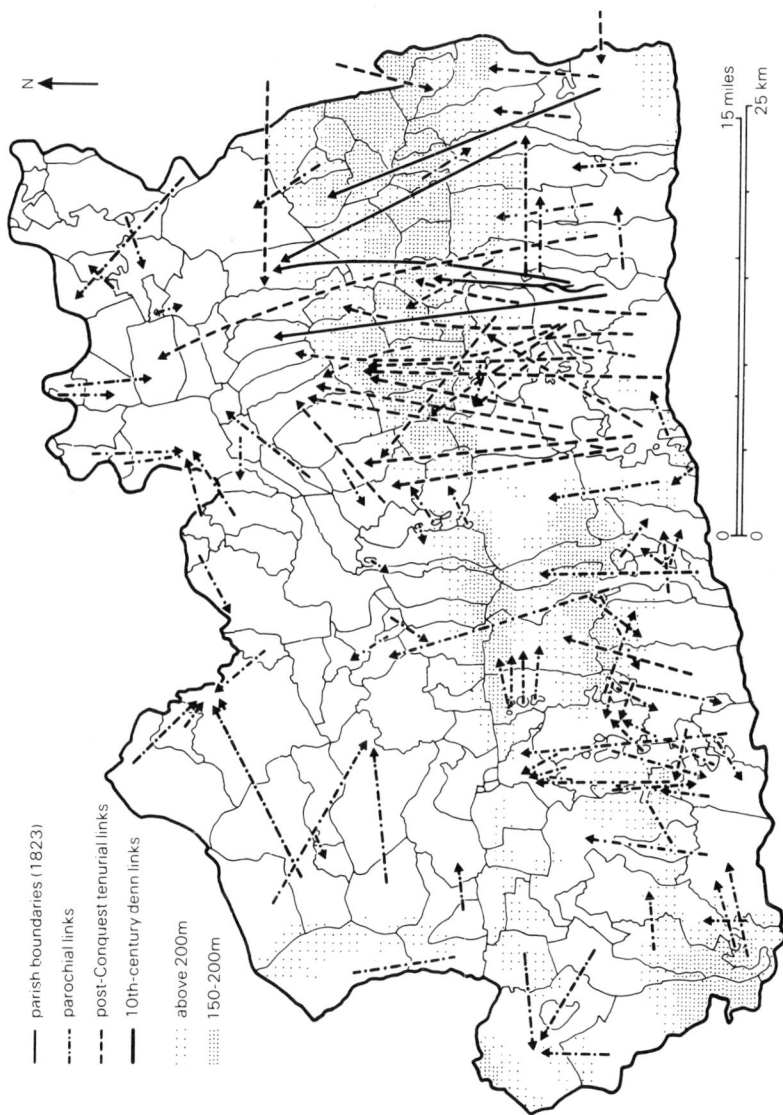

N ←

parish boundaries (1823)

parochial links

post-Conquest tenurial links

10th-century denn links

above 200m

150-200m

15 miles

25 km

Figure 7.2. Surrey: manorial and parochial outliers. (After Blair, *Early Medieval Surrey*, fig. 5.)

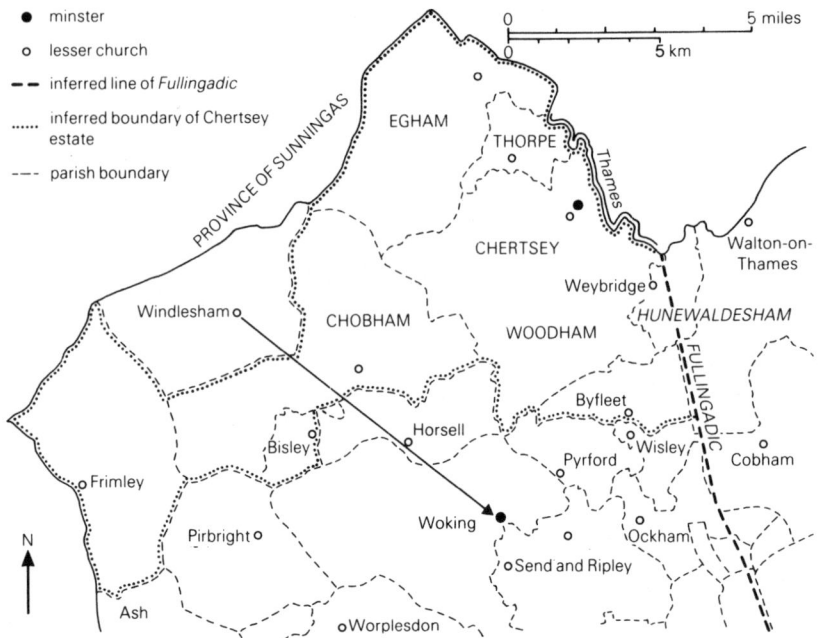

Figure 7.3. The Chertsey estate and its environs. Places mentioned in Frithuwold's charter are in capitals.

The Kentish -*ge* names, Eastry, Lyminge and Sturry, all denote areas much smaller than Surrey; we should remember the relative lateness of the shire system, and ask whether Surrey may not have grown into its eleventh-century boundaries. For Bede it was not a *provincia* but merely a *regio*.[12] The Chertsey charter, in a terminology different from Bede's, calls Frithuwold 'provinciae Surrianorum', and refers to the 'terminus alterius provinciae quae appellatur *Sunninges*' as though Surrey and the Sonning territory were of like kind. As an alternative to the other possibilities it is worth suggesting that the original 'southern province' simply comprised the two *regiones* west of *Fullingadic* – that part of the later county, in other words, which looked northwards and north-westwards to Staines and Sonning in the Thames valley, not eastwards to Kent. The foundation of Chertsey minster under king Egbert in *c.* 666 implies that the land west of *Fullingadic* had been Kentish less than ten years before Frithuwold's gift, and the permanent enlargement of Surrey at the expense of Kent could well have been Frithuwold's work. The reference in the charter to land opposite the port of London[13] shows that his realm extended along the whole Thames boundary of the later county.

What emerges most strongly in the last analysis is the stability of the early *regiones*: organic entities combined and recombined like building bricks to form more transient political territories. The topographical statements in Frithuwold's charter deal not with the boundaries of his kingdom, but with those of the *regio* from which the land which he grants is to be carved: the 'ancient ditch' eastwards and the boundary of the next *regio* north-westwards. It was within this kind of framework that kings of Frithuwold's generation met a demand, unprecedented and perhaps never equalled, for land to endow monasteries.

THE CHERTSEY GRANT IN CONTEXT: THE ENDOWMENT OF MINSTERS AND THE ORIGINS OF MULTI-VILL ESTATES

The twin monasteries of Chertsey and Barking were founded by Eorcenwold for himself and his sister in about 666.[14] Thus Frithuwold's grant does not actually represent the foundation of a monastery, but rather the strengthening of one which had been founded some years earlier and in a different political context. The charter's statements that Frithuwold grants 200 hides at Chertsey and five at Thorpe, but that 'the land is, taken together, 300 hides', are usually dismissed as scribal confusion, but it makes equally good sense to interpret them as meaning that the monastery already had ninety-five hides. It is a mark of the early Church's transcendence over political division that kings who were enemies in the secular world could be persuaded thus to augment each other's religious endowments.

The fact that Bede mentions Eorcenwold's monasteries may mean that they were unusually rich and important; but there is a sense in which they were but two of many, typical and characteristic of their age. Because they were later reformed and re-endowed they tend to be classified as monasteries in a strict, later medieval sense, in contrast to the mass of secular minsters with their groups of priests and parochial territories. When applied to the late seventh century, this contrast is anachronistic. There was in practice no rigid line between 'monastic' and 'parochial'. Rather there was an urgent need to establish a network of well-endowed communities which would maintain learned and pious monks and nuns, while also providing a base from which to convert the countryside. Monasteries were not founded in isolation from the secular world, but in accordance with carefully directed schemes which had regard to practical considerations, including the distribution of royal *villae* and resources.[15] The formation of a minster network was the next logical stage after the conversion of a king and his court; this seems to be the point of king Oswiu of Northumbria's vow in 654 to give twelve little estates to found monasteries, six in Bernicia and six in Deira.[16] Such projects must have been pursued under episcopal and monastic encouragement – an encouragement doubtless the more vigorous after archbishop Theodore's arrival in 668.

It was Eorcenwold's task, like that of his colleagues, to promote this rapid expansion of the monastic network on as consistent a basis as was possible in so fragmented and unstable a political world.[17] Chertsey and Barking were founded respectively under Kentish and East Saxon rulers; within twenty years Eorcenwold had procured one Surrey estate from Frithuwold for Chertsey, and another (at Battersea) from Cædwalla of Wessex for Barking.[18] His hand has also been detected in Cædwalla's grant of land to endow Farnham minster in 685×7 (fig. 7.4).[19] If Eorcenwold was indeed 'the source or channel of diplomatic ideas in south-eastern England',[20] he was probably no less vigorous in obtaining the endowments which his diplomas secured for posterity.

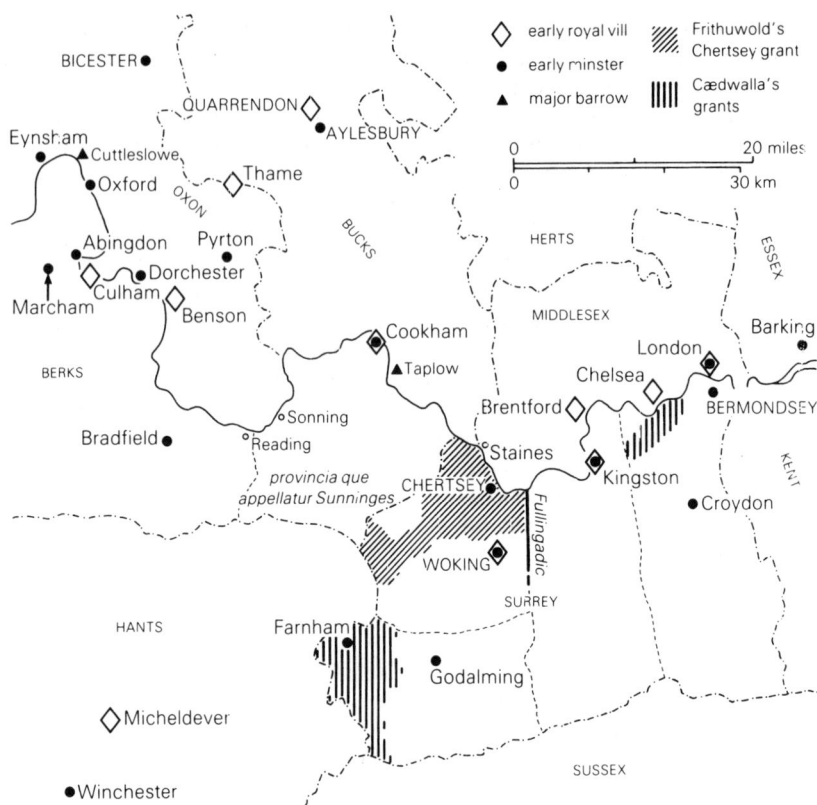

Figure 7.4. The Thames valley in the seventh and eighth centuries. Places associated with Frithuwold and his family are in large capitals.

The granting of big estates by charter, a new and direct consequence of minster building, was to reach within three generations a scale which Bede viewed as alarming and excessive.[21] The pressure on kings' resources must have been considerable: large slices of territories, hitherto administered from royal *villae*, were permanently alienated for the support of new monastic centres. The main Chertsey estate (fig. 7.3) is an exceptionally good illustration of this process. Its boundaries[22] were, with small exceptions, those of the later Godley hundred: it included, that is, the whole north-western corner of Surrey except Windlesham chapelry. But Windlesham was an outlier of Woking manor, hundred and minster parish, cut off from Woking by the Chertsey estate but served as late as the twelfth century by a Woking priest.[23] The explanation for this anomaly is clearly economic: the heathland on the fringe of the *regio* was apportioned in such a way as to give Frimley to Chertsey but leave Windlesham as a detached pasture of the parent royal vill at Woking. The only likely contexts for this apportionment are either the foundation of the monastery *c.* 666, or Frithuwold's gift of 672×4 augmenting the original estate around Chertsey.

Research on shires, sokes and multi-vill manors has been synthesized in a series of papers by Professor G.R.J. Jones, who proposes the 'multiple estate' as a model defining the archetypal land management units of early England.[24] Work in this area, including Jones's, has perhaps failed to distinguish adequately between tribal, political and administrative *regiones* on the one hand, and estates as units of exploitation on the other. To neglect this distinction risks conflating two successive stages, for it is often clear that estates were secondary to *regiones* and a product of the Conversion era. Though among the best, the Chertsey charter is but one of many illustrations that even large and complex middle Saxon estates were carved out of pre-existing territories with established systems of internal division and assessment. The archiepiscopal estate of South Malling[25] bore a similar relationship to the territory of the *Meallingas*, as perhaps did Cædwalla's Farnham estate (fig. 7.4)[26] to that of the *Godhelmingas*. Bundles of townships, already named, hidated, and defined within a hierarchical system of royal control, were regrouped into new entities made stable by perpetual book right. It was this permanence which made the great monastic estates so decisively new: alien grafts on to a mature native stem.

Finally, it is worth noting the statement that the charter was executed 'iuxta villam Friðeuuoldi iuxta supradictam fossatam *Fullingadic*'. Again this is unusually explicit evidence for what seems to be a widespread phenomenon – the foundation of minsters on sites which, although near royal vills, were set apart at a certain distance from them.[27] Whether Frithuwold's vill lay east or west of *Fullingadic* is not stated; if the former, it is even possible that he had his headquarters in the Iron Age hillfort on St George's Hill, immediately east of the ditch line.[28] But it seems equally likely that the vill was the administrative centre of the Woking *regio*: on the western side of the ditch but south of the land granted to Chertsey. Modern Woking lies four miles from the line of *Fullingadic*, so it would be necessary to hypothesize a lost palace site a little further east.

WHO WAS FRITHUWOLD?

It is an attractive proposition that Frithuwold was last in a line of native Surrey kings, soon to sink into oblivion under the heavy hand of Mercia. The charter does not, however, exactly call him sub-king of Surrey, but says rather that he is 'of the province of the men of Surrey' and a sub-king of Wulfhere. This suggests that he was in some way particularly identified with Surrey, and perhaps that his family was of Surrey origin, but it need not mean that he was merely a local ruler. Indeed, the cumbersome and elliptical phrase may be an indication that his position was more complex.

In a paper of 1983 Patrick Wormald suggested that Frithuwold was 'probably not a scion of an otherwise unknown Surrey dynasty but a relative of the Frithuric who attested his [Chertsey] charter [as first witness] and himself disposed of huge Middle Anglian estates'.[29] This was the Friduric *princeps* who in 675×91 gave land at Breedon-on-the-Hill, Leicestershire, to Medeshamstede to found a daughter monastery;[30] and further evidence for a link between the two men can be adduced from the pattern of monastic patronage and dependence. Hædda, abbot of Medeshamstede, is also addressed in a papal privilege of 708×15 as 'abbot and priest of the two monasteries founded in the name of St Peter . . . in places called Bermondsey and Woking',[31] and a twelfth-century list indicates that Breedon, Woking, Bermondsey and Repton minsters were dependencies of Medeshamstede.[32] Woking and Bermondsey lay in territory which had presumably been ruled by Frithuwold, and their sharing of an abbot with a distant monastery founded by Frithuric can hardly be coincidence. These minsters clearly represent the second stage of Christian activity in Surrey after the primary foundation at Chertsey. Equally clearly, the sponsors of this movement were great noblemen with interests extending far into Middle Anglia.

One further piece of evidence, never before considered in this context, implies that Frithuwold ruled an area extending well beyond the boundaries of Surrey. It is late and dubious, but deserves consideration both because of its independence from the Chertsey traditions and because of its general consistency with the late seventh-century world. The fragmentary twelfth-century lives of St Osgyth of Aylesbury, reconstructed by D. Bethell and discussed by C. Hohler,[33] included these statements about Osgyth's birth and childhood: she was a daughter of Wilburh, sister of king Wulfhere of Mercia, by a 'king Fredeswald'; she was born in her father's palace at Quarrendon, Buckinghamshire, on a site well known to the locals because its holiness prevented grass from growing there; and she was brought up by her aunt St Eadgyth at Aylesbury, where her church was later established. Osgyth, Wilburh and Eadgyth clearly belong to that 'holy cousinhood'[34] of late seventh-century princesses which, to judge at least from later hagiographies, produced so many of the first monastic heads. So the Osgyth story fits into a recognizable context, though one which might be invented. The topographical details are, however, encouraging. Aylesbury is an Iron Age hillfort, Quarrendon a village just outside it; this relationship between a minster in an ancient enclosure and a royal vill on open ground nearby is a frequently recurring one.[35] Osgyth's *Vita* introduces another of her aunts, St Eadburh – probably to be identified with the lady of that name enshrined at Bicester,[36] the next minster from Aylesbury going westwards along Akeman Street. It also inspires a degree of confidence that Wilburh shares a name element both with her alleged sister Eadburh and with another (better attested) sister of Wulfhere, Cyneburh abbess of Castor. It is eminently likely that Wulfhere founded a network of minsters on the fringes of Mercia and placed them in the charge of his numerous surplus sisters.

The names Fredeswald and Frithuwold are effectively the same. If this contemporary and brother-in-law of Wulfhere existed at all, it can hardly be doubted that he was the same man as the sub-king of the Chertsey charter; equally, nothing is more likely than that such a man would be given his overlord's sister in marriage. The hagiographical sources place Frithuwold and Frithuric in the same social and monastic milieu as the holy ladies, and both men were enshrined in their turn at their own monasteries of Chertsey and Breedon (see ch. 17). It is, moreover, interesting to speculate on possible connections with two contemporary noble ladies who also had *Frith-* names: Frithogyth, wife of king Æthelheard of Wessex, who went to Rome in 737;[37] and Frithuswith ('Frideswide'), whose activities seem to have centred around the Eynsham area and who was reputedly buried at Oxford in 727.[38] These scraps of tradition may be the only surviving evidence for a powerful sub-royal dynasty.

To take the Quarrendon story seriously entails greatly enlarging Frithuwold's realm, to include not merely Surrey but a swathe of the Thames valley and Chilterns extending up into northern Buckinghamshire (fig. 7.4). If it seems rash to propose so large a principality on so slender a basis, it must be acknowledged that there is room for it. The Middle Angles lay to the north and east; the Middle Saxons extended well into Hertfordshire but not necessarily far, if at all, into Buckinghamshire. If these two *provinciae* were indeed late and artificial amalgams of tribal territories, formed in a context of Mercian overlordship, there is no reason why Wulfhere should not have created a third such *provincia* for Frithuwold. The lack of any clear record is hardly surprising, for the principality must have been very short-lived – perhaps only formed in *c.* 670 and abandoned by the mid-680s. Wulfhere's ratification of the Chertsey charter at Thame, more than thirty miles from Chertsey, is worth recalling in the context of the present hypothesis. If Frithuwold's kingdom extended to the modern Oxfordshire/Buckinghamshire boundary, where Thame lies, there may have been some symbolic appropriateness in this choice of a royal vill on the frontier between land in Wulfhere's direct control and land ruled by his sub-king.

This investigation well illustrates the difficulty of understanding the relationships between tribal territories and delegated power under the seventh-century overkingships. We are still left uncertain whether the original Surrey was (i) a heterogeneous group of *regiones*, some looking towards Kent and Sussex and others towards the Thames valley; (ii) merely that fraction of its eventual self which lay west of *Fullingadic*, the southern part of an early unit of which the northern part was perhaps the Staines or *Wixan* territory (as suggested by Keith Bailey on p. 120); (iii) the southern part of a putative 'greater Middlesex', probably an artificial creation of the late seventh century but perhaps more stable than this and a century or so older; or (iv) the southern part of a different artificial Mercian province, created by Wulfhere for his client and brother-in-law Frithuwold. None of these definitions can be ruled out; some are compatible with others, and none is incompatible either with the late seventh-century political entity proposed in this paper or with more localized kinds of power at earlier dates. Frithuwold's province, like those of the Middle Angles and Middle Saxons, shows how hard it is to distinguish the organic from the transitory elements that went into the making of Anglo-Saxon kingdoms.

8 The Middle Saxons

KEITH BAILEY

I

The history of the London area between 400 and 700 remains largely obscure. Only after 670, when Mercia was in the ascendant, do we glimpse the realities behind the struggle for control of the city and its hinterland. There is no evidence for early rulers in the area north of the Thames which lay between the kingdoms of the East and West Saxons and included the later county of Middlesex and adjacent parts of Hertfordshire bounded by the Rivers Thames, Colne and Lea and the belt of wooded hill country north of the two latter streams (fig. 8.1). The extent of the Middle Saxon province is difficult to define precisely because later shire boundaries in the area are clearly not related to primitive units. Hertfordshire and Buckinghamshire were probably created in the 910s to support Edward the Elder's newly created *burhs*.[1] Little is known of the early history and archaeology of the southern parts of either county, and it is difficult to know their precise relationship with Middlesex, save to say that they seem to belong to the same essentially Saxon cultural milieu.[2] Whether or not these lands formed part of an earlier homogeneous unit, for example the *territorium* of Roman London,[3] is a question outside the scope of this chapter.

The province included a strip of eastern Hertfordshire, roughly between the valley of the Stort and Ermine Street, forming a wedge between Middle Anglian peoples around Hitchin and in Cambridgeshire, and also a salient in the west of the county as far as Hemel Hempstead. Although apparently not of Dark Age date, the Middlesex Grim's Dyke which closely parallels the later county boundary north of Harrow may mark the limits of the *territoria* of London and *Verulamium*, and seems to have continued to act as a dividing line in the post-Roman period, despite East Saxon expansion to the north-west.[4] The boundary of the diocese of London continued to reflect the position at the time of the Conversion,[5] with much of north-east Hertfordshire and north-west Essex in the archdeaconry of Middlesex.[6] There is, however, no evidence of the bishops of London having had jurisdiction in south Buckinghamshire. The Domesday record of a link between Burnham and the minster church at Staines, when both estates were held by Westminster abbey, is unlikely to predate the tenth-century monastic revival.[7] The western boundary of the Middle Saxon territory has therefore been located along the prominent valley of the Colne, and thence along the later Hertfordshire–Buckinghamshire boundary around the Hemel salient. When the Tribal Hidage was compiled, south Buckinghamshire seems most likely to have belonged to the *Ciltern-sætan*, along with northern Hertfordshire and parts of Oxfordshire.[8]

It is not certain that the area around *Verulamium* was included in the Middle Saxon province when it came under Anglo-Saxon rule, apparently towards the end of the sixth century.[9] There is no evidence that East Saxon

Figure 8.1. The Middle Saxon province (based on Anglo-Saxon charter evidence and the boundary of the medieval diocese of London, but using modern parish boundaries).

kings held sway in this area, although they may have done so before the Chiltern region came under Mercian control *c.* 660. It was, however, occupied by the *Wæclingas*, one of the groups which seem so characteristic of the Middle Saxon area in the seventh–eighth centuries.[10] The status of the Christian site at *Verulamium* in the seventh century is unclear, although it does not seem to have attracted an early royal minster foundation, possibly due to recurrent East Saxon paganism.[11]

London was the most important port and administrative centre of Roman Britain and later medieval England but sometimes occupied a peripheral position in the Anglo-Saxon period. During times of peace and prosperity the economic role predominated, whereas in times of unrest and political fragmentation, the Thames resumed its role as a barrier.[12] Even though very early Anglo-Saxon settlement is known at sites such as Mitcham (Surrey) and Mucking (Essex),[13] there is little evidence to indicate how and when the city and its immediate environs came under English control. The port and market centre were apparently refounded outside the Roman walls in the area later called Aldwych, 'the old *wic*', although there is little evidence that this happened before 700.[14]

The walled city was not, however, entirely abandoned during this period. A bishop was established at St Paul's in 604,[15] and early references to the monastic complex as *Paulesbyrig* suggest that it was considered in some sense as a fortified enclosure.[16] A recent paper by Tim Tatton-Brown has suggested that St Paul's was located at the convergence of three important routes within the walls leading west to the *wic* whose market place lay at the junction of the Strand and Drury Lane;[17] this seems to predate the establishment of the extramural commercial centre, however, unless Bede's description of London as an important market *c.* 600 can be believed.[18] The location of the cathedral precinct within the walls was no doubt inspired by the Roman background of Augustine's mission and possibly the influence of Æthelberht of Kent, who may have built the hall mentioned later in the seventh century.[19] If the centre of post-Roman administration had been the Roman fort at Cripplegate, this may also have helped to determine the siting of St Paul's.

London only reappears in the historical record at the end of the formative period of Anglo-Saxon kingship, leaving much doubt not only about the fate of the Roman city after the Britons fled there following the battle of *Crecganford* in '457',[20] but also about the political organization of the fifth-century Saxons attested by cemeteries and their relationship with an apparently strong residual British power around St Albans and with the emergent Anglo-Saxon kingdoms.[21] It cannot be overemphasized that there is still no evidence, documentary or archaeological, for any indigenous royal power in fifth- and sixth-century Middlesex, whatever meaning is given to the term 'Middle Saxons' (which is only recorded at the end of the seventh century). The rest of the chapter examines the early occurrences of this name and their significance, and evidence for early groups in this region, whose names are remembered in later charters and placenames but of whom nothing else is known.

II

The first reference to 'Middle Saxons' occurs in a charter of 704 granting land at Twickenham to Waldhere, bishop of London, in *provincia quae nuncupatur Middelseaxan*.[22] By analogy with other uses of this term, the area described could be anything from a tribal unit, such as that of the *Sunningas* in Berkshire, to one of the major kingdoms.[23] This estate was granted by Swæfred of the East Saxons (*c.* 694–before 709) and the *comes* Pæogthath, and confirmed by the Mercian kings Coenred and Ceolred whose power was already a reality in the London area. Surviving grants by East Saxon kings are extremely rare, but south-west Middlesex was apparently under their control *c.* 700. The name 'Middle Saxons' suggests that it may have been given by the incoming Mercians to the groups living north of the Thames between the kingdoms of the East and West Saxons, an identifiable province within the former.

A fragmentary grant of land in the *pagus* of *Hæmele* in Hertfordshire by Offa king of the East Saxons to bishop Waldhere in 704×9 shows that East Saxon power also extended well into the Chilterns,[24] but when and how this occurred is not known. The name Hemel refers to a district rather than a place, describing its physical characteristics.[25] The politics of this region during the late sixth and seventh centuries were confused, belying the apparently simple situation portrayed by the Tribal Hidage, where the *Cilternsætan* appear to have occupied the belt of country from eastern Hertfordshire to the Goring Gap.[26] The impact of the battle at *Biedcanford* in 571, and of the expansion of Kentish power under Æthelberht after *c.* 580 on any residual British power around St Albans, is not recorded. The expansion of West Saxon power seems, however, to have been confined to the vales to the north of the Chilterns, and it may well be that the East Saxons extended their power into this region betwen 590 and 615, possibly under the aegis of Æthelberht of Kent. The Roman villas in the area show its agricultural potential,[27] and *Hæmele* may have been an earlier territorial unit annexed by the Saxons. The use of the term *pagus* is unusual and might reflect the late survival of Romano-British administrative arrangements hereabouts.[28]

A charter of Offa dated 764 (*recte* 767)[29] concerns an exchange of thirty hides at Harrow *in Middil Seaxum* for land in *Ciltinne* with abbot Stithberht.[30] Grants at Botwell (831) *in provincia Middelsaxanorum* and at Sunbury (962) (*on*) *Middel Seaxan*,[31] and late copies of charters for Yeading (757) *in provincia Midelsexorum* and the Hendon area (959) (*in*) *Middelsexan*,[32] confirm the impression that the Middle Saxon area was a *provincia*, and that it included the later county of Middlesex. The almost complete dearth of charter evidence for the neighbouring counties does not preclude the possibility that the Middle Saxons covered the wider area defined in fig. 8.1. Whatever the precise area, it was clearly far smaller than that of the Middle Angles, whose combined entries in the Tribal Hidage total 17,100 hides, exceeding that of major kingdoms such as Kent and more than twice that of smaller kingdoms such as those of the South and East Saxons.[33] The common factor is that both were geographical groupings of smaller tribes and peoples, not necessarily possessing kings.[34]

The Middle Saxons are not mentioned in the Tribal Hidage, whose compilation may be reasonably attributed to the period 670–90.[35] This leaves two possibilities – first, that this was the homeland of one of the hitherto unidentified tribes, the *Noxgaga* or the *Ohtgaga* being the most likely candidates on geographical grounds,[36] or, second, that it was included within the total for another unit which was seen as having effective control of this area. From the evidence of Bede and the charters, the only kingdom which could meet this requirement at the time was that of the East Saxons. They controlled the London area at least from the reign of Saberht (590×616), their first effective king, who appears to have been a protégé of Æthelberht of Kent during the latter's bretwaldaship in southern England.[37]

The Tribal Hidage's assessment of the East Saxons is 7,000 hides, typical of the minor kingdoms.[38] Although highly speculative, a comparison with the Domesday assessment of about 2,700 hides for Essex alone[39] seems to show a greater discrepancy than might be expected from other areas which had changed little in geographical extent over the centuries.[40] This lends support to the view that the Middle Saxon province, amounting to about 1,400 hides in 1086, was assessed with Essex in the Tribal Hidage in the same way that the eastern hundreds of Surrey seem likely to have been included in the Kentish assessment.[41] If Surrey, the 'south district', had ever been part of Middle Saxon territory, it had clearly ceased to be so by 670, and possibly even a century earlier when Ceawlin of Wessex and Æthelberht of Kent contended at *Wibbandun* in 568 for control of the lands south of the Thames in the hinterland of London. Although Kent was defeated, there is no evidence of a West Saxon presence in the London area around 600.[42]

III

Archaeology and placenames assist little in assessing how the Middle Saxons might have been governed in the fifth and sixth centuries, for no burial indicative of royal status has been found, unless the Tæppa buried at Taplow (Bucks.) in the early seventh century governed this district under East Saxon or Kentish overlordship.[43] There are no names indicative of primitive administrative arrangements other than the tribal groups discussed in the next section. It seems probable that any authority in the London region after 410 would have moved to a more easily defended position, possibly the Roman fort at Cripplegate.[44] The fate of smaller towns such as *Pontes* (Staines), *Noviomagus* (Crayford) and Braughing is obscure.[45] Archaeological evidence points to extensive early Saxon occupation on the fertile terraces of the Thames and its tributaries, at sites such as Mitcham,[46] Shepperton,[47] Hanwell,[48] Mucking[49] and Croydon,[50] but the more intractable claylands of Middlesex itself seem largely unused at this time. There is little evidence of early Germanic settlement in the St Albans district. The temporary demise of London as a port and market meant that its immediate vicinity was no longer an attraction to peasant farmers compared with other areas of light soils. They may indeed have been deterred by the presence of Saxon settlers, possibly mercenaries placed to defend the walled city in depth. There is little evidence near London for continuity of site occupation or overlap between Britons and Saxons such as has been found in the Chiltern area.[51]

The earliest Saxon settlers around London were probably controlled by some

British authority,[52] which would have restricted the scope for any but the most localized rulers. Each group was probably semi-autonomous within this administrative framework, although this is not to say that there were no social or trading links between the various Germanic groups.[53] Not until the collapse of British power in the area, which may have occurred at any time after *c.* 460,[54] would the opportunity have arisen for these early settlers to coalesce into larger units with rulers of higher status. This could have been achieved by agreement or conflict between the groups, or by imposition of control from outside the area. Most of the later evidence suggests a tendency for the latter to occur, as the larger kingdoms sought to fill the political vacuum which appears to have arisen periodically around London before about 700. The sources point to a constant state of flux, for example between Kent and Wessex in the 560s[55] and between the East and West Saxons and Mercia after 650.[56] This would have tended to suppress any emergent native dynasty, just when it might be expected to appear in the records.

Even had such rulers managed to gain overall control of the Middle Saxon area after the final breakdown of British power, it would still not be surprising if no trace of it were to be found in subsequent records. The origins and development of even substantial kingdoms such as that of the East Saxons are little less obscure.[57] It may be that the expansionist rule of Æthelberht acted as some kind of catalyst in the formation of the East Saxon state.[58] Whether he had been instrumental in refounding London as a trading centre and had annexed its hinterland before giving it over to Saberht of the East Saxons, or whether the latter had directly absorbed the Middle Saxon groups, is not recorded in the surviving sources. In either case it seems most likely that the Middle Saxons prior to *c.* 580–600 remained a loose confederation, without kings, an easy prey for powerful neighbours expanding from their original centres of power. In the same way Surrey fell under the control of Ceawlin and Æthelberht in the 560s, creating an administrative dichotomy within the later county which lasted for at least a century.[59]

The position of London becomes clearer about 600, when it was said to be the 'metropolis' of the East Saxons.[60] As an emerging trading and communications centre, it was a natural magnet for both Kent and the East Saxons. Ceawlin of Wessex was unable to advance his own influence as far as London; some of the sixth-century Saxon occupation in west Middlesex may, however, relate to his expansionism.[61] Kentish and East Saxon interests dominated the London area during much of the seventh century but after *c.* 660 it was absorbed into the Mercian sphere of influence.

London, although the third diocese created by the Augustinian mission, was intended by pope Gregory for the seat of the metropolitan. Vigorous East Saxon paganism ensured that it did not come to occupy a prominent role in church affairs until the emergence of Eorcenwald in the 660s.[62] His term as bishop of London (675–93) coincided with the reforms of archbishop Theodore, which emphasized the creation of a full structure of diocesan bishops and the regulation of the affairs of the church through frequent synods.[63]

Eorcenwald, probably a member of the Kentish royal house,[64] was active throughout the London area, establishing minsters at Chertsey in the 660s under Kentish patronage and at Barking for his sister Æthelburh, possibly before the great plague recorded *c.* 664 when part of the East Saxon people once more lapsed into pagan ways.[65] Chertsey was additionally endowed by the *subregulus* Frithuwold under Mercian overlordship in the 670s.[66] Barking was endowed with estates not merely in Essex, but also in Kent, Surrey and Middlesex.[67]

In 688–94 Eorcenwald was described as 'my bishop' by Ine of Wessex.[68] Wessex seems to have gained control of north-eastern Surrey under Cædwalla in the late 680s, when he granted an estate at Battersea to Barking minster,[69] although it is not clear that this control extended north of the Thames. These events imply that Eorcenwald's jurisdiction extended beyond the later diocese of London and that he occupied a central position in relations between the four kingdoms in the area. It seems that northern Surrey at least was not annexed to the diocese of Winchester until the West Saxon sees were reorganized in 705–6.[70] It is probably no coincidence that many early synods took place in this region, at Hatfield, Hertford, Brentford, Chelsea and later London itself, all of them lying close to the boundaries of the Middle Saxon province.[71] Wulfhere extended Mercian overlordship to the area round London after *c*. 665, both north and south of the Thames. There is no record of conflict in this region, which may reflect the diplomatic skills of Eorcenwald, although the incursion of West Saxon power across Surrey after 685 shows that the system was still inherently unstable. Many of the earliest charters for the region are concerned with granting substantial tracts of royal patrimony to religious foundations, and the pattern of grants, from Chertsey and Twickenham in the west to Barking and Erith in the east, implies a conscious policy by Eorcenwald and his successor Waldhere. By 1066 there was hardly any royal land within a ten-mile radius of London.[72]

Placenames provide some evidence of possible rulers in the Middle Saxon area. Sunbury may be named after Sunna, the eponymous founder of the *provincia quae appellatur Sunninges*, whose territory lay in Berkshire west of the lands granted to Chertsey in the mid-670s.[73] Such a move across the Thames may date from the burgeoning of Wessex under Ceawlin between 560 and 580.[74] Links with Britons in this area are suggested by the names Bedfont, containing the element *funta, and Ashford, containing *ecles ('the ford by the (British) church').[75] The former Roman town at Staines by an important river crossing has traces of early Saxon settlement, and was still the focus of a large tract of territory in 1086 which contained four berewicks.[76] This territory may have been the northern equivalent to that granted by Egbert of Kent and Frithuwold to Chertsey abbey. Placename evidence suggests considerable British survival in that part of Surrey,[77] and John Blair suggests (above, p. 107) that this may have been the original *suther ge* ('south district') which later gave its name to the whole of Surrey. If the Staines area, or possibly the wider territory of the *Wixan* (see below), was the 'north district', the latter name did not survive to be recorded in charters; nor did it give its name to the province of the Middle Saxons.[78]

IV

Most evidence of early political units in this area relates to small groups, many of them with *-ingas* names derived from shadowy figures of indeterminate status and date. Charters often show that these groups were still remembered in the second half of the eighth century, and that they had covered wider areas than merely those places which bear their names today. The evidence for each of these peoples will be examined briefly, proceeding in a roughly clockwise fashion. Their approximate locations are shown on fig. 8.2.

In northern Hertfordshire, occupying a strip of land between Ermine Street and the present Essex boundary, lay the territory of the *Brahhingas* (modern Braughing).[79] Braughing was a minor Roman town, one of many in the canton of the Catuvellauni, and an important road junction.[80] Significantly, the site of the town lies on Wickham Hill, the only example of a *wīchām* name in Middle Saxon territory and one suggestive of early contact between Britons and Saxons.[81] If the Romano-British and Anglo-Saxon territories were broadly similar, this is likely to represent the takeover of a functioning agricultural system, even though the market centre soon fell into decline with the end of the money economy in the early fifth century.[82] Ten hides at Braughing were leased by bishop Ceolberht of London to Sigric *minister* after 825,[83] and it has been suggested that he may have been Sigeric II, the last recorded king of the East Saxons.[84] If so, the links between this district and the East Saxon kingdom proper must have lasted for almost three centuries before finally breaking down in the face of the Danish conquest after 880. This area of Hertfordshire remained in the archdeaconry of Middlesex.[85]

The *Beningas*, 'people of the [River] Beane',[86] gave their name to modern Bengeo. Hertford, venue of the synod of 672 and later the location of two *burhs*,[87] probably lay in this territory. The only indication of early Anglo-Saxon settlement in the area is at Ware, where a Romano-British farm site produced some grass-tempered pottery, although the name Epcombs in Hertingfordbury probably indicates early contact between the two peoples.[88]

The large parish of Hatfield was also the scene of an important synod under Theodore in 679 and may have had a minster church and possibly a *villa regalis*.[89] It clearly lay in a frontier zone, and it is not certain whether it lay within Middle Saxon territory or that of the *Hicce* or the *Cilternsætan* of the Tribal Hidage. The name, meaning 'heathy open country', contrasts with the relatively densely wooded areas of north Middlesex and the Chilterns and is reminiscent of Hatfield Chase, the tract of land between Lindsey and Northumbria.[90]

On the later border between Middlesex and Hertfordshire lay another substantial territory. In the former shire this became the Half Hundred of Mimms or Hundred of Edmonton, but its medieval meeting place at South Mimms, remote from the main centres of population,[91] makes it probable that the territory had reached further north, notably including North Mimms itself. The name of the group was apparently the *Mimmas*.[92] Enfield was the largest parish in Middlesex and had a church in 1086, albeit only endowed with one virgate, with a potentially early dedication to St Andrew, and it may once have been a minster serving this district.[93] The relatively low hidation of the area may reflect its original royal status, and large parts became a hunting preserve, the later Enfield Chase.[94] Like Braughing, Tottenham and probably the *Beningas*, this territory lies across Ermine Street, the Roman road from London to Lincoln. There was a roadside settlement at Enfield.[95] Nearby Cheshunt combines the elements *cæster* and **funta* ('the fortification by a

boundary of the Middle Saxon province

Roman road: certain course

Roman road: possible course

● minster church ?

□ villa regalis ?

▲ Latin loan-word placename

○ other places named in text

N

BRAHHINGAS

Braughing □ ▲

▲

St Albans □ ● Hatfield   BENINGAS

Hertford ◉

HÆMELE □

○ Waltham

MIMMAS

Watford   ● Enfield

Rickmansworth ○

▲

GUMENINGAS

Tottenham ○

(WIXAN) Kingsbury □

Harrow ●

○ Uxbridge   GEDDINGAS

Hayes ●

LULLINGAS   ● London   ○ Stepney   ● Barking

Westminster ●

Brentford □   GILLINGAS

Chelsea   Thames

Isleworth ○   Fulham ●

Staines ▲   ▲

STÆNINGAS

Sunbury □   ▲

Chertsey ●

| 0 | | 10 miles |
| 0 | | 15 km |

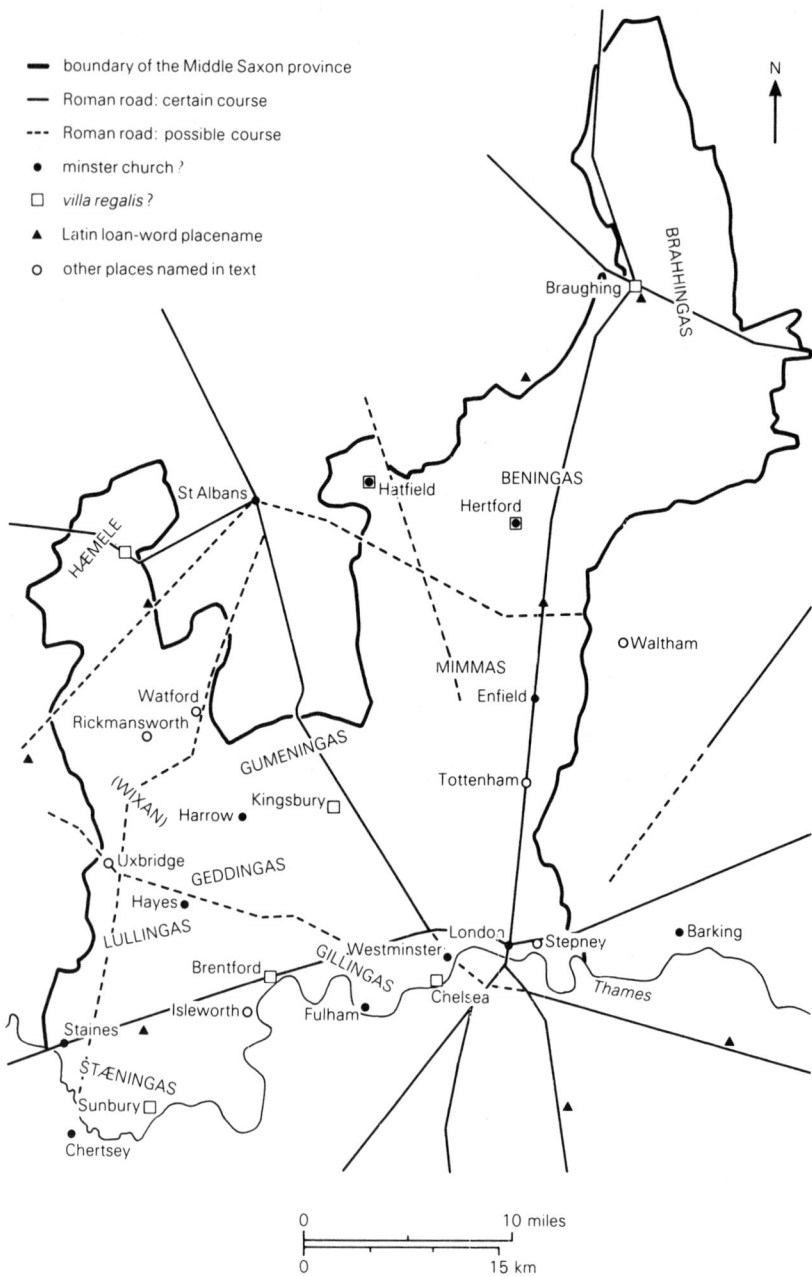

Figure 8.2. Middle Saxon groups and major centres (based on all surviving charter references to the Middle Saxons and to places in the area of their province).

spring'),[96] which suggests early contact between British and Anglo-Saxon peoples. It has been suggested that the area on the Essex bank of the Lea facing Edmonton Hundred, known as the Half-Hundred of Waltham, formed part of the same major division within the East Saxon kingdom, and if so it seems unlikely that such a connection could have arisen after c. 700.[97]

Southwards along the Lea valley there is some evidence that another territory may once have covered parishes later in Essex and Middlesex. Tottenham and Walthamstow both had Domesday renders of five ounces of gold, unique in these counties, and both were held by earl Waltheof in 1066, his only estates in the region.[98] The name *Tottenhale* (now Tottenham Court) may indicate that the territory extended much further south at one time, almost to the outskirts of London.[99] A later medieval reference to Tottenham-shire, made when some of the area was held by the Scottish kings, may contain a memory of an early territory, or may merely be the use of a typically northern term for a jurisdiction.[100]

South-east Middlesex was occupied by the bishop of London's great estate of Stepney, covering the land between the Thames, the Lea and Ermine Street and lying across the major Roman road to Colchester. There is no early evidence for its acquisition by the bishops, although the episcopates of Eorcenwald and Waldhere provide a likely context for the creation of an important estate in church hands at the approaches to London. This territory may have been named from the *Wæppingas*, although it is not certain that Wapping is an *-ingas* name.[101] Like Fulham to the west, the Stepney estate possessed detached woodland, which suggests that a small-scale version of the Wealden transhumance economy was operating in the Middle Saxon area.[102]

The *Gillingas*, ''Gilla's people' (modern Ealing), are mentioned in a grant of ten hides by Æthelred of Mercia to Waldhere, bishop of London in 693×704, *in loco quae dicitur Gillingas* for the advancement of monastic life in the city of London.[103] In 1086 Ealing was part of the bishop of London's great Fulham estate, which included the later parishes of Fulham, Acton, Ealing and Chiswick, and a detached woodland at Finchley. Fifty hides at Fulham had been granted to the bishops of London by Tyrhtil, bishop of Hereford, in 704×9.[104] The territory of the *Gillingas* may have included the whole south-western corner of Ossulstone Hundred, north and south of the London–Silchester road on which lay the Roman settlement at Brentford, which seems to have had a *villa regalis* in its vicinity by 700. In 705 a council was held there to resolve a dispute between the East and West Saxon kings,[105] and a synod was held there in 781.[106] Brentford's position on the Thames and a main highway gave it a nodal importance. Fulham became an episcopal residence and may have had a minster serving this district, although no evidence of one has survived. A seventh-century foundation is, however, unlikely to have survived the overwintering of the Danish army there in 879–80.[107]

Isleworth, an estate of fifty-three hides, was granted to Eorcenwald by Æthelred of Mercia, and then to Barking abbey c. 677.[108] At nearby Twicken-ham a thirty-hide estate was granted by Swæfred of Essex to Waldhere, bishop of London, in 704,[109] although it was in royal hands again by 790 when Offa granted it to Christ Church, Canterbury, for the clothing of the brethren.[110] These two estates seem likely to have been part of one territory originally, yet again lying strategically across a principal Roman road from London.

Hounslow Hundred in 1086 contained only two estates, Isleworth and Hampton, although these included several other settlements.[111] The unit which was broken up in the late seventh century did not remain in the hands of the church for both estates were held by earl Asgar in 1066.[112] The name of this territory has not survived, although the *Gislhere* from whom Isleworth takes it name alliterates with the *Gilla* and *Geddi* of Ealing and Yeading, and together they may represent a group of related early Saxon leaders in west Middlesex.[113]

The memory of an early group in the Hayes area survives in a grant of sixty hides *on linga hæse*, 'the heathland of the Lingas', a name which has not yet been satisfactorily interpreted.[114] The most obvious explanation is that it should be read as *Lullingas*, a group whose tree lay on the boundary of nearby Botwell.[115] Hayes was a Canterbury estate acquired by archbishop Wulfred from his relative the priest Werhard,[116] and it has been suggested that they, along with the Wihtred who received an estate at nearby Yeading, belonged to a noble family with its roots in Middlesex.[117] Werenberht *minister*, who was involved in an exchange of lands at Roxeth in nearby Greenford in 845,[118] may have been a member of the same clan, as might Waldhere, bishop of London from 693 to 705×16; it is impossible to say, however, whether they represent the later generations of some Middle Saxon noble house, or if they had risen to prominence in the area under Mercian kings after 660. If the latter is the case, then they may just represent another of Wulfhere's sub-kingdoms such as that ruled over by Frithuwold in Surrey and Buckinghamshire.

The *Geddingas* (modern Yeading), mentioned twice in charters, are another group located on the low-lying claylands and terraces of west Middlesex, sandwiched between the *Gumeningas*, *Gillingas* and *Lullingas*. Æthelbald of Mercia granted seven hides *in regione quæ dicitur Geddinges* to his *comes* Wihtred and Ansith his wife.[119] In 795 Offa granted a sixty-hide estate at Hayes and Yeading to Christ Church, Canterbury, and Yeading formed part of Hayes parish in the medieval period.[120] The use of the term *regio* suggests a considerably larger unit than the seven hides granted to Wihtred, and it seems likely that the *Geddingas* and the *Lullingas* between them occupied most of the southern part of the later Elthorne Hundred. The rudimentary boundaries of Æthelbald's grant show that the estate lay north of the *Fiscesburna* (Yeading Brook) and south of a *via publica*, except where it extended two *iugera* north of the latter. This would place the public way near the line of the road from Ealing and Greenford to north-west Middlesex, which is not known to be a Roman road but which was evidently in existence linking estates by the mid-eighth century. Greenford is described as *illam famosam villam* in 845.[121] The Hayes and Yeading estates lie across the Uxbridge Road which, although not known as a Roman road, later connected London with Oxford and may have been one of the strategic routes from London which seem to have attracted early Germanic settlement, evidence of which has been found at Hanwell.[122] Such a road would fill up the apparently empty sector between the Silchester and St Albans roads.

Gumeninga hearh, 'the pagan sanctuary of Guma's people', gave its name to Harrow,[123] and was important enough to be remembered two centuries after the Conversion. Harrow was a Canterbury estate, acquired after a dispute between Coenwulf of Mercia and archbishop Wulfred between *c*. 820 and 825 and held temporarily by his kinsman Werhard.[124] This estate, comprising various smaller units, was assessed at 104 hides, whereas the Domesday assessment was 100 hides, suggesting that the four additional hides granted by abbess Cwoenthryth in 825 had not been retained with the rest of the estate. It is not clear whether the *Gumeningas* were restricted to this area, or whether they occupied the whole of Gore Hundred which lay astride Watling Street and may have been another of the strategically placed units covering the Roman roads radiating from London. Harrow had a priest with one hide of land in 1086, which probably denotes minster status.[125] The hamlet of Preston probably commemorates the priests who served the *parochia*.[126]

Apart from the posting station and pottery making centre at Brockley Hill, there was some kind of Roman settlement in this area at Kingsbury whose church incorporates Roman material and bears a potentially early dedication to St Andrew.[127] No Anglo-Saxon settlement is yet known there, but the name may denote a *villa regalis* occupying a strategic position overlooking the crossing of the Brent by Watling Street. Unusually for Middlesex part of Kingsbury remained in royal hands long after the Harrow estate had been granted to the church. The ancient common wood belonging to Kingsbury was still remembered in the eleventh century, when the monks of Westminster were allowed the third pig and penny from the pannage.[128] In a charter of 957 there is a reference to the *cinges inwuda*, implying that part of it had been reserved for the king's use, perhaps the two-thirds excluded from the later grant.[129] The boundaries of a later grant of land in this area mention the *kincges mearce*,[130] the north-western boundary of Hendon between Barnet and the River Brent. Taken together these references suggest a continuing royal presence in this area until at least 980. The *eald tunsteall* which lay further north on the western side of Watling Street may represent either an earlier Anglo-Saxon settlement or another Roman one.[131]

The early administrative history of the strip of land along the western frontier of the Middle Saxons, from Hemel Hempstead and Harefield in the north to Staines on the Thames, is relatively less clear than for most of the province. *Hæmele* seems to have been the north-western extremity of East Saxon territory. The later parish was very large (12,000 acres) and may represent one of the *pagi* of the territory of *Verulamium*, while the names Bedmond (Herts.) and Chalfont (Bucks.) are further examples of names in the London region derived from **funta*, which are seen as indicative of early contact between Britons and Saxons, related in part to the Roman road system.[132]

Nearby Rickmansworth, while it appears only by inference in a suspect grant of Ecgfrith of Mercia to St Albans in 796,[133] was also a very large parish (about 10,000 acres), and together with Watford (10,800 acres) may represent the territory of another Middle Saxon group. All three areas had very low assessments in Domesday Book in relation to their size and resources,[134] which may point to their once having been royal, possibly East Saxon, estates. If the *Wæclingas* who occupied the St Albans area itself were a Middle Saxon group, they would fill the gap between the groups identified here in north-west and north-east Hertfordshire, which would reduce the status of the Middlesex Grim's Dyke to that of an internal boundary during this period.

Uxbridge, Waxlow and Uxendon, respectively the bridge, *leah* and hill of the *Wixan*, cover a wide area in north-west Middlesex.[135] The name also occurs in the Tribal Hidage, relating to a Middle Anglian group usually placed in the Fens.[136] There is, however, no known connection between them, and it seems to be stretching the evidence too far to relocate them in Middle Saxon territory, although the two groups may possibly have had common antecedents. The Middlesex *Wixan* are not mentioned in surviving charters, and some at least of their area seems to have been occupied by other groups in the eighth century. If they occupied the area of the later Hundreds of Elthorne and Hounslow, whose Domesday assessment was about 330 hides, they would have been equivalent to one of the smallest Tribal Hidage groups, and may represent an earlier stratum of administrative grouping amongst the Middle Saxons which broke down when the province was absorbed by the East Saxons or Mercia. The *-ingas* groups which proliferate in charters may mark the break-up of the *Wixan*, either into their original constituents or into new units, to form the great estates of the middle Saxon period. Apart from the centres of these smaller groups, no *villa regalis* has been identified in this area, although Ruislip enjoyed a special status in the later medieval period and may have derived this from an earlier importance.[137]

Staines was the focus of another unit, possibly part of the original *Wixan* territory. It had a minster church of uncertain date.[138] The name of this territory, which covered most if not all of the later Spelthorne Hundred, is not known and could have been either *north ge* ('northern district' in contrast to Surrey) or *Stæningas* from the name of its chief place. (The later medieval London property of this estate was known as *Stæninghaga*.)[139] Possible continuity from the Roman period in this region has already been discussed. A larger unit comprising the northern and southern districts may once have centred on Chertsey and Staines, including western Middlesex and north-western Surrey, and may account for the location of an important seventh-century minster at the former. The role of the *Sunningas* and Frithuwold in this part of Middlesex is not clear.

The only significant gaps in this pattern of territories are to the north and west of London itself, where the reviving commercial centre may be expected to have had some estates. Some of this area may have been included in the twenty-four-hide estate granted to St Paul's by Æthelberht in 604 *iuxta murum*.[140] Chelsea may have been the centre of a royal estate. It was the meeting place for several synods,[141] and its location close to the Thames and to several of the Roman roads radiating from London may have supported an as yet undiscovered settlement which formed the basis of an Anglo-Saxon *villa regalis*. One pointer to its former status is the name of its detached woodland, Kensal, 'the king's wood' (O.E. *cyning, holt*).[142] The monastery at Westminster, whose foundation is variously attributed to Saberht, the first Christian king of the East Saxons, and to Offa of Mercia,[143] had large estates in the corridor along Watling Street as far as Hendon by 1086; although how and when it acquired many of them is obscured by monastic forgeries, they represent another substantial diminution of the former royal patrimony in Middlesex.[144]

V

Most of the Middle Saxon province was occupied by the eighth century by groups of people assessed at between thirty and 100 hides. While this falls far short of the apparent threshold of 300 hides which qualified still independent tribes for a place in the Tribal Hidage (although the *Wixan* may represent such a group), these units nevertheless represent the basic building blocks of the Anglo-Saxon kingdoms. As such they have been found across much of England, recorded in charters and placenames. They sometimes form the basis of middle Saxon great estates, but in other cases disappear early as administrative entities.[145] The progressive disintegration of these territories into ever smaller units as lands were granted away, originally by kings and later by ecclesiastics and laymen, is clearly shown in this region, where virtually no royal land was left in 1066.

The processes by which the units which formed the subject of seventh- and eighth-century grants had originally come into existence are unclear; there are, however, examples such as Braughing and Staines, which hint at some kind of continuity from the Roman era. Elsewhere in the East Saxon kingdom the Rodings display such continuity, although in this case it may be from a villa estate rather than from a minor town.[146] If there is any common denominator between these territories it seems to be a strategic location across the Roman roads radiating from London, often centred on roadside settlements, although how this relates to the presumed disposition of Saxon mercenaries by Roman and post-Roman administrations in the fifth century is not clear. The area of these territories and the evidence of Domesday Book show that they were equipped with extensive agricultural and other resources, and several had the kind of distant woodland links characteristic of the Wealden area.[147] Each unit covered up to ten later parishes, although in some cases, such as Enfield and Harrow, the ancient minster parishes did not succumb completely to the tendency to disintegrate. It seems probable that most Middle Saxon territories had minster churches, created by the joint actions of kings and bishops, although not necessarily at the same location as the *villae regales*.[148]

The example of the *Wixan* implies that the *-ingas* groups recorded in the charters represent a secondary stage in the creation of an administrative framework in the seventh-century landscape, replacing earlier, more amorphous, tribal units. Evidence from the West Midlands suggests that this was also occurring in other regions.[149] Similar groups are found in the heartland of the East Saxon kingdom, for example the *Berecingas* who occupied the south-western corner of Essex and whose name superseded *Beddanhaam*, the original name of Æthelburh's nunnery.[150] Nearby were the *Hæferingas* (modern Havering) and the *Eppingas/Uppingas*, 'the people of the upland'. Further east lay the *Hrothingas* (Rodings), and all these groups seem to share the tendency to lie athwart Roman roads which has been noted in the Middle Saxon province.[151]

If each of these units had once been ruled independently, coming together in loose confederations only as occasion demanded, their central places were potential *villae regales* for incoming kings, although the retention of any estates in the Middle Saxon area by East Saxon or Mercian kings was exceptional. Under Eorcenwald and his successors vast estates were granted to support the recently established diocese and its minsters, although it was not unknown for prominent laymen to be rewarded with small estates after the province had been annexed by Mercia. It is this tendency for early disintegration of royal lands in the Middle Saxon area which probably accounts for the lack of relationship between the names of the later hundreds and the great manors, and indeed for the absence of hundredal manors of the sort which are common in former West Saxon lands.[152] Apart from Mimms/Edmonton, Middlesex hundreds are not named from estates, but from the hundred meeting places. The radical changes which took place in Hertfordshire after 900 make the hundreds there especially artificial, although Cashio is named from a place in Watford, and Braughing and Hertford are named from places of long-standing importance.

Contrary to Stenton's view,[153] it seems on balance that no local dynasty emerged to rule the Middle Saxons before they were absorbed into the kingdom of the East Saxons, probably in the 590s. The area became a province of that kingdom, containing small territorial units which seem to have preserved their identities even in the absence of significant geographical constraints, although the well-wooded claylands of Middlesex and also the Chilterns may have made each group a little more isolated and self-contained than appears at first sight. This apparent failure of the Middle Saxons to develop into a kingdom in the second half of the sixth century probably reflects the continual pressure from powerful neighbours seeking to control London.

By analogy with other areas Middle Saxon kings might have been expected to emerge after 550. There is no record of this having happened, despite the favourable survival of charters and other sources. The rulers of the smaller units which comprised the Middle Saxon province were no doubt defeated in unrecorded conflicts or bought off with gifts of money and land by successive Kentish, East Saxon, West Saxon and Mercian kings, leaving little trace apart from a few placenames and chance references in surviving charters.[154]

9 Essex, Middle Anglia, and the expansion of Mercia in the South-East Midlands

DAVID DUMVILLE

As seen through the written sources, the earliest secular history of Anglo-Saxon England is overwhelmingly the early history of English kingship, its rudimentary administration, and its relationship with named population groups or territories.[1] To that extent, to ask about the origins of Anglo-Saxon political units might seem to be to put a question wholly about the beginnings of kingship among the English. About a decade ago an attempt was made to suggest that the origins of the many Anglo-Saxon polities of the early Middle Ages could be explained, at least partially, without reference to kingship. Scholars have shown little inclination to follow this up, the circumstances in which Anglo-Saxon kingships came into existence remaining largely undebated. For the moment it is sufficient to note that the surviving written evidence is inadequate to allow us to speak about the various areas of England with equal conviction (or lack of it). The gaps in our written evidence are both chronological and geographical, thus posing major problems for the historian; and, for the moment, I pause only to mention the generic gaps, and the omissions due to political bias, and to observe that even were we to state the kind of information which we ideally want about this period the early Christian Anglo-Saxons (to whom we owe such information as we now possess) might for a variety of reasons have proved incapable of supplying it for posterity's benefit.

I turn, then, to consider the types of historical source material available to us for the earliest era of Anglo-Saxon England. While, to a very limited extent, the sources vary from area to area or political unit to political unit, certain types of source material tend to recur and some individual sources, such as the Tribal Hidage and Bede's Ecclesiastical History, offer testimony concerning more than one part of the country. The basic fact is that we have no English written evidence, whether in Latin or the vernacular, which antedates the seventh century (unless, that is, one wishes to invoke the occasional brief inscription carved in runes). For English literacy in the Roman alphabet was, as far as can reasonably be seen, a function of Anglo-Saxon Christianity. Contemporary evidence for the fifth- and sixth-century Anglo-Saxons must therefore come from the Celts or from the Christian population of the west European continent or the East Roman Empire. Some invaluable testimony is gained thus, but there is little in it which bears on the detailed questions of internal political organization in early Anglo-Saxon England. At the very best, therefore, we are using seventh-century English evidence for the preceding two centuries. But in fact there is precious little relevant seventh-century testimony; it is in texts of the eighth and ninth centuries (and even later) that we meet much of the evidence which we must use when discussing the origins and early history of Anglo-Saxon kingdoms. Some of these texts show very easily that, in part at least, they depend on lost sources of the seventh century. But in other cases no line of transmission between the information reported and the source in which it occurs is readily identifiable, and therefore no certain estimate may be made of the historical value of the information in question.

The problems of dealing with partial record and non-contemporaneous information are therefore acute for any historian who wishes to investigate the pre-Christian period of English history; and these problems are only partially ameliorated when one comes to consider the Christian seventh century. But from seventh-century and later sources much incidental information can be gleaned, which helps one to gain some understanding of the problems of social and political organization. Concerning the fifth and sixth centuries, on the other hand, the information at our disposal is largely evidence which someone in the Anglo-Saxon period has seen fit to collect, edit and publish. Insufficiently often has it been asked in whose interest and for what reason has such information been published. Happy accidents of transmission may assure the survival to a later era of historical matter first assembled during the earliest Christian generations in England, but the motives of the original writers need to be investigated and understood. In the seventh century, it must be remembered, many churchmen had an acute vested interest in the survival, and indeed prosperity, of the dynasty ruling in their locality.

It will have been noticed that I have been speaking of kings and kingdoms, and therefore of political, indeed dynastic, history, rather than of settlement history. Apart from Bede's famous excursus on the Angles, Saxons and Jutes who were said to have come to Britain under the leadership of Hengist and Horsa, the literary sources have little to say about settlement history and little enough, indeed, about the peoples frequently represented as constituting political units. Dynastic history looms particularly large in both Northumbrian and West Saxon record. In the former it has very largely obliterated knowledge of the details of the dynastic rulers of Deira, and has cast Northumbrian history in a Bernician mould. In the latter case the record embodied in the common stock of the Anglo-Saxon Chronicle has led a long succession of writers to attempt a national settlement history of Wessex on the basis of what is in fact a dynastic origin legend, while others – in exasperation with an apparent clash between the archaeological and literary record – have entirely rejected the Chronicle's testimony on any fifth- or sixth-century matter; yet others have attempted reconciliations which invent two West Saxon dynasties and thus move us progressively away from the testimony of our only sources. All genealogical records, and some regnal lists, represent manipulations of historical information in the service of political ideology, and the same may be true of retrospective chronicling.

The early histories of the various Anglo-Saxon kingdoms have seemed different in both quality and quantity of information. For some kingdoms we have little or no more than a dynastic pedigree or slightly more ramified genealogy. Under such circumstances information about origins may amount to no more than being told, as for Bernicia, that Esa was the first of his line to come to Britain and that Ida, his grandson according to the Bernician royal pedigree, was the first king, or as for East Anglia that Wehha was the first to reign over the East Angles, but that Wuffa, his son according to the East Anglian royal pedigree, was the dynastic ancestor. In the Kentish context we can see something more of the complexities which may lurk behind such bland statements. The early medieval dynasty seems, on Bede's evidence, to have been known as the *Oiscingas*, after a son or grandson of that Hengist whom Bede names as one of the leaders of the first groups of arriving Anglo-Saxons. An external source, the Ravenna Geography, may tell us, if one interpretation of its evidence be accepted, that Oisc was a principal leader of Germanic migrants into Britain. There are also chronological difficulties about the place later assigned to him in Kentish history. In this case we are in possession of just enough evidence to put us on our guard about simple statements of local dynastic origins, while the complex archaeology of early Kent warns us further of the difficulties inherent in attempting to relate the fragmentary, legendary, dynastic information to the realities of settlement. And rather earlier I mentioned the notably more extensive account of the alleged early history of the ninth-century West Saxon royal dynasty which we meet in the Anglo-Saxon Chronicle. For Wessex we are fortunate in possessing two other native sources of information – groups of dynastic genealogies, and a regnal list, interspersed with genealogical information, which I have called the West Saxon Genealogical Regnal List. This latter is an Alfredian text of somewhat earlier date than the common stock, datable to 892, of the Anglo-Saxon Chronicle. But what consideration of it allows is the wholesale rubbishing of the Chronicle's chronology for the century 495–597. While that may be seen as gain, in clearing away ninth-century disinformation, it does not help us significantly in any attempt to understand the origins of the kingdom. Relative abundance of ninth-century information may not, therefore, be an aid to the historian who seeks to understand the sixth-century origins of an Anglo-Saxon kingdom.

For the areas with which this chapter is concerned such information is notoriously lacking. This fact presents at once advantage and disadvantage. The absence of a Midland or East Anglian chronicle dealing with the early Anglo-Saxon period throws us back on dynastic pedigrees, which are for this area remarkably uninformative about the pre-Christian period. The history of England between the Thames–Severn and Humber–Mersey lines therefore begins in the seventh century. Before that, for two centuries, we are dealing with an effectively prehistoric situation. This does not mean of course that we cannot make deductions about aspects of sixth-century life from information about circumstances in the seventh: indeed, some seventh- and eighth-century evidence positively encourages us to do so. But the liberating effect of having no inherited dynastic origin legend to control one's perceptions of an area's early history should not be underrated or allowed to pass without recognition or welcome.

Certainly in the Midlands, then, and in fact likewise in most areas of what was to become England, neither narrative nor documentary sources will carry us back to the origins of most Anglo-Saxon kingdoms. What they will allow us to see – indeed, what in some cases for partisan reasons they positively encourage us to see – is the creation of overkingdoms, the larger units ruled by kings, which were coming into existence above all in the seventh century. Our seventh-century (and later) sources will sometimes permit us to penetrate behind that stage of kingdom building to an earlier stage of overlordship. But historical research, as opposed to archaeological or linguistic studies, will rarely permit us to approach the creation of the most primitive units of English government. Much of the fifth and sixth centuries is, in terms of *English* history, a lost era, a dark age. And the relationship between settlement and social and political organization in that period is one of the toughest interdisciplinary problems which we face.

In this way, then, our historical sources bring us to the era which textbooks of Anglo-Saxon history have long taught us to call the period of the Heptarchy. The Heptarchy is a difficult concept for the present-day historian to reconcile himself to. No two scholars are likely to count the same kingdoms among their seven, and this poses a genuine historiographic problem. If we cannot agree on a heptarchic head count, the implication is that we are not agreed about the nature of seventh- and eighth-century Anglo-Saxon kingdoms and that we are perhaps failing to see fundamental distinctions (which certainly existed). In the hope of provoking discussion on this matter, it is proposed that we adopt one of two solutions. On the one hand we could speak of an Anglo-Saxon Pentarchy, comprising Northumbria, Mercia, East Anglia, Kent and Wessex. The criterion by which these kingdoms are selected is that at the beginning of the First Viking Age, *c.* 800, in that period which marks the beginning of the end of the dominance of the Midland overkingship of Mercia (a hegemony which is such a marked feature of the late seventh century and the eighth), this Pentarchy represents the kingdoms which have some capacity for independent action. In Kent that is in danger of becoming vestigial, and in East Anglia it might appear so too until the events of the late 820s (and after) display only too clearly the strength of East Anglian local sentiment and institutions. But these five kingdoms are all clearly distinguishable in our sources as having life in them *c.* 800 and as being fairly clearly overkingships in origin. In the course of the sixth to eighth centuries they had all played major roles in English history. And in the Tribal Hidage the four of these kingdoms which lie south of the Humber are the four major units of hidation (15,000–100,000). On the other hand, unless we delete Kent from the list and speak of the Tetrarchy, which was what the Great Viking Army met when it came to England in 865, we must abandon any attempt to highlight a few select kingdoms as dominating the early historical era of Anglo-Saxon England, and recognize instead that we are in fact dealing with a plethora of kingdoms of very varying size and status: in addition to the five already named, one could mention Bernicia, Deira, Lindsey, the Magonsæte, the Hwicce, all of the minor Midland peoples named in the Tribal Hidage, Essex and Sussex. But even then one would have to admit that separate kingships are visible in some divisions of Kent, Essex, Wessex and perhaps Bernicia, that East Anglia appears to be an overlordly creation, and so on. Many of these units represented different levels of kingly government and political organization. Unless, therefore, we wish to throw away any general principle of order among this chaos, the Pentarchy or the Tetrarchy, but not the Heptarchy, may have something to recommend it.

One of the most insistent problems in this connection is the nature of the biological, or racial, relationship between Anglo-Saxon rulers and their peoples. That some groups took their name from their place of settlement is well-known: the king of Kent ruled the 'people dwelling in Kent' (*Cantware, Cantuarii*), which may be an indication of sub-Roman continuity and/or an avoidance of a convenient racial label, such as West Saxons, East Angles and so on. Did the ruling dynasty wish to avoid calling a racially heterogeneous population the East Jutes? Likewise, in Hampshire the Jutish groups were known as the *Wihtware* (in Wight, again showing latinate continuity of name) and *Meanware* (on the mainland). Bede could write of the frontier between the northern and southern *Angli* as being marked by the River Humber. In the end it seems that only the *East* Angles adopted the racially defined name, but there is a sufficiency of evidence that the Northumbrians and Mercians remembered that they were Angles; and when the frontier territory, which I shall be discussing further, between the East Angles and Mercians was being organized by its Mercian conquerors, its people were given the collective name of the Middle Angles. The West Angles were therefore the Mercians, notwithstanding the fact that their own name reflected their frontier origins in the north-west of what was to become Greater Mercia. From the late seventh century, after Lindsey (yet another Romano-British name serving as an Anglo-Saxon territorial name) had come firmly into Mercian control, the Humber does indeed become the major frontier zone in northern England and we hear of Northumbrians and Southumbrians on either side of it. Traces of an older nomenclature survive, however, for in a number of sources we hear of *Humbrenses*, the people living around the Humber, a waterway which apparently joined rather than divided. To the north of the Humber, as also in Lindsey, the invaders seem to have adopted a Celtic nomenclature, although the precise Celtic etymologies of Deira and Bernicia remain unclear. All these were Anglian peoples: to the Welsh they were *Eingl* (Angles), but also *Lloegrwys* (men of the border) and *Saesson* (*Saxones*, the general Late Latin and British name for the hated marauders from the North Sea).

In two famous passages Bede stressed in varying degrees the racial complexity of the Germanic settlers of Britain. Placename evidence has allowed the complications of a hypothetical distribution map to multiply enormously. In terms of the historical source material, to make identifications between kings, the areas in which the peoples whom they ruled lived, and the tribal or racial affiliations of those peoples, is difficult enough in the seventh century, a serious problem as we go back into the sixth, and desperate in any hypothesis about what was happening in the fifth. For at the moment when we begin to use artefactual evidence to decide the racial affiliations of the objects' users, not only do we run into a new range of theoretical difficulties but – even allowing those to take a back seat – we have to confront the likelihood of complex population movements quite out of contact with the distributions measurable from seventh-century and later sources.

In the racial names which we can plot on a map of seventh-century England, as in the dialect maps which a student of Old English language might draw, we see a reflection of the eventual relative stabilization of population distribution. The terminology – East Angles, West Saxons and of course the more specifically (British) geographical names for peoples constituting political units – is a statement of a complex Germanic polity now completely established on British soil. All the inhabitants of seventh-century East Anglia would not have been of Anglian descent, nor all those of Wessex of pure Saxon stock, but such names must have been of sufficient general acceptability among (in these cases) the East Anglian and West Saxon nobility to have allowed them to develop in common usage. But we should always keep in mind that the groups of settlers in any given area may have been racially very heterogeneous, associated by circumstances or by religion (for example) rather than by ethnic links, and in any case contaminated over a long period by the advent of further settlers.

Here, indeed, we are contemplating the origins of English settlement and the very beginnings of Anglo-Saxon political organization. But the chronological gap between those beginnings and the political units which we can detect in the seventh century as English historical sources first become available – especially when taken together with the general lack of interest of seventh-century (and later) Christian writers in the details of earlier local political history – is generally ruinous of direct attempts to gain any understanding of specific political development in the fifth and sixth centuries. For my purposes, then, the period of origins will be taken to be that from the arrival of the Germanic peoples in Britain until the emergence of the Anglo-Saxon Pentarchy in the late seventh century. On the whole, any attempt to comprehend that period of development in political terms has to proceed backwards, jocularly taking the late seventh century as relatively firm ground.

We may turn at last, then, to the geographical area on which the remainder of my chapter will concentrate. I shall be particularly concerned with Essex, Middle Anglia and (of necessity) in some measure East Anglia. The unifying factor is provided by Mercian expansionism, which is such a marked feature of political life in the English Midlands in the seventh and eighth centuries. It is difficult to draw a line around any kingdom or group of kingdoms of this period in order to study them in isolation. In this case Kent and Wessex might seem to demand admission to our group. In spite of the geographically devolved nature of early English political power, there was between kingdoms constant military and diplomatic interaction which seems to have created political chain reactions. For all that, I hope to focus attention on the advertised area – the northern Home Counties and the south-east Midlands.

We must begin with that principal theme of seventh-century Southumbrian history, the expansion of Mercia to the point where its rulers dominate the whole of Midland England, become a major power in the South-East (that is, for these purposes, Kent, Surrey and Sussex), and from time to time have considerable influence in and over Wessex. The Mercians may be seen expanding their hegemony, presumably largely by force of arms, in three principal directions from their original settlement area around the River Trent: (i) north-eastwards, into the Peak district, Lindsey and Elmet (in this last case, therefore, into Deira, an area in which – as we know from Bede's Ecclesiastical History – Mercian rulers showed considerable interest throughout the seventh century); (ii) south-eastwards, into the East Midlands and the Home Counties; (iii) south-westwards, into east-central and south-eastern 'Wales' and north-west Wessex. It is with the second of these movements that we must now be concerned; yet the larger context must be kept in mind both to allow consideration of possible comparanda and to remind us that the creation of a Midland hegemony was achieved by a remarkable series of expansionist campaigns in a number of directions almost simultaneously. The resources and the reputations of the rulers who led these campaigns must have been considerable.

Mercian domination of the Midlands meant the subordination of a substantial number of peoples from whom tribute and military service would henceforth be drawn. When Bede tells us of the thirty *duces regii*, 'royal military commanders', who accompanied Penda, king of Mercia, at the battle of *Winwed* in November 655, he is undoubtedly referring to the rulers of these subject peoples. It is, to say the least, a curious coincidence that the document known as the Tribal Hidage, apparently a list of peoples in the Southumbrian English sphere of influence in the seventh century, contains the names of thirty-four peoples having separate assessments, including the Mercians proper and the three major peoples of England south of the Thames. Among those thirty *duces regii* at *Winwed* was Æthelhere, king of the East Angles.

The distribution of the peoples named in the Tribal Hidage is of some further interest in this connection. It has often been observed that the groups named fall into three categories: (i) the four major Southumbrian kingdoms – Mercia, East Anglia, Kent and Wessex – with assessments of 30,000, 30,000, 15,000 and 100,000 hides respectively; (ii) intermediate units, six with a typical assessment of 7,000 hides (including Lindsey, Essex and Sussex), but including also four other groups with assessments ranging from 2,000 to 5,000 hides; (iii) finally, twenty minor units with hidations extending from 300 to 1,200. What needs to be stressed is that, of the twenty minor peoples, those which can be identified are overwhelmingly distributed in the East and South Midlands. It is the local detail concerning the Midlands which has convinced most historians that we have to do with a Mercian document. But, I repeat, that concentration on numerous small units pertains only to the East and South Midlands. Two questions arise as a result. Were forms of social and governmental organization different in the West and North Midlands from what they were in Middle Anglia (for that is essentially the area in which these small units congregate)? Secondly, was the compiler of the list locally more knowledgeable about the East Midlands than about any other area?

To take the second question first, if we admitted a positive answer we could allow the possibility that the Tribal Hidage was an East Anglian compilation. But it has to be admitted, I think, that the general distribution of information in this document makes a Mercian origin the only probable option. What is more, if it were East Anglian, we should have to go back to the reign of Rædwald and the period of the later 610s and earlier 620s. This does not seem at all appropriate.

If we ask instead about varying forms of socio-political organization, two possible approaches open up. We might care to think that as Germanic settlement in Britain extended westward, so the resulting political units either grew larger or were merely administrative creations of larger parent units, major kingdoms like Mercia and Wessex. The Tribal Hidage would then give an accurate representation of the development of Germanic settlement in the English Midlands. Alternatively, we might think that the larger units, of (say) 2,000 hides and more, had themselves in many (if not all) cases arisen by the aggregation of a number of smaller units.

The correct answer comes immediately into view, for we know from other sources both that a good number of the medium-sized units named in the Tribal Hidage had subdivisions of apparent original separateness and that some of the most westerly Anglo-Saxon political units lived, from their earliest appearances in English sources, under the rule of kings (and dynasties) which display no trace of having been planted by the fiat of an administrative overlord. The variety of political organization which we encounter in the seventh century (by comparison with what we see in the eighth) should be a sufficient warning to us against assuming that the sixth century would be no more complex and varied in that respect. There is every possibility that the larger units seen in the Tribal Hidage, in other seventh-century sources and in Bede's works, would in an earlier century have appeared as many minor ones. The relative rapidity with which the West Midlands are traversed in the Tribal Hidage may therefore suggest that this area had already been brought securely under Mercian domination. If we can accept the seventh-century chronology of the Anglo-Saxon Chronicle, we shall note that Penda seems to have been victorious against the West Saxons in a battle at Cirencester (in the territory of the Hwicce) in 628, and that in the mid-640s he was able to drive king Cenwalh from his West Saxon throne into temporary East Anglian exile. It looks as though the first major and successful phase of Mercian expansion within England was that directed south-westwards, and that the West Saxons were those who incurred loss as a result.

Mercian military and diplomatic campaigning against Northumbria was a central fact of English politics from c. 630 to c. 680. By the end of that period Northumbrian attempts to dominate southern neighbours had been finally beaten off, while the Mercian efforts to destabilize Northumbria by detaching Deira and drawing it into a Southumbrian alliance had also failed. Although archbishop Theodore's mediation between Ecgfrith of Northumbria and Æthelred I of Mercia after the battle of the Trent (679) could not, of course, bring perpetual peace between the kingdoms, no longer was a struggle between them to be one of the determinants of English politics.

Mercia became a more and more formidable adversary for the Northumbrians as its Midland base expanded and the military and economic resources upon which its kings could draw consequently grew. As is well known, the principal crises with Northumbria occurred in 633–4, 642, 651–5, 658, c. 665, 674 and 679. In between these major distractions, however, a continuing and ultimately successful thrust of Mercian policy was directed south-eastwards, to the subjugation of those peoples who collectively came to be known as the Middle Angles and to the overawing (and eventual conquest) of East Anglia and Essex. The 'Middle Angles' are, in effect, the aggregation of the minor peoples, named in the Tribal Hidage, who were situated geographically – and therefore politically – between East Anglia and Mercia.

If we look for geographical definition of Middle Anglia, we gain two main pieces of information. An entirely separate ecclesiastical diocese for the Middle Angles was not established until 737, but when it was created the see was placed at Leicester. Of the constituent units of Middle Anglia we meet, outside the Tribal Hidage, only the Gyrwe. They inhabited the Fenland border but were by the later seventh century in the Greater Mercian ecclesiastical diocese. That they constituted a kingdom of their own is made clear by Bede who wrote that bishop Thomas, the first English bishop of East Anglia

(647×53), came *de prouincia Gyruiorum*, 'from the kingdom of the Gyrwe'. They inhabited at least what is now northernmost Cambridgeshire, one of their *regiones* including Peterborough. In the tenth century Crowland abbey (Lincs.) could be described as lying *on middan Gyrwan fenne*. Æthilthryth, daughter of king Anna of East Anglia, was briefly married to one Tondberht, *princeps* (a troublesome word) of the South Gyrwe; that she was then remarried *c.* 664 to Ecgfrith, son and heir apparent of the powerful Oswiu, king of Northumbria, suggests that Tondberht's own status may have been royal. And we may wish to take their original separateness as a group, which to me (though not to all historians) would imply the existence of a tribal kingship, as confirmed by their appearance in the Tribal Hidage; and it may be that their appearance there in two halves, North and South, implies *two* kingdoms at some stage.

The Middle Angles make two major types of appearance in Bede's Ecclesiastical History, as a secular socio-political unit and as a people to whom a bishop ministered. They are included among the Germanic peoples who settled in Britain, but their principal occurrence in Bede's History is because of their providing a kingdom for Peada, son of king Penda of Mercia, in the period 653–5, a time in which Peada became Christian, married a Northumbrian princess and allowed missionaries to preach in Middle Anglia. Bede summarizes this by saying 'Middilengli, sub principe Peada, fidei mysteriis sunt inbuti': 'the Middle Angles, under the *princeps* Peada, were initiated into the mysteries of the Faith'. In his main account Bede begins with much the same statement, but continues, 'Since he was an excellent young man, most worthy of the name and station of king, he was preferred by his father to the kingship of that people.' He was converted to Christianity in Northumbria, married to a daughter of king Oswiu and sent home with four missionary priests. Bede tells us that, 'Uenientes ergo in prouinciam, memorati sacerdotes cum principe praedicabant Uerbum . . .', 'Coming therefore into the kingdom, the aforementioned priests with the *princeps* preached the Word . . .' It is clear that Penda had created Peada king of the Middle Angles.

When, a couple of years later, Penda was dead and Oswiu was supreme in the Midlands, the Mercians themselves received Christianity. At that juncture the Irish missionary priest Diuma was created first bishop of the Middle Angles and of the Mercians. Bede tells us that 'a shortage of bishops made it necessary that one bishop should be set over both *populi*'. In recounting Midland episcopal succession down almost to his own time Bede is usually careful to remind his readers that the bishops (whose seat was eventually established at Lichfield in Mercia) served these two distinct peoples; indeed, it subsequently emerges that Lindsey was also among his and his immediate successors' charges. Although the Middle Anglian see of Leicester was not established until 737, in the period 690×3 (and in fact probably for a period of some eleven years) St Wilfrid 'was managing the bishopric of the Middle Angles'.

The Middle Angles do not appear as a single people in the Tribal Hidage, and we may wish to draw one of two different conclusions from this. We can deduce from Bede that Middle Anglia, as a royal unit, was a short-lived Mercian creation, made by Penda for his son Peada, and that after 655 (or at any rate after Peada's murder in April 656) it ceased to exist politically. Some further arguments to the same effect were convincingly offered by Wendy

Davies in 1973. Its name may then have been perpetuated in ecclesiastical administration only. This is a possible but not wholly satisfying solution to our problem, notably in view of Bede's continuing references to a *prouincia* (that is, kingdom) of the Middle Angles with constituent *regiones*. Alternatively we could argue that the Tribal Hidage reflects the circumstances of a period when all these peoples had not been welded into a single unit, in other words before 653. In all this, however, we must not mislead ourselves into mistaking what was happening. In making Peada king of the Middle Angles Penda was not thereby suppressing all the local, indeed tribal, kingships of the region: we must remember the thirty *duces regii* who accompanied him with their forces at the battle of the *Winwed* two years later.

We must return to the larger context which we surveyed earlier. The Tribal Hidage allots to Mercia proper and to East Anglia an equivalent hidation: 30,000. In principle, then, these were units of equivalent political and economic standing. But a largely unwritten part of the history of Mercia in the mid-seventh century must be the incorporation of all the small, independent peoples of the south-eastern Midlands. When Penda gave Peada the kingdom of the Middle Angles in 653 he must have been placing him in newly dominated territory as a minor, or intermediate, overlord subordinate to himself. The Mercians' original principal rivals for this territory must have been the East Angles who would therefore have become hereditary enemies. The East Angles' potential for expansion is demonstrated very clearly in 617 when Rædwald must have been master of the East Midlands in order to have launched his successful surprise attack on Æthilfrith of Northumbria. This scenario helps to account for the vehemence with which Penda continued to assault East Anglia from the 630s until 654 (the Anglo-Saxon Chronicle's date) when he killed king Anna. Thereafter for a century and a half East Anglian power was broken, almost all subsequent kings being Mercian dependants, notable for their submissiveness and (after Æthelhere, killed at *Winwed* after one year's reign) their longevity. Mercian possession of Middle Anglia was now secure. We may perhaps compare this process with the Mercian struggle against Northumbria for control of Lindsey, Elmet and Deira, which resulted by the late seventh century in the firm establishment of the Humber boundary. This whole context, it seems to me, defines the date of the Tribal Hidage as being without doubt the period from *c.* 635 to *c.* 680; at any later date the same conditions no longer applied.

Is it in fact possible, on the evidence which I have been discussing, to shorten this time-scale? Juxtaposition of the dates 653 for the establishment of the overkingdom of Middle Anglia and 654 for the death of what was to be the last independent East Anglian king for several generations suggests that this was a time of momentous developments in Midland England. Whether the Mercian establishment of Middle Anglia provoked king Anna into a fatal reaction or whether Penda decided that one more assault on East Anglia would serve to secure his son's new position, we cannot say. Before Penda's death, none the less, Mercian dominance over the Midland (or, in Bede's terms, South Anglian) peoples was assured. No doubt all this fell apart on Penda's death in November 655, notwithstanding Oswiu's new dominance of Mercia. But it was to be restored by Penda's son Wulfhere before very long.

Is the Tribal Hidage to be dated thus to the period from the mid-630s to the early 650s, in other words to the reign of Penda? Not the least difficulty in the way of accepting this is that Mercia had no Christian institutions in that period; formally speaking, Mercian government was illiterate and one would hesitate greatly before invoking early oral transmission for a document such as this. If this was not a governmental document, but rather a descriptive text of ecclesiastical origin, comparable limitations are imposed on dating.

If, then, establishment of a date in the second quarter of the seventh century seems impracticable, we are left with the reign of Wulfhere (658–75) and the early years of Æthelred I (675–704), allowing of course (which some historians would be unwilling to do) that *c.* 680 is the latest likely date for the Tribal Hidage. Within this chronological frame the only period which seems to make sense, in terms of an overkingship territorially described as in the Tribal Hidage, is the early 670s (or just possibly the late 660s, about which we know very little). Stenton in 1918 convincingly displayed the evidence for regarding Wulfhere in that period as overlord of all the Southumbrian English, as Stephanus (in his Life of St Wilfrid) stated that he had been in 674. Perhaps this period is close enough to the first attempt to establish a Middle Anglian mesne overkingdom for us to accept that there were still (up to twenty years later) good reasons for listing their constituent peoples separately rather than under the group name *Middilengle.*

Before we leave them, two further questions must be asked, about the geographical spread and the name of the Middle Angles. I have already remarked that the Gyrwe are the only Tribal Hidage people named explicitly as a constituent of the Middle Angles. Bede tells us of a *regio quae uocatur in Feppingum,* in which bishop Diuma died, and places it among the Middle Angles. Unfortunately this locality has not been identified. In the margin of the earliest – that is, eleventh-century – manuscript of the Tribal Hidage, by the side of the tribal name *Færpingas,* an Old English annotator has written *is in Middelenglum.* Here perhaps is another indication of a Middle Anglian tribe; yet whether the *Feppingas* and the *Færpingas* were one and the same is a nice question. Seventh- and eighth-century written evidence seems to have no further positive contribution to make; negatively, some frontiers can be drawn, as for example by reference to Bede's remark that the *regio* of Ely lay in East Anglia. In general, however, we have to try to clutch at some straws of much later evidence for further guidance as to the extent of Middle Anglia.

Two potentially misleading testimonies may be considered. In the late ninth century, the Middle Anglian episcopal see at Leicester was transferred, presumably as a result of the conditions created by Scandinavian activity in the Midlands, to Dorchester-on-Thames; from there a bishop continued to minister to the East and South Midlands until the see was at length transferred to Lincoln in 1072. It is a possible, but by no means necessary, deduction that in the later ninth century bishop Ceolred or bishop Alhheard transferred his see to the most southerly limit of his diocese, that is to say, that Middle Anglia did in fact stretch southwards as far as the Thames. There seems to me to be a good deal to be said for this view. The whole area east of the Hwicce and south-east of the Mercians proper seems to have been served by this ecclesiastical diocese, and in seventh-century terms this was the area which the Mercians had to bring under tribute if they were to deny the resources of these minor peoples to, in particular, the West Saxons and the East Angles and consequently aggrandize themselves.

Perhaps connected with the move from Leicester to Dorchester is another item of potential interest. The tenth-century list of saints' resting places notes that the remains of bishop Diuma, whose death Bede placed among the Middle Anglian *Feppingas*, then lay buried at Charlbury in Oxfordshire. Either that place lay in the *regio* of the *Feppingas* or else Diuma's relics were removed to the supposed relative safety of the Middle Thames in the late ninth century. In either event there is perhaps an implication that Middle Anglia included part of Oxfordshire.

I conclude, then, very provisionally that Middle Anglia (as constituted in 653 and as represented from 737 by its own ecclesiastical diocese) is likely to have been bounded by Wessex to the south, Essex to the south-east, East Anglia to the east, Lindsey to the north, Mercia proper to the north-west and the Hwicce to the south-west. In other words, it was a very substantial, yet relatively compact, chunk of Midland England.

Why were the Middle Angles so-called? It seems to me that the use of the term 'Middle' is almost a guarantee of relative lateness. East, West, North and South at least have the chance of being used in an effectively absolute way geographically (by reference to the compass, as it were). But 'Middle' implies definition in terms of surrounding units or peoples. It is at the very least curious that the two early Anglo-Saxon uses of this term in administrative or people-names – Middle Anglia and Middlesex, the Middle Angles and the Middle Saxons, that is to say – appear in circumstances where Mercian intervention is writ large in our source material. Certainly in the case of the Middle Angles we can see the creation by the Mercians in the mid-seventh century of a convenient unit representing an agglomeration of formerly independent peoples of very varying sizes and relative importance in a broad band of territory separating Mercia from East Anglia, Essex and Wessex. In the case of the Middle Saxons one again sees the hand of Mercian overlordship at work. If the Middle Saxons had existed as a separate unit in the third quarter of the seventh century, one might have expected archbishop Theodore to have provided them and the East Saxons with separate bishops. On such negative evidence we might assign the creation of Middlesex to the closing years of the seventh century or the opening years of the eighth. This of course raises questions of the prior status of the Middle Saxons. Were they formerly just a division of the East Saxons, with or without such a single group-name? Was Middlesex inhabited by a group of peoples once under East Saxon overlordship but not having any primitive connection with Essex? Or was it a political creation intended simply to provide London with an administrative hinterland, in other words neither more nor less than the portion of Essex annexed by the Mercian overlords to their Greater Mercian Empire which they were busily creating in the seventh and eighth centuries?

Unfortunately, the question cannot be answered without going yet farther afield, to Surrey. As, etymologically, 'the southern *ge* (distinct administrative division)', it looks naturally across to Middlesex. But *-ge* is an old element, perhaps unlikely (although I doubt that it is possible to be firm about this) to have been productive in seventh-century England. If Middlesex was once part of Essex, then Surrey is naturally explained as Essex's southern *ge* and the connection old. The interest of some seventh- and eighth-century East Saxon kings and princes in West Kent (perhaps a Saxon rather than a Jutish region) would be more easily explained in this context. In political circumstances where one can see as much development as we have already done it would be foolish to go further and speak of an 'original connection'. *Originally*, that is to say in the fifth and earlier sixth centuries, we cannot speak of any unit being connected with any other; we probably cannot even credibly define (from later historical sources) what the units were in that period. That is the province of the archaeologist and the historical geographer.

Whether a king or kings of the East Saxons fought at the *Winwed* under Penda's command in 655 is quite unknown, but as the Mercians gained an ever more secure hold on the peoples of the south-eastern Midlands, they would come increasingly into contact with the East Saxons. This is certainly apparent already by the latter half of the reign of Wulfhere (658–75) when they had fallen under his lordship. His role in the granting of the Surrey charter of 672×4 indicates his overlordship there. From 704, the last year of the reign of king Æthelred I of Mercia, a brief series of five documents attests to the overlordship of Æthelred and his successor Coenred (704–9) in Essex. Already in the last decade of his reign we find Æthelred granting land in Middlesex (at Ealing) without reference to an East Saxon king. This sets a pattern by which Æthelbald (716–57) and his successors may be found making grants concerning London and other parts of Middlesex without any thought of a reference to the kings of Essex. The conclusion has long since been drawn that it was at this period that Middlesex was annexed and brought under the direct rule of the Mercian kings, whether in Ceolred's time or in Æthelbald's. But the way the wind was blowing was apparent already in the decade to 704, and the reference in a document dated 704 to the *prouincia Middelseaxan* may be an indication of this. As far as I know, there is no indication of the Mercian kings behaving in a similarly high-handed fashion in the other parts of Essex.

For approximately the first half of the reign of Æthelred of Mercia (675–704) Essex may have been beyond the reach of the Mercians. A period of West Saxon overlordship in Cædwalla's reign (685–8) was followed by at best uneasy relationships with Wessex. The East Saxons could not avoid being caught up in the south-eastern power struggles of this period, some of which were no doubt of their own making. In 689–90 East Saxon royals were active in Kent while acknowledging Æthelred's lordship. From the point at which they eventually passed under Æthelred's control there is no clear evidence that the East Saxon kings were other than wholly loyal dependants of the Mercian rulers. For that very reason, perhaps, their native kingship was the longest to survive (certainly well into the 820s) of any of those peoples who remained part of the Midland hegemony.

The seventh century had seen the East Saxons accepting (however unwillingly) a notable variety of overkings, as well as enjoying some brief periods of freedom of action. Their dependence on the king of Kent seems to have been a personal link to Æthelberht I, the Southumbrian overlord, which did not continue after his death. That period is followed by one of apparent independence and wars with Wessex which continued sporadically through the century and into the next, Surrey (it seems) being the obvious bone of contention. But as each new overlord managed to establish himself over the peoples of the Southumbrian English, so Essex must have been (and at times in our sources visibly was) brought under varying control – East Anglian, Northumbrian and Mercian. East Anglian influence in Essex seems to have been reasserted at some point between 655 and 664, perhaps as an intermediate overlordship under ultimate Northumbrian control and therefore in the period 655–8, after which East Anglia and Essex would no doubt have come fairly rapidly under Mercian domination.

In the end the history of Essex in this period was one of being tugged politically and religiously between rival neighbours and also (sometimes distant) overlords. When some measure of stability was achieved, perhaps after *c.* 690, Mercian dominance was so absolute that Essex could be permanently deprived of a major chunk of itself in a measure which seems almost unprecedented in the records of early Anglo-Saxon history. London and its hinterland, what came to be called Middlesex, were to be part of Mercia thenceforth for two centuries. The link with Surrey was thereby weakened, the southern province now becoming a prey to the competing influences of Mercia and Wessex.

In its internal governmental structure, Essex from the beginning of its recorded history to at least the mid-eighth century presents an unusually complex spectacle. Shared kingship was a frequent occurrence. I do not want to rehearse again what Barbara Yorke has only recently done in her extremely useful historical survey of the East Saxon kingdom and its rulers. What does need to be considered briefly is the possible natures of the shared rule and the evidence for internal administrative or popular divisions of the kingdom.

East Saxon kingship in the seventh and early eighth centuries presents a fairly extensive paradigm of joint rule. When Essex first appears in the historical record at the beginning of the seventh century, it is apparently ruled by one king, Saberht, albeit under the *potestas* of the Southumbrian overlord, Æthelberht I of Kent. However, Saberht was succeeded by his three sons as joint rulers; Bede calls them all 'kings'. Their joint rule was sufficiently unified that they could all agree to expel bishop Mellitus, and they all subsequently led the military force which was destroyed by the Gewisse.

Half a century later, during 664×9, after a number of sole rulers we find the kingship again divided, this time between two rulers, Sigehere and Sebbi; *socius eius et coheres regni*, 'his colleague and the joint inheritor of the kingship', is Bede's phrase to describe the relationship of one to the other. Some twenty years later Sigehere seems still to have been active, for we find him in West Kent after 686 (perhaps in a subordinate role to Cædwalla of Wessex). Sigehere's interest may, after his death when Sebbi was sole ruler of Essex, have been assumed by Swæfheard son of Sebbi who is found as a king in these confused years of Kentish history. Sebbi was succeeded in Essex *c.* 694×9 by his sons Sigehard and Swefred, but it is possible that these two were associated as kings with their father before his death. In a charter of *c.* 690 all three attest a transfer of land by one Oithilred, *parens* ('father' or 'subject') of king Sebbi, but of course the possibility remains that their signatures represent subsequent additions or confirmation. On the other hand, in the first decade of the eighth century we find Sigehard acting in Middlesex without reference to another East Saxon king and Swefred behaving similarly in what is now Essex. That Essex as a whole had more than one ruler in this period is proved by the famous letter of Waldhere, bishop of London, who refers in 705 to *nostrique patriae regnatores* ('the rulers of our country').

An interesting light is thrown on East Saxon kingship by Bede's account of the joint pilgrimage to Rome in 709 of Coenred of Mercia and Offa of Essex. Bede reports that in Essex Offa, son of a previous joint ruler, Sigehere, was seen as (in Colgrave's translation) 'a youth so lovable and handsome that the whole race longed for him to have and to hold the sceptre of the kingdom'. In short he was the heir apparent to the East Saxon throne. A charter issued within the previous five years purports to show Offa as king of Essex making a grant in Hertfordshire (in other words in Middle Saxon territory); if genuine, this would suggest that Offa was already associated in the kingship before the demise of his predecessor or predecessors. His father had been dead for almost twenty years, he was not at all closely related to the present ruler (while king Swefred's brother and co-ruler king Sigehard had a son Sigemund who was father of a later ruler, Swithred), and the likely presence of other candidates are all factors which combine to make his position as heir apparent rather striking. We may wonder if in this kingdom, where joint-kingship was regularly known, the succession rules were not rather more complex than elsewhere. The possibility remains, however, that Offa had built up a powerful political position for himself within Essex and that other candidates were thereby discouraged (or were rendered ineligible on other grounds).

Having briefly examined the evidence for shared kingship, we may now properly ask in what ways royal authority was divided; such a division must also have had implications for, or must itself result from, arrangements for succession to the throne. This must all be looked at within a comparative English framework.

Territorial division seems attested in Kent and Sussex as well as in Essex, although the evidence is of varying quality. In Kent the division between East and West Kent seems to be as old, or almost as old, as the English settlements; such a division seems to be reflected in our sources for the seventh and eighth centuries. Notwithstanding this, Kent retained its political and territorial unity, and kings (who by no means always seem to be related by blood) attest and confirm their colleague's actions. On the occasions when Kent had more than two rulers, we may suspect that another system of division operated simultaneously and wonder whether the six lathes (*regiones*) of Kent should be seen as related to the royal divisions. In Sussex the six rapes may have been the local equivalent of the Kentish lathes, but this is a proposition fraught with difficulty. The Hastings area none the less seems to have maintained its identity within Sussex throughout the historical Anglo-Saxon period: a Northumbrian chronicler noted that in 771 Offa of Mercia conquered the *gentem Hestingorum*. We may perhaps choose to relate this factor to the multiple kingship attested in seventh- and eighth-century Sussex, and the conjectured plurality of dynasties in that kingdom. However, we must remember that, as in Kent, kings are found attesting one another's grants; there is no evidence of an ultimate fragmentation of the South Saxon nation, whatever the nature of the divisions of royal power. For Essex the evidence of territorial division is even less conclusive. It turns largely on the question of the places of Middlesex and Surrey within the East Saxon kingdom. As is well known, Surrey had its own *subregulus*, Frithuwold, in the 670s; he is shown, by the charter from which he is known, to be a dependent of Wulfhere of Mercia. Referring to the same period, Bede called Surrey a *regio*, which is his term for a division of a kingdom. Frithuwold could have been a Mercian royal appointed by Wulfhere; but unless the district had a tradition of separate kingship it is unlikely that such an appointment would have been made. In other words, whether Frithuwold was a native or a Mercian, his appearance is none the less an argument for a tradition of kingship in Surrey. Given that and the connection with Essex, we might choose to argue that the repeated divisions of the East Saxon kingship are reflected in the independent evidence for territorial divisions. This might be supported by reference to East Saxon involvement in Kent, especially West Kent. If Sigehere of Essex was responsible for the conquest of part or all of Kent before 690, then the appearance of his co-ruler's son as a king of Kent may represent an aspect of the division of royal power among the East Saxons. There are, however, too many uncertainties for that line of argument to be given much weight. And on the other hand the close joint action of Saberht's sons, as reported by Bede, suggests committee rule rather than territorial division.

An alternative type of division is suggested by Bede's wording in his account of the state of Christianity in Essex in the 660s. He reports the apostasy of king Sigehere *cum sua parte populi* ('with his part of the people'), while Sebbi, his colleague, remained faithful; Wulfhere of Mercia, their overlord, heard of the apostasy of *prouinciae ex parte* ('part of the kingdom'). This may imply territorial division, but another possibility is suggested by comparative evidence from among the Burgundians and Irish, where a joint ruler might be king of scattered parts of the population rather than of a territorial block within it.

Finally, we may consider joint rule, of which there may be several varieties. Committee rule of two or more kings seems most plausibly attested for the Hwicce and perhaps (sometimes at least) for Essex and even Sussex. When three sons succeeded a single ruler (as after Saberht in Essex, after Wihtred in Kent in 725, and perhaps among the Hwicce in the 750s at least), they may have ruled as a committee, but that is not to say that they were all equal. There is room for the suspicion that the eldest may have been at least *primus inter pares*: this seems very likely in the case of the Hwicce. Another variety of joint rule is the deliberate association by one king of another ruler with him; in all the identifiable cases, the associated ruler was both subordinate and responsible for a separate unit (often a conquered one) within the kingdom. It is interesting that we do not seem to have any evidence for this practice in Essex.

In cases of divided kingship the principles of succession may have required different solutions. Among the various instances there is some suggestion that a brother's sons may have enjoyed special rights in respect of succession. But examination of other instances (for example, Swefred of Essex succeeds in Kent, perhaps to Sigehere, his father's co-ruler; Offa of Essex, Sigehere's son, is heir apparent to the sons of his father's co-ruler) suggests that a wider range of factors was at work, and that political (and military) circumstances dictated the choice of successor(s) or co-ruler(s) from among a wide range of possible candidates.

Two principal risks might seem to be involved in such divisions of kingship.

Territorial fragmentation of the original unit by secession or gradual acceptance of political separation was, however, avoided. Various other medieval situations may be compared (for example, Merovingian Francia, or the Anglo-Norman 'Empire') where, in spite of political division and redivision (and notwithstanding consequent internecine hostilities), a presumption of unity is retained which preserves the 'national' unit from fission. Whether the feeling for unity derived from a racial consciousness or loyalty to an original dynasty is difficult to say. The eventual detachment of Middlesex and Surrey from Essex may seem to contradict this view, but the possibility does of course remain that Middlesex (including Surrey) was originally independent of Essex and that its detachment from Essex represented no more than a change in external overlordship of the area; we may compare therefore the way in which seventh-century Lindsey was now part of Northumbria, now part of Mercia. That is not the necessary conclusion, however. External domination and eventual annexation constituted another risk of territorial division of a kingdom, although the two processes are not necessarily connected. Wessex lost first the Hwicce and then Oxfordshire to Mercia. Indeed, a whole kingdom, such as Sussex, could be gobbled up by an external power. We might wonder whether such division of royal power as is evidenced in Essex, Kent and Sussex did not contribute to these kingdoms' inability effectively to withstand external aggression; in some cases, such as that of Hlothhere and Eadric in late seventh-century Kent, it may have invited foreign intervention; but obviously relative size and geographical factors will be recognized as the principal considerations in this respect.

We may in fact see here, therefore, the beginnings of one distinction between kingship and overkingship in the seventh- (and eighth-) century context. Kingship of a country may be divisible, but the nation itself remains a unity. This must have implications for us as we try to see beneath the surface evidence for the constitution of the earliest attested Anglo-Saxon kingdoms and to conjecture something of their origins.

An overkingship may be created and held by an individual ruler, but it is difficult to transmit to a successor, since it has no natural unity; only a long, continuous period of enforcement, and the vigorous reduction of factors tending to emphasize the separate identity of the constituent parts, could hope to create a kingdom from an overlordship. With this in mind scholars have to interrogate the records for the earliest attested Anglo-Saxon kingdoms to see whether there are hints of earlier socio-political forms.

As for Essex, whatever its relationship with Mercia in the period 674×c. 730 may have been (and the evidence on this matter is very complex), its kings still seem to have been capable of independent political action. They were embroiled with both Cædwalla and Ine of Wessex, apparently for supremacy in south-eastern England. East Saxon power in Kent is probably chronologically defined by the burning of Mul, Cædwalla's brother, in 687 and the payment to Ine of compensation for it in 694. Early in his reign (688–726) Ine controlled Surrey, and it is unclear whether he might have enjoyed power also in Middlesex or elsewhere in Essex. But West Saxon exiles are found in Essex in 705 and in Surrey in 722. These years saw, therefore, a major power struggle in the South-East in which the kings of Essex played a notable part. While they were losing Middlesex to Mercia, they sought to wrest Kent (and no doubt to save Surrey) from Wessex. The overlordship of Æthelbald of Mercia, established by 731, effectively ended East Saxon independence, however.

In the East Midlands the principal political development in the seventh century, and especially its second quarter, was the struggle between Mercia and East Anglia for hegemony over this substantial region and over Essex in the extreme south-east of the area. While East Anglia was dominant its power could reach even Northumbria. But as its power was reduced, East Anglia itself became a prey to Mercian aggression: such was the effect of that onslaught that it was not to revive as an independent power until the first half of the ninth century. As for Mercia, once its dominance of the peoples of the East and South Midlands was assured, the great kingdom which we have long since come to think of as Mercia – in fact Greater Mercia – began to coalesce. To map out the information presented by the Tribal Hidage does much to clarify one's perceptions of both the geography and the politics of this process. Middle Anglia provided the Mercians' gateway to East Anglia and Wessex, and Essex the gateway to the South-East.

It is worth remarking that Mercia seems to have been by a substantial margin the latest of the major kingdoms to come together as a single unit. The other kingdoms of the so-called 'Heptarchy' seem to have been formed anything up to about a century earlier. For the student of eighth-century (or later) Mercian government, this history (or lack of it) may be a significant fact. And that the political unit came together relatively late may even help to explain why we have no annals or chronicle for the Midlands. At the time when such a record might first have been created, there was no single Midland unit or dynasty to give coherence and focus.

The Tribal Hidage map of the Midlands provides, on a large scale, one model for the development of Anglo-Saxon kingdoms in the fifth- to seventh-century period. It is not necessarily to be followed, but it does suggest how in the sixth century an overlordship of intermediate size might have been created by the bringing together of a substantial group of minor kingdoms. As to the origins of those minor peoples, the existence of subdivisions – *regiones* in Bede's term – within their territories does suggest that they were not always primary themselves. At what point the mass of Angles, Saxons, and other West Germanic groups in this region began to coalesce into small units with kingly government is unknown. The archaeologist now produces the raw data which must be interpreted effectively, and may eventually bring order into that whole question of the first creation of minor 'kingdoms'. Whether this creation was occurring already in the fifth century or only in the sixth is a question to which no answer can be given by the historian. The archaeologist and the historical geographer have much to teach us about this dark period.

On the origins of settlement in Essex and the South and East Midlands I cannot (and shall not) comment here. Of the origins of English kingship there, little can be said. But of the origins of Greater Mercia one can in fact say a good deal, as I have tried to show in this chapter.

10 Kingship and material culture in early Anglo-Saxon East Anglia

MARTIN CARVER

An early kingdom may take many forms in the imagination, and the character of an investigation will change depending on which of these forms is chosen. At one extreme it may be a community over which an individual enjoys powers of social and economic dictatorship, but which has no clear territorial boundaries; at another it may be a territory, occupied by a society which does not acknowledge allegiance to any individual. Kings may be war leaders, or theocratic legislators, or wishful thinkers. We could agree by way of compromise that a kingdom existed in early Anglo-Saxon England when a bounded territory can be found over which an individual and his family enjoyed the right of jurisdiction and the routine extraction of at least part of the surplus. In this definition a king inherits an entitlement to dues from all the land in the territory; so whereas any lord can take rent, only a king can tax.

No discipline will find such a thing easy to observe, even supposing it existed, so that the origins of 'kingly' behaviour will be difficult to locate in time and space. On the other hand there will be a general consensus that the period from the fifth to the seventh century in England was crucial for the social, ideological and economic development which allowed the early kingdoms at least to be named. So whether or not territories, kings or subjects are visible in that period is not so important as the character of the community that is actually discernible. Both archaeologists and historians have views on the perceived character of that society and on how to make them more credible. One version of the problem may be summarized in two questions: did Anglo-Saxon society become more stratified after the settlement of the fifth century? And if it did, why? The early English farmer, traditionally portrayed as an independent if superstitious pioneer from a free *Heimat*, seems to have become a royal subject with remarkable acquiescence; was it economic constraint, caused by the exhaustion of the new easy resources, or the development of class consciousness, or the emulation of neighbouring politics, or Christianity, which provoked a change in his status? Or was the free German always a myth, fertilized by the silence of the record? This chapter is an attempt to reconcile two rather different theoretical approaches to this problem, one owed to historians and projected back from the time of Domesday Book, and the other owed to archaeologists and projected forwards from prehistory. The whole exercise is extremely risky, and undertaken more out of curiosity than expertise in either field (or indeed in the early East Anglia to which the two approaches will be applied).[1]

ARCHAEOLOGICAL APPROACHES – NATURAL RESOURCES

The evidence presently at the disposal of archaeologists consists broadly of natural resources, settlements and cemeteries. In the context of this investigation the questions to be answered will be, 'Are resources increasing, decreasing or irrelevant?' and 'Do the settlements and cemeteries show any sign of increasing social stratification over the period?' The first of these questions is provoked by a debate (if as yet a relatively quiet debate) between those who believe that changes in natural resources cause social change and those who do not. The battle lines are not as clearly drawn as, say, in the Brenner debate which considers changes in social relations at the end of the Middle Ages, but positions are often implicit and certainly underlie much of the environmental and landscape archaeology being conducted at present.[2] For one set of protagonists the resources of the land are finite, and the English settlers during their first three or four centuries reached the limit of agricultural expansion allowable by their technology. Pressure on land then caused stratification of society; submission and tenancy became the only strategy available to the once free pioneer. The alternative view is that the carrying capacity of the land was never, indeed has never been, reached and that even if it had been, the result would not inevitably be social stratification caused by deprivation and stress.

In trying to test for one or other of these positions, one could hope for independent testimony from the study of vegetation, and here it appears that the potential resources remained remarkably static. Rackham insists that the major episodes of forest clearance were over before the Anglo-Saxons arrived, and so they cannot be seen as gradually increasing the quantity of land under cultivation (at the expense of woodland) during the first millennium. While allowing a general clearance to continue, Jones sees it as a continuance of Roman resource management, completed in the north and west by the sixth century and by implication long before that in the south and east. Landscape changes did of course happen all over the country, but not all in one direction. Work by environmentalists at Hockham Mere in East Anglia, supported by thirteen radiocarbon dates, has shown a change from pastoral to arable farming in c. 300, from arable to pasture in c. 600 and back to arable a century later. Jones sees the first-millennium landscape as a patchwork of different kinds of agricultural exploitation – arable, pasture and coppice woodland – operating in different places at different times.[3]

It is also difficult to be certain whether climatic changes had any palpable effect on resources, or acted as a cause of social or economic change on a major scale; and this difficulty is not only caused by imprecisions of dating. It seems to be agreed that the climate deteriorated from the relative warmth enjoyed by Roman Britain to a cold wet sixth century, in which glaciers in Norway and the Alpine regions reached points as low as they did during the later 'little ice age' of the seventeenth century. However, there is less certainty that a cold wet climate makes people miserable (whatever one's own feelings on the subject), let alone that climatic decline causes economic decline. Murphy suggests that higher precipitation in the late sixth and early seventh centuries may have *increased* the yield on good soils, and allowed expansion on to those (amongst which one could cite the Sandlings of Suffolk) which were normally too well drained.[4] Whatever changes we observe in the general socio-economic structure of the region (as opposed to small areas within it), it will be difficult to blame them wholly on a changing environment.

DETECTING RANK AND IDEOLOGY

The second part of the archaeological inquiry is directed to the matter of social stratification, which we believe can be observed in settlements and cemeteries. Modern East Anglia has one of the most professional and effective archaeological communities in the country, active over many decades; but even so here, as elsewhere, the corpus of evidence is currently meagre in content and eccentric in distribution. Many fieldworkers, among them the best, will say that any reasonable interpretation at the level I am attempting is many decades away, even supposing the maintenance of a national will to carry out the strategic research necessary. However, the approach followed here is not so much analytical or empirical, which would certainly require a larger data base; it makes use instead of old fashioned and hopefully legitimate analogy, where such attributes as we can observe in the material culture are compared with those of better documented (or better analysed) examples. The strengths and weaknesses of this approach will be self-evident.

It is believed, for example, that settlements which show a development from a group of unbounded buildings of roughly equal size to a heterogeneous group where one is larger than the others (and has a fence around it) are showing social as well as (or instead of) functional changes – in other words, that changes in the use of space reflect changes in the relations of society. Similarly in cemeteries the concentration of grave-goods in fewer graves (if genuinely observable) can be read as the concentration of wealth into fewer hands amongst the living; or at the least that the distribution and variety of burial practice in a cemetery reflect the complexity of the society which built it. The debate about the interpretation of these ranking phenomena has been in train for a number of years, but the aspect of it most important in the present context is the matter of its interpretation as social history. Ranking may be visible in settlement and cemetery alike, but may represent an ideological statement rather than a social fact: the community wishes to project an image of itself rather different from the reality, and is using material culture to do it. The egalitarian character of the (in fact hierarchical) Christian dead is one example that has been cited in support of this idea. It will not be enough to observe ranking; it will be necessary to give it a particular context before deciding what it might mean. The archaeological interpreter has therefore been encouraged to pursue a kind of source criticism long familiar to historians, where the particular bias, fraud or propaganda being employed is no less interesting than the factual implications themselves.[5]

EVIDENCE FOR SETTLEMENT – EARLY EAST ANGLIA

Settlement locations and the settlement pattern have been and are being mapped by an increasingly intensive use of field survey, including surface collection of pottery and metal detection. The region is fortunate in having a pottery sequence which is virtually continuous over the first millennium. The fifth- to seventh-century gap, aceramic in most kingdoms, is here filled by a series of hand-made stamped and incised wares culminating in Ipswich ware, the manufacture of which is thought to begin in the seventh century. The use of metal detectors helps to correct the bias introduced by uneven pottery distribution, to provide supporting evidence for its date, and also to qualify the equation between types of pots and types of people. Given the vast area of the region there is, naturally enough, a debate in progress over what kind of strategy at which scale will most successfully reveal the settlement pattern. The leaders of the Kingdom of East Anglia Project have pursued a programme of intensive field research (incorporating all periods of settlement) within six pre-selected sample areas in Norfolk and Suffolk.[6] The results of this and earlier work are currently being reviewed, and it would be premature to attempt a detailed geography. In general there appears to be little indication of continuity from Roman settlements, and in south-east Suffolk at least (the Sandlings) there is a marked intensification of settlement founding in the late fifth and sixth centuries. The seventh century is a period of some redeployment (sometimes termed the seventh-century shuffle), when established occupation advanced on to the clay uplands of Suffolk for the first time since the Roman period. A further period of expansion is seen in the ninth century. The pattern seems to refer mainly to small dispersed hamlets or farmsteads rather than nucleated villages.[7]

Few of the inhabited areas that have been located have been examined and published in any detail, and in those that have it is not easy to detect trends of the type we seek. West Stow in Suffolk was occupied over the whole period considered here (c. 400–650). Seven halls (or houses) and seventy sunken-floored buildings were excavated, but analysis has demonstrated that this was not the contemporary complement of any village. By associating the huts and houses West shows that no more than four houses (each with an attendant group of between four and seventeen huts) were likely to have been standing at any one time, four farming units constituting a small hamlet, perhaps the workplace and residence of an extended family unit. In the later phase of the life of this settlement there is a boundary between properties, a faint echo, or pre-echo, of the more determined signalling of private property detectable elsewhere. At North Elmham in Norfolk large-scale excavations have revealed three phases of middle Saxon settlement, beginning perhaps in the late seventh century. The principal components (with slight variations in each phase) were two hall-houses, a bakehouse, a well, a street and, by phase 2 at least, a number of boundary ditches. Arguing for planned properties by the eighth century, the excavator proposes a grid of large square tenements perhaps laid out in association with the establishment of the see of North Elmham and the construction of the first cathedral there.

Wicken Bonhunt, though in Essex rather than East Anglia, remains one of the few early-middle Saxon settlements we have seen in the east of England. In

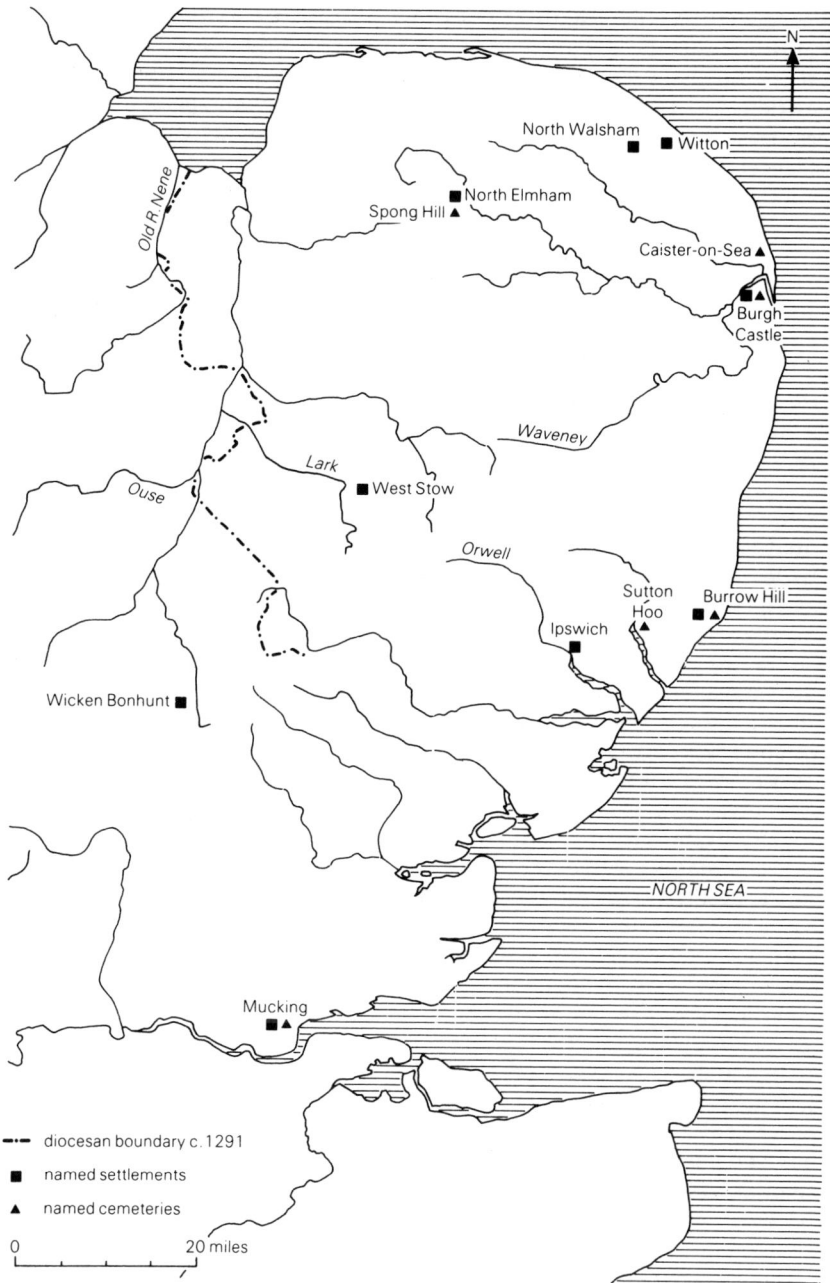

N

North Walsham
Witton
North Elmham
Spong Hill
Caister-on-Sea
Burgh Castle
Old R. Nene
Waveney
Lark
West Stow
Ouse
Orwell
Sutton Hoo
Burrow Hill
Ipswich
Wicken Bonhunt
NORTH SEA
Mucking

—·— diocesan boundary c. 1291

■ named settlements

▲ named cemeteries

0   20 miles

Figure 10.1. East Anglia and its environs, showing places mentioned in the text. (The boundary of the diocese of Norwich, which probably closely mirrors that of the Anglo-Saxon dioceses of the kingdom of East Anglia, is shown at its late thirteenth-century extent.)

this new settlement of sixth- to seventh-century date on a former Roman and prehistoric site, the alignment of the twenty-eight buildings and the boundary ditches suggest a regulated layout from the earliest phase. Less certainly a partitioned hall-house (belonging to a second middle Saxon phase), implies at least some internal ranking. More significantly, perhaps, there was a very large and specialized assemblage of animal bones associated with the first phase, and a nine-post granary with the second, both possible signs of surplus being collected and stored.[8]

Wealthy sites of seventh-century and later date perhaps represent something of the new mood. Rich seventh-century finds including coins have been obtained from sites near Barham and Coddenham in Suffolk. Brandon in Suffolk, which comprises two dozen rectangular post-hole and beam-slot buildings including a church and cemetery, is notable for its engraved book plaque depicting an evangelist's symbol and its three styli.[9] Burrow Hill, also in Suffolk, has produced foodstuffs, rather individual home-made pottery together with Ipswich ware and French imports, and coins of Beonna (fl. 758) and later date. Brandon and Burrow Hill, both 'island' sites, have been interpreted as monasteries rather than seigneurial establishments. But the criteria used for these identifications are not decisive, and excavations at Burgh Castle, associated with the documented early monastic site of *Cnobheresburg*, have done little to show what an early East Anglian monastic plan ought to look like. However, there seems no reason to doubt that this small Roman fort was the one given to Fursa, and the curious oval grooves – whether huts or pens – may have formed part of his establishment.[10]

If the introduction of boundaries and alignments has been recognized as a tentative sign of regulation and privacy in seventh-century property, far more has been made of the social changes implied by the development of the very large settlement at Ipswich. Although Ipswich shows no clear regulation of property in the seventh century (when the occupation apparently begins), it shares the status of a trading centre with *Hamwih*, near modern Southampton, which does. *Hamwih*'s streets and property boundaries led to the assumption that a hierarchy was needed to make it work, and this analogy has been transferred to Ipswich. Ipswich was receiving pottery and lava querns at the hands of Frankish traders from the Rhineland, who presumably took away something (for example wool) from East Anglia in exchange. Hodges sees the early trading links with the Franks not only as direct (rather than, say, via Kent or London) but also as dependent on the individual initiative of East Anglian leaders. Ipswich supplied pottery to Wicken Bonhunt, Burrow Hill and most other middle Saxon settlements in the East Anglian region – indeed this is how they have mainly been recognized. But it appears that these settlements were not otherwise dependent on Ipswich for their trade relations; Wicken Bonhunt and Burrow Hill both received a range of French pottery additional to the French and Rhenish types which dominate the Ipswich imports.[11]

If some progress has been made towards knowing the plans of settlements and their distribution, a still more valuable new departure has been the exploration of how far the land itself was exploited. The intensity of field walking carried out in the parish of Witton (Norfolk) has allowed the pottery deposited within settlements to be distinguished from that deposited during manuring, which has offered in turn a measure of the land under cultivation at a particular time. On this basis the fifth- to sixth-century settlement at Witton had a mere 40ha under the plough, which Wade sees as symptomatic of a period in which 'a small population had the use of a very large territory'.[12] In the seventh century there was a slight shift in the position of the settlement, which had grown in size. By then the area under cultivation had doubled to 80ha, and it nearly doubled again (150ha) in the ninth century.

Whether originating from a putative mother centre at Walsham or independently founded, this *tun* community is seen to be in being and farming on a small scale, with no reference to the Romano-British settlement landscape, within the fifth century. Of itself, however, the archaeological record cannot be said to indicate who was living in such settlements, whose hand was on the plough, or where he came from.

CEMETERIES

Less reticence in identifying peoples has been exercised in the interpretation of the cemetery evidence, which Myres, for example, has tried to reconcile with ethnic zones.[13] As with the settlement sites there are in East Anglia numerous fifth- to seventh-century cemeteries whose location is known; but there is only a handful of examples for which the internal structure and population are reasonably clear, and from these alone will it be reasonable to infer rank and ideology. Of the East Anglian cemeteries that have been located twenty-four mainly comprise cremations and thirty-four mainly inhumations, seventeen are mixed, and a further thirty-seven contacts have been made with undefined burial grounds.[14] About half a dozen of these have earth mounds, while a much larger number probably once had them on the analogy of Spong Hill. The distribution of the cemeteries is riverine, like the settlements, but there is no certainty that cemetery and settlement are generally adjacent (as at West Stow and perhaps Spong Hill) or generally separated.[15]

Two scholars have recently used the evidence of grave-goods to offer revolutionary hypotheses about when the English territories were settled, and from where. According to Böhme troops stationed in Britain in the later fourth century included Franks, Alamans and East Germans, transferred from garrisons on the Danube frontier and in Gaul. Within these imperial forces was a contingent of Saxons and, later, one of Anglians from southern Denmark. The military rhythm of redeploying personnel and garrisons appears to have been unruffled by Constantine III's bid for power in 407, the diagnostic military equipment being found all over central, eastern and southern Britain, including East Anglia, until the mid-fifth century. However, a new development of the early fifth century is the additional presence of equal-arm brooches, supporting-arm brooches and early cruciform brooches, with a source area mainly in the Lower Elbe (or the traditional Saxon region of north Germany) and in Schleswig-Holstein, which is perhaps to be considered Anglian. This cultural material, which Böhme sees as representing the settlement of non-military free Germans with their families (bringing with them their traditional burial rite of cremation) is confined to the region of East Anglia. The new settlement zone is ringed by Kent, Wessex and the Midlands, where objects of quoit-brooch style and late Roman military equipment continue to indicate an essentially British society. In the mid-fifth century the military organization with its transferable mercenaries finally broke down. In the second half of the fifth century new cemeteries indicate arrivals of fresh contingents from Saxony and south Denmark, this time to settle in the upper Thames and upper Avon area of the Midlands – in areas until then Romano-British and outside the original settlement area of East Anglia.[16]

Böhme's work will be assessed in future years in more expert hands than the present writer's, but even on first acquaintance it clearly has important implications for the present discussion. In this interpretation East Anglia is the part of Britain which is first settled by Anglo-Saxon peoples – up to fifty years before Wessex or Kent and perhaps up to 100 years before Northumbria or the West Midlands. East Anglian settlers can therefore have worked loose from the Roman administration while it was still effective in surrounding territories. And in this case one would not expect continuity of estate management to be of the same type or degree in East Anglia as, say, in Gloucestershire.[17] For some fifty years around the mid-fifth century whatever social formations developed in East Anglia in the absence of the late Roman ethos would be watched and influenced by the surrounding communities, where that ethos was still alive. If equations can really be made between brooch types and place of origin, East Anglia can have recognized itself as a seperate territory, if not a kingdom, as early as the early fifth century. Within the territories surrounding East Anglia, fifth-century kingdoms can also have formed, in this case thoroughly British in nature and origin. However, if there was such a kingdom in fifth-century East Anglia, it had no recorded name. The north folk and the south folk (whether themselves actually Anglian or Saxon in origin) could hardly have called themselves East Angles until there were Angles to the west of them, up to a century after the initial settlement.

In the next two centuries (the sixth and seventh), the crucial arguments for the identity and movement of peoples are those of John Hines, who has introduced the idea of a continuing contact, in the form of exchange, migration or ideology, with the lands of Scandinavia, especially south-west Norway. As before the links are expressed in the form of grave-goods – particularly *tracht*, the dress worn for burial. Metal sleeve- or cuff-clasps to fasten shirt or trousers have a distribution concentrated in Norfolk and south-west Norway, with groups in the Swedish Uppland, Denmark and elsewhere in Anglian England, particularly Humberside. Square-headed brooches (which characterize the Anglian areas in the sixth century) are seen as Scandinavian in origin and C-bracteates (gold or gilt disc pendants with somewhat enigmatic iconography) as a south Scandinavian invention: 'The bracteate wearing habit, whatever beliefs it may imply, could then have been principally established in Anglian England, initially in East Anglia, by the personal relationships between Anglian England and the southern Denmark/Schleswig-Holstein area implicit in Bede's Anglian invasion of the fifth century.'[18]

It has to be said that the grave-goods being used to imply migration from Norway to East Anglia in the sixth century are no less valid in context or quantity than those used to describe migration from north Germany to East Anglia in the fifth – although the latter case has the advantage that it was also attested in written sources. Of the alternative mechanisms for interaction trade has been more favoured by some (although it would be a less satisfactory explanation for the clothes implied by the sleeve clasps); and ideological exchange, where parallel burial customs are adopted on either side of the North Sea, has perhaps received less emphasis than it should. Hines does consider the effect of long-range ideological influence for the final phase of pagan burial in East Anglia, epitomized by the barrow cemetery at Sutton Hoo with its ship burial and other rituals. He agrees that Swedish influence permeates the Sutton Hoo assemblage (as demonstrated by Bruce-Mitford) but sees ship burial itself as having a more likely origin in Norway. The link with Swedish Uppland *appears* strong because that is where the principal and most affluent Scandinavian power centre had emerged at the time of East Anglia's own period of demonstrative wealth. He also argues that such episodes of demonstrative burial are a 'migration characteristic' confined to insecure parvenus.[19] However, a specific seventh-century migration at any social level from Uppland or Norway he considers as unlikely.

Some have taken issue with components of Hine's model, doubting for example the feasibility of crossing the North Sea in open rowing boats,[20] but the overall thesis is as persuasive as it is valuable. Following the fifth-century period of settlement, direct contact with lands in Denmark, south-west Norway and Swedish Uppland was continuous and at times intense. It may have involved migration; it may have involved trade; it should certainly have involved ideological interaction. The poverty of the archaeological evidence as a whole allows the speculation that such contact continued beyond the seventh century into the eighth and ninth. Speculating further (since the North Sea grew no wider in the interim), it is possible that the Viking army which chose East Anglia as its bridgehead in 865 and stayed there for a year, 'securing the horses necessary for their further movements', would not have been either alien or unwelcome among all the local inhabitants.[21]

As with settlement studies the main archaeological arguments for deducing rank, ideology and social change from cemeteries have to be drawn not from a corpus of grave-goods but from large-scale excavations; and, as before, we have only a handful of examples, although among them are the best Anglo-Saxon England has to offer. It is inevitable that cemetery studies, not only in East Anglia but in England as a whole, are dominated by the excavations of Catherine Hills and the Norfolk Archaeological Unit at Spong Hill. These have brought to light 2,000 cremations and fifty-eight inhumations, of which four are surrounded by ring ditches implying barrows. The burials are being published in expeditious and exemplary fashion by their excavator as a data base for all to use.[22] There is no certain chronology at Spong Hill for cremation or inhumation, which may begin and continue together throughout the life of the cemetery; but Böhme, bolder than many, puts chamber-grave 40 (with its implied barrow) and a group of cremations into the early fifth century.[23] The implication of this is that the richer and most complex type of burials co-exist with the simpler from the first era of Anglo-Saxon settlement. The simpler burials too, in this case cremations, also manifest uneven access to resources. In his study of the Anglo-Saxon cremation rite from Spong Hill and elsewhere Julian Richards has demonstrated correlations between urn and content which imply that the social identity of the buried person was being advertised through the funerary apparatus. The distribution of attributes throughout his sample population (over 2,000 burials) suggests a variety of status within a broad cultural conformity – 'a society in an intermediate stage, midway between an anarchistic tribe and a hierarchical structured kingdom'.[24] It appears that the Spong Hill cemetery was ranked, and that the community that built it was socially stratified from the earliest phase of the settlement and remained so.

The cemetery at Snape in Suffolk, which has recently been the subject of exploratory excavation, also has cremations, inhumations with grave-goods, small barrows (probably with chamber-graves) and large barrows (up to 12m across), at least one of which, excavated in 1863, contained a boat. The Snape repertoire appears, therefore, both to parallel Spong Hill, which reaches back to the earliest period of settlement, and to presage Sutton Hoo (16km away), which reaches into the final phase of non-Christian burial.[25].

The perceived character of the Sutton Hoo cemetery has changed markedly since the research campaign of the Sutton Hoo Research Trust began there in 1983.[26] Four of its eighteen known burial mounds have been examined; two (nos. 3 and 4) originally contained cremations, one in a bronze bowl, the other on an oak tray. The other two were more elaborate. Mound 1 covered a 90ft (27m) long oak clinker-built rowing boat with a central wealthy grave group which is artistically and symbolically outstanding. Mound 2, the excavation of which was completed in 1986, had contained a chamber-grave with accoutrements, apparently sealed or roofed by a clinker-built vessel 6–20m long. The discovery (nearby in 1987 beneath a small barrow) of an infant burial in an oak coffin with a spear and buckle suggests that status could by then be inherited. Some 0.3ha of an eventual 1ha sample has now been excavated at Sutton Hoo both around the barrows and beside them; and yet no certain Anglo-Saxon cremations and no inhumations with conventional grave-goods have been found. On the other hand twenty-five unaccompanied bodies have been found in twenty-two graves showing a great variety of postures. At least ten are thought to have been examples of ritual killing. There is a coin date of *c.* 625 (for the ship burial) and three radiocarbon dates from flat graves of 620±90, 746±79 and 750±70.[27] The cemetery was also found to be lying over a prehistoric settlement (mainly Neolithic and Beaker) which should have been evident as earthworks when the first Anglo-Saxon barrows were constructed. The Sutton Hoo site appears therefore to be late (seventh-century and later) and specialized, confined apparently to prestigious burials accompanied by sacrifice of humans and animals. Superseding some earlier cemetery, perhaps that at Snape, Sutton Hoo would appear at present to be an example of *Separierung*, a burial ground for the élite.

Sutton Hoo and Spong Hill reinforce the point made by Jankavs, that arguments for ranking cannot be reliably based on groups of partially excavated cemeteries,[28] since the aristocracy are by definition a small proportion of the whole and may be buried on the periphery, as at Spong Hill, or by themselves, as at Sutton Hoo. Spong Hill in particular shines a sombre warning light over any attempts to read social change from grave-goods between the fifth and seventh centuries. Some attempts have nevertheless been made, and carry a fairly consistent message to the effect that throughout the sixth century, and particularly towards its end, wealth, whether scored as deposited grave-goods or as the effort of a constructed tomb (i.e. barrow), appears to manifest an increasingly inequitable distribution.[29] If there is a consensus in favour of this having happened, there is less agreement on what it might mean. Battle lines can be discerned between those who believe that cemeteries were becoming more ranked because society was becoming more unequal, and those who believe that burial is simply a signalling apparatus reflecting ideological commitment, self-opinion or competition but not, or at least not necessarily, changes in social formation – which may remain static or evolve in the reverse of the direction being signalled.[30]

Some support for the ailing case for real social change can be found by analogy with the contemporary and better documented Norway, with which East Anglia, as we have seen, may have shared an ideological outlook. Bjorn Myhre has been able to argue for increasing social stratification, this time in the fourth and fifth centuries, not from burial evidence alone but from hillforts, settlement morphology and the provision of boat-houses. Not the least relevant aspect of Myhre's work is that the material culture suggests not only social stratification but the formation of territories. The process begins quite suddenly in *c.* 300, and by the sixth century ten territories can be discerned. Each is defined by a wealthy burial cluster and a hillfort group; each has access to the mountains (with their fur and iron), the uplands, the fertile coast and the sea. Each of these territories also approximates to the administrative boundaries that survived in historical Norway. Examination of the patterning within these 'chiefdom' territories reveals earlier 'sub-chiefdoms' and, later on, upland centres for middlemen who may have gained political independence through control of the mountain resources. Myhre sees economic success (through exchange with the Roman Empire) as a cause rather than a result of the formation of such territories.[31]

In Norway the variety of consistent evidence makes it harder to argue that no social change had actually occurred. Progressively unequal social relations are also argued by Michael Parker-Pearson for Denmark, where the evidence is rather different from that for either south-west Norway or East Anglia.[32] The Danes went through a phase of wealthy barrow building in the first and second centuries, but by the fifth and sixth centuries (following a period of unrest) wealth was sacrificed in votive bog deposits. These are less certainly attributable to an individual, but settlement studies suggest a contemporary expression of marked ranking within communities in the form of the inequitable use of space in buildings and settlement plans. Parker-Pearson sees the sacrificial deposits as a sign of accumulated capital, whose role is symbolic rather than economic: 'Its consumption can be understood as a kind of reinvestment if it is directed to win support of supernatural forces, such as deities and ancestors.'[33] Social hierarchies and ideological hierarchies are also created through the potlatch process. Support won from the living by gifts and feasting creates debtors. But by additionally assuming responsibility for debts to the gods the prosperous acquire more than worldly capital. A social class may achieve both economic and ideological domination essentially through the same mechanism, which Parker-Pearson describes as 'the privatization of the gods'.

These analogies, although valuable, do not really help us decide whether in East Anglia it was social stratification that took place in the sixth century or merely a change in the degree to which existing hierarchies were signalled in material culture. Theoretical arguments applied by Stephen Shennan to the Beaker period are important for us here.[34] Beaker burial in round barrows had a wide impact, and is seen as evidence of the ideological dominance of (the idea of) individual wealth and status; but a distinction is drawn between western Europe, where social stratification had already occurred, and central Europe, where it apparently had not. The same set of phenomena can be interpreted in one context as a change in the mode of operation of the power base (western Europe), but in another as the actual onset of a stratified society. It is possible that Christianity, for example, may have operated in a similar way to Beaker ideology, in some cases being adopted because of unequal social relations, in others provoking those relations. Shennan's thesis relies on having an independent monitor for the settlements: in Spain the site of Los Millares is used to suggest the existence of pre-Beaker social differentiation, while in north Germany such differentiation is deemed to be absent on the evidence of a dispersed settlement pattern. As we have seen, such evidence as we have for East Anglia aligns it more with the central European analogy. The stratification of society appears to be close in time to the arrival of Christianity – probably too close indeed to distinguish cause from effect.

ARCHAEOLOGICAL SYNTHESIS

The balance of these arguments can be used to offer a hypothesis as follows. East Anglia was settled in the early fifth century by immigrants from north Germany, particularly from the Saxon and possibly some Anglian areas. It was the first part of England to be settled by Anglo-Saxon immigrants. Later immigrants included (more certainly) contingents from Anglian areas of south Denmark, many of whom passed through East Anglia to the Midlands and Northumbria. Both East Anglia and the Humberside area experienced further immigration in the sixth century, now from south-west Norway, and at this time ideological contact was strong between East Anglia, Norway, Denmark and the Uppland area of Sweden.

These contacts are reflected in the grave-goods, the *tracht*, which signal some sense of regional identity in the fifth century and more clearly in the sixth. Within this region farmers of small estates enjoy widespread economic independence in a dispersed settlement pattern. The social units may be small – the size of a parish – but a social hierarchy may already be present within them (Spong Hill). However, towards the end of the sixth century there is an increase in cemetery ranking, culminating in at least one separate élite burial ground at Sutton Hoo. The symbolism employed at the latter site is elaborate and eclectic, the use of ship burial, human sacrifice and purpose-built regalia within a former prehistoric earthwork, all indicating a major exercise in legitimation inspired by a Scandinavian or at least non-Roman ideology and directed at and from a local territory.[35] Whether this territory was very local (i.e. a Sandlings province) or a recently named East Anglia, or both, remains uncertain. Some evidence for the new political mood can be drawn from the fencing of properties, seigneurial settlements and the newly established trading centre at Ipswich. The fact that Ipswich, like Sutton Hoo, is sited at the south-east corner of a supposed East Anglian territory may mean that the most important attribute of the centres of power was not centrality but access to the influential cultural arena of the North Sea.[36]

If social formations did indeed change, as can be argued from the archaeological record, the change is not so much from a more egalitarian to a less egalitarian community, but a change of structure within a high-ranking peer group from local to regionalized independence. What reasons can be suggested for this? Some have argued for stress induced by scarcity of resources, proposing in effect that by the end of the sixth century available land or good land has been taken up through uncontrolled reclamation, a decrease in the viability of the total holding due to climatic deterioration, gift, or division by partible inheritance. As we have seen, the evidence in favour of an environmental trigger for stress is not strong, besides which an exactly opposite cause (i.e. economic prosperity) is diagnosed for the onset of social differentiation in south-west Norway. In archaeology, as in history, the debate is thrown back into the cauldron of human relationships themselves – the contradictions and conflicts generated within society.

One line of argument, similar to that advanced by Parker-Pearson, involves the redistribution of wealth through debt creation, and will be pursued in the final part of this chapter. Another, inspired by the work of other prehistorians, notably Colin Renfrew, proposes the mutual influence of neighbouring communities as a fundamental motor for socio-economic change. In this process territories, which are not yet states but have an element of central control (early state modules), develop mutually in dynamic equilibrium by exchange of goods, by warfare against each other or by imitating each other's status and status symbols ('competitive emulation' and 'symbolic entrainment') and by borrowing other cultural and ideological innovations from each other.[37] Peer polity interaction, as this process is named, is a useful descriptive (rather than explanatory) device which could be applied to Anglo-Saxon England, provided the heterogeneous character of its peoples in the fifth to seventh centuries is recognized. The kingdoms may certainly have developed in imitation of each other, although the peer polities in this case would be those of west, south and north Britain, south-west Norway, Sweden and Denmark, as well as those of the Heptarchy and France.[38] An important additional implication is that the motivation for equipping a community with the material trappings of kingship, or indeed with badges denoting nationhood or ethnicity, may be no reflection of a new political formation but another case of signalling as an offensive or defensive strategy. Renfrew gives the nice example of how Tonga avoided being a British colony, becoming instead an independent state within the Empire, through the simple expedient of providing itself with a prime minister, a state seal, a coat of arms and a flag.[39] On the face of it the projected Anglian origins of East Anglia in the sixth century and the Sutton Hoo regalia are potential candidates for such pantomime diplomacy.[40] Peer polity interaction has the disadvantage that it is difficult to observe archaeologically, since the same material record is required to show that polities are distinct and that they interact.[41] The Norwegian evidence might be held to support the description better than that from early Anglo-Saxon England, where territorial boundaries are so difficult to observe archaeologically. Whether this is because there were no early polities in England, or because there was always too much interaction between them, remains unknown.

Common sense would suggest that an early East Anglian would acknowledge power at three levels: he would owe emotional allegiance to his family (perceived as local), economic allegiance to his landowner, where this was different, and ideological allegiance to his tribe or *folc*. It could be argued that a kingdom could hardly exist without capturing the ideological allegiance of its occupants, implying that orthodoxy, whether heathen or Christian, was a necessary attribute of kingship. It could also be argued that a kingdom could hardly exist without economic inequity; and since the ultimate source of wealth was land, control of the land and its yield was a necessary prerequisite to the formation of a kingdom. The regulated extraction of surplus in the form of obligation, rent, fee or tax must predate the formation of the English kingdoms. On this crucial matter the evidence of documents will probably be more potent.

DOCUMENTARY EVIDENCE

The historical debate occupies similar ground to the less well-known theoretical discussions amongst archaeologists, and similar positions can be discerned. For some the Anglo-Saxon peasant was initially free and suffered a gradual loss of liberty; for others he was initially unfree – and either stayed that way or became freer. Neither side denies the existence of kings; but for some, kings were a common attribute of the immigrant peoples, and for others an invention of the sixth century in which past reality is disguised by ideological canvassing.

Thus Stenton decided that 'the central course of Old English social development may be described as the process by which a free peasantry, at first composed essentially of free men, acknowledging no lord below the king, gradually lost personal and economic independence'.[42] This view, the product of generations of scholarship, was qualified by T.H. Aston who put forward evidence for the existence of Anglo-Saxon landlords, demesne and rented land – in short the essential ingredients of the manor – from at least the seventh century.[43] In the late seventh-century laws of Ine of Wessex the land which is called *gesett land* is that which is rented out. The term used in later East Anglia is *landsetti*, and may reflect as early a usage as in Wessex. Aston feels that the laws imply that settlers of *gesett* land are taxpayers (*gafolgeldan*) to the king, and the quantity of land sublet is therefore subject to royal regulation.[44]

In a postscript published in 1983 Aston postulates the existence of lordships in the period immediately after the first Anglo-Saxon settlement. Subsequently new estates could be established as offshoots, or acquired whole (for example by conquest in the west). If new estates were not an option, and population increased, partible inheritance would tend to decrease the size of holdings; but 'lords . . . normally pursued a positive policy of not allowing fragmentation to proceed beyond a certain point'. This may have been for social reasons. Since a tenure of five hides over three generations was required in order to acquire thegnly status, a family would have an incentive to pass the estate to the eldest son and leave other members of the family to become his tenants.[45] An additional incentive could be that viable mixed farming would normally require arable, pasture, meadow, water and arguably woodland, and a holding would quickly become economically unbalanced if one or more of these components were lost by division or alienation to another owner.

Thus, runs the argument, although groups of rent-free holdings existed and long remained an option on marginal land, the manor with its tied tenants was a feature from the earliest Anglo-Saxon period. Aston sees no clear beginning to the social structure composed of king, lord, tenant and slave, but assumes that it must have been in existence before the seventh century.[46]

There are some grounds therefore for believing that unequal social relations existed before the seventh century and perhaps as early as the fifth-century settlement itself. But it might be doubted that kingship on any scale was a natural concomitant of the Germanic immigration.[47] For East Anglia no royal person is named before Weahha, who belongs most probably to the sixth century.[48] Even then it remains uncertain whether Weahha, Rædwald and other later East Anglian kings were monarchs who did actually legislate and tax, and, if so, in what context. In history, as in archaeology, many of the trappings of early monarchy have been questioned recently as reflections of reality. Laws, genealogies and titles such as 'Bretwalda' may have been conceits, contrivance designed to win status rather than recognize it.[49] It is here that it is difficult to reconcile archaeological and documentary evidence in the seventh century, since the one speaks so little of individuals and almost ceases at the point where the other, which talks of little else, begins. But it can hardly be insignificant that both can be used to assert the same thing. Christianity may have changed the rules of evidence for us and the rules of ideological display for the Anglo-Saxons, but there seems no reason to doubt at least that there were territorial leaders operating in the late sixth century, who were named as kings by the early seventh century and had by then access to regular revenue.

Those who believe that the documented (like the archaeological) attributes of kingship have a strong element of wishful thinking and self-promotion will prefer to see such kings as fairly recent appointments, anxious to stabilize the larger territories over which they had gained economic control. One way to pursue this goal was to convert to Christianity, although, as Angenendt has shown, it was by no means a straightforward political decision.[50] The benefits of centuries of affiliation with the pagan homelands would not be thrown away lightly, perhaps particularly in East Anglia where affiliation is thought to have continued more deliberately than elsewhere. The mechanism of leaving a high ranking member of the royal family unbaptized to represent the pagan faction may have worked on occasion, but equally may have contributed to division. It seems probable that Penda's visits to East Anglia, which were hardly social calls, should be seen in the light of interfactional struggles within East Anglia. However, the great advantage of conversion for the royal family was the stabilization of the new territory, particularly so if it then became coincident with a diocese. The person of the king and his territorial boundaries were sanctified, legitimized and protected, at least in the eyes of neighbouring Christian monarchs, and direct political support was symbolized by the royal godfather who raised the new recruit from the font.[51] After some hesitation East Anglian royalty eventually made up its mind. Soon one of its members was acting in turn as godfather to a neighbouring king, and the heathen temple used by Rædwald was finally abandoned half a century later.[52]

CONCLUSIONS

In so far as these diverse viewpoints can be reconciled, a picture can be constructed of how the East Anglian kingdom began to be formed. The region is the earliest settled by Germanic immigrants – in the early fifth century. There are few clues for discontinuity, but fewer for continuity, institutional or otherwise, with late Roman territorial arrangements. If late Roman Germanic mercenaries had already been rewarded with estate ownership, it hardly shows and the settlement pattern must have been redrawn. Germanic landlords defined or redefined estates which they farmed by employing or enslaving Britons, or encouraging their displacement by Germanic kinsmen from the homelands or from other territories with whom they shared an ideology. Later Germanic arrivals therefore had an opportunity to settle as tenants rather than as landowners. In default of better evidence the expectation is of a dispersed pattern of new small settlements occupied by independent landlords controlling estates of indeterminate size which were continually subject to expansion, partition (through inheritance) and aggregation.[53] If Witton, for instance, is such an estate, it may be a colonizing venture or a division of a notional pre-existing estate (i.e. of Walsham). The fact that such an estate was initially not fully exploited does not mean that it was not fully owned. If Spong Hill represents the cemetery for a territorial unit, which is by no means certain, it implies a population for it of 400 persons. And if expectations of any early social hierarchy are to be satisfied by cemetery evidence, then Spong Hill's aristocracy may be represented by its inhumations. The members of such an upper class family, a dozen or so of whom would be alive at the same time on this hypothesis, would be masters or mistresses of a considerable establishment.[54]

These early pioneers, doyens of a fifth-century enterprise culture whose -hams and -tons were distributed along the valleys of the Lark, Waveney and Sandlings river systems, had within 200 years, it seems, been largely overtaken by a manorial system of landholding under a king. In one sense at least this implies a corporate decrease of liberty, since there were fewer landowners owning more land apiece. And even accepting Aston's general thesis that a hierarchy from lord to slave already existed in our hypothetical pioneer estates, there must have been further polarization of social relations before the seventh century, by which time an aristocratic peer group had apparently broken free of local management duties and could indulge full-time in status competition.

The mechanism which allowed these changes must have involved a redistribution of surplus as well as an increase of surplus, and it is here that Chris Wickham's recent analysis may prove valuable. His discussion of the relative role of tax and rent in the transition from the ancient mode to that of feudalism is drawn mainly from early medieval Mediterranean sources ('By now we know nothing about Britain'); but the model can certainly be applied to England too. The ancient mode required the tenants of an estate to find both tax and rent from the surplus generated. Even assuming that this surplus was reasonably constant, the proportion owed in rent could be increased by powerful landlords in exchange for protecting their tenants from tax demands. If tax is ended, then even if the total surplus actually declines, both landlord and tenant initially enrich themselves at the expense of the state. Thereafter the tenant is feeding the landlord's rather than the state's finances. But if tenants then cannot find cash, they must offer rent in kind; defaulting on rent in kind, they must offer themselves in service. By the fourth century those of the upper classes who have preferred the acquisition of land to the uncertain benefits of official appointments now survive on estates where the feudal system already operates in everything but name. New Germanic landlords may take over, by conquest, extortion or otherwise, such estates as going concerns; if setting up new estates, they have the example of Roman provincial neighbours to follow.[55]

Accepting this thesis for England, the Anglo-Saxon successor estate cannot of course have looked quite like the late Roman 'feudal villa' on the one hand or the medieval manor on the other. If there were slaves, they are not easily distinguished in the archaeological record; those working the land are more readily identified with the numerous dead in the pagan cemeteries, the majority of whom from the fifth century have grave-goods of some kind, if only a bespoke cinerary urn. Such grave-goods must represent private property, derived from a proportion of the surplus, equated to the value of the individual, perhaps even directly related to his or her *wergeld*, and converted into pottery, metalwork and other items of *tracht*. Analogous to the modern national costume, the *tracht* was a special dress, which may have been worn seldom in life and can be seen as an offering made at death in acknowledgement of ideological allegiance to the supernatural nation to which these settlers believed they belonged.[56] As such, grave-goods may be seen as an analogue, an alternative, to tax. To continue the hypothesis, grave-goods would no longer have been deposited if tax, as a concomitant of kingship, had been reimposed in the seventh century. At this point ideological allegiance would be transferred from the supernatural nation to a new terrestrial one personified by the king.[57]

The process expected in the sixth century, therefore, will be an increase in the number of tenants and a decrease in the number of freeholders. Owners who are failing economically will be tempted to become tenants; and tenants who are failing economically will be tempted to acquire subtenants on their holdings and bring more of it into cultivation. Economic failure can of course be provoked by other things than overpopulation or bad weather, for which we have in any case only marginal clues. Tenants losing economic independence may eventually also lose their ability to accumulate private property in the form of *tracht*, but the family may keep its self-esteem by offering, as well as their labour and their lives in war, their religious and emotional loyalty to their lord. Lords themselves may have achieved their status as masters of relatively small territories containing clusters of tenants supported by geography or, less probably, ethnicity. We would expect to find in the sixth century proto-manorial centres of Wicken Bonhunt type for these territories, with the hall and granary as the essential attributes. The process of aggregation and associa-tion of estates through dues owed to a particular lord would have continued so that blocks of territory could be identified of increasing size. The 'Sandlings province' may have been one such territory, and by the end of the century the economic unit at the disposal of a single family had presumably become as large as the East Anglian region.

The problem is not so much whether this process resulted in the kings who are visible in seventh-century kingdoms, but when it did. If a competing peer group with elected or hereditary kings was a possibility from the earliest settlement, then we must explain why we cannot see this in the archaeological evidence before the seventh century. If a territory and its leader existed then, neither has left a clear reflection in the material culture before this date.

Of course this may have been so; before the late sixth century status in life may have required no halls or palaces, and was lost on death to the common fate just as in later Christianity. This would be to say that material culture, far from being a coded tranformation of a society's ideology, had at that time no social role at all. This is contradicted by the vocal and diverse character of Anglo-Saxon grave-goods. It is less contrived to say that the model which best fits the archaeological and documentary evidence (as argued here) is that kings and kingdoms in England were an innovation of the late sixth century, and that the innovation was signalled by the disappearance of grave-goods and the return of a centralized 'taxation' system. Only when they fell under such economic control, perhaps, would the people of Anglian lands become attractive targets for Christian missions from France and Italy.

The first kings of East Anglia were confronted with an urgent political problem: the stabilization of their newly acquired territory against others of a similar size. One reaction was to indulge in heavy signalling of kingly status and tradition, legitimizing the ethnic consistency of the new region, and their own family claim to it, with genealogies, laws and regalia; but ideological pressure from the Roman Christian missions was a related political issue, from which no one could stay aloof for long. On the one hand, these missions were a threat, imposed by a resurgent 'cultural empire', to the long-term ideological and (possibly) economic affiliations between East Anglia and the Scandinavian countries across the North Sea. On the other, they offered the tempting prospect of surer legitimation. The upper class might also wish to see the ideological power of the king held in check through delegation to a priesthood. East Anglian royalty thus vacillated between these positions, at one time building an exaggerated pagan monument at Sutton Hoo as a sign of ideological defiance and solidarity with the North. Indeed, it may be that East Anglia never fully abandoned its sympathy with the Scandinavian lands.[58]

11 The formation of the Mercian kingdom

NICHOLAS BROOKS

The Mercians stand out as by far the most successful of the various early Anglo-Saxon peoples until the later ninth century when they succumbed to the Viking military threat. Yet precisely because Mercia eventually failed, its history remains obscure. Indeed, despite the kingdom's early political prominence there are virtually no Mercian written sources. Not only is there no Mercian chronicle but there was not even a single Mercian among the informants whom Bede consulted when preparing his Ecclesiastical History.[1] Some fragments of annals, purportedly of seventh- or eighth-century origin, recording the creation of the Mercian kingdom have indeed been rescued by Professor Wendy Davies from oblivion among the later compilations of Henry of Huntingdon, Roger of Wendover and Matthew Paris in which they had been incorporated; but they seem to be East Anglian rather than Mercian in their focus,[2] and the date of their composition remains to be determined.[2] No Mercian ecclesiastic has left us a letter collection, as have the West Saxon Boniface and the Northumbrian Alcuin, though both of these on occasion corresponded with Mercians. We might indeed consider that the 159 Latin diplomas issued in the name of Mercian rulers should qualify as Mercian sources, but almost all of them concern estates in kingdoms that fell under Mercian rule – Kent and the territory of the Hwicce above all – rather than in Mercia itself, and they seem to have been drafted and written by local ecclesiastics rather than by Mercians.[3] Even the coins which bear the names of Mercian kings were minted in south-eastern England or in East Anglia. Their circulation was indeed much wider, but what they can tell us of the Mercian kingdom, though important, is limited.[4] The Anglo-Saxon royal genealogies, which used to be attributed to the court of king Offa, have now been rebaptized the 'Anglian Collection' by Dr Dumville and with some important caveats have been accorded a Northumbrian provenance.[5] Finally there is the mysterious Tribal Hidage. Though historians have disputed its date and interpretation, there has been some consensus that it is a Mercian tribute list.[6] Yet if it is indeed a tribute list rather than a general register of hidage assessments capable of serving a variety of purposes, then it seems unlikely to have been Mercian; for the first people whose hidage assessment is listed are the Mercians themselves – '30,000 hides'. An early medieval king did not impose tribute upon his own kingdom. A Northumbrian origin for the Tribal Hidage deserves consideration since it could explain both the document's overall form and the fact that the Elmetsaete are included while both the Deirans and the Bernicians are omitted.

Be that as it may, our knowledge of the Mercians certainly depends to an astonishing degree upon information preserved by their neighbours, their enemies and those whom they conquered. Such people had little reason to record or to develop any coherent account of the origin of the Mercian kingdom. The historian investigating Mercian origins has therefore to draw conclusions from uncertain, incomplete and hazardous materials.

LOCATING THE MERCIANS

The people known to us as the Mercians (O.E. *Mierce*, Latin *Mercii*), the 'borderers' or 'dwellers on the march', have certainly been so-called since the early eighth century. That is, for example, the only name known to Bede. It is true that the late Dr Hunter Blair argued that the term *Suþanhymbre* ('Southumbrians'), which is used sparingly by annals which derive from a Northumbrian compilation of the early eighth century, was indeed an early name for the Mercians;[7] but there is no reason to suppose that the name ever had any currency outside Northumbria. It seems more likely to have been coined late in response to the name *Norðanhymbre* for the Deiran and Bernician peoples when united in one kingdom. Thus the legends on Mercian coins describe their kings only as *Rex* or *Rex Merciorum*, never as 'kings of the Southumbrians'.[8] Similarly the drafters of Mercian charters did not, it would seem, know of this or any other antique name when they sought to vary the regnal styles of Mercian kings. (We may contrast the way that West Saxons occasionally refer to their rulers as kings 'of the Gewisse').[9] Similarly Bede, 'Eddius' Stephanus and the Anglo-Saxon Chronicle all confidently refer to the 'Mercians' from the very first occasion that they need to mention them.[10] So far as we can tell, therefore, 'the Mercians' is the only and the original name of the people. To understand their origin we therefore need to locate the boundary from which they took their name.

When Bede described Rædwald of East Anglia's defeat of Æthelfrith in 616 by the River Idle, he stated that the battle on the east bank of the river was *in finibus gentis Merciorum* (fig. 11.1).[11] But the location of the north-eastern boundary of the Mercian kingdom there in Bede's day is no indication of the whereabouts of the original *mearc* from which they were named. At first sight the Tribal Hidage provides a better chance of resolving the problem, since in allotting 30,000 hides to the land of the Mercians it goes on to specify the territory as that 'which is called the first (land) of the Mercians' (*þær mon ærest myrcna hæt*). By identifying the neighbouring peoples on all sides that are listed in the Tribal Hidage we can therefore locate the territory that the compiler considered to be 'original Mercia'. On the west we appear to have the Wreocensæte and Westerne; on the north the Pecsæte, the Elmetsæte and the Lindesfaran with Hatfield; on the east a host of small East Midland peoples including the Gyrwe, Spalde, Gifle, Hicce and so forth; and on the south the Hwicce, the Arosæte and the Færpingas (fig. 11.1). Few scholars believe that it is now possible to define the boundaries of these peoples (and therefore of 'original Mercia') exactly, but there is a measure of agreement on their general location.[12] Though some substantial peoples, such as the *Wigesta* (900 hides), the *Nox* and *Oht gaga* (5,000 and 2,000 hides), the *Hendrica* (3,500 hides), and the *Unecungga* (1,200 hides), still defy identification, it would seem that the

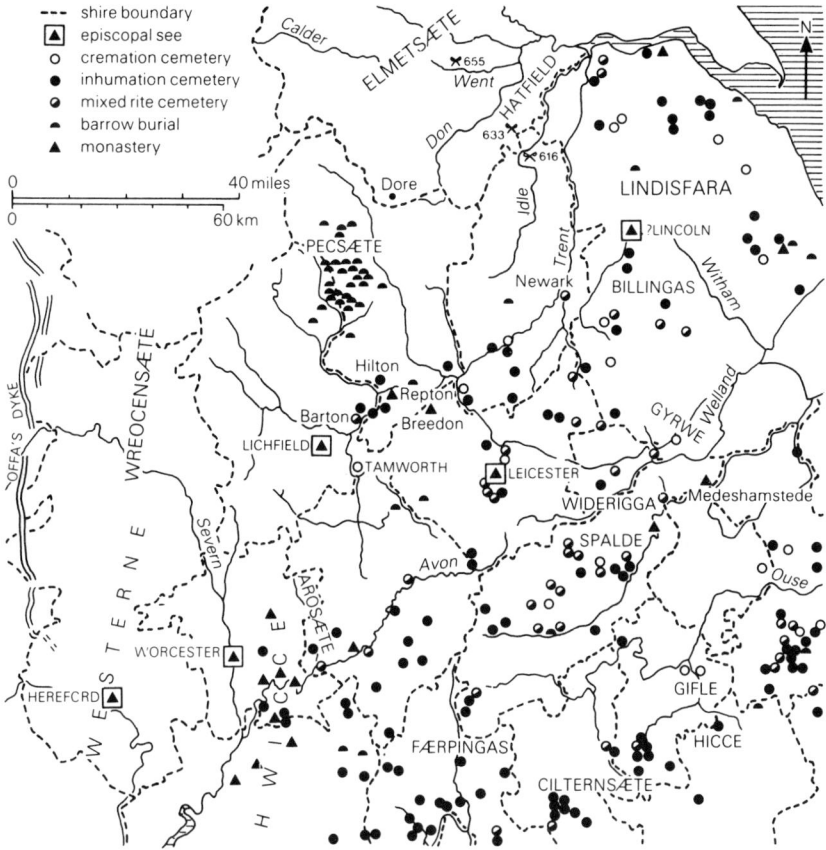

Figure 11.1 Mercia and its neighbours.

'original Mercia' of the Tribal Hidage may have comprised much of the modern counties of Staffordshire, Leicestershire and Nottinghamshire together with south Derbyshire and northern Warwickshire. Whether it extended any further would be disputed. This extensive tract of Midland England, this 'first Mercia', may, however, itself have already been an agglomeration of earlier unrecorded peoples created primarily by military means. It is certainly difficult to envisage when or how the whole of this area was a frontier.

More helpful perhaps is Bede's statement that, at the time of the brief supremacy of Oswiu of Northumbria following his victory at the River *Winwæd* in 655, the 'North Mercians' were divided by the River Trent from the 'South Mercians', and that the two groups were assessed at 7,000 and 5,000 hides respectively.[13] We cannot tell whether the North and South Mercians together occupied a smaller territory than the 'original Mercia' of the Tribal Hidage or were merely less heavily assessed. Nor are we told whether the division of the Mercians was ancient or was a temporary arrangement imposed by Oswiu; but the fact of the division does suggest that the Trent flowed through the heart of the Mercian kingdom. Moreover it is in the vicinity of the

Middle Trent that the principal historical foci of the Mercian kingdom are to be found (fig. 11.1). Thus the Mercian bishopric was established at Lichfield under Chad c. 669 (and it remained there until the Norman Conquest even though Lichfield was itself neither a former Roman town nor an Anglo-Saxon one). Also in the Middle Trent was the Mercian royal monastery of Repton, apparently already established by the late seventh century; and it was nearby at the royal vill of Tamworth that successive eighth- and ninth-century Mercian kings most frequently gathered their *fideles* to celebrate the major Christian festivals.[14] In the absence of evidence for earlier foci elsewhere it is surely in or near this Mercian heartland that we must locate the 'march' from which the Mercians were named. For this reason it seems best to side with Stenton and earlier scholars in supposing that the Mercians were originally a 'border people' because they were settled on the frontier with the Welsh Britons. Hunter Blair's iconoclastic notion that the *Mierce* somehow took their name from the important boundary between the Northumbrians and the *Sutangli* – that is the no man's land in North Derbyshire and South Yorkshire from Dore to the River Don, then to the Idle and the Humber (fig. 11.1), an area that is singularly devoid of pagan Anglo-Saxon cemeteries – has held the field for a generation.[15] But it entirely lacks positive supporting evidence – whether toponymic, historical or archaeological – and should therefore be set aside.

By contrast the Middle Trent valley is an area with numerous pagan Anglo-Saxon cemeteries, not only cremation cemeteries but also several of mixed rite and a number of inhumation cemeteries as well. They stretch from Newark, Holme Pierrepoint and Cotgrave (Nottinghamshire) in the east via Kingston-upon-Soar (Notts.) and Melbourne and Hilton (Derbyshire) in the centre and then to Caves Inn and Stapenhill (Leicestershire), Barton under-Needwood and Stretton (Staffs.) in the west. Unfortunately the River Trent cuts through the modern and medieval administrative boundaries – of counties and municipalities – which determined the establishment of museums and archaeological societies in Victorian times and more recently of archaeological units. As a result the Trent valley cemeteries have never been studied as a group. Such work as has been done in the last generation suggests that these proto-Mercian settlements were relatively small, relatively late (beginning in the sixth century rather than the fifth) and relatively poor. It has also suggested that the settlers reached the Middle Trent mainly from the east via such valleys as that of the Leicestershire River Soar and ultimately from the rivers that drain into the Wash.[16]

KINGDOM AND DYNASTY

This conclusion, uncertain though it must be in the absence of any systematic modern study, has the merit of having been propounded *before* Professor Davies so boldly reconstructed various entries in twelfth- and thirteenth-century annalistic compilations into a coherent account of the settlement and conquest of both East Anglia and Mercia under numerous chiefs (*proceres*) in the early sixth century, that is initially in 527 (or rather in 515, as she would have us correct it).[17] So far as Mercia is concerned, subsequent entries in these compilations purport to record the foundation of a Mercian kingdom by Crida

(Creoda) in 585 and the succession of his son Pypba on Crida's death in 588, of Cearl (the first Mercian king mentioned by Bede) in 594 or 597, and of Penda by the year 610. Despite Professor Davies's tentative advocacy of the historicity of this material, it cannot be said that it is yet clear that what lies behind these scattered entries in the works of Henry of Huntingdon, Roger of Wendover and Matthew Paris is anything more important than some inventive conjectures by an English monk, perhaps as late as the early twelfth century, on the basis of the names available in Bede, the Mercian royal genealogy and the Anglo-Saxon Chronicle. On such an interpretation it would not be surprising that they should more or less fit the fragments of information that we have on the early history of Mercia; for the compiler of these entries may have had access to the same sources as are available to us.

The family (*egregia stirps*) to which Creoda, Pypba and Penda belonged traced their descent in the early eighth century from Icel and therefore came to be known as Iclingas.[18] Icel may have been regarded as the founder of the line because he was the first member of the family in Britain. According to the Mercian royal genealogies preserved in the 'Anglian Collection' of the end of the eighth century there were just five generations spanning the period from Icel to that of the Mercian brothers Penda and Eowa in the first half of the seventh century (Icel–Cnebba–Cynewald–Crida (Creoda)–Pypba–Penda).[19] Depending upon how we resolve the chronological *cruces* of Penda's reign and on whether we allow twenty-five or thirty years per generation we could therefore calculate a *floruit* for Icel at any time of our choice between c. 450 and 525. According to the genealogy the Iclingas were descended (via a number of heroes of poetry and myth) from the Germanic war god Woden. Such a claim was presumably an assertion of the Mercian dynasty's martial qualities. As in other kingdoms descent from Woden was part of the propaganda that accompanied the process by which certain dynasties brutally arrogated the kingly title and status to themselves and demoted other families whose past was no less prestigious to be merely *principes, reguli, subreguli, praefecti, duces, ealdormen* and the like.[20] These centralizing and aggrandizing tendencies seem to have been stronger in England than they were in early medieval Ireland with its 150-odd *tuatha*, each with its own *rí* (king), or in Wales where we have evidence for about a dozen early kingdoms. Be that as it may, Midland England at the beginning of the seventh century is likely to have had much more in common with the multiplicity of rulers and states in the contemporary Celtic world than it was to have in the eighth or ninth centuries. There is no reason to suppose that the Iclinga dynasty, until it produced a war leader of genius, namely the pagan king Penda, was necessarily any more (or any less) royal than the ruling houses of any of the small Midland peoples which were separately recorded in the Tribal Hidage and assessed at 300 or 600 hides each.[21]

There is one other potential clue to the early activity of the Iclinga dynasty which has been strangely neglected in recent years. In 1927 Stenton drew attention to the concentration of placenames in Worcestershire and Warwickshire which apparently preserve the rare personal names of Penda and his father Pypba.[22] In more recent times scholarly fashion has swung against the early emphasis on interpreting placenames in terms of personal names. Topographical names now arouse greater interest and topographical explanations tend to be sought when etymologies are uncertain. Stenton, however, had already warned his readers against the automatic association of these placenames with the Mercian leaders known to us. But their regional distribution is unlikely to be accidental and some such explanation as Stenton's, that these personal names must have become popular among Anglian settlers and lords in the West Midlands because of the success of the dynasty, is necessary. At least at second hand the placenames are therefore likely to reflect the activities of the Iclinga dynasty, and it is worth extending the enquiry to all the names in the Mercian royal genealogy between the eponymous Icel and Penda:

Icel	Ickleton (Cambs.), Ickleford (Herts.) and Icklesham (Sussex)
Cnebba	Knebworth (Herts.).
Cynewald	Kinwalsey (Warwicks.)
Creoda	Credenhill (Herefs. and Wilts.), Curbridge (Oxon.), Curdworth (Warwicks.) and Kersoe and *Creodan ac* (Worcs.).
Pypba	Publow (Somerset), Pedmore, Pepper Wood and Pepwell (Worcs.) and possibly Peplow (Shropshire).
Penda	Penley (Flintshire), Pinbury (Gloucs.), Peddimore (Warwicks.) and Pinvin and *Pendiford* (Worcs.).

Such a list must be used with caution.[23] Where there is only a single extant placename, as is the case for Cnebba and Cynewald, its location is unlikely to be significant – particularly when the second element (e.g. *gehæg* in Kinwalsey) suggests a much later origin than the sixth or seventh century. Equally the temptation to build elaborate conjectures about the origins of the dynasty upon the existence of two Icel names in the East Midlands should be resisted, since the location of both places on the Icknield Way warns us that alternative etymologies are possible. None the less it is clear that placenames formed from Creoda, Pypba and Penda are concentrated in the West Midlands, especially in the south-west (that is in, or on the fringes of, the later territory of the Hwicce). They are not found elsewhere. Such a distribution may suggest that the late accounts of the creation of a Mercian kingdom by Creoda and of its subsequent rule by Pypba and Penda do indeed represent some form of dynastic tradition, as Professor Davies has suggested. For the placenames certainly indicate that these three personal names achieved a unique popularity in this area, while the earlier names in the genealogy did not. The names may commemorate a particular and early phase of Anglian colonization.

PENDA *c.* 626–655

Thus far we may dimly and very tentatively hope to pierce the gloom of Mercian origins. The achievement of Penda in forging a greater Mercian kingdom stands out more clearly from the sources. It cannot, however, be placed in its proper historical context unless some attempt is made to understand and explain the conflicting evidence for the duration of his reign. While there is unanimity that Penda met his death in battle against the Northumbrian king Oswiu, we have three separate dates for the commencement of his reign vouched for by independent authorities. Indeed we might have a fourth were we to accept Professor Davies's conjecture that behind the Anglo-Saxon Chronicle, Henry of Huntingdon and Roger of Wendover lies a source (either an annal or a regnal list) which allotted him a reign of fifty years and therefore supposed that Penda's reign began in 605 or 606.[24] That, however, would be to build a hypothesis upon the most improbable element in the latest of our three principal sources for Penda's reign. Since there are, as we shall see, simpler explanations available, it is best to concentrate attention upon the three sources that do exist:

1. The Anglo-Saxon Chronicle, compiled at the end of the ninth century, states under the year 626: 'And Penda held his kingdom for 30 years and he was 50 years old when he succeeded to the kingdom.'[25] Since the same source records that Penda 'perished' (*forwearþ*) in 655 (rather than 656), it is clear that we should not press the '30 years' too exactly.
2. In his Ecclesiastical History Bede described Cadwallon's defeat of Edwin of Northumbria at the battle of Hatfield in 633 and recounted that Penda, a *vir strenuissimus* of the Mercian royal line, had aided Cadwallon and from that time had himself ruled the Mercians for twenty-two years with varying fortune (*varia sorte*).[26]
3. Finally the *Historia Brittonum* in its so-called 'Northern British' section records: 'Penda, the son of Pypba, reigned ten years. He first freed (*separavit*) the kingdom of the Mercians from the kingdom of the Northerners (*Nordorum*) . . . He fought the battle of *Cocboy*, in which fell his brother Eowa, king of the Mercians (and) son of Pypba, and Oswald king of the Northerners.'[27]

Here then we have three independent and apparently contradictory versions of Penda's reign – namely that it lasted thirty, twenty-two or ten years respectively. Given that it is difficult to accept the Chronicle's assertion that Penda was already 50 years old in 626, given the low opinion in which the *Historia Brittonum* has been held by historians, and given the difficulty in reckoning only ten years from the battle of *Maserfelth/Cocboy* where Oswald was slain to that of *Winwæd/Campus Gai* where Penda himself fell, it is perhaps not surprising that historians have tended to stick to Bede's account. The other dates have been largely forgotten and Eowa has been neglected, except by Professor Davies who wrote of Penda and Eowa as joint rulers. But if we bear in mind that none of these sources is Mercian, then we should be less surprised that they record contradictory information about Penda. Not only may his reign have been perceived differently by his West Saxon, Northumbrian and Welsh neighbours, but they also only had reason to record those of his activities which brought him into military contact with their own peoples. We should also observe that Bede's statement that after Hatfield (633) Penda ruled the Mercians with mixed fortune could indicate that his reign was intermittent, which would allow it to have had a new beginning after his defeat of Oswald at *Maserfelth/Cocboy* (642).

Greater difficulties are presented by the 626 annal in the Anglo-Saxon Chronicle. As H.M. Chadwick pointed out long ago, if Penda had indeed been aged 50 in 626 he would have been almost 80 at the battle of the *Winwæd*. Yet it is difficult to believe that he could have been termed *vir strenuissimus* at Hatfield in 633 when he would already have been 57, or that his eldest son

Peada should have been a young man (*iuvenis*) in 653, or that another son, Wulfhere, should have still been *adulescens* when he was brought out of hiding in 658, while a third son, Æthelred, who was to retire to a monastery as late as 704, was apparently even younger still; it would be strange too that Penda's sister should have married Cenwalh of Wessex between 642 and 645 at a time when her brother was nearly 70.[28] Individually none of these items is impossible, but cumulatively they suggest that the Chronicle's chronology has had the effect of making Penda a generation too old.

If we re-examine the 626 annal with this in mind it becomes significant that, although its purpose ought to be to record Penda's accession, in fact it only states the length of his reign and his age, both of which more naturally belong to a record of the end of his reign or to a regnal list. The Chronicle's source may have recorded this information in some such brief form as: *Penda mortuus est xxx^{mo} anno regni sui, aetate L.* In calculating from his death at the *Winwæd* (655) that Penda must have acquired the throne in 626, the chronicler could simply have misapplied Penda's age to his accession. In other words what the Chronicle should have written under 626 was: 'Penda (succeeded to the kingdom and) reigned 30 years and was 50 years old *when he died.*' This simple emendation would solve all the chronological problems of Penda's career and would have him reigning (intermittently) from the age of about 20 until his death in battle aged 50. It is easier to suppose that the *strenuissimus vir* who was an ally of Cadwallon in the defeat of Edwin at Hatfield was 27 years of age than that he was already 57; by the same token it is easier to believe that the victor of *Maserfelth* was 36 rather than 66, and that the great warrior king who led thirty *duces regii* to the *Winwæd* and left young children among his heirs was a man of 50, not a doddering octogenarian.

There is a little more information to be elicited from the evidence for his accession. The Welsh sources, that is both the *Historia Brittonum* and the *Annales Cambriae*, regard Penda's reign as lasting from his victory at *Cocboy/Maserfelth* to his defeat at the battle of the field of *Gai* (i.e. Bede's *Winwæd*).[29] Hence when the *Historia* states that at *Cocboy* Oswald king of the Northerners and Eowa king of the Mercians were killed, its assumption is probably that Eowa was ruling the Mercians until his death in that battle and that Penda succeeded him as a result. We should therefore hesitate to follow Professor Davies in supposing that Eowa had ruled jointly with his brother Penda – common though shared kingship was in the Anglo-Saxon kingdoms of the seventh and eighth centuries. Rather Eowa's reign may have been one of the periods in Bede's twenty-two years when Penda's fortunes were low. Here we need to bear in mind the *Historia*'s statement that Penda first *separavit* the kingdom of the Mercians from the Northerners. There is some exaggeration of Penda's achievement here, for the Mercian king Cearl can scarcely have been subject to the Northumbrian Æthelfrith when he allowed his daughter Cwenburh to marry the exiled Deiran prince Edwin.[30] None the less the author of the *Historia* would seem to have believed that before the battle of *Cocboy/Maserfelth* the Mercians and their king Eowa had indeed been subject to control by the Northumbrian king Oswald. We should therefore beware assuming that Eowa was killed fighting alongside his brother Penda. If Eowa had indeed been a Northumbrian puppet, it is more probable that he fought alongside his overlord to maintain his throne against his brother.

By such means the bare bones of Penda's career begin to emerge. There seems no reason to reject the Chronicle's suggestion that Penda had acquired the Mercian throne in (or about) 626, for the West Saxons had reason to remember him. The battle which he fought against the pagan West Saxon kings, Cynegils and Cwichelm, at Cirencester in 628 (according to the Chronicle) is likely to have been a West Saxon defeat since they then 'came to terms'.[31] Thereafter the people later known as the Hwicce were under Mercian rather than West Saxon lordship. It may have been then that the personal names Creoda, Pypba and Penda became popular in this territory.

By 633 Penda was extending his and his people's ambitions as a junior client of the great British war lord Cadwallon of Gwynedd. It was presumably Penda's Mercians who were the 'pagans' who after Edwin had been killed at Hatfield burnt his royal vill of *Campodonum* and the church that had been newly built there.[22] The Hatfield campaign and its brutal aftermath were indeed what first caused Penda's rule to be remembered in Northumbria.

How long Penda enjoyed the spoils of that campaign, however, how long, that is, he survived in power after Oswald's destruction of Cadwallon at 'Heavenfield' in the following year, is uncertain. He certainly attempted to ingratiate himself with Oswald by murdering Edwin's son Osfrith who had fled to his protection; but we do not know that Penda was still ruling the Mercians in 635 when Oswald sponsored the baptism of Cynegils of Wessex at Dorchester and married Cynegils's daughter.[33] Other recorded activities of Penda – such as his slaying of the East Anglian kings Ecgric and Sigberht in battle, or the marriage of his sister to Cenwalh of Wessex, or his devastation of Northumbria and of the royal centres of Bamburgh and Yeavering[34] – cannot be precisely dated. They may all have occurred after his defeat of Oswald at *Maserfelth/Cocboy* and should perhaps be seen as attempts to undo the Northumbrian regime step by step and to replace it with Mercian lordship. Certainly it was his overthrowing of Northumbrian control and his victory at *Cocboy* that impressed themselves upon Welsh memories as marking the beginning of Penda's rule.

Eowa's rule of the Mercians, which we have interpreted as belonging to the political system of Oswald, may therefore have lasted from *c.* 635 to his death at *Cocboy/Maserfelth* in 642. Nothing is known of his reign, but it provides a possible historical context for some evidence that is otherwise difficult to explain. Thus it may have been at this time and under Oswald's direction that the territory of the Hwicce was established under a dynasty whose members' personal names over several generations could indicate that they were linked to, or descended from, the Bernician royal dynasty, that is Oswald's own family.[35] Pushing conjecture even further we might suggest that the establishment of a kingdom of the Hwicce had the corollary that Eowa was not allowed the whole territory that Penda had been ruling before 634×5; his reduced kingdom may have been restricted to the 'first land of the Mercians' which the Tribal Hidage assessed at 30,000 hides.[36] One of the functions of the Tribal Hidage, indeed, in allocating 7,000 hides to such peoples as the Hwicce (*Hwinca*), the Wrekin-dwellers (*Wocen sætna*), the Westerne and the Lindisfaran, and multiples of 300 hides to a host of smaller Midland peoples, would seem to be to assert that such peoples were no longer part of the Mercian kingdom. No longer were the Mercians to be a great and growing warrior folk on the border; but henceforth, restricted to their previous boundaries, they would just be one Anglo-Saxon kingdom surrounded by others. Divide and rule is the apparent philosophy underlying the Tribal Hidage. The assessment of this remaining core of the Mercian kingdom at a massive 30,000 hides, however, suggests that there was also a penal element in the exactions of the Northumbrian overlord, whether this was Oswald himself (634–42) or one of his successors Oswiu or Ecgfrith, who were briefly dominant in the south from 655 to 658 and from *c*. 674 to *c*. 678 respectively.

Finally and most hesitantly we need to take some account here of Old Welsh poetry. It is unlikely that there will ever be a consensus on how to interpret and evaluate poems that are only extant in manuscripts of the thirteenth century and later, but whose subject matter concerns heroes and warfare of the sixth or seventh century. The date of original composition, the length of the oral transmission and the period when these poems were first written down are all highly uncertain. Those who go 'in search of' the true songs of Aneirin, Taliesin or Llywarch Hen meet problems in every way comparable to those encountered in the search for the historical Troy or Roland or indeed Arthur. Poetry and legend make dangerous tools for the historian when they have been subject to adaptation and corruption over so long a period and when the context of the composition of the extant works is so uncertain.[37] Widely accepted rules of thumb, such as that poems in which the enemy are the English must reflect the conditions of the ninth century or later, clearly rest upon the shakiest of historical and critical foundations. Moreover those like the present writer who have no command of the Welsh language, old or modern, seek to assess the evidence and the scholarly debate at their peril.

When all the necessary reservations have been made, however, it deserves to be noted that the battle of *Cocboy* long continued to be of interest to Welsh poets. A poem attributed to the late eleventh- or early twelfth-century poet Cynddelw depicted it as a struggle between Oswald and the men of Powys;[38] while a stanza of the *Canu Llywarch Hen*, dated by some to the ninth century, has Cynddylan (of Powys) present at the battle as an ally.[39] More important is the *Marwynad Cynddylan* or lament for Cynddylan whose death in battle had brought an end to his dynasty. If Dr Rowland's recent study is correct in claiming that this elegy was composed very shortly after Cynddylan's death, then its statement that 'When the son of Pyb [*i.e. either Penda or Eowa*] desired, how ready he [*Cynddylan*] was!' could provide a welcome early support for the alliance between Cynddylan and Penda that might be deduced from the later poetry.[40] Whether she is right to suppose that Cynddylan's death was at the battle of *Gai/Winwæd* rather than at *Cocboy/Maserfelth*, it is certainly clear that Welsh support played a part in determining Penda's fortunes at the critical moments of his career. In 633 he had attached his Mercians to the cause of Cadwallon of Gwynedd; in 642 he regained his kingdom at *Cocboy* probably with the support of Cynddylan of Powys; and in 655 Cadafael of Gwynedd was certainly, and Cynddylan possibly, among the thirty *duces regii* whom he led to the disaster of the *Winwæd*.[41]

We do not know whether the alliance between Mercia and certain Welsh kingdoms survived Penda's death. The absence of any record of Mercian–Welsh hostilities until the Welsh victories of the early eighth century[42] does not indicate that peace was the norm. Lacking Mercian sources we have no record of how the territories of the Magonsæte and the Wreocensæte were established under English rule;[43] the silence of the *Annales Cambriae* may only reflect their sparse record for that period (or their natural reluctance to record Welsh defeats). Nor need we suppose that king Eowa had shared his brother's close relations with the Welsh. Indeed Eowa's reign provides a possible context for Morfael's great raid on *Caer Lwytgoed* which is recounted in a difficult passage of the *Marwynad Cynddylan*. We learn that Morfael carried off 1,500 cattle and five herds of swine and gave no protection to the bishop or the book-holding monks there.[44] Such swashbuckling raiding from which even the churches of one's enemies were not exempt remained typical of Welsh princely activity as late as the twelfth and early thirteenth centuries when the extant manuscript of the poem was written.[45] But if the Morfael episode genuinely belongs to the lament for Cynddylan and if the poem was indeed composed in the mid-seventh century, then its account of a Welsh raid on Mercia is of prime importance. The name *Llwytgoed* ('grey wood') refers to the woodland from which both the Romano-British fortified town of *Letocetum* (now Wall, Staffs.) and the nearby Anglo-Saxon episcopal see of Lichfield (Bede's *Liccidfelth*) take their name. But *Caer Lwytgoed* ('the fort of the grey wood') must refer to *Letocetum*, whose Roman walls still stood some 12 feet high in places in the eighteenth century, rather than to Lichfield which could not have been a *caer* since its defences are no earlier than the twelfth century.[46] Morfael was, however, raiding right into the heart of the Mercian kingdom and carrying off much of its movable wealth. If he was a contemporary of Cynddylan and therefore of the pagan Mercian king Penda, it is difficult to understand the presence at Wall of a bishop and monks. It is conceivable that Penda might have permitted British clergy to continue at Wall to serve the needs of any British subjects of his kingdom; but the poet is unlikely to have reported so glowingly an attack on Penda's Mercia, that is on his hero's ally. Nor is there any hint that the raid was subsequent to (and in revenge for) the deaths of Cynddylan and Penda. Mercia under king Eowa, the puppet of the Northumbrian overlord who had slain Cadwallon and was the enemy of Cynddylan, is a much more probable target for Morfael's raid. In that event the bishop and monks at Wall are likely to have been Northumbrians or 'Scots' installed by Oswald.[47]

Such are the sorts of conjecture to which the *Marwynad Cynddylan* may lead us if we accept it as an early source. It suggests that Wall (*Letocetum*) had some role in the early development of Christianity in Mercia, and this may help to explain both the choice of Lichfield by Chad and Wilfrid as the site for the Mercian see and Theodore's acceptance of it. Girt by forest and marsh Lichfield was perhaps the nearest approximation Chad could find to an island 'Lindisfarne' in the sea-less Mercian kingdom. But it is at Wall rather than at Lichfield that archaeologists should seek the sub-Roman and early Christian roots of the Mercian kingdom. Above all, however, the *Marwynad Cynddylan* supports the conclusion that has emerged from our re-examination of the exiguous sources, namely that Penda's fortunes and in consequence relations between Mercia and the Welsh kingdoms in his day were more uneven and tortuous than has hitherto been supposed. Amid much uncertainty we can none the less recognize that Penda of Mercia bestrode the political stage like a Colossus. He it was who made the *Mierce* into a great kingdom dominating the whole of Midland England. He it was who found new ways of exploiting their frontier situation. Had the eventual demise of Mercia and his own paganism not combined to prevent his memory from being cultivated, Penda might have been known to us in English poetry, like some early El Cid, as a great war leader who had made nonsense of the ethnic and religious divisions of his day.[48]

12 Defining the Magonsæte

KATE PRETTY

Now the existence on the Welsh Border of a little kingdom ruled by an Anglian dynasty as early as the second half of the 7th century is a fact deserving close attention. It has implications which have not been squarely faced by our historians.[1]

In 1961 and 1964 H.P.R. Finberg published three papers which stand as the basis of our interpretation of the establishment of Anglo-Saxon control over the central Welsh Border. His commentary on the unpublished Testament of St Mildburg[2] and his analysis of the fragmentary evidence for the family of king Merewalh[3] were followed by a paper setting out his views on relationships between the Mercians and the Welsh along the border in the seventh and eighth centuries.[4] Other writers have tended to accept his suggestion that the family of king Merewalh were the 'princes of the Magonsæte' and have gone on to assume, perhaps too easily, that the whole of the large and complex area, eventually fixed as the see of Hereford, was under their domination.

In their skeletal histories of the early Anglo-Saxon annexation of the Welsh borderland Finberg and Stenton[5] rarely speculate on what preceded the seventh-century record. Finberg was perplexed by the origins of Merewalh's kingdom and the circumstances which had 'set him up as ruler over this delectable countryside'.[6] This chapter aims to explore those origins. The fifth and sixth centuries cannot be easily reconstructed from historical sources alone. However, recent evidence from archaeology, coupled with a change in current opinion about the nature of the end of Roman rule in western Britain, allows us to suggest new possibilities for understanding the changing patterns of power along the border.

In this chapter some of these current issues will be looked at, particularly the continuity of land ownership, the problems of identifying late Roman and Anglo-Saxon land and the question of racial identity. The historical and archaeological evidence taken together reveal something of the nature of political power, seen in the patterns of assessment such as the Tribal Hidage, in the patterns of royal land given to the church, in the patterns of administrative and ecclesiastical foci from the fourth century onwards and in the emergence of rulers, secular and religious, whose names, families and activities pin down the shifting network of historical and archaeological 'facts'. Merewalh and his family and their activities between about 625 and 735 represent one of the few patches of coherent history in four centuries of obscurity, and it is tempting to tie all possible loose ends into their story as other historians have done since the Middle Ages. From such ties stems the frequent equation of Merewalh and his dynasty with the Magonsæte, a people from a district which Finberg himself admits may not have covered the whole diocese in the seventh century.[7] Between the Magonsæte, who emerge by name only in the ninth century, and Merewalh there are two centuries dominated by other names and people. Before Merewalh lie two centuries of late Roman or British rule which must be explored before we can understand the origins of his kingdom.

The earliest Anglo-Saxons to the west of the Severn in Shropshire and Herefordshire were late arrivals in an area which had been on the fringes of the Roman civilian zone. It is necessary to understand the late Roman configuration, politically and geographically, before looking at the nature of these arrivals. In the late fourth century each major river valley running east–west to the Severn contained a Roman town, which presumably acted as a focus for fiscal, judicial and economic practices, with satellite villas in the surrounding hills (fig. 12.1). The largest town lay to the north at *Viroconium* (Wroxeter), where the Rivers Tern and Severn meet and where the Watling Street crosses the Severn. South of Wroxeter was *Bravonium* (Leintwardine) in the Teme valley, and further south on the Wye, near its confluence with the Lugg, lay *Magnis* (Kenchester), while the lower Wye was controlled by *Ariconium* (Weston-under-Penyard). These settlements were linked by a major Roman road which, running through the Church Stretton Gap, provided a north–south route across the prevailing east–west system of wooded ridges and fertile stream valleys. Each settlement presumably administered a defined hinterland or territory; and while Gloucester controlled the crossing of the lower Severn, access into the northern Severn plain and modern Powys could be controlled by Wroxeter.

The late history of the city of *Viroconium* and its hinterland may be of particular importance in our understanding of late Roman and post-Roman developments in the Welsh borderland. Although Wroxeter lies immediately to the north of the Hereford diocese and outside the area assigned to the Magonsæte, fieldwork at Wroxeter and in the settlement area of the Wreocensæte suggests a framework of events which may help to interpret the pattern of change farther south. This must be tentative but such models may be the only way forward to further enquiry. Only at Wroxeter is there extensive archaeological evidence for the nature of fifth- and sixth-century occupation in a Roman town. Here in the old city centre, on public land where once the Basilica of the Baths stood, a large wooden framed building was constructed on Classical lines. The choice of the site may have been dictated by the ease with which the building could be secured or enclosed in the shell of the Baths' precinct walls. If this re-use represents the privatization of public land by someone both influential and with the ability to command considerable labour, as it would seem to do, then it is a significant change. Stratigraphic evidence at Wroxeter suggests that this part of the town was in use for at least 100 years after the Roman withdrawal, but the site was presumably abandoned by the time a burial, radiocarbon dated to AD 610±50, was inserted into the layers over the building.[8]

The area excavated at Wroxeter covers less than an acre of this 220-acre city; there is little other fifth-century evidence except for a re-used Roman tombstone, dug up on the rampart bank, which carries the inscription CVNORIX MACVS MAQVI COLINE. Jackson has dated this to the last quarter of the fifth century.[9] Its formula has been used to suggest an Irish presence at Wroxeter, though whether this could be regarded as administrative or ecclesiastical is

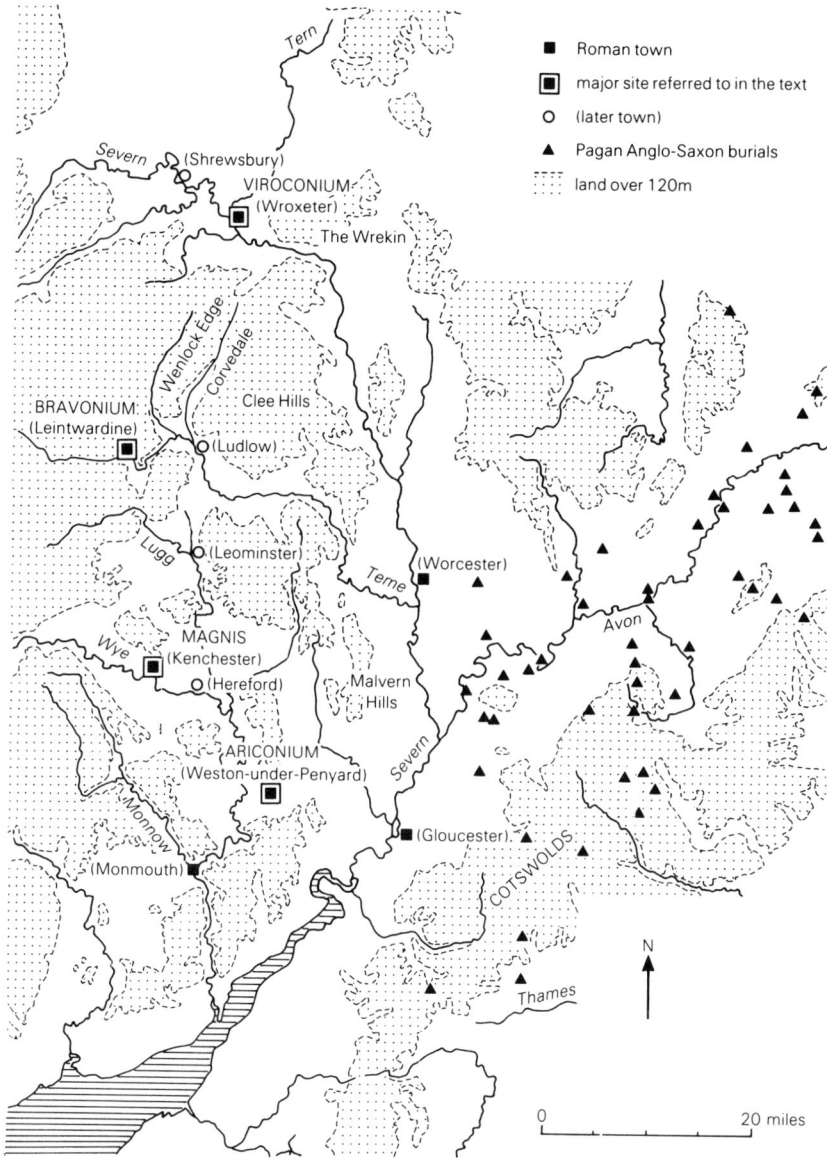

Figure 12.1. The topography of the West Midlands, showing Roman towns and early Anglo-Saxon cemeteries.

unclear.[10] No definite Roman church is known from the city, but in the corner of the ramparts, near the medieval village, is a church with a simple rectangular nave, built with stone from the Roman town.[11] Its construction date is unknown but is possibly seventh century. The reason for its siting has yet to be explained, but it represents the only evidence for Anglo-Saxon building in the Roman town area. Otherwise the city became wholly deserted and was eventually replaced as a political centre by Shrewsbury.[12] Wroxeter, then, in spite of being occupied by a powerful presence in the fifth and sixth centuries, is rare among the *civitas* capitals of lowland Britain in that it eventually lost its central status. This may have been for pragmatic reasons stemming from the difficulty of defending a 220-acre site surrounded by an earthern rampart. Alternatively its abandonment may have been political and may reflect a deliberate break in continuity on the part of the Anglians who eventually came to power in the area.

These Anglo-Saxon incomers became part of the Wreocensæte, whose name derives from the Wrekin (as does that of *Viroconium*);[13] they are assessed at 7,000 hides in the Tribal Hidage.[14] Whether they took their name from the hill or the city they must have been the inhabitants of the old hinterland of *Viroconium*, and as such they are likely to have been as much British as Anglo-Saxon in origin. Their territory seems to have been administered from the Mercian heartland in the east: their churches were under the jurisdiction of the see of Lichfield, and there are records of estates along the Watling Street being granted to Medeshamstede.[15] The only archaeological evidence for an early Anglo-Saxon presence in the Wrekin area is the Yeavering-type, undated, cropmark near Atcham about half a mile from the Anglo-Saxon church of St Eata. There may be some significance in the location of both these sites a mile away from the Roman city if incoming Anglo-Saxons were respecting an existing land-holding. Yet, as we have seen, the stone church in the corner of the ramparts at Wroxeter may represent Anglo-Saxon annexation of late Roman land, or possibly of British royal land (perhaps in a local collapse following the battle of *Maserfelth* in 642). This is suggested by Finberg, who believed with Sir Ifor Williams that the Llywarch Hen poems could be linked to the Wroxeter area in the seventh century.[16] This could explain why, as far as we know, the Wreocensæte were not administered as a separate sub-kingdom under Mercian control (as were the kingdoms of Merewalh and the Hwicce), but remained under the direct control of Mercia, both politically and ecclesiastically. Direct control may have been a political necessity, to prevent Northumbrian incursion and to impose an Anglo-Saxon presence in a sensitive area. This too might explain the abandonment of Wroxeter as a local centre.

In most of Herefordshire and Shropshire the fifth and sixth centuries are even less well documented than in the Wroxeter area. In the centuries after Roman rule had ceased we can perhaps assume that the British population was relatively stable and owed allegiance to hereditary ruling families. These families, whose status had been recognized, but masked, during the Roman occupation when they served as administrators, emerged as kings when the Imperial superstructure was removed. There are no direct references to a continuation of Roman formulae or practices, no fathers who had 'worn the purple' or memorials to 'protectors' in the area of the kingdom of Powys. Nevertheless Vortigern and his descendants like Cyndyllan suggest the existence of British kingdoms in the centuries after the Roman withdrawal. Their centres are unknown, but one may propose that in each of the Roman towns down the border – *Viroconium, Bravonium, Magnis* and *Ariconium* – the old public land was taken over, perhaps enclosed as was the Baths Basilica at Wroxeter, and used as the centre of a small kingdom. There are parallels in the re-use of Roman town centres by Anglo-Saxon kings.[17] The best model for such kingdoms in western Britain is *Ergyng* (Archenfield, whose name comes from *Ariconium*), reconstructed by Wendy Davies from the charter memoranda of the Book of Llandaff.[18]

The rulers of these kingdoms are exemplified by the kings of Bath, Cirencester and Gloucester who were defeated in 577 at Dyrham, the first time that Anglo-Saxons are seen to approach the British western territories. When and how Anglo-Saxon settlers crossed the Severn is still problematic. No pagan Saxon burial has been found on the west bank of the Severn. Indeed, eastwards in the Cotswold area the burials peter out before reaching the flood plain. Farther north there are large cemeteries around Bredon Hill near the Avon–Severn confluence, but none farther west.[19] It could be argued from this that Anglo-Saxon settlers were not present in any great number in the late sixth century in any of the western British kingdoms which grew up in the former Roman *civitates*. The complete absence of pagan burials makes it appear either that there were *no* Anglo-Saxons in Herefordshire or Shropshire in the late sixth century or that any incoming settlers had already been converted to Christianity before they arrived west of the Severn. It has been suggested elsewhere that the rarity of seventh-century burials in the West Midlands as a whole may arise from the strength of Christianity in the western kingdoms where Anglo-Saxon settlers were quickly converted.[20]

The lack of pagan burials, then, can be construed either as a lack of Anglo-Saxon settlers before the seventh century or possibly as evidence of an early conversion through the British church during the late sixth century. Thus the base of Finberg's 'little kingdom ruled by an Anglian dynasty' may have been wholly British in origin or have been made up of converted Anglo-Saxon settlers. When and where the Anglo-Saxons settled beyond the Severn and how many of them there were will be explored later in this chapter. At present there is no archaeological evidence for their presence and we must rely on the historical record.

The historical record suggests that the outcome of the battle of Dyrham and the transference of power to the Anglo-Saxons in the lower Severn valley seem to have had little effect farther north and west; but sixty-five years later the balance of power in the middle Severn valley was upset after the battle of *Maserfelth* at which the successful British and Mercian alliance defeated the Northumbrians. Finberg has suggested that Penda's supremacy after *Maserfelth*, reinforcing his earlier victory over the West Saxons at Cirencester, allowed him either to endow or to confirm a considerable territory west of the Severn on a previously unknown man. This is Merewalh, who became the first named Anglo-Saxon to rule in the border area.[21]

What are we to make of Merewalh, whose name means 'illustrious Welshman'? According to Goscelin he was the third son of Penda and *rex Westehanorum*, and elsewhere was called *Westan-Hecanorum rex*.[22] Merewalh was thus termed a king, as were his sons by his first marriage. We know about the family primarily from Goscelin's Life of St Mildburg, Merewalh's daughter by his second marriage. Merewalh must have lived between about 625 and 685. He was converted to Christianity after 660 and then took a Christian bride from the Kentish royal family; they had three daughters, all saints, and a son of whom nothing more is known. Merewalh is said to have founded the minster at Leominster and to have provided the land at Wenlock where Mildburg eventually became abbess. He parted from his second wife in 673, when she returned to a Kentish monastery. Merewalh was said by Goscelin to have been buried at Repton where he too may have retired to a monastery.[23]

Mildburg became abbess of Wenlock about 680 and probably lived to about 727–30. In the Testament of St Mildburg are recorded a number of grants from her brothers Merchelm and Mildfrith.[24] Merchelm is termed *rex* in the charter which put Mildburg in possession of Wenlock, and his brother *regulus* in the monumental inscription set up in Hereford cathedral between 736 and 740 by bishop Cuthbert, according to William of Malmesbury. The whole of Merewalh's family tree is contained within the period 625–735 and then abruptly disappears.[25]

The history of the family of Merewalh, pieced together by Finberg, lies at the centre of any reconstruction of events which led to a change in the power structures of the border area. The ingredients – the tradition of a new kingdom set up under one of Penda's sons, the establishment of a short-lived dynasty, the growing institution of the church, the alienation of royal land to feed that growth and the royal investment in it, and the saintly royal children, disarmed of secular power but enhancing religious reputation – all these echo events not only in other early Anglo-Saxon kingdoms of the seventh century but also in contemporary British kingdoms. One of the central questions posed by Merewalh's story lies in his name and thus his identity. The lack of alliteration of Merewalh's name with Penda's (which, according to Stenton but not Finberg, runs contrary to normal Mercian practice),[26] casts some doubt on whether he was really Penda's son or whether this is hagiographical fiction. If he was not Mercian by birth but possibly attached to Penda by marriage (we know nothing of his first wife, Merchelm's and Mildfrith's mother), then his name suggests that the central border area may already have been his own land, confirmed by Penda as a reward for allegiance or alliance.

Penda's connection with this area is seen only in Goscelin's allegation that he was the father of Merewalh. There is the argument that what he may have done for the Hwicce, namely set up a sub-kingdom, and his establishment of Peada in Middle Anglia mirror the setting up of Merewalh as sub-king over the central border area. There are arguments both for and against the statement that Merewalh was actually Penda's son. On the one hand, Mildburg calls Æthelred her uncle in referring to his assenting to several grants of land by Merchelm and Mildfrith,[27] and Æthelred was undoubtedly one of Penda's sons. Moreover, Merewalh was buried at Repton, as were at least three members of the Mercian royal family.[28] On the other hand, if the argument can be made that a Northumbrian family was rewarded with the kingship of the Hwicce, following a joint enterprise against the West Saxons, there is a possibility that Merewalh ('illustrious Welshman') really was a Briton, rewarded perhaps for a similar joint enterprise elsewhere, possibly against the Northumbrians at *Maserfelth*. This might well help to explain how he managed to have control of such a considerable area of land in the Leominster area and farther north, in areas where there is no archaeological attestation of early settlement by Anglo-Saxons and no historical record of conquest.

The establishment of Merewalh as king could be seen as the evidence of conquest in itself, so that he represents the first Anglo-Saxon settlement. Alternatively it is possible that Merewalh's power was based on authority stemming from an old established Anglo-Saxon community, already Christian and invisible, or from a British community, either of them centred on a considerable group of estates. Steven Bassett has suggested that the basis of the kingdom of the Hwicce may have been an earlier, much smaller kingdom centred on Winchcombe.[29] Similarly it could be argued that the centre of Merewalh's kingdom lay in a group of estates in the Lugg valley, based either on Leominster, where he founded a minster, or on land around Maund or Marden, an area associated with his family by legend.[30] The latter two placenames may reflect the roots of the district name for the Magonsæte.[31]

The land at Leominster and the lands he alienated to the monastery at *Wininicas* (Wenlock), together with land at *Magana* (Maund), Lyde and along the River Monnow,[32] are our only direct references to land held by Merewalh. Wendy Davies has commented in respect of Archenfield that 'before the eighth century only the kings had powers of perpetual endowment, of alienating land'.[33] It is not clear whether this must be their own land or if they had some rights through kingship over land held by other families. At this early period, however, it seems generally agreed that royal grants were of royal land, so that where we see land given to the church we see the fossil record of royal estates. The distribution of Merewalh's grants holds a particular interest in that this must represent our earliest information on the distribution of part of the estates of a single family. If Merewalh was an incoming Anglo-Saxon the spread is startlingly wide, ranging from an area west of Hereford on the Monnow, through land in the Lugg valley at Maund, Lyde and Leominster, to the northern end of Corve Dale at Much Wenlock. Wendy Davies notes the widespread nature of the grants made in South Wales by individual families,[34] but those families were long established. Merewalh's daughter Mildburg was given land by her half-brothers around Clee Hill and in Corve Dale, while Mildburg herself, according to the Testament,[35] was able to secure her position as abbess of Wenlock by using land at Hampton, which Lord Rennell of Rodd has tentatively identified as part of the Leominster estate.[36] In due course Wenlock claimed, or was given, other estates in the northern part of Hereford diocese,[37] but it is difficult to explain how Merewalh came into possession of the Wenlock site or indeed how his daughter had a connection with Llanfillo, near Brecon, well into British territory.[38] Finberg claims that it reflects the easy relationship between the Mercians and the Welsh in the early eighth century;[39] but if it were true that Mildburg held land there, this would strengthen the possibility that Merewalh or his immediate forebears were British.

Why did Merewalh choose to establish a religious site at Wenlock, in the far north of his territory near the border with the area of the Wreocensæte? Below the Cluniac priory at Much Wenlock Humphrey Woods has recently discovered the standing wall of a Roman building. Plaster had fallen from this wall to be covered by a midden radiocarbon dated to AD 660±90, and above the midden level the wall had been replastered in or after the seventh century.[40] Mr Woods has interpreted the building as a disused Roman villa, whose standing walls attracted the seventh-century builders of the monastery to choose the site for their foundation. However, he also advances the hypothesis that 'the "apsed" room excavated by Cranage[41] became a church', observing that the fact that the first Cluniac church 'exactly respects the axis of the

Roman buildings suggests that it was deliberately superimposed on the earlier building because of its sacred nature'.[42] Clearly with such a limited opportunity for excavation it was impossible to investigate fully the significance of these sequences. The single radiocarbon determination for material in the midden layer would support a date equivalent to the Mildburg or Liobsynde phase or possibly take it back to an earlier, pre-Saxon, occupation. The finds are also equivocal: material in the form of scrap glass dated to the sixth century was residual in thirteenth century deposits.

It is tempting to ask if the Wenlock site, with its Welsh name *Wininicas* used late into the Anglo-Saxon period, had really been abandoned or if it was a British ecclesiastical site. No evidence for continuity from the Roman period exists, but Mr Woods cites Ligugé, where the ruined basement room of a Roman villa became the site of a fourth-century church, as a possible analogue.[43] The case for its being a pre-seventh-century British site may be enhanced by the suggestion that at both Leominster and Hereford there were British churches preceding later Anglo-Saxon foundations. Some truth may lie behind the story that the arm-bone of St David was treasured at Leominster (*Llanllieni*) because, according to Rhygyfarch, he had founded the church there.[44] D.A. Whitehead, writing of the early history of the church of St Guthlac on Castle Green, Hereford,[45] reviews the evidence for the Anglo-Saxon royal foundation's being a refoundation of an earlier Celtic minster and quotes Stenton's statement about 'primitive upland minsters ... of high antiquity whose origins must be sought during the earliest phases of British Christianity'.[46]

Wendy Davies has established that in *Ergyng* land was being alienated to the church from the middle of the sixth century, and she notes the possibility that the bishopric associated with Welsh Bicknor may represent the transfer of a late Roman see based at *Ariconium*.[47] Whitehead refers to the statement in the Iolo MSS that Geraint (son of Erbin, who died about 540), founded the church at *Caerfawydd* (Hereford)[48] and that the bishop of *Caerfawydd* was among the seven bishops who disputed with St Augustine in 602 or 603.[49] Were there similar dioceses at *Viroconium* and *Magnis* providing a network of late Roman, then British, religious *loci*? All in all the evidence suggests that behind the visible Christian network celebrating the Anglo-Saxon kings' rise to power, both politically and ecclesiastically, there lay a shadowy network of Celtic Christianity which was deliberately overlaid for political and spiritual reasons. Whether or not Merewalh was a Christian before 660, his conversion, marriage to a Christian princess and land giving to the church have all the hallmarks of a shrewd politician publicly following the prevailing Anglian trend. Whether he was British by birth or an Anglo-Saxon colonist rewarded by the Mercian royal family for services rendered, he and his family became the very model of early Anglo-Saxon kingship in the early seventh century.

Both Lord Rennell of Rodd[50] and June Sheppard[51] have written in detail of the Lugg valley estates, the probable heartland of Merewalh's family holdings and a possible parallel for Steven Bassett's putative early kingdom based on Winchcombe. Lord Rennell has described the vast Domesday estates of Leominster, arguing for a British core in the Land of Lene; while June Sheppard has concentrated on the Marden estate between the Lugg and the Frome. Both Lord Rennell and Sheppard see this area as the original *Magana* from which the

Magonsæte took their name. Within a three-mile radius are Marden (possibly *Magewurdin* in 1177), which may give *'Magene* enclosure', and the Maunds – Rosemaund, Maund Brian and Upper Maund Common (*Magene* in Domesday). Margaret Gelling has written extensively about the derivation of the name Magonsæte which she says 'is more difficult to explain than most names of this type'.[52] Its actual meaning may be associated with the Welsh word for 'the rocks', and one of the possible derivations is directly from *Magnis* (Kenchester), itself possibly coined with reference to the rocky outcrop of Credenhill with its hillfort. In the same way the name for the Wreocensæte stems from the word which produces both the Wrekin and *Viroconium*. *Magnis* is about four miles away from Marden and about six miles from the Maunds.

To achieve this derivation Gelling has been concerned to bridge the gap between early Anglo-Saxon and late Roman or British speakers who would have needed to transmit the name as *Magnis* before 550 if it was to survive as the etymological base for Magonsæte. She hypothesizes federate Germans stationed in southern garrisons like Caerwent whose descendants passed the name through folk tradition.[53] As we have seen at Wroxeter there is no problem in taking late Roman or British use of Roman towns through to the mid-sixth century, particularly perhaps as private estates. Kenchester, however, is much less well known archaeologically than Wroxeter; excavations by Heys and Thomas suggest that occupation in the town may have gone on into the fifth century with a narrowing of the west gate and a recutting of the ditch.[54] As at Wroxeter, where the Old Work still stands as a tangible local reminder of the Roman city, so too there were standing ruins at Kenchester which Leland saw in the sixteenth century and Stukeley in the seventeenth.[55] As with Wroxeter it is impossible to guess the size of the territory controlled by *Magnis* in its Roman heyday, but one with a radius of five miles is not too large to have assumed the name of the Roman town.

The district name may be even older and may precede the Roman administration; both Sheppard[56] and Della Hooke[57] have argued that it is the late Iron Age which stamps the territorial pattern on this part of the border. Sheppard argues that the Iron Age hillfort at Sutton Walls, overlooking the Marden estate, established an administrative focus in the area, while Credenhill has been claimed as the focus for the area west of the Lugg. Although the importance of these Iron Age centres must be acknowledged (the Wrekin and Croft Ambrey being other significant examples), it is uncertain that the late Iron Age pattern outweighs the Roman one. The major Roman centres are strategically situated away from the hillforts for logistical and political reasons. Although it has been argued above that the British population may have retained their familial loyalties throughout the Roman occupation, the practice of Roman organization, literacy and religion must have augmented the Iron Age pattern so that it is to a refocused, recent, late Roman past that we look rather than to a pattern six centuries earlier. There may be a coincidence of hillforts and Anglo-Saxon centres for reasons which stem not from a long-term recognition of the continuity of the administrative focus, but from the avoidance of the immediate hinterland of Roman towns by the Anglo-Saxons, who settled in the gaps between Roman administrative centres and so sometimes coincided with the hillforts which the Romans themselves had chosen to avoid. Fig. 12.2 shows the pattern of positive and negative evidence for Anglo-Saxon land-holding in the east–west valleys. The negative areas are particularly interesting in that they cannot all be explained by highland and woodland (though they may simply represent areas for which we have no surviving records). Some, like Wroxeter, the Teme valley around *Bravonium*, and Kenchester, may be delimiting areas which were too strongly held by British magnates to be accessible to early Anglo-Saxon secular domination,

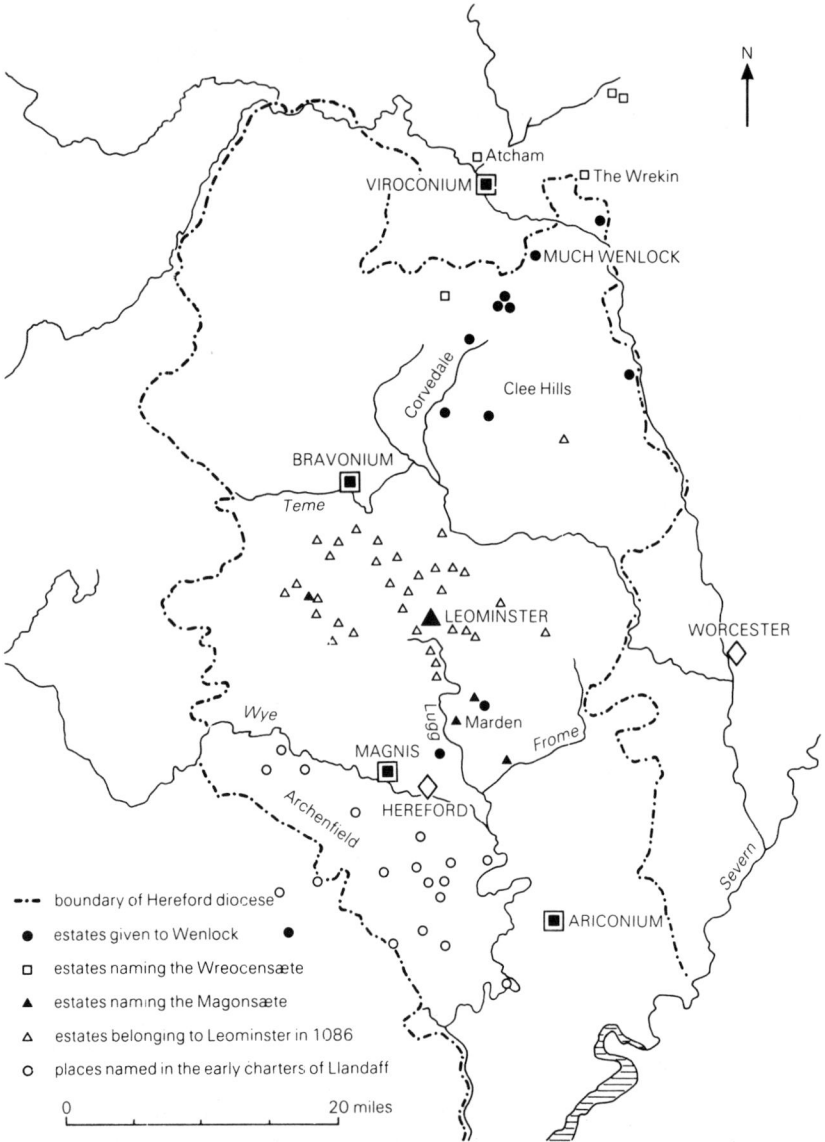

Figure 12.2. The Welsh border in the Anglo-Saxon period.

although they may have been subsumed later under the religious umbrella of the early dioceses.

This brings us back to the question of an original Anglo-Saxon settlement, if indeed there was one, and how it can have been effected. In the Tribal Hidage the people living in the area south of the Wreocensæte and west of the Hwicce were known as the Westerna and assessed at 7,000 hides. Their name gives no hint of where they might be geographically located. They have been equated with the *populis qui ultra amnem Sabrinam ad occidentem habitant* named by Bede,[58] and with the *Westan Hecanorum* and *Westehanorum* whose king was also called the *rex West-Anglorum*.[59] Who were their eastern counterparts? Hart commented on the possibility that the Western Hecani might be the 'West Hwicce' who had crossed the Severn to establish colonies.[60] In support of this Stevenson notes that the Appendix to 'Florence' of Worcester's *Chronicon ex Chronicis* states that Worcester was 'the ancient metropolis of the Hwiccii or Magesetenses', and speculates that the Eastern Hecani, if they existed, would have been found in the diocese of Worcester.[61] Like Stenton, who commented that 'There is no evidence to support the suggestion . . . that the Magesaetan formed part of the Hwicce, and the fact that each of these peoples had its own bishop in the seventh century is decisive against their identity',[62] Stevenson felt that 'the statement that the Hwicce and the Magesaetan were identical conflicts with what we know of their history'.[63] But if we were to recognize a pre-Pendan phase of Anglo-Saxon settlement, then there would be less objection to the Hwicce having a western settlement in Herefordshire before the sees of Worcester and Hereford were established. The most likely way for Anglo-Saxon settlers to establish themselves in Herefordshire was for them to have come from the Worcester area where the pagan burials of Wyre Piddle and Upton Snodsbury are the most westerly of all Anglo-Saxon burials in the Severn valley north of the confluence with the Avon.[64]

Any early land-taking should postdate 577 when Gloucester was taken and, to be pre-Pendan, predate 628. During this fifty-year period there was plenty of time for Merewalh's predecessors, if they were Anglo-Saxon, to have taken possession of a set of estates in the Lugg valley, and even to have pushed northwards to take land north of the Teme valley in the area around Wenlock where Mildburg was given land. But the latter point is unlikely. If one were to speculate, it would be to suggest that these early territorial units, British or Saxon, were quite small, and that Merewalh's rise to a wider power followed his instatement by Penda, perhaps as a result of Penda's success in the north which may have given the latter a claim to south Shropshire as far as the Teme valley. The existence of numerous small kingdoms might also explain why more than one folk name can be found in this area, and would raise the distinct possibility that the Western Hecani and the Magonsæte were separate until the see of Hereford was founded.

There can be no direct equation between them. The Hecani are glossed in one source as *Hecana quae nunc Hereford dicitur*[65] and elsewhere the bishops' lists under Hecana are *Magesetensium sive Herefordensium*,[66] so that Hereford is identified with both names at a late stage, possibly as a rationalization or possibly reflecting the fact that the two folk groups were incorporated into one see. Merewalh's relationship to both names is equivocal. His identification with the Magonsæte is based on the alliteration of the names and the possibility that some of his family estates lay in the area of *Magana*. His identification with the Hecani is solely based on 'Florence' of Worcester.[67] It is puzzling that the first mention of the Magonsæte (as *Magonsetum*) is not until 811 when they are associated with land at Yarkhill, not far from Marden;[68] then they appear again in 823–5 when an ealdorman of the *Magansetum* gave land, possibly in Archenfield, to St Peter's, Gloucester.[69] In 958 king Edgar gave land at Staunton-on-Arrow, at the western end of the great Leominster estate, which was said to be *in pago Magesætna*.[70] Finally, the Anglo-Saxon Chronicle records that in 1016 the Magonsæte with ealdorman Eadric were the first to fly from the battlefield at Ashingdon.[71] These four references, together with the glosses mentioned above, are our only evidence for the existence of the Magonsæte. This suggests that the Magonsæte in the strict sense are to be identified only with the Lugg valley and Leominster. This leaves us with the possibility that the Hecani are to be found somewhere else, perhaps in south Shropshire in Corve Dale and around Clee Hill, although if they were the West Hwicce this would seem unlikely.

With the establishment of the diocese of Hereford by 680, which united and delimited the Anglo-Saxon kingdom between the Wreocensæte in the north and Archenfield in the south, we see an attempt at religious control of that whole area which has come to be seen as the kingdom of the Magonsæte.[72] The date and name of Hereford's first bishop are disputed, but Hillaby prefers to see Tyrthel as the first incumbent,[73] whose term of office (693–704) probably coincided more or less with Mildfrith's rule in the Hereford area. Tyrthel and his successors, as well as Mildfrith and his wife Cwenburg, were buried in Hereford according to William of Malmesbury.[74] A recollection of Mildfrith's rule is incorporated in the legend of the death of St Æthelbert who was killed at Sutton, a *villa regia* of the Mercian kings in south Herefordshire, in the eighth century. In the legend St Æthelbert's body is brought in slow procession from Sutton, identified as Sutton Walls in the *Magana* heartland, through Lyde (once owned by Mildburg) to Hereford for burial.[75] Although Mildfrith must have been long dead, the story reinforces the identification of some of the names and places which are associated with the family in the seventh century. Neither Mildfrith nor Merchelm witnesses the gift of land made by king Ceolred to Mildburg in a charter of 709–16;[76] by then we must assume that they were dead although their sister survived another thirty years.[77] In the early years of the eighth century Coenred had problems with the Welsh,[78] and it may be that this was a result, or a cause, of the end of Merewalh's short-lived dynasty.

Early in this chapter it was suggested that the key issues surrounding the early Anglo-Saxon takeover of the Welsh border were continuity and racial identity. Using archaeological and geographical techniques we are beginning to be able to see the shadowy outlines of the political organization of the three centuries between the official Roman withdrawal and the appearance of the see of Hereford. The evidence for continuity exists at Wroxeter and perhaps at Kenchester and Much Wenlock. It may also be present at Marden where June Sheppard's analysis suggests an older settlement element below the later Anglo-Saxon layout.[79] Superimposed upon this continuum is the evidence for an early British church network, characteristically located between late Roman settlements rather than within them. Since there is no strong evidence for depopulation we must assume that individual polities grew up in the fifth and sixth centuries, some in the Roman towns, others between them, and it is these interstitial polities which cause the greatest difficulty in determining racial identity. The Leominster and Marden estates, and the land in Corve Dale and around Clee Hill, may have been British or Anglo-Saxon in the late sixth century. This chapter has tried (perversely, some may think) to suggest that Merewalh was not Anglo-Saxon by birth but a Briton who aped Anglo-Saxon practices for political ends. If so, then his family lands may have been in the Lugg valley from time out of mind. If not, then the migration of the Anglo-Saxons into this area was insidious and possibly uncontested. Actual numbers of immigrants are impossible to assess. The preponderance of Welsh speakers may be reflected in the name of the third or fourth bishop of Hereford, Wealhstod ('interpreter'),[80] and Whitehead notes that Gruffydd ap Llewellyn regarded Herefordshire as part of the ancient patrimony of the Welsh princes.[81]

In 1934 Stenton wrote that 'The early history of the district known at least since the eleventh century as Herefordshire is impenetrably obscure'.[82] Archaeology, geography and history together now provide some chinks of light into that obscurity. We now accept that continuity of rural land use is more likely than not, that the Anglo-Saxon incursion was not into a vacuum but perhaps into a series of weak spots, and that strongholds of late Roman or British character were likely to have influenced the disposition of these Anglo-Saxon settlements. In some areas, like Archenfield, early Anglo-Saxon domination was never achieved. In other places the rulers of what had been late Roman towns may have been some of the slowest to give way. All along the border in each river valley we might be able to predict sixth-century polities based on Roman towns, British ecclesiastical centres and possibly old villa estates. The Anglo-Saxon policy under the Mercians was to weld these together so that separate units were indivisible, lumped under an administrative and religious superstructure. This chapter tries to demonstrate, albeit speculatively, that it may be possible by looking more closely at each element to disentangle the confused muddle of Mercians and Welsh along the border.

13 The early history of western Mercia

MARGARET GELLING

It should be said at the outset that the materials are not available which would enable a firm account to be given of the origins of the western part of the great Mercian kingdom of the middle Saxon period. Of the types of evidence which could be used, directly relevant archaeology is virtually restricted to the Avon valley in south Warwickshire, though the puzzling phenomenon of post-Roman Wroxeter and the new evidence for a Roman presence at Much Wenlock must also be considered. History is restricted to traditions and to copies of documents connected with St Mildburg. Placenames, though abundant and ubiquitous as ever, may acquire a dangerous dominance in the absence of their natural partners. A final element of confusion is contributed by Welsh literary works, of disputed date, which offer a story in contradiction to everything else. An attempt will be made to present the problems, but there are probably no objective grounds for preferring any of the possible alternative solutions.

The region I am considering comprises the counties of Cheshire, Staffordshire, Shropshire and Warwickshire. Worcestershire is the core of the sub-kingdom of the Hwicce, and requires separate consideration both for that reason and on account of the different quantity and quality of its documentation. It is impossible to discuss Shropshire without encroaching on the sub-kingdom of the Magonsæte, but no attempt will be made to appraise the evidence for events in the southern part of that kingdom.

It will be useful to consider in some detail the geography of the area, as this is likely to have been a factor of major importance in its post-Roman history. The region is predominantly low-lying. The Pennines intrude into north Staffordshire and into the eastern edge of Cheshire. The Welsh mountains take up a large area of south-west Shropshire and a small portion of the north-west. In south-east Shropshire there is the large massif of the Clee Hills. Further east, in Staffordshire and Warwickshire, there is the modestly elevated Birmingham plateau which occasionally, as in Cannock Chase, the Clent and Lickey Hills, and at Barr Beacon, rises too high for settlement.

Outweighing these high areas, there is a great deal of low ground. Some of this lies in the river systems of the Trent, Severn and Avon; and in addition to this Cheshire and north Shropshire constitute a single great plain which extends eastwards across the centre of Staffordshire, and in this great area only a few small massifs, like that of the Wrekin and the Ercall, are too high for settlement (except in Iron Age terms).

There are two major watersheds: that which separates the rivers flowing through Cheshire to the Irish Sea from those which flow either to the North

Sea via the Trent or to the Bristol Channel via the Severn; and the one which separates the feeders of the Trent and Severn from each other. The Trent/ Severn watershed meanders across Warwickshire, emphasizing the artificial nature of that county as an administrative unit. Otherwise the two watersheds coincide with county boundaries to a noteworthy degree. Considerable stretches of the southern boundary of Cheshire (which is the northern boundary of Staffordshire and Shropshire) follow the divide between the drainage to the Irish Sea and the tributaries of the Trent and Severn. A good deal of the Shropshire/Staffordshire boundary follows the narrow ridge separating the headstreams of the Penk from those of the Stour, which is the watershed between the feeders of the Trent and Severn.

The area of our four counties contains only limited patches of marsh and heath. Dr Graham Webster[1] speaks of 'lakes and great bogs' on the north Shropshire plain, but the largest of the lakes is that which gives name to the town of Ellesmere – a very modest feature compared to the waters of the Lake District. The biggest of the bogs is the moss, about four miles long and two miles wide, on the boundary between Shropshire and the detached portion of Flintshire. This is called Fenn's Moss in Flintshire (preserving its sixteenth- and seventeenth-century name of *The Fens*), and Whixall Moss or Wem Moss in Shropshire, from the parishes in which it lies. It is small compared to the fens of Lincolnshire, Huntingdonshire and Cambridgeshire, or to the moors of Yorkshire. There are some particularly interesting smaller marshes, like the Weald Moors in Shropshire and the basin which gives name to Wigmore in Herefordshire, but these are not serious barriers to movement. The Romans put a road across the last-named marsh.

Areas of heath are mostly small. Dunsmore Heath in south Warwickshire is about four miles long and not much over a mile broad. Hine Heath in Shropshire is perhaps four miles square. Rudheath in Cheshire was quite large in medieval times, perhaps five miles by four. There are stretches of heathland in Cannock Chase. But many other heaths are of a size to be contained within a parish or shared by a small group of parishes. The great heaths of Suffolk are on a different scale.

Another potential bar to communications and easy expansion of settlement is forest. There was plenty of woodland in south Staffordshire and north Warwickshire, but it was of a sort to be considered as a valuable resource, probably never to be seen as a great barrier, unlike the Weald in south-east England. Many of the designated 'forests' of the post-Conquest period in our area were heathland, like the Wirral and Rudheath in Cheshire and the Long Mynd in Shropshire.

So we have in western Mercia a large region with little obstacle to penetration and settlement. It is not defensible to the east, north-west, or south. Convenient crossing places on the River Severn are quite numerous. There is no corridor of land which could be defended with dykes, like that which takes the Icknield Way into East Anglia, and there is no great barrier like the Weald of Kent and Sussex. Sir Frank Stenton spoke of the forests of Morfe and Kinver as if they were a barrier on the western edge of the Mercian heartland;[2] but with Watling Street running from the vicinity of Tamworth and Lichfield to Wroxeter, there was no serious impediment to westward movement.

This is a region in which there is no natural refuge, either for British people to form an enclave or for a defeated ruler to bide his time, like Alfred at Athelney. There are many secluded settlement sites (this is the reason for the frequent use of the generic *hop* in Herefordshire and Shropshire placenames), but each would only support a small community. A settlement site like that of Ratlinghope would be a bunker rather than a rallying point in time of war. The only natural boundary is that on the west, formed by the mountains of Wales.

In the Roman period the greater part of the region fell within the province of the Cornovii, whose capital was at Wroxeter. Materials do not exist which would enable a firm boundary to be discerned between the Cornovii and the people to the east of them, or between the Cornovii and the Dobunni of the Severn valley, and there is probably no way of knowing how far north their territory extended. (The people to the east of the Cornovii were referred to until recently as the Coritani, but it is now suggested on the basis of an inscribed tile that their true name was Corieltauvi.) This part of Britain lies beyond the region in which Roman villas are numerous, and evidence for rural settlement in the period is scarce. There can be no useful estimate of population density or, as Dr Webster expresses it, 'the extent to which the land was used in the Roman period'.[3] Dr Webster lists only eight buildings 'which could be described as villas',[4] and other habitation sites can seldom be ascribed to this period. Aerial photography cannot usually distinguish Iron Age from Romano-British farmsteads.

Some indication of the degree to which the countryside was developed at the end of the Roman age can, however, be deduced from surviving placenames. These tell us which parts of the region were forest or swamp at the time of the change to English speech; and there is a general probability that most of the areas not so designated were under cultivation and had been so throughout the centuries of Roman rule. The Weald Moors, since the name means 'uncultivated marsh', had perhaps reverted from agricultural use. Names containing the Old English generics *æcer*, *feld* and *land* may indicate the appropriation for arable purposes of land previously used for communal stock-grazing.[5] Some of the names in -ley probably refer to new English settlements in forest clearings, though many (particularly in north Warwickshire) are more likely to describe pre-English settlements with a forest environment.[6] There was certainly room for expansion of settlement after the Roman period, but there can be no question of a deserted landscape awaiting Mercian colonization. Many, perhaps even a majority, of the land-units known from medieval times are likely to represent arrangements which go back to the Iron Age. Some evidence for ancient 'multiple estates' in Shropshire and Herefordshire is discussed by Della Hooke.[7]

For an indication of political conditions at the end of the Roman period one turns to Philip Barker's excavations at Wroxeter. Here we have the well-known evidence for timber buildings, placed on carefully laid rubble platforms, eventually fronting a street which was made by the deposition of sieved silt. These buildings were constructed in the early fifth century, after the demolition of the latest Roman structures. They include a winged corridor house with a central entrance, which is an essentially classical type, and smaller buildings surrounding it.

There has been general agreement among authorities on Roman Britain that these buildings at Wroxeter constitute evidence for a highly organized hierarchical society continuing well into the fifth century. There is no sign of a Germanic presence, and there is none of the imported pottery which is the commonest evidence at this date for contacts with people closer to the Irish Sea and the Bristol Channel. There is, however, a tombstone, found outside the walls of the Roman town, commemorating 'Cunorix macus maqui coline', which has been dated by Professor Kenneth Jackson to 460–75.[8]

Some of the assertions which have been made on the basis of this tombstone seem unconvincing. Professor L. Alcock envisaged Cunorix as the furthest inland manifestation of the Irish immigration for which there is evidence in the form of Ogham and Latin inscriptions in parts of Wales, particularly Dyfed, Brycheiniog and the upper Usk valley.[9] But the Wroxeter stone is surely too far removed and too isolated to be seen as part of that corpus. Mr Barker speaks of the tombstone as 'probably Christian' and says that it 'implies the presence of a Latin-speaking community in the city'.[10] In fact the stone offered an obvious opportunity for Christian symbolism if the people commissioning it had wished this; and the Latin is minimal. Perhaps Cunorix was a guest, an Irish visitor to a British ruler, whose hosts had sufficient courtesy and just sufficient literacy to give him a memorial in the style appropriate to his nationality. Some evidence may yet be found for the practice of the Christian religion in Wroxeter; but the absence so far of casual finds, like the metal bowls with chi-rho signs embossed or scratched on them from Wall and Caerwent, is surprising.

Perhaps the only certainty about the person who held court in the timber mansion at Wroxeter is that he was not anticipating trouble. Whatever else fifth-century Wroxeter may have been, it was not a citadel. Any place which succeeded *Viroconium* as the centre of government for this part of the Marches was likely to be in a more easily defended position. The Wrekin hillfort has yielded no trace of post-Roman occupation; and common sense seems to rule out this inconvenient site as a political centre for people who had long ceased to think in the extravagant terms of Iron Age society. The strongly fortified lowland site called The Berth north of Shrewsbury is frequently mentioned in this connection. Another possibility is Shrewsbury itself, with its promontory site in a bend of the River Severn. The transfer of political power to Shrewsbury certainly took place at some time between the fifth and ninth centuries, but there is plenty of scope for an intermediate seat. Air photographs have revealed great timber buildings, resembling those of the Northumbrian royal centre at Yeavering, in a field called Frog Hall near Atcham; this, like Wroxeter, is an indefensible site.

There is doubtless good evidence that the rulers of a large part of our area between 400 and 500 did not feel so threatened by insurrection or invasion that they were moved to abandon the Roman city. The Anglo-Saxons must have seemed far away to the east and any Irish immigrants or raiders comfortably distant to the west.

The story of Wroxeter may take us to *c.* 500, but the history of the region is a total blank for a long time after that. The obscurity of the sixth century is impenetrable. Something is known of events in the seventh century, but historians' views of these have been unduly influenced by Welsh poetry which purports to deal with the loss of the eastern part of the kingdom of Powys to the English. It is generally assumed that the kingdom of Powys evolved from the canton of the Cornovii. The poems of most relevance are the cycle known as *Canu Heledd* and the elegy known as *Marwnad Cynddylan*.

The dominant factor in the political life of central England in the middle decades of the seventh century was the violent hostility between the Anglian kingdoms of Mercia and Northumbria. The Welsh kingdoms of Gwynedd and Powys were caught up in the warfare, and they participated as allies of Mercia. But at a later date poetic traditions were formed in which vague memories of seventh-century battles were falsely seen as part of the process by which the lands in Shropshire which had once been the eastern part of Powys had become part of greater Mercia.

A poem associated with the *Canu Heledd* cycle refers to the battle of *Maes Cogwy*, the name given in Welsh sources to the battle which Bede calls *Maserfelth*. It is *Bellum Cocboy* in the *Historia Brittonum* and in the *Annales Cambriae*. It happened in 642, and the poet's statement that Heledd's brother Cynddylan was an ally there suggests that the whole saga of Cynddylan was set in the seventh century. This was the battle in which king Penda of Mercia defeated and killed king Oswald of Northumbria, and Cynddylan's role there, if it were a historical fact, could only have been as an ally of Penda. The *Canu Heledd* cycle, however, is a lament for the loss of Cynddylan's kingdom to English enemies who could only be Mercians. There is no way in which the *Canu Heledd* poems can represent genuine historical traditions of seventh-century events. Many scholars have accepted them as a historical source, but there have been dissentient voices, most notably Ifor Williams,[11] whose views were taken up by H.P.R. Finberg[12] as offering the only means by which a sensible reconstruction could be made of the seventh century in Shropshire. A new discussion of the poems by Dr J. Rowland in a forthcoming book will probably release historians from any obligation to try to make sense of *Canu Heledd*.[13] Dr Rowland also provides a convincing explanation of the *Marwnad Cynddylan* and the battle which it describes near Lichfield. Any historical events which underlie the poem were part of the war between Mercia and Northumbria.

The occurrence in *Canu Heledd* of a number of Shropshire placenames shows that when these poems were composed, in the ninth century or perhaps later, the people of Powys knew that their kingdom had once extended over that county. It seems reasonably clear that the River Tern in eastern Shropshire was remembered as their ancient boundary. But before discussing the Shropshire names which occur in *Canu Heledd* it is desirable to consider the evidence concerning the site of the battle of *Cogwy/Maserfelth*, and the almost universally accepted identification with Oswestry.

Oswestry is an Old English name meaning 'Oswald's tree'. It is not recorded till *c.* 1180 (when it appears in Shrewsbury abbey's cartulary as the name of the site of a Norman castle), but it is a type of name which can confidently be ascribed to the pre-Conquest period. In the Domesday Survey the castle had a French name, *Luvre*, and the manor in which it stood was called *Meresberie*. This last survives as modern Maesbury, the name of a hamlet two and a half miles south of Oswestry, and it means 'manor of the boundary'. The estate later acquired a French name, *Blancmuster*, and a Latin one, *Album Monasterium*, both meaning 'white collegiate church'. The French and Latin names alternate with *Oswaldestre* in records till 1300, after which

Oswaldestre becomes the commonest one. Maesbury is well documented in the late thirteenth and early fourteenth centuries as one of the settlements in this large estate, and it seems clear that the centre of administration shifted from Maesbury in the southern part to Oswestry on its northern edge when the Norman castle was built there.

If there had been no question of an association with king Oswald of Northumbria, Oswestry would have seemed a normal specimen of a well-evidenced type of placename in which the genitive of an Old English personal name (frequently dithematic) is combined with the word *tree*. Thirty-eight examples which are either settlement names or names of meeting places are known,[14] and an uncounted number is to be found in the boundary clauses of Anglo-Saxon charters. Situation on a boundary is a marked characteristic of these names. The present writer believes the original *Oswaldestrēow* to have been a boundry marker on the northern edge of Maesbury. The Welsh and English traditions which made this the site of the battle of 642 may have been encouraged by a superficial resemblance between the name *Maserfelth*, by which Bede refers to it, and *Meresbyrig*. There was similar tradition at a place called Oswald's Tump in Marshfield in Gloucestershire.[15]

The church at Oswestry was dedicated to St Oswald probably because the placename suggested him as the appropriate saint. There are parallels for this, such as Atcham (Shropshire), Boston (Lincolnshire) and Warburton (Cheshire). The association was doubtless fostered by the priests who served there. The church is called *Ecclesia Sancti Oswaldi* in 1121 in the Shrewsbury cartulary, and this is by implication the earliest record of the placename. The interpretation of Oswestry as 'cross of St Oswald' becomes explicit in the late twelfth century, when Gerald of Wales translates it as 'the tree of St Oswald', and in the thirteenth century the Welsh form *Croes Oswallt* appears in records. But the battle of 642 is called *Maserfelth* by Bede and *Maes Cogwy* in the Welsh poetry, and nothing corresponding to those names is to be found in this neighbourhood. There can be no way of demonstrating that the battle did not take place at Oswestry, but there is no firm evidence to show that it did. The occurrence of the personal name Penda in Penley (Flintshire), some ten miles from Oswestry, is of very doubtful relevance. Penley was translated into Welsh as *Llannerch Banna*,[16] using the correct Welsh equivalent (Panna) of Penda; but this does not prove that the reference is to the king. Penda is the first element of other names, such as Pinbury (Gloucestershire), Pinley (Warwickshire) and Pinvin (Worcestershire), and it is probable that other Mercians were called by it.

The contexts in which placenames occur in *Canu Heledd* are mostly vague, but there is a precise reference to Baschurch (Shropshire), which is said to be the burial place of Cynddylan. The name is translated into Welsh as *Eglwysseu Bassa*, and Dr Rowland has pointed out to me that the use of the plural 'churches' suggests that the poet imagined the place as a Celtic *clas* with many small shrines. The poet's choice of Baschurch as Cynddylan's resting place may have been partly due to the presence in the parish of the great earthwork called The Berth. Traditions of Dark Age activity there were perhaps current in the ninth century as they were in later times. The poet may also have wanted a -church placename for this context, and these are rare in England, Whitchurch being the only other one in Shropshire.

Baschurch is in the western half of Shropshire. The name *Tren*, which occurs frequently in the poems, is considered to be the River Tern in the eastern part of the county. Sometimes in the poems *Tren* seems to be a district name: Cynddylan is said to have defended *Tren*, his patronymy, and the English are said to come through *Tren*. In other stanzas *Tren* is a settlement – an unfortunate, splendid, desolate town. It also occurs as a river name in some stanzas in which it is mistakenly said to flow into the Roden.

One stanza refers to Ercall. This is a placename, probably of English origin, which belongs to two settlements, High and Child's Ercall, which are six and a half miles apart and on either side of the River Tern. There is also a large hill called The Ercall, which is part of the same massif as the Wrekin, and lies six miles south-east of High Ercall. If, as seems probable, Ercall (Old English *Earcaluw*) was a district name, the statement in the poem that 'the sod of Ercall is on brave men' could be a general reference to fighing over the eastern part of the north Shropshire plain.

In another stanza Heledd says that she has looked out from *Dinlle Ureconn*. This is naturally interpreted as a reference to the Wrekin, but the form *Ureconn* can only be based on the English development of the ancient British name *Uricon*, since the British name would have become *Gwrygon* in Welsh.

There are two other placenames in *Canu Heledd* which require consideration here: *Pengwern* and *Drefwen*. *Pengwern* is frequently named as the central place of Cynddylan's kingdom, his ruined hall being *Llys Bengwern* in the first stanza. There is a comprehensive discussion in Dr Rowland's book of the identifications which have been offered for *Pengwern*. The earliest is that of Gerald of Wales, who stated that it was Shrewsbury; but no convincing case has been made for this or for any other identification. *Drefwen* has frequently been considered to be a Welsh version of Whittington, near Oswestry. It is the subject of a poem in the cycle, each stanza of which begins 'Drefwen . . .' One stanza says it is 'on the slope of the woods', another describes it as 'in its valley', and the final two stanzas say it lies 'between Tren and Rhodwydd' and 'between Tren and Trafal'. *Rhodwydd* and *Trafal* present difficult prob¹ ⹂ms, also comprehensively discussed by Dr Rowland; but however they are interpreted neither phrase constitutes a useful description of the whereabouts of *Drefwen*. If it is Whittington it is a slightly incorrect translation, as the English name is more likely to be 'settlement associated with a man named Hwīta' (Old English *Hwītingtūn*) than '[at the] white settlement' (*Hwītantūne*). This is not a serious objection to the identification. Whittington is called *Trefwen* in 1254, in the Valuation of Norwich, and the name may well have been considered to mean 'white settlement' by both English and Welsh speakers from the ninth century onwards. Dr Rowland, however, suggests very plausibly that *Drefwen* is not a name but a descriptive term meaning 'fair town'.

Perhaps the only fragment of historical information to emerge from the Welsh poetry is that the River Tern was remembered as the eastern boundary of Powys before Shropshire became part of Mercia. The poems cannot be taken as evidence for a Mercian conquest in the seventh century. Warfare in the region at that date was between the English kingdoms of Northumbria and Mercia, with Welsh forces participating as allies of the latter.

There is no record of a conquest of western Mercia in English sources. At the battle of Chester (613×16) king Æthelfrith of Northumbria defeated a British

army led by a son of the king of Powys;[17] and this victory was accompanied by
the slaughter of a host of British monks from the monastery of Bangor Iscoed.
Æthelfrith may have had plans for adding Powys to his kingdom, but if so they
perished with him when he was killed by Rædwald of East Anglia in 616. There
is no way of knowing how far east the British kingdom of Powys extended at
the date of the battle of Chester. It is possible that the area which later became
Shropshire was already part of Mercia. It was certainly not conquered by
Penda, though it may well have been part of the greater Mercian kingdom
which he put together between *c*. 630 and the middle of the century. Penda's
frenetic warfare was conducted against Wessex, Northumbria and East Anglia.
No record suggests that he ever fought against the Britons of Wales, and kings
of Gwynedd accompanied him on two vital occasions, the killing of Edwin of
Northumbria in 633 and the campaign which ended in the defeat at the
Winwæd in 654. The kingdom of the Magonsæte, comprising Herefordshire
and south Shropshire, was created by Penda for one of his sons, who took the
name Merewalh, 'famous Welshman', presumably as a compliment to his
subjects.

Probably the areas which later became Herefordshire and Shropshire were
absorbed into Mercia by agreement. There seem to have been two ruling
houses in Powys,[18] and a federate structure might have facilitated the accession of part of the kingdom to Mercia. Penda cannot have fought and conquered
all the peoples who were included in his kingdom. For the most part it must
have consisted of self-interested allies; and the price of keeping their allegiance
would be the aggressive warfare by which he won and maintained his status
and from the spoils of which he rewarded his followers. The problem of where
Penda obtained an army for his first recorded victory against the West Saxons
at Cirencester might be solved by assuming that he had the support of the
Welsh people of the West Midlands.

There is no reason to think that the British rulers who were contemporary
with Penda resented the Mercian overlordship of lands which had recently
been British, or that they saw him as a threat to their kinsmen whose lands
marched with his. They would surely have felt resentment on behalf of their
countrymen if those lands had been conquered in the manner adumbrated in
the Welsh poetry. There is much in the history of seventh-century Britain
which indicates that the bearing of long-lasting grudges after military defeat
was an essential ingredient of politics.

The greater Mercia which Penda created is set out in the tax list known as
the Tribal Hidage. The opening statement, *Myrcna landes is thrittig thusend
hyda* ('of the land of the Mercians [the tax] is of thirty thousand hides'), is
glossed by the phrase *thær mon ærest myrcna hæt*. The text only uses *land*
twice, but all the tribal names listed are in the genitive, suggesting that the
word should constantly be supplied by the reader. It is certainly essential in the
phrase *is in middelenglum Færpinga*. If *land* is to be supplied in the phrase
thær mon ærest myrcna hæt, the correct position seems to be after *myrcna*,
and this would give the phrase the meaning 'which is called the first land of the
Mercians'. The reconstructed term *Ærest Myrcnaland* is in fact a district name
meaning 'original Mercia'. Most of this district must have been contained in
the later county of Staffordshire, where hidage assessments in the tenth and
eleventh centuries were extremely low; and as pointed out by Stenton the

figure of 30,000 cannot be taken seriously.[19] The area may have comprised Northern and Southern Mercia, lying on either side of the River Trent, to which Bede ascribed 7,000 and 5,000 hides respectively.[20] It must be considered to centre on Tamworth and Lichfield, and it probably did not extend far to the south of Birmingham.

The Tribal Hidage names two administrative districts of the West Midlands immediately after the opening statement about the tax due from the Mercian heartlands. The next statements are *Wocen sætna is syfan thusend hida. Westerna eacswa.* The emendation of *Wocen* to *Wrocen* is universally accepted, and the Wreocensæte are the people of the north Shropshire plain, named from the Wrekin which (as in other instances of such group names) is on the border of their territory. The Westerne are said by Stenton to be 'probably . . . in Cheshire and north Staffordshire'.[21] If this is correct, the Magonsæte do not appear in the list. If, on the other hand, Westerne is an earlier name for the Magonsæte, the document does not include the people of Cheshire. (It does not seem likely that Cheshire can be included in the Wreocensæte, as the marginality of the Wrekin would then become extraordinary.) Whether the Westerne be located in Cheshire or in Herefordshire, these two groups are as far west as the document goes. The only other people listed who may fall within our area of study are the Arosæte, a people allotted 600 hides, who can plausibly be placed by the River Arrow, a tributary of the River Alne which rises a few miles south of Birmingham and joins the Alne at Alcester (Warwickshire). They cannot be placed on the River Arrow in Herefordshire, as that (in spite of having the same modern spelling) is *Erge* in a document of 958. A possible objection to placing them south of Birmingham is that they would then be in the old diocese of Worcester, and this is thought to be coterminous with the territory of the Hwicce, who (misspelt *Hwinca*) are separately listed in the Tribal Hidage.

The best historical record of events in the later seventh century in western Mercia is probably the tradition concerning the foundation of the priory of Wenlock in Shropshire.[22] This was preserved because a colony of French monks who were established there after the Conquest commissioned Goscelin, a professional hagiographer, to compile a life of St Mildburg, the foundress of the house. St Mildburg was one of the daughters of king Merewalh of the Magonsæte, who was allegedly the third son of Penda; and the foundation can be placed *c.* 685. Goscelin's account includes a copy of an autobiographical statement, professedly drawn up by Mildburg herself towards the close of her life. This includes the texts of several charters by which endowments were given to Mildburg's monastery by her brothers, by king Ceolred of Mercia and by the abbot of *Icanho* of which Wenlock was a daughter house. These are in essence genuine charters of the late seventh and early eighth centuries, but some of the placenames have been 'modernized', so that they appear in post-Conquest forms. This applies to *Lydas* (probably Lyde, Herefordshire), *Clie* (Clee, Shropshire) and *Cheilmers* (Chelmarsh, Shropshire), and it is possible that these English names replaced Welsh ones in the original documents. The monastery itself is referred to as *Wininicas*, a name used also in a charter of 901.[23] The compiler of this charter and Goscelin are both likely to have been using the foundation charter of *c.* 685, which was presumably preserved at Wenlock. *Wininicas* defies complete explanation, but *Win-* must surely be Welsh *gwyn*, 'white'. The monastery is called *Wenlocan, Wynlocan* in a ninth-century text giving the burial places of saints.[24]

Wenlock has always been explained as a Welsh name meaning 'white monastery'; but this presents considerable problems. It is difficult to imagine such a name being coined in the late seventh century in an area where other placename evidence does not suggest the late survival of Welsh speech. If the name had been coined at that date the adjective would have been more likely to come after the noun (as in *Drefwen* in *Canu Heledd*). The word *loc* does not seem likely to have been an active Welsh placename-forming term in the late seventh century. Modern Welsh *llog*, Old Welsh *loc*, from Latin *locus*, 'place', is discussed by Professor G.O. Pierce.[25] Latin *locus* did acquire a religious significance, and it was adopted into Welsh with the meaning 'monastery'; but although well represented in placenames in Brittany, it is exceedingly rare in Wales, and Professor Pierce only cites a single instance in the *Liber Landavensis*. A recent study of the corresponding Cornish word concludes that there is only one instance in Cornish placenames, and points out that the *Lok-* names in Brittany date from the eleventh century or later.[26] It is possible that what we have in Wenlock is rather the English word *loca*, 'enclosed place', which might have been combined with the first syllable of *Wininicas*. The whiteness referred to could be that of the limestone of Wenlock Edge, rather than the monastery buildings. Behind the name Wenlock there may be a pre-English district name meaning something like 'white area'. Rumours in 1986 that a late Roman Christian church had been found beneath the medieval buildings of the priory suggested the exciting possibility that the name went back to Roman times. If so, Wenlock would have had the structure usual in Romano-British names, and it would have seemed reasonable to postulate a transient use of *locus* in the sense 'religious place' at the end of the Roman period. Subsequent information states that the Roman building does not have the features of a church, but the excavator nevertheless considers that the relationship to it of later buildings suggests respect due to an earlier Christian structure.[27] The walls of the Roman building were certainly standing when the seventh-century monastery was built, so it is possible that the name refers to it.

In accordance with the possibility of Wen- being the remnant of a pre-English district name, Wenlock has been shown on fig. 13.1 as the name of the limestone escarpment rather than of the monastery. This is highly speculative, but it seems virtually certain that part at least of the name is pre-English, and it therefore deserves inclusion on the map in one position or the other. The map emphasizes the extreme rarity of pre-English names in this part of Shropshire, and this makes it difficult to envisage the creation of a new name in Welsh c. 685. Even the largest features of the landscape in this area, like the Clee Hills and the River Corve, were renamed in the English language.

An attempt has been made on figs 13.1–5 to plot all names in western Mercia which can be used as indications of linguistic contact between Welsh and English speakers up to the time of the construction of Offa's Dyke at the end of the eighth century. English names containing *walh* and *cumbre* are included. Welsh names of medieval or modern origin in Herefordshire, west Shropshire and parts of Cheshire have not been plotted.

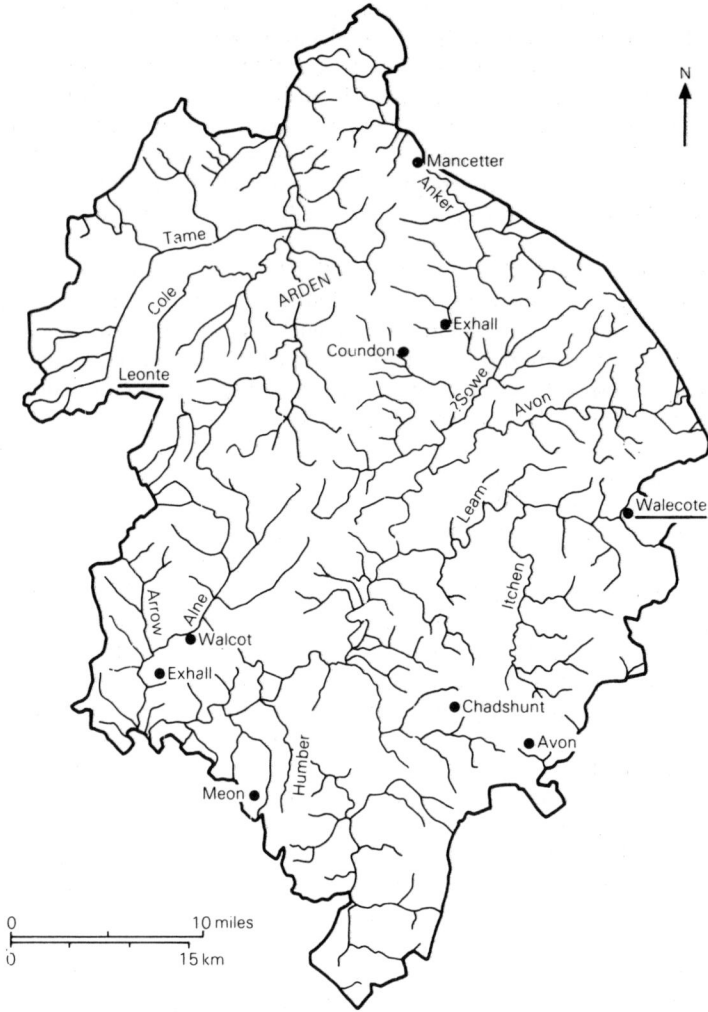

Figure 13.1. Warwickshire: placenames which are pre-English or of related significance.

The absence, except in south Warwickshire, of significant archaeological evidence for an early Anglo-Saxon presence would have seemed consistent with a much denser coverage of pre-English placenames. The facts, however, appear to be roughly as presented on these maps. In the last three decades of placename study much care has been taken to distinguish pre-English names, and it is unlikely that the corpus now recognized will be significantly increased by further research. Items are now more likely to be deleted from these maps than to be added to them.

Surviving pre-English names are extremely sparse in Warwickshire and only a little more frequent in Staffordshire (figs 13.1–2). In these two counties this may reasonably be ascribed to a considerable Anglo-Saxon presence. The pagan

Figure 13.2. Staffordshire: placenames which are pre-English or of related significance.

cemeteries of south Warwickshire and the adjacent part of Worcestershire are not large enough to represent a reservoir from which regions further west could have drawn an English population; but they do provide evidence for a community of Anglo-Saxon farmers from *c.* 500, and they are spread over quite a wide area. Staffordshire has only a few cemeteries along the Trent, in the east of the county; but since this county must contain the greater part of the entity which the Tribal Hidage calls 'Original Mercia', a considerable English presence must be presumed, even if it is not attested by pagan burials. A large

settlement has been excavated at Catholme, north of Tamworth, and this is
dated by radiocarbon to the Anglo-Saxon period and contains houses of Anglo-
Saxon type. Unfortunately the site was characterized by a remarkable scarcity
of diagnostic small finds.

In Cheshire, Shropshire and Herefordshire there is no archaeological trace of
pagan Anglo-Saxons. In Herefordshire (fig. 13.3) the linguistic evidence does
not compel an assumption of English dominance, though it is noteworthy that
English parish names, like Craswall and Knill, occur on the western boundary.
Celtic names which may be considered at least as old as the Roman period are
relatively numerous, however, and it is important to note that some Welsh
names for places of administrative importance, though post-Roman in form,
may be taken to represent a continuous linguistic history. Parish names like
Llanwarne, Llandinabo, Hentland and Tretire, which are interspersed in
Archenfield with more ancient Welsh names like Ross and Pencoyd, are a
different phenomenon from the minor names like Bron-y-wern or Llwyn-y-
mapsis, which are frequent in the westernmost parishes of Shropshire. Some
Welsh names on the Shropshire border are obvious translations from English,
like Trebirt and Treverward representing *Burton* and *Burwarton*.[28] The

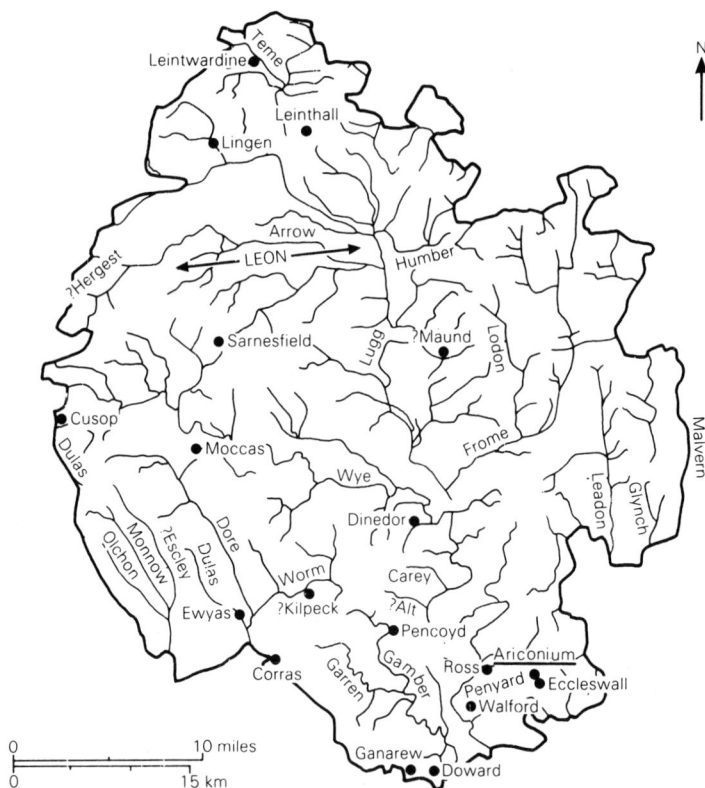

Figure 13.3. Herefordshire: placenames which are pre-English or of related
significance.

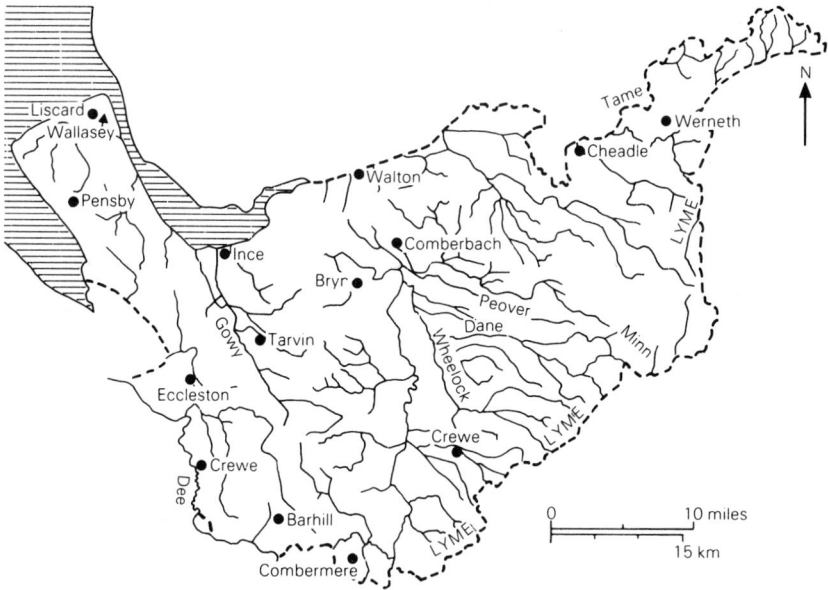

Figure 13.4. Cheshire: placenames which are pre-English or of related significance.

opposite process is manifested in Archenfield by names which are English translations from Welsh, such as Mawfield (*Mais Mail Lochou* in *Liber Landavensis*) and Kenderchurch (*Lanncinitir* in *ibid.*). In Shropshire there is a Walcot in Chirbury parish on the west boundary of the county. This name is now considered to denote a hamlet in which Welsh was still spoken when the surrounding people were using English.[29] The apparent absence of such names from Herefordshire may indicate that Welsh speech was never exceptional there.

In Cheshire and Shropshire (figs 13.4–5) the English language must have prevailed and have been employed for a wholesale replacement of Welsh names by English ones. It seems unlikely that this can have been due to the numerical superiority of English farmers, so it has to be ascribed to the social and administrative superiority of a relatively modest number of Mercians. Administrative usage by Mercian governors may partly explain the loss of Welsh placenames, especially in Shropshire. One of the most striking features of Shropshire placenames is the frequent recurrence of some compounds with *tūn*, a placename element known to have become fashionable in the mid-eighth century.[30]

The 'directional' names, Aston, Weston, Norton and Sutton, occur in Shropshire ten, eight, seven and eight times respectively, and there are five Uptons, four Middletons and ten Newtons. Acton ('oak settlement') occurs eight times, Eaton ('river settlement') six, and Eyton ('island settlement') five. There are four instances of Hatton ('heath settlement'), Mor(e)ton ('marsh settlement') and Wootton ('wood settlement'). It is possible that such names were originally convenient labels used by Mercian administrators when referring to the component parts of large estates. Some, like Eaton and Hatton, could refer to the special contributions made by a place to a larger economic unit. Other names which are not so frequently repeated could have a similar origin: R(u)yton, of which Shropshire has three instances, could have been coined for an ancient settlement   hich embarked on a new type of farming with greater use of rye. Preston, 'estate of the priests', of which Shropshire has five examples, could not have been the earliest name of any settlement. In other English counties it can occasionally be demonstrated that names of the Preston type have replaced earlier English names; in Shropshire, on the other hand, they may have been used by Mercian administrators in preference to locally current Welsh names. If such descriptive compounds were applied to settlements in recognition of their role in a wider economy, they may have come to be perceived fairly gradually as proper names, and have displaced earlier Welsh toponyms. There is only one British name (Lingen, Hereford-

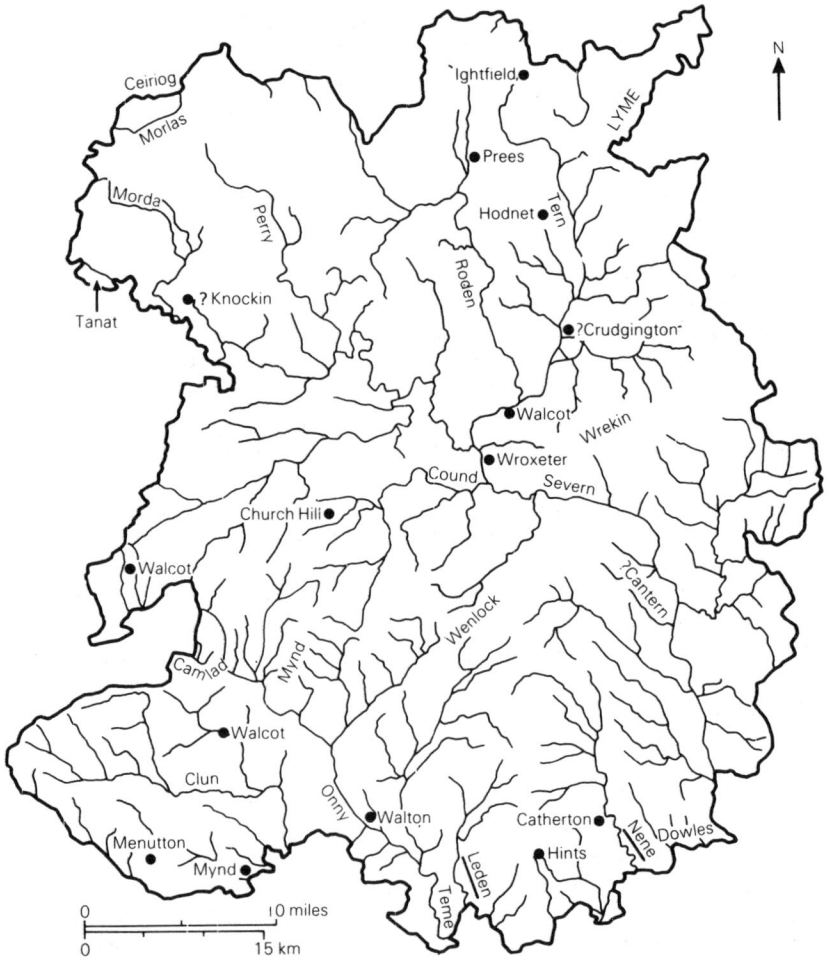

Figure 13.2. Shropshire: placenames which are pre-English or of related significance.

shire) in the Testament of St Mildburg, but, as noted above, a number of names which occur there have forms which are not correct for the late seventh century. As far as we can judge from our sparse records, Welsh names could have persisted in Shropshire until well into the eighth century.

Shropshire has at least a normal share of the type of name which means 'x's estate', like Alcaston ('Alhmund's *tūn*') and Dudston ('Dud's *tūn*'), and also of those in which -*ingtūn* is added to a personal name to give a slightly variant possessive sense, such as 'estate associated with x'. There are four instances of *Dod(d)ingtūn* and three of *Dunningtūn* (the first group have variant modern forms Dodington, Detton, Ditton, Derrington, and great care has been required in the assignment of Middle English spellings). This aspect of the repetitious nature of Shropshire names could be due to the acquisition of these estates by Mercian overlords at a time when the -*ingtūn* formula was fashionable and *Dod(d)a* and *Dunna* were common personal names. In counties where documentation is less sparse it can occasionally be demonstrated that a 'manorial' English name replaced either a British name (as Bibury replaced *Colne* in Gloucestershire in the second quarter of the eighth century) or an earlier type of English name (as Woolstone and Uffington replaced *Æscesbyrig* in Berkshire in the second half of the tenth century).[31] In Shropshire and perhaps also in Cheshire it is a reasonable assumption that some British names were superseded when estates acquired new Mercian overlords.

English placenames which are likely to be at least as old as the eighth century occur in a two-mile-wide belt to the west of the course of Offa's Dyke through Shropshire and Cheshire. In Herefordshire the Dyke runs between Mansell Gamage and Mansell Lacy, two settlements which share the same, English, name. Because of this relationship to English names it used to be thought that some English territory was abandoned by Offa.[32] The most recent study of the Dyke, however, establishes the probability that it was a patrol line, set back from the actual frontier.[33] The earthwork regularly bisects parishes, and most historians today would probably agree that this is an indication that the land-units had been formed before the Dyke was made, and that they continued to operate as units afterwards. It seems likely that English-speaking farmers living to the west of the Dyke continued to work their land under the protection of patrols riding along the earthwork.

Frank Noble believed that some idea of how the frontier operated could be obtained from the study of an Old English text known as The Ordinance concerning the Dunsæte.[34] This text, which dates from the tenth century, sets out laws governing the relationships between Welsh and English people living on either side of a river. The river is not named, but it is obviously the Wye in Herefordshire. There is no internal indication that an earlier text has been adapted, and there is nothing to connect this law code directly with Offa's Dyke; but it does not seem unduly fanciful to postulate a similar codification of frontier relationships at the end of the eighth century.

There may be a trace in placenames along Offa's Dyke of an administrative reorganization at this date. There is a series of names stretching from Oswestry to Hereford which are formed with the suffix -*sæte* ('dwellers'), but which refer to much smaller units than those designated by the names Magonsæte and Wreocensæte, which are probably of greater antiquity. These are shown on fig. 13.6. *Meresæte, Rhiwsæte* and *Stepelsæte* were names of hundredal divisions.

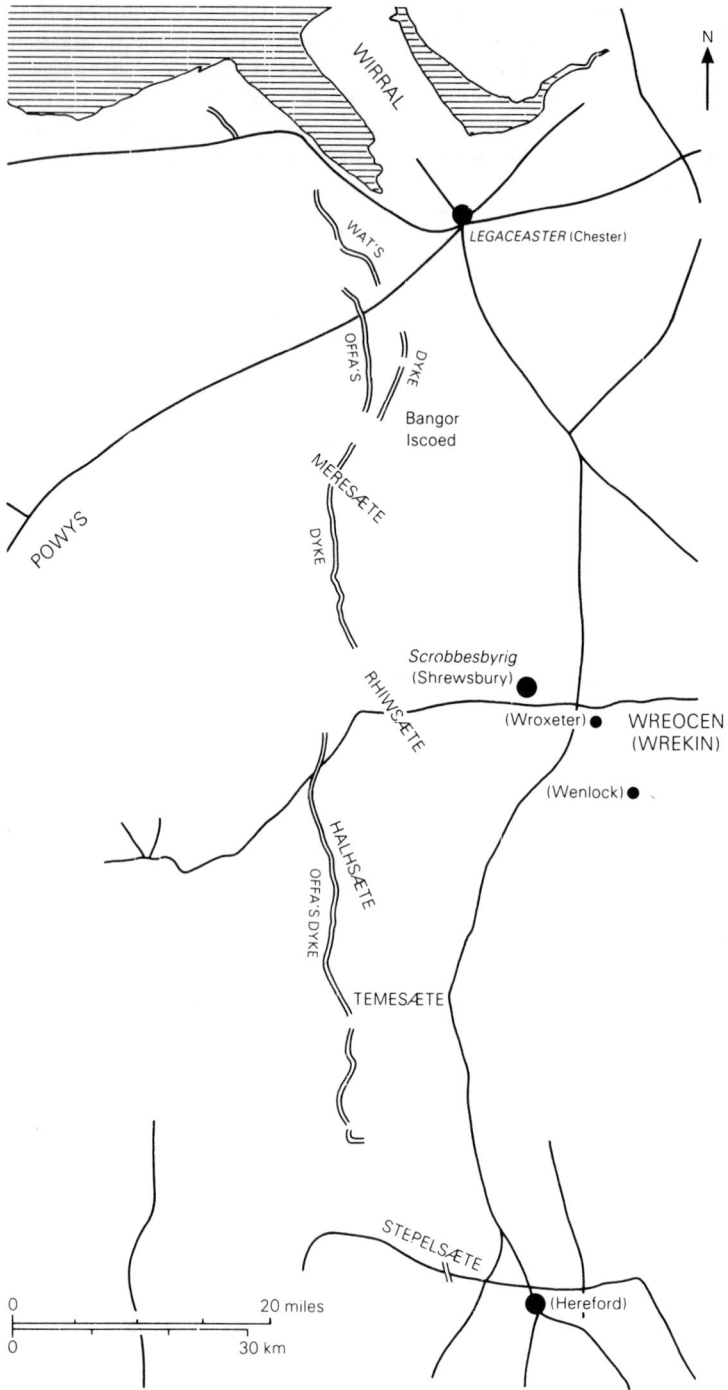

Figure 13.6. -sæte names along Offa's Dyke.

Halhsǽte persisted (in the later form *Alcester*) into the sixteenth century as the name of a district in the parish of Church Stoke (Montgomeryshire). *Temesǽte*, later *Tempsiter*, was the name of the southern portion of the Honour of Clun. There is a degree of regularity in the size and spacing of these units which suggests an arbitrary origin, and they may have been created by the ruler of Mercia when the frontier was defined and arrangements were made for its maintenance.

14 Lindsey

BRUCE EAGLES

The present boundaries of Lindsey are in all probability essentially those of the 7,000 hides of Lindsey and Hatfield which are recorded together in the Tribal Hidage and also those of the diocese of Lindsey which was established in 678.[1] Hatfield was formerly an area mainly of moor and marsh lying immediately west of the Isle of Axholme, an island of Keuper Marl which rises to some 44m above the surrounding fen, and which was the only part of Lindsey west of the River Trent. On all sides Lindsey is defined by river, fen or the sea. In the north Lindsey reaches the Humber estuary and in the east the sea coast. The southern limits are less precisely marked. For the most part the boundary here follows the River Witham, although north and east of Boston the present line takes an erratic course between parishes across the fen. At Lincoln the Witham flows through the Lincoln Gap in the Lincolnshire Cliff. For some 6km to the west the boundary follows the Fossdyke, a canal probably of Roman date cut to link the Trent and Witham which in this section utilized the straightened channel of the River Till. The remaining 11km of frontier follow an irregular course across Tertiary sands and gravels to the Trent at Newton-upon-Trent.[2]

The grain of Lindsey runs markedly from north to south, the main natural divisions following the Vale of Trent and the valleys of the Ancholme and Langworth. The region is dominated by two areas of high ground: the limestone Cliff – in places above 61m – between the Trent and the Ancholme, and the chalk Wolds east of Ancholme which rise to some 170m at their highest, south of Caistor.

In the Roman period Lincoln (*Lindum colonia*) was situated in the northern part of the *civitas Corieltauvorum*, which was centred upon Leicester (*Ratae Corieltauvorum*).[3] The boundaries of the *civitas* on the west and south are very uncertain. In the south the River Nene may have been the limit.[4] The boundary at the north-west is discussed below. The *civitas* would have been divided into smaller administrative units (*pagi*), but none of these has been identified within Lindsey. Lincoln had its own *territorium*; its extent is unknown but a milestone found in Bailgate, Lincoln, whose inscription is possibly to be expanded to read *a L(indo) S(egelocum) m(ilia) p(assuum) XIIII*, may indicate that Littleborough (*Segelocum*) on the Trent lay within the city's territory.[5]

In the fourth century it is probable that Lincoln was a provincial capital.[6] Soon after 197 the emperor Severus had divided Britain into two provinces, Superior (in the south) and Inferior. Diocletian created four provinces, probably by further subdivision. The names of the new provinces are recorded in the *Notitia Dignitatum* and those of their capitals, apparently, in the list of metropolitan bishops who attended the Council of Arles in 314. It seems likely that Britannia Superior was split between Prima (in Wales and the south-west) and Maxima Caesariensis, whose capital was almost certainly at London. Britannia Inferior became Secunda and Flavia Caesariensis. Flavia and Maxima together may have previously formed a short-lived province of Caesariensis.[7] If so, this would indicate that Flavia occupied the southern part of Inferior. Since both Lincoln and York had been in Inferior, it is probable that Lincoln became the capital of Flavia Caesariensis and York of Secunda.

Each new province may have comprised a group of existing *civitates*, whose boundaries it retained. Flavia Caesariensis probably included the territories of both the Corieltauvi and the Iceni. This is suggested by the title of the Count of the Saxon Shore (*comes litoris Saxonici per Britannias*) which shows that his command, which stretched from Portchester, most probably in Maxima Caesariensis, to the Wash, extended through more than one province and therefore into Flavia Caesariensis.[8]

At the north-west Flavia Caesariensis bordered Britannia Secunda.

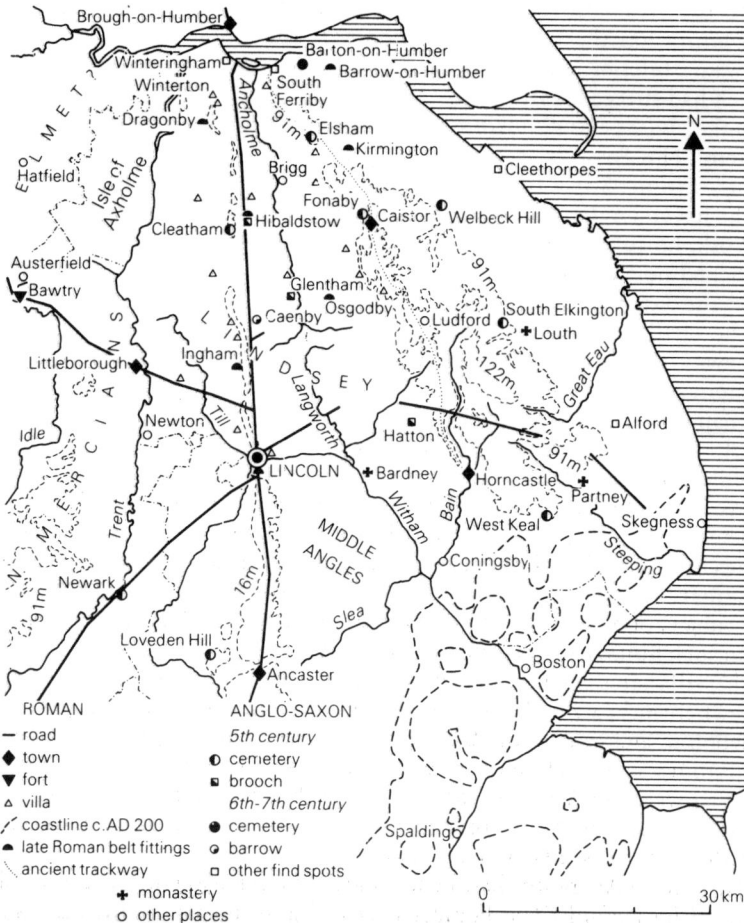

Figure 14.1. Lindsey and its environs, showing Romano-British and early Anglo-Saxon sites mentioned in the text.

Secunda's governor combined both military and civilian duties.[9] By 369 his military functions had passed to the *dux Britanniarum*, whose title apparently implies that Secunda had been subdivided, a change probably to be associated with the creation of a new province of Valentia, whose capital is also likely to have been at York.[10] If the fort – a triple-ditched enclosure of less than one acre – on the River Idle at Bawtry, which limited excavation has shown to have been occupied in the reign of Julian (355–63) or later,[11] was under the *dux*, it may be suggested that the Idle, at that point at least, formed part of the common boundary of Caesariensis and Valentia (and earlier of Secunda). However, since Bawtry is not listed in the *Notitia Dignitatum*, it is possible either that it had been evacuated by the date when the *Notitia* list was compiled, possibly in the early fifth century, or that it had been held by a detachment of the field army, whose units were not included in the *Notitia*.[12] If the argument that the River Idle near Bawtry formed part of the boundary of the Roman military district is accepted, it might reasonably be deduced that there the river also divided the *civitas Corieltauvorum* from the *civitas Brigantum*, on the likely assumption that the whole of the latter was in Britannia Inferior (and in the provinces of Secunda and probably Valentia, which had succeeded it).

In the *civitas Corieltauvorum* Lincoln served as a focus for the Roman road system. The Fosse Way connected Lincoln with Leicester and the south-west.[13] Ermine Street from London led northwards along the limestone ridge to the haven on the Humber at Winteringham. The direct route from London to York, however, avoided the Humber crossing and, 7km north of Lincoln, branched north-west from Ermine Street to pass along Tillbridge Lane and cross the Trent at Littleborough *en route* to Doncaster (*Danum*).[14]

The chalk Wolds were similarly served by a through-route. This was a ridgeway, not a metalled Roman road, which kept close to the generally steep western escarpment of the Wolds, less high in the north. Caistor High Street is the name given to it between Horncastle in the clay Wolds and Caistor; further north, as far as the Humber at South Ferriby, this native route is known as Middlegate Lane. The clay Wolds are an area of generally high ground, reaching above 91m, and are characterized by an extensive cover of chalky boulder clay.

The relative prosperity of the chalk Wolds and the limestone Cliff in Roman times is indicated by the distribution of villas in Lindsey.[15] There is very little information about most of them. Only one, at Winterton on the Cliff, has been the subject of modern and meticulous excavation,[16] and most are known only from such hints as tesserae or hypocaust tile found scattered in modern arable. Eight villa sites have been recognized on the Cliff and six on the Wolds. Elsewhere just two are known in the Vale of Trent, one in the clayland near the Ancholme and one on the Liassic escarpment. The Lias, where a variety of limestones, clays and ironstone are mostly overlaid by blown sand, rises above 61m between the Vale and the Cliff in north-west Lindsey. There is no villa known in the clay Wolds, the Steeping valley to their south-east, the eastern dip-slope of the Wolds, or the marshes.

The Vale of Ancholme had a wide marshy floor between, to the west, slopes covered by Oxford Clay, boulder clay and gravels and, to the east, similar deposits with Kimmeridge Clay and extensive blown sands. Crossing places are few; the shortest of them is at Brigg. Although no Roman road has been recognized there, it is likely that one existed for the route is continued north-east by a natural passage through the Wolds, the Kirmington Gap. Other crossings of the Vale are suggested by two metalled Roman roads, one of which branched north-east from Ermine Street at Fillingham and another which left Lincoln by the east gate and headed towards the River Langworth. The valley must have suffered from the inundations which resulted from the general rise in sea level at the end of the Roman period.[17] Later on the journey across the Vale near its mouth at the Humber was apparently made by ferry. Domesday Book records two ferries at South Ferriby on the east bank of the Ancholme, and it is likely that one crossed the Humber and the other the Ancholme itself to Winteringham.[18] Finds of the sixth century and later, together with others of Romano-British date, have been exposed in cliff falls at South Ferriby,[19] and a spiral-headed pin, likely to be of the seventh century, and probably a styca of Eanred (c. 835) are recorded from Winteringham.[20] At Glentham, however, a fifth-century cruciform brooch[21] has been recovered from the area of a Romano-British settlement near the river, and there is a seventh-century gold pendant[22] from the same site.

The recognition of the Cliff and the western parts of the Wolds as the most prosperous parts of Lindsey in the Roman period may help to explain the disposition of late Roman defences. At Lincoln there is some evidence to suggest that interval towers were replaced by solid internal platforms.[23] The defences there would have presented a formidable obstacle to barbarian raiders who had arrived at the Wash and approached along the Witham. On the Wolds at Horncastle the Roman walls, which are of the later third century or later, have contemporary projecting towers.[24] They were built on a new site, adjacent to an unwalled settlement of some 135 acres which was occupied throughout the Roman period. The military site lies on a naturally defensible terrace at the confluence of and between the Rivers Bain and Waring, tributaries of the Witham. It has recently been recognized that silts of an estuarine type (probably late Roman or later date) on the Bain at Coningsby may well mark an inlet of the sea, only some 9km south of Horncastle.[25] Horncastle was therefore of strategic defensive importance. Less is known of the similar fortifications at Caistor, where there was also an extramural settlement of unknown extent. Caistor dominates the Ancholme valley, and the construction of these defences indicates the military importance which was attached to it and the main north–south route along the Wolds. It has been suggested that Caistor and Horncastle, together with perhaps a site lost off Skegness and with Brough-on-Humber, served as a northern extension of the system of Saxon Shore forts, and provided defence for the coastline and its hinterland between the Wash and the Humber.[26]

Other late Roman defensive measures are less easily discerned. A possible source of evidence is the chip-carved belt equipment of the second half of the fourth century.[27] Such items, particularly buckle loops, are fairly widespread in north Lincolnshire.[28] Some of the wider buckles of Types II and III were certainly associated with the *cingulum*, the broad leather belt worn by officers and officials.

Two buckles of Type IIIA were probably imported. One from Hibaldstow, a site on Ermine Street and probably a posting station, was recovered during excavations from a layer of rubble overlying a third- to fourth-century building.[29] The other is from a probable rural settlement at Ingham, west of Ermine Street; the site has produced coins of the House of Valentinian.[30] Insular buckles of Type IIA are known from Dragonby,[31] Kirmington[32] and Lincoln.[33] The site of Dragonby on the Liassic escarpment near Scunthorpe was a settlement occupied in the Iron Age and throughout the Roman period. Kirmington was also an extensive settlement; it lies where an ancient route along the Wolds, defined for almost its entire length by parish boundaries and roughly parallel to the present Middlegate Lane, crosses the Kirmington Gap, a natural passage through the Wolds. The piece from Lincoln was found unstratified during excavations in 1968 at the west gate of the lower walled area at The Park. A buckle from Barrow-on-Humber[34] is akin to Type IIC. It is a surface find, and from the same field there are a crossbow brooch and a pot, buried c. 395, which contained a hoard of silver *siliquae*.

The belt buckles of Type I are much narrower than those of Types II and III. Some examples have been found in female Anglo-Saxon graves. A Type IA buckle is known from Osgodby, a settlement on the road from Fillingham.[35] Two other examples of IA and one of IB are from Kirmington.[36]

It is difficult to know how many of these buckles belonged to soldiers.[37] Units of the *comitatenses*, the field army, when in Britain may have been billeted from time to time at Lincoln. Other places such as Hibaldstow may have had an official function. However, it is possible that some buckles were worn by other civilians, who copied military and civil service fashion.[38]

There is evidence for some survival of the Romano-British population after the early fifth century. Romano-British sites and others of the pagan Anglo-Saxon period, which vary in their nature from the chance discovery of potsherds or other objects to excavated hut remains or burials, have been recognized within or immediately adjacent to medieval and later settlements in all the regions of Lindsey. In many cases there is a likelihood that the places have been continuously occupied.[39] At Hibaldstow the evidence hints at a local shift in the location of the settlement. St Higebold was buried on *Cecesege* ('Cec's island') near the River *Oncel* (Ancholme), probably Hibaldstow.[40] 'Cec's island' suggests a location in a loop of the river; the Romano-British settlement, where there was a very early Germanic presence (below, p. 208), was on Ermine Street in the same parish but on the high ground to the west. There are also indications that some placenames and river names were passed to the Anglo-Saxons by the native Brittonic-speaking population. Further, the occurrence of the British name Cædbæd in the pedigree of the ruling house of Lindsey may show inter-marriage between Anglo-Saxons and Britons at the highest social level (although not necessarily with a local British family).

The name of Lincoln itself is certainly derived, through Brittonic speech, from the Latin name of the city.[41] Horncastle appears to be a translation of the Roman name *Bannovalium*, where British *banno* means 'horn, spur (of land)'.[42] The river name Trent was certainly borrowed from the British population, and the names Humber, Ancholme and Witham may also have been.[43] There are also three Wykeham names in Lindsey, which have been shown to be derived from O.E. *wīchām*.[44] One belonged to a lost settlement in Nettleton parish immediately south of Caistor. The others were respectively 0.8km and 2.5km south-east of a large Romano-British settlement at Ludford;[45] the nearer instance occurs in the parish of Ludford, the further one in its own small parish of East Wykeham whose bounds suggest that it had once been an integral part of Ludford. The O.E. word appears to have had a specific connection with Latin *vicus*, but it has been pointed out that the usage is quite unspecific and suggests a careless attitude on the part of the Germanic settlers to the proper meaning(s) of the term.[46] *wīchām* may also have been used of a district dependent on a *vicus*.[47]

At Lincoln itself excavations within the Roman forum in the upper walled area at St Paul-in-the-Bail have revealed the site of a wooden church and a Christian cemetery.[48] Much of the outline of the church was uncovered. The building had an apsidal east end and was orientated precisely on the axis of the forum buildings around it. Its floor appears to have utilized the paving of the forum itself, whose slabs had only been lifted (in rather erratic lines) where it was necessary to excavate beneath them for the church's foundations. It was not possible to uncover the west end of the church, but its proximity to the assumed, although very probable, position of the west porticus of the forum suggests that the church was entered from it, and therefore that both church and forum were in use at the same time. A few fourth-century potsherds were found in one of its construction trenches. The location of the church in the very heart of the Roman city emphasizes the official support it must have received. Its discovery also adds weight to the argument for the existence of a bishop of Lincoln in the fourth century.

The cemetery is of a later period, and on general grounds it is likely to belong to a time when Roman burial law, which forbade interment within the city, was no longer upheld. The graves themselves are dated by radiocarbon determination of the age of the bones. The earliest date of AD 370±80 obtained by this method is from a north–south grave, the only one found with this orientation, which was cut into the soft filling of the foundation trench for the wall or partition which had divided the nave of the church from the apsidal chancel. All the other graves were orientated west–east; their dates range from AD 450±80 through every century until the eleventh. All graves were unfurnished and there was no evidence of coffins. One grave was exceptional. The body had been removed from it in antiquity; but the grave pit, which was lined with slabs, was found to have been dug larger than was necessary. In the extra filling at the west end had been concealed a seventh-century bronze hanging bowl,[49] which was crumpled and probably old at the time of deposition. It is possible that the grave, which occupied a central position within the area of the east end of the nave of the former church, probably near the altar, lay within a rectangular timber structure, which was superseded by one of masonry.

The church and the sequence of graves at St Paul-in-the-Bail suggest, therefore, the maintenance of a strong Christian tradition in the centre of the Roman city. If the dating of the graves is reliable it appears to point to a Christian community which had survived since Roman times. In this connection it is pertinent to notice the British name Cædbæd recorded in the Lindsey royal genealogy; he may possibly have been a ruler of a British population at Lincoln itself. Paulinus built a stone church in the city; however, its site is unknown and it was in ruins in Bede's own day.[50]

The discoveries at St Paul-in-the-Bail suggest that the walled area of Lincoln north of the Witham continued to be occupied after the Roman period. It is likely in general that the defences of late Roman towns, as also those of the Saxon Shore forts and doubtless other places which provided a refuge that was both prestigious and secure, attracted the attention of status- and militarily-minded Anglo-Saxon kings.[51]

There was an extramural suburb of Roman Lincoln on the south side of the river. In the later medieval period that area was known as Wigford, a name whose first element is derived from Old English *wīc* – and possibly ultimately from Latin *vicus*, a term which might indicate the suburb's official ranking in Roman times. Alternatively the name may have been given only in the Anglo-Saxon period to a new trading settlement.[52]

At Lincoln archaeological evidence of the Anglo-Saxons in the pagan period is very slight.[53] It is limited to a girdle-hanger and wrist-clasp,[54] both probably of the sixth century, and a seventh-century spiral-headed pin. There is no reliable information about a cemetery. Single finds of pots have been made at the site of a Romano-British pottery kiln at Rookery Lane and at the Roman villa at Greetwell. A small-long brooch, likely to be of the sixth century, was found in the Fossdyke at Carholme.

The earliest object of certain Germanic origin to have been found in Lindsey is from Kirmington. This is a complete *Tutulus* brooch, which dates probably to the second half of the fourth century.[55] This brooch type was worn by women; it originates in north Germany in the area between the Elbe and Weser. Its occurrence at this site, therefore, suggests a Germanic presence in the settlement. The site at Hibaldstow has recently produced a supporting-arm brooch.[56] It is of Böhme's 'Mahndorf' sub-group and is from the Elbe-Weser region. This brooch was part of female dress; it dates to c. 400.[57] There is also a second example of this type of brooch from Lindsey. It had been burnt, and was recovered as a loose find from the large Anglian cremation cemetery at Elsham.[58] The brooch belongs to Böhme's 'Perlberg' group and is of similar origin and date to the other one.

Therefore at two late Roman sites, Kirmington and Hibaldstow, there is now evidence for the probable presence of Germanic women in the population c. 400. The women perhaps arrived as the wives of German soldiers who had been recruited from beyond the imperial frontiers. The immigrants may have been *laeti*, who are recorded on the Continent from the later third century.[59] *Laeti* were groups of barbarians who were offered settlement on deserted land within the Empire in return for a hereditary obligation to military service; they were organized under Roman prefects. At Hibaldstow on Ermine Street they would have been well placed to protect settlements on the Cliff; and at Kirmington on the Wolds, where there had been a Roman fort,[60] Middlegate Lane and the route through Brigg and the Kirmington Gap make a strategic cross-roads. Such groups perhaps continued to be deployed after the final withdrawal of the field army.

The occurrence of the same type of brooch at both Hibaldstow and the Anglian cremation cemetery at Elsham, which shows no sign of Romano-British influence, indicates the possibility of a chronological continuity between those two sites. If even small numbers of Germans were already established at some Roman settlements by c. 400, later immigrants may have been attracted, or even directed, to the same locality. It is possible that there were similar connections between Hibaldstow and the Anglian cremation cemetery at Cleatham in the parish of Manton only 3km to the south-west of it (earlier finds from this site were recorded from just within the northern limit of Kirton-in-Lindsey, the adjacent parish to the south),[61] and also between Kirmington and the cemetery at Elsham, 5km to its north-west. The cemeteries at Elsham and Cleatham are described immediately below.

The Anglo-Saxon cremation cemetery located on Elsham Wold was excavated in 1975 and 1976 in advance of the construction of the A15 approach road to the Humber Bridge. One edge of the site is bounded by Middlegate Lane which is still in use today. Approximately 630 Anglo-Saxon urns and accompanying cremations were recovered. Individual vessels survived in every condition from a few fragments to substantially undamaged pots, but it seems likely that a significant number of urns had been destroyed by ploughing and other activities without leaving a trace. Four inhumation burials of Anglo-Saxon date were also excavated. It is believed that around 95 per cent of the area of the cemetery was excavated; no evidence was found of the cemetery's having being artificially enclosed.

Dating evidence based on metalwork ranges from the early fifth century, in the form of the supporting-arm brooch already mentioned, to fragments of two late sixth-century 'florid' cruciform brooches. Other metalwork includes the burnt front plates from a pair of applied disc brooches, whose decoration incorporates six human masks.[62] Also indicative of the cemetery's having been in use during the fifth century are twenty-nine triangular-backed combs.[63]

Examination of cremated bone from the urns identified twenty-one apparently double burials, of which the great majority were adults buried with younger persons. Only two instances of two adult cremations buried together in one urn were noted, but the obvious difficulty of distinguishing between the cremated bones of adults after they had been put together makes it likely that more double burials took place than can now be determined. Many cremations were accompanied by burnt animal bones; sheep, deer, pig, cattle and some of the horse bones found may represent no more than joints of meat, but at least five deposits contained sufficient horse bones to indicate that whole animals had been cremated.

At the cemetery at Cleatham some fifty to sixty cremation urns were found in 1856 in a slight mound, perhaps a barrow. In 1979 a trial excavation was conducted to determine the degree of plough damage to the site.[64] The area sampled had suffered severely and in many cases only the bases of the urns remained in position. Further excavations since 1984 have uncovered more than 600 urns and thirty-four inhumations from areas where preservation was better. It has proved possible to recover a large number of urns together with the cremated bone they contained. It is already clear that the cemetery was in use from the fifth century until at least the late sixth. The dating brackets are provided by a barred zoomorphic comb[65] and a Group V cruciform brooch.

Three other well-known cemeteries began in the fifth century: Fonaby on Middlegate Lane near Caistor, where there are both cremations and inhumations;[66] South Elkington near Louth, a wholly cremation site with some 290 urns recorded;[67] and West Keal with more than twenty cremation vessels.[68] All three places have produced, for instance, pots decorated with *stehende Bögen*, a design which lasted little after 500.[69] A grave at Welbeck Hill, Irby, whose contents included a wrist-clasp of Scandinavian ancestry, may belong to the late fifth century.[70] Elkington and Irby are on the dip slope of the Wolds, and the site at West Keal in south-east Lindsey lies above an escarpment which rises sharply from the Roman shore line. Other fifth-century material is the brooch from Glentham mentioned above and another cruciform brooch from Hatton in the clay Wolds.[71]

It has been suggested that in the earliest phases of Anglo-Saxon settlement no distinction was made between the peoples who lived on either side of the Humber. However, although the term 'Northumbrian' can be shown to be no earlier than the mid-seventh century,[72] it is not clear that the *Humbrenses* ever included Anglo-Saxons south of the river.[73] The River Humber must have provided one of the main routes of Anglo-Saxon penetration into this part of England. In Lindsey numerous sites of the pagan period are known along its south bank, and there are other indications of the importance of its tributaries, the Trent (p. 211) and the Ancholme (p. 205). From the Wash immigrants to the southern parts of Lindsey would have used the Steeping valley, where a number of early Anglo-Saxon sites have been recorded, and the Witham and its tributaries (p. 205).

The Anglo-Saxon sites of the sixth and seventh centuries are spread throughout Lindsey,[74] but it is noticeable that none occupies the lowest ground. That is so even in the sea marshes, where an Anglian pot from Cleethorpes was found in Beacon Hill mound[75] and potsherds at Burgh-le-Marsh,[76] where the Roman road from Lincoln, having crossed the Langworth, finally reached a settlement above an inlet of the sea. A cruciform brooch is also recorded from Alford.[77]

The first historical event in Lindsey of which a record survives is the mission of Paulinus of *c.* 627. Paulinus's first convert was Blæcca, a *praefectus* at Lincoln.[78] Although this term is usually translated 'reeve', it is used by 'Eddius' Stephanus of Berhtwald nephew of king Æthelred of Mercia.[79] Berht-wald was probably as powerful as others elsewhere who are described as *regulus* or even *rex*. The kingdom of Lindsey may thus have had an early independent existence, and the genealogy of its alleged kings may represent actual rulers.[80] One of their kings may have been buried in a barrow beside Ermine Street at Caenby 18km north of Lincoln, where the contents of the seventh-century grave included ornate fittings, some of silver, probably from wooden chests or boxes.[81] However, it is by no means certain whether all, or indeed any, of the kings in the genealogy ruled the whole of Lindsey, or whether some of those named were no more than contemporary local rulers of unidentified districts. Indeed, it is possible that, in order to facilitate their own political aims of consolidation in the area, the expanding Northumbria and Mercia themselves encouraged the emergence of a single pre-eminent dynasty in Lindsey. It may not be a coincidence that the first and only king of Lindsey who can be identified in another written source is Aldfrith, who witnessed a charter of king Offa of Mercia.

The territory of the kingdom occupied only the northernmost parts of either the *civitas* of the Corieltauvi or the late Roman province of Flavia Caesariensis. Its Anglo-Saxon name (*provincia*) *Lindissi* or *Lindissae,* which was derived from part of Lincoln's official Roman name *Lindum* (*colonia*),[82] may originally have been restricted to that city's southern suburb at Wigford.[83]

There is no evidence that Lincoln ever exercised authority south of the Witham in the post-Roman period. The region was settled by the Middle Angles, who occupied the area between the territories of the East Angles and the Mercians. The Middle Angles were never ruled by a single dynasty and were apparently a loose grouping of small independent peoples.[84] The names of some of them are recorded in the Tribal Hidage, among them the Spaldingas around Spalding and some others near the Wash. To the north-west, west and south-west of these named groups, however, in the Middle Anglian areas dubbed 'Outer Mercia' by C.R. Hart[85] no other tribal names are known, and it is possible that the peoples there came under Mercian domination earlier and had lost their individual identities. The very large Anglian cremation cemetery at Loveden Hill,[86] in use from the fifth century, may have been located close to one early focus of settlement, for Loveden was the name later given to the wapentake in which the cemetery was located. The first recorded ruler of all the Middle Angles was Peada the son of Penda who granted him the title of *rex* or *princeps.*[87] The extent of Middle Anglian territory may be indicated by that of their diocese of Leicester, which was separated from that of the Mercian see of Lichfield in 679.[88]

When Penda was killed in 655, Oswiu of Northumbria gave Peada authority over the South Mercians. South Mercia, assessed at 5,000 hides, was separated by the River Trent from North Mercia, of 7,000 hides.[89] The boundary between the North Mercians and the Middle Angles, however, may not have followed the river itself but rather the line of the Leicester diocese, which in that area is also part of the present boundary of Nottinghamshire. If so, it took a course south and east of the Trent before rejoining the river at Newton-on-Trent. Between Newton and the Isle of Axholme the North Mercians and Lindsey shared a common boundary along the Trent itself. North Mercian territory by this definition would have included Newark. Newark-on-Trent is situated where the Fosse Way passes beside the river on its south bank. The place was therefore of strategic importance, and for that reason Angles may have been established there under British control in the fifth century, the date when burial began at the Anglian cremation cemetery at Millgate which has produced several hundred urns.[90] This burial ground is comparable in its exceptional size to that, even larger, at Loveden Hill. Each of the two largest early Anglian cemeteries in this part of the East Midlands, therefore, began in the fifth century and each was located in a distinct Anglian territory – Newark in that of the North Mercians and Loveden Hill in that of the Middle Angles. The location of these large groups of Angles relates perhaps to the break-up, soon after the end of Roman rule, of a part of the former *civitas* of the Corieltauvi into separate territories, which may have foreshadowed the later political boundaries, one around Newark which was possibly under British rule and another around Loveden possibly under Anglian control. Such putative princedoms, it may be thought, might have effectively prescribed and defined the limits of the kingdom of Lindsey from an early date.

In the seventh century the boundary of the North Mercians reached the Idle[91] and, from the Trent, probably followed that river along the southern side of the Isle of Axholme as far as Bawtry. Beyond Bawtry the territorial limit of the North Mercians may have taken the line of the present boundary between Nottinghamshire and the West Riding of Yorkshire, which is also probably that of the diocese of Lichfield, founded in 669.[92] Until *c.* 617, when Edwin of Northumbria expelled Ceretic,[93] the whole area north-west of the Nottinghamshire county boundary including Hatfield may have been part of the independent British kingdom of Elmet, itself carved out of the old *civitas Brigantum*.[94]

Political dominance over Lindsey in the seventh century passed between Northumbria and Mercia,[95] and appears to have followed upon the military success of either the one or the other in achieving control of the strategically important Tillbridge Lane, part of the main route from Northumbria to the south. In 616 Edwin of Northumbria won a battle at the River Idle, probably where the road crosses the river at Bawtry. A few years later, when Paulinus baptized large numbers of converts in the Trent at *Tiowulfingacæstir*, probably Littleborough on this same road, the political aspect of the occasion and probably of the location is evident from Edwin's attendance. In 633 Penda of Mercia was victorious at the battle of Hatfield. The location of this battle is uncertain, but whether it was fought near Cuckney in Nottinghamshire[96] or near the low-lying carrs of Hatfield Chase immediately north of the Idle, the Northumbrian army is likely to have arrived by this route. Another battle, at the Trent in 679, was won by Æthelred of Mercia.

There are, therefore, indications of several kinds for the influence of British inhabitants in the Anglo-Saxon kingdom of Lindsey. The earliest Germanic immigrants appear to have arrived by *c.* 400 and to have lived in Romano-British settlements almost certainly under native control. Before 500 there are signs of new Anglian communities particularly on the Wolds. Thereafter, the Anglo-Saxons expanded into all parts of the area. In the seventh century Lindsey lay close to the scene of the incessant warfare on the frontier between Mercia and Northumbria. The splendid burial at Caenby is perhaps that of a Lindsey prince, but if so his trappings betoken no true independence. The absorption of the kingdom into that of one of its larger neighbours was soon to be complete.[97]

15 The origins of Northumbria: some aspects of the British background

DAVID DUMVILLE

To ask about the origins of Anglo-Saxon rule in Northumbria is in fact to pose a number of different questions.[1] How and when did Anglo-Saxon settlement originate in Britain north of the Humber? What was the nature of relations between English and Britons in the North in the fifth, sixth and seventh centuries? How and when did the kingdoms of Deira and Bernicia and their royal dynasties come into existence?

Forty years ago, in what came to be seen as a classic paper, 'The origins of Northumbria', my teacher Peter Hunter Blair gave lengthy consideration to some of these problems. His essay was divided into two sections, 'the Gildas tradition' and 'the veracity of Gildas'.[2] The principle of investigating fifth- and sixth-century history with the primary aid of a sixth-century source is of course a reasonably respectable one. However, whether Gildas provides much usable information on this subject is an arguable matter: he is (in any case) a dangerous witness to whom to cede centrality in this matter, as the long disputes over his general credibility and (now) the area of his interests and information attest all too clearly.[3]

Also, forty years ago, the available archaeological testimony to pre-Christian Anglo-Saxon activity in Northumbria was very slight and barely susceptible of useful interpretation. Now it is much more extensive, though particularly so in Deira rather than Bernicia. But pre-Christian Northumbria has perhaps been fortunate in that few attempts have been made to achieve an integrated interpretation of the literary and the archaeological evidence. As we see in the south, such premature essays in undisciplined integration create models which develop lives of their own, improperly influencing subsequent work on the sources proper to the independent disciplines.[4] This chapter, therefore, commences with an examination of the written sources for the earliest history of English settlement and Anglo-British relations in Northumbria, with no presupposition of course that by themselves they can provide a complete or even necessarily an intelligible account of those processes. As a historian I shall deliberately cast no more than an occasional sideways glance at the archaeological testimony.

The chronological boundaries of the first topic to be considered, the origins of Anglo-Saxon settlement north of the Humber, are (broadly speaking) 400 and 550. For the Germanic immigrants and their still pagan descendants this was, one presumes, an effectively illiterate period and for us, therefore, prehistoric. The formal caveat should perhaps be entered here that some of the

early settlers might have been converted to Christianity – and thus theoretically have gained access to Roman-style literacy – particularly if we were to
allow a fourth-century or earlier origin *and* continuity of identity to Germanic
population groups, however small, in the Northumbrian region.)[5] However,
this presumed pre-Christian illiteracy did not of course prevent Northumbrians of a somewhat later era from making statements about persons or
events of the pagan period, and these (although they are very few) must be
subjected to scrutiny. A further complication is that native Britons may be
taken to have had access to literacy throughout this period, certainly in Latin
and very probably in the vernacular also. There is here, then, a very clear
distinction to be drawn between the Britons and the Anglo-Saxons.

Turning to these northern Britons, our principal difficulty – and it is one
which affects almost all the evidence of British origin – is the apparent
continuum of vernacular transmission between the sub-Roman North and
medieval Wales.[6] If there was such a continuum (and it is not easy to deny it) it
is near to impossible to explain how it worked, at least in terms of received
notions of political geography, notwithstanding the calmness with which
students of Welsh literature and north-British history have accepted this
proposition. Such a continuum may have delivered monuments of the northern Britons' literature and learned lore to their fellow countrymen in Wales;
yet it was not to the scholarly safety of petrification that they were delivered,
but rather to the ever changing context of Welsh literary transmission,
whether learned or oral or both, in which politically dictated self-interest and
an active scholarly antiquarianism intervened at least as much as the more
mechanical accidents of transmission.[7]

We may begin, then, with Latin texts of British origin and very briefly with
Gildas's *De excidio Britanniae*. Whether Gildas lived in the North in the first
half and middle of the sixth century and whether he was informed and
concerned largely about northern events are issues which have been debated to
an inconclusive standstill in recent years; it should be admitted that there are
pointers in both directions. What we probably can say is that in Gildas's mind
we can recognize a belief that Anglo-Saxon mercenaries or federates were
introduced into the north-eastern quarter of British (as opposed to Pictish)
Britain to repel the Picts. I have made elsewhere the rough calculation that if
Gildas had expressed his narrative in a way susceptible to simple dating he
would be seen to have been talking (whether rightly or wrongly) about the 480s
– but on this point many views are no doubt possible, and there is in any case a
large question about whether any of Gildas's testimony concerning the period
before his own lifetime is usable.[8] He might also be taken to imply the
beginnings of post-Roman (north-)British kingship in the third quarter of the
fifth century, but the same caveats apply. If by 'the Gildas tradition', as Hunter
Blair called it, we understand the sequence of reported events to which the
hiring of Anglo-Saxons is central – the series of Pictish invasions and their
repulse by the Britons with or without Anglo-Saxon help – we have one partial
framework for the beginnings of sub-Roman history in the North. Nor is it
necessarily an incredible one, until (perhaps) we attempt to put absolute dates
to the sequence of events which it envisages. By the earlier ninth century,
when the *Historia Brittonum* was written in Gwynedd, this outline had
acquired a gloss which gave names to a pair of Anglo-Saxon leaders fighting for

the Britons against the 'northern peoples' (as Gildas called the Gaels and Picts) and associated them with a figure, Hengist, who had himself by the earlier eighth century been recognized (first, perhaps) as leader of the initial Anglo-Saxon settlers and (probably secondarily) as the ancestor of the Kentish royal dynasty.[9] But what the source of this account may be, and what was its significance, remain undemonstrated: until enlightenment can be achieved, the information remains unusable.

Another, and rather different, continuum emerged from Hunter Blair's examination of the literary record – that of the possibility of co-operation between Picts and Saxons from the *barbarica conspiratio* of 367 through the Hallelujah victory campaign of 429 to the revolt of the Saxon federates in the second half of the fifth century.[10] Unless Constantius had read Ammianus we may take the first two to be independent, but Bede's knowledge of Constantius might have led him to embroider with this detail Gildas's account of the third. The possibility of Picto-Saxon *political* interaction must at any rate be kept in mind.

Any kind of interaction between Picts and Saxons requires us to give some consideration to where they might meet – where federate Saxons would be settled in order to deal with the Picts. While the latter might be found fighting in Kent in 367/8, according to Ammianus, routine interception of their invasions would presumably be more naturally placed to the north at least of the Humber and arguably much farther north still. If, therefore, we give any credence to the so-called 'Gildas tradition' we should expect to find Anglo-Saxons in the Northumbrian region by the second half of the fifth century, and so we do – from York to Catterick – on currently accepted archaeological chronology.[11] That physical testimony should be found early in association with major (Romano-)British military centres may be thought consistent with the broad lines of Gildasian interpretation. It is difficult to avoid the impression that rebellion of such strategically located Anglo-Saxon forces would have had the severest effect on the British polity to which they had been attached.

The other Latin text which bespeaks a northern British origin is a source (or perhaps more than one source) of the Welsh group of chronicles now known collectively as *Annales Cambriae*.[12] The ninth- and tenth-century 'Chronicle of Ireland' embodied a set of north-British annals for the years to 780. Likewise the last of a series of Northern notices in *Annales Cambriae* refers to 777. In the eighth century, and to some extent in the later seventh, these annal entries refer to the kingdom of Strathclyde. But in so far as they deal with the period from c. 550 to c. 650 no such bias is apparent, the focus of attention being rather more southerly, on other British kingdoms of the region which is now northern England and southern Scotland.[13] Whether we see here a line of transmission or (instead) more than one source is crucial to know, but once again for the moment enlightenment is not dawning. Nor is it clear whether the notices of the first century of this period are contemporaneous with the events or a later, antiquarian construct. Their occasional annals chronicle wars between named but untitled Britons and between Britons and English. It has been suspected that a few items in the *Historia Brittonum* come from the same source.[14] Other entries in the 'Chronicle of Ireland' which notice British affairs are usually explained as proceeding from the lost annals of Iona. Rarely does any of this information give us much to play with; evidence of this is perhaps provided, for the cynic at least, by the enthusiasm and historical mileage generated by a two-word entry in the Annals of Ulster for 638 – *Obsesio Etin* – supposedly recording the end of the kingdom of Gododdin.[15]

In the interstices between Latin and the vernacular we meet the collections of Welsh genealogies.[16] Our earliest is of the mid-tenth century but preserved in a manuscript of *c.* 1100. Extraordinarily, only two or three of the thirty-two pedigrees which it contains have been subjected to close analysis. In spite of this some large conclusions have been drawn from certain names in the upper (and in principle least reliable) sections of the pedigrees of Northern dynastic lines. In particular the appearance of names of Latin origin has been urged as a reason for thinking the supposedly fourth- or fifth-century characters who bore them to have belonged to a period of Roman political manipulation of the intervallate British peoples. This assumption cuts wildly through a great deal of linguistic and cultural history. We may have heard less in recent years of Padarn Peisrudd, that 'Paternus' whose red cloak (in Hunter Blair's words) 'seems to imply that the man to whom it was given was invested with some kind of Roman authority';[17] but this extraordinary linguistic theorizing still underlies some current discussion of the end of Roman rule in the North. Again, the Welsh genealogical tracts – and there are quite a lot of them – need close study before we dare use any of them for any purpose, but especially before such texts can be offered to the historian of sub-Roman north Britain. In particular we need to know to what extent genealogical doctrines have interacted with vernacular Welsh literature and been formed under pressures of medieval politics.

The vernacular heroic poetry often attributed to the British North of the sixth and seventh centuries is, if accepted as in any sense genuine, a capital source for the period. One might even say that, whatever the status of that poetry, the known transmission in traditional literature of a societal context proper to the founding era of that literature, but subsequently anachronistic, justifies Thomas Charles-Edwards's use of it to describe the heroic ethos of the sub-Roman northern Britons.[18] There is no need to dwell at length here on this poetry and the problems and opportunities which it presents to the historian. The issues have been discussed in a recent volume of papers on the Book of Aneirin.[19] The poems attributed by Ifor Williams to a sixth-century poet Taliesin are looking more and more problematic, as troublesome anachronisms are recognized.[20] On the other hand, study of the *Gododdin* has suddenly started moving rapidly forward again after a generation's lull. Before long, perhaps, we shall know better how to handle it. If we take at face value its attribution to Aneirin and its apparent story-line – of the defeat of an elect force of Gododdin by Deirans at Catterick – it would seem to fit well with the *mid*-sixth-century date given to Aneirin by the author of the *Historia Brittonum*: it is particularly notable that the more archaic B-text of the *Gododdin* never mentions the Bernicians, speaking always of the men of Deira as the enemies of the Votadini/Gododdin. If we envisage the situation as historical, we might think that a major defeat of the Votadini by the Deirans would have opened up the prospect of Germanic settlement in their territory, that is, in what was to become Bernicia.

The difficulties presented for the present purpose by our British sources, as being largely non-contemporary in their present forms though perhaps variously deriving from early witnesses, are above all that they give us no clear sense of the structures of political authority which succeeded Roman, and preceded English, rule in this large region. Not the least of our problems in trying to understand northern British political development is created by uncertainty as to the pre-fifth-century forms of organization. Because roman-ized *civitates* were not formed in this area, the tribal names of the Roman period are infrequently encountered in the largely epigraphic sources, and territorial boundaries are even less clear to us than they are farther south. The political condition of the area between the Walls in the last half century of Roman rule in Britain is especially unclear. Was it dominated by the Picts? Did the rulers of the Roman diocese also determine what happened in *this* area? Or were the native tribes more or less independent? It has generally been thought that the kingdoms of Strathclyde and Gododdin, not to mention the mysterious Rheged, emerged by the mid-fifth century in the aftermath of a Pictish defeat. In so far as this does not arise from reading archaeological evidence in the 'light' of Gildas, it may be thought to derive from an incautious marriage of St Patrick's *Epistola ad Coroticum* with (eighth-century?) infor-mation found only in the Book of Armagh.[21] Generalization on this basis may be a little too simplistic. The Damnonii appear to have occupied what in recent times were the counties of Ayr, Renfrew, Lanark and Dumbarton, and western Stirlingshire too.[22] This defines also territory which we should assign to the early medieval kingdom of Strathclyde, based on Dumbarton: why should this not be the lineal successor of an Iron Age kingdom of the Damnonii? In the east the Votadini may be seen emerging in our post-Roman sources as the Godod-din, in occupation of the territory between Tees and Forth continuing to the region of Manaw (notably Clackmanannshire) around the head of the Forth.[23] Here the old tribal grouping may be seen continuing, albeit perhaps with some internal shifts – if, for example, the abandonment of Traprain Law is to be so interpreted. What, then, of the Novantae of Galloway and the Selgovae of Dumfriesshire and points east? On this model we should perhaps suppose there to have been separate sub-Roman successor kingdoms in south-central and south-western Scotland.

The Hadrianic Wall cut through the southernmost part of the territory of the Votadini in the east, although the northern frontier of the Brigantes cannot have been far to the south and one presumes that the Romans were attempting as far as possible to follow a pre-existing political boundary. The political arrangements in the Roman military zone in what is now northern England are less clear than they might be. Did the Brigantes retain their tribal identity to the end of the Roman period? If so, was this identity in any way connected with the arrangements made for their government by the Romans? Brigantian territory was in effect coextensive with that of Deira (although one must not forget the Parisi of East Yorkshire).[24] Can we therefore suppose that Romano-British political geography more or less fossilized pre-existing native arrange-ments and that in its turn a sub-Roman unit which continued these was subverted by Anglo-Saxon settlers within the territory? As increasingly often, one wonders whether the facts of Romano-British political geography have ultimately influenced the shape of English settlement. Be that as it may, by the mid-sixth century at latest the northern English were being opposed by British leaders with royal titles; if Gildas has been correctly understood, this situation was by no means new at that date.[25]

Finally, in our consideration of the origins of Anglo-Saxon settlement north of the Humber we must turn to the English evidence itself. Bede tells us that the Germanic settlers of Northumbria were Angles,[26] a statement seemingly well supported (particularly in Deira) by the nature of the archaeological record, in so far as that is logically possible. Beyond that, however, he tells us nothing about the English takeover of Deira and Bernicia, nothing (that is) before the 540s for Bernicia and the second half of the sixth century for Deira. Even then his information is of the very thinnest until the time of Æthelfrith (592–616) who was supposedly the first Bernician king to rule Deira also.[27]

The effective totality of the Anglo-Saxon literary evidence bearing on the origins of English settlement north of the Humber amounts to two items, one for each kingdom. In a chronicle fragment derivative of Bede's summary chronicle but written before c. 850, now surviving in a French manuscript at Bern, we are told in a genealogical context under the year 547 that Oessa-Eosa was the first member of the Bernician royal dynasty to come to Britain.[28] According to the sole surviving pedigree, echoed by this annal, he was the grandfather of Ida, founder of the Bernician dynasty, whose reign was supposed to have extended from 547 to 559.[29] The floruit of his grandfather would therefore belong c. 500. And in the *Historia Brittonum* an English item uniquely preserved in a hybrid Welsh-and-Latin guise tells us that Soemil first separated Deira from Bernicia. He was great-great-great-grandfather of that Ælle who was king of Deira from 568 to 598. Soemil therefore (if he enjoyed a historical existence and if the pedigree is correct) flourished in the middle years of the fifth century. If the statement that he separated Deira from Bernicia means anything for the fifth century, it must be that he detached Deira from British rule. Of that we know nothing and can say merely that that was broadly the appropriate period; but anyone who had read Bede's History could have drawn the same conclusion.

Bede's date of 547 for the beginning of Ida's reign, and (by implication) of Bernician kingship, was calculated from the regnal list.[30] On it has been hung a picturesque story for which no early source gives warrant. Bernicia has been thought to have originated as a pirate settlement at Bamburgh rock; but we have no grounds for placing unique beginnings of Bernician settlement there. That view, and another that Bernicia achieved little or no territorial expansion in its first generation, emerged from a Welsh notice in the *Historia Brittonum* that the British king Urien, with three royal allies, besieged the Bernician king Theodric (572–9) on Lindisfarne Island/Holy Island.[31] But these are not necessarily logical deductions from evidence which is in any case hardly first-rate. (In passing, one might wonder whether, if that text's information has any validity for the period from which its ninth-century Welsh author was so distant, the four allied north-British kings should be taken as representing four British nations or tribal confederations in the area.)

The transmitted royal pedigrees for Bernicia and Deira tell us nothing which we can use to help us understand the process of Anglo-Saxon settlement in the North. At best they might be employed to give us a sense of the approximate date at which dynastic continuity began in these kingdoms and of the processes of selection. And unfortunately they seem to tell us nothing of the relationship of early settlement and political organization in Bernicia to those of Deira.

Likewise linguistic evidence largely fails us. Although we know of two Northumbrian dialects, South and North, in effect the literary languages of the churches of Deira and those of Bernicia respectively, it is the almost universal opinion of Germanic philologists that the dialect distinctions within Old English arose in England itself in response to geographical and political factors and were not reflexes of Continental dialect differences.[32]

In summary, then, we may say that our Anglo-Saxon sources of the eighth and ninth centuries tell us that the Northumbrians were of Anglian stock; by the earlier ninth century doctrines had arisen, cast within dynastic terms of reference, that settlement occurred in Deira by the middle of the fifth century and in Bernicia by *c.* 500, and that the historical Bernician dynasty began to rule in 547. Kingship in Deira is visible only from the 560s, but is presumably of greater antiquity than that would imply. On the face of it the fifth century and much of the sixth were largely lost to Anglo-Saxon historical memory in Northumbria's early Christian period. To what extent that is simply a reflection of the overwhelmingly ecclesiastical source material is difficult to tell: we should be better placed to say, no doubt, if we understood more of the transmission of secular historical information about pagan southern England into the late ninth-century Anglo-Saxon Chronicle.[33] For the moment we may reflect that at least we appear to know more of northern than of midland history in the settlement period.

That we do so is due largely to the availability of British (and, to a limited extent, Irish) sources bearing on this period; their survival has to be understood in the context of the relatively late existence of British kingdoms in the Northumbrian region and perhaps of the relatively short span of time in much of Bernicia between English settlement or conquest and the evangelization of the Anglo-Saxons.[34] None the less the British 'survivals', if that is what they are, leave us with more questions than answers. Some we need the Romanists to address. But many detailed questions about Briish political organization in the fifth, sixth and seventh centuries remain effectively unanswerable. Sub-Roman north-British history and pagan Anglo-Saxon settlement history are matters which we shall have to leave largely to the archaeologists; it would of course help if in the course of their activities they could present us with another Yarrowkirk-style inscription or two![35]

Anglo-British relations in the fifth, sixth and seventh centuries were of course largely characterized by hostility. There seems no reason to regard the course of events in the North as essentially different from that in the Midlands or South. As Wendy Davies reminded us in her Oxford O'Donnell Lectures, English aggression is a constant theme in Anglo-British relations: talk of treaties, and of continuity of institutions and population between British and English rule, cannot wish that away. On the British side Welsh heroic poetry leaves us in no doubt of the sixth-century northern hostilities between Briton and Angle. Bede stresses the savage vigour of Æthelfrith of Bernicia and, in return, of Cadwallon of Gwynedd who (Bede thought) wanted to extirpate the entire Northumbrian people.[36] We should not conclude too hastily that Bede overdramatized the sentiments of a century earlier. Similarly, in the later seventh century St Wilfrid's biographer Stephanus leaves us in no doubt as to the effect of continuing English invasion on northern British communities.[37]

All this is not to say of course that political advantage could not be seen in developing temporary links across racial lines. Gildas hints strongly that there were Britons who argued for this course in his own day.[38] Vortigern, wherever and whenever he lived, had found a treaty useful. In the second quarter of the seventh century Venedotians and Mercians opposed Northumbrians (and probably the men of Powys too).[39] In the eighth century, in an era of more settled international politics in the North, we find Mercians and Picts conspiring against Northumbria, and Picts and Northumbrians against Strathclyde.[40] The exigencies of exile also brought Englishmen among the Britons – for example, the Deirans Edwin and Hereric, the former apparently in Gwynedd, the latter in Elmet.[41]

None of these factors must be allowed to blind us to the overall pattern, however, which is of continuing Northumbrian aggression and expansion. It would be perverse to pretend that the result of such expansion was business as usual for the Britons, if under new management. The question is rather how much their future prospects changed, or whether they had any at all, under English rule. The different circumstances (and dates) which have been deduced for the origins of English settlement in Deira and Bernicia must have affected the interaction of Briton and Anglo-Saxon in the two regions, as must the very different histories of the Brigantes and the more northerly British tribes during the Roman period.

One might be forgiven for thinking that the method of English takeover of British kingdoms would be conquest, whether piecemeal or (occasionally) sudden and total. However, one piece of evidence for royal intermarriage between Bernician and Briton has allowed a startlingly different model to be proposed. We know from the *Historia Brittonum* that at least one British writer thought Oswiu, king of Northumbria from 642 to 670, to have had a British wife Rhiainfellt who belonged to the royal line of Rheged. Although no English source directly attests any of these statements, the lady's existence seems to be confirmed by an entry in the Lindisfarne *Liber Vitae*.[42] If her precise origin is correctly stated, we are left to work out the implications of the marriage. Oswiu had been in northern exile until 633/4 and it is of course possible that the marriage dated from that period. If not, however, we must presumably suppose some sort of marriage alliance between Rheged and Bernicia during the reign of his predecessor and brother, Oswald (634–42). From there, however, it is a very large leap to the supposition that this somehow allowed Oswald or Oswiu (who acquired a new, English queen soon after his accession to the throne) to 'absorb' Rheged – presumably either the kingdom of the Novantae or that of the Selgovae – into Bernicia, and an even larger one to generalizing this into a model for Bernician expansion.

The ancient British tribal groupings have been taken as a basis for discussion. That that is inadequate, at least in part, is shown by the existence until the earlier seventh century of the kingdom of Elmet/Elfed in what is now West Yorkshire. The name is known elsewhere, in Durham for example and perhaps in Wales. If it is in some sense tribal, do we have to do with a sub-group of the Brigantes, or is the name of more recent origin? If the former, is one model for the reconstruction of sub-Roman political geography in Brigantian territory the former sub-kingdoms which first-century evidence allows us to glimpse (as Thomas Charles-Edwards has shown)?[43] Without the evidence provided by Bede and *Annales Cambriae*, however sparse it may be, we should never have guessed that the Yorkshire Elmet was a British kingdom, for there is nothing in the placename to demand it, and we should probably have doubted that Britons retained control in this area to a date as late as *c.* 620.

How many lost British kingdoms of the North we are to reckon with is a nice question, therefore. Certainly, if we were to allow ourselves to be beguiled by medieval Welsh learned lore we could imagine, via named characters attributed to the old British North, a good many more than we can now put names to. Even if we restrict ourselves to *Annales Cambriae*, however, we are left to wonder about the events which are there ascribed to the last third of the sixth century, from the battle of Arfderydd in the early 570s, via the deaths of Gwrgi and Peredur attributed to 580, to the death of a king Dunod in the later 590s. Further, there have been suggestions, largely based on interpretations of the poetry attributed to Taliesin, that the medieval Welsh kingdom of Powys at this era extended up into Cheshire and Lancashire, thus explaining more pointedly the battle of the men of Powys with Æthelfrith of Northumbria *c.* 613.[44] The existence of a Powys in Liddesdale has been called in support, notwithstanding the (potentially polygenetic) derivation of this name from the Latin common noun *pagenses*.[45] There is no evidence to support this extended geography, but it was able to be suggested because of the void within our total body of sources.

As elsewhere in Anglo-Saxon Britain, the facts of conquest have submerged most of the evidence for the pre-existing British polities. The glimpses which history has preserved for us derive from the interest of neighbouring societies in northern British affairs and from the still unexplained route by which some north-British literary matter entered the Welsh literary tradition. The Selgovae seem to have been finished off politically by the first half of the seventh century, but the Novantae were not tackled (and then very incompletely) until the later part of that century. The Damnonii in their kingdom of Strathclyde were not assaulted by the English until the late eighth century, by which time the literary record had taken sufficient notice of them for us to understand something of their kingdom; and by the time when the Northumbrians got seriously to grips with the Strathclyders Northumbrian power was already diminishing.

Like most other English kingdoms Deira and Bernicia were founded on the wreckage of British polities of which we know almost or absolutely nothing. The growth which fuelled the development of Northumbria and its brief pan-English hegemony was achieved in part by the advantages derived from constant expansion against the British, particularly to the north and north-west. For a variety of reasons the steam ran out of Northumbrian – principally Bernician – expansion in the eighth century; that development, and the growth of substantial overkingdoms south of the Humber, deprived the northern Anglo-Saxons (who came increasingly to seem as though they lived in another, if yet still English, world) of any real chance of repeating their military successes of the early to mid-seventh century. The origins of the Northumbrian overkingdom – which was from time to time to take on the characteristics of a single, unified kingdom – are to be sought in that brief period from the late sixth century to the late seventh when the thirst for territorial expansion and military aggression could be turned successfully against both English and Britons.[46]

Part 3 Appendices

16 The Tribal Hidage: an introduction to its texts and their history

DAVID DUMVILLE

The text known today as 'The Tribal Hidage' has been transmitted in three different forms. Only one of these, here called Recension A, is found in a manuscript of the Anglo-Saxon period. Reduced fascimiles of that copy have been published on three occasions.[1] The text was printed accurately but indigestibly by W. de G. Birch a century ago.[2]

The sole witness to Recension A is London, British Library, MS Harley 3271,[3] a copy of abbot Alfric's Grammar (fos. 7–90)[4] to which various additions have been prefixed (fos. 1–6) and subjoined (fos. 90–129). The original manuscript belongs, on the evidence of its script, to the first half of the eleventh century.[5] The appended folios contain numerous short texts, the last of which is datable to 1032.[6] Likewise fos. 1–6 (probably the remains of an original quire of eight whose first two leaves have been lost) should be attributed to the first half of the eleventh century. The handwriting of the several scribes represented in the whole codex is stylistically similar throughout.[7] Unfortunately it is not known where in England the book was written.[8] The position of the Tribal Hidage suggests that it may have been a secondary addition to the codex. Fos. 1r–6r are occupied by Latin grammatical matter, now acephalous. This finishes halfway down 6r, the rest of which remains blank. On 6v we meet the Tribal Hidage, followed by a brief Latin text (found elsewhere in a variety of versions) on the stereotypical characteristics of nations.[9] It is to be presumed, then, that our text owes its place in the Harleian manuscript to an antiquarian interest visible also among the other additions to the book.

Recension A is printed here in tabular form, but opposite a full-page reproduction of Harley 3271, f. 6v. As may readily be seen, its text is in Old English throughout; this copy lacks a title. It has been demonstrated by various commentators that the text is far from incorrupt: some of the figures must be in error; one or two names and hidations may have been omitted;[10] certain of the people names are universally regarded as corrupt.[11] And the marginal addition to *Færpinga* is worthy of note.[12]

Recension B appears to be a Latin text. Such hesitation is necessary, for the conclusion depends merely on *continet* (1) and on the repeated words *hidas*, apparently intended to be a first declension Latin accusative plural. This version is known only from Henry Spelman's *Archæologus in modum Glossarii ad rem antiquam posteriorem*, published in London in 1626;[13] his entry 'De Hidis & Hidagiis Anglo-saxonicis' occupies pp. 352–3 (of which a

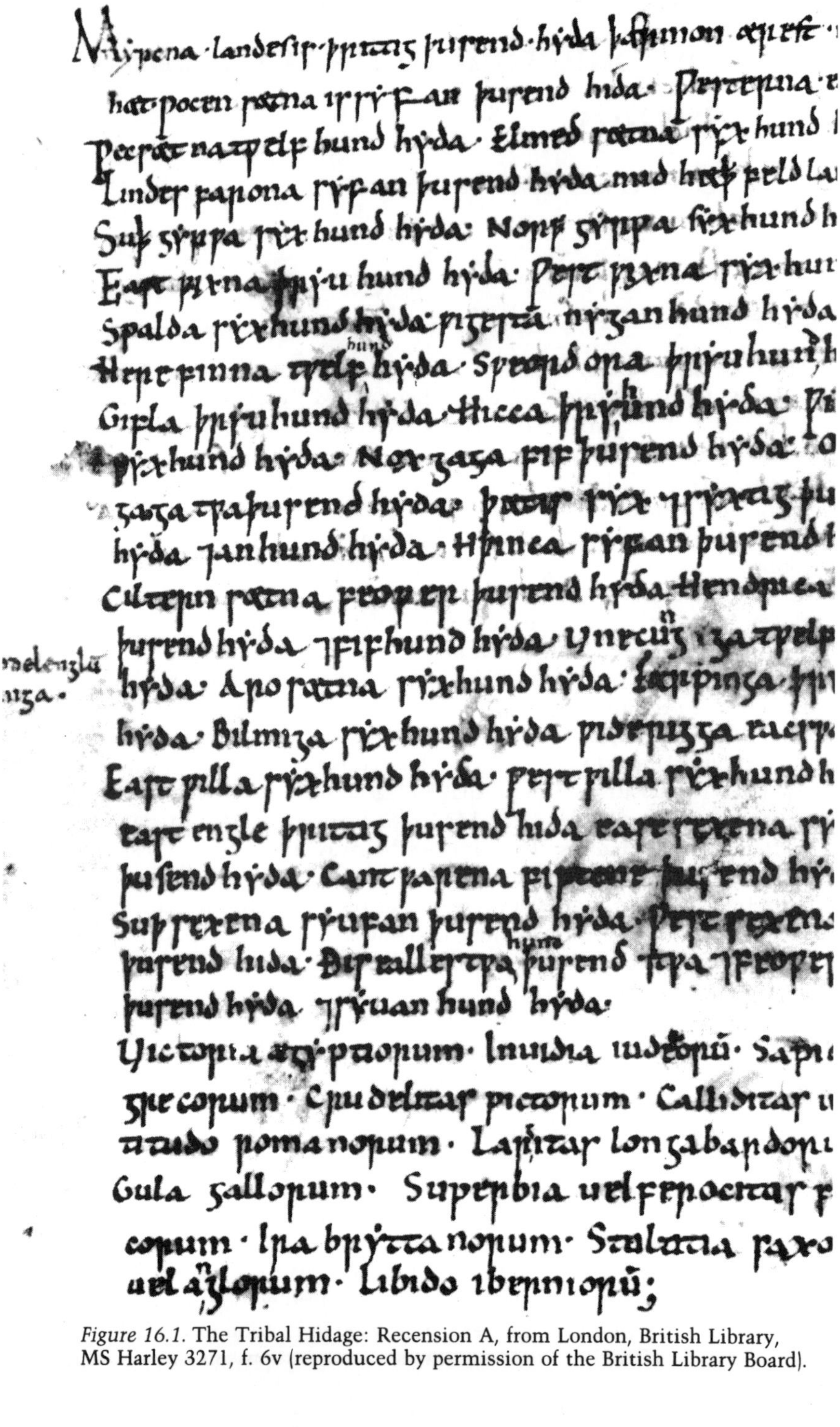

Figure 16.1. The Tribal Hidage: Recension A, from London, British Library, MS Harley 3271, f. 6v (reproduced by permission of the British Library Board).

RECENSION A

(1) Myrcna landes is þrittig þusend hyda þær mon ærest Myrcna hæt.	30,000	(1)
(2) Þocen sætna is syfan þusend hida.	7,000	(2)
(3) Þesterna eac spa.	7,000	(3)
(4) Pecsætna tpelf hund hyda.	1,200	(4)
(5) Elmed sætna syx hund hyda.	600	(5)
(6) Lindesfarona syfan þusend hyda mid Hæþ feldlande.	7,000	(6)
(7) Suþ gyrpa syx hund hyda.	600	(7)
(8) Norþ gyrpa syx hund hyda.	600	(8)
(9) East pixna þryu hund hyda.	300	(9)
(10) Þest pixna syx hund hyda.	600	(10)
(11) Spalda syx hund hyda.	600	(11)
(12) Þigesta nygan hund hyda.	900	(12)
(13) Herefinna tpelf 'hund' hyda.	1,200	(13)
(14) Speord ora þryu hun'd' hyda.	300	(14)
(15) Gifla þryu hund hyda.	300	(15)
(16) Hicca þry 'h'und hyda.	300	(16)
(17) Þiht gara syx hund hyda.	600	(17)
(18) Noxgaga fif þusend hyda.	5,000	(18)
(19) Ohtgaga tpa þusend hyda.	2,000	(19)
þæt is syx 7 syxtig þusend hyda 7 an hund hyda.	66,100	
(20) Hpinca syfan þusend hyda.	7,000	(20)
(21) Ciltern sætna feoper þusend hyda.	4,000	(21)
(22) Hendrica þryu þusend hyda 7 fif hund hyda.	3,500	(22)
(23) Unecu'n'g[a]ga tpelf hund hyda.	1,200	(23)
(24) Arosætna syx hund hyda.	600	(24)
(25) Færpinga þreo hund hyda. '[i]s in Middelenglum Færpinga' (left-hand margin)	300	(25)
(26) Bilmiga syx hund hyda.	600	(26)
(27) Þiderigga eac spa.	600	(27)
(28) Eastpilla syx hund hyda.	600	(28)
(29) Þestpilla syx hund hyda.	600	(29)
(30) East engle þrittig þusend hida.	30,000	(30)
(31) Eastsexena syofon þusend hyda.	7,000	(31)
(32) Cantparena fiftene þusend hyda.	15,000	(32)
(33) Suþsexena syufan þusend hyda.	7,000	(33)
(34) Þestsexena hund þusend hida.	100,000	(34)
	[178,000]	
Ðis ealles tpa 'hund' þusend 7 tpa 7 feopertig þusend hyda 7 syuan hund hyda.		
	242,700 [recte 244,100]	

'. . .'=matter inserted interlineally or marginally
[. . .]=letter(s) erased (23) or physically lost (25)

tione *[ur le cafe* apud Fitzherbert. fol.
94. *Si W. &c. tunc pone I &c. oftenfu-*
rius quare idem I. tres currus pro victuali-
bus et herucfijs ipfius, W. ad partes tranf-
marinas ducendas — facere & fabricare
apud S. affumpfit.&c.

❧ Heftha.] Domefd. Tit. Ceftre.
Quando Rex ipfe ibi veniebat, reddebat ei
vnaquaque carucata CC. hefthas, et vnam
cunam plenam ceruifia, et vnam butyri
rufcam. Heftham intelligo pro capo,
feu gallo caftrato ; vel pullo quopiam
gallinaceo. A Gall. *heftaud,* vndè he-
ftaudean : vt *Chapon, chaponneau.*

❧ Heueward & Heuewarth.] Domefd. Titt. Grentebr. Picot de Grentebr. Heftiton. — *Fi* VIII. *Aueras,*
& VIII Ineward, et iij heneward Vice-
comiti inueniebat. Sic iterum in Ta-
dely ; fed neutro liquidè.

❧ Heyward.] Rei pafcuæ curator.
A Sax. hiᵹ. i. *gramen,* vel heᵹ. i. *fepes*
(quod vtrumque Anglo-Normanni
hey pronuntiant)et peapᵭ.i.*cuftos.* Ho-
die pasfim pro armentario accipitur,
An Heardman.

¶ *De Hidis & Hidagiis An-*
glo-faxonicis.

❧ Hida, et Hyda ; *Scotis,* Hilda.]
Terræ portio , quæ vel ad alimonium
vnius familiæ, vel ad annuum penfum
vnius aratri defignatur. Authoribus
medij temporis; *Manfum, manfio, ca-*
rucata terræ, colonica, &c. Bedâ, *familia.*
A Sax. hyᵭ. non vt Polydorus intelli-
git, pro corio bubulo ; ac fi tantum
contineret foli (iuxta id Virgilij
Æn.1.)

Taurino quantū poffent circundare tergo:
fed ab hyᵭen, pro *tegere.* Sic vt hyᵭ
apud Saxones noftros, idem fit quod
apud Latinos *tectum.* Continet autem
(vt etiam *Manfum, Manerium* et e-
iufmodi) non folùm ipfam domum in
qua habitatur ; fed afcriptos pariter
fundos : quos diftinguens aliàs ve-
Hidelands. tus Bedæ Interpres Saxonicus, hyᵭelanᵭeᵹ, quafi *terras ad hydam feu tec-*
tum pertinentes, appellauit.

Hilda.   Huic eonuenit vox Scotorum *Hilda,*
nam hilᵭen etiam eft *tegere, cooperire.*

Quo ad *hyda* fignificata : dicatur

primò pro ftatione & confugio : nam
fic huᵭae interpretantur Gloff. Cant.
y in *u,* vt fæpè inter Saxones, tranfmu-
tato.

Pro manfo, & *manfione.* Sic vbi dicitur in Charta Ethelwulphi R.circ. An.
Dn. 845. Famulis Dei *femper decimam*
manfionem perdonari dijudicaui: Williel-
mus Malmesburienf. hanc enarrans in
lib.1.de Geft.Regum:*Semperᵹ,*(inquit)
ad finē feculi in omnis fuæ hæreditatis deci-
ma hida, pauperè veftiri et cibari præcepit.

Pro *familia.* Nam quas Beda in Hi-
ftor. Ecclefiaft. *familias* vocat; Autho-
res alij,& Interpres eius Saxonicus (vt
fupra diximus) *hidas,* & hyᵭelanᵭeᵹ
nuncuparunt.

Pro *carucata:* id eft,portione terræ,
ad vnius aratri penfum annuum fuffi-
cienti. Nota hæc & vulgarris fignifi-
catio. Henric. Huntington Hift.lib.6.
in An. Dn. 1008. Regis Edelredi 30.
Fecit Rex parari per totam Angliam ex
310 hidis nauem vnam: & ex octo hidis,
loricam et galeam. Hida autem Anglicè
vocatur terra vnius aratri culturæ fuffici-
ens. Item Author Annalium Wauerli-
enfium in Anno 1083. *Mifit Rex* 5 *Iu-*
fticiarios fuos per vnamquamᵹ fcyram, 1-
prouinciam Angliæ, et inquirere fecit per
iufiurandum quot hide,id eft,iugera a vni a-
ratro fufficientia per annum, effent in vna-
quaᵹ villa. Hoc idem Mat.Paris in eo-
dem Anno, adiungens : *et quot animalia*
poffent fufficere ad vnius hide culturam.

Quantitas *Hidæ* in disfidio eft. Ger- De quan-
uafio Tilberienfi nuncupatus liber, ca. titate Hi-
penult. *Hida*(inquit)*in primitiua inftitu-* de.
tione,ex 100 *acris conftat.*Codex quidam
MS.Abbatiæ Malmesber.(vt ab Agar-
do accepi) fic legit. *Virgata terra conti-*
net 24 *acras : et* 4 *virgatæ conftituunt v-*
nam hidam: et 5 *hidæ, conftituunt feodum*
militare.

Non errauerit igitur qui *Hidam* (vt
carucatam dixerit, vnius aratri penfum
annale: explofo hoc quod afferit Polydorus ; *hidam* effe *menfuram terræ quæ*
20 *continet iugera.*

Angliæ per *hydas* diftributio peran- Angliæ per
tiqua eft : non Aluredo,licèt Infulam *hidas di-*
multifaria infigniuit diuifione, (vt in *ftributa.*
voce *Comitatus,* pa. 169. col.1. often-
dimus) tribuenda. Occurrit enim *hy-*
darum

darum mentio in ll. Regis Inæ (qui supra 100 annos Aluredum præcessit) ca. 14. et *hydarum* nomine antiquius cognoscuntur 12, illæ portiones, quæ 12 Iosephi Aramathiæ comitibus in Glastoniensis monasterij territorio feruntur assignatæ. Veterrimam, etiam apud Franciscum Tatum schedam aliquando vidimus, *hydarum* numerum in plurimis Angliæ regiunculis continentem, vt hic sequitur.

Myrcna continet 30000. Hidas.
Woken-setna 7000. hidas.
Westerna 7000. hidas.
Pec-setna 1200. hidas.
Elmed-setna 600. hidas.
Lindes-farona 7000. hidas.
Suth-Gyrwa 600. hidas.
North-Girwa 600. hidas.
East-Wixna 300. hidas.
West-Wixna 600. hidas.
Spalda 600. hidas.
Wigesta 900. hidas.
Herefinna 1200. hidas.
Sweordora 300. hidas.
Eysla 300. hidas.
Wicca 300. hidas.
Wight-gora 600. hidas.
Nox gaga 5000. hidas.
Oht gaga 2000. hidas.
Hwynca 7000. hidas.
Ciltern-setna 4000. hidas.
Hendrica 3000. hidas.
Vnecung-ga 1200. hidas.
Aroseatna 600. hidas.
Fearfinga 300. hidas.
Belmiga 600. hidas.
Witherigga 600. hidas.
East-willa 600. hidas.
West-willa 600. hidas.
East-Engle 30000. hidas.
East fexena 7000. hidas.
Cant-warena 15000. hidas.
Suth-sexena 7000. hidas.
West-sexena 100000. hidas.
Per *Hidas* abnegare, quid. Vide *Hloth.*

Hidagium.
Hidegild.
Hidagium: tributum quod ex singulis *hidis* colligitur : aliàs *Hidegild* vide *Geldum.* In taxis & tributis persoluendis, mos antiquus fuit regnum per *hidas* describere. Mori dedit originem Rex (opinor) Edelredus An. Dn. 1008. cum aduersus Danos ex 310 *hidis* nauem vnam, ex octo, loricam & galeam præstanda indixisset. Gulielmus Conquestor (vt refert Florentius Wigorn, in An. 1084.) *de vnaquaq, hida per Angliam sex solidos accepit,* vel (vt inquit Mat. Paris in An. 108:.) *– de vnoquoq, aratro.i. hyda terra totius regni.* &c. Gulielmus Rufus ad Normanniam retinendam, *habuit it* (inquiunt ll. Ed. Confess. ca. 11)*ex vnaquaq, hyda* 4 *sol. Ecclesia non excepta.* Henricus I. maritadæ filiæ suæ gratiâ Imperatori : *cepit ab vnaquaque hida Angliæ tres sol.*

Hidare est terram per *hidas* censere: ex quo *hidatus* particip.pro *taxatus* vel ceusui descriptus. **Hidatus.**

℃ Hikenild & Hikenild-streete.] Vide *Ikenild.*

℃ Hilda.] Vide *Hida.*

℃ Himilzorum.] L. Boior. seu Baiwar. Tit. 7. ca. 7. *Si indumenta* (mulieris)*super genucula eleuauerit, quod himilzorum vocant, cum xij sol. componat.*

Hinderl ng.] Contumeliæ vocabulum ab Occiduis Saxonibus profectum : atq; *Dearling* & *Adeling* contrarium. LL. D. Edouardi Confes. ca. 35. in calce. — *in quadam regione Saxoniæ,* Ling, *imago dicitur,* Athel *Anglicè nobilis est, quæ coniuncta sonant,* nobilis imago. *Vnde etiam Occidentales Saxonici, sc₂. Excestrenses, habent in prouerbio summi despectus,* hinderling. *i. omni honestate deiecta & recedens imago,* hoc est, patri omnino dissimilis, *hynþeþ* enim *remotum significat* & *posthabitum.* Vide *Adelingus.*

℃ Hinesar.] Vide *Heinsar.*

℃ Hinniculum.] Spurcum ludi genus, quod damnat S. Augustinus Serm. de Tempore 215. *Si adhuc agnoscatis aliquos, illam sordidissimam turpitudinem de hinnicula vel ceruula exercere : ita durissimè castigate vt eos pæniteat rem sacrilegam commisisse.*

℃ Hioba.] Vide *Hoba.*

℃ Hird.] Vide *Herd* pro *familia.*

℃ Hitha.] Vide *Heda.*

℃ Hiufa, Hiufare.] Vide *Guisare,* & *Wisare* : nam hæc eadem sunt. Scilicet, *Hiusare,* id quod Iurisconsulti *arrestare,* & *sasire* dicunt : *Hiusa,* ipsa arrestum, saisura, & signum quod in facti editur notitiam. Costitut. Caroli M.an. regni 11. — *casu eorum* (viz. iterum decimas subtrahentium) *hæc iuntur, quousq̃, pro ipsa decima sicut supradicta est satisfaciant.* **Hiusare.**

G g 3 *Quod*

Figure 16.2. (pp. 228–9). The Tribal Hidage: Recension B, from Henry Spelman's *Archaeologus* (1626).

reproduction follows here) and embodies a text of the Tribal Hidage. In form and content it corresponds to Recension A rather than Recension C, but differs in one hidation and variously in spelling of the people names.[14] It has been largely ignored in modern scholarly commentary. To imagine that it is a confection of Spelman's era, and to deny that Spelman's source was of Anglo-Saxon date, would be difficult.[15] According to Spelman he drew it from a *ueterrima scheda* which he had seen *apud* Francis Tate;[16] the phrase compels one to think of a single-sheet document. Francis Tate had been the owner of two or three other copies of the Tribal Hidage;[17] but these were texts of Recension C and certainly not the source of what was printed in 1626. It is to be hoped that Tate's *ueterrima scheda* may yet be rediscovered.

Recension C, known at present from six manuscripts of thirteenth- and fourteenth-century date, is certainly a Latin text but is equally clearly an imperfect translation from Old English as the retention of several vernacular words indicates.[18] In some manuscripts it is entitled 'De numero hidarum Anglie in Britannia'. All six witnesses display many corruptions in the people names. The copies of Recension C occur in the context of legal and administrative matter, perhaps suggesting early bureaucratic transmission of this version. It is not possible within the confines of this brief chapter to give Recension C the very full attention which it deserves: I hope to return to the task on another occasion. For the moment reference must be made to the pioneering study published by Wendy Davies in 1974, where the variant readings of this group were recorded and a discussion of them begun.[19] The manuscript sources are as follows:

1. Cambridge, Corpus Christi College, 70+258 (MS 70, pp. 3–4).
2. London, British Library, Hargrave 313 (f. 15v).
3. London, Guildhall, Liber Custumarum, fos. 103–72 & 187–284+Oxford, Bodleian Library, Oriel College 46, fos. 1–108+London, British Library, Cotton Claudius D.ii, fos. 116–23 (Oriel, f. 2v).
4. London, Guildhall, Liber Custumarum, fos. ii, 1–102, 173–86+British Library, Cotton Claudius D.ii, fos. 1–24, 30–40, 42–115, 124–35, 266–77+Oxford, Oriel College 46, fos. 109–211 (Claudius, f. 4v).
5. London, Public Record Office, E. 164/2 (K.R. Misc. Bks. 2: Red Book of the Exchequer) (fos. 29v–30r).
6. Manchester, John Rylands Unversity Library, Latin 155+London, British Library, Additional 14252 (Rylands, f. 3v).

It is apparent from Davies's discussion of her 'Latin group' (my 'Recension C') that behind this text – whose earliest recoverable form needs to be reconstructed – lay an Old English text different from and in at least a few respects superior to that of Recension A.[20]

By a comparison of the three recensions, therefore, it should be possible to carry the history of the text back into the tenth century at least; with the aid of Recensions B and C the eleventh-century text of MS Harley 3271 may be tested and improved. Textual enquiry still seems to offer some hope that our understanding of the Tribal Hidage may yet be improved.

17 The Chertsey resting-place list and the enshrinement of Frithuwold

JOHN BLAIR

For the 'holy cousinhood' of late seventh-century princesses the path to sanctity was almost inevitable. Their fathers and brothers, who founded and endowed their minsters, generally remained secular rulers and were thus less likely to become the objects of cults. But early monastic communities did sometimes venerate the relics of founders as well as those of first abbesses (doubtless the more so if those founders had 'opted out' and ended their days as monks).[1] Frithuwold's presumed kinsman Frithuric was enshrined in his own monastery of Breedon-on-the-Hill,[2] so it is scarcely surprising to find that Frithuwold himself was venerated at Chertsey.

The late Anglo-Saxon list of saints' resting-places survives in two Old English versions and a Latin translation; these were edited by Liebermann and have recently been discussed by David Rollason.[3] At Chertsey they name the late ninth-century saints Beocca and Edor, 'with whom ninety monks were slain by heathen men', but not Frithuwold. However, there existed a separate Chertsey version of the list, now lost, from which John Leland made brief 'excerpta ex veteri codice Ceortesegano' (fig. 17.1); these extracts are printed parallel with the main texts in Table 17.1.[4] Leland's notes are in Latin, but his

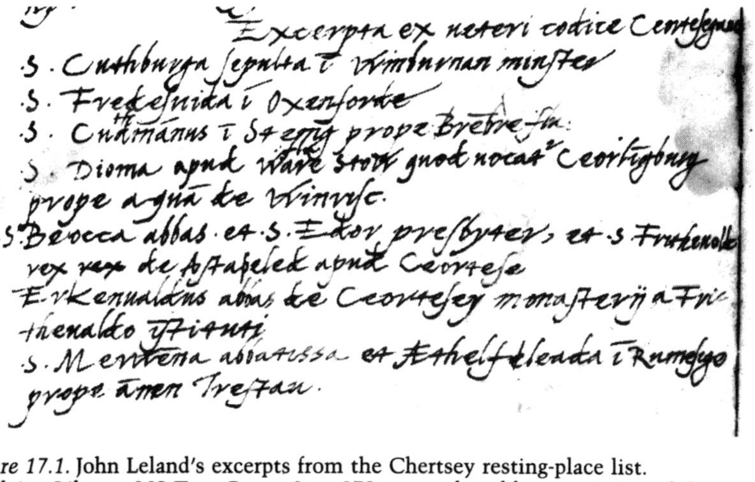

Figure 17.1. John Leland's excerpts from the Chertsey resting-place list. (Bodleian Library, MS Top. Gen. c.2, p. 370a; reproduced by permission of the Curators of the Bodleian Library.)

Table 1. Comparison of the Chertsey resting-place list with related texts (entries in order of Chertsey list)

Liebermann No.	Corpus O.E.	Stowe O.E.	Latin	Chertsey
45	Ðonne resteð Sancte Cuðburh and Cwenburh on Winburnan mynstre, þe ærest þæt minicena lif and þeawas arærde, þe man git on þam mynstre hylt.	Ðonne resteþ Sancte Cuðburh on Winburnan mynstre, þe ærest þæt lif and þeawas arærde þe man gyt on þam mynstre hylt.	Sanctaque Cuðburh in loco qui dicitur Winburnan menster.	S. Cuthburga sepulta in Wimburnan minster.
46	Ðonne resteð Sancte Fryðesweoð on Oxnaforda.	Ðonne resteð Sancte Frydeswyð on Oxnaforda.	Sanctaque Frydeswiða in loco qui dicitur on Oxnaforda.	S. Fredesuida in Oxenforde.
48	Ðonne resteð Sancte Cuðman æt Stæningum on Suðseaxum neah þare ea Bræmbre.	Ðonne resteð Sancte Cuðmann æt Stæningum on Suðsexum neah þære ea Bremre.	Sanctus Cuthmannus vero in loco qui dicitur æt Stæninge requiescit prope amnem Brembre nominatum.	S. Cudmannus in Stening prope Brembre flu.
17	Ðonne resteð Sancte Dionia on þare stowe þe is genemnod Ceorlincburh neah þare ea Wenrisc.	Ðonne resteð Sancte Dioma on þære stowe þe is genemned Ceorlingburh neah þare ea Wenrisc.	Sanctaque Dionia in loco qui dicitur Ceorlingburh prope amnem Wenrise.	S. Dioma apud Ware stow [flu:] quod vocatur Ceorlingburg prope aquam de Winrisc.

Liebermann No.	Corpus O.E.	Stowe O.E.	Latin	Chertsey
49	Ðonne resteð Sancte Beocca abbod and Edor mæssepreost on Cyrtesige þam mynstre; and þar man ofsloh hundeahtatig muneca mid him.	Ðonne resteð Sancte Beocca abbod and Edor mæssepreost on Ceortesige þam mynstre; and þær man sloh hundneogontig muneca: — hæðene menn.	Sanctusque abba Beocca et Edor presbyter in loco qui dicitur Ceortesige, cum quibus sunt monachi xc occisi a paganis.	S. Beocca abbas, et S. Edor presbyter, et S. Fritheuold rex de Astapeled apud Ceortese.
23b	Ðonne resteð Sancte Erconwald se biscop on Lundenbirig.	Ðonne resteð Sancte Ercenwald bisceop on Lundenbyrig.	Sanctusque episcopus Erconwaldus in civitate Lundonia.	Erkenualdus abbas de Ceortesey monasterii a Fritheualdo instituti.
34	Ðonne resteð on Rumesige Sancta Mærwyn, wæs seo forme abbodesse þaes mynstres, and Sancte Balthild regina, and Sancta Æþelflæd, and fela oðre halgan.	Ðonne resteð Sancte Mærwynn abbatissa on Rumesige þam mynstre neah þære ea Tærstan.	Sanctaque Merwinna abbatissa in loco qui dicitur Rumesyge prope amnem Tærstan.	S. Merwenna abbatissa et Æthelfleada in Rumesige prope amnem Trestan.

bungled translation of the standard Charlbury entry, 'Sancte Dionia on þare stowe þe is genemnod Ceorlincburh', as 'S. Dioma apud Ware stow quod vocatur Ceorlingburg', suggests that his exemplar was in Old English. To the normal pair of Chertsey saints Leland adds a third: 'S. Fritheuold rex de Astaþeled'. This is not an otherwise unknown kingdom but a further confusion: *astaþeled* is evidently a late form of the past participle of O.E. *gestaþelian*, 'to found', and the sense of the original passage must have been something like 'St Frithuwold the king who founded Chertsey minster'.[5]

An independent transcript of the entry is preserved in the mid-thirteenth-century Chertsey cartulary, British Library Cotton Vitellius A.xiii. This manuscript deservedly has a poor reputation; many of the charters are crude forgeries, and the narrative passages seem to have been concocted by the scribe, partly from standard national chronicles. The passage describing the sacking of the monastery by the Danes, its colonization and rebuilding under St Æthelwold, and the rediscovery of the relics is none the less of some interest, and since it has never previously been printed it is given here in full:[6]

> Eodem igitur tempore, crescente malicia Danorum et sevitia paganorum, totius fines Britannie conati sunt in exterminium bellis, incendiis, depredationibus et aliis nefandis vastationibus dare. Tandem totam terram fere pervagantes et depopulantes, venerunt ad quoddam monasterium quod est situm apud Cirotis insulam quod nunc dicitur Certeseya in provincia Surrianorum, precipientes monachis ibidem tunc deo servientibus a monasterio egredi, et nisi citius exire volentes mortem iam fere proximam eis ferociter intentantes. Illis autem exire nolentibus nec eorum obsecundare preceptis, omnes gladio interfecti sunt, videlicet XC, quorum corpora in uno loco iuxta vetus monasterium condita sunt. Postea ecclesiam et omnes officinas predicti monasterii igni combusserunt, res, terras, villulas et omnes eorum possessiones omnino depredaverunt. Illi autem in malicia sua perdurantes, repatriare cupientes, iusto Dei iudicio apud Londoniam omnes interfecti sunt, in loco qui dicitur Ecclesia Danorum.
>
> Multis autem labentibus annorum curriculis, reedificatum est monasterium Certeseye tempore venerabilis patris Sancti Ætheluuoldi Wentane sedis episcopi, qui missis nuntiis ad abbatem et conventum Abbendonie precipiendo in virtute obedientie ut ad monesterium supranominatum tresdecim mitteret monachos, quod et factum est. Illis autem apud Certeseyam venientibus, unus illorum electus est in abbatem. Ceperunt ergo reedificare ecclesiam que vocatur nova ecclesia, adepta regis licentia; officine et alie domus reedificate sunt, et in rebus, terris, villis et possessionibus per Sanctum Æth[el]uuoldum pacifice positi sunt.
>
> Post multum vero tempus, cuidam monacho revelatum est ut corpora monachorum a paganis occisa ter divino ammonitus oraculo de loco ubi requiescebant in ligneo feretro honorifice collocarentur; quod et factum est et usque hodie manifestum, sicut in chronicis predicti monasterii Anglico ideomate invenitur: *In Certeseye in þe munstre þer restet Seint Beccan Abbod and Seint Edor messe prest and Seint Fritheuuold king þat staþelede erest þat munstre mid Seint Erkenuualde Abbed þat eft*

iwerþ Bissup on Londone suuiþe holi, and hundnigenti moneches of slagene und heþene men. Acta sunt hec anno dominice incarnationis octingentesimo octogesimo quarto, tempore Ethelredi regis filii regis Etheluulfi quo mortuo regnavit Æluredus filius Ethelwlfi.

[At that time the malice of the Danes and the cruelty of the pagans grew; they tried to bring the whole land of Britain to destruction through wars, burnings, sackings and other villainous outrages. As they ranged through almost the whole land slaying the people, they came to a certain monastery built at 'Ceorot's Island', now called Chertsey, in the province of the folk of Surrey. They ordered the monks serving God there to come out of the monastery, with savage threats of imminent death if they declined to leave more quickly. When the monks refused to come out or obey their commands all ninety of them were put to the sword, and their bodies were hidden in one place beside the old monastery. Then the church and all the monastic building were burnt, and their goods, lands, farmsteads and all other possessions were utterly laid waste. The Danes, persisting in their malice, decided to return home, but by God's just judgement they were all slain at London in the place called 'Danes' Church'.

Many years later the monastery at Chertsey was rebuilt in the time of the venerable father St Æthelwold, bishop of Winchester. He sent messengers to the abbot and convent of Abingdon, ordering them by virtue of their obedience to send thirteen monks to the above-named monastery, which was duly done. They came to Chertsey, and one of them was elected abbot. They obtained the king's permission, and began to rebuild the church which is called 'the new church'; the monastic buildings and other houses were rebuilt, and St Æthelwold put the monks in peaceful enjoyment of their goods, lands, farmsteads and possessions.

Long afterwards it was revealed to a certain monk, warned three times by a divine revelation, that the bodies of the monks killed by the pagans should be honourably gathered from where they lay into a wooden feretory. This was done, and can still be seen today, as is written in English speech in the chronicles of that monastery: *At Chertsey in the minster rest St Beocca the abbot, and St Edor the mass priest, and St Frithuwold the king who first established that minster with St Eorcenwold who was afterwards a most holy bishop of London, and ninety monks slain by heathen men.* These things happened in the year of our Lord's incarnation 884, in the time of king Æthelred son of king Æthelwulf, after whose death reigned Alfred son of Æthelwulf.]

The author's utter confusion is most clearly revealed by his chronology: a refoundation by St Æthelwold as bishop of Winchester (963–84) is said to have happened long before an event which is dated to 884 and in the reign of Æthelred I (865–71). This need not mean that he had no genuine materials or traditions to draw on. The survival of Frithuwold's charter is itself evidence that the community existed continuously in some form between the Viking attack and the Benedictine Reform; one possible rationalization would be to suggest that it was sacked in the time of Æthelred I and reinstated as a minster of secular priests in 884.[7] There was a community at Chertsey at some date between 871 and 889, when it received bequests from ealdorman Alfred.[8] The Anglo-Saxon Chronicle notes that Chertsey was recolonized with monks in 964; Æthelwold was probably involved and may well have brought monks from Abingdon, which he had only left the previous year.[9] The tradition of an 'old monastery' on a different site from the 'new church' is interesting, though it is impossible to be certain that the move really occurred in the tenth century, not in the late eleventh when so many monastic churches were rebuilt. There is at all events a plausible context for an unbroken cult both of the late ninth-century martyrs and of 'St Frithuwold', even if their relics were so thoroughly lost as to require a miraculous invention.

Clearly the cartulary scribe used either the manuscript of the resting-place list which Leland saw or one closely related. The vocabulary of the phrase peculiar to the Chertsey text would be possible at any date between the tenth and early thirteenth centuries; some of the spellings are clearly post-Conquest, but the scribe could have modernized his exemplar.[10] Since he cites the list as an old authority, and since it was a version of a known late Anglo-Saxon text, it can reasonably be accepted as predating the main Chertsey forgeries. The fact that Frithuwold only appears in Chertsey's own version may mean that his cult was obscure, but not that it was spurious; the main texts of the list are very far from being comprehensive and cannot be used for *ex silentio* arguments. Frithuwold's cult is not of a kind likely to have been invented in the post-Reform period, and is best seen as an organic development from his own time in the community which he had endowed.

NOTES

1 In search of the origins of Anglo-Saxon kingdoms

1. This chapter is in most respects the paper which I gave at the conference entitled 'The Origins of Anglo-Saxon Kingdoms' at Oxford in December 1986. I am most grateful to Chris Wickham, Nicholas Brooks and Philippa Bassett for their comments on earlier drafts of it.
2. *Bede's Ecclesiastical History of the English People* (hereafter *HE*), ed. B. Colgrave and R.A.B. Mynors (1969), v, 10; E.A. Thompson, *The Early Germans* (1965), 29–48; J.M. Wallace-Hadrill, *Early Germanic Kingship in England and on the Continent* (1971), 1–20.
3. D.N. Dumville, 'Kingship, genealogies and regnal lists', in *Early Medieval Kingship*, ed. P.H. Sawyer and I.N. Wood (1977), 72–104 (esp. at 91–2).
4. As exemplified in e.g. *The Anglo-Saxons*, ed. J. Campbell (1982), ch. 2; and C.C. Taylor, 'The nature of Romano-British settlement studies – what are the boundaries?', in *The Romano-British Countryside. Studies in Rural Settlement and Economy*, ed. D. Miles (Brit. Archaeol. Reports (hereafter BAR), Brit. series, no. 103, 1982), 1–15.
5. Dumville, 'Kingship, genealogies and regnal lists', 77–96 and refs. cited there; D.P. Kirby, 'Problems of early West Saxon history', *Eng. Hist. Rev.* lxxx (1965), 10–29; D.P. Henige, 'Oral tradition and chronology', *Journal of African History*, xii (1971), 371–89; P.C. Lloyd, 'Yoruba myths: a sociologist's interpretation', *Odu*, 1st ser. ii (n.d. *c*. 1955), 20–8.
6. Since 1951 most scholars have agreed with Whitelock's arguments for an eighth-century date of composition, even if not all of them could accept her case for narrowing it down still further: D. Whitelock, *The Audience of Beowulf* (1951), 24–30, 63–4.
7. K.H. Jackson, *Language and History in Early Britain* (1953), 512, 600; A.L.F. Rivet and C. Smith, *The Place-Names of Roman Britain* (1979), 300, 393; S.R. Bassett, 'Lincoln and the Anglo-Saxon see of Lindsey', *Anglo-Saxon England* (hereafter *ASE*), xviii (forthcoming).
8. J. Campbell, *Bede's Reges and Principes* (Jarrow Lecture for 1979); *idem*, 'Bede's words for places', in *Names, Words, and Graves: Early Medieval Settlement*, ed. P. H. Sawyer (1979), 34–53.
9. Dumville, 'Kingship, genealogies and regnal lists'; *idem*, 'The Anglian collection of royal genealogies and regnal lists', *ASE* v (1976), 23–50.
10. B. Hope-Taylor, *Yeavering: An Anglo-British Centre of Early Northumbria* (1977), 276–324.
11. H.E. Walker, 'Bede and the Gewissae: the political evolution of the Heptarchy and its nomenclature', *Cambridge Hist. J.* xii (1956), 174–86; Kirby, 'Problems of early West Saxon history'; M. Biddle, 'Hampshire and the origins of Wessex', *Problems in Economic and Social Archaeology*, ed. G. de G. Sieveking, I.H. Longworth and K.E. Wilson (1976), 321–42; B.A.E. Yorke, 'The foundation of the Old Minster and the status of Winchester in the seventh and eighth centuries', *Proc. Hants. Field Club & Arch. Soc.* xxxviii (1982), 75–83, and in this volume. And now D.N. Dumville, 'The West Saxon genealogical regnal list and the chronology of early Wessex', *Peritia*, iv (1985), 21–66.

12. A.H. Smith, 'The Hwicce', in *Frankiplegius: Medieval and Linguistic Studies, In Honour of Francis Peabody Magoun, Jn.* (1965), 56–65; D. Hooke, *The Anglo-Saxon Landscape: The Kingdom of the Hwicce* (1985).

13. It must be said, however, that I have no intention of trying to answer all the questions which I posed at the beginning of this chapter.

14. Smith, 'The Hwicce', 59–60; Hooke, *The Anglo-Saxon Landscape*, 12–20.

15. *Taxatio Ecclesiastica Angliae et Walliae auctoritate P. Nicholai IV* (1802), 216–40.

16. The earlier date is given in an appendix to Florence of Worcester's *Chronicon ex Chronicis*, printed in *The Church Historians of England*, ed. J. Stephenson, II.i (1853), 379, and the later one in its main text: *ibid.*, 189. The creation of the diocese is discussed in my forthcoming paper, 'Churches in Worcester before and after the Conversion of the Anglo-Saxons'.

17. e.g. F.M. Stenton, *Anglo-Saxon England* (3rd edn. 1971), 45; H.P.R. Finberg, 'The Princes of the Hwicce', in *idem, The Early Charters of the West Midlands* (hereafter *Early Charters*) (2nd edn. 1972), 167–8.

18. S.R. Bassett, 'A probable Mercian royal mausoleum at Winchcombe, Gloucestershire', *Antiq. J.* lxv (1985), 84.

19. W. Stubbs, 'The cathedral, diocese, and monasteries of Worcester in the eighth century', *Arch. J.* xix (1862), 237–8; Finberg, 'Princes of the Hwicce', 167–70. Finberg suggested that Penda owed his victory of 628 to the assistance of 'a powerful war-band of Northumbrian origin' whose reward was to rule the newly created province. Although ingenious, the argument has only a thin evidential basis. It depends on two assumptions, neither of which need be true. First, Penda may not have been a 'land-less noble . . . fighting for his own hand' (Stenton, *Anglo-Saxon England*, 45), powerless without allies; he may already have been ruling in Mercia by then (W. Davies, 'Annals and the origins of Mercia', *Mercian Studies*, ed. A. Dornier (1977), 20–1). Any alliance against Wessex, moreover, is much more likely to have been with Anglian settlers in the Severn and Avon valleys who had an obvious interest in curtailing West Saxon involvement in the West Midlands. Secondly, Finberg bases a lot on the occurrence of certain names in both the Northumbrian and the Hwiccian dynasties, emphasizing Stubbs's suggestion of a family relationship. This may well be true, but need not imply that the rulers of the Hwicce were an offshoot of the Bernician royal family. Instead, the two dynasties may have shared a common ancestry somewhere in eastern England in the first phases of their settlement in Britain, a notion in keeping with available written and archaeological evidence (*HE*, i, xv; K. Pretty, 'The Welsh Border and the Severn and Avon valleys in the fifth and sixth centuries AD: an archaeological survey' (unpubl. Ph.D. thesis, Univ. of Cambridge, 1975), *passim*). Marriages between members of the various Anglian dynasties would have maintained the link. There seems no good reason why the rulers of the Hwicce should not themselves have been of Hwiccian stock; indeed, if they were, it would be easier to explain how they maintained their position throughout the troubles between Mercia and Northumbria in the seventh century.

20. F.M. Stenton, 'The supremacy of the Mercian kings', *Eng. Hist. Rev.* xxxiii (1918), 433–52.

21. C.S. Taylor, 'The origin of the Mercian shires', in *Gloucestershire Studies*, ed. H.P.R. Finberg (1957), 17–45; Finberg, 'The ancient shire of Winchcombe', in *idem, Early Charters*, 228–35.

22. *Hemingi Chartularium Ecclesiae Wigorniensis*, ed. T. Hearne (2 vols., Oxford, 1723), i, 1–247; N.R. Ker, 'Hemming's Cartulary', in *Studies in Medieval History presented to F.M. Powicke*, ed. R.W. Hunt *et al.* (1948), 49–75.

23. Cited here from *Domesday Book seu Liber censualis Willelmi Primi Regis*, ed. A. Farley (hereafter *DB*) (2 vols., London, 1783).

24. W. de G. Birch, *Cartularium Saxonicum* (hereafter CS) (3 vols., 1885–93), no. 575; P.H. Sawyer, *Anglo-Saxon Charters: An Annotated List and Bibliography* (hereafter S) (1968), no. 1442. Finberg, who alone has commented on this charter, accepts it as an authentic eleventh-century copy: *Early Charters*, no. 86. (For the identification of *Uptune* see *ibid.*, no. 63.) The authenticity of Coenwulf's stipulation, known only from this source, need not be in serious doubt. In the settlement it is recorded that in 897 ealdorman Æthelwulf found it among privileges recorded in the *hereditarios libros* of Coenwulf; these are very probably the ancient privileges stored at Winchcombe which are referred to in the settlement of a dispute in 825, an authentic original charter (CS384): *antiquis privilegiis quae sunt aet Wincel cumbe.* See also W. Levison, 'Winchcombe Abbey and its earliest charters', appendix iv of *idem, England and the Continent in the Eighth Century* (1946), 252 and n.2.

25. *quod nullus heres post eum licentiam haberet hereditatem Cenuulfi quae pertinet ad Wincelcumbe alicui hominum longius donandam vel conscribendam quam dies unius hominis.* On the standard canonical prohibition against alienation of monastic property for more than one lifetime, see N.P. Brooks, *The Early History of the Church of Canterbury* (1984), 175 and n.1 there.

26. CS364, S1861. *aldantune* is identified as Alderton (Glos.) near Winchcombe, rather than Aldington (Worcs.), by H.P.R. Finberg, *The Early Charters of Wessex* (1964), 250. Alderton and Upton were both in Winchcombeshire in the early eleventh century.

27. Bassett, 'A probable Mercian royal mausoleum at Winchcombe', 82–5.

28. *ibid.*, 85, 89–93; H.M. Taylor, 'St Wystan's church, Repton, Derbyshire: a reconstruction essay', *Arch. J.* cxliv (1987), 205–45.

29. He was Offa's fourth cousin twice removed. It is possible that his ancestors included members of the Hwiccian royal family. His recorded genealogy alleges a direct descent from Pybba (Dumville, 'The Anglian collection', 31, 33, 37) from whom, through two of his sons Eowa and Penda, all but one (Beornred) of Coenwulf's predecessors as kings of Mercia are said to be descended. Next to nothing is known, however, about any of his direct male ancestors, and his claim of descent from Pybba is as unsubstantiated as that alleging Merewalh, ruler of the Magonsæte, to have been a son of Penda (Stenton, *Anglo-Saxon England*, 47, n.1; H.P.R. Finberg, 'The princes of the Magonsaete' in *idem, Early Charters*, 217–24, at 217, 219). None of them figures in any land charter – unless Coenwulf's father is the same man as the Cuthbert *princeps* granted land by Beonna, abbot of *Medeshamstede*, in 786×96 (CS271, S1412) and/or the Cuthbert entitled *dux* in the witness lists of three (unreliable) Mercian royal charters of the 790s (CS264, S138; CS280, S151; CS281, S150). It is none the less likely that Coenwulf's 'hereditary land belonging to Winchcombe' and his marked personal interest in the place both derived from a close blood relationship to one or more of the last members of the

Hwiccian royal family known to have had authority in the kingdom. The last three such were the brothers Eanberht (not heard of after 759), Uhtred (not heard of after 775), and Ealdred, whose final recorded act was to witness Offa's memorandum of donation of land at Broadwas (Worcs.) to the church of Worcester in 789 or 790 (CS233, S216; Finberg, 'Princes of the Hwicce', 178–80). Coenwulf's relationship to the Hwiccian ruling dynasty could have been through either of his parents. Certainly his own name, and those of his brothers Cuthred and Ceolwulf and his children Cynhelm and Cwoenthryth (all echoing the strongly predominant C- alliteration of his direct male ancestors, whose names included one in Coen-, one in Cyn- and two in Cuth-), are similarly reminiscent of the names of a number of late seventh- and eighth-century aristocrats of importance in the *provincia* of the Hwicce, of whom some at least were no doubt lesser members of the Hwiccian royal family. For example, the records of the short-lived family monastery at Inkberrow (Worcs.) reveal Cutberht, Cuthswith, Cyneburg and Cussa (CS85, C53; CS153, S95; CS256, S1430; P. Sims-Williams, 'Cuthswith, seventh-century abbess of Inkberrow, near Worcester, and the Wurzburg manuscript of Jerome on Ecclesiastes', *ASE* v (1976), 1–21), the first three of whom were very probably members of the Hwiccian royal family. The only known abbots of the Hwiccian monastery at *Sture* were Cyneberht, *comes* of Æthelbald of Mercia, and his son Ceolfrith (CS154, S89; CS220, S1411; and for Cyneberht's abbacy, CS181, S96). Others, royal or noble, who may have had blood links to the Hwiccian ruling dynasty include the *patricius* Cenfrith (CS58; S73), and the thegn Ceolmund to whom Uhtred granted (or confirmed) land in Kemerton,

Worcs. (*Cyneburgingctun*) in 777×9 (CS232, S57; Finberg, *Early Charters*, 94).

30. CS59, S71; CS117, S1174; CS120, S78; CS124, S79; CS125, S80; CS127, S81; CS134, S83; CS205, S61; CS221, S107; CS235, S118.

31. CS43, S51; CS51, S52; CS76, S76; CS85, S53; CS116, S54; CS122, S1177; CS123, S64; CS183, S55; CS187, S56; CS203, S59; CS218, S63; CS231, S147; CS232, S57; CS238, S62; CS240, S121.

32. Land around Gloucester, for the foundation of a monastery there, and at Pershore, 671 for 674×9: CS60, S70; Tetbury, 681: CS58, S73; Somerford Keynes, 685: CS65, S1169; Henbury and Aust, 691×9: CS75, S77; Fladbury, 691×9: CS76, S76; Wychbold, 692: CS77, S75; Wyre Piddle, 709×16: B.L. Additional MS 34,633, f. 206 (printed by Finberg, *Early Charters*, 203), S1800; land in or near Stoke Prior, 716×17: CS137, S102; part of a building in Droitwich, 716×17: CS138, S97; Three other charters may also be earlier than 727: Wootton Wawen, 716×37: CS157, S94; Woodchester, 716×45: CS164, S103; and Bradley near Inkberrow, 723×37: CS153, S95.

33. Daylesford, 718 for ?727: CS139, S84; Batsford, 727×36: CS163, S101; land in the province of *Husmerae*, 736: CS154, S89; Aston Blank and Notgrove, 737×40: CS165, S99; Wick [Episcopi], 757×75: CS219, S142; Evenlode, 772 for 775: CS209, S109; Sedgeberrow, 778: CS223, S113; Donnington, 779: CS229, S115; land near Salmonsbury, 779: CS230, S114; Cofton Hackett and Rednal [and the unidentified *Waersetfelda*], 780: CS234, S117; Teddington, Washbourne, Cutsdean, and Bredons Norton, 780: CS236, S116; Hampton Lucy [and the unidentified *Faehha leage*], 781: CS239, S120; Icomb, in exchange for Sapey, 781: CS240, S121; Broadwas, 786 or 589 for 789×90: CS233, S126; Westbury-

on-Trym, 793×6: CS274, S139; land probably near Huntingford, 796: CS278, S148. Three other charters may also be of 727 or later: Wootton Wawen, 716×37: CS157, S94; Woodchester, 716×45: CS164, S103; and Bradley near Inkberrow, 723×37: CS153, S95.

34. There are twenty lost charters known about from reliable sources. Six were allegedly issued by rulers of the Hwicce, with or without the association of the contemporary Mercian king in the grant: Withington, 674×704: referred to (hereafter ref.) in CS156, S1429; Twyning, ?*c.* 740: ref. in a codicil to CS217, S1255; Overbury, ?757: in a list of benefactions to the church of Worcester printed in W. Dugdale, *Monasticon Anglicanum*, ed. J. Caley, H. Ellis and B. Bandinel (6 vols. in 8, London, 1817–30), i, 607; Weston-on-Avon, 773: *ibid.* 608; Over, near Gloucester, and Northleach, ?*c.* 780: CS535, S209 & S1782 (in a list of benefactions to St Peter's, Gloucester); Coln St Aldwyn, Chedworth and Nympsfield [and the unidentified *Weapcaurtane*], 779×90: *ibid.* A further fourteen lost charters were allegedly issued by Mercian rulers alone: Hanbury, 657×74: *Hemingi Chartularium*, ed. Hearne, 567, S1822; a shed and two furnaces at Droitwich, 691: Dugdale, *Monasticon*, i, 607; Bredon, 716×17: *ibid.*; Westbury-on-Trym and Henbury, 716×57: ref. in CS273, S146; Yate, 716×57: ref. in CS231, S147; Aust, 716×57: ref. in CS269, S137; Evenlode and Badgeworth, 716×57: ref. in CS535, S209 and S1782; part of a building with two salt furnaces in Droitwich, 716×57: *Hem. Chart.* 565, S1824; Hymelmore (at or near Himbleton), 716×57: *ibid.*, 567, S1825; Wolverley, 718×45: Dugdale, *Monasticon*, i, 607, S1827; Tetbury, 757–96: *Hem. Chart.* 369; *Sture* (near Kidderminster), 757×96: *ibid.*, 564, S1829; Laughern, 781–96: *ibid.*, 515, 574; and ten houses

with salt pits in Droitwich, 796–821: *Hem. Chart.* 516.

35. The only difficulty raised by the lost charters concerns king Æthelbald's charter of 716×17 to his kinsman and companion Eanulf in respect of Bredon, where the latter founded a monastery. Bredon certainly lay within the area of the future Winchcombeshire (Mitton in Bredon parish is one of the places entered in the *Liber Wigorniensis* (f. 111rv) under the heading *Into Wincelcumbe*: CS1111, S1308). If the charter which Dugdale saw was authentic, and if his record of it is reliable (e.g. if he did not omit the name of a Hwiccian co-grantor), then the rulers of the Hwicce would seem to have lost sole control over land in the area concerned – at any rate the prime land beside the Avon – by 716×17 not 727. But that would not be the case if Eanulf, who was Offa's grandfather, was himself a member of the Hwiccian royal family (presumably on his mother's side – even though it has not been customar; to think of transmission through the female line in Anglo-Saxon society) or was married to one. That he was may be indicated by his founding of a second monastery in the diocese of Worcester, on his estate at Westbury-on-Trym, and by the association, as late as 777×9, of Ealdred, *subregulus* of the Hwicce, with Offa in a grant of part of that estate to the church of Worcester (CS231, S147; CS273, S146). It may also be significant that Offa apparently made an important contribution to the development of the monastery at Winchcombe (Bassett, 'A probable Mercian royal mausoleum at Winchcombe', 82–4 and refs. cited there), and that in 780 he gave lands at Teddington Washbourne, Cutsdean and Bredons Norton to St Peter's, Bredon – all later on in Winchcombeshire – stipulating moreover that they were always

to remain in his family's hands (CS236, S116).

36. The area contained at least ten minster churches – eight of them certainly, and the others probably, of middle Saxon origin – but there is hardly any charter evidence of their foundation. For Winchcombe, in existence in Offa's day, see Bassett, 'A probable Mercian royal mausoleum at Winchcombe', 82–5. Withington was founded in 674×704 by Oshere (CS156, S1429; CS217, S1255); and in a charter of 759 Oshere's greatgrandsons Eanberht, Uhtred and Ealdred (Finberg, *Early Charters*, 179) described 10 hides of land at Andoversford in Withington as *terram juris nostri*, 'land of our legal right' (CS187, S56). Nothing is known of the origins of [Bishop's] Cleeve, but Offa and Ealdred together enlarged its endowment in 768–79 (CS246, S141). Bredon was founded by Eanulf, Offa's grandfather (n.35 above). Cheltenham and Beckford were in existence by 803 (CS309, S1431) and Blockley by 855 (CS489, S207). Daylesford was founded in ?727 by the otherwise unknown Baegia on land freed from secular dues by king Æthelbald (CS139, S84) – the earliest charter in respect of land in this area issued by a Mercian king alone. Stanway and Stow-in-the-Wold are shown to be minster churches in 1086: W.J. Blair, 'Secular minster churches in Domesday Book', *Domesday Book. A Reassessment*, ed. P.H. Sawyer (1985), 108 (fig. 7.1).

37. Taylor, 'The origins of the Mercian shires', *passim*.

38. Stenton, *Anglo-Saxon England*, 292–7; Campbell, *Bede's Reges and Principes*, 3–4.

39. *HE* iii, 16, v, 11.

40. W. Davies and H. Vierck, 'The contexts of Tribal Hidage: social aggregates and settlement patterns', *Frühmittelalterliche Studien*, viii (1974), 230–6.

41. B.L. MS Harley 3271, f. 6v, printed as CS297.

42. Stenton, *Anglo-Saxon England*, 296; Davies and Vierck, 'The contexts of Tribal Hidage', 225–7. For a dissenting view, Brooks, below, p. 159, 167–8.

43. I shall give details of these in a future publication.

44. CS220, S1411; D. Ford, 'A note on a "grant by Æthelbald, king of Mercia, to ealdorman Cyneberht, of land at Stour in Ismere, Worcs." ', *J. Eng. Place-Name Soc.* xii (1980), 66–9.

45. CS157, S94.

46. H.M. and J. Taylor, *Anglo-Saxon Architecture* (2 vols., Cambridge, 1965), ii, 685–8. However, it may well no longer be on its original site.

47. S.R. Bassett, 'The Wootton Wawen Project', *West Midlands Archaeol.* xxvi (1983), 69–70; *idem, The Wootton Wawen Project: Interim Report No. 4* (School of History, University of Birmingham, 1986), 13.

48. Or else they were the 'people of the hollow' (O.E. *stoppa*, 'bucket', used in a topographical sense): M. Gelling, 'The placename volumes for Worcestershire and Warwickshire: a new look', *Field and Forest: An Historical Geography of Warwickshire and Worcestershire*, ed. T.R. Slater and P.J. Jarvis (Norwich, 1982), 69.

49. F.J. Byrne, *Irish Kings and High-Kings* (1973), 7–8 and *passim*.

50. P.H. Sawyer, 'The royal *tun* in pre-Conquest England', *Ideal and Reality in Frankish and Anglo-Saxon Society*, ed. P. Wormald (1983), 273–99.

51. T.M. Charles-Edwards, 'Kinship, status and the origins of the hide', *Past & Present*, lvi (Aug. 1972), 3–33, at 8, 29–32, and refs. cited there.

52. Initially and chiefly propagated by G.R.J. Jones, whose views are conveniently summarized in 'Multiple estates and early settlement', in *Medieval Settlement. Continuity and Change*, ed. P.H. Sawyer (1976), 15–40. It is a model for the development of (among others) Anglo-Saxon land-units based on lords, tenants and estates, i.e.

one which assumes that concepts of ownership in early medieval Britain were always those of Roman law (i.e. exclusive ownership of the modern sort by individuals). It begs the question of how the 'multiple estate' originated, beyond declaring it to be a surviving pre-Anglo-Saxon land-unit. The model could appear to have been given considerable support by T.H. Aston's seminal paper, 'The origins of the manor in England *with* A postscript', in *Social Relations and Ideas. Essays in Honour of R.H. Hilton*, ed. T.H. Aston *et al.* (1983), 1–43; but Aston himself begs the questions of what happened to the late Romano-British estate system and what sort of economy lowland Britain had in the Migration Period, and uses only the broadest chronological terms when discussing the origins of Anglo-Saxon lordship. His views cannot be safely projected back into the fifth and sixth centuries. For a revealing discussion of other flaws in Jones's model, see N. Gregson, 'The multiple estate model: some critical questions', *J. Historical Geog.* xi (1985), 339–51, and Jones's reply 'Multiple estates perceived', *ibid.*, 352–63.

53. Partible inheritance is of course entirely appropriate to a social system which allows all (or all male) members of the tribe to enjoy the common stock of land. Its practical applications diminish considerably, however, once land ownership becomes a major determinant of a person's social status.

54. G.W.O. Addleshaw, *The Beginnings of the Parochial System* (St Anthony's Hall (York) Publics. no. 3, 1953); *idem, The Development of the Parochial System from Charlemagne to Urban II* (St Anthony's Hall Publics. no. 6, 1954); C.N.L. Brooke, 'Rural ecclesiastical institutions in England: the search for their origins', *Settimane di Studio del centro Italiano di Studi Sull'alto*

Medioevo, xxviii (Spoleto, 1982), 685–711.

55. Good examples include B.R. Kemp, 'The mother church of Thatcham', *Berks. Arch. J.* lxiii (1967–8), 15–22; J.N. Croom, 'The fragmentation of the minster *parochiae* of south-east Shropshire', in *Minsters and Parish Churches: The Local Church in Transition 950–1200*, ed. J. Blair (1988), 67–81.

56. F.W. Maitland, 'The surnames of English villages', *The Archaeol. Rev.* iv (1889), 237–8.

57. P.H. Reaney, *The Place-Names of Essex* (Eng. Place-Name Soc. vol. xii. 1935), 490–1.

58. *Taxatio Ecclesiastica Angliae et Walliae auctoritate P. Nicholai IV circa* A.D. 1291 (London, 1802), 15b, 18, 21b; P. Morant, *The History and Antiquities of the County of Essex* (London, 1768), 471.

59. DB ii, fos. 3, 19, 35b, 36b, 40b, 49, 50b–51, 52, 55, 57b, 61, 61b–62. A detailed account of the Rodings land-unit and its fragmentation is in preparation.

60. Mapped in Bassett, *The Wootton Wawen Project: Interim Report No. 4*, fig. 7a.

61. For land-units: Taylor, 'The nature of Romano-British settlement'; for settlement and land-use: P.J. Fowler, 'Agriculture and rural settlement', in *The Archaeology of Anglo-Saxon England*, ed. D.M. Wilson (1976), 23–48; for field systems: S.R. Bassett, 'Medieval Lichfield: a topographical review', *Trans. S. Staffs. Arch. & Hist. Soc.* xxii for 1980–1 (1982), 95–8 and refs. cited there.

62. See e.g. S. James, A. Marshall and M. Millett, 'An early medieval building tradition', *Arch. J.* cxli (1984), 182–215 and refs.

63. The argument here briefly summarizes the conclusions of my investigation of the likelihood of a substantial survival of pre-medieval boundaries in the medieval landscape of lowland Britain. It owes a debt to e.g. D.J. Bonney,

244 Notes to pp. 22–4

'Early boundaries in Wessex',
Archaeology and the Landscape,
ed. P.J. Fowler (1972), 168–86,
and Fowler, 'Agriculture and
rural settlement', but opposes
the theses of C.J. Arnold and
P. Wardle, 'Early medieval
settlement patterns in England',
Med. Arch. xxv (1981), 145–9,
and A. Goodier, 'The formation
of boundaries in Anglo-Saxon
England: a statistical study',
ibid., xxviii (1984), 1–21. In
respect of the Rodings there is
some evidence that many
lengths of their parish
boundaries perpetuate pre-
medieval land divisions: W.J.
Rodwell, 'Relict Landscapes in
Essex', in *Early Land Allotment*,
ed. H.C. Bowen and P.J. Fowler
(BAR, Brit. series, no. 48, 1978),
89–98 at 97.

64. On multiple kingship in early
Germanic societies, see I.N.
Wood, 'Kings, kingdoms and
consent, in *Early Medieval
Kingship*, ed. Sawyer and Wood,
18–20; for its practice in one
such society: B.A.E. Yorke, 'The
kingdom of the East Saxons',
ASE xiv (1985), 1–36.

65. As exemplified in the royal
succession in, for instance,
Mercia in the period from the
mid-seventh century to 716 and
Wessex in the ninth century.

66. Byrne, *Irish Kings and High-
Kings*, 28, 35–9.

67. Stenton, *Anglo-Saxon England*,
45.

68. The mechanisms involved –
indeed the process of state
formation itself – have not been
much discussed by medieval
historians, with one or two
exceptions: e.g. R. Hodges, 'State
formation and the role of trade
in middle Saxon England', *Social
Organisation and Settlement:
Contributions from
Anthropology, Archaeology and
Geography* (BAR, Internat. ser.
47, 1978), 439–53; *idem*, 'Peer
polity interaction in Anglo-
Saxon England', in *Peer Polity
Interaction and Socio-political
Change*, ed. C. Renfrew and J.F.
Cherry (1986), 69–78. However,
prehistorians have a lot to say of

direct relevance: e.g. C. Renfrew,
'Introduction', *ibid.*, 1–18; T.
and S. Champion, 'Peer polity
interaction and the European
Iron Age', *ibid.*, 59–68; C.C.
Haselgrove, 'Wealth, prestige and
power: the dynamics of political
centralisation in south-east
England', in *Ranking, Resource
and Exchange*, ed. C. Renfrew
and S. Shennan (1982), 79–88;
and specifically on the factor of
population growth, B. Cunliffe,
'Settlement and population in
the British Iron Age: some facts,
figures and fantasies', in
*Lowland Iron Age Communities
in Europe*, ed. B. Cunliffe and
T. Rowley (BAR, Internat. ser.
48, 1978), 3–24. For a yet broader
perspective, see M. Mann, *The
Sources of Social Power. Volume
1: A History of Power from the
Beginning to AD 1760* (1986), chs.
2–4.

69. *Beowulf*, tr. K. Crossley-Holland
(1968), lines 1684–6, 1882–3.

70. *An Anglo-Saxon Dictionary.
Based on the manuscript
collections of the late Joseph
Bosworth*, ed. and enlarged by
T.N. Toller (1882), 185–6, at
cyning.

71. Except those of J.N.L. Myres,
most recently set out in *The
English Settlements* (*The Oxford
History of England*, vol. Ib.
1986), on which see my review
in *Archives*, xvii (1986), 168–9.
Prevalent current thinking is
well represented by *The Anglo-
Saxons*, ed. Campbell, chs. 1–2.

72. Brooks, below, ch. 4; Biddle,
'Hampshire and the origins of
Wessex'; P.H. Blair, 'The origins
of Northumbria', *Archaeologia
Aeliana*, 4th ser. xxv (1947), 1–
51, at 39–44.

73. The case is made in my paper,
'Great Chesterford and Bonhunt:
the transition from Roman to
Anglo-Saxon control in the Essex
area', read at seminars at the
Universities of Birmingham,
Cambridge, London and
Manchester in 1980–2, and now
redrafted for publication.

74. *ibid.*

75. *The Victoria History of the
County of Essex. III: Roman*

Essex (1963), 86–8; A. Meaney, *A Gazetteer of Early Anglo-Saxon Burial Sites* (1964), 85; V.I. Evison, 'Five Anglo-Saxon inhumation graves containing pots at Great Chesterford, Essex (with a contribution by J.N.L. Myres)', *Berichten van de Rijksdienst voor het Oudheidkundig Bodemonderzoek*, xix (1969), 157–73.
76. Dr M. Gelling, pers. comm.
77. K. Wade, 'A settlement site at Bonhunt Farm, Wicken Bonhunt, Essex', in *Archaeology in Essex to AD 1500*, ed. D.G. Buckley (Council for Brit. Archaeol. Research Rep. no. 34, 1980), 96–102.
78. The evidence is set out in full in my paper 'Great Chesterford and Wicken Bonhunt'.
79. Campbell, *Bede's Reges and Principes*, 4.
80. Davies and Vierck, 'The contexts of Tribal Hidage', 230–6.
81. For the genealogy: R.L.S. Bruce-Mitford, *The Sutton Hoo Ship-Burial. I: Excavations, Background, The Ship, Dating and Inventory* (1975), 693–6; for East Anglian sees: *Handbook of British Chronology*, ed. E.B. Fryde *et al.* (3rd edn. 1986), 216–17.

2 Early medieval kingships in the British Isles

1. D.A. Binchy, *Celtic and Anglo-Saxon Kingship* (1970), is the classic discussion.
2. P. Wormald, 'Celtic and Anglo-Saxon Kingship', in *Sources of Anglo-Saxon Culture*, ed. P.E. Szarmach with the assistance of V.D. Oggins (*Studies in Medieval Culture*, xx, 1986), 151–83.
3. A.H.M. Jones, *The Roman Economy: Studies in Ancient Economic and Administrative History*, ed. P.A. Brunt (1974), 37.
4. The weights used were Roman, the ounce and the scruple.
5. e.g. the Old Welsh glosses on the *De Mensuris et Ponderibus*, ed.

I. Williams, *Bulletin of the Board of Celtic Studies*, v (1929–31), 226–48.
6. Cf. J. Campbell, *Essays in Anglo-Saxon History* (1986), 95–7, 108–16.
7. Bede, *Historia Ecclesiastica* (hereafter abbreviated *HE*), iii, 26, ed. B. Colgrave and R.A.B. Mynors, *Bede's Ecclesiastical History of the English People* (1969), 310.
8. Campbell, *Essays in Anglo-Saxon History*, 95–7.
9. *Vita Wilfridi* (hereafter abbreviated *VW*), c.2, *The Life of Bishop Wilfrid by Eddius Stephanus*, ed. B. Colgrave (1927), 4–6.
10. *HE* ii, 14, 16 (Colgrave's translation of *saepius*, on 188, as 'very frequently' seems to miss the point).
11. See the map in *Karl der Grosse*, general ed. W. Braunfels (1965), vol. i, *Persönlichkeit und Geschichte*, ed. H. Beumann, opp. 312.
12. *VW* c.20, *HE* ii, 5.
13. Cf. *HE* iv, 26, on the recovery of their *libertas* by the Irish of Dál Riata after Nechtansmere, with ii, 5, on their payment of tribute; a similar freeing from servile tribute may be implied by the *libertas* recovered by the Mercians in 658, *HE* iii, 24; *VW* c.20.
14. Ine c.70.1 (*Die Gesetze der Angelsachsen*, ed. Liebermann, 1903–16, i, 118–21). Cf. Liebermann's note *ad loc.*, which regards it as not merely royal. F.M. Stenton, *Anglo-Saxon England* (3rd edn., 1971), 285, considers it to be seigneurial and not royal, but he gives no reason apart from the heaviness of the obligation compared with that in *Cartularium Saxonicum*, ed. W. de G. Birch (3 vols., 1885–99), no. 273 (P.H. Sawyer, *Anglo-Saxon Charters: An Annotated List and Bibliography* (1968), no. 146). Yet it is not obvious that a West Saxon royal render of Ine's day must have been of approximately the same value per hide as a Mercian royal render of Offa's day.

15. *The Fourth Book of the Chronicle of Fredegar with its Continuations*, ed. J.M. Wallace-Hadrill (Nelson Medieval Classics, 1960), iv, 74.

16. J.E. Lloyd, *A History of Wales* (3rd edn., 1939), 465, 540.

17. W. Schlesinger, *Die Enstehung der Landesherrschaft* (1941), 41.

18. e.g. *The Annals of Ulster*, ed. S. Mac Airt and G. Mac Niocaill, i (1983), s.a. 720/1.

19. P. O Riain, 'The *Crech Ríg* or Royal Prey', *Éigse*, xv (1973–4), 24–30.

20. *VW* c.19.

21. R. Geraint Gruffydd, 'Canu Cadwallon ap Cadfan', *Astudiaethau ar yr Hengerdd/ Studies in Old Welsh Poetry*, ed. R. Bromwich and R. Brinley Jones (1978), 29, line 26.

22. *Armes Prydein: The Prophecy of Britain*, ed. I. Williams and transl. R. Bromwich (1972), line 167.

23. *ibid.*, lines 102 and 179.

24. *VW* c.2.

25. *ibid.*, c.3.

26. *HE* iii, 25.

27. *VW* c.17.

28. *HE* v, 24. See also A.T. Thacker, 'Some terms for noblemen in Anglo-Saxon England', in *Anglo-Saxon Studies in Archaeology and History*, ii, ed. D. Brown, J. Campbell and S.C. Hawkes (Brit. Archaeol. Reports, Brit. series, no. 92, 1981), 210–13.

29. *VW* c.60; cf. P.H. Blair, 'The Bernicians and their Northern Frontier', in *Studies in Early British History*, ed. N.K. Chadwick (1959), 170–1. On *princeps* see Thacker, 'Some terms for noblemen', 203–5.

30. *HE* v, 24.

31. Blair, 'The Bernicians', 170–1.

32. *Annals of Ulster*, ed. Mac Airt and Mac Niocaill, s.a. 697/8; *Annals of Tigernach*, ed. W. Stokes, *Revue Celtique*, xvii (1896), 216; *VW* c.19.

33. To judge by his gift of Ripon and his apparent wish to have Wilfrid consecrated as bishop of York 'for his own people': *HE* iii, 25, 28; *VW* cc.7–11.

34. K.H. Jackson, 'On the Northern British Section in Nennius', in *Celt and Saxon*, ed. N.K. Chadwick (1963), 41–2.

35. *HE* iii, 14.

36. *VW* cc.21 (*regnum ecclesiarum*) and 24 (note the *exercitum sodalium regalibus vestimentis et armis ornatum*, 'army of companions adorned with royal garments and weapons').

37. The Continuation of Bede's Chronological Summary, s.a. 737: *Baedae Opera Historica*, ed. C. Plummer (1896), i, 362; *Bede's Ecclesiastical History*, ed. Colgrave and Mynors, 572; see D.P. Kirby, 'Northumbria in the time of Wilfrid', in *Saint Wilfrid at Hexham*, ed. D.P. Kirby (1974), 21, for the dynastic position of Ecgberht's brother Eadberht.

38. *Epistola ad Ecgbertum: Baedae Opera Historica*, ed. C. Plummer, i, 411–13 (cc.8–9); cf. 408 (c.5).

39. *ibid.*, 410 (c.7)

40. See M. Metcalf in *The Anglo-Saxons*, ed. J. Campbell (1982), 62–3.

41. W. Davies, *An Early Welsh Microcosm: Studies in the Llandaff Charters* (1978), 47–8, 101, discusses the evidence for pre-Norman food renders.

42. cf. my *Early Irish and Welsh Kinship* (forthcoming), c.10.

43. *Vitae Sanctorum Britanniae et Genealogiae*, ed. A.W. Wade-Evans (1944), 210.

44. D. Jenkins, *The Law of Hywel: Law Texts from Medieval Wales* (1986), 128–9 and cf. 123–4.

45. These are what E. Mac Neill called 'sept-names'; see the discussion in his 'Early Irish population-groups: their nomenclature, classification, and chronology', *Proc. Roy. Ir. Acad.* xxix (1911), Section C, No. 4, 82–7; F.J. Byrne, 'Tribes and tribalism in early Ireland', *Ériu*, xxii (1971), 128–66, argues that the rise of dynastic names for kingdoms reflects the decline of tribalism.

46. A.P. Smyth, *Celtic Leinster* (1982), 51–2.

47. R.A. Macalister, *Corpus Inscriptionum Insularum Celticarum*, i (1945), no. 40;

F.J. Byrne, *Irish Kings and High-Kings* (1973), 137–8.
48. Widsith, ed. K. Malone (rev. edn., 1962), 23–5; several of the tribal names in -*ingas* in Widsith are not derived from patronymics (e.g. Seringas=Seres, ibid., 198–9).
49. Beowulf, lines 30, 53, etc.; Widsith, ed. Malone, line 29 and pp. 172–3.
50. HE ii, 5, 15; P. Gonser, *Das angelsächsische Prosa-Leben des hl. Guthlac* (1909), 104, translating *Felix's Life of Saint Guthlac*, ed. B. Colgrave (1956), 74 (c.2).
51. Cf. J.N.L. Myres, 'The Angles, the Saxons, and the Jutes', *Proc. Brit. Acad.* lvi (1970), 65–7.
52. HE iii, 21; W. Davies and H. Vierck, 'The contexts of Tribal Hidage: social aggregates and settlement patterns', *Frühmittelalterliche Studien*, viii (1974), 223–93.
53. D.A. Binchy, 'The Saga of Fergus mac Léti', *Ériu*, xvi (1952), 37 (transl. 39); *Bechbretha*, ed. T. Charles-Edwards and F. Kelly (1983), 133–4.
54. D. Ó Corráin, 'Irish regnal succession: a reappraisal', *Studia Hibernica*, xi (1971), 7–39.
55. *The Patrician Texts in the Book of Armagh*, ed. L. Bieler (1979), 160 (Tírechán, 47.4; 48.1); *Bethu Phátraic*, ed. K. Mulchrone (1939), 94–5.
56. Cf. E. Mac Neill, 'The topographical importance of the *Vita Tripartita*', in his *St Patrick* (1964), 206–7.
57. The seventh-century prophecy of the kings of Tara, *Baile Chuind* (ed. G. Murphy, *Ériu*, xvi, 145–51), includes two kings of Cenél nÉogain, Áed Alláin (ob. 612) and Suibne Mend (ob. 628); after 550 it confines the kingship to the Uí Néill; cf. also *Annals of Ulster*, ed. Mac Airt and Mac Niocaill, s.a. 563 and 605 (in the latter a victory of Áed Alláin is described as having been won by the Uí Néill).
58. Byrne, *Irish Kings and High-Kings*, 114–17.
59. ibid., 258.
60. ibid., 108–9.
61. *Patrician Texts*, ed. Bieler, 78–80, 162, esp. the dynastic prophecy in Muirchú, I.xii.3 (p. 80).
62. *Bechbretha*, ed. Charles-Edwards and Kelly, 123–4.
63. Adomnán, *Vita S. Columbae*, ed. A.O. and M.O. Anderson (1961), i, 50; *Patrician Texts*, ed. Bieler, 160 (c.48.3).
64. Kirby, 'Northumbria in the time of Wilfrid', 19–21.
65. D.N. Dumville, 'The Ætheling: a study in Anglo-Saxon constitutional history', *Anglo-Saxon England*, viii (1979), 14–21.
66. HE iv, 12.
67. *Anglo-Saxon Chronicle: Two of the Saxon Chronicles Parallel*, ed. C. Plummer (1891) (hereafter ASC), s.a. 648.
68. *Life of St Guthlac*, ed. Colgrave, 81.
69. HE ii, 20; iv, 15.
70. *Life of St Guthlac*, ed. Colgrave, 73.
71. Stenton, *Anglo-Saxon England*, 202.
72. Even the heir apparent, *tánaise ríg*, is of noble rather than royal status: *Críth Gablach*, ed. D.A. Binchy (1941), para. 29, and my discussion in 'Críth Gablach and the law of status', *Peritia*, v (1986), 62.
73. ASC s.a. 694 (cf. 685–7).
74. See my *Early Irish and Welsh Kinship* (forthcoming), c.2, part (1).
75. Ó Corráin, 'Irish regnal succession', 27–30.
76. VW c.60.
77. The pre-900 examples are *Annals of Ulster*, ed. Mac Airt and Mac Niocaill, s.a. 771, 790, 824, 869, 872, 879. Those s.a. 822, 837, 856 and 870 have *dux* or *toísech* in a different sense, and this may even be true of the earliest ones, s.a. 771, 790 and 824.
78. 'A poem on the Airgialla', ed. M. Ó Daly, *Ériu*, xvi (1952), 179–88. On this and other texts illuminating the relationships between overkings and their client kings see the important paper by M. Gerriets, 'Kingship and exchange in pre-Viking

79. Ireland', *Cambridge Medieval Celtic Studies*, xiii (1987), 39–72.

79. 'A poem on the Airgialla', ed. Ó Daly, stanza 19.

80. e.g. *Corpus Genealogiarum Hiberniae*, ed. M. O'Brien (1962), p. 94 (127 b 18ff.); *Corpus Iuris Hibernici*, ed. D.A. Binchy (1978), 38, line 21.

81. On *census regis* see the early eighth-century *Collectio Canonum Hibernensis: Die irische Kanonensammlung*, ed. H. Wasserschleben (2nd edn., 1885), xvii.10; xxv.9–11, 14. b; xxix.6; xxxii.13 (and footnote b, from the B Recension), 22; xli.8–9; xlii.28; xlviii *passim*. The vernacular equivalent appears to be *cís flatha: Corpus Iuris Hibernici*, ed. Binchy (page and line) 38.21; 54.31; 219.5; 914.22; cf. *cís nemid*, 207.3. Cf. Gerriets, 'Kingship and exchange in pre-Viking Ireland', 52–66.

82. *Collectio Canonum Hibernensis*, ed. Wasserschleben, xxxii.13, 22; xlviii.1; *Corpus Iuris Hibernici*, ed. Binchy, 910.27–28; 912.9–13; 924.22–24=*Bechbretha*, ed. Charles-Edwards and Kelly, para. 49 (j).

83. This may be implied by the canonists' use of the story of Joseph acquiring the land of Egypt for Pharaoh (Gen. 47: 20–6): *Collectio Canonum Hibernensis*, ed. Wasserschleben, xxv.9.g; xlviii.1.

84. Some kindreds are distinguished by being bound to pay such *census: Corpus Iuris Hibernici*, ed. Binchy, 51.32. Similarly, some churches are liable to pay *census: Collectio Canonum Hibernensis*, ed. Wasserschleben, xxix.6; xlii.28.

85. e.g. 'The expulsion of the Déssi', ed. K. Meyer, *Y Cymmrodor*, xiv (1901), 122–3; Gerriets, 'Kingship and exchange in pre-Viking Ireland', 66–7.

86. *Táin Bó Cúailnge, Recension I*, ed. C. O'Rahilly (1976), 1, line 8, for billeting guests on subjects; *Corpus Genealogiarum Hiberniae*, ed. O'Brien, 93 (127 b 13–14), shows the Loíchsi arguing that the *cís* and other dues of the 'seven kindreds of

the Loíchsi' are due to their own overking (the king of the Loíchsi Réta), and *ibid.*, 94 (127 b 43–4), that these dues are not paid to the king of Leinster. The implication is that, in the absence of a special privilege – the *soíre* referred to in *ibid.* (127 b 27) – a subject people would be liable to pay these dues.

87. *Críth Gablach*, ed. Binchy, para. 46; *Dál Caladbuig*, ed. J.G. O'Keeffe, *Irish Texts*, ed. P. Grosjean, J. Fraser and J.G. O'Keeffe, i (1931), 20, para. 8.

88. *Regesta Regum Scottorum*, ii, ed. G.W.S. Barrow (1971), 52–7; for later Irish evidence see e.g. the charters in the Book of Kells: *Notitiae as Leabhar Cheanannais 1063–1161*, ed. G. Mac Niocaill (1961), nos. I, lines 10–11, XII, lines 4, 16.

89. Purveyance (*ag slige, bó slógaid*): *Corpus Iuris Hibernici*, ed. Binchy, 372. 6–9; *Corpus Genealogiarum Hiberniae*, ed. O'Brien, i, 94 (127 b 20, 24). Billeting (*coindem, coindmed, dám ríg*): *Corpus Iuris Hibernici*, ed. Binchy, 850. 8, 10; 1544. 36; 'Poem on the Airgialla', ed. Ó Daly, st. 19. Third share: *ibid.*, st. 24. Special exactions (*forbanda*): *ibid.*, st. 18. Protection, *mund* (*taurrthugud*): *ibid.*, st. 20.

90. For road work (*cartad slige, dénum slige, dénum ráitte*): *Corpus Iuris Hibernici*, ed. Binchy, 381. 30; 580. 7–9; Cogitosus, *Vita S. Brigidae*, c.7, *Acta Sanctorum, Feb.*, i, 140. A.

91. *Cath Maige Mucrama*, ed. M. Ó Daly (1975), para. 6; *Scéla Cano meic Gartnáin*, ed. D.A. Binchy (1963), lines 38–40.

92. Cf. G.W.S. Barrow, 'Pre-feudal Scotland: shires and thanes', in his *Kingdom of the Scots* (1973), 7–68.

93. W. Davies, *Wales in the Early Middle Ages* (1982), 105–7.

94. A.P. Smyth, *Warlords and Holy Men: Scotland AD 80–1000* (1984), c.6.

3 The origins of barbarian kingdoms: the continental evidence

1. 'The English Flag', in *Rudyard Kipling's Verse: Definitive Edition* (1940), 221.
2. S. Reynolds, *Kingdoms and Communities in Western Europe, 900–1300* (1984), 250.
3. Gregory of Tours, *Decem Libri Historiarum*, ed. R. Buchner (Darmstadt, 1977), ii, 9, 10 (80–92).
4. *Gregory of Tours: History of the Franks*, trans. L. Thorpe (1974), 122–3.
5. *Germania*, 7.1. See e.g. E.A. Thompson, *The Early Germans* (1965), 32–41.
6. J.M. Wallace-Hadrill, *The Long-haired Kings and Other Studies in Frankish History* (1962), 154.
7. Thompson, *Early Germans*, 40.
8. P.H. Sawyer, *Anglo-Saxon Charters: An Annotated List and Bibliography* (1968), nos. 58–60; Uhtred appears as a *subregulus* in no. 61.
9. Procopius, *Wars*, trans. H.B. Dewing (7 vols., 1914–28), V.i.26 (vol. iii, 11).
10. Cited by H. Wolfram in 'The shaping of the early medieval kingdom', *Viator*, i (1970), 1–20, whose argument I summarize here.
11. On Athanaric see above all H. Wolfram, *Geschichte der Goten* (Munich, 1979), 68–83.
12. Themistius, *Oratio*, xv.191A, quoted by E.A. Thompson, *The Visigoths in the Time of Ulfila* (1966), 54.
13. Themistius, *Oratio*, x.134D, quoted by Thompson, *The Visigoths*, 46.
14. Bede, *Ecclesiastical History of the English People*, ed. B. Colgrave and R.A.B. Mynors (1969), v, 10 (481–2).
15. J. McClure, 'Bede's Old Testament Kings', in *Ideal and Reality in Frankish and Anglo-Saxon Society*, ed. P. Wormald *et al.* (1983), 76–98.
16. K.F. Stroheker, 'Zur Rolle der Heermeister fränkischer Abstammung im späten vierten Jahrhundert', *Historia*, iv (1955),

314–50, reprinted in *idem, Germanentum und Spätantike* (Zurich, Stuttgart, 1965), 9–29; cf. E. James, *The Franks* (1988), 41–4.
17. Returning to Francia might even be dangerous, as Silvanus was warned; Mellobaudes, on the other hand, was a Roman general who did somehow then become *rex Francorum*: see James, *The Franks*, 41–2, 44.
18. Procopius, *Wars*, trans. Dewing, V.i.9 (vol. iii, 5).
19. Gregory, *Decem Libri Historiarum*, ed. Buchner, ii, 38 (54, 134).
20. *ibid.*, ii, 42 (140–1).
21. R. Wenskus, 'Bermerkungen zum Thunginus der Lex Salica', *Festschrift P.E. Schramm zu seinem 70. Geburtstag*, i (Wiesbaden, 1964), 217–36. On the prince in Cologne cathedral, see J. Werner, 'Frankish royal tombs in the cathedrals of Cologne and Saint-Denis', *Antiquity*, xxxviii (1964), 201–16.
22. M. Rouche, *L'Aquitaine des Wisigoths aux Arabes, 418–781* (Paris, 1979), believes Eudes (Odo) to have been king in Aquitaine, but apparently on no better evidence than the denarii inscribed E.R., which he interprets (p. 379) as EODO REX.
23. On this concept, see H. Wolfram, 'The shaping of the early medieval principality as a type of non-royal rulership', *Viator*, ii (1971), 32–51, and, for more detail, *idem, Intitulatio I: Lateinische Königs- und Fürstentitel bis zum Ende des 8. Jahrhunderts* (Vienna, 1967).
24. E. James, 'La disparition du royaume de Soissons et ses conséquences archéologiques', *Bulletin de Liaison de l'Association Française d'Archéologie Mérovingienne*, x (1986), 28–31, and now James, *The Franks*, 67–71, 79–82.
25. H. Wolfram, 'Gothic history and historical ethnography', *Journal of Medieval History*, vii (1981), 317.
26. Above all R. Wenskus, *Stammesbildung und Verfassung*

(2nd edn., Cologne, Vienna, 1977), and *idem*, 'Probleme der germanisch-deutschen Verfassungs- und Sozialgeschichte im Lichte der Ethnosoziologie', *Historische Forschungen für Walter Schlesinger*, ed. H. Beumann (Cologne, Vienna, 1974).

27. See James, *The Franks*, 235ff.
28. As I do in the opening pages (1–10) of *The Franks*, from which I take the following three paragraphs.
29. P.J. Geary, *Aristocracy in Provence: the Rhône basin at the Dawn of the Carolingian Age* (Stuttgart, 1985), 111.
30. Procopius, *Wars*, trans. Dewing, V.xii.13–19 (vol. iii, 120–3).
31. Ennodius to Libanius, *Epistolae*, 9.23, trans. A.H.M. Jones, *The Later Roman Empire* (1964), 251.
32. W. Goffart, *Barbarians and Romans, AD 418–584: The Techniques of Accommodation* (Princeton, 1980), 35.

4 The creation and early structure of the kingdom of Kent

1. For a survey ranging over much of Europe, see C.J. Wickham, 'The other transition: from the ancient world to feudalism', *Past & Present*, cvi (1985), 3–36.
2. See, for example, A. Dorpalen, *German History in Marxist Perspective* (1985).
3. R. Hodges, 'State formation and the role of trade in Middle Saxon England', *Social Organization and Settlement* (Brit. Archaeol. Reports (hereafter BAR) series, no. 47, 1978), 438–53; *idem*, *Dark Age Economics* (1982); C.J. Arnold, *From Roman Britain to Saxon England* (1984).
4. Bede, *Ecclesiastical History of the English People*, ed. B. Colgrave and R.A.B. Mynors (1969) (hereafter *HE*); *Historia Brittonum*, ed. T. Mommsen (*Chronica Minora*, iii, M.G.H., Auctores antiquissimi, xiii, Berlin, 1898) (hereafter *HB*); *The Anglo-Saxon Chronicle*, trans. D. Whitelock *et al.* (hereafter ASC) (1961); D.N. Dumville, 'The

Anglian collection of royal genealogies and regnal lists', *Anglo-Saxon England*, v (1976), 23–50.
5. W. Levison, *England and the Continent in the Eighth Century* (1946), 270–3, 277, citing *Annales iuv. mai.* (M.G.H., SS, i), 87; *Ann. Lind. et Cant.* (M.G.H., SS., iv), 2; and Fleury annals in L. Delisle, *Catalogue des mss des fonds Libri et Barrois* (Paris, 1888), 70–1.
6. *Die Gesetze der Angelsachsen*, ed. F. Liebermann (3 vols., Halle, 1903–16), i, 3–14.
7. P.H. Sawyer, *Anglo-Saxon Charters: an annotated List and Bibliography* (1968) (hereafter S); W. de G. Birch, *Cartularium Saxonicum* (1885–93) (hereafter CS); *Charters of Rochester*, ed. A. Campbell (*Anglo-Saxon Charters*, i, 1973) (hereafter Campbell, *Rochester*).
8. D.W. Rollason, *The Mildrith Legend* (1982); P. Grierson and M. Blackburn, *Medieval European Coinage, i, Early Middle Ages* (1986), 155–89.
9. S.C. Hawkes, 'Anglo-Saxon Kent c. 425–725', in *Archaeology in Kent to AD 1500*, ed. P. Leach (1982), 64–78; V.I. Evison, *The Fifth-Century Invasions South of the Thames* (1965).
10. A. Everitt, *Continuity and Colonization: the Evolution of Kentish Settlement* (1986).
11. A. Detsicas, *The Cantiaci* (1983).
12. A.L.F. Rivet and C. Smith, *Place-Names of Roman Britain* (1979), s.v.; K. Jackson, *Language and History in Early Britain* (1953), 600, 603.
13. Jackson, *Language and History*, 419–20, 701–5; J.G.F. Hind, 'Elmet and Deira – forest-names in Yorkshire?', *Bull. Board of Celtic Stud.* xxviii (1978–80), 541–52.
14. Everitt, *Continuity*, 93–117.
15. N.P. Brooks, *The Early History of the Church of Canterbury* (1984), 24–5.
16. *HB* c.37.
17. Strabo, *Geography*, ed. G. Aujac (Paris, 1969), iv, 3, 3 and iv, 5, 1; Diodorus Siculus, *History*, ed. C.H. Oldfather (1939), v, 21, 3.

18. Caesar, *De Bello Gallico*, ed. R. du Pontet (1900–1), v, 22; B. Cunliffe, 'Social and economic development in Kent in the pre-Roman Iron Age', in *Archaeology in Kent*, ed. Leach, 40–50; W. Rodwell, 'Coinage, *Oppida* and the rise of Belgic power in SE Britain', in *Oppida in Barbarian Europe*, ed. B. Cunliffe and T. Rowley (BAR, Int. series, no. 11, 1976), 187–367. However, the coins of Tasciovaunus (who seems to have preceded Dumnovellaunus) are limited to the area east of the Medway, and it is there that the 'Belgic' pottery is concentrated.

19. Ptolemy, *Geography*, ed. C. Müller (2 vols., Paris, 1883–1901), ii, 3, 12–13.

20. J.E. Turville-Petre, 'Hengest and Horsa', *Saga Book of the Viking Soc.* xiv (1953–7), 273–90; J. De Vries, 'Die Ursprungssage der Sachsen', *Niedersächsisches Jahrb. f. Landesgesch.* xxxi (1959), 20–37; D.N. Dumville, 'Sub-Roman Britain: history and legend', *History*, n.s. lxii (1977), 173–92; *idem*, 'Kingship, genealogies and regnal lists', in *Early Medieval Kingship*, ed. P.H. Sawyer and I.N. Wood (1977), 72–104; P. Sims-Williams, 'The Settlement of England in Bede and the Chronicle', *ASE* xii (1983), 1–41.

21. *HE* i, 15.
22. *HE* ii, 5.
23. Bede's use of *perhibentur* can be traced in P.F. Jones, *Concordance to the Historia Ecclesiastica of Bede* (1929), s.v.
24. Sims-Williams, 'Settlement of England', 21.
25. *ibid.*, 24–5.
26. H.M. Chadwick, *The Origin of the English Nation* (1907), 44–5; H. Moisl, 'Anglo-Saxon genealogies and Germanic oral tradition', *J. Medieval Hist.* vii (1981), 219–23, 235–6; Sims-Williams, 'Settlement of England', 21–4.
27. A. Faulkes, 'Descent from the Gods', *Mediaeval Scandinavia*, xi (1978–9), 92–125; Moisl, 'AS Genealogies', 215–48; E. Leach,

Genesis as Myth and Other Essays (1969), 25–83; B.A. Agiri, 'Early Oyo history reconsidered', *History in Africa*, ii (1975), 1–16; R. Law, 'Early Yoruba historiography', *ibid.*, iii (1976), 68–89.

28. Moisl, 'AS Genealogies', 215–48. The argument is normally countered by the suggestion that Christians were prepared to invent descent from euhemerized men.
29. Sims-Williams, 'Settlement of England', 35.
30. For various approaches see B. Malinowski, 'Myth in primitive psychology', *Magic, Science and Religion* (1948), 72–124; C. Levi-Strauss, *The Savage Mind* (1966); L. de Heusch, *Le roi ivre ou l'origine de l'état* (Paris, 1972); *The African Past Speaks*, ed. J.C. Miller (1980); R. Law, 'How many times can history repeat itself?', *Internat. J. African Hist. Stud.* xviii(1) (1985), 33–51.
31. J.K. Wallenberg, *Kentish Place-Names* (Uppsala, 1931), 83–4, 286–8, 320–3.
32. F.M. Stenton, *Anglo-Saxon England* (3rd edn., 1971), 207, identified Egbert's father Ealhmund as the Kentish ruler 'Ealmundus' who is the donor of S38 (=CS243); but see my cautionary note: Brooks, *Church of Canterbury*, 349 n.15.
33. *HE* v, 24. After 731 the Chronicle records archiepiscopal successions, the fire at Canterbury in 756 and some eighth-century Kentish royal successions.
34. *The African Past Speaks*, ed. Miller; J. Vansina, *Oral Tradition as History* (1985).
35. *HB* cc.31, 36–8, 43–6.
36. J. Morris, *Age of Arthur* (1973), 37, 80–1.
37. Dumville, 'Sub-Roman Britain', 176–8; *idem*, 'Some aspects of the chronology of the *Historia Brittonum*', *Bull. Board Celtic Stud.* xxv (1974), 439–48; *idem*, ' "Nennius" and the *Historia Brittonum*', *Studia Celtica*, x–xi (1975–6), 78–95.
38. For possible explanations of this name, see Sims-Williams,

'Settlement of England', 29, n.124.

39. Wallenberg, *Kentish Place-Names, passim*; N.P. Brooks, 'Romney Marsh in the early Middle Ages', in *Evolution of Marshland Landscapes*, ed. R.T. Rowley (Oxf. Univ. Dept. for External Stud., 1981), 74–94.

40. Chadwick, *Origin*, 39–44.

41. Widukind of Corvey, *Res Gestae Saxonicae*, ed. K.A. Kehr (M.G.H., Script. rer. Germ. in us. schol., 1904), i, 6–7; *Annales Stadenses* s.a. 917, ed. M. Lappenberg (M.G.H., SS., xvi, 1925), 317. See de Vries, 'Ursprungssage d. Sachsen', 20–37.

42. Dumville, 'Genealogies and regnal lists', 72–104; Moisl, 'AS royal genealogies', 215–48.

43. For a bold suggestion of when these versions may have been current see D.P. Kirby, 'Vortigern', *Bull. Board of Celtic Stud.* xxiii (1968–70), 37–59 at 47–8.

44. *HE* ii, 5; Dumville, 'Anglian Collection', 23–50.

45. Gregory of Tours, *Decem Libri Historiarum*, ed. B. Krusch and W. Levison (M.G.H., Script. rer. merov., i (1), Hannover, 1951) (henceforth *HF*), ix, 26.

46. See the names listed by W.G. Searle, *Onomasticon Saxonicum* (1897).

47. M.T. Morlet, *Les noms de personne sur la territoire de l'ancienne Gaule dès vi au xii siècle*, i (Paris, 1968), s.v.; E. Förstemann, *Altdeutsches Namenbuch, i, Personennamen* (Nordhausen, 1856), s.v.

48. E.T. Leeds, *Early Anglo-Saxon Art and Archaeology* (1936), 41–78; C.F.C. Hawkes, 'The Jutes of Kent', in *Dark-Age Britain: Studies to E.T. Leeds*, ed. D.B. Harden (1956), 91–111; Evison, *Fifth-century Invasions*; J.M. Wallace-Hadrill, *Early Germanic Kingship in England and the Continent* (1971), 24–32; Hawkes, 'Anglo-Saxon Kent', 72–4.

49. *HE* preface; K.H. Krüger, *Königsgrabkirchen der Franken, Angelsachsen und Langobarden bis zum Mitte des 8, Jahrhunderts* (Münstersche Mittelalterschriften, iv, 1971).

50. *HE* ii, 5: 'qui est annus uicesimus primus ex quo Augustinus cum sociis ad praedicandum genti Anglorum missus est'.

51. P.H. Blair, 'The Moore memoranda on Northumbrian history', in *The Early Cultures of North-West Europe [H.M. Chadwick Memorial Studies]*, ed. C. Fox and B. Dickins (1950), 243–59. For Bede's practice in calculating incarnation dates and regnal years, see S. Wood, 'Bede's Northumbrian dates again', *Eng. Hist. Rev.* xcviii (1983), 280–96.

52. *HE* iii, 8; iv, 1, 5.

53. *HE* ii, 5; 'Defunctus uero est rex Ædilberct die xxiiii mensis Februarii post xx et unum annos acceptum fidei atque in porticu sancti Martini intro ecclesiam beatorum apostolorum Petri et Pauli sepultus.' For the chronology of the Augustinian mission, see Brooks, *Church of Canterbury*, 3–11.

54. Fleury annals in Delisle, *Cat. des mss des fonds Libri et Barrois*, 70–1; *Ann. Lind. et Cant.* (M.G.H., SS., iv, 2).

55. *Venerabilis Baedae Historia Ecclesiastica*, ed. C. Plummer (1896), ii, 85; ASC s.a. 565, 616; *Annals of St Neots*, s.a. 565, ed. D.N. Dumville (*Anglo-Saxon Chronicle*, ed. Dumville and S.D. Keynes, xvii), 8.

56. *HE* ii, 5: 'Ædilberct rex Cantuariorum post regnum temporale, quod L et sex annis gloriosissime tenuerat, aeterna caelestis regni gaudia subiit.'

57. G.H. Wheeler, 'Gildas *De Excidio* chapter 26', *Eng. Hist. Rev.* xli (1926), 521.

58. See e.g. *HE* ii, 5: '... Sabercti regis Orientalium Saxonum qui ubi regna perennia petens tres suos filios ... regni temporalis heredes reliquit ...'; *HE* iii, 18: 'Tantumque rex ille [=Sigberct] caelestis regni amator factus est ut ad ultimum ... intraret monasterium ...'; *HE* iv, 14: '... regis Osualdi, qui quondam genti Nordanhymbrorum et regni

temporalis auctoritate et
Christianae pietatis quae ad
regnum perenne ducit . . .
praefuit . . .'; *HE* v, 21 (letter of
abbot Ceolfrith to king
Nechtan): 'Sic enim fit ut post
acceptam temporalis regni
potentiam ipse beatissimus
apostolorum princeps caelesti
regni tibi . . . pandat introitum.'
59. For a comparable muddle over
Penda's age at his accession and
at his death, see below, p. 164–6.
60. *HF* iv, 26: 'Porro Charibertus rex
Ingobergam accepit uxorem de
qua filiam habuit, quae postea in
Ganthia uirum accipiens est
deducta.' For the date of
composition see Gregor v. Tours,
Fränkische Geschichte, ed. R.
Büchner (Deutscher Verlag der
Wissenschaften, c. 1955), p. xxi.
61. P. Stafford, *Queens, Concubines
and Dowagers: the King's Wife
in the Early Middle Ages* (1983),
35–6, 38, 67–8, 73–4.
62. *HF* ix, 26: 'Anno quoque quarto
decimo Childeberti regis [=588–
9], Ingoberga regina Chariberti
quondam relicta migrauit a
saeculo . . . relinquens filiam
unicam, quam in Canthia regis
cuiusdam filius matrimonio
copulauit.' My interpretation of
the details of the chronology was
reached independently (cf.
Brooks, *Church of Canterbury*,
5–6) but is largely parallel to
that of I.N. Wood, 'The
Merovingian North Sea',
*Occasional Papers on Medieval
Topics*, i (1983), 15–16, though I
am not inclined to follow him in
thinking that Frankish court
praise means that Frankish
overlordship was real.
63. ASC s.a. 568, 593. For
Æthelberht's overlordship after
Ceawlin see *HE* ii, 5.
64. Wood, 'Merovingian North Sea',
16.
65. *Laws of Æthelberht*, cc.2, 3, 5
(*Gesetze der Angelsachsen*, ed.
Liebermann, i, 3–8). For the
organization of itinerating royal
households see T. Charles-
Edwards, above, 28–33.
66. Everitt, *Continuity*, 69–92.
67. Brooks, *Church of Canterbury*,
24–5.

68. B.A.E. Yorke, 'Joint kingship in
Kent, c. 560–785', *Archaeologia
Cantiana*, xcix (1983), 1–20.
There are some important
revisions of the order and dates
of early eighth-century Kentish
kings in S.E. Kelly, 'The pre-
Conquest history and archive of
St Augustine's Abbey,
Canterbury' (unpubl. Univ. of
Cambridge Ph.D. thesis, 1986),
233–7, 312.
69. S.C. Hawkes, 'Anglo-Saxon
Kent', 70–4.
70. J.K. Wallenberg, *Place-Names of
Kent* (Uppsala, 1934), 139, was
cautious; A.H. Smith, 'Place-
names and the Anglo-Saxon
settlement', *Proc. Brit. Acad.* xlii
(1956), 82, and *idem, English
Place-Name Elements* (Eng.
Place-Name Soc. xxvi, 1956), ii,
256, accept derivation from -*ge*.
71. *Domesday Book seu Liber
censualis Willelmi Primi Regis*,
ed. A. Farley (2 vols., London,
1783) i, f. 1a.
72. J. Bosworth and T.N. Toller,
Anglo-Saxon Dictionary (rev.
edn. A. Campbell, 1975), s.v.; the
Rochester bridgework document
is A.J. Robertson, *Anglo-Saxon
Charters* (1939), no. 52, and the
estates and territorial units
assigned to the repair of sections
of the bridge are identified by
G. Ward. 'The lathe of Aylesford
in 975', *Arch. Cant.* xlvi (1934),
7–26.
73. J.E.A. Jolliffe, *Pre-Feudal
England: the Jutes* (1933), 39–72.
74. S1180 (=CS141); S125 (=CS248);
S30 [=Campbell, *Rochester*, no.
4); S157 (=Campbell, *Rochester*,
no. 16).
75. S128 (=CS254); S1264 (=CS332);
S31 (=CS199).
76. Jolliffe, *Pre-Feudal England*.
77. J.E.A. Jolliffe, 'The hidation of
Kent', *Eng. Hist. Rev.* xliv (1929),
613–14; and *Pre-Feudal England*,
44–6.
78. *ibid.*, 46.
79. R.H.C. Davis, *Kalendar of Abbot
Samson* (Royal Hist. Soc.
Camden 3rd ser. lxxxiv, 1954);
G.W.S. Barrow, 'Pre-feudal
Scotland: shires and thanes', in
The Kingdom of the Scots (1973),
7–68; G.R.J. Jones, 'Multiple

estates and early settlement', in
English Medieval Settlement, ed.
P.H. Sawyer (1979), 9–34;
W.J. Ford, 'Some settlement
patterns in the central region
of the Warwickshire Avon',
ibid., 143–63.
80. K.P. Witney, *The Jutish Forest*
(1976), especially 31–55.
Witney's further revisions of
Jolliffe's 'original lathes' are in
his *Kingdom of Kent* (1982), 52–
60, 236–8. For an early, vigorous
and for the most part well-
justified criticism of Jolliffe's use
of sources see G. Ward's review
in *Arch. Cant.* xlv (1933), 290–4.
81. S546 (=CS880); for the later
manorial history of Reculver see
*Hoath and Herne: The Last of
the Forest*, ed. K.H. McIntosh
and H.E. Gough (1984). For my
understanding of the details of
the bounds I am indebted to
information from Mr Gough, Mr
P.R. Kitson, Mr T. Tatton-Brown
and Mrs M. Sparks.
82. e.g. Ickham: 14 sulungs in S123
(=CS247), 4 in DB; Mersham: 5
sul. in S328 (=CS496)+9 in S332
(=CS507), 6 in DB; Teynham: 30
hides in S1258 (=CS291), 12 sul.
in S1613 (=CS301), 5½ in DB;
Warehorne: 5 sul. in S282
(=CS396), 1 in DB.
83. *Arch. Cant.* xlv (1933), 290–4.
84. S25 (=CS191); S36 (=Campbell,
Rochester, no. 10); S177
(=CS348).
85. Jolliffe, *Pre-Feudal England*, 46,
and Witney, *Kingdom of Kent*,
236, arguing from S128 (=CS254)
and S168 (=CS335).
86. S31 (=CS199); the *regio* of the
Merscuare appears in a tenth-
century interpolation to the text
of S168 (=CS335); ASC s.a. (796
for) 798.
87. Robertson, *AS Charters*, 52; S27
(=Campbell, *Rochester*, no. 3).
88. Jolliffe, *Pre-Feudal England*, 45–
50, and Witney, *Jutish Forest*, 32,
35, 42, 249–51, citing S168
(=CS335), S169 (=CS341), S170
(=CS340), S178 (=CS353) and
S300 (=CS459).
89. I am most grateful to David
Dumville, Simon Keynes, David
Kirby, Chris Wickham and
Patrick Wormald for their

comments on earlier drafts of
this chapter, which have helped
me to make many corrections
and improvements. I remain
alone responsible for the views
expressed and for errors that
persist.

**5 The kingdom of the South
Saxons: the origins**

1. A new edition of the Selsey
charters is currently being
prepared for publication. I am
grateful to Dr Simon Keynes for
the opportunity to see the text of
two of its introductory chapters
(on the kingdom and the church
in Sussex).
2. W. Davies and H. Vierck, 'The
contexts of Tribal Hidage: social
aggregates and settlement
patterns', *Frühmittelalterliche
Studien*, viii (1974), 223–93.
3. Bede, *Historia Ecclesiastica
Gentis Anglorum* [hereafter *HE*],
iv, 13 (B. Colgrave and R.A.B.
Mynors, *Bede's Ecclesiastical
History of the English People*
(1969), 372–3).
4. *HE* preface (Colgrave and
Mynors, *Bede*, 4–5).
5. P.H. Sawyer, *From Roman
Britain to Norman England*
(1978), 110–11.
6. Beowulf, lines 2194–6 (F.
Klaeber, *Beowulf and the Fight
at Finnsburg* (3rd edn., 1950),
82).
7. *HE* iv, 13: 'quae post cantuarios
ad austrum et ad occidentem
usque ad occidentales saxones
pertingit' (Colgrave and Mynors,
Bede, 372–3).
8. *HE* iv, 16: 'contra medium
australium saxonum et
geuissorum interposito pelago
latitudinis trium milium quod
vocatur soluente' (Colgrave and
Mynors, *Bede*, 384–5).
9. *HE* iv, 13 (Colgrave and Mynors,
Bede, 372–3); see also Anglo-
Saxon Chronicle (hereafter ASC)
s.a. 661 (D. Whitelock, D.C.
Douglas and S.I. Tucker, *The
Anglo-Saxon Chronicle* (1961),
21).
10. M.G. Welch, *Early Anglo-Saxon
Sussex* (Brit. Archaeol. Reports

(hereafter BAR), Brit. series, no. 112, 1983), 260; S.C. Hawkes, H.R. Ellis Davidson and C.F.C. Hawkes, 'The Finglesham Man', *Antiquity*, xxxix (1965), 32, n.62.

11. *HE* iv, 15–16 (Colgrave and Mynors, *Bede*, 380–3).
12. *HE* iv, 13 (Colgrave and Mynors, *Bede*, 372–3).
13. Welch, *Sussex*, 261: *(ge)mære dun*.
14. *Vita Sancti Wilfridi* (hereafter *VSW*), c.41 (B. Colgrave, *The Life of Bishop Wilfrid by Eddius Stephanus* (1927), 82–3).
15. B. Cunliffe, *The Regni* (1973), 23.
16. Davies and Vierck, 'Tribal Hidage', esp. 238–40.
17. *Symeonis Monachi Opera Omnia, ii, Historia Regum*, ed. T. Arnold (Rolls Series, no. 75, 1885), 44 (c.47).
18. ASC s.a. 1011, 1049D (Whitelock, *Chronicle*, 91, 114).
19. Welch, *Sussex*, 247–50, text fig. 10.9.
20. P.H. Sawyer, *Anglo-Saxon Charters. An Annotated List and Bibliography* (1968) (hereafter S), nos. 43, 45, 1173.
21. C.T. Chevallier, 'The Frankish origin of the Hastings Tribe', *Sussex Archaeol. Colls.* civ (1966), 56–62.
22. S108.
23. S24.
24. S1193: G. Ward, 'The Saxon Charter of Burmarsh', *Archaeologia Cantiana*, xlv (1933), 135, 137–9.
25. S.H. King, 'Sussex', in *The Domesday Geography of South-East England*, ed. H.C. Darby and E.M.J. Campbell (1962), 414.
26. *ibid.*, 407–8, fig. 119: rapes centred on Arundel, Bramber, Lewes, Pevensey and Hastings.
27. *HE* iv, 13 (Colgrave and Mynors, *Bede*, 372–3).
28. *VSW* c.41 (Colgrave, *Wilfrid*, 82–3); F. Aldsworth, ' "The Mound" at Church Norton, Selsey, and the site of St Wilfrid's church', *Sussex Archaeol. Colls.* cxvii (1979), 103–7.
29. A. Down, *Chichester Excavations*, ii (1974), 7–15; Welch, *Sussex*, 499–502.
30. J. Munby, 'Saxon Chichester and its predecessors', in *Anglo-Saxon*

Towns in Southern England, ed. J. Haslam (1984), 315–30.
31. Welch, *Sussex*, 269.
32. *VSW* c.42 (Colgrave, *Wilfrid*, 84–5): Chiltington and Andred (derived from *Anderitum*).
33. *HE* iv, 15 (Colgrave and Mynors, *Bede*, 380–1).
34. Sawyer, *Roman Britain*, 49.
35. *HE* iv, 15 (Colgrave and Mynors, *Bede*, 380–1).
36. S45.
37. ASC s.a. 710 ADE (Whitelock, *Chronicle*, 26).
38. S43, S45, S1173.
39. Athelstan *rex* with Æthelthryth *regina* (S42), Æthelberht *rex* (S44, S46, S47), Osmund *rex* and *dux* (S44, S48, S49, S108), Oswald *dux* (S108), Oslac *dux* (S108, S1184), Ælfwald *rex* and *dux* (S50, S108, S1184), and Ealdwulf *rex* and *dux* (S50, S1178, S1183).
40. Welch, *Sussex*, 270.
41. They also feature prominently in the Bernician royal house of Northumbria.
42. S50.
43. S108.
44. B. Cunliffe, *Excavations at Portchester Castle, ii, Saxon* (1976), 49–52, 303.
45. Welch, *Sussex*, 124–6, 276, fig. 68a–c.
46. *ibid.*, 404–5, 408–18.
47. G.R.J. Jones, 'Multiple estates and early settlements', in *Medieval Settlement*, ed. P.H. Sawyer (1976), 26–35.
48. Welch, *Sussex*, 276.
49. C.E. Blunt, 'The coinage of Athelstan, 924–939: a survey', *British Numismatic J.* xlii (1974), 48, 115. I am grateful to Dr M. Archibald for this reference.
50. J. Campbell, 'Bede's words for places', in *Names, Words and Graves: Early Medieval Settlement*, ed. P.H. Sawyer (Leeds, 1979), 34–54; L. Alcock, *Economy, Society and Warfare among the Britons and Saxons* (Cardiff, 1987), 162–3, 244–5.
51. Welch, *Sussex*, 255–7.
52. M.G. Welch, Ballot note, *Antiq. J.* lxvii (1987), 364–5.
53. ASC s.a. 477 (Whitelock, *Chronicle*, 11).
54. e.g. F.M. Stenton, *Anglo-Saxon*

England (3rd edn., 1971), 17–18: S232, S1291. Far from confirming the existence of the Chronicle's *Cymenesora* on Selsey (s.a. 477) the charter's *Cumeneshora* may have been borrowed from the Chronicle in the tenth century.

55. ASC s.a. 485 (Whitelock, *Chronicle*, 11).
56. Welch, *Sussex*, 255–7.
57. ASC s.a. 491 (490 in F) (Whitelock, *Chronicle*, 11).
58. *HE* ii, 5 (Colgrave and Mynors, *Bede*, 148–9).
59. e.g. J.N.L. Myres, *Anglo-Saxon Pottery and the Settlement of England* (1969), map 8.
60. Welch, *Sussex*, 257–8, on Henry of Huntingdon and Roger of Wendover.
61. *VSW* c.13 (Colgrave, *Wilfrid*, 26–9).

6 The Jutes of Hampshire and Wight and the origins of Wessex

1. *Venerabilis Baedae Opera Historica*, ed. C. Plummer (1896), ii, 28. The reference is to J.R. Green in *The Making of England* (1882). For an excellent survey of the historiography of the Anglo-Saxon settlements see P. Sims-Williams, 'The Settlement of England in Bede and the *Chronicle*', *Anglo-Saxon England*, xii (1983), 1–41. In this paper citations from the Anglo-Saxon Chronicle are taken from *Two of the Saxon Chronicles Parallel*, ed. C. Plummer and J. Earle (2 vols., 1892, repr. 1952), and those from Bede's *Historia Ecclesiastica* (*HE*) come from *Bede's Ecclesiastical History of the English People*, ed. B. Colgrave and R.A.B. Mynors (1969).
2. There are obviously a large number of works which could be cited here, but see in particular E.T. Leeds, *The Archaeology of the Anglo-Saxon Settlements* (1913, repr. 1970).
3. See in particular G.J. Copley, *The Conquest of Wessex in the Sixth Century* (1954), J.N.L. Myres, *Anglo-Saxon Pottery and the Settlement of England* (1969) and *The Anglo-Saxon Settlements* (1985), and J. Morris, *The Age of Arthur* (1973).

4. K. Harrison, *The Framework of Anglo-Saxon History to* A.D. *900* (1976); Sims-Williams, 'The Settlement of England'; D.N. Dumville, 'The West Saxon Genealogical Regnal List and the Chronology of Early Wessex', *Peritia*, iv (1985), 21–66.
5. H. Moisl, 'Anglo-Saxon royal genealogies and Germanic oral tradition', *J. Med. History*, vii (1981), 215–48. Even Gildas's account may have been influenced by such stories: P. Sims-Williams, 'Gildas and the Anglo-Saxons', *Cambridge Medieval Celtic Studies*, vi (1983), 22–3.
6. There are three main accounts of the foundation of Kent: *HE* i, 15; the annals 449–88 in the Chronicle; and the Kentish entries in the *Historia Brittonum*. Bede appends a brief section on the settlement of the Saxons, Angles and Jutes to his extracts from c.23 of Gildas's *De Excidio Britanniae* (*Gildas: the Ruin of Britain and Other Works*, ed. and trans. M. Winterbottom (1978), 26–7), in which he appears to claim that Hengest and Horsa were the Germanic leaders invited into the country by Vortigern, and that the events described by Gildas took place in Kent. Bede may have been the first to link Hengest and Horsa with Gildas's account, though it is also possible that he was drawing on a tradition already current in Kent. See further N. Brooks in this volume.
7. The Germanic leaders of Gildas's account arrived with three ships (c.23). In the Chronicle the West Saxons who arrived in 514 also came in three ships, but Cerdic and Cynric came in 495 with five ships. For the chronological

connections between the Kentish and West Saxon traditions see below.

8. *Nennius: British History and the Welsh Annals*, ed. and trans. J. Morris (1980), c.38, p. 69. However, it cannot be demonstrated that this work was known in Wessex in the ninth century. On the problem of Stuf's and Wihtgar's relationship to Cerdic and Cynric, see below.

9. *Cerdicesora* also appears in the annal for 514 when 'the West Saxons' are said to land there, and *Cerdicesford* is also named in the annal for 508 when the district of *Natanleaga* is defined.

10. In 530 Cerdic and Cynric are said to have captured the Isle of Wight and killed men at *Wihtgaræsbyrg*.

11. *HE* ii, 3. The etymology of this name is extremely complex: E. Ekwall, *The Concise Oxford Dictionary of English Place-Names* (4th edn., 1960), 390. As H.M. Chadwick wrote on the Cerdic and Cynric annals in the Chronicle, 'The analogy of similar stories in other lands would lead us to infer that the personal names had been created out of the place-names . . . It is the uniformity of the above list which excites suspicion' (*The Origin of the English Nation* (1924), 21).

12. M. Gelling, 'Latin Loan-Words in Old English Place-Names', *ASE* vi (1977), 10–11. There are a number of placenames in the Portsmouth Harbour area which contain this element, including *Porteceaster* (Portchester), the Saxon Shore fort which the Romans called *Portus Adurni*. The present settlement of Portsmouth appears to date from the twelfth century, so the Chronicle reference presumably refers literally to the mouth of the harbour: J.E.B. Gover, 'Hampshire place-names', unpublished MS in Hampshire R.O., 24.

13. Ekwall, *Dictionary of English Place-Names*, 'Nately Scures', 336.

14. L. Alcock, '*Her gefeaht with Walas*: aspects of the warfare of Saxons and Britons', *Bull. Board Celtic Studies*, xxvii (1977), 416–17. Excavations have suggested that a Roman fort underlies the castle at Carisbrooke: S. Rigold, 'Recent investigations into the earliest defences of Carisbrooke Castle, Isle of Wight', in *Chateau-Gaillard*, iii, ed. A.J. Taylor (1969), 128–38. So far it is the only known site on the island which the Saxons are likely to have described as *byrig*. The report on subsequent excavations at Carisbrooke by Chris Young is eagerly awaited.

15. A.L.F. Rivet and C. Smith, *The Place-Names of Roman Britain* (1979), 487–8.

16. The Tribal Hidage is probably of seventh-century date, but the earliest manuscript of it is eleventh-century: W. Davies and H. Vierck, 'The contexts of Tribal Hidage: social aggregates and settlement patterns', *Frühmittelalterliche Studien*, viii (1974), 223–93, *passim*. Bede knew the inhabitants of Wight as the *Uictuarii* (*HE* i, 15) and one might have expected the O.E. version of their name to be *Wihtwara*, analogous to *Cantwara* for the inhabitants of Kent: Sims-Williams, 'Settlement of England', 30.

17. For instance, Copley, *The Conquest of Wessex*, 158–68.

18. Chadwick, *Origin*, 25–6.

19. F.M. Stenton, *Anglo-Saxon England* (3rd edn., 1971), 24–5. There are other problems connected with the existence of Cerdic as the founder of the West Saxon house, not the least being that his name seems to be British in origin: K. Jackson, *Language and History in Early Britain* (1953), 554, 557, 613–14, 653, 689.

20. *The Chronicle of Æthelweard*, ed. A. Campbell (1962), 12. Campbell doubted whether Æthelweard's identification was

correct (see under *Cerdicesford* in his index, p. 59).

21. Stenton, *Anglo-Saxon England*, 22–3.
22. The annal for 500 does not appear in the Chronicle. See further below.
23. Harrison, *Framework*, 127–30, but see further below.
24. Dumville, 'West Saxon genealogical regnal list'.
25. The confusion arises because the reign of Ceol (Ceawlin's successor) is said to begin in 591, but Ceawlin's expulsion is dated to 592.
26. Dumville prefers the reading '7' for Ceawlin's reign and argues for 538/9 for the beginning of Cerdic's reign, which allows him to propound a theory of a triplication of events whereby the West Saxon dates were extended backwards not by one cycle of nineteen years, but by two. The argument is ingenious, but the original readings of the Regnal List cannot be known for certain. Sims-Williams, 'The Settlement of England', 31, favours a discrepancy of twenty-seven or twenty-eight years between Chronicle and Regnal List and, following Chadwick (*Origin*, 22, n.4), suggests a confusion between *Anno Passionis* and *Anno Domini* to explain the difference between the two sources.
27. Chadwick, *Origin*, 22, n.4.
28. In *HE* i, 15 and v, 24 Bede places the *adventus* at some point between 449 and 556 when Marcianus and Valentinianus ruled as co-emperors. The date range seems to be the result of his own calculations based on Gildas's account; see Sims-Williams, 'The English Settlement', 19–21.
29. Æthelweard also has the annal for Port (*Chronicle*, ed. Campbell, 11), so it is possible that the 500 annal was omitted by mistake from the Chronicle archetype but was known to Æthelweard, in which case the annal for Port in 501 would not

have any significance for the duplication of the annals. The fact that the Chronicle has a duplicated West Saxon arrival in 519 (i.e. 500+19) could imply the existence of a 500 annal behind the Chronicle calculations. The different dates for the arrival of Cerdic and Cynric in Æthelweard and the Regnal Table, on the one hand, and the Chronicle, on the other, are puzzling and have not been satisfactorily explained. See Dumville, 'West Saxon genealogical regnal list' and n. 35 below. It may be that the date of 500 was arrived at independently. Sims-Williams suggests a calculation based on the (supposed) date of Mount Badon ('The Settlement of England', 38–9), but it may just have been an attractive round number to which events could be related (e.g. 'the kingdom of Wessex began about 500'). If a date of 500 were already popular by the late ninth century, it could be that some of the apparent distortions in the dating sequence were the result of a desire to incorporate the date into a chronology that was chiefly established by other means.
30. The Chronicle, in fact, records the advent of the West Saxons in 514 at *Cerdicesora*, where Cerdic and Cynric are supposed to have arrived in 495, followed by a victory over the British by Stuf and Wihtgar. The Chronicle does not state that Stuf and Wihtgar were leading the West Saxons, although that could be what its account wished to imply.
31. There are good grounds for doubting the historical value of the Kentish dates and genealogical information: Sims-Williams, 'The settlement of England', 21–9.
32. *HE* ii, 5. Bede's table of overlords was reproduced in the Chronicle s.a. 829.
33. The Chronicle records Ceawlin's expulsion from Wessex in 592, but his

successor Ceol is said to have begun to reign in 591. On these bases, using the reign lengths of the Regnal Table, Ceawlin's accession would have been in 584/5 or 574/5. However, see Dumville, 'West Saxon genealogical regnal list'. For doubts about the validity of Bede's date of 560 for the accession of Æthelbert, see Brooks in this volume.

34. 534=560−26 years: twenty-six years is the reading of some, but not all, of the Regnal Table texts, and the entries for 534 in A, E and Æthelweard state that Cynric ruled for that amount. However, the other Regnal Table texts and B, C and F read twenty-seven years, and Dumville (*ibid.*) prefers twenty-seven as the reading of the Regnal Table archetype. 519=534−15 years, whereas the reading of the Regnal Table archetype was sixteen years. The discrepancy of one year in both instances could be explained by a confusion of ordinal and cardinal numbers.

35. 534−39=495; however, if it were believed that Cerdic had reigned forty years, rather than that he had died in his fortieth year, then the date of 494 would be reached, which of course is the date given by Æthelweard and the Regnal Table.

36. See above. n. 87.
37. *HE* i, 15.
38. *Asser's Life of King Alfred*, ed. W.H. Stevenson (1904, repr. 1959), c.2, p. 4, and for comments on their relationship with Cerdic and Cynric see 170–2. Asser also reproduces an erroneous ninth-century view that the Jutes were of the same stock as the Goths; see Stevenson, *ibid.*, 169–70, and *Alfred the Great*, ed. S. Keynes and M. Lapidge (1983), 229–30.
39. *HE* i, 15.
40. Sims-Williams, 'The settlement of England', 25.
41. C. Arnold, *The Anglo-Saxon Cemeteries of the Isle of Wight* (1982), 97–109, and Myres,

English Settlements, 113–28.
42. Chessell Down grave 45: Arnold, *Anglo-Saxon Cemeteries*, 26–8, 50–72, 106–7.
43. *HE* iv, 16.
44. When Wulfhere granted control of the island to the king of the South Saxons *c.* 661, the Isle of Wight had come under the jurisdiction of bishop Wilfrid who was acting as bishop of the South Saxons, as Bede relates in iv, 13.
45. Davies and Vierck, 'The contexts of Tribal Hidage', *passim.* The Tribal Hidage was probably drawn up in the second half of the seventh century, but date and provenance are problematical. The *Wihtgara* have an assessment of 600 hides in the Tribal Hidage, whereas Bede places their assessment in Cædwalla's reign at 1200 hides (*HE* iv, 16), which has led to some reluctance in equating the *Wihtgara* with the Isle of Wight and some ingenious solutions (see J.H. Brownbill, 'The Tribal Hidage', *English Historical Review*, xl (1925), 497–503). However, the name *Wihtgara* was definitely associated with the Isle of Wight (see above) and there is no reason why Cædwalla should not have put a heavier burden of assessment on the island than Wulfhere had chosen to do. It should be noted that the assessment quoted by Bede is exactly twice that given in the Tribal Hidage. As David Hinton has observed in a discussion of these problems the inclusion of Wight as a province independent of Wessex must date the original text of the Tribal Hidage to before the reign of Cædwalla: D. Hinton, 'Hampshire's Anglo-Saxon origins', in *The Archaeology of Hampshire*, ed. S. Shennan and T. Schadla-Hall (1981), 56–65.
46. *HE* i, 15.
47. *HE* iv, 16.
48. *ibid.* Bede says that the River *Homelea* (Hamble) ran *per*

*terras Iutorum quae ad
regionem Geuissorum
pertinent.*

49. *HE* iv, 13.
50. P. Hase, 'The development of
the parish in Hampshire'
(unpubl. Univ. of Cambridge
Ph.D. thesis, 1975), 96–123,
303–7. Of course there can be
no certainty that the minster
parishes preserve earlier
boundaries, but there is good
evidence to suggest that the
southern Hampshire minsters
were established in the late
seventh century, that is, within
less than fifty years of the
events here described. See also
M.J. Hare, 'The Anglo-Saxon
Church of St Peter, Titchfield',
*Proc. Hants. Field Club and
Archaeol. Soc.* xxxii (1975),
5–48.
51. Gover, 'Hampshire place-
names', 63a.
52. However, as Hase,
'Development of the parish',
110–22 indicates, there is some
uncertainty about the minster
provision for the Portsmouth
area.
53. *HE* iv, 16.
54. Hase, 'Development of the
parish', 69–71.
55. *HE* iv, 16.
56. Gover, 'Hampshire place-
names', 41, 199. There can be
no doubt that the placename
Stone is a more accurate
rendering of Bede's *ad Lapidem*
(*æt Stane* in the O.E. version of
HE) than Stoneham. Stoneham
is represented today by the two
parishes of North and South
Stoneham, but originally the
name seems to have been
applied to a large area in the
vicinity of Southampton which
may have included *Hamtun*
within its bounds: Hase,
'Development of the parish',
152–61. Stoneham seems to
have been an important royal
estate at an early period,
whereas little is known of
Stone, so there has been a
tendency to favour the equation
of Stoneham with Bede's *ad
Lapidem*: see *Venerabilis
Baedae Opera Historica*, ii,

229, and G.B. Grundy 'The
Saxon land charters of
Hampshire with notes on place
and field names', *Archaeol. J.*
3rd ser. xxxiii (1926), 241–52.
57. I.D. Margary, *Roman Roads in
Britain* (2nd edn., 1967), 95–6.
58. Hase, 'Development of the
parish', 73–95. Hase proposes
that the minster of Redbridge (a
district name) was located at
Eling.
59. *Florentii Wigorniensis Monachi
Chronicon ex Chronicis*, ed. B.
Thorpe (2 vols., 1848–9), ii, 44–
5: 'in Nova Foresta, quae lingua
Anglorum Ytene nuncupatur'.
The occasion of the reference
was the death of William
Rufus. In i, 276 Florence refers
to William II's death as having
occurred 'in provincia Jutarum,
in Nova Foresta'.
60. Gover, 'Hampshire place-
names', 67.
61. P. Colebourn, *Hampshire's
Countryside Heritage: Ancient
Woodland* (1983), 21–2.
62. R. Welldon Finn, 'Hampshire',
in *The Domesday Geography of
South-East England*, ed. H.
Darby and E. Campbell (1962),
figs. 89, 90, pp. 289, 292.
63. The barrow bearing this name
is recorded in the bounds of a
tenth-century charter: *Anglo-
Saxon Charters: An Annotated
List and Bibliography*, ed.
P.H. Sawyer (1968) (hereafter S),
no. 359.
64. J. Campbell, *Bede's Reges and
Principes* (Jarrow Lecture for
1979), 1–2.
65. One can note here the name
East Seaxnatune (S283), modern
Exton, which lies on the west
bank of the River Meon,
opposite Meonstoke. The name
is often interpreted as '*tun* of
the East Saxons', but 'eastern
tun of the Saxons' is also a
possibility, indicating an
eastern expansion of (West)
Saxons into what was
predominantly Jutish territory.
66. The only large cemetery to
have been excavated which
definitely lay within Jutish
territory in Hampshire is
Droxford in the Meon valley:

F. Aldsworth, 'Droxford Anglo-Saxon Cemetery, Soberton, Hampshire', *Proc. Hants. Field Club and Arch. Soc.* xxxv (1979), 93–182. Although there are parallels between grave-goods from the Droxford cemetery and from the Jutish cemeteries on the Isle of Wight (Aldsworth, *ibid.*, and Arnold, *Anglo-Saxon Cemeteries, passim* and esp. 102–10), there are also parallels with material from South Saxon cemeteries (M. Welch, *Early Anglo-Saxon Sussex* (Brit. Archaeol. Reports, Brit. series (hereafter BAR), no. 112 (1983)) and from the (presumably) Saxon cemeteries of Portway, near Andover (Hants.) (A.M. Cook and M.W. Dacre, *Excavations at Portway, Andover, 1973–1975* (1985)) and Charlton, near Downton (Wilts.) (S.M. Davies, 'The excavation of an Anglo-Saxon Cemetery (and some prehistoric pits) at Charlton Plantation, near Downton', *Wilts. Archaeol. Mag.* lxxix (1984), 109–54).

67. Presumably a substantial number of the inhabitants were of Romano-British descent and the number of Germanic migrants may have been relatively small: C. Arnold, *Roman Britain to Saxon England* (1984), 121–41.

68. Davies and Vierck, 'The contexts of Tribal Hidage', 224–36, 288–92. The Latin texts derive from two different exemplars and their variant readings for the 'Ochtgaga' are given here. The 'Ochtgaga' entry is followed by a sub-total for the preceding eighteen entries.

69. In *HE* ii, 5 'Octa' appears as the grandfather of king Æthelbert I, but in various versions of the Anglian collection 'Ocga' is the son of Hengist (D.N. Dumville, 'The Anglian collection of royal genealogies and regnal lists', *ASE* v (1976), 23–50). 'The Kentish Chronicle' included in the *Historia Brittonum* relates how Hengist invited his son

'Octha' and the latter's cousin Ebissa to Britain, and 'Octha' is also given as the son of Hengist in the Kentish regnal list in the *Historia Brittonum*, which is closely related to the pedigree in the Anglian collection (*Historia Brittonum*, 69 and 77).

70. The provinces of Lindsey, the Hwicce, the South Saxons and the East Saxons are all assessed at 7,000 hides in the Tribal Hidage, that is, the total of the *Noxgaga* and *Ohtgaga* entries. Clearly the *Noxgaga* and *Ohtgaga* were substantial units.

71. Davies and Vierck, 'Contexts of Tribal Hidage', 236, 279.

72. *ibid.*, 257–9, 275–9.

73. *HE* iii, 24 refers to the North and South Mercians as units of 7,000 and 5,000 hides respectively which were divided from each other by the River Trent. For the early role of the Humber as uniting rather than dividing settlements on opposite banks and parallel instances, see Myres, *The English Settlements*, 174–7.

74. *HE* iv, 16. In *HE* v, 7 Bede says that Cædwalla abdicated in the third year of Aldfrith's (of Northumbria) reign, i.e. 688, and that he had ruled his people for two years.

75. *Two Chronicles*, i, 38–9.

76. *HE* iv, 13. According to Bede, king Æthelwalh's baptism occurred shortly before Wilfrid's arrival in the province.

77. *Two Chronicles*, i, 32–5.

78. *ibid.*, 32–3.

79. *HE* iii, 7.

80. *HE* iii, 28. See also B.A.E. Yorke, 'The foundation of the Old Minster and the status of Winchester in the seventh and eighth centuries', *Proc. Hants. Field Club and Arch. Soc.* xxxviii (1982), 75–83.

81. If the interpretation of Winchester's being very close to the northern Jutish border is correct, it is interesting to note the care which was taken to block the Southgate in the city which could suggest that particular attention was being paid to an enemy further south:

M. Biddle, 'Excavations at Winchester, 1971: tenth and final interim report; Part I', *Antiq. J.* lv (1975), 109–19.

82. *Two Chronicles*, i, 34–5.

83. Bede explains the division of the bishopric as the result of Cenwalh's desire to have a Saxon-speaking bishop (*HE* iii, 7), but as he appointed another Frank (Agilbert's nephew Leuthere) as bishop a few years later the explanation is not entirely convincing. It is, however, likely that Wulfhere's successes in the upper Thames valley were an additional factor in causing the transfer of the West Saxon see from Dorchester to Winchester: Copley, *The Conquest of Wessex*, 137–8.

84. C. Arnold, 'Wealth and social status: a matter of life and death', in *Anglo-Saxon Cemeteries*, ed. P. Rahtz, T. Dickinson and L. Watts (BAR, Brit. series, no. 82, 1980), 81–142, contrasts the differences in wealth and complexities of social structure that can be seen between cemeteries of coastal areas like the Isle of Wight and those of inland areas like Wiltshire and the Thames valley in the late sixth and early seventh centuries. He suggests that West Saxon aggression against the coastal areas was fuelled by a desire to share in the latter's commercial advantages.

85. See *Excavations in Hamwic, Volume One*, ed. A.D. Morton (forthcoming) for a full discussion of the dating evidence for the origins of the settlement.

86. A useful summary of the present state of knowledge of the Anglo-Saxon *wics* is to be found in T. Tatton-Brown, 'The topography of Anglo-Saxon London', *Antiquity*, lx (1986), 21–8. See also M. Biddle, 'Towns' in *The Archaeology of Anglo-Saxon England*, ed. D.M. Wilson (1976), 112–20.

87. It has been argued that the Geuissae were a separate body

of Saxons based in Winchester, who eventually joined with the main group of West Saxons in the Thames valley: R.G. Collingwood and J.N.L. Myres, *Roman Britain and the English Settlements* (2nd edn., 1937), 403–4, and Copley, *Conquest of Wessex*, 137. However, the claim is not repeated in Myres's latest edition of his work, *The English Settlements*, and he presumably accepted the article of H.E. Walker, 'Bede and the Gewissae: the political evolution of the Heptarchy and its nomenclature', *Cambridge Hist. J.* xii (1956), 174–86, which showed that there was a chronological distinction between Bede's use of West Saxon and Geuissae, but not a geographical one.

88. *HE* iii, 7.

89. *HE* iii, 7 and v, 19.

90. *HE* iv, 16 and v, 7.

91. *HE* v, 7.

92. S235. Patrick Wormald points out (pers. comm.) that the West Saxons conspicuously avoided describing themselves as 'West' Saxon and it was only outsiders who used the qualifying 'West'.

93. *Two Chronicles*, i, 16–17, s.a. 552 and 556.

94. Myres, *The English Settlements*, 149–62.

95. *ibid.* and D.P. Kirby, 'Problems of early West Saxon history', *Eng. Hist. Rev.* lxxx (1975), 10–29, for attempts to reconcile the evidence.

96. Sims-Williams, 'Settlement of England', 331–4, and Dumville, 'West Saxon genealogical regnal list'.

97. H. Sweet, 'Some of the sources of the Anglo-Saxon Chronicle', *English Studies*, ii (1879), 310–12, and J. Bately, 'The compilation of the Anglo-Saxon Chronicle, 60 BC to AD 890: vocabulary as evidence', *Proc. Brit. Academy*, lxiv (1978), 102–3.

98. S.C. Hawkes, 'The early Saxon period', in *The Archaeology of the Oxford Region*, ed. T. Rowley *et al.* (1986), 64–108.

99. *HE* iii, 7.

100. *Asser's Life of King Alfred*, c.2, p. 4. Osferth, a royal kinsman who received estates in king Alfred's will and was a leading ealdorman in Wessex in the early years of the ninth century, may also have been related to Osburh: see *Alfred the Great*, ed. Keynes and Lapidge, 177, 322 n.79.

101. This can only be supposition. The Chronicle's text contains few clues and the Kentish and South Saxon material is not known outside it, though other versions of the foundation of Kent are known, as noted above. Bately, 'The compilation of the Anglo-Saxon Chronicle', 93–129, concluded that there were a few features which marked the annals 449–584 from the rest of the Chronicle and could indicate a Latin source behind some of the entries, but that what was more striking was the unitary nature of the Chronicle's annals so that there could have been 'a single compiler for the bulk of the section 60 BC to the early ninth century' (p. 114). In other words, any distinctive features of the Kentish, South Saxon and Jutish entries could have been lost during the act of compilation, particularly if translation from Latin into Old English was involved. Kent became a West Saxon dependency after Egbert's conquest of the province in 825, and the West Saxons could have acquired written sources about its early history after this date as well as the incentive to bring the histories of the two kingdoms closer together. See also Brooks in this volume, where he argues that the West Saxons are more likely to have received oral traditions from Kent than written annals.

102. *Two Chronicles*, s.a. 755, i, 46–7.

103. B.A.E. Yorke, 'The bishops of Winchester, the kings of Wessex and the development of Winchester in the ninth and early tenth centuries', *Proc.*

Hants. Field Club and Arch. Soc. xl (1984), 61–70.

104. I would like to thank Chris Arnold, Mark Brisbane and Michael Hare for reading an earlier draft of this chapter and providing much helpful advice. However, they do not bear any responsibility for errors remaining and do not necessarily agree with all the chapter's conclusions.

7 Frithuwold's kingdom and the origins of Surrey

1. P.H. Sawyer, *Anglo-Saxon Charters: An Annotated List and Bibliography* (hereafter S) (1968), no. 1165. The authenticity of this charter (which is preserved in a thirteenth-century transcript) has been much debated, but despite obvious modifications the core of the text stands up to criticism. The main points in its favour are (a) that it shares a preamble with Hodilred's charter for the sister foundation at Barking, and belongs to a distinctive group of early charters associated with Eorcenwold (see P. Wormald, *Bede and the Conversion of England: the Charter Evidence* (The Jarrow Lecture, 1984), 9–11); and (b) that the witness list, the simple Latin boundary clause, and the references to *subreguli, provinciae*, the port of London and Frithuwold's *villa*, are all distinctively appropriate to a late seventh-century context. The strictures of A. Scharer, *Die angelsächsische Königsurkunde in 7. und 8. Jahrhundert* (Wien, 1982), 129–31, are therefore over-severe.

2. Translation from *English Historical Documents I*, ed. D. Whitelock (2nd edn., 1979), no. 54.

3. This section is based on J. Blair, *Landholding, Church and Settlement in Early Medieval Surrey* (Surrey Arch. Soc., forthcoming), c.1, where further supporting evidence will be found.

4. For the Wealden economy see esp. K.P. Witney, *The Jutish Forest* (1976); F.R.H. du Boulay, 'Denns, droving and danger', *Archaeologia Cantiana*, lxxvi (1961), 75–88; A. Everitt, *Continuity and Colonisation: The Evolution of Kentish Settlement* (1986); Blair, *Landholding, Church and Settlement*, c.2.

5. cf. J.E.A. Jolliffe, *Pre-Feudal England: the Jutes* (1933).

6. Witney, *Jutish Forest*, 35–8, 66–77; A. Everitt, 'River and wold', *J. Historical Geog.* iii (1977), 1–19; D. Hooke, *Anglo-Saxon Landscapes of the West Midlands: The Charter Evidence* (1981), 48–50.

7. Evidence in Blair, *Landholding, Church and Settlement*, mainly cc.1,2,4.

8. As suggested by Jolliffe, *Pre-Feudal England*, 45; the argument is developed in Witney, *Jutish Forest*, 40, and Blair, *Landholding, Church*.

9. For which see M. Gelling, *The Place-Names of Berkshire*, iii (Eng. Place-Name Soc. 1976), 841.

10. Later boundary clauses in S1165 and S621, discussed by J.E.B. Gover, A. Mawer and F.M. Stenton, *The Place-Names of Surrey* (Eng. Place-Name Soc. 1934), 105–6n, 114n, 119n, 132n.

11. For some earlier comments on this problem see *Place-Names of Surrey*, xiv–xv; J.N.L. Myres, *The English Settlements* (1986), 106n; F.M. Stenton, *Anglo-Saxon England* (3rd edn., 1971), 58; G.J. Copley, 'Stane Street in the Dark Ages', *Sussex Archaeol. Colls.* lxxxix (1950), 98–104; Gelling, *Place-Names of Berkshire*, iii, 813–14, 820–2, 840–1.

12. Bede, *Historia Ecclesiastica* (hereafter *HE*) (ed. C. Plummer, 1896), iv, 6; cf. J. Campbell, 'Bede's *Reges* and *Principes*', in idem, *Essays in Anglo-Saxon History* (1986), 86–7, for Bede's use of *regio* and *provincia*.

13. For which see T. Dyson, 'London and Southwark in the seventh century and later', *Trans.*

London and Middlesex Arch. Soc. xxxi (1980), 83–95. However, the subsequent archaeological discovery of the middle Saxon *wic* of London along the Strand now suggests that the Chertsey land lay opposite it on the south bank.

14. *HE* iv, 6.

15. These sentences summarize arguments set out more fully in J. Blair, 'Secular minster churches in Domesday Book', in *Domesday Book: a Reassessment*, ed. P.H. Sawyer (1985), 114–19; J. Blair, 'Minster churches in the landscape', in *Anglo-Saxon Settlements*, ed. D. Hooke (1988), 35–58; P.H. Hase, 'The mother churches of Hampshire', in *Minsters and Parish Churches: the Local Church in Transition 950–1200*, ed. J. Blair (Oxford Committee for Archaeology, 1988), 45–8.

16. *HE* iii, 24.

17. For Eorcenwold see especially Wormald, *Bede and the Conversion*, 9–11.

18. S1248; discussed in C.R. Hart, *The Early Charters of Eastern England* (1966), 135–41, 144, and Blair, *Landholding, Church and Settlement*, c.1.

19. S235; discussed in Blair, *Landholding, Church and Settlement*, c.1.

20. Wormald, *Bede and the Conversion*, 10.

21. Bede's Letter to Egbert, trans. *English Historical Documents I*, 804–7; see, most recently, the discussion in Wormald, *Bede and the Conversion*, 19–24.

22. See n. 10.

23. *Bracton's Notebook*, ed. F.W. Maitland, ii (1887), 586–8.

24. The numerous works of Jones and his predecessors are conveniently surveyed in a recent critique and in Jones's response: N. Gregson, 'The multiple estate model: some critical questions', *J. Hist. Geog.* xi (1985), 339–51; G.R.J. Jones, 'Multiple estates perceived', ibid., 352–63. The current dominance of the multiple estate model is well-illustrated by several papers in *Studies in Late*

Anglo-Saxon Settlement, ed. M.L. Faull (1984).
25. G.R.J. Jones, 'Multiple estates and early settlement', in Medieval Settlement, ed. P.H. Sawyer (1976), 26–35.
26. S235.
27. See Blair, 'Minster churches in the landscape'.
28. See Blair, 'Early Medieval Surrey'.
29. P. Wormald, 'Bede, the Bretwaldas and the origins of the Gens Anglorum', in Ideal and Reality in Frankish and Anglo-Saxon Society, ed. P. Wormald (1983), 112.
30. F.M. Stenton, 'Medeshamstede and its colonies', in Preparatory to Anglo-Saxon England, ed. D.M. Stenton (1970), 182; A. Dornier, 'The Anglo-Saxon monastery at Breedon-on-the-Hill, Leicestershire', in Mercian Studies, ed. A. Dornier (1977), 157–8.
31. W. de G. Birch, Cartularium Saxonicum, i (1885), no. 133.
32. Dornier, 'Anglo-Saxon monastery at Breedon', 159–60.
33. C. Hohler, 'St Osyth and Aylesbury', Records of Buckinghamshire, xviii (1966–70), 63–4, 66; D. Bethell, 'The Lives of St Osyth', Analecta Bollandiana, lxxxviii (1970), 75–127.
34. James Campbell's phrase: 'Some twelfth-century views of the Anglo-Saxon past', in idem, Essays in Anglo-Saxon History, 218.
35. See Blair, 'Minster churches in the landscape', where the case of Aylesbury and Quarrendon is discussed and illustrated.
36. Hohler, 'St Osyth', 63–4.
37. Anglo-Saxon Chronicle, s.a. 737 (ed. D. Whitelock et al. (1961)).
38. J. Blair, 'Saint Frideswide reconsidered', Oxoniensia, lii (1987), 71–127.

8 The Middle Saxons

1. 'Anglo-Saxon Chronicle (60 BC–AD 1042)', English Historical Documents, c. 500–1042 (hereafter E.H.D.), ed. and trans.
D. Whitelock (2nd edn., 1979), 211, 213.
2. Victoria County History (hereafter V.C.H.), Bucks., i (1905), 195–205; V.C.H. Herts., i (1902), 251–62; V.C.H. Middx., i (1969), 74–9.
3. M. Robbins, Middlesex (1953), 14; R. Merrifield, London, City of the Romans (1983), 127–39.
4. R. Ellis, 'Excavations at Grim's Dyke, Harrow, 1979', Trans. London & Middlesex Archaeol. Soc. (hereafter T.L.M.A.S.), 33 (1982), 173–6, and refs. cited there.
5. C. Brooke and G. Keir, London 800–1216: The Shaping of a City (1975), 16–17.
6. The Phillimore Atlas and Index of Parish Registers, ed. C. Humphery-Smith (1984), Map 16: Hertfordshire.
7. Domesday Book: Buckinghamshire, ed. J. Morris (hereafter D.B.) i, 145d. Both East Burnham and Staines were Westminster abbey estates at this time, so the link between them may date only to the period since c. 960.
8. W. Davies and H. Vierck, 'The contexts of Tribal Hidage: social aggregates and settlement patterns', Frühmittelalterliche Studien, viii (1974), 233; C. Hart, 'The Tribal Hidage', Trans. Royal Hist. Soc., 5th ser. xxi (1971), 151.
9. B. Yorke, 'The kingdom of the East Saxons', Anglo-Saxon England, xiv (1985), 28; H.M. Chadwick, Studies on Anglo-Saxon Institutions (1905), 271.
10. J.E.B. Gover, A. Mawer and F.M. Stenton, The Place-Names of Hertfordshire (1938), 86–7; B. Cox, 'The place-names of the earliest English records', J. Eng. Place-Name Soc. (hereafter J.E.P.N.S.), viii (1975–6), 37, 62.
11. Bede's Ecclesiastical History of the English People, ed. B. Colgrave and R.A.B. Mynors (1969) (hereafter H.E.) i, 7 (martyrdom) and i, 18 (St Germanus's visit); M. Gelling, The Early Charters of the Thames Valley (1979), passim for grants by Offa in

Hertfordshire and other counties which seem to represent the founding or refounding of the monastery at St Albans.

12. J. Morris, *Londinium* (1982), 264–5; R. Merrifield, *London, City of the Romans* (1983), 12–14.

13. H.F. Bidder and J. Morris, 'The Anglo-Saxon Cemetery at Mitcham', *Surrey Archaeol. Collns.* (hereafter *Sy.A.C.*) lvi (1959), 51–131; M.U. Jones, 'An early Saxon landscape at Mucking', *Anglo-Saxon Settlement and Landscape*, ed. T. Rowley (Brit. Archaeol. Reports, Brit. series (hereafter BAR), no. 6, 1974), 20–35.

14. T. Dyson and J. Schofield, 'Saxon London', *Anglo-Saxon Towns in Southern England*, ed. J. Haslam (1984), 289, 292; M. Biddle, 'London on the Strand', *Popular Archaeology*, vi (1984), 23–7; A. Vince, 'The Aldwych: Saxon London Discovered', *Current Archaeology*, xciii (1984), 310–12. This use of *wic* to denote a trading centre (unfortified) is common in the seventh and eighth centuries, e.g. *Hamwic*, Ipswich, Wijk-bij-Duurstede and *Quentavic* (Boulogne).

15. *H.E.* ii, 3.

16. P.H. Sawyer, *Anglo-Saxon Charters, An Annotated Handlist and Bibliography* (1968) (hereafter S), nos. 1790, 1786; M. Gibbs, *Early Charters of the Cathedral Church of St Paul, London*, Camden Soc., 3rd ser. lviii (1939), 17, 18.

17. T. Tatton-Brown, 'The topography of Anglo-Saxon London', *Antiquity*, lx (1986), 21–30. I am grateful to John Blair for this reference.

18. *ibid.*, 22–4, fig. 2.1.

19. Dyson and Schofield, 'Saxon London', 290; *E.H.D.* 395 (Laws of Hlothhere and Eadric, 16, 16.1).

20. *E.H.D.* 154. The date is merely an approximation, albeit a reasonably close one in this case.

21. K. Branigan, *The Catuvellauni*

(1987), 190–6; Merrifield, *London*, 262.

22. S65, surviving in a probably late eighth-century copy.

23. J. Campbell, *Essays in Anglo-Saxon History* (1986), 86–7; see S1165 for *Sunningas*; *H.E.* iii, 19: *provinciam Orientalium Anglorum*; *H.E.* iii, 24: *provincia Merciorum*.

24. S1784; Gibbs, *Early Charters*, J 9.

25. From O.E. **hamol, 'broken, undulating country': see B. Cox, 'Place-names and the earliest English records', 22.

26. J. Rutherford Davis, *Britons and Saxons* (1982), 10, 108; Davies and Vierck, 'Tribal Hidage', 233.

27. Branigan, *Catuvellauni*, 102–10.

28. P. Salway, *Roman Britain* (1981), 535.

29. S106; *E.H.D.* 500–1.

30. *Ciltinne* used to be identified with the Chilterns in the vicinity of High Wycombe, but Margaret Gelling (*Early Charters of the Thames Valley*, 99) has shown that it is more likely to represent the district of Chiltington in Sussex. Stithberht also witnessed a grant in Sussex: S108.

31. S188 (Botwell); S702 (Sunbury).

32. S100 (Yeading); S1293 (Hendon).

33. Hart, 'The Tribal Hidage', 143–6.

34. Davies and Vierck, 'Tribal Hidage', 228, 240.

35. *ibid.*, 227.

36. Hart, 'The Tribal Hidage', 147–8.

37. Yorke, 'Kingdom of the East Saxons', 17; *H.E.* ii, 3; Chadwick, *Anglo-Saxon Institutions*, 277.

38. The *Wrocensætna, Westerna, Lindisfarona*, Hwicce, and East and South Saxons are all assessed at 7,000 hides, while the *Noxgaga* and *Ohtgaga* together amount to this figure.

39. The estimated figure varies around 2,700 hides: H.C. Darby, *The Domesday Geography of Eastern England* (1952), 221.

40. The Domesday assessment for Lindsey was 2,007 carucates (Darby, *Domesday Geography of Eastern England*, 39); and for Sussex it was 3,193 hides: *The Domesday Geography of South-East England*, ed. H.C. Darby and E.M.J. Campbell (1962), 429.
41. K.P. Witney, *The Kingdom of Kent* (1982), 27, 45, 48.
42. Not until the reign of Cædwalla (685–8) does Wessex seem to have held sway over any part of London's hinterland.
43. E.T. Leeds, *The Archaeology of the Anglo-Saxon Settlements* (1913), 67; V.C.H. *Bucks.* i, 200–3. Many of the artefacts from this burial have Kentish or East Saxon parallels.
44. Merrifield, *London*, 246.
45. Branigan, *Catuvellauni*, 175–6; Morris, *Londinium*, 315, 333.
46. Bidder and Morris, 'The Anglo-Saxon Cemetery at Mitcham'.
47. R. Canham, 'Excavations at Shepperton Green', *T.L.M.A.S.* xxx (1979), 97–124; R. Poulton, 'A Saxon cemetery at Upper West Field, Shepperton', *ibid.*, xxxiii (1982), 177–85.
48. V.C.H. *Middx.*, i (1969), 76–7.
49. M.U. Jones, 'An early Saxon landscape at Mucking', 20–35.
50. J. Morris, 'A gazetteer of Anglo-Saxon Surrey', *Sy.A.C.* lvi (1959), 137–9, 152–4.
51. Branigan, *Catuvellauni*, 171–5.
52. Morris, *Londinium*, 334.
53. J.N.L. Myres, *The English Settlements* (1985), 101–2.
54. There is no mention of London after the *Crecganford* entry in the Anglo-Saxon Chronicle s.a. 457.
55. *E.H.D.* 157.
56. *E.H.D.* 165, 166–7; *H.E.* iv, 12–13.
57. Yorke, 'Kingdom of the East Saxons', 12, 16; Chadwick, *Anglo-Saxon Institutions*, 271–2; *H.E.* i, 25.
58. Saberht of Essex was the son of Æthelberht's sister Ricula: *H.E.* ii, 3.
59. Witney, *Kingdom of Kent*, 25, 56–7.
60. *H.E.* ii, 3.
61. M. Sharpe, *The Middlesex District in Saxon Times* (1916), 8.
62. D. Whitelock, 'Some Anglo-Saxon bishops of London', Chambers Memorial Lecture, 4 May 1974 (University College London, 1975), 5.
63. F.M. Stenton, *Anglo-Saxon England* (2nd edn., 1947), 131–6.
64. Eorcenwald's name contains a Frankish element rarely found in England except in a Kentish context; cf. W.G. Searle, *Onomasticon Anglo-Saxonicum* (1897), 230–1, but also Yorke, 'Kingdom of the East Saxons', 15.
65. Yorke, 'Kingdom of the East Saxons', 19; *H.E.* iv, 6.
66. S1165.
67. S1246.
68. *E.H.D.* 399, Prologue to the 'Laws of Ine' (688–694); Chadwick, *Anglo-Saxon Institutions*, 278.
69. S1248.
70. Yorke, 'Kingdom of the East Saxons', 28–9.
71. Hertford: *H.E.* iv, 5; Hatfield: *H.E.* iv, 17; W. de G. Birch, *Cartularium Saxonicum* (hereafter CS) (3 vols., 1885–99), no. 1330; Chelsea: *E.H.D.* 180, S123, S125, S128, S130, S131, S136, S158, S1430; Brentford: *E.H.D.* 792–3.
72. The king had only four insignificant holdings in Middlesex, nothing in the relevant parts of Hertfordshire and little in south-west Essex: *D.B.* i, 127a, 132a–133b; ii, 2b, 3a, 5a.
73. S1165; M. Gelling, *The Place-Names of Berkshire*, iii (1976), 814, 841; J.E.B. Gover, A. Mawer and F.M. Stenton, *The Place-Names of Middlesex* (1942), 22.
74. In the absence of any notice of a battle involving Ceawlin in the Middle Saxon area in the Anglo-Saxon Chronicle, it seems possible that a West Saxon takeover of parts of later Middlesex and south Buckinghamshire took place *c.* 570, between the battles at *Wibbandun* (568) and *Biedcanford* (571).

75. M. Gelling, *Signposts to the Past* (1978), 83–4.
76. *D.B.* i, 128c: Staines had had four berewics since before 1066; P. Jones, 'Saxon and Early Medieval Staines', *T.L.M.A.S.* xxxiii (1982), 191–2.
77. Chertsey combines a British personal name *Ceorot* with O.E. *ieg*, while in the same area lay Walton, *Wealas huthe* and *Wealagate*, respectively the settlement, landing place and gate of the Britons: J.E.B. Gover, A. Mawer and F.M. Stenton, *The Place-Names of Surrey* (1934), 105–6; K. Cameron, 'The meaning and significance of O.E. *walh* in English place-names', *J.E.P.N.S.* xii (1979–80), 41, 45.
78. On *ge* see A.H. Smith, *The Place-Name Elements*, i (1970), 196–7.
79. *PN Herts*, 189.
80. Branigan, *Catuvellauni*, 18–20, 87–9.
81. M. Gelling, 'English place-names derived from the compound *wīchām*', *Med. Archaeol.* xi (1967), 87–104.
82. Morris, *Londinium*, 310–11.
83. S1791; Gibbs, *Early Charters*, J 16.
84. Yorke, 'Kingdom of the East Saxons', 24.
85. *Atlas*, ed. Humphrey-Smith, Map 16: Hertfordshire.
86. *PN Herts.*, 215.
87. *E.H.D.* 211, when two *burhs* were built, one on each bank of the Lea, indicating an important bridgehead.
88. Branigan, *Catuvellauni*, 176; Gelling, *Signposts*, 77, fig. 2.
89. *H.E.* iv, 17; CS1330; as at Hertford, there is no direct evidence of a minster here, although its choice for a synod suggests at least some kind of seventh-century church.
90. *PN Herts.*, 126.
91. *V.C.H. Middx.*, v (1976), 128–9; *D.B.* i, 129d. Most of the hundred was held by Asgar the Staller before the Conquest, perhaps reflecting part of the former royal lands which had, unusually for Middlesex, not been broken up prior to the

tenth and eleventh centuries.
92. *PN Middx.*, 76; *PN Herts.*, 65; S. Doree, *Domesday Book and the Origin of Edmonton Hundred* (Edmonton Hundred Historical Society, Occ. Paper 48, 1986), 13, 20–30.
93. *D.B.* i, 129d; Doree, *Edmonton Hundred*, 10.
94. Enfield had a park in 1086: *D.B.* i, 129d; D.O. Pam, *The Story of Enfield Chase* (1984).
95. G. Gillam, *Prehistoric and Roman Enfield* (Enfield Arch. Soc. Res. Rep. 3, 1973).
96. *PN Herts.*, 220; Gelling, *Signposts*, 84.
97. Doree, *Edmonton Hundred*, 14.
98. *D.B.* i, 130d; ii, 92a.
99. *PN Middx.*, 143. The lord of Tottenham owed service to the bishop of London *c.* 1130: G. Barrow, *The Kingdom of the Scots* (1973), 9–10.
100. Barrow, *Kingdom of the Scots*, 10; *V.C.H. Middx.*, v, 324–6.
101. *PN Middx.*, 152.
102. K. MacDonnell, *Medieval London Suburbs* (1978), 12–14.
103. S1783; Gibbs, *Early Charters*, J 7.
104. S1785; Gibbs, *Early Charters*, J 6.
105. CS115, *E.H.D.* 792–3; Whitelock, 'Bishops', 10; *Two Thousand Years of Brentford*, ed. R. Canham (1978), 148–50.
106. CS235, CS241.
107. *E.H.D.* 196.
108. S1246.
109. S65.
110. S132.
111. *V.C.H. Middx.*, iii (1962), 83.
112. *D.B.* i, 130a–b.
113. *PN Middx.*, xiv, 27, 40, 90.
114. *PN Middx.*, 40.
115. S188.
116. S132.
117. N. Brooks, *The Early History of the Church of Canterbury* (1984), 141–2.
118. S1194.
119. S100.
120. S132.
121. S1194.
122. *V.C.H. Middx.*, i (1969), 76–7. For Uxbridge Road see J. Cotton, J. Mills and G. Clegg, *Archaeology in West Middlesex* (1986), 63; Stratford Bridge,

where Uxbridge Road crosses the River Pinn at the eastern end of the town, may indicate a Roman road on this axis, although it may refer to the road from *Verulamium* to the Thames at Laleham discussed by the Viatores, *Roman Roads in the South-East Midlands* (1964), 125–36, 382–6.

123. *PN Middx.*, 51–2; S106; *E.H.D.* 461–2.
124. S1436; Gelling, *Early Charters of the Thames Valley*, 102–4.
125. J. Blair, 'Secular minster churches in Domesday Book', in *Domesday Book. A Reassessment*, ed. P.H. Sawyer (1985), 109; *D.B.* i, 127a.
126. *PN Middx.*, 53.
127. Robbins, *Middlesex*, 306; V.C.H. *Middx.*, v (1976), 83–4.
128. S1121: writ of 1044×51.
129. S645; grant by Eadwig to Lyfing *minister* in 957.
130. S1451 (972×8).
131. S1451; S645.
132. Branigan, *Catuvellauni*, 103–10; Gelling, *Signposts*, 84–6, and Viatores, *Roman Roads*, 140–3, 375–6; both places lie on the *Verulamium*–Silchester road.
133. S151.
134. *D.B.* i, 136d (Hemel, 10 hides); 136a (Rickmansworth, 15 hides; Cashio, 20 hides).
135. *PN Middx.*, xiv.
136. Hart, 'The Tribal Hidage', 143–4; Davies and Vierck, 'Tribal Hidage', 232.
137. Cotton *et al.*, *Archaeology in West Middlesex*, 74–5.
138. P. Jones, 'Saxon Staines', 191; *D.B.* i, 145d.
139. S1142; Dyson and Schofield, 'Saxon London', 306–8.
140. Gibbs, *Early Charters*, no. 11 (writ of 1066×87, referring to an alleged grant by Æthelberht).
141. *E.H.D.* 180; S128, S130, S131; S150 was issued at Chelsea in 796.
142. *PN Middx.*, 162.
143. P. Hunting, *Royal Westminster* (1981), 16; S124.
144. Offa granted estates at Cashio and St Stephen's (Herts.) and Stanmore (Middx.) to St Alban's abbey in 793 (S136). At Aldenham (Herts.) nine out of ten hides in 1086 belonged to Westminster abbey, granted by Offa in 785 (S124); the other hide was held by St Alban's: *D.B.* i, 135b, 135d.
145. G.R.J. Jones, 'Multiple estates and early settlement', in *English Medieval Settlement*, ed. P.H. Sawyer (1979), 9–34.
146. P.H. Reaney, *The Place-Names of Essex* (1935), 490–1; W. Rodwell, 'Relict Landscapes in Essex', *Early Land Allotment*, ed. H.C. Bowen and P.J. Fowler (BAR 48, 1978), 89–98, esp. 97–8.
147. K.P. Witney, *The Jutish Forest* (1976); W.J. Blair, 'Land-holding, church and settlement in Surrey before 1300' (unpubl. Oxford Univ. D.Phil. thesis, 1982).
148. J. Blair, 'Minster churches in the landscape', in *Anglo-Saxon Settlements*, ed. D. Hooke (1988), 35–58.
149. D. Hooke, *The Anglo-Saxon Landscape: The Kingdom of the Hwicce* (1985), *passim*.
150. C. Hart, *The Early Charters of Essex* (2nd edn., 1971), 9.
151. E. Ekwall, *The Concise Oxford Dictionary of English Place-Names* (4th edn., 1960), 167, 226. *PN Ess.* 22, 111. Ambersbury Banks, an Iron Age earthwork and an *Ambros-*name (which may indicate post-Roman importance), lies in Epping: J. Morris, *The Age of Arthur* (1973), 100–1.
152. H. Cam, 'Manerium cum hundredo: the hundred and the hundred manor', in *idem*, *Liberties and Communities in Medieval England* (1944), 82–9.
153. Stenton, *Anglo-Saxon England*, 53–4.
154. I should like to thank John Blair and the editor for comments on earlier drafts of this chapter and for helpful suggestions which have considerably improved it, although any errors and contentious opinions remain the responsibility of the author.

9 Essex, Middle Anglia and the expansion of Mercia in the South-East Midlands

1. Owing to unforeseeable personal circumstances Dr Dumville was not able to provide notes to accompany this chapter. The editor is grateful to him for his kindness in allowing it to be published in its present form.

10 Kingship and material culture in early Anglo-Saxon East Anglia

1. This chapter is a development of the one given at the Oxford conference, where I was something of a last-minute stand-in. I hope I have managed to enliven the debate about East Anglian origins without in any way appearing to claim expertise. I am most grateful to Steven Bassett, Chris Wickham, John Newman, Catherine Hills, Tania Dickinson, Norman Scarfe and Keith Wade, who kindly read and commented on an earlier draft.
2. T.H. Aston and C.H.E. Philpin, *The Brenner Debate: Agrarian Class Structure and Economic Development in Pre-industrial Europe* (1985).
3. O. Rackham, *The History of the Countryside* (1986); M. Jones, *England Before Domesday* (1986); P. Murphy, 'Environmental archaeology in East Anglia', in *Environmental Archaeology: A Regional Review*, ed. H.C.M. Keeley (1984), 13–42.
4. H.H. Lamb, *Climate, History and the Northern World* (1982), ch. 9; R. Murphy, 'Iron Age to late Saxon land use in the Breckland', in *Integrating the Subsistence Economy*, ed. M. Jones (British Archaeological Reports (hereafter BAR), Int. Series, no. 181, 1983), 177–208.
5. R. Chapman, 'Death, culture and society: a prehistoric perspective', in *Anglo-Saxon Cemeteries 1979*, ed. P.A. Rahtz *et al.* (BAR, Brit. Series, no. 82, 1980), 59–80, for the analytical

approach. I. Hodder, 'Social structure and cemeteries: a critical appraisal', *ibid.*, 161–70; developed further in *idem*, *Symbols in Action* (1982) and *The Present Past* (1982), for a structuralist approach. J.D. Richards, *The Significance of the Form and Decoration of Anglo-Saxon Cremation Urns* (BAR, Brit. series, no. 166, 1987), gives a useful summary of the significance of different approaches to cemetery interpretation. In this chapter 'rank' is used to mean 'unequal social relations' (a continuous grading) rather than specific and separated social positions.
6. K. Wade in *Bulletin of the Sutton Hoo Research Committee*, iv (1986), 61–2.
7. Wade, *ibid.*, 29; J. Newman, *Bulletin of the Sutton Hoo Research Committee*, v (forthcoming).
8. S.E. West, 'West Stow: the Anglo-Saxon village', *East Anglian Archaeology* [hereafter *EAA*], xxiv (1985); P. Wade-Martins, 'Excavations in North Elmham Park 1967–72', *EAA* ix (1980), 1–661; K. Wade, 'A settlement site at Wicken Bonhunt, Essex', in *Archaeology in Essex to AD 1500*, ed. D.G. Buckley (Council for British Archaeology [hereafter CBA] Res. Rep. 34, 1980), 96–102.
9. For Brandon: Suffolk County Council, *Suffolk Archaeology 1987* (plan and text). J. Newman, R. Carr: pers. comm. D.M. Wilson, *Anglo-Saxon Art* (1984), Pl. 123, for the plaque.
10. V. Fenwick, 'Insula de Burgh: excavation at Burrow Hill, Butley, Suffolk, 1978–81', *Anglo-Saxon Studies in Archaeology and History*, iii (1984), 35–54; S. Johnson, 'Burgh Castle, excavation by Charles Green 1958–61', *EAA* xx (1983), 1–129.
11. R. Hodges and D. Whitehouse, *Mohammed, Charlemagne and the Origins of Europe* (1983), 95; R Hodges, *Dark Age Economics* (1982).

12. K. Wade in 'The archaeology of Witton, near North Walsham', *EAA* xviii (1983), 69. The Roman infrastructure (e.g. roads) may of course have continued in use without continuity of settlement site.

13. J.N.L. Myres, *The English Settlement* (1986), and see comments in Hills, *op. cit.* in note 15, and S.R. Bassett, review in *Archives*, lxxv (1986), 168–9.

14. J.N.L. Myres and B. Green, *The Anglo-Saxon Cemeteries of Caistor-by-Norwich and Markshall, Norfolk* (Society of Antiquaries Res. Rep. 30, 1973), 258–60.

15. C. Hills, 'The archaeology of Anglo-Saxon England in the pagan period: a review', *Anglo-Saxon England*, viii (1978), 297–329; and *idem*, 'Economic and settlement background to Sutton Hoo in eastern England', *Vendel Studies* (Statens Historiska Museum, Stockholm, 1983), 99–104.

16. H.W. Böhme, 'Das ende der Romerherrschaft in Britannien und die angelsachsische Besiedlung Englands im 5 Jahrhundert', *Jahrbuch des Romisch-Germanischen Zentral museum*, xxxiii (1986), 466–574, esp. 558–9. Hills, 'Archaeology of Anglo-Saxon England', already noted the problems of attributing military or ethnic status to much of the metalwork used by Böhme. Richards, 'Anglo-Saxon cremation urns', 194, argues that 'a high level of contact and conformity between peoples practising the new burial rite indicates its common origin'.

17. e.g. H.P.R. Finberg, 'Roman and Saxon Withington' in *idem*, *Lucerna: Studies on Problems in the Early History of England* (1964).

18. J. Hines, *The Scandinavian Character of Anglian England in the Pre-Viking Period* (BAR, Brit. series, no. 124, 1984), 241. Hills, 'Archaeology of Anglo-Saxon England', 313–16, points out that Anglian distinctions in grave-goods belong mainly to the sixth century rather than to the fifth.

19. Hines, 'Scandinavian character', 285. R.L.S. Bruce-Mitford, *The Sutton Hoo Ship Burial*, I (1975), 693, expanded in *idem*, 'The Sutton Hoo ship burial: some foreign connections', *Settimane di studio del centro Italiano di studi sull'alto medioevo*, xxxii (Spoleto, 1986), 143–218, esp. 195–210.

20. As observed by M.G. Welch, 'Reflections on the archaeological connections between Scandinavia and eastern England in the Migration period', *Studien zur Sachsen-forschung*, vi (1987), 251–9, who also questions Hines's dating.

21. F.M. Stenton, *Anglo-Saxon England* (3rd edn., 1971), 247.

22. C.M. Hills *et al.*, 'The Anglo-Saxon Cemetery at Spong Hill, North Elmham, Part I, Catalogue of cremations', *EAA* vi (1977); 'Part II, Catalogue of cremations', *EAA* xi (1981); 'Part III, Catalogue of inhumations', *EAA* xxi (1984); 'Part IV, Catalogue of cremations', *EAA* xxxiv (1987). See also Hills, 'Archaeology of Anglo-Saxon England', for an overview.

23. Böhme, 'Das ende der Romerherrschaft', abb. 59. Hills, 'Archaeology of Anglo-Saxon England', 41, suggests grave 40 as the founder burial of a 'small new separate cemetery whose occupants were in some way different from the rest of the community'. Dickinson (pers. comm.) would see the shield boss (her type 3) as not earlier than *c.* 525.

24. Richards, 'Anglo-Saxon cremation urns', 197. For the status role of the barrow in Anglo-Saxon England see J.F. Shephard, 'The social identity of the individual in isolated barrows and barrow cemeteries in Anglo-Saxon England', in *Space, Hierarchy and Society*, ed. B. Burnham and J. Kingsbury (BAR, Int. series, no. 59, 1979), 47–80, and M.O.H. Carver, 'Sutton Hoo in context', *Settimane di studio del centro Italiano di studi sull'alto medioevo*, xxxii (Spoleto, 1986), 77–123.

25. R.L.S. Bruce-Mitford, *Aspects of Anglo-Saxon Archaeology* (1974), 114–69; W. Filmer-Sankey, 'Snape Anglo-Saxon cemetery: first interim report on the 1986 trial excavation', *Bulletin of the Sutton Hoo Research Committee*, v (1987).

26. R.L.S. Bruce-Mitford, *The Sutton Hoo Ship Burial*, I–III (1975–83) is the definitive account of the ship burial. For the research design, methodology and results of the new campaign see *Bulletin of the Sutton Hoo Research Committee*, i–v (1983–7). For a new (summary) interpretation of the site see Carver, 'Sutton Hoo in context'.

27. *Bulletin of the Sutton Hoo Research Committee*, iv (1986), 75.

28. P. Jankavs, '"Social image"="cemetery image". Some generalization problems. The 3rd–8th centuries on Gotland', in *Similar Finds? Similar Interpretations?*, ed. C.A. Moberg (1981), 1–56.

29. C. Arnold, 'Wealth and social structure: a matter of life and death', in *Anglo-Saxon Cemeteries 1979*, ed. Rahtz et al., 81–142; idem, 'Stress as a stimulus for socio-economic change: Anglo-Saxon England in the seventh century', in *Ranking, Resource and Exchange*, ed. C. Renfrew and S. Shennan (1982), 124–31; Shephard, 'Social identity'.

30. The point was made (innocently) in Carver, 'Context', 101, but has been studied by e.g. R. Chapman, 'Death, culture and society: a prehistoric perspective', in *Anglo-Saxon Cemeteries 1979*, ed. Rahtz et al.; and, from the second viewpoint, Hodder, *Symbols in Action*; idem, 'Social structure and cemeteries: a critical appraisal', in *Anglo-Saxon Cemeteries 1979*, ed. Rahtz et al., 161–9; and see Richards, 'Anglo-Saxon cremation urns', 12–14, for a discussion of the principles and their application.

31. B. Myhre, 'Boat houses as indicators of political organization', *Norwegian Archaeol. Review*, xviii (1985), 36–60; idem, 'Chieftain graves and chieftain territories in south Norway in the migration period', *Studien zur Sachsenforschung*, vi (1987), 166–87. In a number of studies B. Ambrosiani has also proposed early estates, comprising aristocratic graves in burial mounds, settlement, fortified place, and latterly church, for Uppland in Sweden, which may itself have been a territory of the type of the East Anglian kingdom by the seventh century: Ambrosiani, 'Aristocratic graves and manors in early medieval Sweden', in *In Honorem Evert Baudou*, ed. M. Backe et al. (Umeå, 1985), 109–18; P. Sawyer, 'Settlement and power among the Svear in the Vendel period', *Vendel Studies*, ii (1983), 117–22, is reluctant to see the 'Svealand' as subject to a coherent power by the seventh century, and prefers 'a stage of social organization where relatively small units of lordship were the norm' (p. 119). This view seems to correspond to the model of sixth-century East Anglia developed here.

32. M. Parker Pearson, 'Economic and ideological change: cyclical growth in the pre-state societies of Jutland', in *Ideology, Power and Prehistory* ed. C. Tilley and D. Miller (1984), 69–92.

33. *ibid.*, 70.

34. S. Shennan, 'Ideology, change and the European early Bronze Age', in *Symbolic and Structural Archaeology* ed. I. Hodder (1982), 155–61.

35. Carver, 'Context', and see R. Bradley, 'Time regained: the creation of continuity', *J. British Archaeol. Assoc.* cxl (1987), 1–17, for an elaboration of the argument that the choice of prehistoric monuments by later (e.g. Anglo-Saxon) people may be deliberate.

36. For a 'Sandlings province' see *Bulletin of the Sutton Hoo Research Committee*, iv (1986). A special character for south-east East Anglia has also been argued

from cemetery evidence:
Fenwick, 'Insula de Burgh', 37.
The idea of Christian innovators
and pagan reactionaries
developing in close confrontation
to each other may also be
observable on the Yar estuary.
At Burgh Castle a 'Christian'
cemetery orientated east–west
lies in the supposed monastery
established by Fursa: see
Johnson, 'Burgh Castle'. Across
the water at Caister-on-Sea, a
contemporary cemetery shows
quite different burial practices,
including those using boat
pieces; these are also present at
Burrow Hill (Fenwick, 'Insula de
Burgh'); A. Meaney, *A Gazetteer
of Early Anglo-Saxon Burial
Sites* (1964).

37. *Peer Polity interaction and
Socio-political Change*, ed.
C. Renfrew and J.F. Cherry (1986),
esp. C. Renfrew, 'Introduction'.

38. In attempting to apply the peer
polity idea to Anglo-Saxon
England, R. Hodges tends to
overlook the possibility of peer
polities in Scandinavia:
R. Hodges, 'Peer polity
interaction in Anglo-Saxon
England', *ibid.*, 69–78. A rather
more applicable model is
provided by T. Champion and
S. Champion, 'Peer polity
interaction and the European
Iron Age', *ibid.*, 59–68.

39. Cherry and Renfrew, 'Epilogue
and prospect', *ibid.*, 154.

40. Hodges sees these kings as more
rooted in tradition: 'Their fathers
had been elected to power by the
aristocracy within the kingdom,
but they themselves aspired to
establish dynasties ... The
church offered a means of
altering the social roles, while
traditional legitimacy was
endorsed by a final, quite
spectacular burial rite (as at
Sutton Hoo) when the son
sought recognition for his rights
through the lavish disposal of
traditional and Frankish-
Christian imported goods in the
pagan cemetery' (Hodges, 'Peer
polity', 76). This attractive
generalization can be questioned
in a number of particular

aspects. Elective kingship must
be doubly hypothetical when the
existence of a kingdom is itself
uncertain. Neither is it obvious
why a king should not gain
power by exactly the same
strategies of wealth or debt
accumulation as other members
of the aristocracy. Inherited
power could be achieved without
the assistance of the church (e.g.
see P. Sawyer, 'Settlement and
power', 122). Burials such as
Sutton Hoo (not that there are
many) can hardly be traditional,
at least not in Anglo-Saxon East
Anglia where both ship burial
and regalia are themselves
innovations.

41. Champion and Champion, 'Iron
Age', 59.

42. Stenton, *Anglo-Saxon England*, 470.

43. T.H. Aston, 'The origins of the
manor in England', reprinted
with a postscript in *Social
Relations and Ideas*, ed.
T.H. Aston *et al.* (1983), 1–43.

44. *ibid.*, 10, 11.

45. *ibid.*, 38.

46. *ibid.*, 15.

47. J.M. Wallace-Hadrill, *Early
Medieval History* (1975), 181–2.

48. D. Dumville, 'Kingship,
genealogies and regnal lists', in
Early Medieval Kingship ed.
P.H. Sawyer and I.N. Wood
(1977), 72–104.

49. Dumville, *ibid.*, 81, Wallace-
Hadrill, *Early Medieval History*,
213–14, and P. Wormald, '*Lex
Scripta* and *Verbum Regis*:
legislation and Germanic
kingship from Ewic to Cnut',
ibid., 105–38; and *idem*, 'Bede,
Bretwaldas and the origin of the
Gens Anglorum', in *Ideal and
Reality in Frankish and Anglo-
Saxon Society*, ed. P. Wormald
(1983), 99–129. The role of the
church in general and Gregory in
particular in creating the image
of the English nation is
persuasively claimed in the last
of these; but although it may
have been important to use the
church to stabilize the new
kingdoms (see below), the church
was surely not necessary for the
creation of rich powerful individuals
aspiring to control territory.

50. A. Angenendt, 'The conversion of the Anglo-Saxons considered against the background of the early medieval mission', *Settimane di studio del contro Italiano di studi sull'alto medioevo*, xxxii (1986), 747–92.

51. Angenendt, *ibid.* and refs. cited there.

52. See F.M. Stenton, 'The East Anglian kings of the seventh century', in *The Anglo-Saxons: Studies in Some Aspects of Their History and Culture Presented to Bruce Dickens*, ed. P. Clemoes (1959), and D. Whitelock, 'The pre-Viking church in East Anglia', *Anglo-Saxon England*, i (1972), 1–22, for sources. Temples are virtually unknown archaeologically, and those that have been claimed are treated with some scepticism by O. Olsen in e.g. 'Is there a relationship between pagan and Christian places of worship in Scandinavia?' *The Anglo-Saxon Church*, ed. L.A.S. Butler and R.K. Morris (CBA Res. Rep. 60, 1986), 126–30. Rædwald's temple, perhaps at Rendlesham or Sutton Hoo, thus falls readily into the same context as that at Uppsala: not a traditional construction but one provoked by the onset of ideologically acquisitive Christian missions. If it was made of timber and survived until Alduulf's boyhood, as reported by Bede, it may have remained standing, and therefore in use, for fifty years after the death of Rædwald.

53. These landlords resemble Stenton's 'independent master of a peasant houshold ... subject to no lord below the king', except that they had no king to be subject to (cf. Stenton, *Anglo-Saxon England*, 277 .

54. Complete cemeteries have been excavated at Mucking II (W.T. Jones, 'Early Saxon cemeteries in Essex', in *Archaeology in Essex to AD 1500*, ed. Buckley, and Wasperton (Birmingham University Field Archaeology Unit, unpublished) but do little

to reinforce these speculations. Mucking II had 336 inhumations and 468 cremations, but the existence of adjacent Mucking I, an incomplete group of c. sixty inhumations orientated east–west, makes any guess about the size of territory served or social ranks within it more insubstantial than usual. The Wasperton cemetery's 200 inhumations and twenty cremations may suggest a live population of forty, two or three of whom on the evidence of grave-goods were of high rank. This cemetery is also continuous in burial practice from 'late Roman' (fourth and fifth centuries) to 'Anglo-Saxon' (sixth and seventh centuries), thus endorsing Böhme's picture.

55. C. Wickham, 'The other transition: from the ancient world to feudalism', *Past & Present*, ciii (1984), 3–36.

56. By the sixth century this was perceived as Anglian and signalled as such in grave-goods. Hills, 'Archaeology of Anglo-Saxon England', points out that regional differences are noticeable, if at all, in the sixth century rather than the fifth. This supports the notion that being Anglian is not a fact based on ethnic derivation but a sixth-century idea used to enhance a new polity. That some commonality of material culture existed at all suggests that the polity may have had a pre-Christian economic root based on landholding, rather than being solely an invention of Gregory's church (cf. Wormald, 'Bede, *Bretwaldas* and the origins of the *Gens Anglorum*'). But the archaeological evidence is suggestive rather than decisive.

57. This is not to assume that grave-goods, in the period that they were used, always necessarily indicated fiscal status or debt or freedom from debt. But I am assuming, without arguing it in detail, that the burial rite is ideologically meaningful – in other words, an intelligent act.

D. Bullough, 'Burial, community
and belief in the early medieval
West', in *Ideal and Reality*, ed.
Wormald, 177–201, argues that
the juxtaposition of apparently
Christian and pagan burial rites
may signify indifference, but it
could equally be held to argue
conflict. The arguments are still
stronger for interpreting
'Christian' grave-goods in pagan
burials as a sign of pagan
chauvinism, not compromise.
See Carver, 'Context', and
W.Y. Adams, *Nubia, corridor to
Africa* (1977) for this
interpretation applied to the
contemporary X-group in Nubia.
58. cf. F.M. Stenton, 'The Danes in
England', *Proc. British Academy*,
xiii (1927), 203–46; R.H.C.
Davis, 'East Anglia and the
Danelaw', *Trans. Royal Hist.
Soc.* 5th ser. v (1955), 23–9.

**11 The formation of the Mercian
kingdom**

1. *Bede's Ecclesiastical History of
the English People*, ed.
B. Colgrave and R.A.B. Mynors
(1969) (hereafter *HE*), preface.
This chapter follows Bede's
chronology as interpreted by
S. Wood, 'Bede's Northumbrian
dates again', *Eng. Hist. Rev.*
xcviii (1983), 280–96.
2. W. Davies, 'Annals and the
origin of Mercia', in *Mercian
Studies*, ed. A. Dornier (1977),
17–29.
3. P.H. Sawyer, *Anglo-Saxon
Charters: An Annotated List
and Bibliography* (1968)
(hereafter S), nos. 67–226. For
local production of early
charters, see P. Chaplais, 'The
origin and authenticity of the
royal Anglo-Saxon diploma',
J. Soc. Archivists, iii (1965–9),
48–61, and N.P. Brooks, *The
Early History of the Church of
Canterbury* (1984), 167–70,
327–30.
4. A convenient modern survey
with full references may be
found in P. Grierson and
M. Blackburn, *Medieval
European Coinage, I, Early*

Middle Ages (5th–10th Centuries)
(1986), 155–89, 270–93.
5. D.N. Dumville, 'The Anglian
collection of royal genealogies
and regnal lists', *Anglo-Saxon
England*, v (1976), 23–50.
6. Printed below, 227, and in W. de
G. Birch, *Cartularium
Saxonicum* (3 vols., 1885–93)
(hereafter CS), no. 297. The
principal modern discussions are
C.R. Hart, 'The Tribal Hidage',
Trans. Royal Hist. Soc. 5th ser.
xxi (1971), 133–57; W. Davies
and H. Vierck, 'The contexts of
Tribal Hidage: social aggregates
and settlement patterns',
Frühmittelalterliche Studien, viii
(1974), 223–93; H.R. Loyn, *The
Governance of Anglo-Saxon
England 500–1087* (1984), 34–40.
For tribute see T. Reuter,
'Plunder and tribute in the
Carolingian Empire', *Trans.
Royal Hist. Soc.* 5th ser. xxxv
(1985), 75–94.
7. P.H. Blair, 'The Northumbrians
and their southern frontier',
Archaeologia Aeliana, 4th ser.
xxvi (1948), 98–126 at 105–12,
citing the Anglo-Saxon
Chronicle (ed. D. Whitelock *et
al.*, 1961) (hereafter ASC), 'E' s.a.
449, 641, 697, 702.
8. Grierson and Blackburn,
Medieval European Coinage,
I, 279; H. Pagan, 'Coinage in
southern England, 796–874', in
Anglo-Saxon Monetary History,
ed. M. Blackburn (1986), 46.
9. H.E. Walker, 'Bede and the
Gewisse', *Cambridge Historical
J.* xii (1956), 174–86. For *rex
Geuis(s)orum* in early West
Saxon charters, see S256, S262
whose authenticity is discussed
by H. Edwards, 'The authority of
the earliest West Saxon charters'
(unpubl. Glasgow Univ. Ph.D.
thesis, 1985), 407–8.
10. *HE* ii, 12, 14, 20; *The Life of
Bishop Wilfrid by Eddius
Stephanus*, ed. B. Colgrave
(1927), c.14; ASC s.a. 655, 657.
11. *HE* ii, 12.
12. C.R. Hart's bold attempt ('Tribal
Hidage') to define the boundaries
has not been accepted, but there
is much common ground
between him and the work of

Davies and Vierck and of Loyn (cited above in n. 6), of D. Hill, *Atlas of Anglo-Saxon England* (1982), map 136, and of D. Hooke, *Anglo-Saxon Territorial Organization: The Western Margins of Mercia* (Univ. of Birmingham, Dept of Geography, Occas. Paper 22, 1986), 1–45.

13. *HE* ii, 24.

14. For Lichfield see *HE* iv, 3 and *Life of Wilfrid*, ed. Colgrave, c.15, and below, p. 169 and n. 46. For Repton see the grant of Frithuric of 675×92 (S1805), which is discussed above by J. Blair (above, ch. 7) and also by A. Dornier and by A. Rumble in *Mercian Studies*, ed. Dornier, 158, 169–72. Early charters whose witness lists indicate meetings of the Mercian witan at Tamworth in 781, 790, 799, 808, 840, 841, 845, 849, 855 and 857 are S121, S133, S155, S163, S192, S193, S198, S199, S207, S208.

15. Blair, 'Southern frontier', 112–26.

16. A. Meaney, *A Gazetteer of Early Anglo-Saxon Burial Sites* (1964), *passim*; M. Fowler, 'Anglian settlement of the Derbyshire-Staffordshire Peak District', *Derbyshire Archaeol. J.* lxxiv (1954), 134–51; A. Ozanne, 'The Peak dwellers', *Medieval Archaeol.* vi–vii (1962–3), 15–52; T.H. McK. Clough, A. Dornier and R.A. Rutland, *Anglo-Saxon and Viking Leicestershire* (1975). For more recent work see M.W. Bishop, 'An Anglian cemetery at Cotgrave, Notts.', *Trans. Thoroton Soc.* lxxxviii (1984), 16–17; S. Losco-Bradley and H.M. Wheeler, 'Anglo-Saxon settlement in the Trent valley: some aspects', in *Studies in Late Anglo-Saxon Settlement*, ed. M.L. Faull (1984), 101–14. J.N.L. Myres, *The English Settlements* (2nd edn., 1986), 182–6, largely follows his original account of 1935.

17. Davies, 'Annals', 22–3.

18. *Felix's Life of Saint Guthlac*, ed. B. Colgrave (1956), c.2.

19. Dumville, 'Anglian Collection', 33. For the earlier (pre-Icel) stages of this genealogy, see *idem*, 'Kingship, genealogies and regnal lists', in *Early Medieval Kingship*, ed. P. Sawyer and I. Wood (1977), 72–104 at 93, and H.M. Chadwick, *The Origin of the English Nation* (1907), 111–43.

20. J. Campbell, *Bede's Reges and Principes* (Jarrow Lecture for 1979) (reprinted in *idem*, *Essays in Anglo-Saxon History* (1986), 85–98).

21. Davies and Vierck, 'Tribal Hidage', 224–41. For Ireland see F.J. Byrne, *Irish Kings and High-Kings* (1973), and G. MacNiocaill, *Ireland before the Vikings* (1972); for Wales, W. Davies, *Wales in the Early Middle Ages* (1981), 85–116.

22. *The Place-Names of Worcestershire*, ed. A. Mawer and F.M. Stenton (Eng. Place-Name Soc. iv, 1927), xxii.

23. It has been compiled on the basis of the volumes of the Eng. Place-Name Soc. supplemented by E. Ekwall, *The Concise Oxford Dictionary of English Place-Names* (4th edn., 1960). I am most grateful to Margaret Gelling for advice on these names.

24. Davies, 'Annals', 21.

25. ASC s.a. 626.

26. *HE* ii, 20.

27. *Historia Brittonum*, ed. T. Mommsen (*Chronica Minora Saec. IV–VII*, iii, M.G.H., Auctores Antiquissimi, xiii, Berlin, 1898) (hereafter *Hist. Britt.*), c.65.

28. Chadwick, *Origin*, 15, referring to *HE* ii, 20, iii, 7, 21, 24, and v, 13.

29. *Hist Britt.* cc.64–5; *Annales Cambriae*, s.a. CC, CCXII (=644, 656), ed. E. Phillimore, *Y Cymmrodor*, ix (1888), 141–83.

30. *HE* ii, 14.

31. ASC s.a. 628.

32. *HE* ii, 14. Compare Bede's use of the term 'pagan' in *HE* ii, 20.

33. *HE* ii, 20, iii, 7.

34. For Bamburgh see *HE* iii, 16; for Yeavering *HE* ii, 14 and B. Hope-Taylor, *Yeavering: An Anglo-British Centre of Northumbria* (1977).

35. W. Stubbs, 'The cathedral, diocese and monasteries of

Worcester in the 8th century',
Archaeol. J. xix (1862), 237–8;
H.P.R. Finberg, 'The princes of
the Hwicce', in *idem, Early
Charters of the West Midlands*
(1961), 167–80. But compare the
argument of S. R. Bassett, above,
238, n.19.

36. CS297A.

37. For varying assessments see
I. Williams, 'The poems of
Llywarch Hen', *Proc. Brit. Acad.*
xviii (1932), 269–301; reprinted
in *idem, The Beginnings of
Welsh Poetry*, ed. and trans.
R. Bromwich (1972); R.
Bromwich, 'The character of
early Welsh tradition', in *Studies
in Early British History*, ed.
N.K. Chadwick (1954), 83–136;
D.P. Kirby, 'Welsh bards and the
border', in *Mercian Studies*, ed.
Dornier, 31–42; D.N. Dumville,
'Palaeographical considerations
in the dating of early Welsh
verse', *Bull. Board of Celt. Stud.*
xxvii (1976–8), 246–52; *idem*,
'Sub-Roman Britain: history and
legend', *History*, lxii (1977),
173–92; Davies, *Wales in Early
Middle Ages*, 209–12.

38. I. Williams, 'A reference to the
Nennian Bellum Cocboy', *Bull.
Board Celt. Stud.* iii (1926–7),
59–62; for the earlier date see
J. Rowland, 'A study of the Saga
Englynion' (unpubl. Ph.D. thesis,
Univ. Coll. of Wales,
Aberystwyth, 1982), 325.

39. *Canu Llywarch Hen*, ed.
I. Williams (1935), 48.

40. *Marwynad Cynddylan*, in *ibid.*,
50–2; a widely available
translation is in J.P. Clancy,
Earliest Welsh Poetry (1970),
87–9, and a much more scholarly
text and translation in Rowland,
'Saga Englynion', 303–7. Dr
Dumville would date the poem
no earlier than the ninth
century: 'Sub-Roman Britain',
186.

41. *Hist. Britt.* c.65: 'Solus autem
Catgabail, rex Guenedotae
regionis, cum exercitu suo evasit
de nocte consurgens; quapropter
uocatus est Catgabail
Catguommed.'

42. F.M. Stenton, *Preparatory to
Anglo-Saxon England: Collected*

Papers, ed. D.M. Stenton (1970),
357–63.

43. For attempts to bring
archaeological and onomastic
evidence to bear, see the
chapters of K. Pretty and
M. Gelling in this volume.

44. *Marwynad Cynddylan*, in *Canu
Llywarch Hen*, ed. Williams, 11.

45. Welsh politics of that later
period are now superbly analysed
by R.R. Davies, *Conquest,
Coexistence and Change: Wales
1063–1415* (1987).

46. For *Lwytgoed*, Lichfield and
Letocetum see M. Gelling,
Signposts to the Past (1978), 57,
and A.L.F. Rivet and C. Smith,
*The Place-Names of Roman
Britain* (1979), 436–7; for
Letocetum see J. Gould,
'Letocetum, Christianity and
Lichfield', *Trans. S. Staffs.
Archaeol. & Hist. Soc.* xiv
(1973), 29–31; for Lichfield see
C.C. Taylor, 'Origins of
Lichfield, Staffs.', *ibid.*, x (1968–
9), 43–52, S.R. Bassett, 'Medieval
Lichfield: a topographical
review', *ibid.*, xxii (1982), 93–121
at 12–13, and J. Campbell, 'The
Church in Anglo-Saxon towns',
Studies in Church History, xvi
(1979), 119–35 at 120.

47. A similar suggestion but in the
context of Oswiu's recovery of
Oswald's relics is made by
Rowland ('Saga Englynion', 343).

48. This chapter has benefited
greatly from the comments of
Steven Bassett, David Dumville,
Margaret Gelling and Patrick
Wormald. I am, however, alone
responsible for any errors and for
the form of the argument.

12 Defining the Magonsæte

1. H.P.R. Finberg, 'Mercians and
Welsh', *Lucerna* (1964), 72.

2. H.P.R. Finberg, 'St Mildburg's
Testament', in *idem, The Early
Charters of the West Midlands*
(hereafter *ECWM*) (1961), 197–217.

3. H.P.R. Finberg, 'The princes of
the Magonsæte', *ECWM*, 217–25.

4. Finberg, 'Mercians and Welsh',
66–82.

5. F.M. Stenton, 'Pre-Conquest

Herefordshire', in *Preparatory to Anglo-Saxon England*, ed. D.M. Stenton (1970), 195–202.

6. Finberg, 'Mercians and Welsh', 72.

7. Finberg, 'Princes of the Magonsaete', 219, n. 2.

8. P.A. Barker, K.B. Pretty *et al.*, 'Excavations on the Baths Basilica at Wroxeter, 1986–7', *Britannia* (forthcoming).

9. R.P. Wright and K.H. Jackson, 'A late inscription from Wroxeter', *Antiq. J.* xlviii (1968), 296–300.

10. P.A. Barker, 'Excavations on the site of the Baths Basilica at Wroxeter, 1966–74', *Britannia*, vi (1965), 115.

11. See also Barker *et al.*, 'Baths Basilica at Wroxeter'.

12. M.O.H. Carver, 'Early Shrewsbury: an archaeological definition in 1975', *Trans. Shropshire Arch. Soc.* lix (1973–4), 225–63.

13. M. Gelling, *Signposts to the Past* (1978), 57.

14. W. de G. Birch, *Cartularium Saxonicum* (3 vols., 1885–93), no. 297.

15. Finberg, *ECWM*, 147.

16. Finberg, 'Mercians and Welsh', 79.

17. M. Biddle, 'Towns', in *The Archaeology of Anglo-Saxon England*, ed. D.M. Wilson (1976), 103–12; P. Dixon, 'Life after Wroxeter', in *From Roman Town to Norman Castle: Essays in honour of Philip Barker*, ed. A. Burl (University of Birmingham, 1988), 37–9.

18. W. Davies, *An Early Welsh Microcosm: Studies in the Llandaff Charters* (1978).

19. K.B. Pretty, 'The Severn Basin in the 5th and 6th Centuries AD', (unpublished Ph.D. thesis, University of Cambridge, 1975).

20. *ibid.*

21. Finberg, 'Mercians and Welsh', 73.

22. Finberg, 'Princes of the Magonsæte', 217, n. 1. and refs. cited there.

23. *ibid.*, 217–25.

24. Finberg, 'St Mildburg's Testament', 205.

25. Finberg, 'Princes of the Magonsæte', 217–24.

26. F.M. Stenton, *Anglo-Saxon England* (2nd edn., 1946), 47; Finberg, 'Princes of the Magonsæte', 219, n. 2; *idem*, 'Mercians and Welsh', 71.

27. Finberg, 'St Mildburg's Testament', 205.

28. M. Biddle, 'Archaeology, architecture, and the cult of saints in Anglo-Saxon England', in *The Anglo-Saxon Church*, ed. L.A.S. Butler and R.K. Morris (Council for British Archaeology (hereafter CBA) Res. Rep. 60, 1986), 16, 22.

29. S.R. Bassett, 'A probable Mercian royal mausoleum at Winchcombe, Gloucestershire', *Antiq. J.* lxv (1985) 84, and above, 6–7, 17.

30. Finberg, 'Princes of the Magonsæte', 221.

31. Gelling, *Signposts to the Past*, 102–5.

32. Finberg, 'St Mildburg's Testament', 205.

33. Davies, *An Early Welsh Microcosm*, 162.

34. *ibid.*, 98.

35. Finberg, 'St Mildburg's Testament', 204.

36. Lord Rennell of Rodd, 'The Land of Lene', in *Culture and Environment*, ed. I.Ll. Foster and L.A. Alcock (1963), 315.

37. Finberg, *ECWM*, 148.

38. Finberg, 'Mercians and Welsh', 74.

39. *ibid.*, 75.

40. H. Woods, 'Excavations at Wenlock Priory, 1981–6', *J. Brit. Archaeol. Assoc.* cxl (1987), 36–76.

41. D. Cranage, 'The Monastery of St Mildburge at Much Wenlock', *Archaeologia*, lxii (1922), 105–32.

42. Woods, 'Excavations at Wenlock Priory', 59.

43. A.C. Thomas, *Christianity in Roman Britain to AD 500* (1981), 166–7.

44. Finberg, 'Princes of the Magonsæte', 220, n. 3; J.W. James, *Rhygyfarch's Life of St David* (1967), 33.

45. D.A. Whitehead, 'Historical introduction', in *Hereford City Excavations. Volume I: Excavations at Castle Green*, ed.

R. Shoesmith (CBA Res. Rep. 36, 1980), 1–6.
46. Stenton, *Anglo-Saxon England*, 149.
47. Davies, *An Early Welsh Microcosm*, 157.
48. Whitehead, *Hereford City Excavations I*, 4.
49. D.A. Whitehead, 'The historical background to the city defences', in *Hereford City Excavations. Volume II: Excavations on and close to the defences*, ed. R. Shoesmith (CBA Res. Rep. 46, 1982), 90.
50. Rennell of Rodd, 'Land of Lene', 323.
51. J.A. Sheppard, *The Origins and Evolution of Field and Settlement Patterns in the Herefordshire Manor of Marden* (Queen Mary College, London, Dept. of Geography, 1979).
52. Gelling, *Signposts to the Past*, 102.
53. *ibid.*, 105.
54. F.G. Heys and M.J. Thomas, 'Excavations on the defences of the Romano-British town at Kenchester', *Trans. Woolhope Nat. Field Club*, xxxvii (1961–3), 165, 167.
55. *The Itinerary of John Leland in or about the Years 1535–1543*, ed. L.T. Smith (5 vols., 1964), v, 102; *Victoria County History of Herefordshire*, i (1908), 176.
56. Sheppard, *Manor of Marden*, 36.
57. D. Hooke, *Anglo-Saxon Territorial Organisation: The Western Margins of Anglo-Saxon Mercia* (Univ. of Birmingham, Dept. of Geography, Occas. Paper 22, 1986), 9.
58. *English Historical Documents c500–1042*, ed. D. Whitelock (1955), 682.
59. Finberg, 'Princes of the Magonsæte', 217, n. 1. and refs. cited there.
60. C.R. Hart, 'The Tribal Hidage', *Trans. Royal Hist. Soc.* 5th ser. xxi (1981), 140–1.
61. *Asser's Life of King Alfred*, ed. W.H. Stevenson (1904), 229.
62. Stenton, 'Pre-Conquest Herefordshire', 194, n. 5.
63. *Asser*, 229, n. 2.
64. Pretty, *The Severn Basin in the 5th and 6th centuries AD*,

Appendix; but see also a ref. to a possibly Anglo-Saxon cemetery at Bromfield in S.C. Stanford, *The Archaeology of the Welsh Marches* (1986), 178–9.
65. P.H. Sawyer, *Anglo-Saxon Charters: An Annotated List and Bibliography* (1968) (hereafter S), no. 167.
66. *Florentii Wigorniensis Monachi Chronicon ex Chronicis*, ed. B. Thorpe (Eng. Hist. Soc. no. 13, 1848), 265.
67. *ibid.*, 238.
68. S1264.
69. S1782.
70. S677: 'in the district of the Magonsæte'.
71. *The Anglo-Saxon Chronicle*, ed. D. Whitelock *et al.* (2nd edn., 1965), 96.
72. J.G. Hillaby, 'The origins of the diocese of Hereford', *Trans. Woolhope Nat. Field Club*, xxviii (1976), 44.
73. *ibid.*, 33.
74. *Willelmi Malmesbiriensis monachi de gestis pontificum Anglorum libri quinque*, ed. N.E.S.A. Hamilton (Rolls Series, no. 52, 1870), 299.
75. Finberg, 'Princes of the Magonsæte', 221–2.
76. S1800.
77. Finberg, 'Princes of the Magonsæte', 220.
78. Whitehead, *Hereford City Excavations II*, 13.
79. Sheppard, *Manor of Marden*, 31–2.
80. Finberg, 'Mercians and Welsh', 77, n. 3.
81. Whitehead, *Hereford City Excavations I*, 15.
82. Stenton, 'Pre-Conquest Herefordshire', 193.

13 The early history of western Mercia

1. G. Webster, *The Cornovii* (1975), 1.
2. F.M. Stenton, *Anglo-Saxon England* (3rd edn., 1971), 40.
3. Webster, *The Cornovii*, 79.
4. *ibid.*, 83.
5. M. Gelling, *Place-Names in the Landscape* (1984, 230–49).
6. *idem*, 'Some notes on

Warwickshire place-names',
*Trans. B'ham & Warwicks.
Arch. Soc.* lxxxvi (1974), 59–79
at 68.

7. D. Hooke, *Anglo-Saxon
Territorial Organisation: The
Western Margins of Mercia*
(Univ. of Birmingham, Dept. of
Geography, Occas. Paper 22,
1986).

8. R.P. Wright and K.H. Jackson, 'A
late inscription from Wroxeter',
Antiq. J. xlviii (1968), 296–300.

9. L. Alcock, *Arthur's Britain*
(1971), 268.

10. P. Barker, *Wroxeter Roman City.
Excavations 1966–1980* (1981), 18.

11. I. Williams, 'The poems of
Llywarch Hen', *Proc. Brit.
Academy*, xviii (1932), 269–302;
idem, Canu Llywarch Hen
(1935).

12. H.P.R. Finberg, *Lucerna* (1964),
66–73.

13. J. Rowland, *The Welsh Saga
Englynïon* (forthcoming). I have
benefited greatly from an
exchange of views with Dr
Rowland.

14. Gelling, *Place-Names in the
Landscape*, 212–13.

15. A.H. Smith, *The Place-Names of
Gloucestershire*, pt 3 (Eng. Place-
Name Soc. xl, 1964), 61.

16. B.G. Charles, *Non-Celtic Place-
Names in Wales* (1938), 214.

17. Stenton, *Anglo-Saxon England*,
78.

18. W. Davies, *Wales in the Early
Middle Ages* (1982), 101–2.

19. Stenton, *Anglo-Saxon England*,
295.

20. *Bede's Ecclesiastical History of
the English People*, ed.
B. Colgrave and R.A.B. Mynors
(1969), iii, 24.

21. Stenton, *Anglo-Saxon England*,
296.

22. H.P.R. Finberg, *The Early
Charters of the West Midlands*
(1972), 197–216.

23. P.H. Sawyer, *Anglo-Saxon
Charters: An Annotated List
and Bibliography* (1968), no. 221.
In *Lucerna* (74, n.1) Finberg says
that *Wininicas* is the correct
reading, both in the 901 charter
and in the Life of St Mildburg.
The name has more frequently
been transcribed as *Wimnicas*.

24. D.W. Rollason, 'Lists of saints'
resting-places in Anglo-Saxon
England', *Anglo-Saxon England*,
vii (1978), 89.

25. G.O. Pierce, 'The evidence of
place-names', *Glamorgan
County History*, ii (1984), 487
and n.131 on 492.

26. O.J. Padel, *Cornish Place-Name
Elements* (Eng. Place-Name Soc.
lvi/lvii, 1985), 151–2.

27. H. Woods, 'Excavations at
Wenlock Priory, 1981–6', *J. Brit.
Archaeol. Assoc.* cxl (1987),
36–75.

28. M. Gelling, 'The place-name
Burton' (paper presented to
seminar on Anglo-Saxon
Weapons and Warfare, Oxford,
January 1987; publication
forthcoming).

29. K. Cameron, 'The meaning and
significance of Old English *walh*
in English place-names', *J. Eng.
Place-Name Soc.* xii (1980), 1–53.

30. B. Cox, 'The place-names of the
earliest English records', *ibid.*,
viii, 63.

31. M. Gelling, *Signposts to the Past*
(1978), 181–2.

32. Stenton, *Anglo-Saxon England*,
214.

33. F. Noble, *Offa's Dyke Reviewed*
(Brit. Archaeol. Reports, Brit.
series, no. 114, 1983).

34. A facsimile of the text and a
translation are printed in *ibid.*

14 Lindsey

1. F.M. Stenton, 'Lindsey and its
Kings', in *Essays in History
Presented to R. Lane Poole*, ed.
H.W.C. Davis (1927), 136–50;
W. Davies and H. Vierck, 'The
contexts of Tribal Hidage: social
aggregates and settlement
patterns', *Frühmittelalterliche
Studien*, viii (1974), 223–36,
288–92; C. Hart, 'The kingdom
of Mercia', in *Mercian Studies*,
ed. A. Dornier (1977), 43–61. For
the foundation of the see of
Lindsey: *Bede's Ecclesiastical
History of the English People*,
ed. B. Colgrave and R.A.B.
Mynors (1969) (hereafter *HE*), iv,
12.

2. The geographical background to

Romano-British and early Anglo-Saxon settlement and communications in Lindsey is described in B.N. Eagles, *The Anglo-Saxon Settlement of Humberside*, Brit. Archaeol. Reports (hereafter BAR), Brit. series, no. 68, parts i and ii (1979), 1–10, 149–87.

3. R.S.O. Tomlin, 'Non Coritani sed Corieltauvi', *Antiq. J.* lxiii (1983), 353–5. The new name appears in a graffito on a tile found at *Tripontium* on Watling Street.

4. J.B. Whitwell, *The Coritani. Some Aspects of the Iron Age Tribe and the Roman Civitas*, BAR, Brit. series, no. 99 (1982), 58.

5. R.G. Collingwood and R.P. Wright, *The Roman Inscriptions of Britain* [RIB], i (1965), no. 2241.

6. This paragraph is based largely upon J.C. Mann, 'The administration of Roman Britain', *Antiquity*, xxxv (1961), 316–20.

7. S.S. Frere, *Britannia: A History of Roman Britain* (rev. edn., 1978), 241.

8. Mann, 'Administration', 319.

9. *ibid.*, 319.

10. M.W.C. Hassall, 'Britain in the Notitia', in *Aspects of the Notitia Dignitatum*, ed. R. Goodburn and P. Bartholomew, BAR, Int. series, no. 15 (1976), 109.

11. 'Roman Britain in 1956. I. Sites explored', *J. Roman Studies*, xlvii (1957), 209.

12. Frere, *Britannia*, Fig. 11 (map on 264–5).

13. J.B. Whitwell, *Roman Lincolnshire* [History of Lincolnshire, ed. J. Thirsk, vol. ii, 1970], 44–57, for this and other Roman routes in Lindsey.

14. A.L.F. Rivet, 'The British section of the Antonine Itinerary', *Britannia*, i (1970), Fig. 7.

15. Eagles, *Anglo-Saxon Humberside*, Figs. 118, 120, 122.

16. I.M. Stead, 'Winterton Roman villa: an interim report', *Antiq. J.* xlvi (1966), 72–84. A report on the later excavations by R. Goodburn is in preparation.

17. Eagles, *Anglo-Saxon Humberside*, 149–54.

18. *The Lincolnshire Domesday and the Lindsey Survey*, transl. and ed. C.W. Foster and T. Longley (Lincoln Record Soc. xix, 1924), 105–6. Information on the ferry routes was kindly given by Mr G.C. Knowles.

19. Full bibliography in Eagles, *Anglo-Saxon Humberside*, 393.

20. The spiral-headed pin is in Scunthorpe Museum. The coin of Eanred is described in M. Blackburn, C. Colyer and M. Dolley, *Early Medieval Coins from Lincoln and its Shire c 770–1100* (Lincoln Archaeol. Trust (hereafter L.A.T.) Mono. series, no. VI–1, 1983), 7–8. The date of spiral-headed pins is discussed in A.P. Detsicas and S.C. Hawkes, 'Finds from the Anglo-Saxon Cemetery at Eccles', *Antiq. J.* liii (1973), 281–6.

21. J. Hines, *The Scandinavian Character of Anglian England in the Pre-Viking Period*, BAR, Brit. series, no. 124 (1984), 245.

22. A.J. White, 'A 7th-century Anglo-Saxon Gold Pendant from Glentham, Lincs.', *Med. Archaeol.* xxvi (1982), 142–4.

23. M.J. Jones, *The Defences of the Upper Roman Enclosure* (L.A.T. Mono. series, no. VII-1, 1980).

24. N. Field and H. Hurst, 'Roman Horncastle', *Lincs. History & Archaeol.* xviii (1983), 47–88.

25. B.B. Simmons, 'Iron Age and Roman coasts around the Wash', in *Archaeology and Coastal Change*, ed. F.H. Thompson (Soc. Antiquaries Occas. Paper, n.s. i, 1980), 56–73.

26. Field and Hurst, 'Roman Horncastle', 85–7.

27. S.C. Hawkes and G.C. Dunning, 'Soldiers and settlers in Britain, fourth to fifth century', *Med. Archaeol.* v (1961), 1–70.

28. K.A. Leahy, 'Late Roman and early Germanic metalwork from Lincs.', in *A Prospect of Lincolnshire, being collected articles on the History and Traditions of Lincolnshire in honour of Ethel H. Rudkin*, ed. N. Field and A. White (1984), 23–32.

29. Leahy, 'Metalwork from Lincs.', item no. 4.
30. *ibid.*, item no. 6.
31. *ibid.*, items nos. 2 and 3.
32. *ibid.*, item no. 7.
33. *ibid.*, item no. 13.
34. C. Atkins, A. Hatt and B. Whitwell, *The Excavation of a Romano-British Aisled Building at Deepdale Barrow-on-Humber 1981* (Humberside Archaeol. Unit Occas. Report no. 1), n.d.
35. Leahy, 'Metalwork from Lincs.', item no. 14.
36. *ibid.*, items nos. 9, 10 and 8.
37. The arguments for a relatively small army in Britain in the fourth century are set out in S. James, 'Britain and the late Roman army', in *Military and Civilian in Roman Britain. Cultural Relationships in a Frontier Province*, ed. T.F.C. Blagg and A.C. King, Brit. series, no. 136 (1984), 161–86.
38. C. Hills, 'The archaeology of Anglo-Saxon England in the pagan period: a review', *Anglo-Saxon England*, viii (1979), 297–308.
39. Eagles, *Anglo-Saxon Humberside*, 178–82 (list).
40. *HE* iv, 3; E. Ekwall, *The Concise Oxford Dictionary of English Place-Names* (4th edn., 1960), 238; D.W. Rollason, 'Lists of saints' resting-places in Anglo-Saxon England', *Anglo-Saxon England*, vii (1978), 89.
41. K. Cameron, *The Place-Names of Lincolnshire. Part I* (Eng. Place-Name Soc. lviii, 1985), 1–3.
42. C. Smith, 'The survival of Romano-British toponymy', *Nomina*, iv (1980), 30.
43. K.H. Jackson, *Language and History in Early Britain* (1953), 503 (Trent), 510, 511, 519 (Humber), map 220, 221, 558 (Ancholme and Witham).
44. M. Gelling, 'English place-names derived from the compound *wīchām*', *Med. Archaeol.* xi (1967), 87–104.
45. Field and Hurst, 'Roman Horncastle', 84.
46. Smith, 'Survival of Romano-British toponymy', 34.
47. P.H. Sawyer, *From Roman Britain to Norman England* (1978), 159.
48. The account which follows is based upon a draft report prepared by the Lincoln Archaeol. Trust, which Messrs M. Jones and D. Stocker have been kind enough to allow me to use.
49. B. Gilmour, 'The Anglo-Saxon church at St Paul-in-the-Bail, Lincoln', *Med. Archaeol.* xxiii (1979), 214–18.
50. *HE* ii, 16.
51. M. Biddle, 'Towns', in *The Archaeology of Anglo-Saxon England*, ed. D.M. Wilson (1976), 103–12.
52. S.R. Bassett, 'Lincoln and the Anglo-Saxon see of Lindsey', *Anglo-Saxon England*, xviii (forthcoming); Cameron, *Place-Names of Lincolnshire*, 45–6.
53. It is summarized in P. Everson, 'An Anglo-Saxon brooch from Lincoln', *Lincs. History & Archaeol.*, xii (1977), 81–2.
54. 'Archaeology in Lincolnshire and South Humberside, 1983', compiled by A.B. Page, *ibid.*, xix (1984), 99.
55. P. Everson and G.C. Knowles, 'A *Tutulus* brooch from Kirmington, Lincolnshire (S. Humberside)', *Med. Archaeol.* xxii (1978), 123–7.
56. V.I. Evison, 'Supporting-arm brooches and equal-arm brooches in England', in *Studien zur Sächsenforschung*, ed. H.-J. Hässler (Hildesheim, 1977), 127–47.
57. Leahy, 'Metalwork from Lincs.', item no. 5.
58. Information about the cemetery at Elsham was kindly provided by Mr G.C. Knowles in advance of his own publication.
59. Frere, *Britannia*, 252, 267.
60. D.N. Riley, 'Roman defended sites at Kirmington, S. Humberside and Farnsfield, Notts., recently found from the air', *Britannia*, viii (1977), 189–92.
61. 'Proceedings at the meetings of the Archaeological Institute April 3 1857', *Archaeol. J.* xiv (1857), 275–6.
62. V.I. Evison, 'Early Anglo-Saxon

applied disc brooches. Part 1: On the Continent. Part II: In England', *Antiq. J.* lviii (1978), 266–7.

63. S. West, 'West Stow. The Anglo-Saxon village', *East Anglian Archaeol.* xxiv (2 vols., 1985), 126–8.

64. The excavation was conducted by Mr K. Leahy who kindly furnished information about the site.

65. K. Leahy, 'Kirton in Lindsey: Anglo-Saxon cemetery', *Lincs. History & Archaeol.* xv (1980), 72–3. C.M. Hills, 'Barred zoomorphic combs of the migration period', in *Angles, Saxons, and Jutes. Essays presented to J.N.L. Myres*, ed. V.I. Evison (1981), 96–125.

66. A.M. Cook, *The Anglo-Saxon Cemetery at Fonaby, Lincolnshire. Based on a Catalogue of the Material by S.C. Hawkes* (Occas. Papers in Lincs. History and Archaeol. no. 6, 1981).

67. G. Webster and J.N.L. Myres, 'An Anglo-Saxon urnfield at South Elkington, Louth, Lincs. (by G.W.), with an account of the pottery (by J.N.L.M.)', *Archaeol. J.* cviii (1951), 25–64.

68. Eagles, *Anglo-Saxon Humberside*, 399.

69. ibid., 122–3.

70. Hines, *Scandinavian Character*, 93.

71. J. Reichstein, *Die kreuzförmige Fibel (Zur Chronologie der späten römischen Kaiserzeit und der Völkerwanderungszeit in Skandinavien, auf dem Kontinent und in England)* (Offa-Bücher, xxxiv, 1975), 97, 152 no. 824.

72. J.N.L. Myres, 'The Teutonic settlement of northern England', *History*, xx (1935), 250–62.

73. P.H. Blair, 'The Northumbrians and their southern frontier', *Archaeologia Aeliana*, 4th ser. xxvi (1948), 98–126.

74. Eagles, *Anglo-Saxon Humberside*, Fig. 124.

75. J.N.L. Myres, 'The Anglo-Saxon pottery of Lincs.', *Archaeol. J.* cviii (1951), 97.

76. 'Archaeology in Lincolnshire and South Humberside, 1976', compiled by A.J. White, *Lincs. History & Archaeol.* xii (1977), 71.

77. 'Archaeology in Lincolnshire and South Humberside, 1981', compiled by A.J. White, *ibid.*, xvii (1982), 71.

78. *HE* ii, 16.

79. *The Life of Bishop Wilfrid by Eddius Stephanus*, ed. B. Colgrave (1927), c.40; J. Campbell, 'Bede's words for places', in *Names, Words, and Graves: Early Medieval Settlement*, ed. P.H. Sawyer (1979), 42, n.12.

80. Stenton, 'Lindsey and its Kings', 136–50; D.N. Dumville, 'Kingship, genealogies and regnal lists', in *Early Medieval Kingship*, ed. P.H. Sawyer and I.N. Wood (1977), 90; J. Campbell, *Bede's Reges and Principes* (Jarrow Lecture for 1979), 4.

81. G. Speake, *Anglo-Saxon Animal Art and its Germanic Background* (1980), 39, 42.

82. For the Anglo-Saxon name of Lindsey see Ekwall, *O.D.E.P.* 299.

83. The point is argued by Mr S.R. Bassett in his forthcoming paper, 'Lincoln and the Anglo-Saxon see of Lindsey', to which he has kindly allowed me to refer.

84. F.M. Stenton, *Anglo-Saxon England* (2nd edn., 1947), 42.

85. Hart, 'Kingdom of Mercia', 47.

86. K.R. Fennell, 'The Anglo-Saxon cemetery at Loveden Hill (Hough-on-the-Hill) Lincolnshire and its significance in relation to the Dark Age settlement of the East Midlands' (unpublished D.Phil. thesis, Nottingham Univ. 1964).

87. Campbell, *Bede's Reges and Principes*, 3.

88. Hart, 'Kingdom of Mercia', 49.

89. *HE* iii, 24.

90. Eagles, *Anglo-Saxon Humberside*, 412.

91. *HE* ii, 12.

92. Ordnance Survey, map of *Monastic Britain (South Sheet)* (1950). Cf. above, p. 204.

93. *Nennius. British History and the*

Welsh Annals, ed. and trans.
J. Morris, 1980, c.63.

94. G.R.J. Jones, 'Early territorial
organization in Gwynedd and
Elmet', *Northern History*, x
(1975), 3–27.

95. C. Plummer, *Venerabilis Baedae
Opera Historica* (2 vols., 1896),
ii, 155.

96. S. Revill, 'King Edwin and the
battle of Heathfield', *Trans.
Thoroton Soc.* lxxix (1975), 40–9.

97. I would like to thank Mr S.R.
Bassett, Mr S. James, Mr M.J.
Jones, Mr G.C. Knowles, Mr K.
Leahy and Dr P. Stafford, all of
whom kindly read this chapter
in draft and to whose many
stimulating ideas I have tried to
do justice. Mr Jones and Mr D.
Stocker generously provided
details of the excavation at St
Paul-in-the-Bail, Lincoln, in
advance of their own
publication, as did Mr Knowles
and Mr Leahy respectively of the
cemeteries at Elsham and
Cleatham. My colleague Mr
M.C. Corney prepared the map
and to him my warm thanks are
also due.

**15 The origins of Northumbria:
some aspects of the British
background**

1. A version of this chapter was
originally delivered at a
conference (at the University of
Leeds in July 1987) to mark the
tenth anniversary of the lecture
series published as *Early
Medieval Kingship*, ed. P.H.
Sawyer and I.N. Wood (1977).
I am indebted to Ian Wood for
his invitation to contribute. I
had originally intended to
publish this chapter in the form
of an extended treatment of the
written sources for the origins of
Northumbria, but unforeseen
circumstances have prevented
me from so doing. I hope to
return to the more thoroughly
English dimension of the
question in due course. In the
meantime my gratitude is due to
Steven Bassett for giving this
shorter study (of British aspects

of early Bernician and Deiran
history) a comfortable home
within the present volume.

2. 'The origins of Northumbria',
Archaeologia Aeliana, 4th ser.
xxv (1947), 1–51, reprinted in his
Anglo-Saxon Northumbria (1984).

3. Gildas's works may be most
readily consulted in the edition
and translation by M.
Winterbottom, *Gildas: The Ruin
of Britain and Other Works*
(1978). For recent (and less
recent) controversies see *Gildas:
New Approaches*, ed. M. Lapidge
and D. Dumville (1984) and the
literature cited therein.

4. I have discussed some of these
problems in 'Sub-Roman Britain:
history and legend', *History*, n.s.
lxii (1977), 173–92, and
'Kingship, genealogies and regnal
lists', in *Early Medieval
Kingship*, ed. Sawyer and Wood,
72–104. For a slightly later
period see also my 'Textual
archaeology and Northumbrian
history subsequent to Bede', in
*Coinage in Ninth-century
Northumbria*, ed. D.M. Metcalf
(1987), 43–55.

5. For this point cf. my remarks in
'New Angles on the Saxon
Shore', *Times Literary
Supplement* (4 July 1986), 741.

6. The classic statement of this
'apparent continuum' is by
I. Williams, *The Beginnings of
Welsh Poetry* (1972), 70–88,
reprinting a paper of 1950.

7. Cf. D.N. Dumville, '"Beowulf"
and the Celtic world', *Traditio*,
xxxvii (1981), 109–60, and the
literature cited there.

8. 'The chronology of *De Excidio
Britanniae*, Book I', *Gildas: New
Approaches*, ed. Lapidge and
Dumville, 61–84.

9. D.N. Dumville, 'The historical
value of the *Historia Brittonum*',
Arthurian Literature, vi (1986),
1–26; on Bede's Hengist, see
T.M. Charles-Edwards *apud* J.M.
Wallace-Hadrill (n.30 below),
212–15.

10. For some remarks on Picto-
Saxon alliance see E.A.
Thompson, *Saint Germanus of
Auxerre and the End of Roman
Britain* (1984), 39–46.

11. See L. Alcock, 'Gwŷr y Gogledd: an archaeological appraisal', *Archaeologia Cambrensis*, cxxxii (1983), 1–18.
12. On these see K. Hughes, *Celtic Britain in the Early Middle Ages. Studies in Scottish and Welsh Sources* (1980), 67–106, and K. Grabowski and D. Dumville, *Chronicles and Annals of Mediaeval Ireland and Wales. The Clonmacnoise-group Texts* (1984), 207–26.
13. Cf. M. Miller, 'The commanders at Arthuret', *Trans. Cumberland & Westmorland Antiq. & Archaeol. Soc.* n.s. lxxv (1975), 96–118.
14. Cf. D.N. Dumville, 'On the north British section of the *Historia Brittonum*', *Welsh Hist. Rev.* viii (1976–7), 345–54.
15. K.H. Jackson, 'Edinburgh and the Anglian occupation of Lothian', in *The Anglo-Saxons. Studies in Some Aspects of their History and Culture presented to Bruce Dickins*, ed. P. Clemoes (1959), 35–42.
16. *Early Welsh Genealogical Tracts*, ed. P.C. Bartrum (1966). Cf. M. Miller, 'Forms and uses of pedigrees', *Trans. Hon. Soc. of Cymmrodorion* (1978), 195–206, and *idem*, 'Royal pedigrees of the Insular Dark Ages: a progress report', *History in Africa*, vii (1980), 201–24.
17. 'The origins of Northumbria', 29.
18. 'The authenticity of the Gododdin: an historian's view', in *Astudiaethau ar yr Hengerdd (Studies in Old Welsh Poetry) cyflwynedig i Syr Idris Foster*, ed. R. Bromwich and R.B. Jones (1978), 44–71.
19. D.N. Dumville, 'Early Welsh poetry: problems of historicity', in *Early Welsh Poetry: Studies in the Book of Aneirin*, ed. B.F. Roberts (1988).
20. *The Poems of Taliesin*, ed. I. Williams and J.E.C. Williams (Dublin, 1968); cf. S. Lewis, 'The tradition of Taliesin', *Trans. Hon. Soc. of Cymmrodorion* (1968), 293–9, and Dumville, 'Early Welsh poetry'.
21. E.A. Thompson, 'St Patrick and Coroticus', *J. Theological Studies*, n.s. xxxi (1980), 12–27.
22. W.J. Watson, *The History of the Celtic Place-names of Scotland* (1926), 24.
23. K. Jackson, *The Gododdin: The Oldest Scottish Poem* (1969), 69–75.
24. H. Ramm, *The Parisi* (1978); see 124–38 on the late Roman and sub-Roman periods.
25. For Gildas on the origins of sub-Roman British kingship, cf. Dumville, 'The chronology', 69–70, 83.
26. *Bede's Ecclesiastical History of the English People* (hereafter *HE*), ed. B. Colgrave and R.A.B. Mynors (1969), i, 15.
27. Cf. M. Miller, 'The dates of Deira', *Anglo-Saxon England* (hereafter *ASE*), viii (1979), 35–61.
28. ed. D.N. Dumville, 'A new chronicle-fragment of early British history', *Eng. Hist. Rev.* lxxxviii (1973), 312–14.
29. For the pedigree see D.N. Dumville, 'The Anglian collection of royal genealogies and regnal lists', *ASE* v (1976), 23–50, at 30, 32, 35.
30. J.M. Wallace-Hadrill, *Bede's Ecclesiastical History of the English People. A Historical Commentary* (1988), 201.
31. See my forthcoming paper, 'Some notes on the treatment of Northumbrian history 547–616 in the *Historia Brittonum*'.
32. A. Campbell, *Old English Grammar* (1959; rev. imp. 1962), 3–11; T.E. Toon, *The Politics of Early Old English Sound Change* (New York, 1983).
33. F.M. Stenton, 'The foundations of English history', in *Preparatory to Anglo-Saxon England*, ed. D.M. Stenton (1970), 116–26, at 116–22.
34. P.H. Blair, *The World of Bede* (1970).
35. The inscriptions of northern Britain have been reproduced by R.A.S. Macalister, *Corpus Inscriptionum Insularum Celticarum* (2 vols., Dublin, 1945–9).
36. *HE*, i, 34 and ii, 2; ii, 20 and iii, 1.
37. Stephanus, *Vita Wilfridi*, c.17

(ed. and trans. B. Colgrave (1927), 34–7.
38. *De excidio Britanniae*, iii, 92; cf. Dumville, 'The chronology', 81–2.
39. *HE*, ii, 20, for Gwynedd, Mercia and Northumbria.
40. *Continuatio Bedae*, s.a. 740, 750 (Picts and Mercians); *Historia regum*, s.a. 756 (Northumbrians and Picts).
41. On Hereric, see *HE*, iv, 23.
42. Cf. K.H. Jackson, 'On the northern British section in Nennius', in *Celt and Saxon. Studies in the Early British Border*, ed. N.K. Chadwick (1963; rev. imp. 1964), 20–62, at 41–2.
43. T. Charles-Edwards, 'Native political organization in Roman Britain and the origin of MW *brenhin*', in *Antiquitates Indogermanicae*, ed. M. Mayrhofer *et al.* (Innsbruck, 1974), 35–45.
44. *The Poems of Taliesin*, ed. Williams and Williams, lix–lx.
45. For the etymology, see K. Jackson, *Language and History in Early Britain* (1953), 91, 443–4.
46. For discussion of the name 'Northumbria(n)', its antecedents and chronology, see J.N.L. Myres, 'The Teutonic settlement of northern England', *History*, n.s. xx (1935–6), 250–62, and T.M. Charles-Edwards *et al.*, *apud* Wallace-Hadrill (as n.30), 226–8.

16 The Tribal Hidage: an introduction to its texts and their history

1. J. Brownbill, 'The Tribal Hidage', *Eng. Hist. Rev.* xl (1925), 497–503, opp. 497; R.H. Hodgkin, *A History of the Anglo-Saxons* (3rd edn., 2 vols., 1952), ii, 389 (pl. 53); Michael Wood, *Domesday. A Search for the Roots of England* (1986), 88 (Wood's photograph shows less of the marginale than does Brownbill's).
2. W. de G. Birch, *Cartularium Saxonicum: A Collection of Charters relating to Anglo-Saxon*

History (3 vols., 1885–93), i, 414–15, no. 297.
3. N.R. Ker, *Catalogue of Manuscripts Containing Anglo-Saxon* (1957), 309–12, no. 239.
4. This text was composed 992×1002: *Ælfrics Grammatik und Glossar*, ed. Julius Zupitza (Berlin, 1880).
5. Ker, *Catalogue*, 309. Note this date, not 'around AD 1000' (Wood, *Domesday*, 86) or 'early eleventh century' (Davies, as n. 19 below, 288–9).
6. Ker, *Catalogue*, 311 (item 23).
7. *ibid.*, 311–12.
8. The original book (the copy of Ælfric's Grammar) was evidently not the work of a scriptorium of the highest standards, in view of the lack of distinction of scripts for Latin and Old English in that text (*ibid.*, 312; cf. 201–2 on no. 158). On this practice see Ker, *ibid.*, xxv–xxvii, and T.A.M. Bishop, *English Caroline Minuscule* (1971), nos. 11, 22, 28.
9. The standard (but inadequate) edition is that of Theodor Mommsen, *Chronica Minora saec. IV. V. VI. VII.* (3 vols., Berlin, 1891–8), ii, 389–90; for brief comment see D.N. Dumville, '"Nennius" and the *Historia Brittonum*', *Studia Celtica*, x–xi (1975–6), 78–95, at 83 and n.4; a full study of the versions of this text is required.
10. Inasmuch as the figures do not add up to the grand total stated, there are clearly errors in the text – perhaps simply of addition or of corruption of figures. The last stated total (242,700 hides) is 1,400 too few. Yet the discrepancies of hidations between the three witnesses also give pause in this respect. Finally, it has been argued by P.H. Sawyer, *From Roman Britain to Norman England* (1978), 111, that the West Saxons with their 100,000 hides are a late addition to the text; it is noteworthy that they are absent from Recension C.
11. The first, obvious example is that of *Wocensætna* for W⟨r(e)⟩ocensætna (2). Cf. also

Herefinna (13), Hwinca (20), Færpinga (25), Bilmiga (26). For discussion see Davies, as n. 19 below, 230–6.

12. For further discussion of this name see my paper 'Essex, Middle Anglia, and the expansion of Mercia in the South-East Midlands', above, 123–40.

13. On Spelman see the article by William Carr in *Dictionary of National Biography*, liii, ed. S. Lee (1898), 328–33; cf. F.M. Powicke, 'Sir Henry Spelman and the "Concilia"', *Proc. Brit. Academy*, xvi (1930), 345–79. I have examined two forms of the *Archæologus*: the copy from which pp. 352–3 are reproduced here has the error *enrrantur* in the seventeenth line of the title page, but the form in which this is corrected to *enarrantur* has an identical text of the Tribal Hidage.

14. *Hendrica 3000 hidas* (B), against 3,500 (A). On spellings, note especially (B/A) *Eyfla/Gifla* (15), *Wicca/Hicca* (16), *Wight-gora/Wiht gara* (17), *Aroseatna/Arosætna* (24), *Fearfinga/Færpinga* (25), *Belmiga/Bilmiga* (26), *Witherigga/Widerigga* (27).

15. But just that has been done by C. Hart, 'The Tribal Hidage', *Trans. Royal Hist. Soc.* 5th ser. xxi (1971), 133–57, at 133, n.1.

16. See the article by A.F. Pollard in *Dictionary of National Biography*, lv, ed. Lee (1898), 376–7. Tate was a member of Middle Temple and the Society of Antiquaries, and author of a wide variety of historical tracts and collections unpublished in his lifetime. He died in 1616.

17. N.R. Ker, *Books, Collectors and Libraries. Studies in the Medieval Heritage* ([1985]), 139–40, 142. It is noteworthy (*ibid.*, 139) that Tate had two books (containing the Tribal Hidage) formerly owned by William Fleetwood, Recorder of London (*ob.* 1594); Harley 3271 had also been owned by Fleetwood, but remained in the possession of his family a century later (Ker, *Catalogue*, 312).

18. *eac* (3); *mid* (6); *eac swa* (27, 29); *peat is ealles* (concluding sentence).

19. See W. Davies and H. Vierck, 'The contexts of Tribal Hidage: social aggregates and settlement patterns', *Frühmittelalterliche Studien*, viii (1974), 223–93, at 224–41 and esp. 288–92. Hart, 'The Tribal Hidage', 133, n.1, inexplicably thought the Latin texts to be 'of no independent value'.

20. Davies and Vierck, 'The contexts', 290.

17 The Chertsey resting-place list and the enshrinement of Frithuwold

1. Cf. C. Stancliffe, 'Kings who opted out', in *Ideal and Reality in Frankish and Anglo-Saxon Society*, ed. P. Wormald (1983), 154–76.

2. *The Chronicle of Hugh Candidus*, ed. W.T. Mellows (1949), 60. Hugh Candidus's list of resting-places is also discussed by L. Butler, 'Two twelfth-century lists of saints' resting-places', *Analecta Bollandiana*, cv (1987), 94–103.

3. F. Liebermann, *Die Heiligen Englands* (Hannover, 1889); D.W. Rollason, 'Lists of saints' resting-places in Anglo-Saxon England', *Anglo-Saxon England*, vii (1978), 61–93.

4. Bodl. MS Top.Gen.c 2 p. 370a; printed in *Johannis Lelandi Antiquarii Collectanea*, ed. T. Hearne (2nd edn., 1774), iii, 409.

5. For this point I am extremely grateful to Miss Celia Sisam.

6. B.L. MS Cotton Vitellius A.xiii fos. 34v–35v. I am grateful to Dr Alan Thacker for helpful suggestions regarding this passage.

7. For the likely context see J. Blair, 'Secular Minster Churches in Domesday Book', in *Domesday Book: A Reassessment*, ed. P.H. Sawyer (1985), 117–25, and *idem*, introduction to *Minsters and Parish Churches: the Local*

Church in Transition 950–1200
(1988), ed. J. Blair, 1–19.
8. S1508.
9. Anglo-Saxon Chronicle, s.a. 964.
    A. Thacker, 'Æthelwold and
    Abingdon', in *Bishop Æthelwold:
    his career and influence*, ed B.

Yorke (1988), 58–9, comments
that colonization from Abingdon
is especially likely in the cases
of the four foundations named in
this annal, Chertsey included.
10. For these points I am extremely
    grateful to Mr Malcolm Godden.

Index

The following abbreviations have been used. (1) pre-1974 counties: Bk = Berkshire; Bu = Buckinghamshire; Ca = Cambridgeshire; Ch = Cheshire; Db = Derbyshire; E = Essex; Gl = Gloucestershire; Ha = Hampshire; He = Hertfordshire; Hf = Herefordshire; IoW = Isle of Wight; K = Kent; Le = Leicestershire; Li = Lincolnshire; M = Middlesex; Mg = Montgomeryshire; Mn = Monmouthshire; Nb = Northumberland; Nf = Norfolk; No = Nottinghamshire; Nt = Northamptonshire; O = Oxfordshire; Sf = Suffolk; Sh = Shropshire; So = Somerset; St = Staffordshire; Sx = Sussex; Sy = Surrey; Wa = Warwickshire; Wi = Wiltshire; Wo = Worcestershire; Y = Yorkshire. (2) other: anc. = ancestor; archb. = archbishop; b. = bishop; dau. = daughter; E. = East; f. = father; k. = king; ks. = kings; R. = River; S. = South; St. = Saint; W. = West; w. = wife.

Abingdon (Bk), 234–6
Acton (M), 117
Ad Lapidem, 90
Adomnán, 36
adventus Saxonum, 57, 87–8
Ægelesthrep, battle of, 60, 62
Aegidius, 46
Ælfwald, k. of S. Saxons, 80
Ælfwine, k. of Northumbrians, 31
Ælle, k. of Deira, 218
Ælle, k. of S. Saxons, 60, 81, 83
Æsc, son of Hengist, 58, 60, 62–3, 87; see also Oisc/Oeric
Æthelbald, k. of Mercians, 18, 66, 118, 135, 139
Æthelberht, k. of Kent, 55, 58, 60–1, 64–9, 73–4, 81, 87, 92, 110–13, 120, 135–6
Æthelbert, k. of E. Angles, 182
Æthelburh, abbess of Barking, 113, 121
Æthelfrith, k. of Northumbrians, 160, 166, 191, 218–19, 221
Æthelheard, k. of W. Saxons, 106
Æthelhere, k. of E. Angles, 129, 132
Æthelred, k. of Mercians, 37, 117, 130, 133, 135, 166, 176, 210, 212
Æthelred, k. of W. Saxons, 235
Æthelwealh, k. of S. Saxons, 78–81, 83, 90, 92
Æthelweard, ealdorman, 86–7, 94
Æthelwold, b. of Winchester, 234–6
Æthelwulf, k. of W. Saxons, 95, 235
Æthilfrith, k. of Northumbrians, 132
Æthilthryth, w. of Tondberht *princeps*, 131
Agilbert, b. of Dorchester-on-Thames, 93
Aidan, 28
Airgialla, the, 36, 38–9
Alamanni/Alamans, the, 39, 41–2, 46–7, 147
Alans, the, 50

Albinus, abbot of St. Augustine's, Canterbury, 59, 65
Alcester (Wa), 192
Alcester (Mg), 201
Alcuin, 159
Alderton (Gl), 8
Aldfrith, k. of Lindsey, 210
Alford (Li), 210
Alfred, k. of W. Saxons, 79, 81, 95, 186, 235
Alfred, ealdorman, 236
Alfriston (Sx), 81
Alhfrith, son of k. Oswiu, 32
Alhheard, b. of Leicester, 133
Alne, R., 192
Ambrose, St., 43
Ammianus Marcellinus, 42–3, 215
Ancholme, R., 202, 204–6, 210
Anderitum see Pevensey
Andhun, *dux regius* of S. Saxons, 79–80
Aneirin, The Book of, 168, 216
Anglo-Saxon Chronicle, 40, 55, 60–3, 65, 75, 81, 84–9, 91–6, 124–5, 130, 132, 160, 163, 165–7, 182, 219, 236
Anna, k. of E. Angles, 131–2
Annales Cambriae, 166, 169, 188, 215, 221
Annales Stadenses, 63
Annals of Ulster, 216
Ansehis, *princeps*, 59
Ansith, w. of *comes* Wihtred, 118
Apple Down (Sx), 75
Aquitaine, 46, 50
Arborychoi/?Armoricans, the, 49
Archenfield, 175, 177, 182–3, 196–7; see also Ergyng
Arfderydd, battle of, 221
Ariconium see Weston-under-Penyard
Arosæte/Arosætna, the, 26, 160, 192, 227
Arrow, R. (Hf), 192
Arrow, R. (Wa), 192

Aruald, k. of Wight, 89
Asgar, earl, 118
Ashford (M), 114
Ashingdon (E), battle of, 182
Asser, 88
Atcham (Sh), 174, 187, 189
Athanaric, 43
Athelstan, k. of England, 30, 80
Augustine, archb. of Canterbury, 60, 65,
    110, 178
Austrasia, 29
Avon, R. (Ha), 94
Avon, R. (Wa), 17, 148, 175, 181, 184
Aylesbury (Bu), 106
Aylesford/*Ægelesford* (K), 60–2, 69–70,
    73

Bamburgh (Nb), 167, 218
Bangor Iscoed (Flintshire), 191
Barbury Castle (Wi), 94
Barham (Sf), 146
Barking (E), 21, 103, 113–14, 117
Barnet (He), 119
Barrow-on-Humber (Li), 206
Baschurch (Sh), 189–90
Bath (So), 175
Battersea (M), 103, 114
Bawtry (Y), 204, 212
Beddanhaam, 121
Beddingham (Sx), 80
Bede, 4–5, 17–18, 26, 28–9, 32, 34, 37,
    39, 42–4, 47, 55, 57–61, 65–8, 75, 81,
    85, 87–96, 102–4, 110, 112, 123–5,
    127–34, 136–8, 140, 148, 159–61, 163,
    165–6, 181, 188–9, 192, 207, 215, 218–
    19, 221
Bedfont (M), 114
Bedmond (He), 119
Bengeo (He), 115
Beningas, the, 115
Beocca, St., 231, 234–5
Beonna, k. of E. Angles, 146
Beornheth, *subregulus*, 32, 37
Beowulf, 4, 33, 43, 75
Berecingas, the, 121
Berhtfrith, *praefectus, secundus a rege
    princeps*, 31–2, 38
Berhtred/Berht, *dux regius*, 31–2, 37
Berhtwald, *praefectus*, 210
Bermondsey (M), 106
Bernicia/Bernicians, the, 5–6, 29, 32, 36,
    57, 103, 124–7, 159–60, 167, 213, 216,
    218–21
Bertechramnus/Bertram, of Bordeaux, 48
Berth, The (Sh), 187, 189
Bertha, w. of k. Æthelberht, 66–7
Berthun, *dux regius* of S. Saxons, 79
Bexhill (Sx), 78
Bicester (O), 106
Bieda, son of Port, 86, 89

Biedcanford, battle of, 111
Bilmiga, the, 227
Birinus, b. of Dorchester-on-Thames, 93
bishop(s), 26, 32, 36, 48, 73, 89, 93, 108,
    113–15, 117, 130–1, 133–4, 169, 178,
    181–3, 207
Bishopstoke (Ha), 91, 93
Bishops Waltham (Ha), 90–1
Blackheath Hundred (Sy), 100
Blæcca, *praefectus*, 210
Bóinrige, kingdom of, 36
Bonhunt *see* Wicken Bonhunt
Boniface, 159
Book of Llandaff/*Liber Landavensis*,
    175, 193, 197
bookland, 20
book right, 105
Bosham (Sx), 78–9
Boston (Li), 189, 202
Botwell (M), 111, 118
Boyne, R., 33, 35
Brahhingas, the, 115
Brandon (Sf), 146
Braughing (He), 112, 115, 121–2
Bravonium see Leintwardine
Breedon-on-the-Hill (Le), 105–6, 231
Brentford (M), 117
    synod of, 114
Brétach, the, 34
bretwaldaship, 112, 155
Brigantes, the, 212, 217, 220
Brigg (Li), 204, 208
Britons, the, 4, 6, 21 50, 81, 84, 93,
    110–14, 117, 119, 148, 156, 169, 172,
    174–9, 181–3, 185–6, 191, 206, 211–
    12, 213–22; *see also* Celts, Welsh
Brittany, 193
brooches, 147–8, 205–6, 208–10
Broomy (Ha), 72
Brough-on-Humber (Y), 205
buckles, 205–6
Burgh Castle (Sf), 146
Burgh-le-Marsh (Li), 210
Burgundians, the, 45, 47, 50–1, 138
burials, 55–6, 68, 75, 80–1, 88–9, 92, 94,
    110, 142–3, 146, 147–52, 156–8, 162,
    175, 181, 195, 206–9, 211
    of royalty, 46, 91, 93–4, 106, 112,
        149–52, 176, 182, 210, 212, 231
    gravegoods, 56, 64, 89, 143, 147–50,
        152, 157–8, 210
Burmarsh (K), 78
Burnham (M), 108
Burrow Hill (Sf), 146
Byfleet (Sy), 100

Cadafael of Gwynedd, 168
Cadwallon, k. of Gwynedd, 30, 165–9,
    219
Cædbæd, ?k. of Lindsey, 206–7

Cædwalla, k. of W. Saxons, 37, 61, 78–80, 89–90, 92–6, 103, 105, 114, 136, 139
Caenby (Li), 210, 212
Caerwent (Mn), 179, 187
Cæsterwara, the, 73, 98
Caistor (Li), 202, 204–6, 209
Campodonum, 167
Canterbury (K), 5, 24, 57, 65, 68–9, 72, 78, 83
    Christ Church, 72, 117–18
    St. Peter and St. Paul's, 65
Cantiaci/Cantii, the, 57
Cantware, the, 68, 72, 127, 227
Canu Heledd, 188–90, 193
Canu Llywarch Hen, 168, 174
Carholme (Li), 208
Carisbrooke (IoW), 86
Carthage, 45–6
Cashio (He), 122
Categirn, son of Vortigern, 62
Catholme (St), 196
Catterick (Y), 215–16
Catuvellauni, the, 115
Cearl, k. of Mercians, 163, 166
Ceawlin, k. of W. Saxons, 61, 67, 81, 86–7, 94, 96, 112–14
Cecesege (?Hibaldstow), 206
Celts, the, 47–8, 123, 127; *see also* Britons, Welsh
cemeteries *see* burials
Cenél Conaill, 36
Cenél nÉogain, 34–7
Cenél nGabráin, 39
Cenwalh, k. of W. Saxons, 37, 93, 96, 130, 166–7
Ceolberht, b. of London, 115
Ceolred, k. of Mercians, 111, 135, 182, 192
Ceolred, b. of Leicester, 133
Cerdic, k. of W. Saxons, 84–9, 91, 94–5
Cerdicesbeorg, 91, 94
Cerdicesford[a], battle of, 85–6, 91, 94
Cerdicesleaga, battle of, 85–6
Cerdicesora, battle of, 85–6, 89
Ceretic, 212
Chad, b. of Lichfield, 93, 162, 169
Chadwick, H.M., 63, 165
Chalfont (Bu), 119
Charford (Ha), 86, 89, 91, 94
Charibert, k. of Franks, 66–7
Charlbury (O), 134, 234
Charlemagne, K. of Franks, 29, 44
Chart (K), 72
charters, 6, 8, 17, 19, 29, 33, 42, 55, 70–3, 75, 78–81, 93, 97–8, 100, 102–5, 107, 110–12, 114–15, 119–22, 135–7, 159, 182, 192, 210, 235
Chelmarsh (Sh), 192
Chelsea (M), 120
    synod of, 114, 120

Chertsey (Sy), 97–8, 102–7, 113–14, 120, 231, 234–6
Chesell Down (IoW), 89
Cheshunt (M), 115
Chester, battle of, 191
Chichester (Sx), 75, 78–81, 83
Childeric, k. of Franks, 45–6, 49
Chilperic, k. of Franks, 40
Chilterns, the, 107, 110–12, 115, 122
Chirbury (Sh), 197
Chiswick (M), 117
Chobham (Sy), 97
Chonodomarius, Alamannic leader, 42
Christianity, 36, 44, 49, 52, 55, 60, 78, 90, 123, 131, 141, 152, 155, 169, 175, 178, 187, 214
'Chronicle of Ireland', the 215
Church, the, 4, 20, 29, 89, 175
Church Norton (Sx), 79
Cilternsætan, 108, 111, 115, 227
Cirencester (Gl), 175
    battle of, 130, 167, 175, 191
civitas/civitates, 24, 41, 46, 57, 78–9, 83, 174–5, 188, 202–4, 210–12, 217
Cleatham (Li), 209
Clee (Sh), 192
Clee Hill(s) (Sh), 177, 182–4, 193
Cleethorpes (Li), 210
Clovis/Chlodovechus, k. of Franks, 45–6, 48–9, 52
Cnebba, anc. of Mercian ks., 163–4
Cnobheresburg, monastery of, 146
Cobham (Sy), 100
Cocboy, battle of, 165–8, 188; *see also* *Maes Cogwy*, *Maserfelth*
Coddenham (Sf), 146
Coenred, k. of Mercians, 111, 135, 137, 182
Coenwulf, k. of Mercians, 8, 72, 118
coins/coinage, 28, 32, 55, 57, 80, 146, 150, 159–60, 205–6
Colmán, 28
Cologne, 46
Columba, St., 36
comitatus, 37
Connor, 36
Constantinople, 28, 43
Constantius, author of *Vita Germani*, 215
Corieltauvi/Coritani, the, 186, 202, 204, 210
Cornovii, the, 186, 188
Corve, R., 193
Corve Dale (Sh), 177, 182–3
Crayford/*Cræganford* (K), battle of, 60–2, 112
Crecganford, battle of, 60, 62–3, 110
Credenhill (Hf), 179
Creoda/Crida, anc. of Mercian ks., 162–4, 167

Crowland (Li), 131
Croydon (Sy), 100, 112
Cruithni/Cruithin, the, 36
Cúl Raithin/Coleraine, 36
Cumeneshora, 81
Cunorix, died at Wroxeter, 172, 187
Cutha, k. of W. Saxons, 61, 87
Cuthbert, b. of Hereford, 176
Cuthred, nephew of k. Cenwalh, 37
Cwenburg, w. of Mildfrith *regulus*, 182
Cwenburh, w. of k. Edwin, 166
Cwichelm, k. of W. Saxons, 167
Cwoenthryth, abbess, dau. of Coenwulf,
   8, 119
Cymeneshora, 81
Cynddylan of Powys, 168–9, 174, 188–
   90
Cyneburh, abbess of Castor, 106
Cynegils, k. of W. Saxons, 167
Cynewald, anc. of Mercian ks., 163–4
Cynewulf, k. of W. Saxons, 96
Cynhelm, son of k. Coenwulf, 8
Cynric, k. of W. Saxons, 84–9, 94–5

Dál Riata, 29, 39
Damnonii, the, 217, 221
Danes, the, 33–4, 151, 234–5; *see also*
   Vikings
Daniel, b. of Winchester, 75, 89–90
Danube, R., 41, 43, 147
Darent/*Derguentid*, R., 62
'Darent' (unidentified *urbs*), 80
David I, k. of Scotland, 39
Deira/Deirans, the, 5, 24, 29, 57, 68,
   103, 124, 126–8, 132, 159–60, 213,
   216–21
Denmark, 147–9, 151–3
diocese(s), 6, 26, 68, 79, 89, 92–4, 96,
   108, 113–14, 122, 130–1, 133–4, 155,
   162, 169, 171–2, 174, 178, 181–2, 192,
   202, 211–12
Diodorus Siculus, 57
Diuma, b. of Mercians and Middle
   Angles, 131, 133–4, 234
Dobunni, the, 186
Domesday Book, 7, 21, 69–73, 79–80,
   90, 108, 112, 117, 119–21, 141, 178,
   188, 205
Doncaster (Y), 204
Donnington (Sx), 79
Dorchester-on-Thames (O), 92–4, 96,
   133–4, 167
Dore (Y), 162
Dover (K), 78
Dragonby (Li), 206
Drefwen, 'fair town', 190, 193
Druim Alban, 39
Dumbarton, 217
Dumnovellaunus, Belgic ruler in Kent, 57
Dunod, k., 221

dux/duces, 37–8, 41–2, 79–80, 163
   dux Britanniarum, 204
Dyfed, 39
dynasties, royal, 6–8, 17–18, 29, 32–9,
   83, 122, 124–5, 137, 140, 163, 167,
   171, 210
   dynastic segmentation, 33–9, 137,
   155
Dyrham (Gl), battle of, 175

Eadbald, k. of Kent, 65
Eadberht, abbot of Selsey, 79
Eadburh, ?abbess of Bicester, 106
Eadgyth, abbess of Aylesbury, 106
Eadred, k. of England, 72
Eadric, k. of Kent, 55, 68, 139
Eadric, ealdorman, 182
Eafa/(Eaba), w. of Æthelwealh, 79–80
ealdorman, 6, 42, 163, 182, 236
Ealdwulf, k. of S. Saxons, 80
Ealing (M), 117–18, 135
Eanfled, w. of k. Oswiu, 29, 31
Earconberht, k. of Kent, 65
East Anglia/East Angles, the, 17, 26, 33–
   4, 71, 125–34, 136, 140, 141–58, 162,
   191, 211, 227
Eastbourne (Sx), 75
East Meon (Ha), 90–1
Eastry (K), 69, 71, 102
East Saxons/Essex, 24, 62, 68, 103, 108,
   110–15, 117, 119–22, 126, 128–30,
   134–40, 144, 227
Eaton (Sy), 97, 100
Ebbsfleet (K), 60–1
Ebissa, kinsman of Octha, 85
Ecgberht, b. of York, 32
Ecgfrith, k. of Northumbrians, 29–32,
   130–1, 168
Ecgfrith, k. of Mercians, 8, 119
Ecgric, k. of E. Angles, 167
'Eddius' Stephanus, 133, 160, 210, 219
Edgar, k. of England, 182
Edmonton Hundred (M), 115, 117, 122
Edor, St., 231, 234–5
Edward the Elder, k. of W. Saxons, 108
Edwin, k. of Northumbrians, 29–30,
   165–7, 191, 212, 220
Egbert I, k. of Kent, 65, 97, 102, 114
Egbert, k. of W. Saxons, 61
Egham (Sy), 97
Eilne, kingdom of, 36
Ellesmere (Sh), 185
Elmet, kingdom of, 128, 132, 212, 220–1
Elmetsæte, the, 159–60, 227
Elsham (Li), 208–9
Elthorne Hundred (M), 118, 120
Ely (Ca), 133
Enechglas, 33
Enfield (M), 115, 121
Ennodius, 50

Éogan, son of Niall, 34–5
Eóghan, 35
Eorcenwold, b. of London, 97, 103, 113–14, 117, 121, 234–5
Eowa, k. of Mercians, 163, 165–9
Epcombs (He), 115
Episford, battle of, 62–3
Eppingas/Uppingas, the, 121
Ercall (Sh), 184, 190
Ergyng, 175, 178; *see also* Archenfield
Erith (K), 114
Ermanaric, Gothic warrior king, 64
Esa, anc. of Bernician ks., 125
Essex *see* East Saxons
Ethelwald, nephew of k. Oswiu, 32
ethnicity, 34, 47–9, 127–8, 147, 153, 157–8, 171
Eunapius, 43
Evesham (Wo), 8
extended family, 20, 22–4, 26, 100, 111–12, 120, 122, 133, 154
Eyhorne (K), 70
Eynsham (O), 106

Færpingas, the, 133, 160, 191, 225, 227
Farnham (Sy), 93, 103, 105
Farnham Hundred (Sy), 100
Faversham (K), 57, 71–3
federates, 50, 179, 214–15
Féni, the, 34
Feppingas, the, 34, 133–4
feudal mode of production, 55, 156–7
Fight at Finnesburh, 34
Fillingham (Li), 205
Fínán, 28
Finberg, H.P.R., 6–7, 41, 171, 174–7, 188
Finchley (M), 117
'Florence' of Worcester, 91, 181–2
folc, 154
folkland, 20
Fonaby (Li), 209
food renders, 28–33, 38–9
feorm, 31
Forest of Bere, 91
Francia, 89, 93, 139, 153, 158
Franks, the, 30, 40–1, 45–51, 64, 146–7
Fredegar, 30
Friduric/Frithuric, *princeps*, 105–6, 231
Frimley (Sy), 104
Frithogyth, w. of k. Æthelheard, 106
Frithuswith ('Frideswide'), 106
Frithuwold, *subregulus*, 97–8, 100, 102–7, 114, 118, 120, 137–8, 231, 234–6
Fulham (M), 100, 117
Fullingadic, 97–8, 100, 102, 105, 107
Fursa, 146

Gaels, the, 215
Gaul, 45, 47, 49–50, 147
Geddingas, the, 118

genealogies, royal, 4–5, 34–5, 38, 55, 59–60, 63–4, 67, 75, 88, 124–5, 155, 158–9, 163–4, 176, 206–7, 210, 216, 218
Genseric, *Heerkönig*, 44
Gerald of Wales, 189–90
Gewisse/Geuissae, the, 75, 78–9, 90, 93–4, 96, 136, 160
Gifle/Gifla, the, 160, 227
Gildas, 40, 51, 58, 88, 213–15, 217–18, 220
Gillingas, the, 117–18
Glentham (Li), 205, 210
Gloucester (Gl), 6, 172, 175, 181
Godalming (Sy), 100
Godalming Hundred (Sy), 100
Gododdin, kingdom of, 216–17
Gododdin, the, 216
Godhelmingas, the, 100, 105
Godley Hundred (Sy), 100, 104
Gore Hundred (M), 119
Goscelin, 175–6, 192
Goths, the, 43–4, 50–1, 59
Great Chesterford (E), 25, 41
Gregory I, pope, 113
Gregory of Tours, 40–2, 45–6, 48, 64, 66–7
Grim's Dyke (M), 108, 119
Guildford (Sy), 100
Gumeninga hearh, 118
Gumeningas, the, 118–19
Gundobad, Burgundian k., 45
Gundulf, 48
Guthlac, St., 37
Gwrgi, 221
Gwynedd, kingdom of, 39, 191, 214, 220
Gwyrangon, British k., 57
Gyrwe, the, 130–1, 133, 160
South Gyrwe, 131, 227
North Gyrwe, 137, 227

Hædda, abbot of Medeshamstede, 105
Hæferingas, the, 121
Hæmele, territory of, 111, 119
Hæstingas, the, 78
hagiography, 34, 55, 106, 176, 182, 192
Halhsæte, the, 201
Hamble, R., 90–1
Hampton (Hf), 177
Hampton (M), 118
Hamtun, 96
Hamtunscir, 96
Hamwih/Hamwic, 93, 96, 146
Hanwell (M), 112, 118
Harefield, (M), 119
Harrow (M), 108, 111, 118–19, 121
Hastingford (Sx), 78
Hastingleigh (K), 78
Hastings (Sx), 21, 78, 80, 83, 137
Hatfield (He), 115
synod of, 114

Hatfield, battle of, 160, 165–7, 202, 212
Hatfield Chase (Y), 115, 212
Hatton (Li), 210
Havering (E), 121
Hayes (M), 118
Hayling Island (Ha), 90–1
'Heavenfield', battle of, 167
Hecani, Western, the, 175, 181–2
Hemel Hempstead (He), 108, 111, 119
Hemming's Cartulary, 7
Hendon (M), 111, 119–20
Hendrica, the, 160, 227
Hengist, 57–60, 62–4, 87–8, 95, 124–5
Henry of Huntingdon, 159, 163, 165
Heptarchy, the, 126, 140, 153
Herefinna, the, 227
Hereford (Hf), 171–2, 176–8, 181–2, 199
Hereric, nephew of k. Edwin, 220
Herne (K), 72
Hertford (He), 115, 122
    synod of, 114
Hertingfordbury (He), 115
Hibaldstow (Li), 205–6, 208–9
Hicce, the, 115, 160, 227
Higebold, St., 206
Highdown (Sx), 81, 83
Historia Brittonum, 55, 57, 60–4, 85,
    165–6, 188, 214–16, 218, 220
Historia Regum, 78
Hitchin (He), 108
Hlothhere, k. of Kent, 55, 68, 139
Hoath (K), 72
Hockham Mere (Nf), 142
Hollingbourne (K), 70
Hoo (K), 71–2
Horncastle (Li), 205–6
Horsa, 58–60, 62, 87, 95, 124
Houndslow Hundred (M), 118, 120
Howare, territory of, 72
Hreutford, 'reed ford' (Ha), 90
Hrothingas, the, 23–4, 121
Humber, R., 17, 29, 81, 127, 132, 162,
    202, 204–5, 210, 213, 215, 218, 221
Humbrenses, the, 127, 210
hundred(s), 72, 100, 104, 112, 115, 117,
    119–20, 122, 199
Hunewaldesham (Sy), 98
Hurstbourne Tarrant (Ha), 91, 94
Husmerae, province of, 18, 42, 98
Hwicce, the, 6–8, 17–18, 26, 34, 42, 79–
    80, 126, 130, 133–4, 138–9, 159–60,
    164, 167, 174, 176–7, 181–2, 184, 192,
    227

Icanho, 192
Icel, anc. of Mercian ks., 163–4
Iceni, the, 203
Icklesham (Sx), 78
Iclingas, the, 34, 37, 163–4
Ida, k. of Bernicia, 65, 125, 218

Idle, R., battle at, 160, 162, 204, 211–12
Ine, k. of W. Saxons, 30, 80, 114, 139
Ingham (Li), 206
Ingoberga, mother-in-law of k.
    Æthelberht, 66–7
Inis Eóghain (Inishowen), 34–5
inter-marriage, 21, 47–9, 67, 89, 206,
    220
Iona, 36, 215
Iona Chronicle, 3
Ipswich (Sf), 93, 144, 146, 152
Irby (Li), 210
Ireland, 18, 23, 28, 32–9, 163
Irish, the, 42, 138
Irminric, f. of k. Æthelberht, 64, 67
Isle of Wight, 59, 75, 78–9, 86, 88–96,
    127
Isleworth (M), 117–18
Italy, 45, 51, 158
Iurminburh, w. of k. Ecgfrith, 64

joint-kings, 23, 31–2, 37, 136–9, 165–6
Jolliffe, J.E.A., 41, 71–3
Jordanes, 59
Julius Caesar, 57
Jutes, the, 88–96, 124, 127
Jutland, 88

Kenchester (Hf), 172, 174, 178–80, 182
Kent, 3, 5, 18, 24, 34, 37, 55–74, 78–9,
    83–4, 87–8, 92–3, 95–6, 98, 100, 102,
    107, 111–14, 122, 125–9, 135–9, 146–
    8, 159, 215, 227
Keymer (Sx), 81
Kidderminster (Wo), 18
king lists, 5, 65, 67, 75, 124–5, 165, 218
Kingsbury (M), 119
Kingsham (Sx), 79
kingship, terminology of
    archon, 43
    basileus, 43
    basiliskos, 43
    cyning, 24, 43
    princeps, 17, 37–8, 42, 46, 59, 105,
        131, 163, 211
    regalis, 41–3
    regulus, 17, 42–3, 163, 176, 210
    reiks, 43–4
    rex, 31, 38, 41–7, 80–1, 83, 176,
        210–11
    rhix, 43
    rí, 38, 163
    rí ruirech, 38
    rí tuaithe, 43
    ruiri, 34, 37–8
    subregulus, 17, 31–2, 37–8, 41–3,
        46, 114, 137, 163
    theoden, 43
    thiod-cyning, 43

thiudans, 43
thiudareiks, 43
thungingus, 46
tuath, 18, 163
  other royal terms:
    dux regius, 31–2, 37–8, 42, 79, 83,
      129, 132, 166
    praefectus, 31–2, 37, 42, 71, 163,
      210
    procer, 162
    regalis socius, 29
Kingston (Sy), 100
Kingston-by-Lewes (Sx), 80
Kirmington (Li), 206, 208–9
Kirton-in-Lindsey (Li), 209

Laigin, the, 34; *see also* Leinstermen
Langworth, R., 205, 210
lathe(s), 69–73, 98, 100, 137
laws, 29–30, 42, 48, 55, 67–9, 71, 154–5,
  158, 199, 207
Lea, R., 108, 117
Leicester (Le), 130–1, 133–4, 202, 204,
  211
Leinster, 33
Leinstermen, 30, 34; *see also* Laigin
Leintwardine (Hf), 172, 174, 180
Leland, John, 179, 231, 234, 236
Leominster (Hf), 175–8, 182–3
Letocetum, 169; *see also* Wall
Leuthere, b. of Winchester, 93
Lewes (Sx), 80–1, 83
Lex Salica, 46
Liberius, 50
Liber Wigorniensis, 7
Lichfield (St), 131, 162, 169, 174, 185,
  188, 192, 211–12
Lichfield Gospels, 33
Life of St. Cadog, 33
Life of St. Mildburg, 175
Life of Wilfrid, 29, 31–2, 75, 78, 133
Limenware/Limenwara, the, 72, 98
Lincoln (Li), 5, 133, 202–8, 210–11
  St. Paul-in-the-Bail, 207
Lindesfaran, the, 160, 167
Lindisfarne (Nb), 28, 218, 220
Lindsey, kingdom of, 5, 29, 33, 126–9,
  131–2, 134, 139, 202–12, 227
Lingen (Hf), 199
Liobsynde, abbess of Wenlock, 178
Littleborough (Li), 29, 202, 204, 212
Llanfillo (Brecknockshire), 177
Lombards, the, 47, 51
London, 57, 62–3, 68, 93, 97, 100, 102,
  108, 110–14, 119–22, 134, 136, 146,
  203–4, 234–5
  Aldwych, 110
  Cripplegate, 110, 112
  Drury Lane, 110
  St. Paul's/*Paulesbyrig*, 110, 112

The Strand, 110
  synod of, 114
Lothar, k. of Franks, 66
Lothian, 32
Lough Foyle, 34–5
Lough Neagh, 36
Loveden Hill (Li), 211
Lugg, R., 172, 177–9, 181–2
Lullingas, the, 118
[*Caer*] *Lwytgoed*, 169
Lyde (Hf), 177, 182, 192
Lyminge (K), 57, 71, 102
Lymington (Ha), 90
Lympne (K), 69, 78–9

MacCairthínn, descendant of Enechglas,
  33
Mægla, son of Port, 86, 89
Maesbury (Sh), 188–9
Maes Cogwy, battle of, 188–9; *see also*
  Cocboy, *Maserfelth*
Magana/Maund (Hf), 177–9, 182
Mag Line, kingdom of, 36
Magnis see Kenchester
Magonsæte, the, 126, 169, 171–83, 184,
  191–2, 199
Mag Tóchuir, kingdom in, 34
Maitland, F.W., 21
Manaw, 217
manorialism, 20
manors, 20, 98, 105, 122, 154–7
Marcomer, *regalis Francorum*, 41
Marden (Hf), 177–9, 182–3
Marden (Sx), 75, 78
Marwynad Cynddylan, 168–9, 188
Maserfelth, battle of, 165–8, 174–6, 188–
  9; *see also* Cocboy, Maes Cogwy
Masuna, *rex gentium Maurorum et*
  Romanorum, 46
Matthew Paris, 159, 163
Meallingas, the, 98, 105
Mearcredesburna, R., battle at, 81
Medeshamstede, 105–6, 174; *see also*
  Peterborough
Mellitus, b. of London, 136
Meon, R., 75, 90–1
Meonware/*Meanware*, the, 75, 78–9, 90–
  3, 127
mercenaries, 24–5, 121, 147–8, 156, 214
Merchelm, *rex*, son of Merewalh, 176,
  182
Mercia/Mercians, the, 3, 6, 8, 17–18, 27,
  29–30, 33–4, 37, 44, 78, 97, 100, 105–
  8, 110, 113–14, 118, 120–2, 126–36,
  138–40, 159–70, 171, 174–7, 183–4,
  188–92, 195, 197–9, 201, 210–12, 220,
  227
Meresæte, the, 201
Merewalh, k. of Magonsæte, 171–2,
  174–8, 181–3, 191–2

Merovingians, the, 39, 46
Merscware, the, 72
Middle Angles, the, 26, 37, 100, 106–7, 120, 127–34, 140, 191, 211
Middle Saxons/Middlesex, 62, 107, 108–22, 134–7, 139
Migration Period, 3, 5, 19, 21, 23–4, 47
Mildburg, abbess of Wenlock, 171, 175–8, 181–2, 184, 192
Mildfrith, regulus, son of Merewalh, 176, 182
Milton Regis (K), 69, 73
Mimmas, the, 115
Mimms, Half Hundred of (M), 115, 122
Mimms, North (He), 115
Mimms, South (M), 115
minster church(es), 19, 78–9, 90, 97, 102–6, 108, 110, 113, 115, 117, 120–2, 146, 162, 166, 175–8, 191–3, 231, 234, 236–7
Mitcham (Sy), 110, 112
Molesey (Sy), 97, 100
monasteries, Anglo-Saxon see minster church(es)
Monnow, R., 177
Morfael, 169
Mucking (E), 110, 112
Mul, brother of k. Cædwalla, 37, 61, 139
'multiple estate', 20, 71, 104, 186
multiple kingship see joint-kingship
mund, 39, 68

Natanleaga, district of, 85–6
Natanleod, legendary British k., 85
'Nennius', 61
Netley Marsh (Ha), 85, 89, 91
Nettleton (Li), 206
Newark-on-Trent (No), 211
New Forest (Ha), 91
New Winchelsea (Sx), 78
Niall, 35
Nidd, R., 31
Normandy, 79
North Elmham (Nf), 144
North Sea, the, 149, 152, 158, 184
Northumbria/Northumbrians, the, 17, 30–2, 38, 103, 124, 126–7, 130–2, 136–7, 139–40, 148, 152, 159–60, 162, 165–7, 169, 176, 188, 190–1, 210, 212, 213–22
Norway, 148–9, 151–3
Nothhelm/Nunna, k. of S. Saxons, 80
Notitia Dignitatum, 202, 204
Novantae, the, 217, 220–1
Noxgaga, the, 92, 112, 160, 227

Octha/Octa/(Ocga), anc. of Kentish ks., 60, 63–4, 85, 92
Oessa/Eossa, anc. of Bernician ks., 218

Offa, k. of E. Saxons, 111, 137–8
Offa, k. of Mercians, 8, 78, 80–1, 83, 111, 117–18, 120, 137, 159, 199, 210
Offa's Dyke, 193, 199
Ohtgaga, the, 92, 112, 160, 227
Oisc/Oeric, son of Hengist, 58–60, 63–4, 125; see also Æsc
Oiscingas, the, 34, 59–60, 63, 125
Oithilred, parens of k. Sebbi, 136
Old Sarum (Wi), 94
Old Saxons, the, 3, 44
Ordinance Concerning the Dunsæte, 199
origin legends, 5, 58–64, 69, 73, 81, 83–8, 95–6, 124–5
Osburh, w. of k. Æthelwulf, 95
Osfrith, son of k. Edwin, 167
Osgodby (Li), 206
Osgyth, ?abbess of Aylesbury, 106
Oslac, k. of S. Saxons, 80
Oslac, pincerna, 95
Osmund, dux, 80
Ossa/Oese, anc. of Kentish ks., 63–4
Ossulstone Hundred (M), 117
Ostrogoths, the, 45, 50
Oswald, b. of Selsey, 78
Oswald, dux, 80
Oswald, k. of Northumbrians, 30, 165–9, 188–9, 220
Oswestry (Sh), 188–9, 199
Oswine, k. of Northumbrians, 32
Oswiu, k. of Northumbrians, 29, 31–2, 103, 131–2, 161, 164, 168, 211, 220
overking(ship) see overlord(ship)
overlord(ship), 31, 34, 81, 94, 98, 100, 106–7, 114, 126, 128, 130, 132–6, 138–40, 161, 166–8, 174, 191, 199, 211–12, 221
Oxford (O), 80, 106

Pactus Legis Salicae, 48
Padaran Peisrudd/'Paternus', 216
Pæogthath, comes, 111
Pagham Harbour (Sx), 78–9
Paris, 40, 45
Parisi, the, 217
partible inheritance, 20, 153–4, 156
Patrick, St., 36, 217
Paul the Deacon, 51
Paulinus, archb. of York, 29, 207, 210, 212
Peada, k. of Middle Angles, 131–2, 166, 176, 211
Peak District, the, 128
Pecsæte/Pecsætna, the, 160, 227
Penda, k. of Mercians, 6, 23, 37, 96, 129–33, 135, 155, 163–70, 175–6, 181, 188–9, 191–2, 211–12
Pengwern, 190
Penwalh, f. of Guthlac, 37

people
  gens, 41, 47, 68, 78, 91, 137, 160
  natio, 41, 89
  populus, 41
Peredur, 221
Peterborough (Nt), 131; *see also*
  Medeshamstede
Pevensey (Sx), 78, 80–1, 83
Picts, the, 29–32, 39, 214–15, 217, 220
Pipba, k. of Mercians, 163–5, 167–8
placenames, 5, 17, 21, 24, 60–1, 78, 85–
  6, 88, 90–1, 110, 112, 114, 120, 122,
  127, 163–4, 177, 179, 184, 186, 188–
  90, 192–4, 196–9, 201, 206, 221
  -ge, 69, 71–2, 100, 102, 114, 120,
    134
  -ingas, 21, 23, 114, 117, 120–1
  tun 8, 19, 25, 67–8, 197, 199
  wic, 93, 110, 208
  wīc-hām, 115, 206–7
  Latin loan word placenames, 25,
    114–15, 119
Plummer, Charles, 84
poetry, 30, 94, 168–70, 187–91, 216, 219,
  221
Port, legendary Jutish leader, 85–7, 89,
  91, 95
Portchester (Ha), 80, 203
Portesmupa/Portsmouth (Ha), 85, 89–90
pottery, 115, 144, 146, 187, 206–11
Powys, kingdom of, 168, 174, 187–8,
  190–1, 220–1
Preston (in Harrow) (M), 119
Procopius, 40, 43, 45, 49
province, 89–93, 95–6, 102, 105, 107–8,
  111–12, 114, 121–2, 152, 157
provincia/provinciae, 17–18, 26, 91, 102,
  107, 111, 114, 131–2, 135, 138, 211
Ptolemy, 57
Pytheas, the navigator, 57

Quadi, the, 42
Quarrendon (Bu), 106–7

Rædwald, k. of E Angles, 129, 132, 155,
  160, 191
Rainham (K), 71–2
rape(s), 79, 83, 98, 37
Ravenna Cosmograi her, 59
Ravenna Geography, 125
Reading (Bk), 21, 100
Reculver (K), 72
Redbridge (Ha), 90–1
reeve, 31, 42, 71, 210
Regino of Prüm, 47
regio/regiones, 17–19, 21, 26, 71–3, 98,
  100, 102, 104–5, 107, 118, 131–4, 137–
  8, 140
regnal lists *see* king-lists
Regni, the, 57

regnum, 41, 46
Renatus Profuturus Frigeridus, 41
rent, 154–7
Repton (Db), 8, 106, 162, 176
Rheged, kingdom of, 32, 217, 220
Rhiainfellt, w. of k. Oswiu, 32, 220
Rhine, R., 40–1, 46, 48
Rhiwsæte, the, 201
Rhodri Mawr, 39
Rhygyfarch, 178
Richborough (K), 57
Ricimer, uncle of k. Gundobad, 45
Rickmansworth (He), 119
Ripon (Y), 31
Rochester (K), 57, 68–73, 78, 85
Roding, R., 21
Rodings, the (E), 21, 121
Roger of Wendover, 159, 163, 165
Roman Britain, 4, 24, 110, 142, 171–2,
  174, 186, 193, 202–4, 217
Roman emperors
  Anastasius, 45
  Constantine I, 43
  Constantine III, 147
  Julian, 46
  Marcian, 60
  Valentinian, 60
Roman Empire, 28, 41, 44, 51–2, 151
  Western Empire, 5, 44–5
  Eastern Empire, 123
Romans, the/'Rome', 40–2, 44–6, 48–51
Rome, 28, 93, 106, 137
Romney Marsh, 63, 72
Rotherfield (Sx), 119
Roxeth (in Greenford) (M), 118
royal vill *see villa regia*
Ruislip (M), 120

Saberht, k. of E. Saxons, 113, 120, 136,
  138
St. Albans (He), 110–12, 119
Salians, the, 48
Salisbury (Wi), 94
Sandlings, the (Sf), 143–4, 152, 156–7
Sarre (K), 89
Saxons, the (continental), 30, 44, 47, 63
Saxony, 3
Scandinavia, 89
Scotland, 215
Scots, the, 39, 169
Sebbi/Sæbbi, k. of E. Saxons, 68, 136,
  138
see(s) *see* diocese(s)
Selgovae, the, 217, 220–1
Selsey (Sx), 75, 79–81, 83
Serapio, Alamannic leader, 42
settlements, excavated, 142–4, 146–7,
  151, 172–4, 186–7, 196, 206
Severn, R., 172, 175, 181, 185–7
Shepperton (M), 112

shires, 6, 79, 83, 96, 102, 104, 108, 117
Shrewsbury (Sh), 174, 187, 190
Sigeberht, k. of E. Angles, 167
Sigebert, k. of W. Saxons, 96
Sigehard, k. of E. Saxons, 136–7
Sigehere, k. of E. Saxons, 68, 136–8
Sigemund, f. of k. Swithred, 137
Sigered, k. of E. Saxons, 68
Sigeric II, k. of E. Saxons, 115
Sigric, *minister*, 115
Snape (Sf), 150
Soemil, anc. of Deiran ks., 218
Solent, the, 75, 84, 90, 92, 96
Sonning/*Sunninges* (Bk), 21, 97, 100,
    102, 111, 114, 120
Southampton (Ha), 80, 91
Southampton Water, 90–1
South Downs, 75, 78, 81, 83
South Elkington (Li), 209–10
South Ferriby (Li), 204–5
South Malling (Sx), 80, 105
South Saxons *see* Sussex
Southumbrians, 127–30, 133, 135–6, 160
Spalda/Spalde/Spaldingas, the, 26, 160,
    211, 227
Spelthorne Hundred (M), 120
Spong Hill (Nf), 147, 149–50, 152, 156
Stæningas, 120
Staines (M), 102, 107–8, 112, 114, 119–21
Staunton-on-Arrow (Hf), 182
Stenton, F.M., 6, 23, 122, 133, 154, 162–
    4, 171, 176, 181, 183, 185, 192
Stepelsæte, the, 201
Stepney (M), 117
Stevenson, W.H., 181
Stithberht, abbot, 111
Stoke (K), 72
Stone (Ha), 90
Stoneham (Ha), 90
Stoppingas, the, 18–19, 21, 23, 42, 98
Strabo, 57
Strasburg, battle of, 42
Strathclyde, kingdom of, 215, 217,
    220–1
Stuf, legendary anc. of ks. of Wight, 85–
    6, 88, 95
Sturry (K), 71, 102
sub-kings, 31, 97, 105–7, 176
Sulpicius Alexander, 41
Sunbury (M), 111, 114
Sunno, *regalis Francorum*, 41
Surrey, province of, 68, 92–4, 97–107,
    112, 114, 118, 120, 128, 134–5, 137–9,
    234–5
Sutton-at-Hone (K), 69, 73
Sutton Hoo (Sf), 5, 149–50, 152–3, 158
Sutton Walls (Hf), 179, 182
Sussex/South Saxons, the, 60, 62, 75–83,
    90, 92–4, 98, 107, 111, 113, 126, 128–
    9, 137–9, 227

Swæfheard, k. of E. Saxons, 68, 136
Swæfred/Swefred, k. of E. Saxons, 111,
    136–8
Sweden, 148–9, 152–3
Sweordora, the, 227
Swithred, k. of E. Saxons, 137
Syagrius, *rex Romanorum*, 46
synod(s), 113–15, 117, 120

Tacitus, 42–4
Taliesin, 168, 216, 221
Tamworth (St), 162, 185, 192, 196
Taplow (Bu), 112
tax(es), 50–2, 141, 154, 156–8, 191–2
Teme, R., 172, 180–1
Temesæte/Tempsiter, 201
Tern, R., 172, 188, 190
Testament of St. Mildburg, 171, 176–7,
    199
Thame (O), 97, 107
Thames, R., 97–8, 100, 102, 107–8, 110,
    112, 114, 117, 120, 133–4, 148
Thanet (K), 60, 62
Themistius, 43
Theodore, archb. of Canterbury, 68, 103,
    113, 115, 130, 134, 169
Theodoric, Ostrogothic k., 43, 45
Theodric, k. of Bernicia, 218
Thomas, b. of E. Angles, 130
Thorpe (Sy), 97, 103
Thuringians, the, 30, 47
Tiowulfingacæstir, 212
Tírechán, 34, 36
Tír Eóghain (Tyrone), 35–6
Titchfield (Ha), 90–1
Tondberht, *princeps*, 131
Tottenhale/Tottenham Court (M), 117
Tottenham (M), 115, 117
tracht, 148, 152, 157
trade, 110, 112–13, 115, 146, 148–9, 153
trading centre, 93, 110, 112–13, 115,
    146, 208
Trent, R., 128, 161–2, 185, 192, 195,
    202, 204, 206, 210–12
    battle of, 130
Tribal Hidage, the, 17–18, 26, 34, 44, 75,
    78, 86, 89, 92, 108, 111–12, 115, 120–
    1, 123, 126, 129–33, 140, 159–61, 163,
    167–8, 171, 174, 191–2, 195, 202, 211,
    225–30
tribe *see* extended family
tribute, 29–30, 32–3, 39, 129, 159
Trinovantes, the, 24
Tripartite Life, the, 34
Twickenham (M), 111, 114, 117
Tyrthel/Tyrhtil, b. of Hereford, 117, 182

Uecta, anc. of Kentish ks., 58–9, 88
Uhtred, *regulus* of Hwicce, 42
Uictgisl, anc. of Kentish ks., 58–9, 88

Uictuarii, the, 88
Uí Enechglais, the, 33
Uí Néill, the, 30, 35–6, 38–9
Uitta, anc. of Kentish ks., 58–9, 88
Ulaid, the (men of Ulster), 34
Ulfila, 43
Unecungga, the, 160, 227
Upton (in Blockley) (Gl), 8
Urien, British k., 218
Uxbridge (M), 119
Uxendon (M), 119

Vandals, the, 44, 46
Venedotians, the, 220
Verulamium, 108, 110, 119
Vikings, the, 28, 126, 149, 159, 234–5;
  see also Danes
villa regia/regalis/regis, 28–9, 39, 79,
  103–7, 117, 119–21, 162, 167–8, 182
Viroconium see Wroxeter
Visigoths, the, 43, 45, 47, 50
Vortemir, son of Vortigern, 62
Vortigern, 57–8, 62–3, 174, 220
Votadini, the, 216–17

Wæclingas, the, 110, 119
Wæppingas, the, 117
Waldhere, b. of London, 111, 114, 117–
  18, 136
Wales, 28, 33, 163, 187, 191, 193, 214
Wall (St), 169, 187; see also *Letocetum*
Wallington (Sy), 100
Walsham (Nf), 147, 156
Waltham, Half Hundred of, 117
Walthamstow (E), 117
Waltheof, earl, 117
Walton-on-Thames (Sy), 100
Wantsum channel, the, 63
Wapping (M), 117
Warburton (Ch), 189
Ware (He), 115
Watford (He), 119, 122
Wattus, k. of S. Saxons, 78, 80
Waxlow (M), 119
Weald, the, 58, 70–2, 75, 78, 81, 83, 98,
  100, 185
Wealhstod, b. of Hereford, 183
Wehha/Weahha, k. of E. Angles, 125,
  155
Welsh, the, 30, 39, 47, 127, 162, 165,
  167–9, 171, 177, 182–3, 190–1; see
  also Britons, Celts
Welsh Bicknor (Hf), 178
Wenlock/*Wininicas* (Sh), 175–8, 181–2,
  184, 192–3
Weowara, the, 98
Werenberht, *minister*, 118
wergeld, 37, 157
Werhard, priest, 118
Wessex/West Saxons, the, 3, 5–6, 18, 24,

27, 37, 44, 60–1, 75, 79–80, 84–96,
  108, 111–14, 117, 122, 124–30, 134–6,
  139–40, 147–8, 154, 160, 165, 167,
  175–6, 191, 227
Wester (K), 69
Westerna/Westerne, the, 160, 167, 181,
  192, 227
West Keal (Li), 209–10
Westminster abbey, 108, 119–20
Weston-under-Penyard (Hf), 172, 174–5,
  178
West Stow (Sf), 144, 147
Westwood (K), 72
Weybridge (Sy), 100
Whitchurch (Sh), 189
Whittington (Sh), 190
Wibbandun, battle of, 61, 67, 87, 112
Wicken Bonhunt (E), 25–6, 41, 144, 146,
  157
Wickham Hill (He), 115
Widerigga, the, 227
Widsith, 33
Widukind of Corvey, 63
Wigesta, the, 160, 227
Wigford (Li), 208, 211
Wigmore (Hf), 185
Wihtgar, legendary anc. of ks. of Wight,
  85–6, 88, 95
Wihtgara/Wihtware, the, 86, 92, 127,
  227
Wihtgarabyrg, 85
Wihtred, k. of Kent, 55, 138
Wihtred, *comes*, 118
Wilburh, sister of k. Wulfhere, 106
Wilfrid, St., 29, 31–2, 64, 78–9, 83, 131,
  169, 219
Willa, East and West, the, 26, 227
William of Malmesbury, 176, 182
Winchcombe (Gl), 6, 8, 17, 26, 177–8
Winchcombeshire, 6–8, 17–18, 26
Winchester (Ha), 24, 89, 91–4, 96, 114
Winchester Hill (Ha), 91
Windlesham (Sy), 104
Wine, b. of Winchester, 92–3
Wingham (K), 57
Winteringham (Li), 204–5
Winterton (Li), 204
Winwed/Winwæd, battle of, 129, 132,
  135, 161, 165–6, 168, 191
Wipped, thane, 61–2
Wippedesfleot, battle of, 60, 62–3
Witham, R, (Li), 202, 205–6, 208, 210–11
Witton (Nf), 146–7, 156
Wixan, the, 107, 114, 119–21, 227
Woccingas, the, 100
Woden, 58–60, 88, 163
Woking (Sy), 100, 104–6
Woking Hundred (Sy), 100, 104
Woodham (Sy), 97
Wootton Wawen (Wa), 18–19

Worcester (Wo), 6, 8, 181, 192
    church of, 8, 17
Wotton Hundred (Sy), 100
Wrekin, the (Sh), 167, 174, 179, 184,
    187, 190, 192
Wreocensæte, the, 160, 167, 169, 172,
    174, 177, 179, 181–2, 192, 201, 227
Wroxeter (Sh), 172–4, 178–80, 182, 184–
    7
Wuffa, k. of E. Angles, 125
Wuffingas, the, 34
Wulfhere, k. of Mercians, 75, 79, 90,
    92–3, 97, 105–7, 114, 132–3, 135, 137–
    8, 166

Wulfred, archb. of Canterbury, 118
Wye (K), 69
Wye, R., 172, 199
Wykeham (Li), 206–7

Yarkhill (Hf), 182
Yeading (M), 111, 118
Yeavering (Nb), 5, 29, 167, 187
York (Y), 24, 203–4, 215
Yppelesfleot, 60
Ypwinesfleot/Heopwinesfleot, 60, 62
Ytedene, 'valley of the Jutes', 90
Ytene, 'of the Jutes', 91
Ytingstoc (Bishopstoke, Ha), 91, 93